ANNE BEAN
SELF ETC.

EDITED BY ROB LA FRENAIS

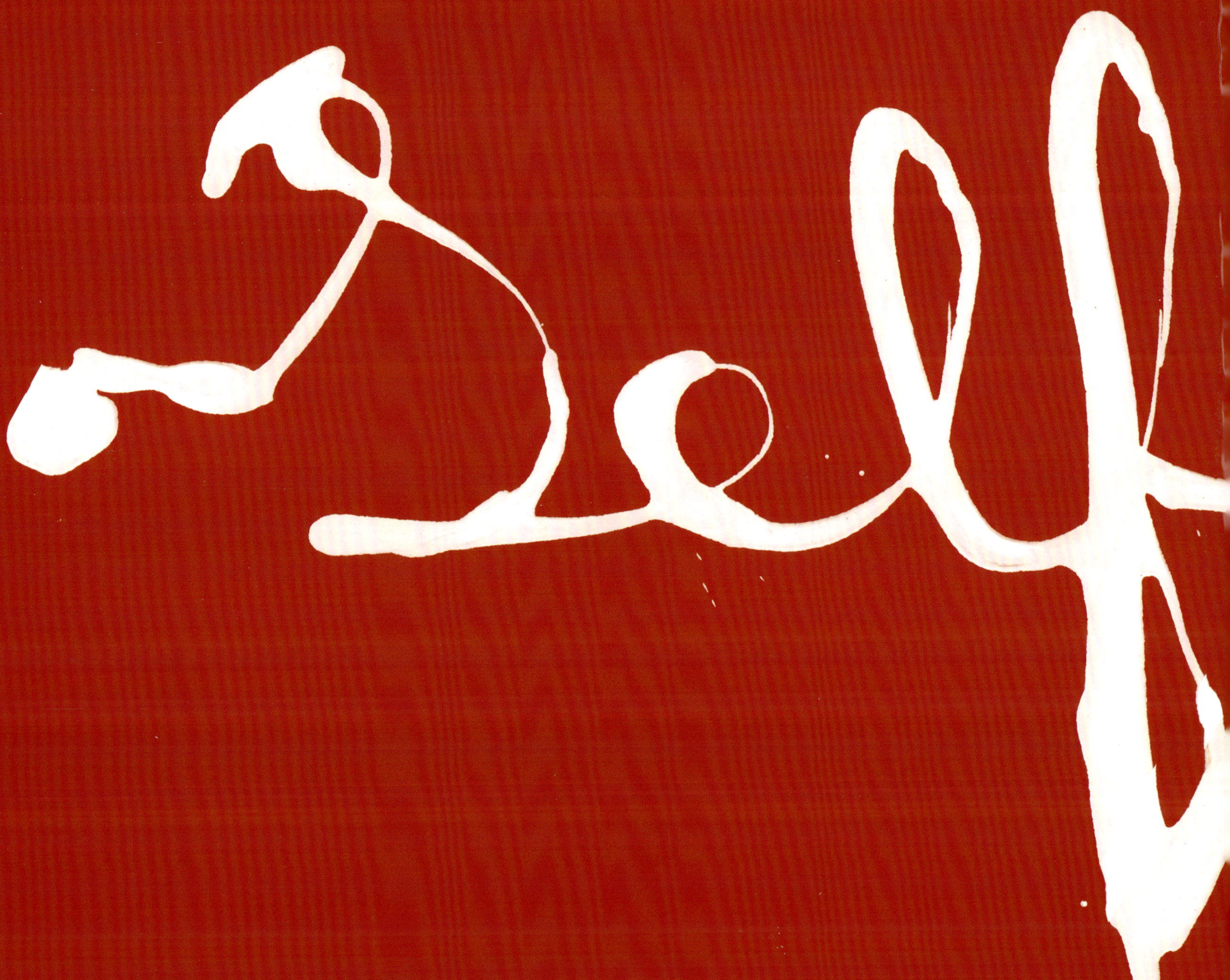
Self

I
CONTAIN MY
ENTIRE PAST
& FUTURE
MY BIRTH
& DEATH
ABSOLUTELY
& COMPLETELY
RIGHT NOW

AN AWARENESS
LIVINGSTONE
ZAMBIA
1965

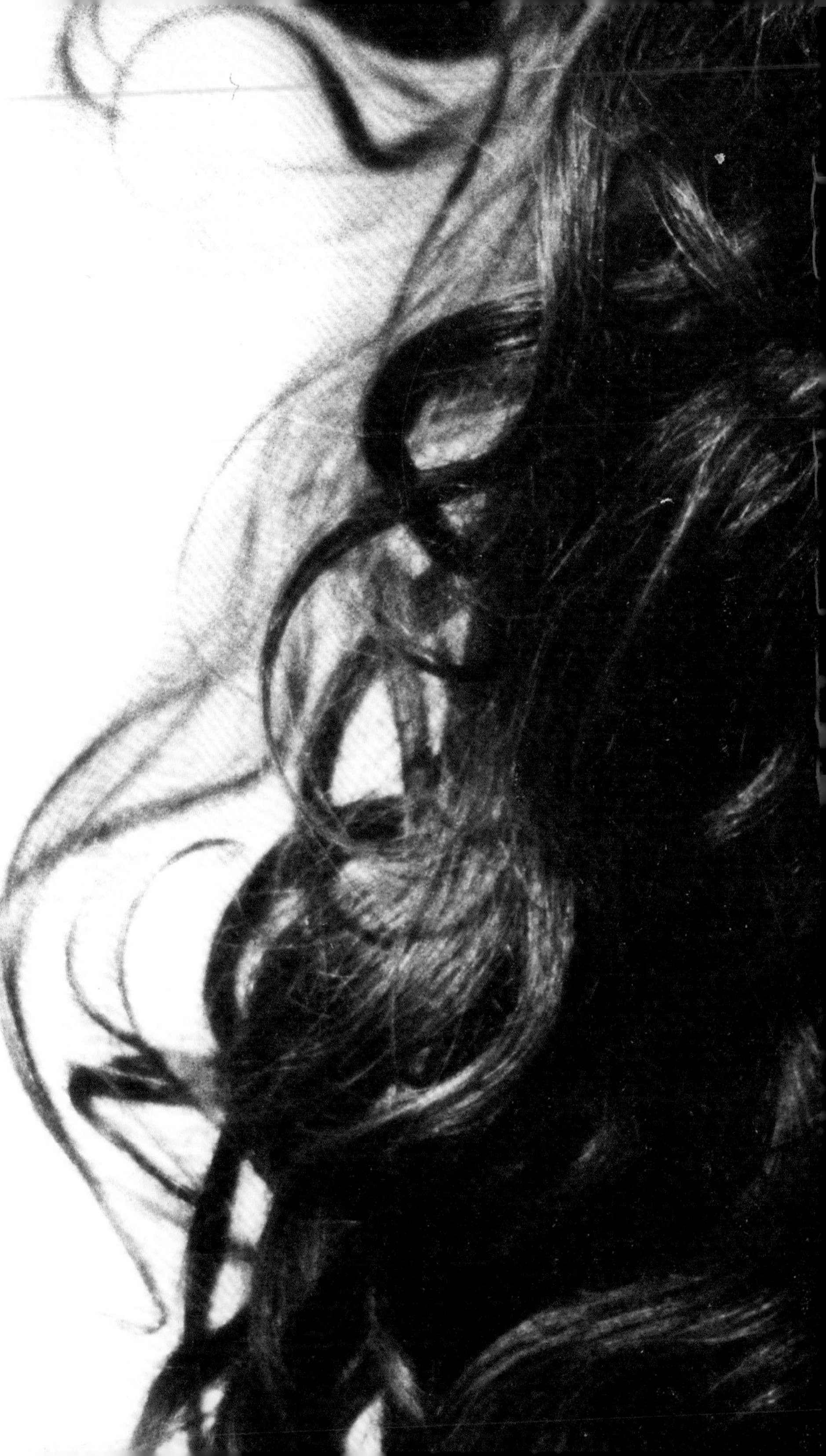

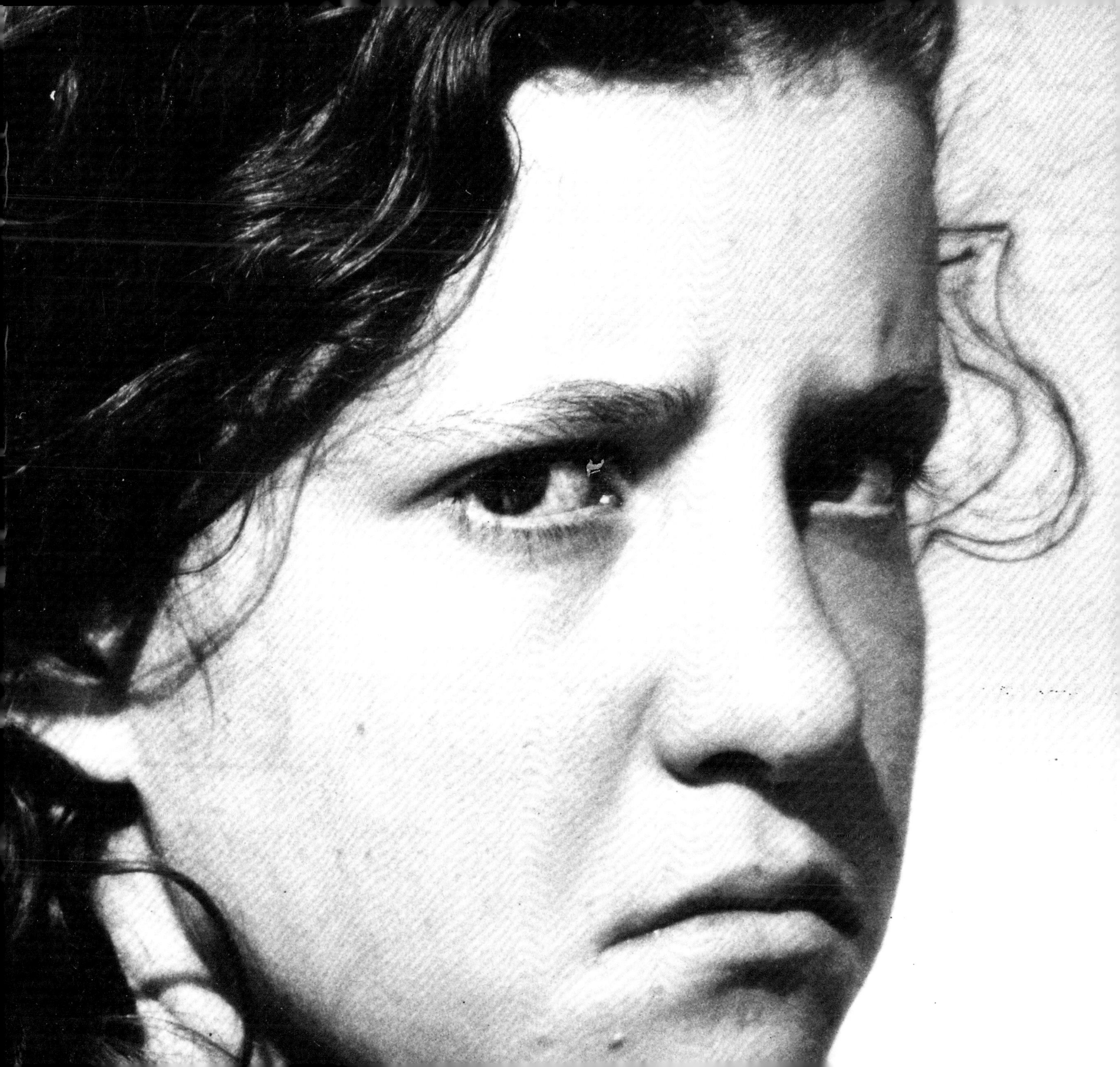

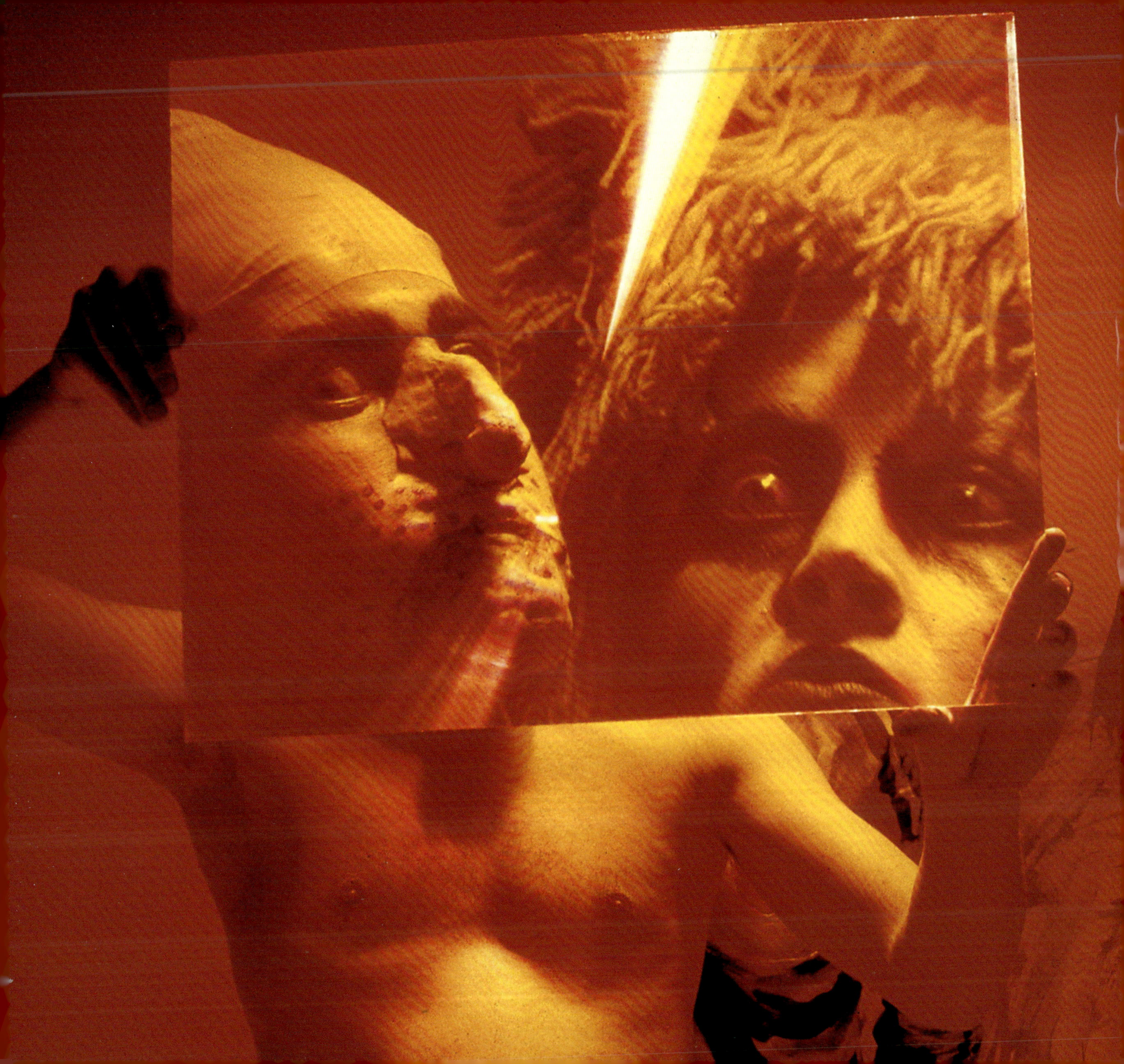

CONTENTS

INTRODUCTION
ROB LA FRENAIS

'Now all you artists don't rack your brains what it's all about', the showgirl in Union Jack sequins said as she left (described in an email from Anne Bean about her recent event *MoCa to Mega* in 2018 while we were compiling this book). *Anne Bean: Self Etc.* was meant to be a monograph about the massive body of work that is Anne Bean's artistic activity since the 1960s but that would imply that it has finished. The artist, like me, born in the very early 1950s, seems to have just started, not finished.

Nearly all of these essays – mainly, newly commissioned – seem to follow a theme of stripping back the art: the un-paintings, un-art, un-performances, and anti-art aspects of the life-art of Anne Bean. A running thread concerns her various selves, not only her embodied self who emerged in the last years – Chana Dubinski – but also the 'self and the others', the now dead and not-yet-dead ones, the micro-selves contained within Bean's consciousness. Bean is insistent that the 'self' is fluid, that the 'etc' is as significant as the 'self' it multiplies. She lives the lives as others walk the walk in her 'wilfully untenable acts', as Dominic Johnson puts it in his opening essay.

'Nothing is True – All is Permitted', reportedly uttered by the Master of the Assassins, Hassan-i Sabbah, could be the motto of her venturings – except for the fact that despite her apparent ability to put herself in sometimes physical, if not psychic danger in the random circumstances she finds herself in, she is also a regular, vulnerable human, who – as she says in 'The Audience as Battery', our interview in this book – 'does not want to be an art sacrificial lamb'.

These essays, then, explore the various selves of Anne Bean. Like Gurdjieff's exercise of 'self-re-membering', referred to in Dominic Johnson's essay, we are indeed 'racking our brains' wondering what the 'self' is all about. Lynn MacRitchie explores the 'self and the others' in her juxtaposition of Anne Bean's work and a group of influential female artists who are no longer alive but live on in our lives and in Bean's. I have tried, in my essay, to assemble the mischievous versions of memory that were created by moments of collaboration with her, where the 'critic' – which I am – becomes fuel for creation and destruction. In two interviews, the voices of Bean and her long-term collaborators, Richard Wilson and Paul Burwell can be heard, Burwell being also one of Anne's many 'selves' beyond his death.

Voices can be heard from elsewhere – the artist Poshya Kakl describes how meeting Bean in Iraqi Kurdistan changed her life and gave her permission to make performance art in a place of danger. Guy Brett invokes the spirit of Ana Mendieta in a comparison with Anne Bean's later work. Finally physicist and philosopher Ezra Rubinstein makes the important point that the many selves of Bean align pretty appositely with our current understanding of quantum entanglement and cosmology.

These texts are all tied together by visual essays and interventions composed by the artist herself, to ultimately freeze-frame a moment in the complex construct that is the life and work of Anne Bean. It is there, hopefully to be enjoyed, to enliven, to disturb, to tease, to scare, to amuse and finally challenge the notion of the many *et ceteras* that seem to define the 'self'.

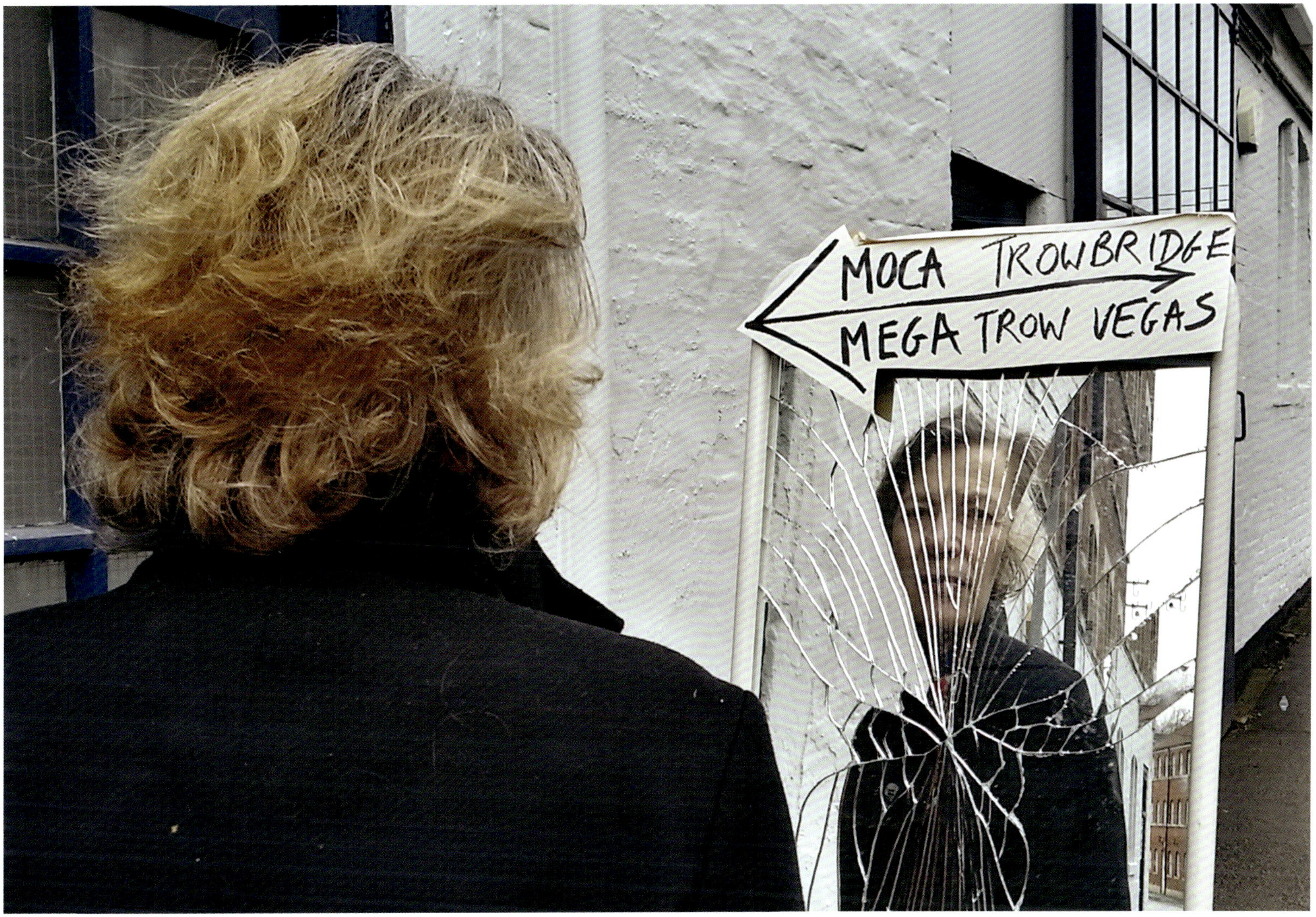

Above: Anne Bean, *MoCa to Mega,* an installation at Moments of Consciousness and..., Trowbridge, alongside *Trow Vegas* tour with local artist Meg Mosley. Photo: Peter Fink

p. 6: Anne Bean, untitled performance with the Kipper Kids, Los Angeles, 1979. Photo: Elisa Leonelli

pp. 10-11: Anne Bean, *She Perceiving Her* with Manuel Vason, River Thames, 2016

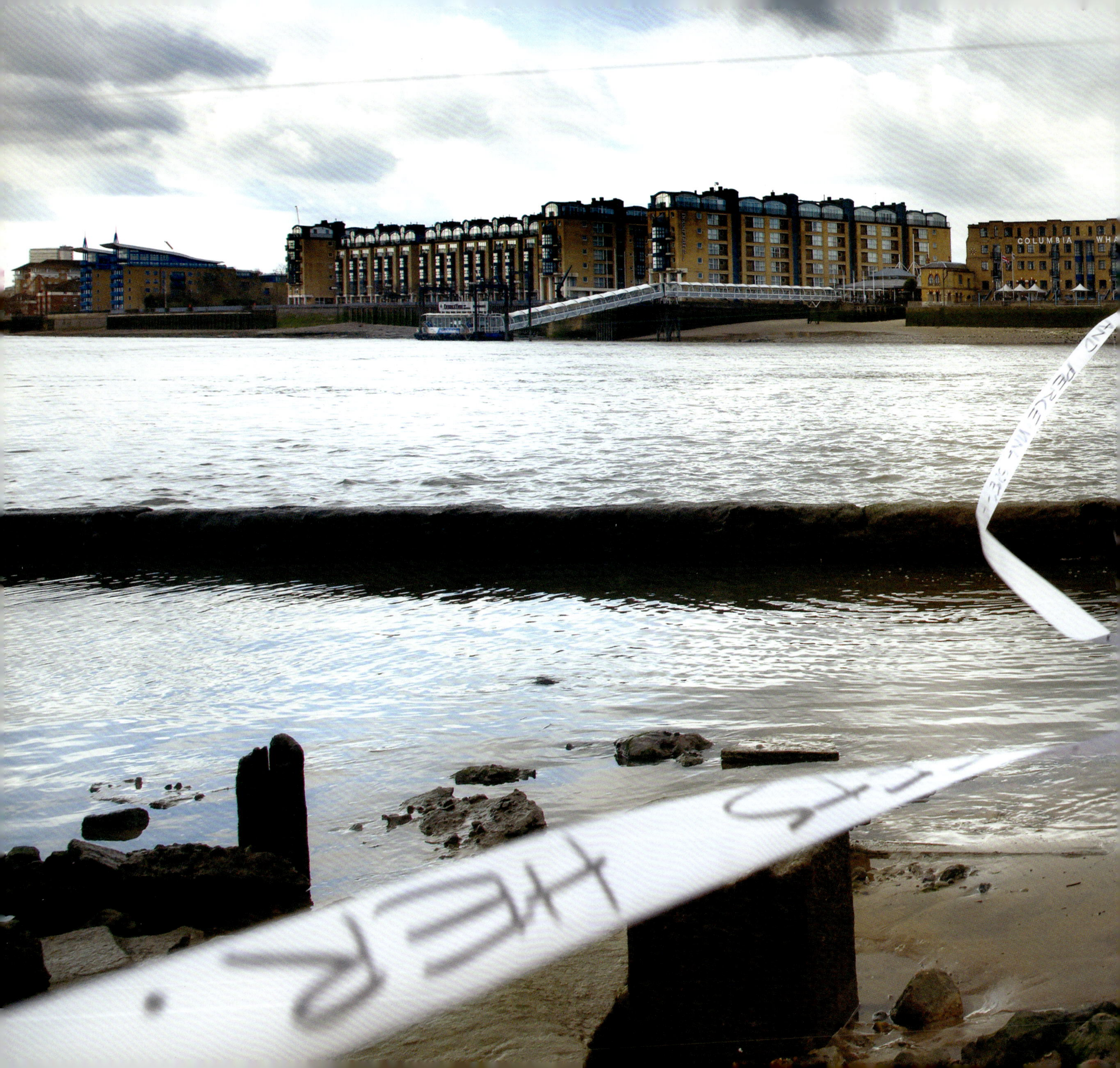
COLUMBIA
HER.

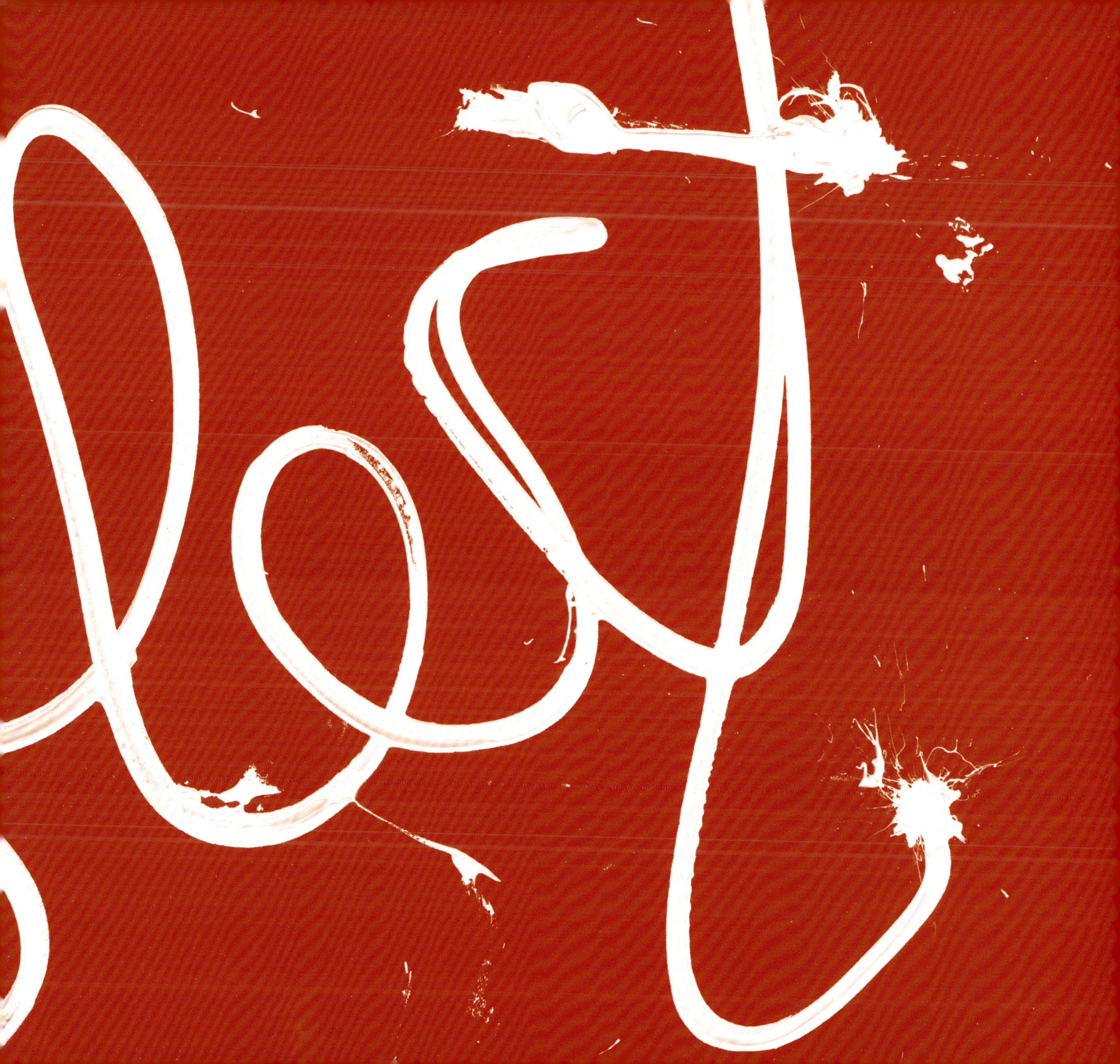

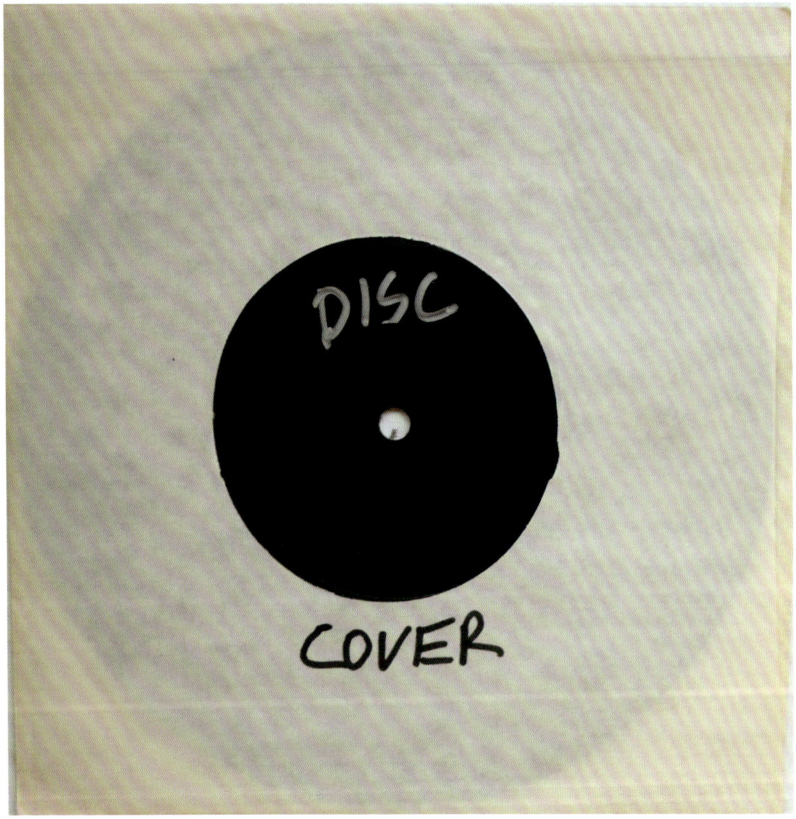

Low Flying Aircraft (1979), a single by PULp MUSIC (Anne Bean and Paul Burwell)

SELF ETC APPEARED IN REFLECT
TIME WENT BACKWARDS FOR EMIT
TAPS SCRAMBLED PAST
A YEAR BECAME A YEARNING
A DRESS BECAME A REDRESS
ANXTIONS HELD ANXIOUS ACTIONS
WAR REVERSED TO RAW
A WOUND UNWOUND
A LEAD MAN IS ALSO A LEAD MAN
WAKE AWOKE, TRACKING TURBULENCE AND VIGILS
AUTOBITUARY AND ORBITUARIES
RABBITEARS FUSED RABBI TEARS AND RABBIT EARS
A TEAR IS A TEAR
LIVE IS ALSO LIVE
A TRANSPECTIVE
DISC COVER

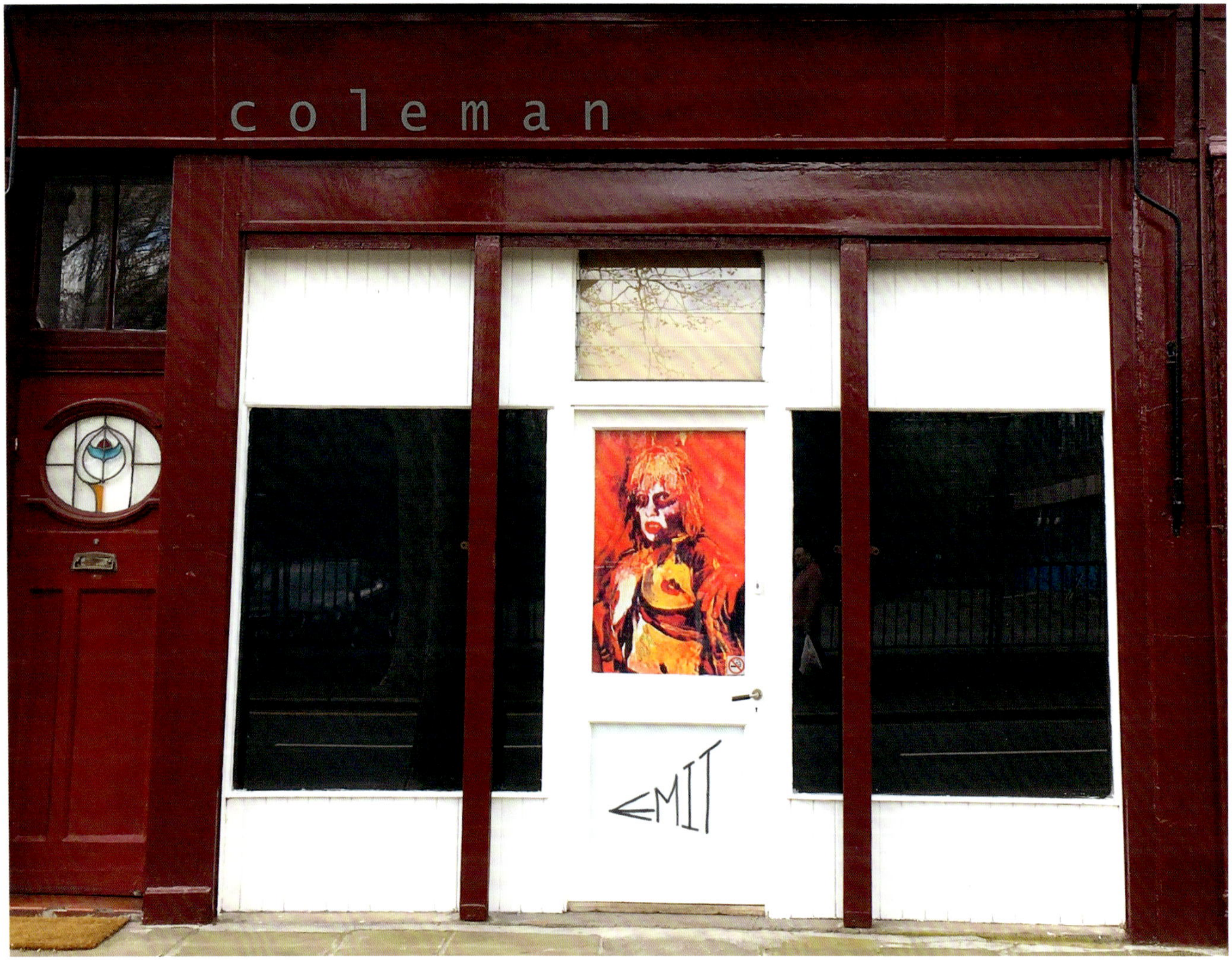

Above: EMIT exhibition, Coleman Project Space, London, 2017. Photo: Anne Bean

Opposite: Anne Bean, *LIVE LIVE*, Live Art Development Agency, launch of new space, 2017. Photo: Alpay Beler

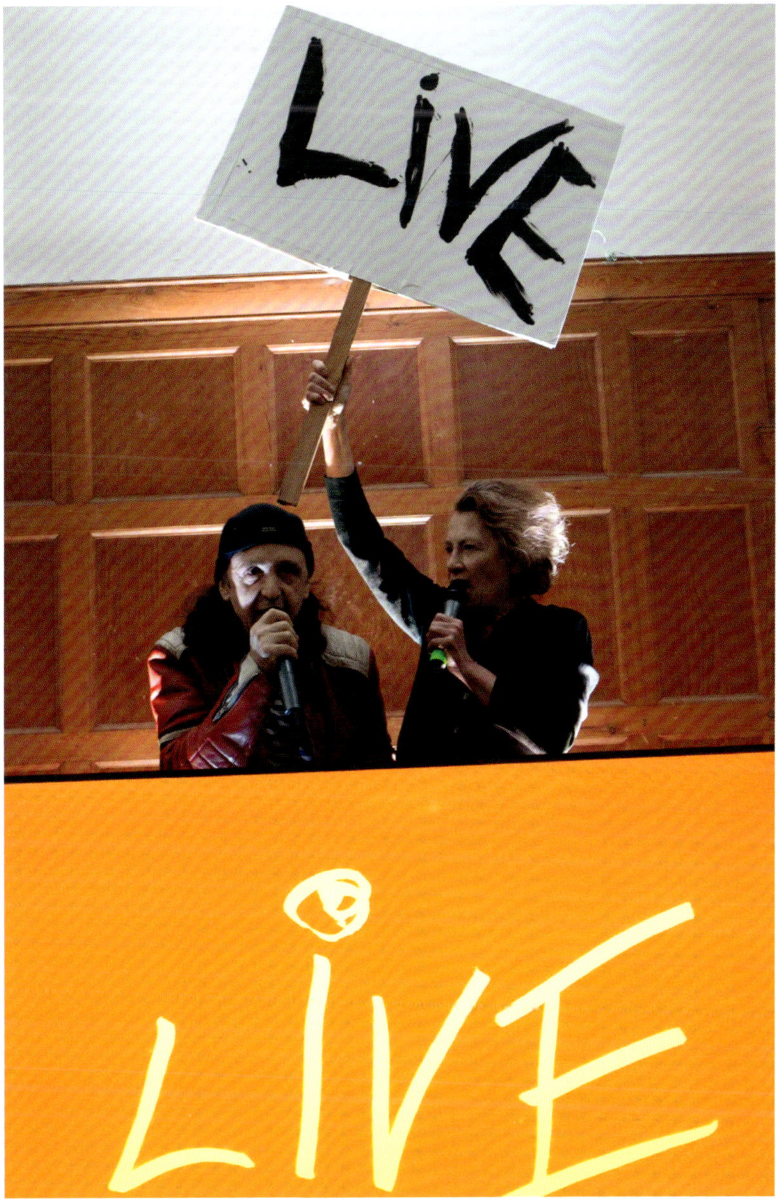
LIVE
LIVE

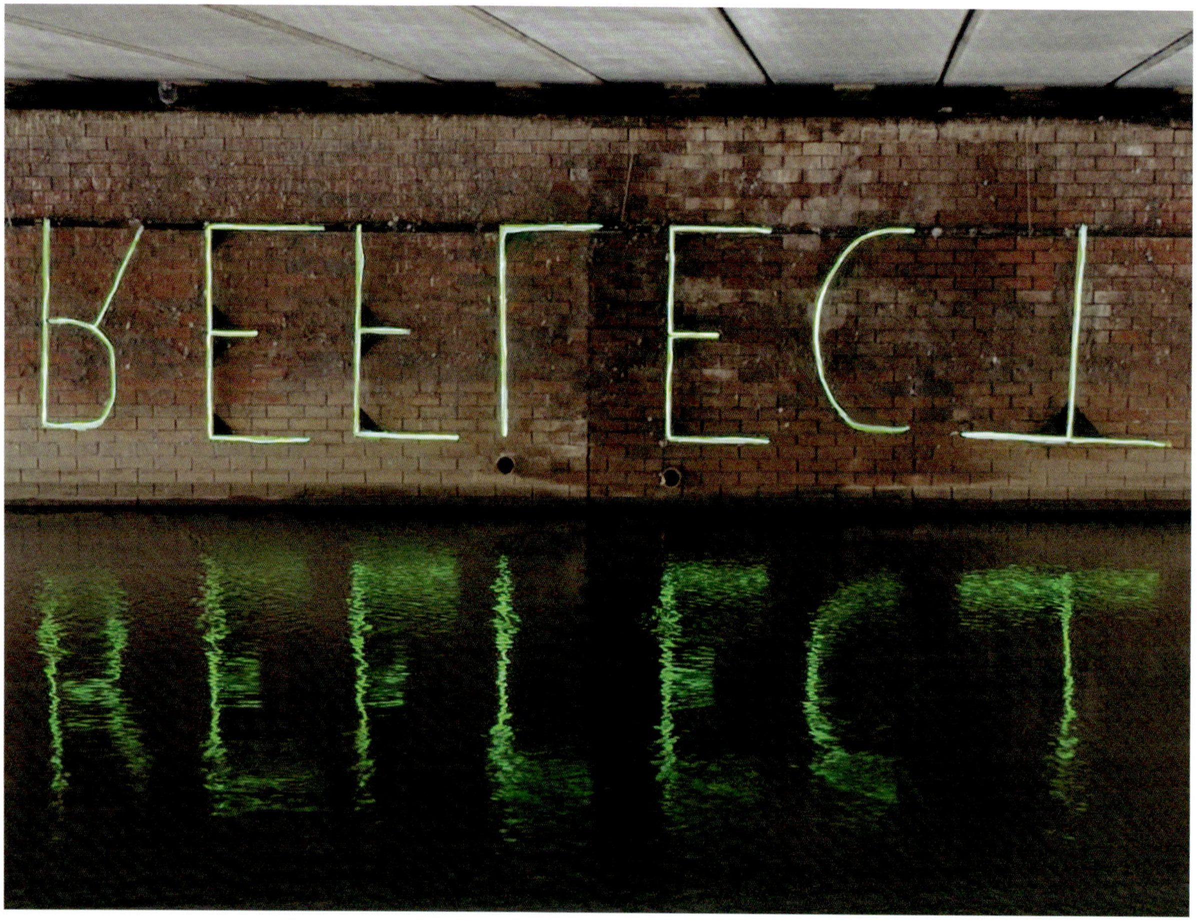

Anne Bean, *Reading Water*, under Forbury Bridge, Reading, 2016

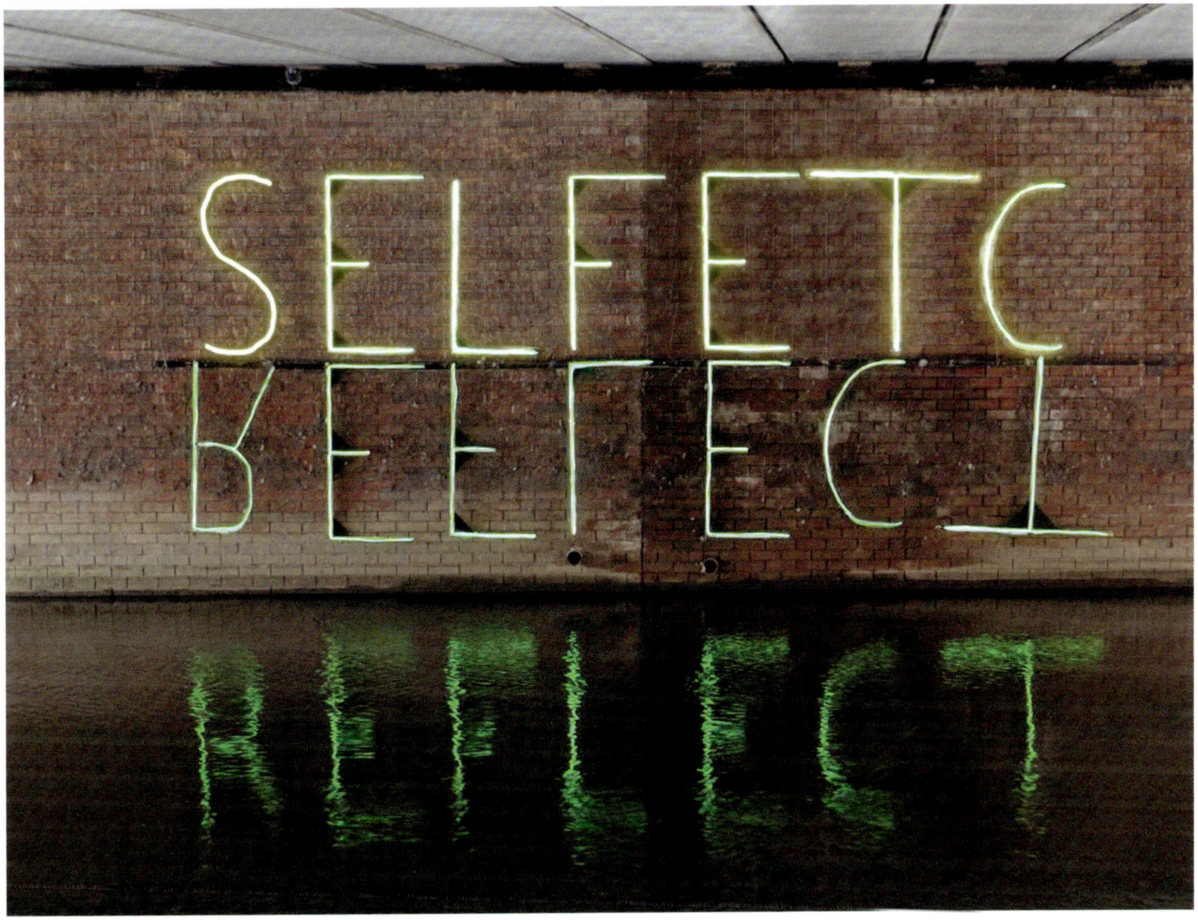

Anne Bean, annotated image of *Reading Water*. I saw 'SELFETC' emerging as I contemplated an upside-down 'REFLECT'

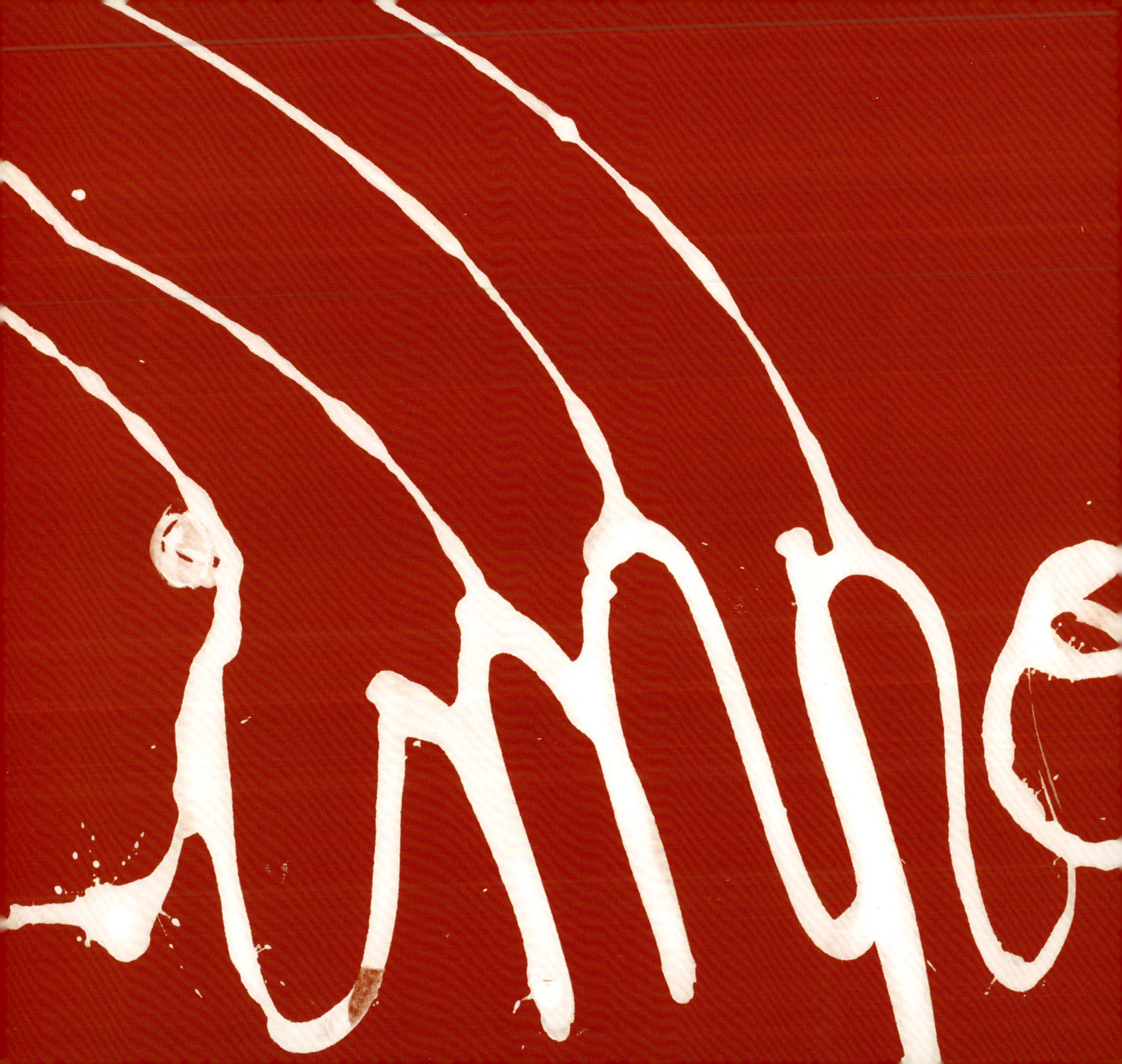

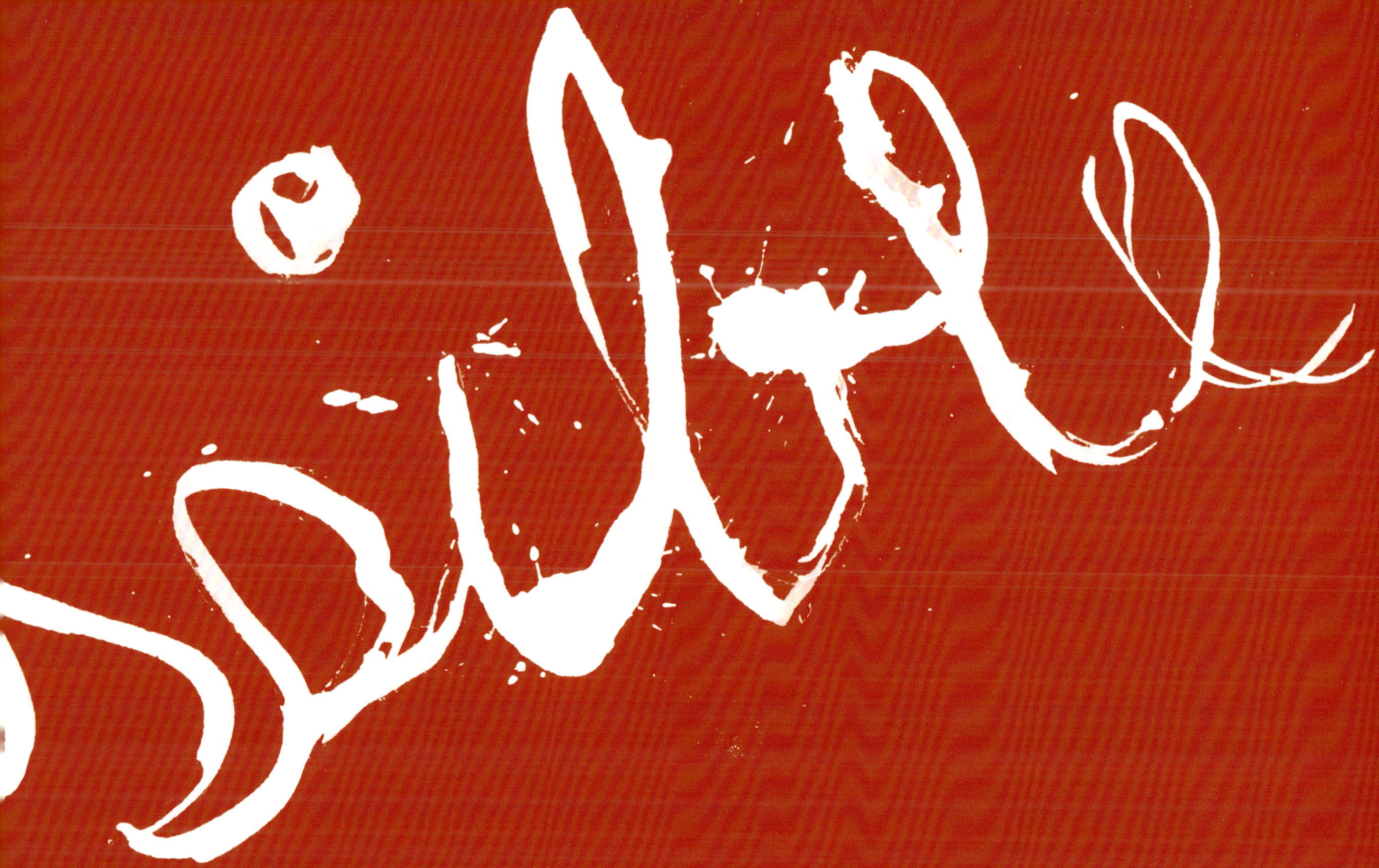

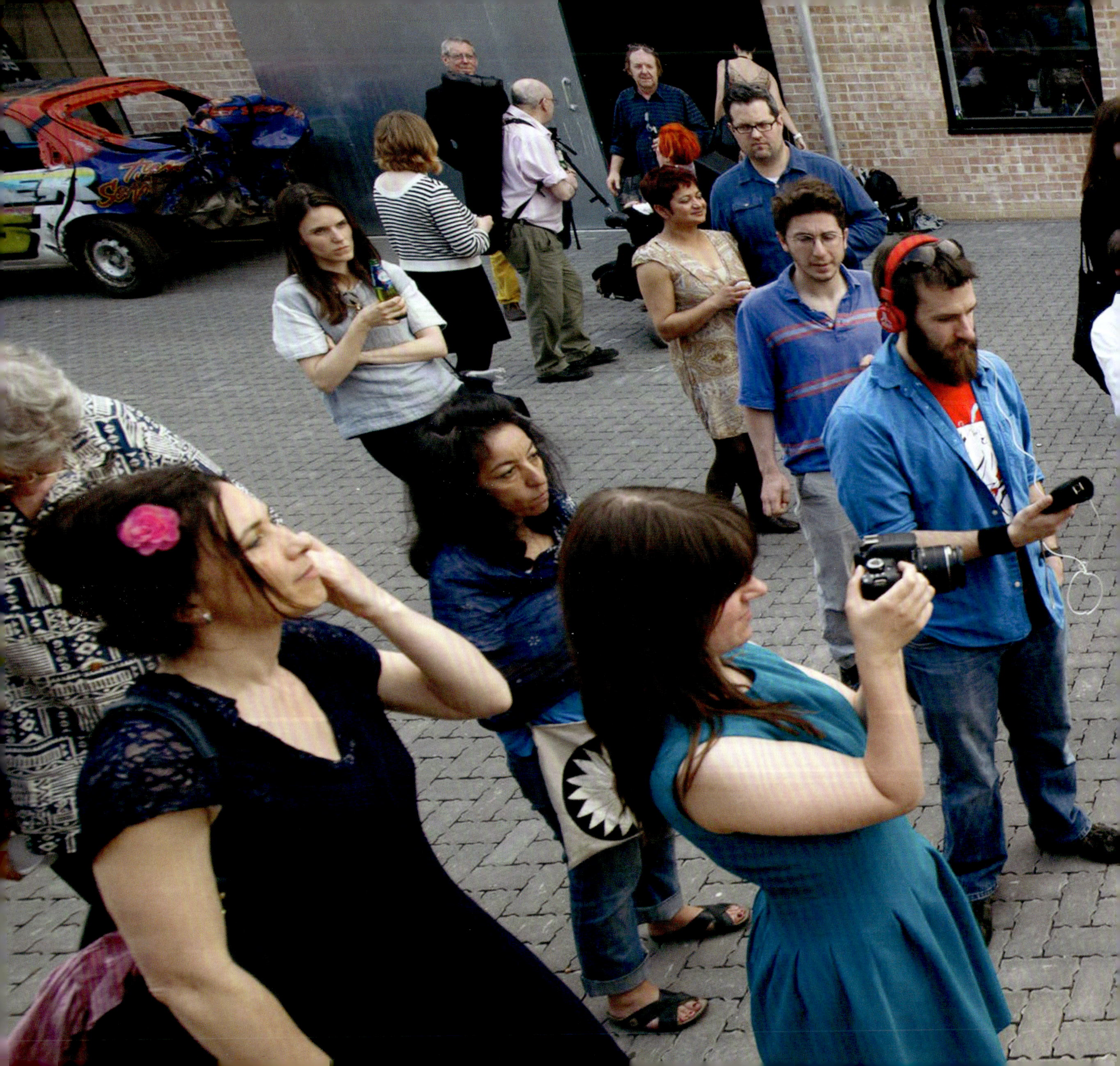

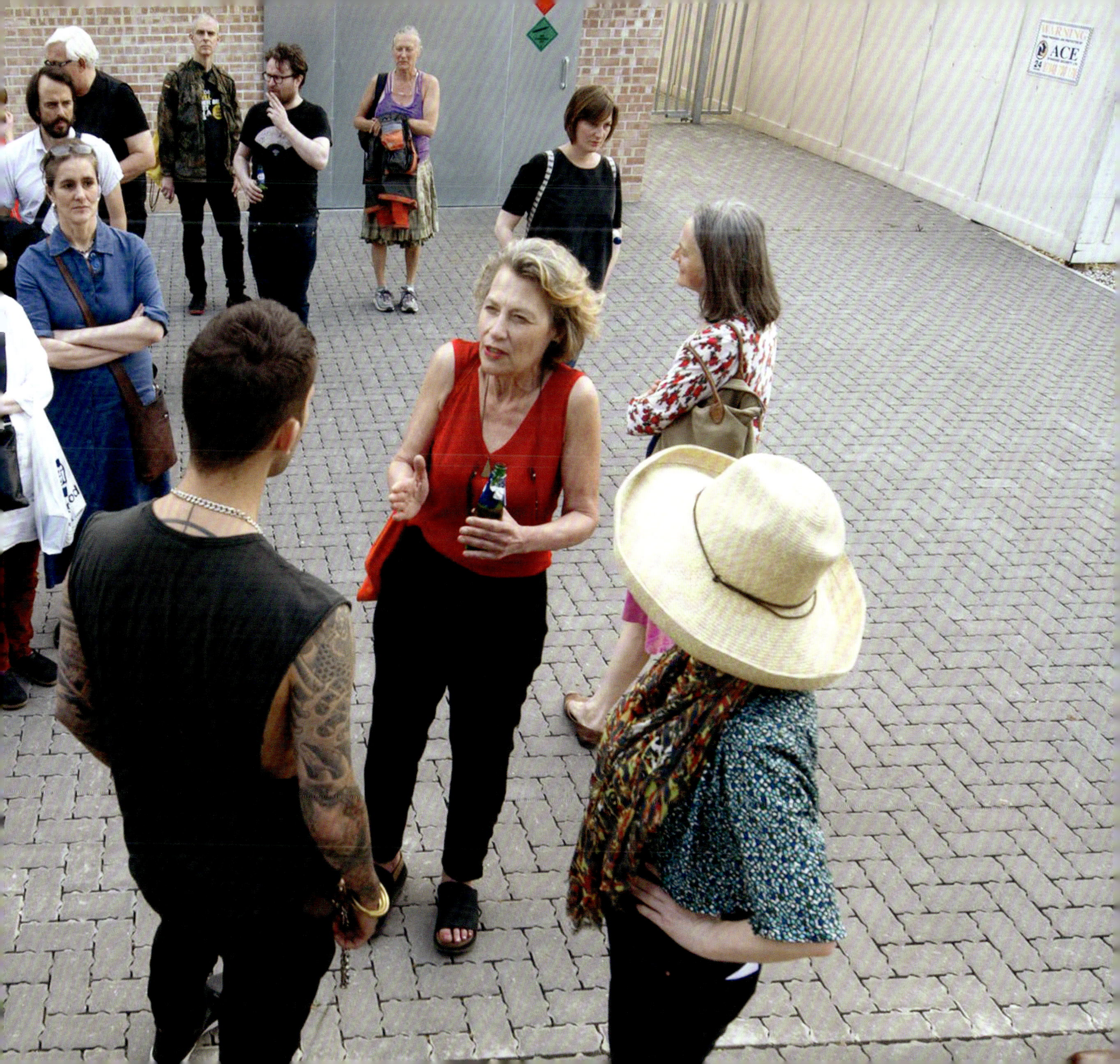
WARNING
ACE

IMPOSSIBLE THINGS: THE LIFE ART OF ANNE BEAN IN THE 1970S

DOMINIC JOHNSON

You can't force a story that doesn't want to be told.
— **Eileen Myles**

The Whitechapel Gallery Archive holds a letter to Anne Bean from the curators of *A Short History of Performance Vol. 1* (2002) a major retrospective of performance art of the 1960s and 1970s.[1] In the form letter – also sent to Yoko Ono, Carolee Schneemann, Paul McCarthy, Vito Acconci, Stuart Brisley, Gilbert & George and others – Andrea Tarsia and Iwona Blazwick invited Bean to 're-live a small number of pivotal performances, once again bringing them in direct relation with an audience.' Bean replied with a postcard to Tarsia to politely decline, writing: 'I have to be honest and say that I don't consider any of my work either renowned or pivotal in the sense of this "season".'[2] More than mere humility, Bean's refusal signals a conviction about the status of her performances, the nature of the relationship between her performances as a continuum, and the role of the continuum as an anchor for the broader edifice of a life.

In Anne Bean's practice since the late 1970s, the principles of her work and their attendant values have remained more or less consistent: her performances are never scripted in advance beyond a basic score, never repeated or re-performed (though sometimes 'reformed', or returned to and reinterpreted anew), and inconsistently documented. Working principles include her refusal or emphatic side-lining of photographic and audio-visual documentation; practices of differing durations, from the very short to the very long, necessitating a definite refusal of the convention of theatrical or cinematic time; the use of *povera* ('poor') or pedestrian materials, including found or pre-loved objects; and the disavowal of a signature style. Bean often refrains from making key decisions until the day of a performance – decisions that then remain provisional, and may be abandoned in the course of a performance, should its undertaking seem to require it.

Taken together, Bean's performances, public interventions, drawings, videos, and writings are actively pursued as a 'continuum,' and she strives to diminish the distinctiveness or iconicity of each, in favour of a democracy of forms and effects. No single performance may take precedence over another, nor may it be pulled free from the complications of the life from which it grows. In an interview, Bean tells me,

> By being a continuum, art includes all the life 'in between'. It's just the truth of it. That's how the work happens, in among other practices of life. So, those moments in a life that happen to have a photograph or a bit of video attached, they are simply butterflies caught in a net. ... The work, and the life, and everything in between – the *fluidity* of it – all of it is equally valid.[3]

She invents a new term to define her work: 'I tend to say "life art," she explains, adding, '[m]aybe one doesn't need any nomenclature at all.' As a summation of her orientation to art, she continues to ask, 'How can one seamlessly integrate one's work into just living?'[4] A life can no longer, here, be represented as left unadulterated by what is done in or as art. Nor might individual butterflies be picked from the net, and subjected to scrutiny as evidence of her or its significance. As she writes in a note on her web archive, pursuing the theme: 'The flight is the thing. Not the pinned butterflies.'

Amid Bean's mutually connective series of works of the 1970s, my attention is drawn to her iconoclastic series *Imposters*, which she performed as interventions in Reading in 1970, and in London from 1971. Dressed in variously eccentric attire – slightly emphatic versions of her everyday experiments in pedestrian couture – Bean and friends would create 'im-posters' – impossible posters, non- or anti-posters – first by wheat-pasting large blank sheets to walls, also by pasting sheets featuring a single suggestive word, and subsequently by 'cancelling' existing posters by overlaying them with new images and texts.

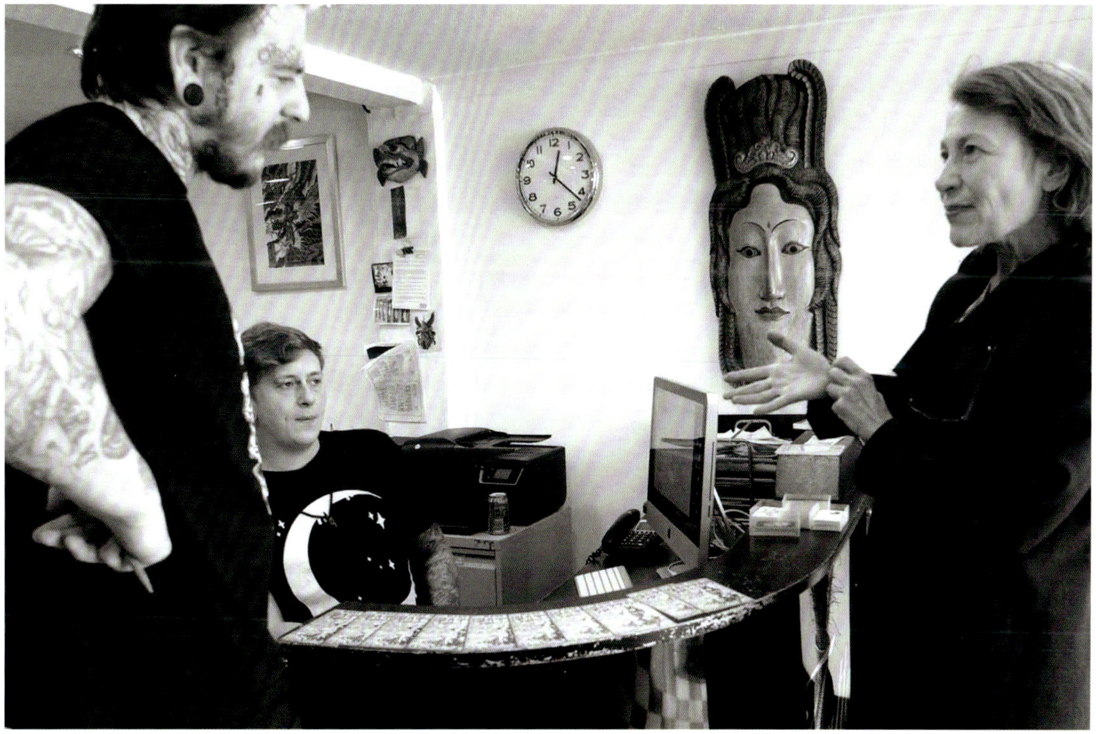

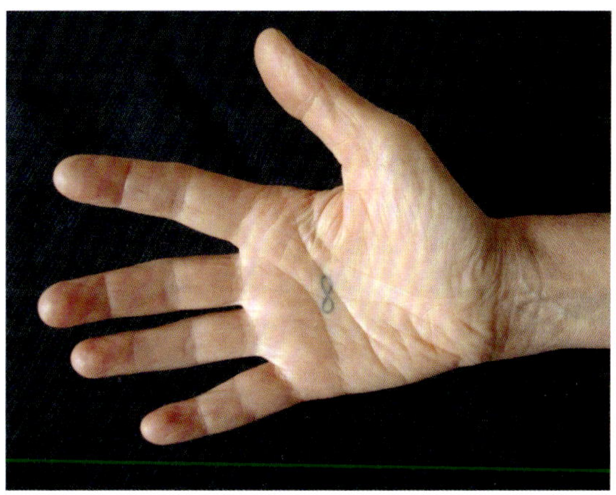

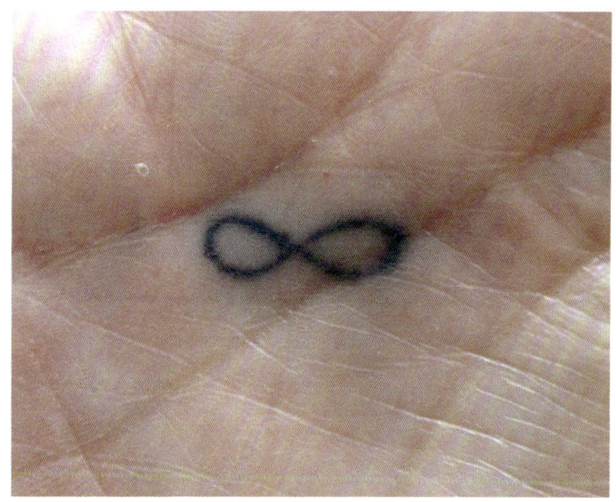

Top: Anne Bean, *Holding Infinity in the Palm of my Hand* (tattoo), Brick Lane Tattoo Parlour, 2015. Photo: Markéta Luskačová

Bottom: Anne Bean, *Between Heart and Head Line* (tattoo). Photo: David Caines

pp. 22-3: Anne Bean, *The ABCD ness of it All: Ceci n'est pas une performance* (by chance with Dominic Johnson and Elyssa Livergant). Part of Aaron Williamson and Kate Mahony's season *Sculpture-Performance: Acme Artists Now*, Purfleet, 2014. Photo: Hugo Glendinning

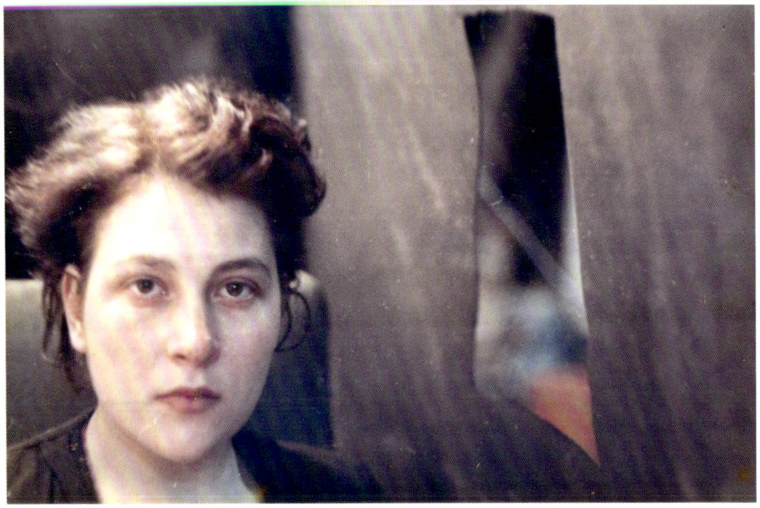

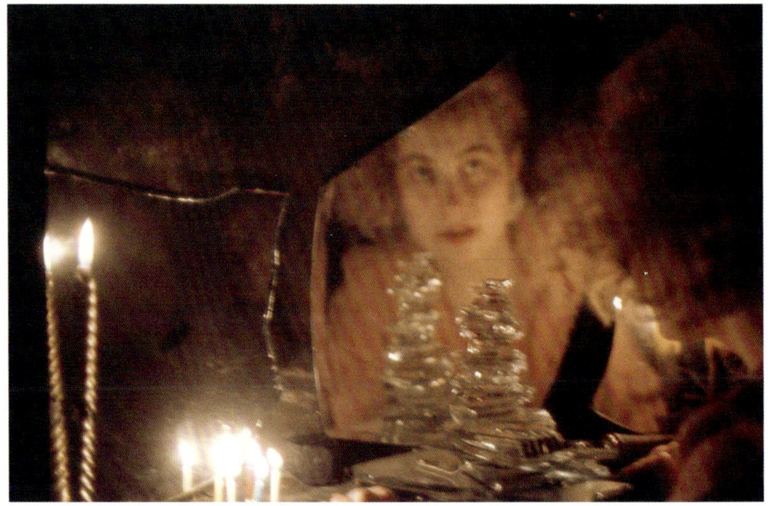

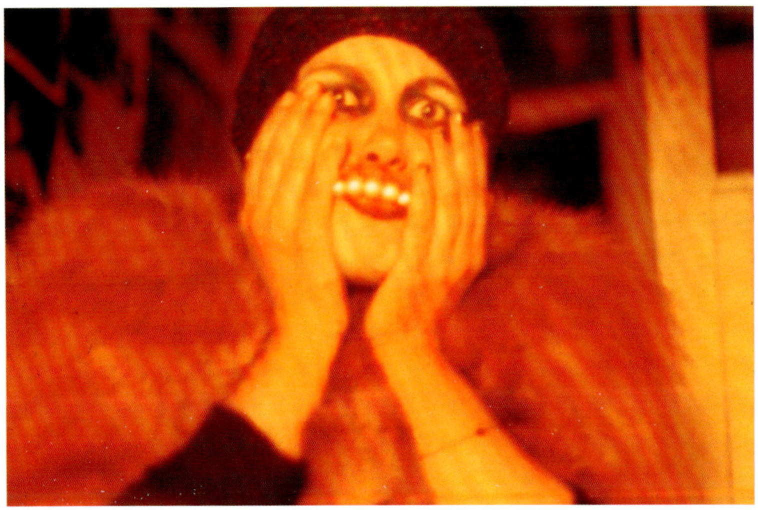

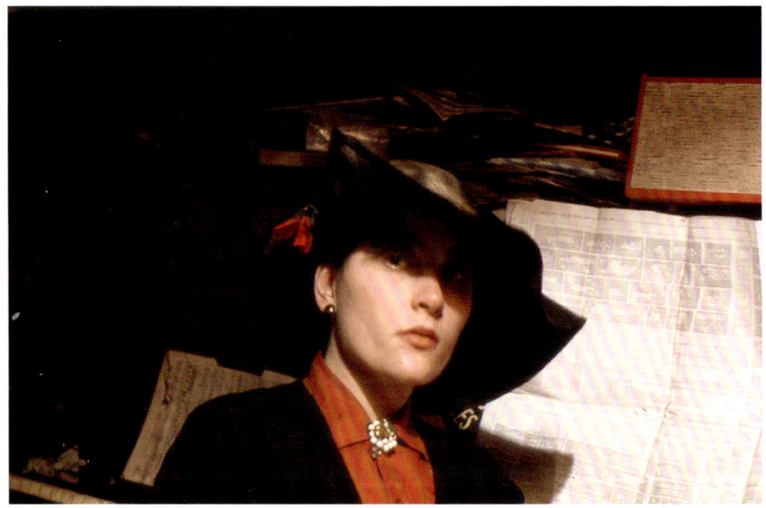

Top left: Anne Bean, *Until the Flowers Die*, a 24-hour event for BA dissertation project, *What is Art and What am I Doing in It?* Photo: Martin von Haselberg

Top right: Anne Bean, *A Party*, Bill's Bargain Shop, Reading, 1971. The performance began in complete darkness and everyone was invited to bring a candle and a mirror. Photographer unknown

Bottom left: Anne Bean, *Between Gritted Teeth*, Reading, 1971. Trying to keep pearls in place in my mouth, whilst singing the Buck Owens song *(All I Gotta Do is) Act Naturally.* Photographer unknown

Bottom right: Anne Bean, score for *Irma*, a 1969 experimental opera by Tom Phillips, Fred Orton and Gavin Bryars (an interpretation with Rod Melvin), Reading, 1971. Photo: Alastair Brotchie

In one such action, in East London in 1971, Bean searched out posters for the Whitechapel Gallery's first *East London Open* exhibition. In 1971, it used the tagline 'Who Selects the Selectors?' to foreground the ideological constraints of curatorial and institutional practice, suggesting that the gallery's selection of curators conditions and sustains aesthetic imperatives at the institutional level. Regardless, Malcolm Jones' submission to the Whitechapel's open call was rejected on what Bean remembers as 'practical reasons' that complicated or exceeded the 'open' nature of the exhibition.[5] In an elliptical response, Bean, Malcolm Jones, Natasha Lawrence, and Martin von Haselberg sought out the advertisements for the exhibition and covered them with new posters featuring an image of Jones' work stencilled with the word 'cancelled' across it in black letters. Approached for suspected vandalism, Bean – wearing a powdered face, lace bonnet, and flowing smock – attempted to explain to a policeman the semiotic trouble posed by the action: as the poster had been rendered an 'im-poster', or impossible object, she explained, one could not be held liable for its damage. The 'poster', now cancelled at an ontological level, had ceased to exist and could no longer be subject to vandalism. Von Haselberg's photographs show the uniformed policemen writing down Bean's and Lawrence's explanations on a small pad. Baffled by the artists' philosophical expositions of the former poster's thorny ontological status, he let Bean and company go with a caution.

Bean's works in performance often proposed such ontological trouble. In *Digging a Hole in Water* (1973), Bean performed a *kōan*: a Zen practice of active meditation devoted to the inauguration of 'great doubt,' akin to the riddle of one hand clapping. Invited to perform at Essex University, Bean asked a number of her peers to present a *kōan* towards a curriculum of non-standard intellectual experiments, a kind of anti-university premised on performance. Her own action involved the impossible attempt to dig through the surface and density of a lake. In a document from the action, Bean stands half-submerged, slinging a shovelful of water, engaged in a Sisyphean task of apparent meditative intensity that lasted some three hours. The sole photograph that survives it is the only material change Bean can hope to achieve in the action; any significant transformation in the moment is registered in her commitment to the impossible action, and the effects on her concentration, belief, or thought that her commitment might engender. Like the *Imposters* series, *Digging a Hole in Water* was explicitly interventionist in activating the urban environment, and relational in its provocation of a philosophical conversation with an incidental audience: passers-by, or a policeman. In other performances, Bean foregrounds more explicitly her political agency, engaging with risk, negative affects, and personal culpability.

In its secrecy or humility, the work of Anne Bean is *formally* enigmatic, and materially hidden – or *occulted* – from view, hence her refusal, or incapacity, to invoke a single work's iconicity in the ways required by the Whitechapel. Bean's framing of her work suggests her commitment to *being insignificant*, to remaining beyond the pale, without significance, and without renown. How and with what effects might an artist choose insignificance, or invisibility, as their working principle? How do the effects of one's commitment, in this regards, differ from the passive situation of being ignored or actively overlooked, by institutions of art, art history, and art criticism?

In a public discussion with the Kipper Kids in 2003, at the National Review of Live Art, Bean reiterated her position: 'I feel nothing we've done has been significant.' One of the Kipper Kids, Martin Von Haselberg replies, 'Thanks a lot, Anne!', prompting peals of laughter from the audience. Bean clarifies her position, mollifying the perceived insult that enables the joke, by explaining their collective ethos in the 1970s:

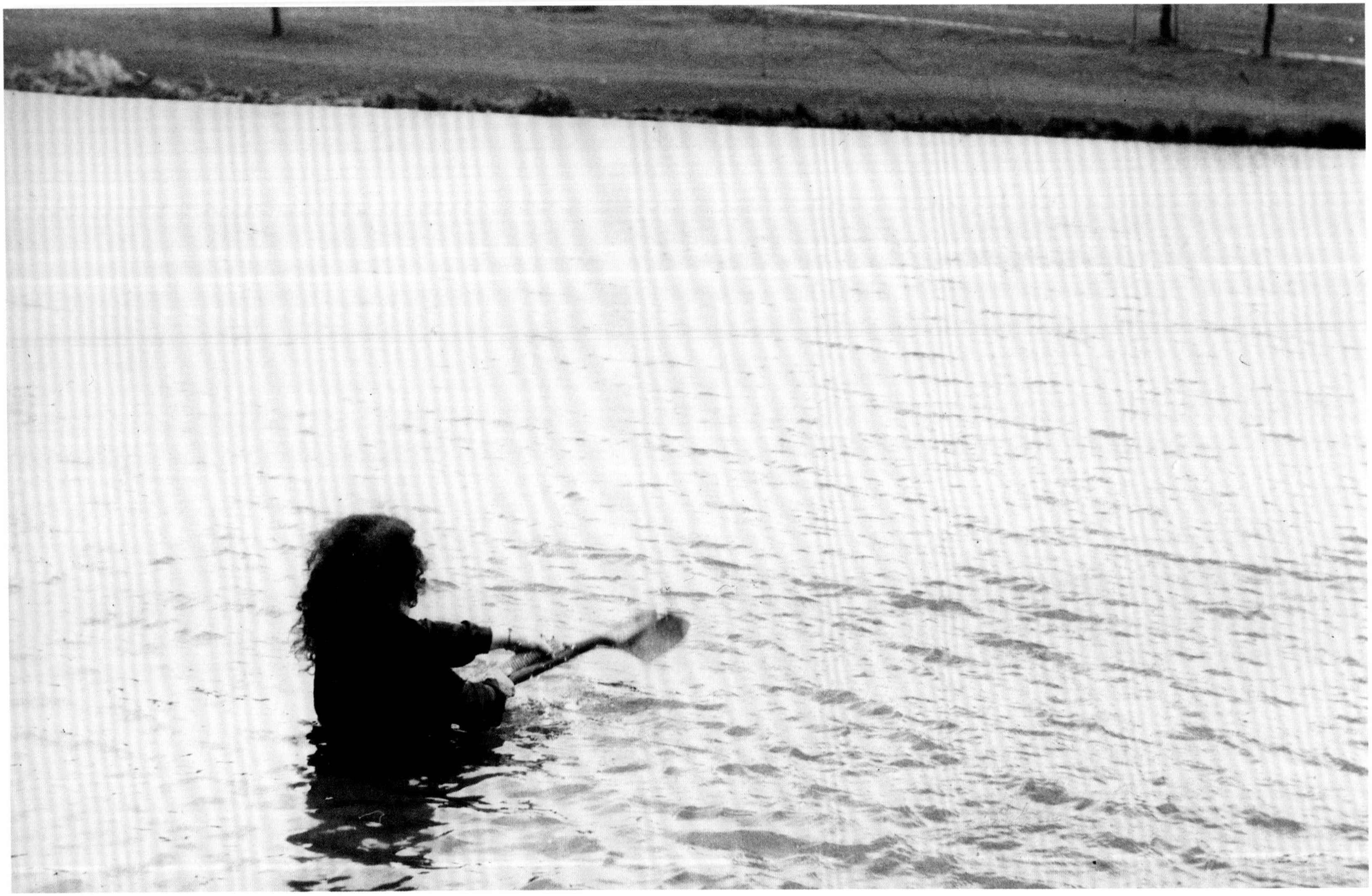

Anne Bean, *Digging a Hole in Water*, Lakeside, Essex, 1973. Photo: Martin von Haselberg

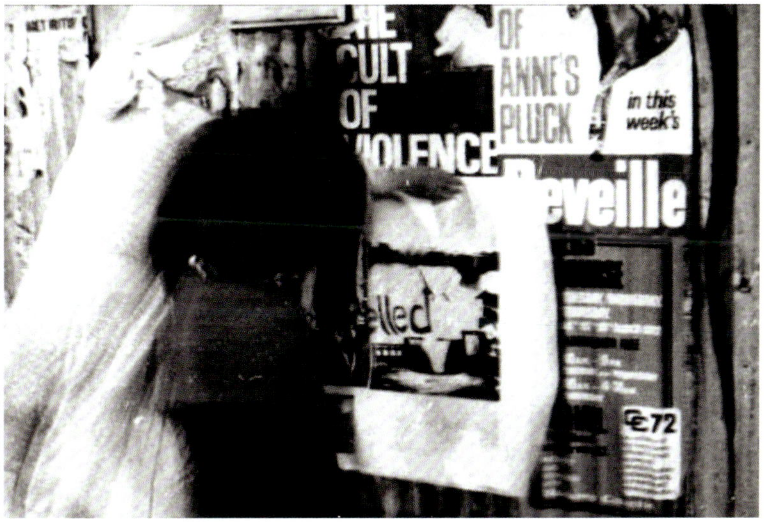

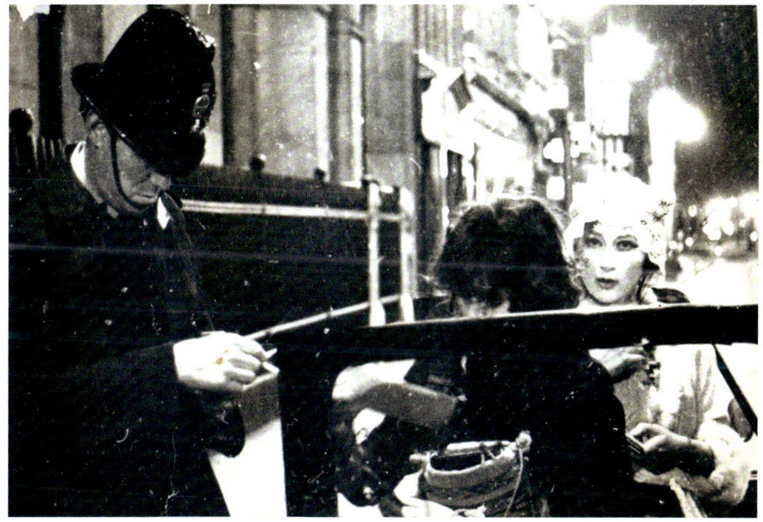

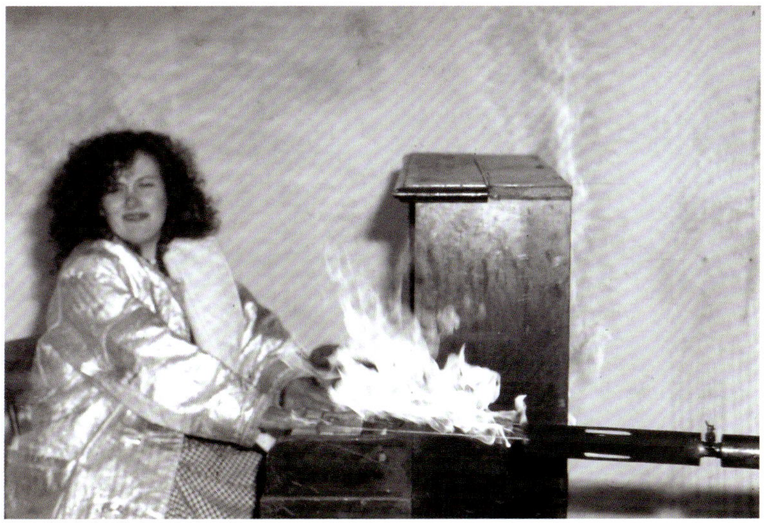

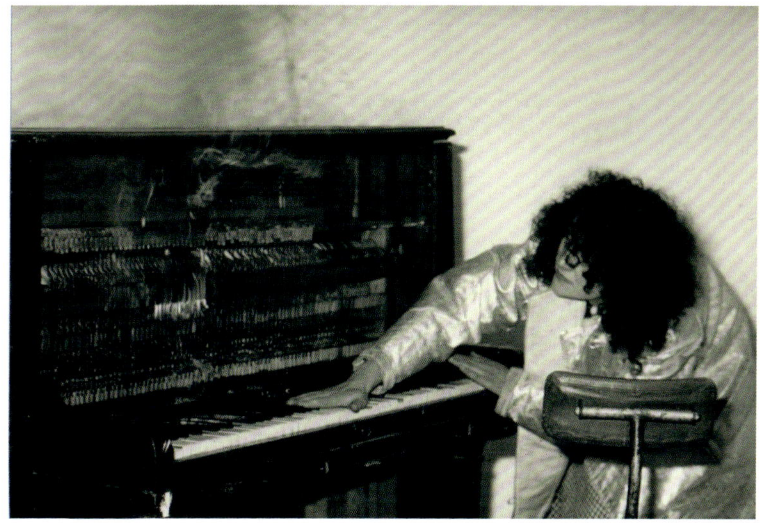

Top: Anne Bean with Natasha Lawrence, *Imposters*, London, 1971. Photos: Martin von Haselberg

Bottom: Anne Bean, Paul Burwell and Stephen Cripps, *Burning Piano*, Butlers Wharf, London, 1979. Photo: Chris Bishop

> I think it was about *not* being significant, about small gestures, about being together, about trying things out, about risking and experimenting. It was about present time, and not documenting, about free floating and being open to different situations and ... explorations ... I think there was very much an attitude [among us] of things being of the moment, and not of the marketplace.[6]

Bean performs a paradoxical, ambivalent, or enigmatic project towards being both historically *impersonal*, and creatively, personally *singular*. She suspends her own significance, or dominance, while attempting to become unorthodox and therefore fully oneself. The tension signals Bean's anti-masculinist, anti-capitalist, and anti-spectacular stance as an artist – the seeking of a non-position, or invisible position without *station*. Moreover, I argue, her performances draw upon and internalise a set of esoteric reference points and unfamiliar ways of being, thinking and doing that are metaphysical in nature or form, and inscrutable at heart. This speaks to Bean's apparent elision from broader histories of art and performance, for Bean's practice of art finds itself at a conceptual limit: a limit of the visible and the intelligible. She mandates her own work's willed insignificance, and undermines its receptiveness to criticism and historicity.

The pursuit of an impossible practice in performance finds form in Bean's prolific continuum of works since the late 1960s. In the countercultural rhetoric of the 1970s, she sought to *actualise* herself, not in a final, authentic fashion, but as a perpetual work-in-progress, as though this unfinished work of the self could be the subtle, provisional triumph of a deconditioned subjectivity. This argument entails a strange or perilous route through and about her work, and an esoteric direction in which to pursue the performance of extremity, taking in the theosophy of G. I. Gurdjieff – in which she was thoroughly immersed at the time – to end with a restatement of the persistence of her refusal to be fixed or found by history.

Throughout the continuum of her work and life, Bean sustains the dream of a democratic acceptance of any practice, action, or thing as the stuff of art. In 1969, Bean had immigrated to England from South Africa, and studied under the tutelage of the painter Rita Donagh at Reading School of Art. Donagh told Michael Bracewell that Bean embodied 'the feeling that anything could be art,' which was particularly current in the late 1960s and early 1970s, when Bean studied under her. Donagh continues, 'it was just how you did it, and what you did. Anne really understood that everything she did was her creative work'.[7]

The animation of all that which the self comes into contact with – as a vitalist imperative of sorts – involves Bean's subordination of self to chosen materials in performance, in the 1970s and after: to the slow *durée* of melting ice, the drip of honey, wilting flowers, the freezing of skin in snow; or the quick and dangerous temporalities of flames, fireworks, explosions, breaking glass, or the swirling undertows of a river in which her body might spontaneously drown while swimming in her lover's boat's wild wake. Each animated material, in encounter with Bean's body, seems bigger than she, much older, bolder, additionally vital, or more profound than the merely human, in whose wake she wants to move, without station.

Disappearance, enigma, and ineffability are particular germane to art after modernism. Especially after 1960, there is almost nothing to find in art, and certainly no intrinsic meaning, and no coherent subject-position outside of language from which to look. For Amelia Jones, the enigmatic nature of performance art, specifically, relies on its incessant slippage into the past, including in the duration of its experience as a live event, as well as when one engages with its documentation. Moreover, its elusiveness depends on the formal impossibility of subjective 'presence' to the material. Jones writes,

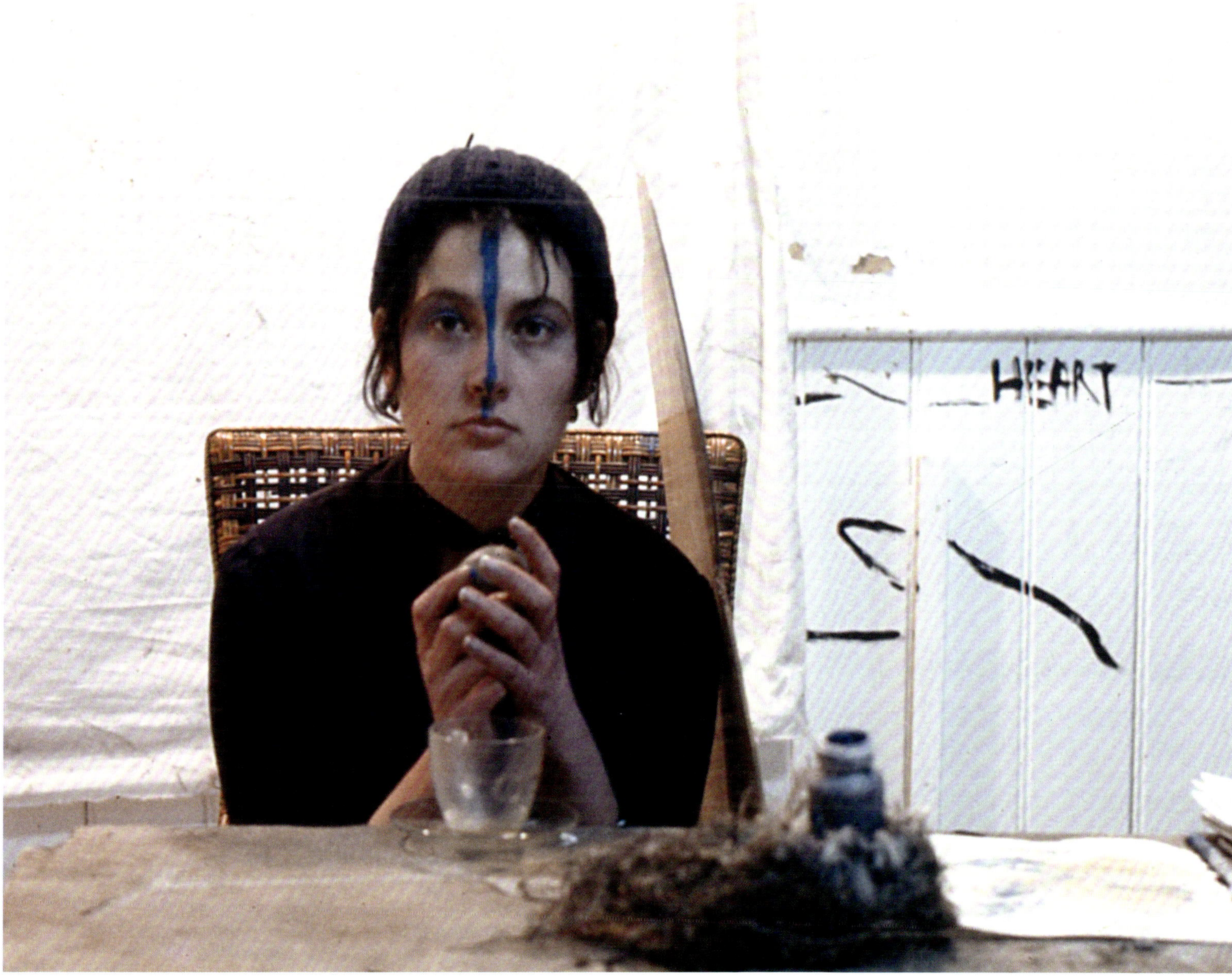

Above: Anne Bean, *Between Heart and Head*, Reading, 1971. Making a series of drawings and objects that were distinguished by coming from either the heart or the head. Photographer unknown

pp. 32-3: Anne Bean and the Kipper Kids, untitled performance at The Masque, Hollywood, Los Angeles, 1978. Photo: Elisa Leonelli

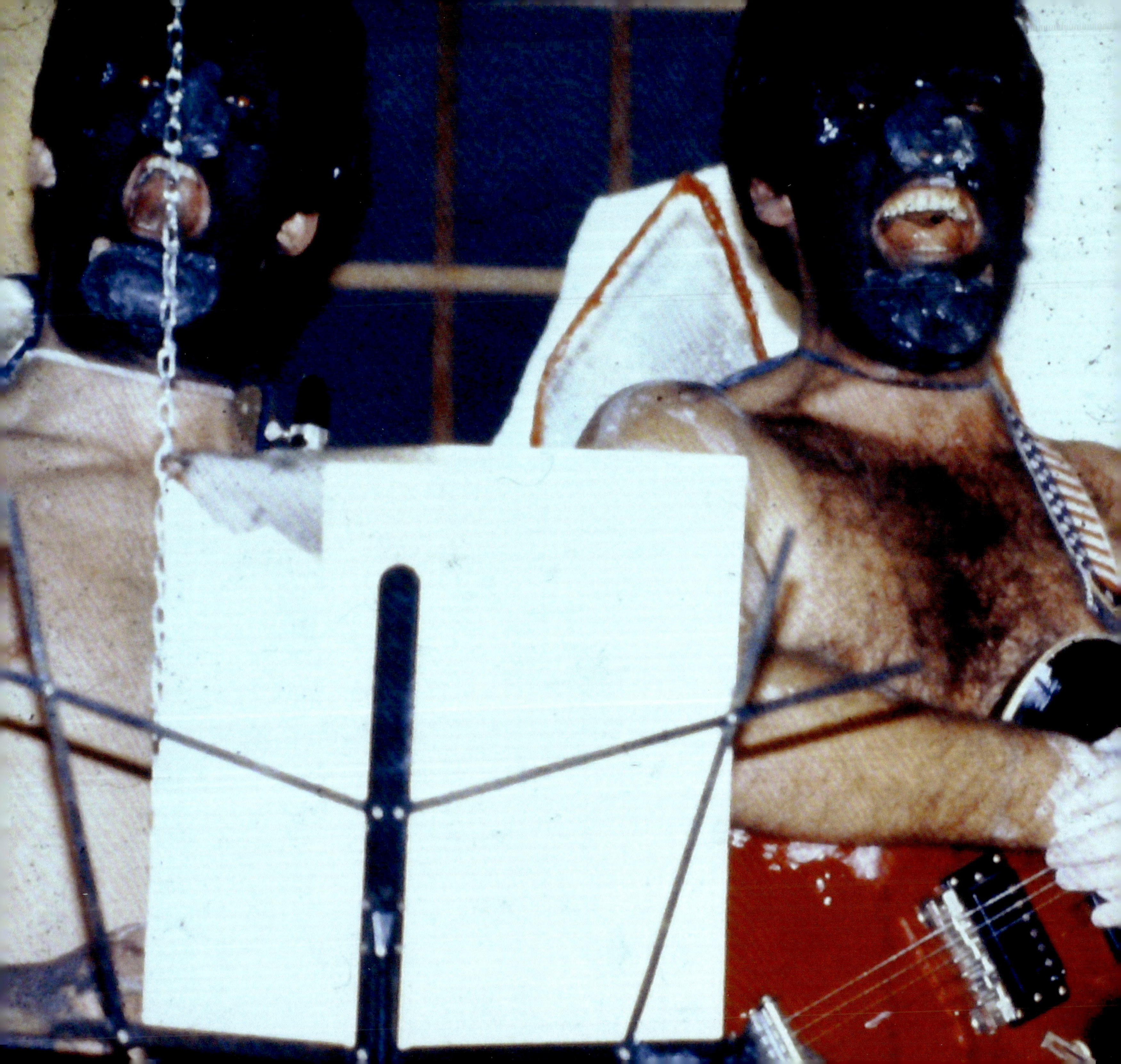

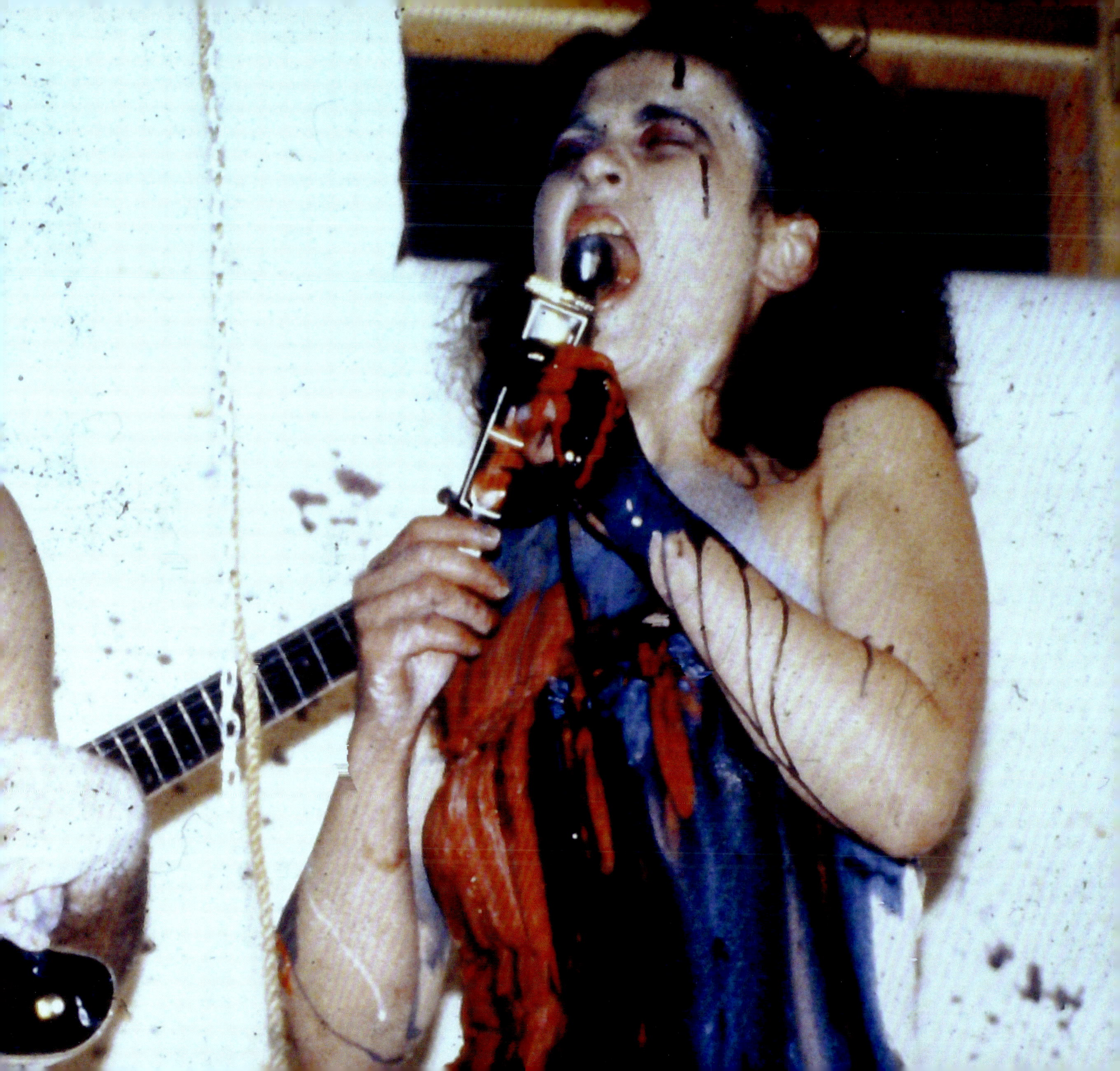

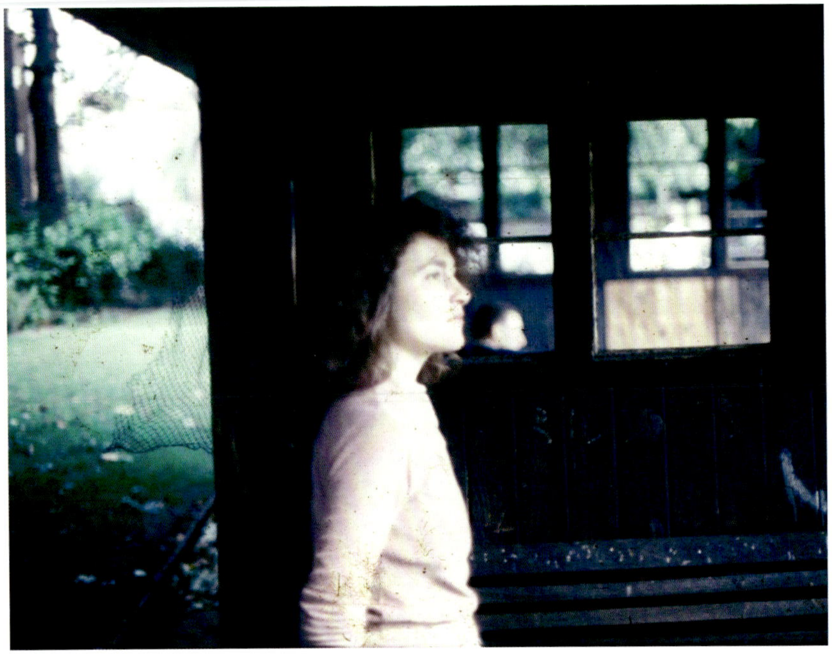

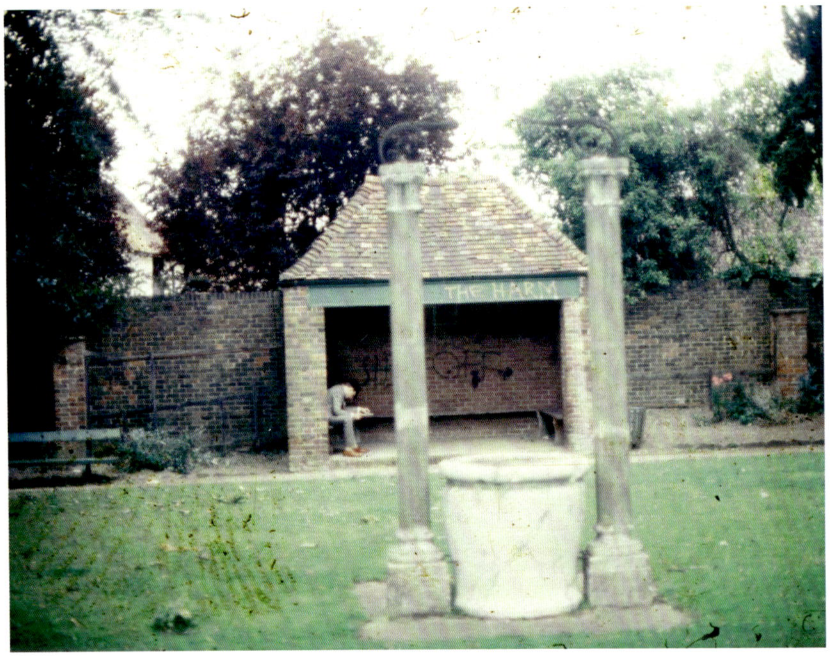

Anne Bean and Peter Davey, process images for *Anxtions*,
presented at Helen Chadwick's Hayward Annual, London, 1979

> We engage with art or performance because we want confirmation of (our own) presence, paradoxically by relating to works produced by another in the past. We want to defer endlessly the 'eternal return', the way in which we are continually opened to the other … even as we want fullness within our own enunciation of self. We seek this in performance art by clinging to a notion of the 'original event'. But … there is no original event; or, strictly speaking, there 'was' an event, but it was never … fully 'present'.[8]

For Jones, the claims of performance to authenticity, hermeneutic fullness, and pure presence – or, at least, the claims of artists and critics, and the silent claims of certain works themselves – signal an 'impossible' ambition at the core of performance. This central enigma is accentuated, Jones notes, by uncritical attempts to reclaim or master the lost object or event, which belie 'the impossibility of that fantasy of a return,' to authenticity, to an origin, or to presence.[9]

Necessarily, on account of Bean's absolute refusal of the significance of individual works and projects, and the terms upon which she affirms the radical continuity between performances, and between her work and her life, it is untenable, or at least counterproductive, fully to isolate particular instances of art from the broader wash in which they swim. While Bean categorically refuses the habitual disciplinary approach of selecting and iconicising a case study, the attempt to bring the continuum under scrutiny as a whole – to see Bean's work as demanding our attention, despite her secrecy – requires an attempt, at least, to depict some fragments of the continuum as it existed in the 1970s. Here and elsewhere, the described actions are to be recalled or encountered as a number of sites of difference along a continuum: as contiguous artefacts dotted around the interconnected skeins of a web.

Born in 1950 in Livingstone, Northern Rhodesia (then a British colony, and since 1964, the Republic of Zambia), Bean's earliest performances framed her conflicted identity as a white, Jewish woman in colonial Africa. Specifically, these took place after 1968, when Bean left Livingstone to study fine art in South Africa at the University of Cape Town. During her time there, Bean made *Net Blankes* (1969), a response to Apartheid, in which she sat on benches for 'Whites Only' (the English translation of her original title in Afrikaans), with parts of her body painted black: the palms of her hands, or one side of her face. The performances evaded the mimetic minstrelsy of blackface while asking how much of a person – their skin, constitution, or sense of self – must be black before one is excluded from segregated spaces. Bean put herself at risk in the actions: she recalls, 'I was always threatened, taken in for questioning and moved on by the police,' yet nevertheless felt 'strong, angry, scared'.[10] The works were intuitive – and perhaps naïve, in the sense that her conservative education in Cape Town, and the pioneering nature of her actions did not admit her much knowledge of the emergent historical genealogy of performance art (or of the racial politics of her image-making).

The performance series may have had little material efficacy, beyond the posing of an oblique question to passers-by, but it enabled Bean to address a political question that possessed her, and to mediate a problem that curtailed her happiness or subjective coherence. No documentation exists of these performances, and this transient or ephemeral nature prevents them from circulating or persisting beyond their status as hearsay, or legend.

After moving to England, Bean continued to mine the political efficacy of performance art, as interventions into public space, or as private performances for small, often invited audiences.

In *Raw/War* (1971), performed in London, Bean sliced the tip of her finger with a blade. Standing before a large sheet of plate glass, she used the same finger to write 'RAW' in blood, turned the glass around to reveal an approximation of the word 'WAR', and rammed her head against the glass until it shattered, lacerating her scalp. She painted her face with the issuing blood, along with spittle and pigment. For Bean, *Raw/War* enabled her to imagine the fear and danger in a way that created a relation (she tells me) of 'direct simpatico with a fearful situation, like hiding in a building with the windows being blown in.'[11] While performance can never fully approximate such an experience, the use of physical wounding, disruptive effects, and formal unpredictability create a relation of vague equivalence that is provocative for herself and for her witnesses.

In a similarly abrupt, undocumented performance series in 1970, Bean realised that walking with a dog allows one to shout a de-contextualised word (the dog's name) in public without the particular affront that other loud interruptions seem to cause. She acquired a dog, named it 'Mortality', and walked it at various public spaces, including Heathrow Airport, Glasgow Central Station, a street market in London, and the countryside, and created stealth performances by screaming the dog's name – 'MORTALITY!' – to the surprise, amusement, and probable annoyance of passers-by. The resulting series, *Mortality* (1970) used performance to shock incidental audiences into questioning social decorum, the proper and improper usages of public space, and perhaps one's own habitual relations (also governed by law, ritual and decorum) to life and death.

From 1976, she lived and worked in Butlers Wharf with the artist Paul Burwell, who used drumming as a sculptural technique to create performances on both an intimate and industrial scale. Situated on Shad Thames, Butlers Wharf was a converted studio complex where Bean and Burwell cohabited with artists including Derek Jarman, Andrew Logan, Richard Wilson, and Stephen Cripps – until the buildings were destroyed by fire in 1979. (With Wilson and Burwell, she would go on to form the influential sound experiment Bow Gamelan Ensemble in 1983). At Butlers Wharf, Bean recalls the way performance overtook or otherwise merged with daily practices of living, actively to blur the hierarchical distinction between art and life:

> [M]any days would be spent with whatever was in the kitchen, in true laboratory style – seeing if bacon dripping fat on to different surfaces would make different sounds, or throwing poems into a liquidiser to reform texts, or whatever, until one's whole life became a sort of laboratory. I have mostly lived my life in that mode.[12]

With what effects does an artist refuse to privilege the slices in time explicitly given over to the production of 'art', and the things so produced? And what is the effect upon the remaining swathes of time that constitute the day, the night, the week, month, or year? If such an endeavour – the creation of a continuum between works of art, and between art and life – is 'impossible,' what are the stakes of committing oneself to the pursuit of wilfully untenable acts, to redefine the world of one's experience? How is such an impossible or untenable project the basis for the blurring of 'art' and 'life', and what is the shape and texture of the 'life art' so inaugurated? What are the specifically cultural and theoretical contexts that make this praxis an ontological reality? Put simply, what was it, in the spirit of the times, that allowed Bean to seek to obliterate the distinctions between her works, and between her works and her life, and what was it that enabled her to think the benefits of such an endeavour?

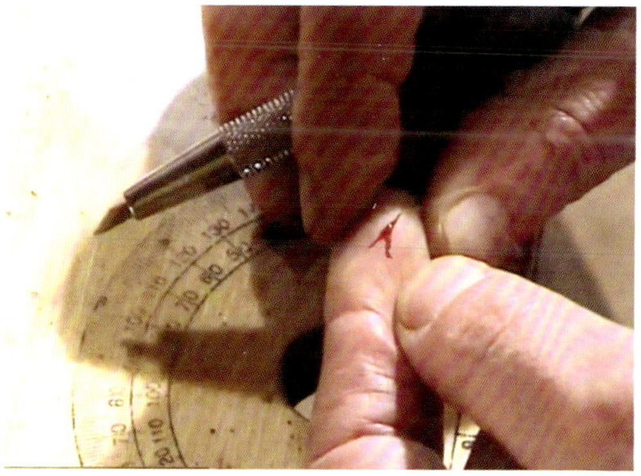

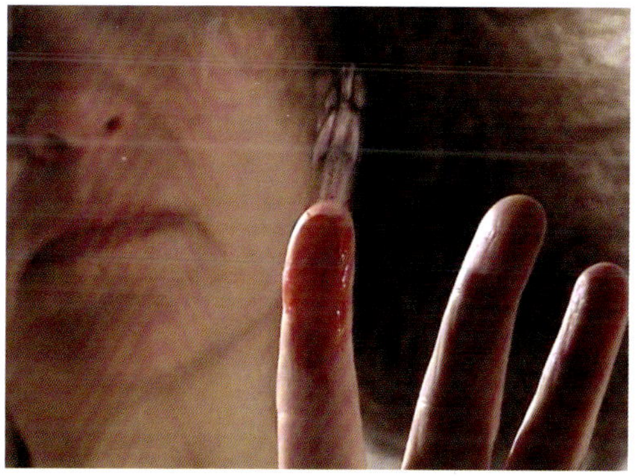

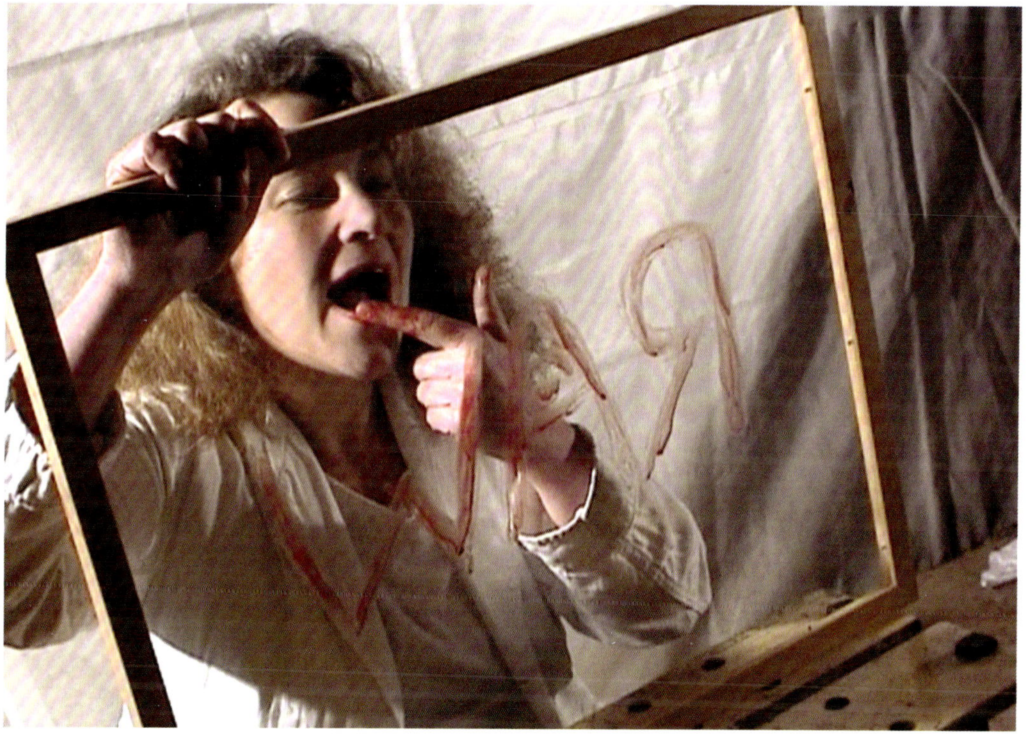

Anne Bean, *Raw/War* reformed as a *Shadow Deed* in 1998 for *Autobituary* (2006). Still from video by Lee Merrill-Sendall

p. 38: Anne Bean, street wear (*Moodier*), 1979. Photo: Elisa Leonelli

p. 39: Anne Bean, streetwear (Anne Archy of the Moodies), 1973. Photo: Joe Gaffney

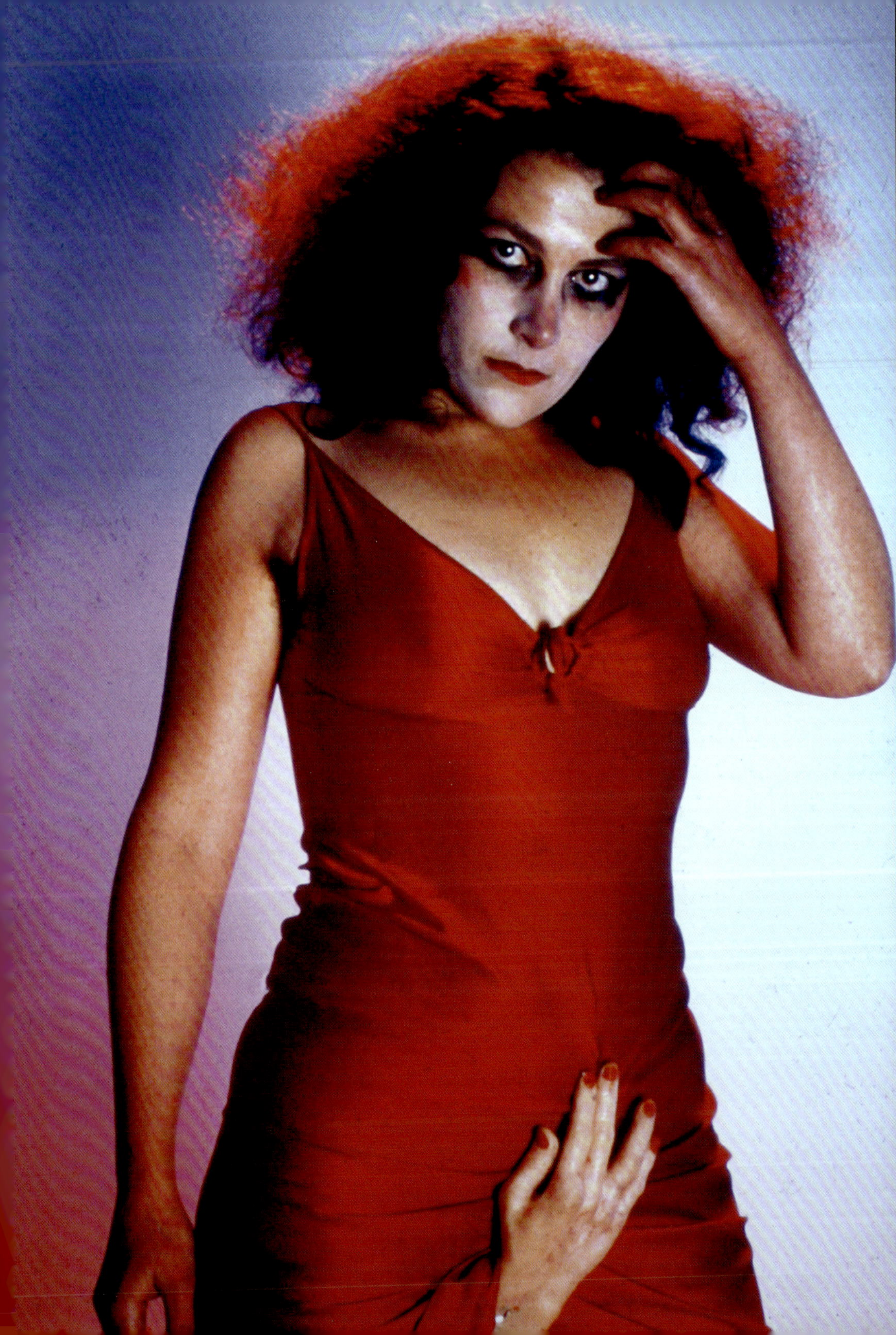

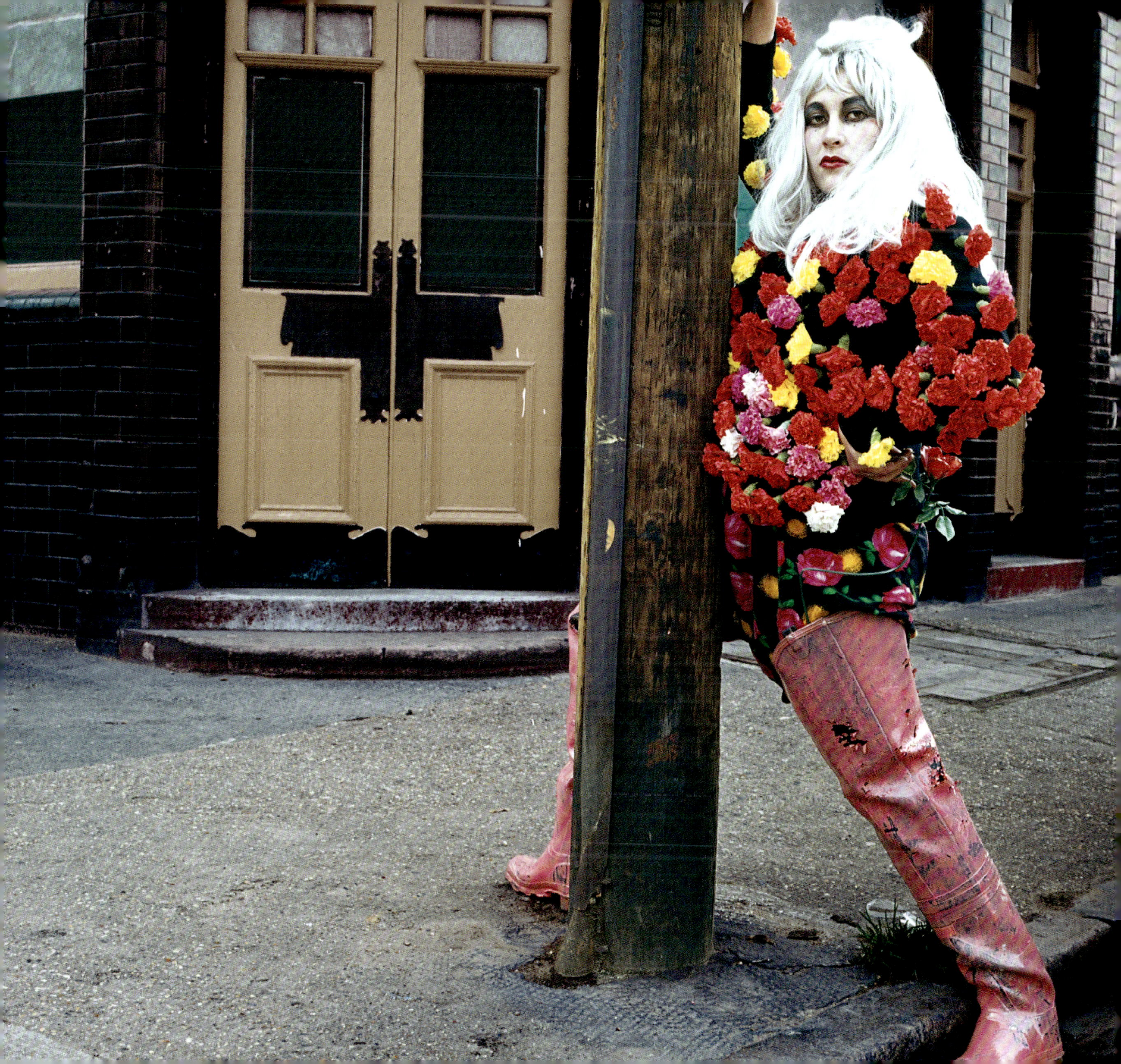

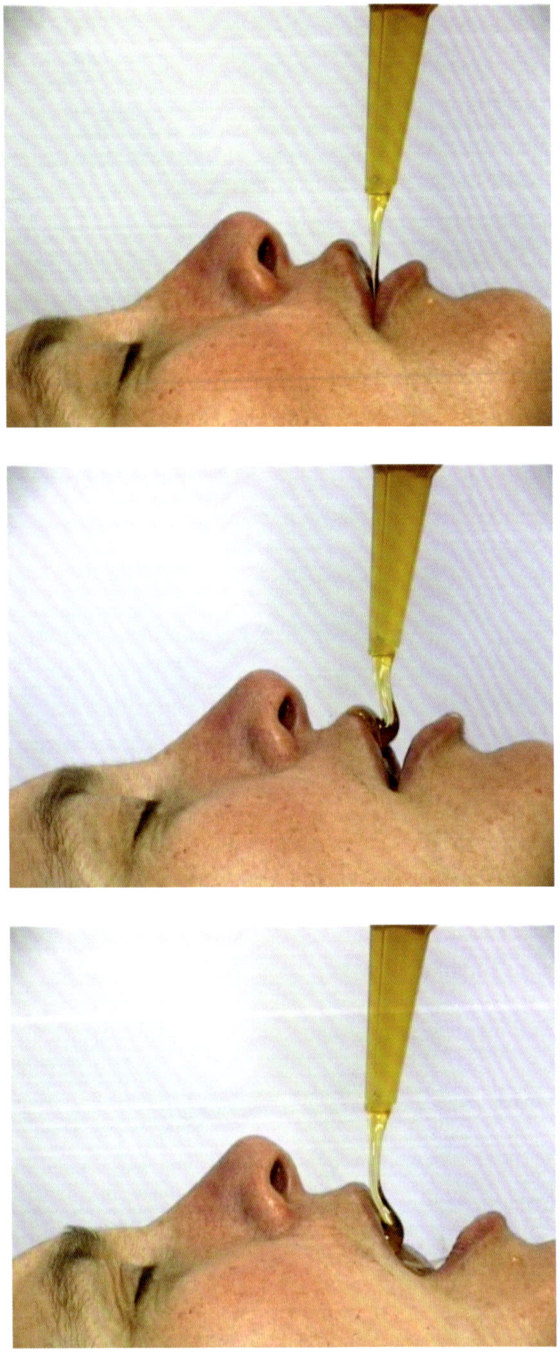

Anne Bean, *Honey Tongued* reformed as a *Shadow Deed* in 1997 for *Autobituary* (2006). Still from video by Chris Bishop

Cosmic arisings

In the early 1970s, Anne Bean lived in a co-operative setting with a number of other artists, including the Kipper Kids, the painter-philosopher Chris Millar, Malcolm Jones, Peter Davey and Jonathan Harvey (Director of Acme Gallery). This loose collective took the name Bernsteins, after the derelict chemist's shop in which they lived together, in Mile End Road in East London. Bean recounts,

> We acquired an old building in the East End in 1972, a semi-legitimate squat. We spent a lot of time there, asking what we were trying to do, philosophically and conceptually ... We were reading Gurdjieff and Ouspensky, and thinking seriously about being and doing, wakefulness and mindfulness.[13]

Their collective art of living entailed long and committed conversations, extensive reading, and intermittent undocumented actions, generally in private or in secluded semi-public places. Bean clocked up 'thousands of hours' of conversation, she recalls, over terrestrial days and astral weeks, on topics concerning philosophy, theosophy, the occult, and art; their research developed initially through an enthusiasm for P. D. Ouspensky's writing, and subsequently through close readings of Gurdjieff. These and other occult thinkers, including Austin Osman Spare and Aleister Crowley, enabled Bean to privilege performance as a practice of self-actualisation – a countercultural project of the 1970s that named the search for fuller or deeper selfhood through rituals of social de-conditioning and active self-fashioning.

As Bean recalls of her time at Reading in the early 1970s, and after, 'Gurdjieff was a seminal influence,' because he influenced a 'pre-punk thought,' namely that 'everything's unreal,' and 'everything's an illusion,' so 'you can create your own being. It's called "self-re-membering"'.[14] Bean's small group took seriously this work of 'self-re-membering,' in the course of their research into the occulted word of human experience – as demonstrated by Bean's pilgrimage to Gurdjieff's Institute for the Harmonious Development of Man, at the Château du Prieuré commune in Paris (and, later, her 'brief' experiment in Scientology, during which she lived for six months at Saint Hill, the cult's British headquarters in East Grinstead, West Sussex).[15] This turn of mine to Gurdjieff and the occult is warranted, methodologically, as a means of thinking how Bean aestheticised the full continuum of her life and works; moreover, when artists embraced ephemerality, and sought means and methods to produce art against the prevailing tendency towards permanence, commodification and institutionalisation, what countercultural models of thinking were available, viable, or in vogue? My turn to *occulture* also allows me to consider a precise context for the way Bean demands her own insignificance, as we turn, as she warrants, towards a debased theory or wilfully unsubstantial method.

George Ivanovich Gurdjieff was born in Alexandropol in the Greek Caucasus (now Armenia) in 1866, and came to wide public attention from around 1915, on account of his 'sacred dances', his lectures on the occulted life, and his general school of thought – first in Moscow, then in Paris and London, and through national tours in the United States, until his death in 1949.[16] He had an imposing appearance, with what Ouspensky described as 'the face of an Indian raja or an Arab sheik,' and an overall attire that 'produced the strange, unexpected, and almost alarming impression of a man poorly disguised'.[17] Celebrated by his disciples as a true mystic, guru, and philosophical genius, Gurdjieff is dismissed by many others as a cultist, showman, and crackpot. A huckster or otherwise, Gurdjieff cultivated actively an aspect of charlatanism about himself. As Ouspensky recalled, 'no ordinary demands could be made of [Gurdjieff] ... He might say one thing today and something altogether different tomorrow, and yet, somehow, he could never be accused of contradictions; *one had to understand and connect everything together*'.[18]

The latter sentiment must have seemed profound for Bean. In the early 1970s, Bean and her collaborators in Bernsteins were grappling with an arcane book of Gurdjieff's called *Beelzebub's Tales to his Grandson: An Objectively Impartial Criticism of the Life of Man*. Dictated by the guru in the 1920s, and published posthumously in 1950, this tome of 1135 pages is written in a circumambulatory, arcane, and funny manner. They also read Ouspensky's analytic portrait of Gurdjieff, *In Search of the Miraculous* (also published in 1950). *Beelzebub's Tales* is framed by a profoundly ambitious prolegomena, in which Gurdjieff sets out his attempt '[t]o destroy, mercilessly and without any compromise whatsoever, in the mentation and feelings of the reader, the beliefs and views, by centuries rooted in him, about everything existing in the world'.[19] In the book, Beelzebub circles the universe in a spaceship called the *Karnak*, and imparts a copious, novelistic and sometimes baffling account of the occulted life of man to his grandson, Hassein. As Hassein listens to his grandfather's ceaseless schoolings, he tells Beelzebub, 'Things I never thought of before are now a-thinking in me'.[20]

I want to take seriously Bean's statement about studying Gurdjieff for lessons about 'being and doing, wakefulness and mindfulness,' and towards active 'self-re-membering'.[21] This entails me to pursue Gurdjieff's account of the 'definite and peculiar psychic data crystallized in my common presence during my preparatory age,' and to provide an honest engagement with the critical potential of 'mindfulness,' as an actualizing of new ways of thinking and being, and of 'wakefulness'.[22] It would be convenient to laugh at Gurdjieff and his followers, and patronising to excuse Bean her youthful diversion. So what if Gurdjieff seemly intellectually weightless, unserious, insane? I will account briefly for Gurdjieff's school of thought and its implications, and pursue some of his apparent influence on Bean's unique approach to art and performance in the 1970s, including her appropriation of what Ouspensky calls 'the connectedness of everything [Gurdjieff] said,' or, how 'his ideas were not detached from another, as all philosophical and scientific ideas are, but made one whole'.[23]

The core of Gurdjieff's philosophy is to propose methods for unlearning or de-habituating inhibition. He writes of the accumulation of 'mentation by form' – or thought by ritual or rote – by which an individual relies upon an idea that is 'fixed as a result of specific local influences and impressions,' and which 'evokes in him by association the sensation of a definite "inner content",' or 'habitual meaning.' De-habituating thought – actualizing 'mindfulness' – requires a thinker to become aware of received mentation by form, and to forge 'a different "inner content",' for a given word, object, practice, or thought.[24]

In his attempt to de-habituate thought and language, and to avoid or retrain 'mentation by form,' Gurdjieff introduces new words to explain his idiosyncratic worldview, and devises a series of 'cosmic laws' about the shape and structure of consciousness and corporeality. 'Actualization' is a key term. Gurdjieff's most influential construction, however – including for Bean and her co-conspirators, is the esoteric ethic of 'being-partkdolgduty,' or the 'ilnosoparnian process' of mind, the formal terms for what Bean describes, above, as 'self-remembering'. Being-partkdolgduty marks the achievement of a 'subjective being-conviction' formed by processes of social and linguistic de-programing, as a state of grace from convictions that depend exclusively upon the opinions of others. 'Self-calming', or docility, is productively undermined in Gurdjieff's teaching, in order to accrue personal sensitivity to 'instinctive sensing of reality'; the process of self-actualisation seeks to energise the subject, and revivify her or his relation to the world, in part through the destruction or neutralisation of 'sane logic'.[25]

Opposite: Anne Bean filming *Ubu* with Alastair Brotchie, Graham Challifour, Rod Melvin, and Stuart Smith. Photo: Ren Pesci

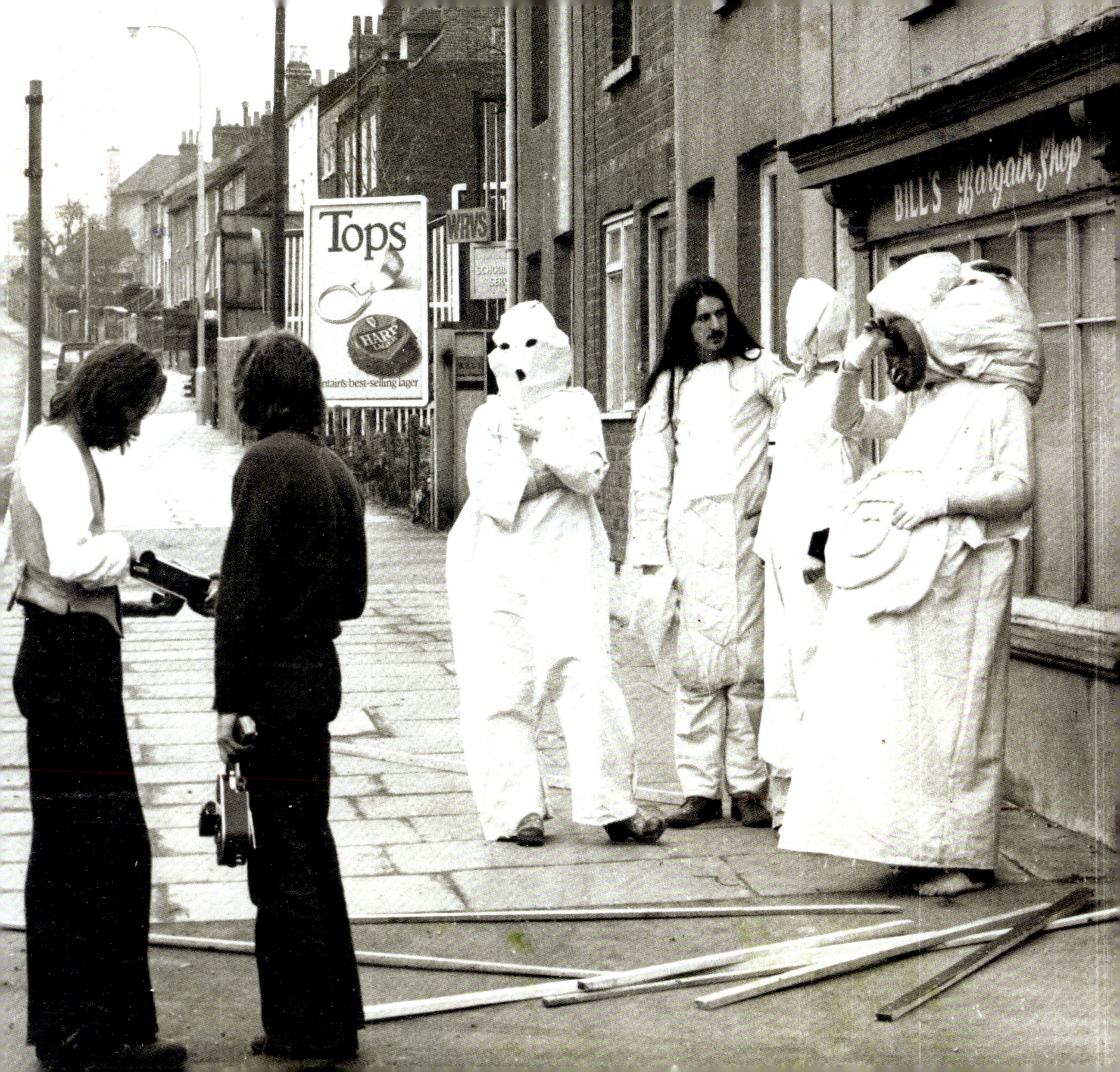
Tops
HARP
best-selling lager
WRVS
BILL'S Bargain Shop

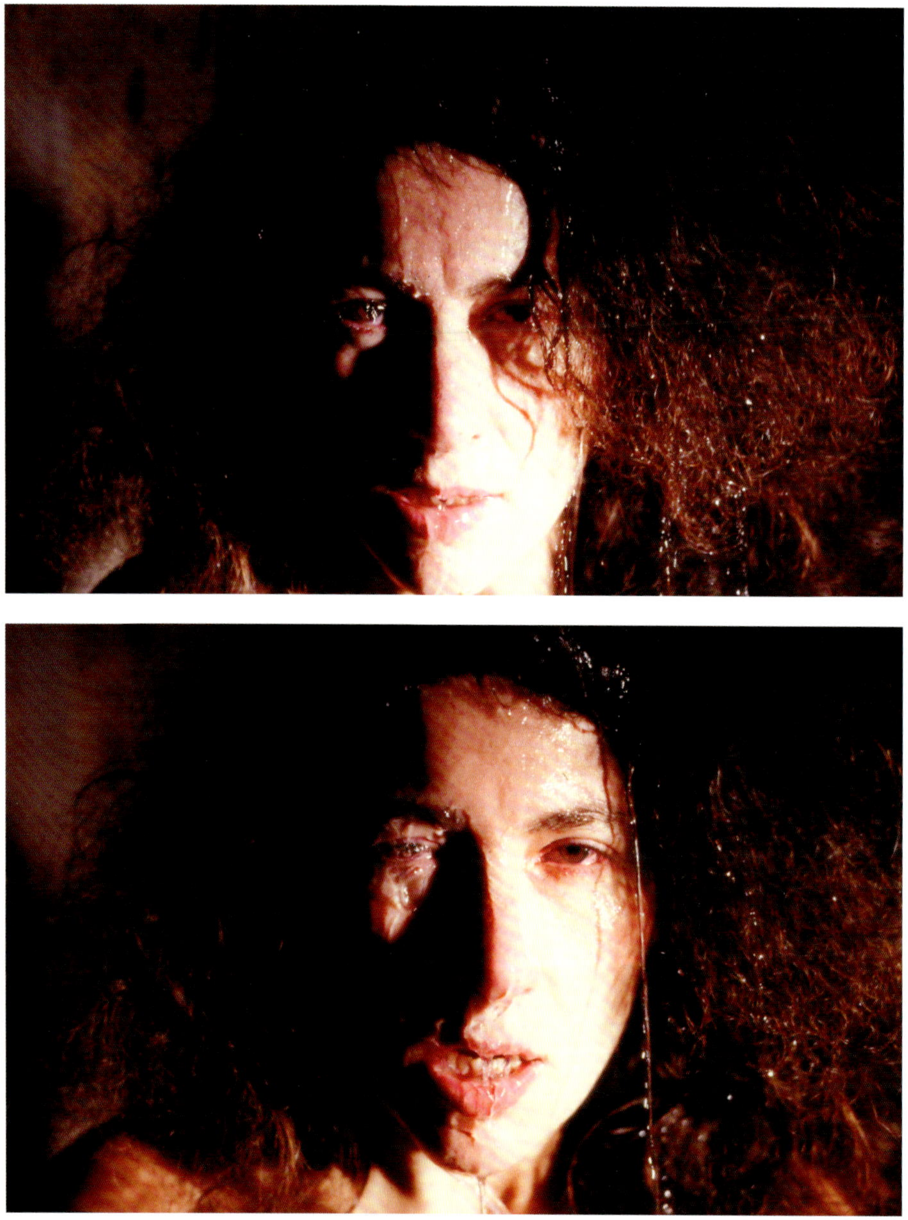

Anne Bean, *Tearing my Hair, Tearing my Eyes*, Reading, 1972. I splash my face and pull my hair with soapy water so my eyes redden and tear up and a small pile of hairs are produced. Photographer unknown

Many of Bean's works in the period enact this sense of a refusal of sane logic in the service of a specialised, alien, but individually necessary action. For example, in *Homecoming* (1972), Bean purchased 20 pounds of sea salt, and several sacks of sand, travelled to the shore, and emptied them on Peacehaven Beach, Sussex. She undertakes the arduous task of transporting the materials, carrying them across the beach, and piling up pyramids of sand and salt on the shore. She waits as the sea laps upwards with the tide, reclaiming the sea's constitutive elements, namely the salt that distinguishes it from other bodies of water, and the sand upon which we might stand. The action is pointless in practical terms, incidental, and a miniscule contribution in the grand ecological sense of how much the beach might need or register these activities. Yet, *Homecoming* refuses the very logic of productivity or accountability. No account can make biochemical sense of the contribution Bean makes to the elemental makeup of the Sussex sea or coastline. Yet the poetry of *Homecoming* is profound, even if its profundity is directed towards a private operation upon the performing self – and precisely because it is written or spoken in a minor key. Its wilful insignificance is accentuated by Bean's refusal to document the action.

This resistance to registering as a permanent trace or as wilfully significant art – and the deliberate use of great labour to achieve slight shifts in the makeup of one's environment – also appears in the work of Bean's peers in the 1970s. For example, in *Sweeping the Sea* (1975), the British artist Annabel Nicolson swept a shoreline in Southampton, on the south coast of England, over several hours. Performed as a poetic exploration of a seemingly impossible task – of cleaning or sorting the sand and pebbles or of brushing away the lapping waters – the piece had no formal audience, beyond the walkers and beachcombers who happened to pass by – and is documented by a single, ghostly photograph of Nicolson lunging her broom into the shallow shifting tide. 'On a grey day in July she was seen sweeping the sea', the artist writes in a note on the performance, '[p]erhaps it was deliberate this trick of making herself part of the background of being just slightly out of focus'. Her reflection on the action gives a sense of being unfocused in time, of evading full recognition even by those who pass her by, in her immersion on the beach, and afterwards in our encounters with her documents. Writing in the third person, she also gives the impression of having difficulty in identifying with or laying claim to her own action.

Provocatively, for Gurdjieff, being-partkdolgduty is inhibited – not facilitated – by art, even though the theosophist humbly describes himself, early in his book, as 'simply, a teacher of dance'.[26] Importantly, Gurdjieff assumes a constitutive difference between 'art' – codified as a normative and inhibitive set of practices, styles, and institutions – and instinctive aesthetic sensing, or *aisthesis*. His manifesto on art describes a means to revalue the practice of art at a remove from the 'terrestrial' values attributed to a new form of aesthetic practice that would be integrated into the path to being-partkdolgduty. He calls this art of actualisation 'afalkalnas', and defines it as 'various works of man's hands which have entered into the everyday life of people,' including rituals, ceremonies, and occult occurrences.[27] As A. R. Orage writes, in his influential commentary on *Beelzebub's Tales*, according to Gurdjieff '[a]n artist should not be a special kind of man, but every man should be a special kind of artist'.[28]

Gurdjieff's position (and Orage's commentary) directly anticipates formal developments in the new art that became more fully recognised later in the 1950s (the decade Gurdjieff's book first appeared) and into the 1960s. In the early 1960s, Fluxus proposed a model for making art based on seemingly simple or usefully transparent games and pedestrian instructions, particularly in the work of George Maciunas, George Brecht and Yoko Ono: 'Art is not merely a duplication of life', Ono proclaimed in 1966. 'To assimilate art into life,' she continues, 'is different from art duplicating life'.[29]

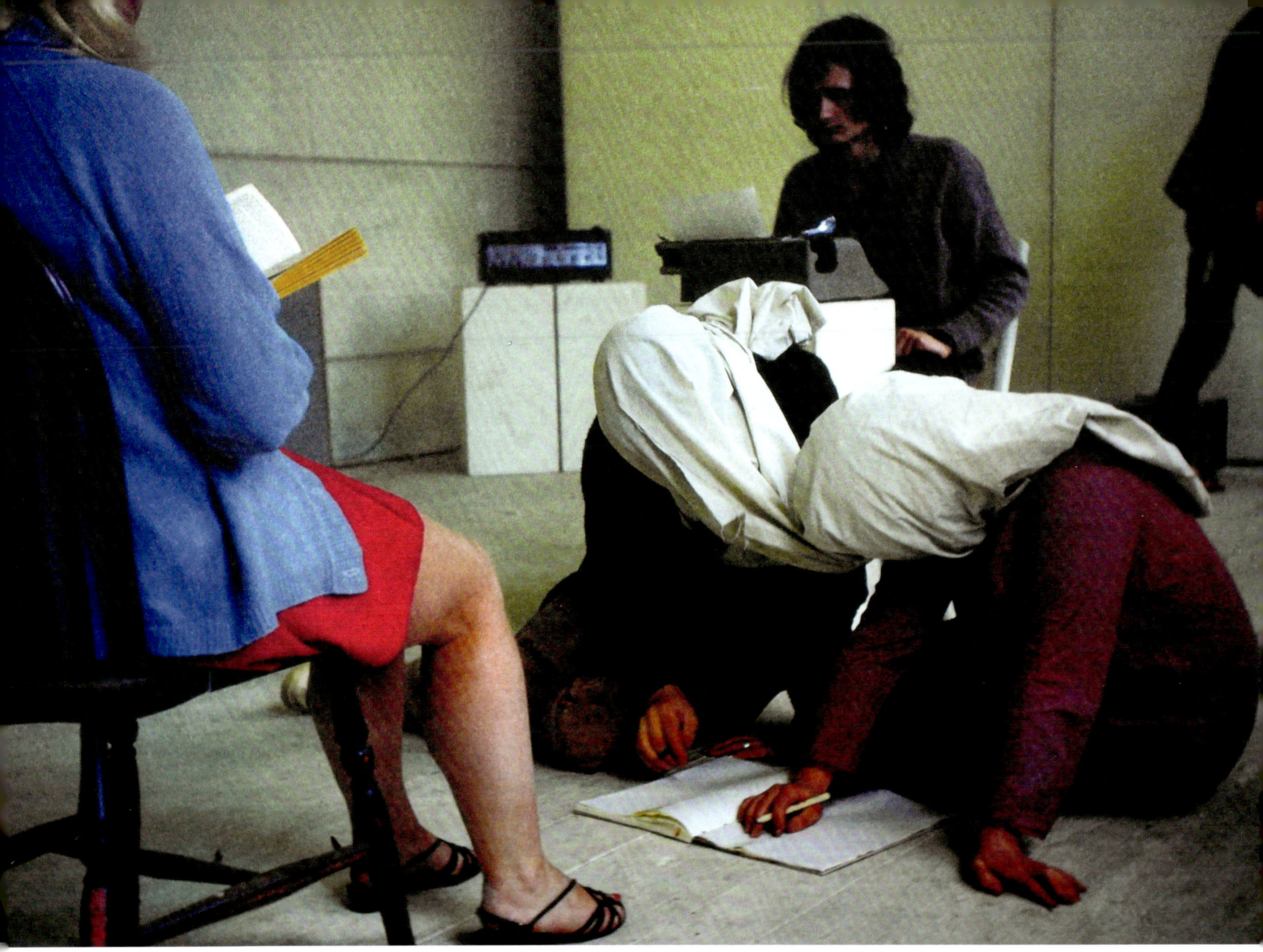

Above: Anne Bean and collaborators, blindfolded drawings during *White Room*, Reading, 1970. Photo: Phil Winder

Opposite: Anne Bean, *Drawing Life* reformed as a *Shadow Deed* in 2002 for *Autobituary* (2006). Still from video by Chris Bishop

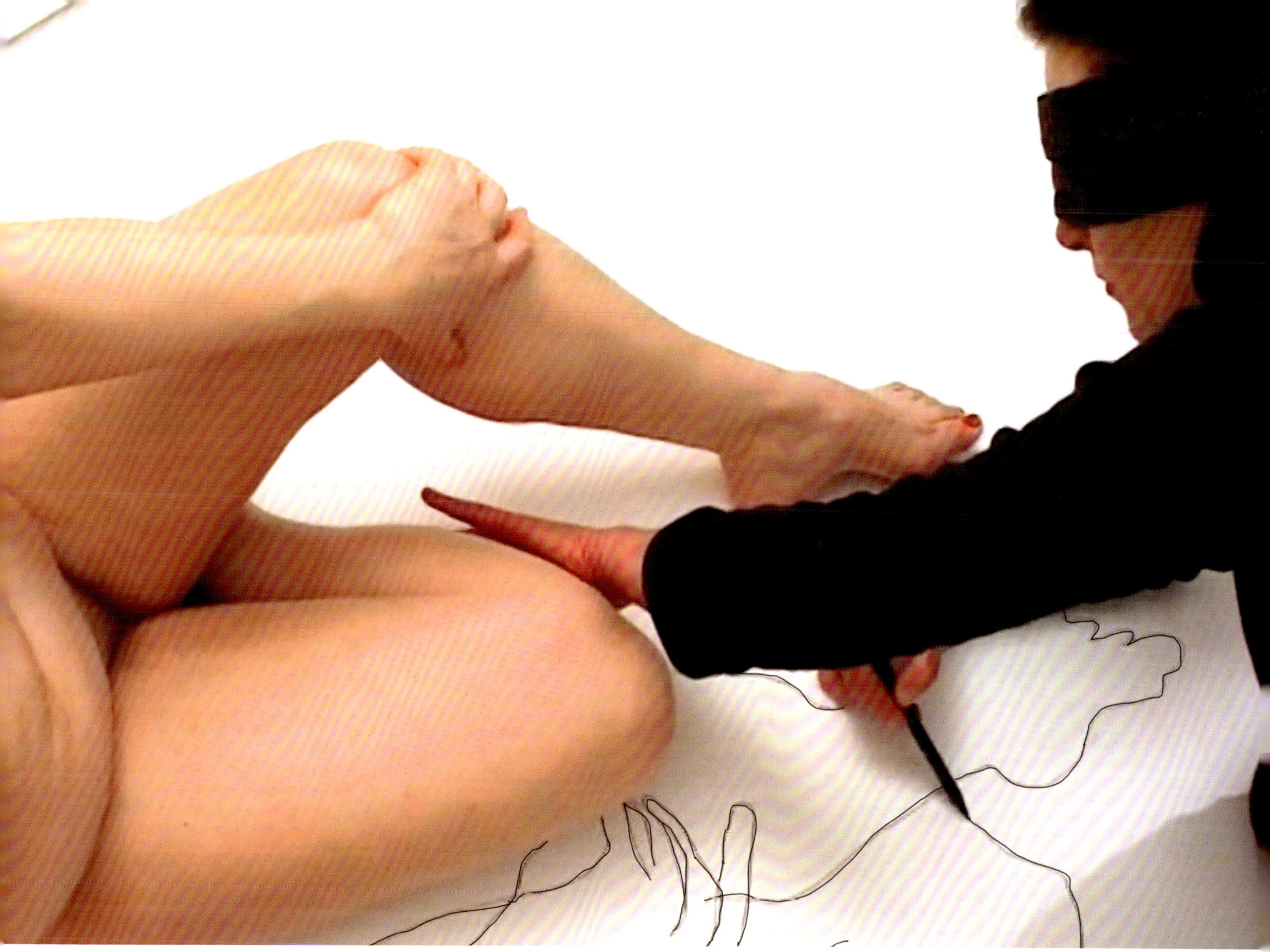

Similarly, Gurdjieff anticipates the 'social sculpture' (*soziale Plastik*) of Joseph Beuys, which held that 'Sculpture = Everything' and – in his much-quoted (and frequently misunderstood) credo – that 'every human being is an artist'. Beuys' slogans stood in for his more complicated equivalences and less quotable theses concerning the utopian potential of art, such as his statement in 1971 that 'Art equals man equals creativity equals freedom. Every man is creative, and hence he is free. Freedom and creativity make him fundamentally able to determine, to form, and to change. This is true both in the realm of art – whose task is to create awareness of such possibilities – and in society'.[30] In practical terms, for Beuys creativity was to be detached from the production of stable objects and epitomised by or assimilated into all aspects of human life, such that '[e]ven the peeling of a potato can be a work of art if it is a conscious act'.[31] Of a piece with these developments, and emerging from his own spectacular 'sacred' dances, Gurdjieff's theorisation of progressive art entails the strategic invocation of what he terms 'reciprocal thrusts' between the artist-performer and the members of the audience. These produce 'inexactitudes' of meaning – or sites of ambivalence. In its ambivalence or strangeness, a performance action may provoke 'cosmic arisings', or the 'common integral vibration', as he puts it – namely, a transformative experience of vacillation in response to performance.[32]

Bean's 'life art' performances of the 1970s, then, are not illustrations of theosophy or philosophy per se, despite her serious readings in the occult. Rather, her works inhabit the key principles of such a theosophy, including the ambition towards art as a process not of aesthetic production but of aesthetic sensing (a 'cosmic arising'). As such, she searches out, through performance, the possibilities, potentialities, dead ends, and new realities associated with being and doing for art. Further approaches furnished by Gurdjieff include, moreover, the incitement of reciprocal thrusts between the artist and the audience, and the commitment to try to let meaning go. These spaces of productive confusion provoke what Gurdjieff calls 'inexactitudes', situations of blurred or impossible meaning that do not allow the viewer or participant to rely upon habituated thought. So, when Bean performs *Shouting 'Mortality' as I Drown* (1973), the durational commitment to the task and her refusal to document the live action (though it was subsequently performed to camera) may complement or confirm a commitment to these preceding principles. Naked in a bath of water, the artist submerges her head and face and screams 'mortality', repeatedly, through the water, creating a muffled, gargled sound. As her action progresses, Bean incrementally comes closer to drowning. At the point when the artist is too tired to continue, and she brings herself as close as bearable to drowning, she articulates the nature of mortality, as a property of bodies, in which one's finitude can be foreclosed, or embraced, by the commitment of a body to testing its own vital limits, or by external factors beyond one's control. Its strangeness or excess is warranted, after Gurdjieff, by the possibilities for self-actualisation it engenders.

I believe in nothing but

Methodologically speaking, Bean poses problems for those of us who seek to engage with her continuous history as a 'life artist'. Prior to the publication of the present book, her personal archive had had little or no material existence, beyond the selected images and cryptic texts she publishes on her website (and the possibility of a suitcase of slides she alluded to, but declined me access). From conversations with Bean, I understand her propensity towards ephemerality, and her attitude of resistance towards institutional custodianships and intellectual capture. Yet while writing, I contacted her regardless, pushing my luck perhaps, to ask for access to whatever she may have saved from her early work, be it notes, journals, sketchbooks, or documents. She replied in an email: 'Numerous electro-chemical archives and repositories abound [but] all paper work, sketch books etc. have been ditched at various junctures. I mourn not'. Her archival process is not a reverent one. It entails active destruction, and casual disregard for posterity,

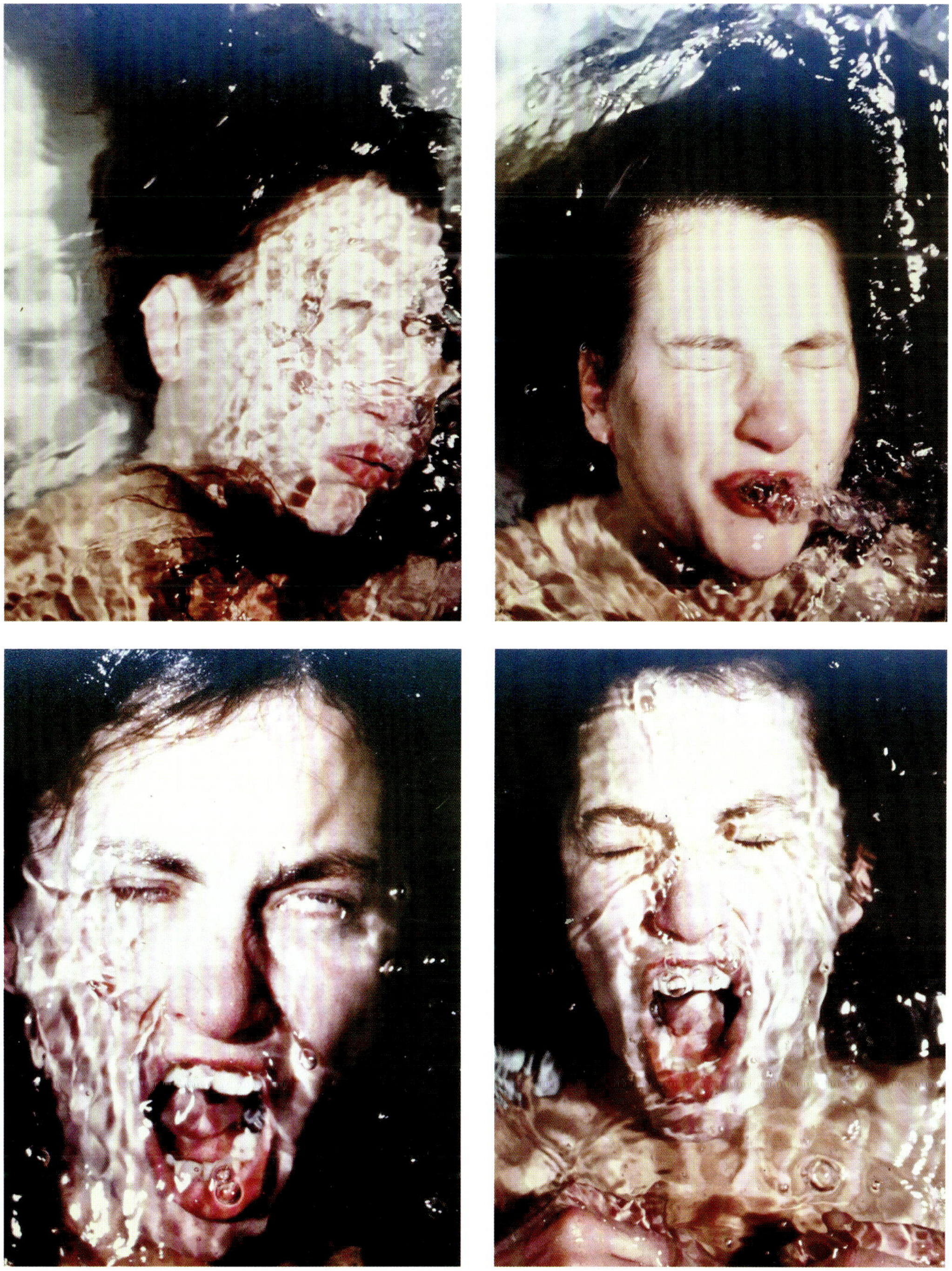

Anne Bean, *Shouting 'Mortality' as I Drown* (1973), performed for camera in 1977. Photos: Chris Bishop

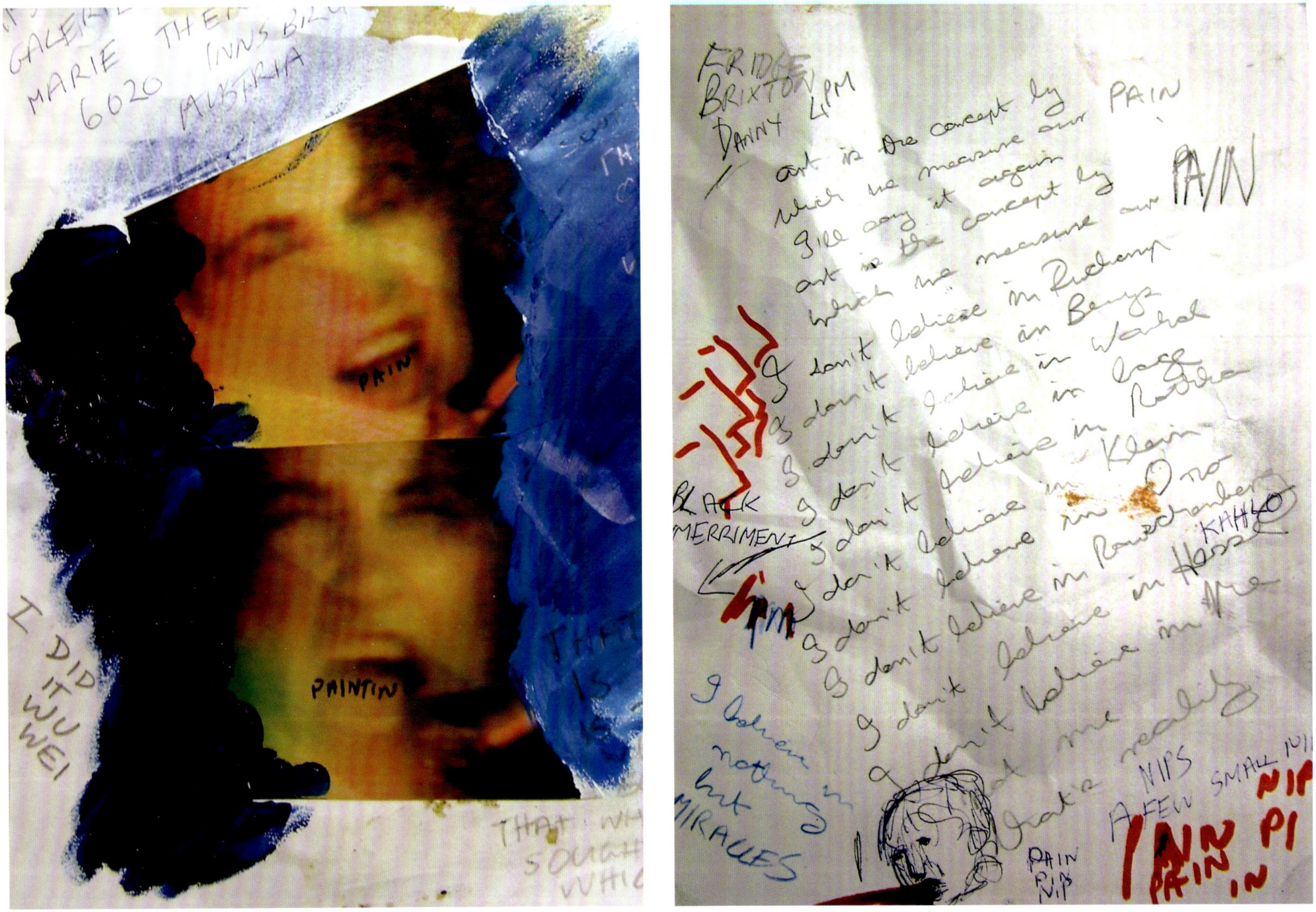

Anne Bean, pages from notebooks, ca. 1979.

orthodoxy, administrative care, or being preserved or revered as a 'seminal' artist.

A week after the 'I mourn not,' I received a further email from Bean, containing a number of scans of sketches retained by her friend, collaborator and sometimes partner, the late Paul Burwell, whose posthumous papers she does keep. Bean writes that the sheets with collaged photos, watercolour washes, and pencilled aphorisms were 'crumpled up, possibly pulled out of bins by him [Burwell]'. One of the pieces, made by Bean in the late 1970s, consists of a written declaration:

> Art is the concept by/ Which we measure our PAIN/
> I don't believe in Duchamp/ I don't believe in Beuys/
> I don't believe in Warhol/ I don't believe in Cage/
> I don't believe in Rothko/ I don't believe in Klein/
> I don't believe in Ono/ I don't believe in Rauschenberg/
> I don't believe in Hesse/ I don't believe in the/ Not me/
> That's reality/ I believe in nothing but/ MIRACLES

The manifesto is a stark statement of refusal, an active negation of – or suspension of belief in – primary figures of progressive art after modernism, many of whom privileged performance in their critical practices of art (most were still active at the time of her writing). Bean's dissidence, she suggests, extends to everything outside her, negating the existence (or importance) that seems, cumulatively, to constitute external reality: 'I don't believe in the/ Not me/ That's reality'. Beyond her Oedipal figures (and, strictly, in some cases, peers) whose authority is bluntly refused in the list, Bean stakes her belief in that which exceeds rational belief: 'I believe in nothing but/ MIRACLES.' The *search for the miraculous*, amid so many negations, may be an impossibly counterintuitive logic in which to invest, exclusively, the entirety of one's capacity towards belief. But there, she suggests, lies the magic of the exercise. Perhaps she writes the manifesto as an exorcism of sorts, a *sigil*, as if to act out and thus to manifest her heretical relation to art, and to art history. The totemic function of the writing underwrites both her historical exceptionalism and an occult fantasy of herself as a miracle-maker who seeks to congeal into reality a series of impossible fictions.

Bean's anxiety about ending up *significant*, or being held by history, is sustained across the five decades of her artistic becoming. She has stated that her project since the 1960s has consisted of an attempt to become an 'a-artist' (as in a-theist) – a person who commits oneself to aesthetic sensing without believing in the condition of art as a discrete phenomenon, or in the artist as a stable identity. As an a-artist (or an an-artist), Bean overhauls the Beuysian democratic standard: rather than advocating for the utopian ideal in which *every human being is an artist*, she holds out for a future horizon of consciousness in which 'no-one is an artist', for 'the "art" space is implicitly part of living'.[33] The actualisation or 'self-re-membering' of oneself as a distinctive personality, or as *a non-entity of distinction*, beyond or even against one's identity as an artist, is an imaginative effect of her reinvention of art and life on a vital continuum. *You can't force a story that doesn't want to be told.*

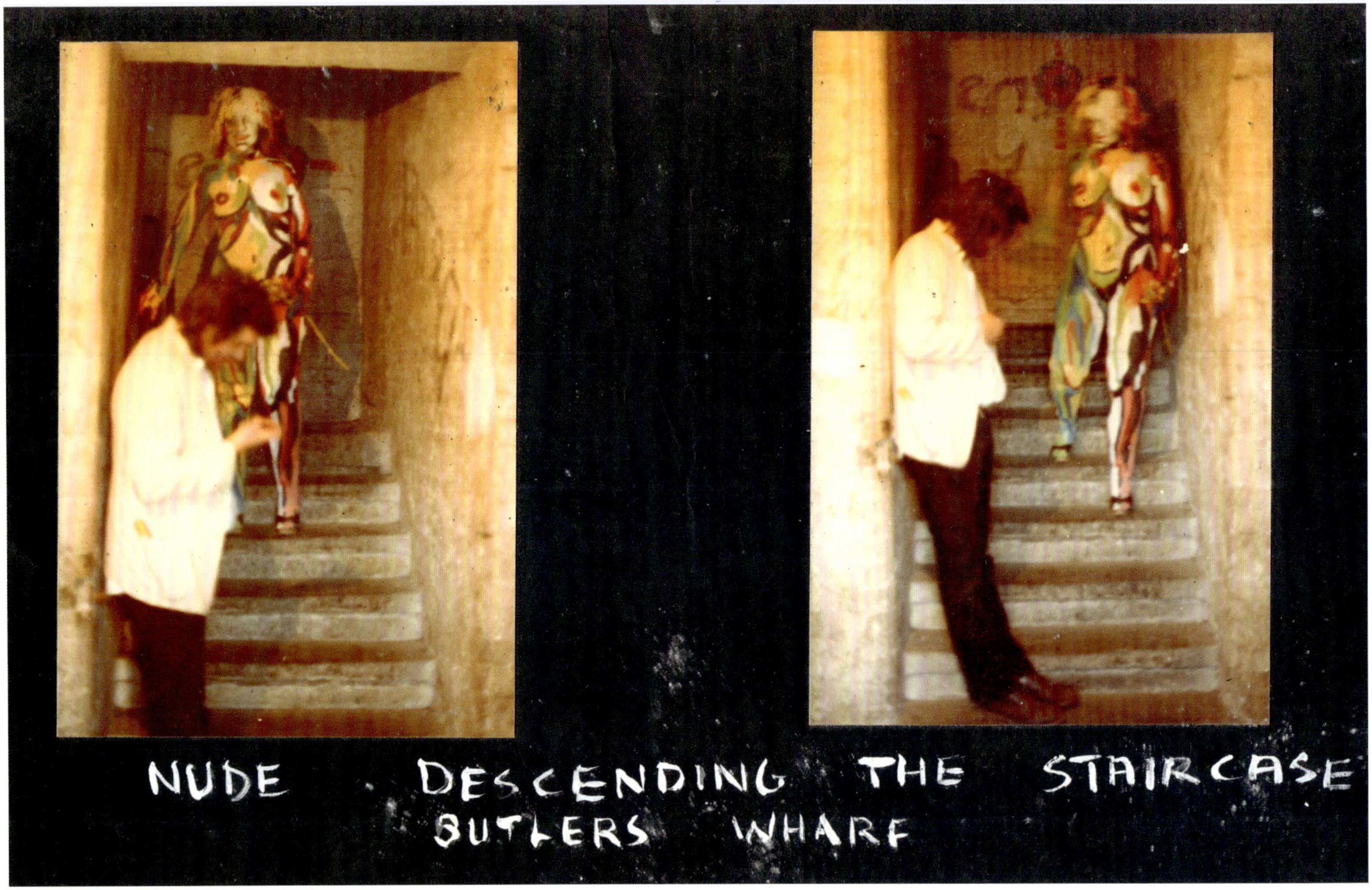

Above: Anne Bean and Stephen Cripps, *Nude Descending the Staircase*, Butlers Wharf, London, 1978. Photo: Paul Burwell

1 This essay is revised and excerpted from a full chapter of the same name in Dominic Johnson, *Unlimited Action: The Performance of Extremity in the 1970s* (Manchester and New York: Manchester University Press, 2018).

2 Anne Bean, postcard to Andrea Tarsia, 18 March 2002, *Short History of Performance Vol. 1*, Exhibition Folder, Whitechapel Gallery Archive, Foyle Reading Room, London.

3 Dominic Johnson, 'Hiding in Plain Sight: An Interview with Anne Bean' in *The Art of Living: An Oral History of Performance Art* (Basingstoke and New York: Palgrave Macmillan, 2015), pp. 41-64 (p. 64). Emphasis in original.

4 Ibid., p. 56.

5 Anne Bean, 'Holding Infinity in the Palm of your Hand' (performance-lecture), *Performance and Politics in the 1970s*, organised by Dominic Johnson and Nicholas Ridout, Whitechapel Gallery, London, 31 May 2015.

6 Anne Bean, the Kipper Kids and Nikki Milican, 'Meet the Artists', unpublished presentation, *National Review of Live Art*, 2003. A002555 National Review of Live Art Video Archive, Theatre Collection, University of Bristol.

7 Michael Bracewell, *Re-Make/Re-Model: Art, Pop, Fashion and the Making of Roxy Music, 1953-1972* (London: Faber and Faber, 2007), p. 263.

8 Amelia Jones, 'Notes on a (Impossible/Eternal) Return' in *Notes on a Return*, ed. by Sophia Yadong Hao and Matthew Hearn (Sunderland: Sunderland Art Gallery), pp. 7-12 (p. 11).

9 Ibid., p. 12.

10 Bean published an untitled statement on *Kinship International Strategy on Surveillance and Suppression*, www.kisss.org.uk/KISSS/launch.html (accessed 14 December 2015, URL no longer active).

11 Johnson, 'Hiding in Plain Sight', p. 61.

12 Ibid., p. 60.

13 Ibid., p. 51.

14 Bracewell, *Re-Make/Re-Model*, p. 265.

15 Chris Millar, 'Profile: Anne Bean – A Portentous Event in Earshot of Braying Donkeys', *Performance Magazine* 20-1 (December-January 1983), 4-8. Bean reminds me that although her experiment may have seemed brief (some six months) in practice, it was also *eternal*: she signed a form committing her soul to Scientology for 'a billion years'.

16 P. D. Ouspensky, *In Search of the Miraculous: Fragments of an Unknown Teaching* (London: Routledge/Kegan Paul, 1950), p. 16.

17 Ibid., p. 7.

18 Ibid., p. 36. Emphasis added.

19 G. I. Gurdjieff, *Beelzebub's Tales to his Grandson: An Objectively Impartial Criticism of the Life of Man*, trans. by Jeanne de Salzmann (New York and London: Viking Arkana, 1992), frontispiece.

20 Ibid., p. 72.

21 Johnson, 'Hiding in Plain Sight', p. 51.

22 Gurdjieff, *Beelzebub's Tales*, p. 24.

23 Ouspensky, *In Search of the Miraculous*, p. 28.

24 Gurdjieff, *Beelzebub's Tales*, pp. 14-15.

25 Ibid., p. 127.

26 Gurdjieff, *Beelzebub's Tales*, p. 46.

27 Ibid., p. 420.

28 A. R. Orage, *Commentaries on G. I. Gurdjieff's All and Everything: Beelzebub's Tales to his Grandson*, ed. by C. S. Nott (Aurora: Two Rivers Press, 1985), p. 93.

29 Yoko Ono, 'To the Wesleyan People' in *Theories and Documents of Contemporary Art: A Sourcebook of Artists' Writings*, ed. by Kristine Stiles and Peter Selz (Berkeley: University of California Press, 1996), pp. 736-39 (p. 738).

30 Carmen Alonso, 'Joseph Beuys 1968-1972' in *Joseph Beuys: Parallel Processes* (Düsseldorf: Shirmer/Mosel, 2010), pp. 190-1 (p. 191).

31 Joseph Beuys, 'Interview with Willoughby Sharp' in *Energy Plan for the Western Man: Joseph Beuys in America*, ed. by Carin Kuoni (New York: Four Walls Eight Windows, 1990), pp. 77-92 (p. 87).

32 Gurdjieff, *Beelzebub's Tales*, p. 421.

33 Rob La Frenais, 'What's in a Name? Anne Bean Interviewed', *Art Monthly* 398 (July-August 2016), 1-5 (p. 4). The interview is republished in a different version in this book.

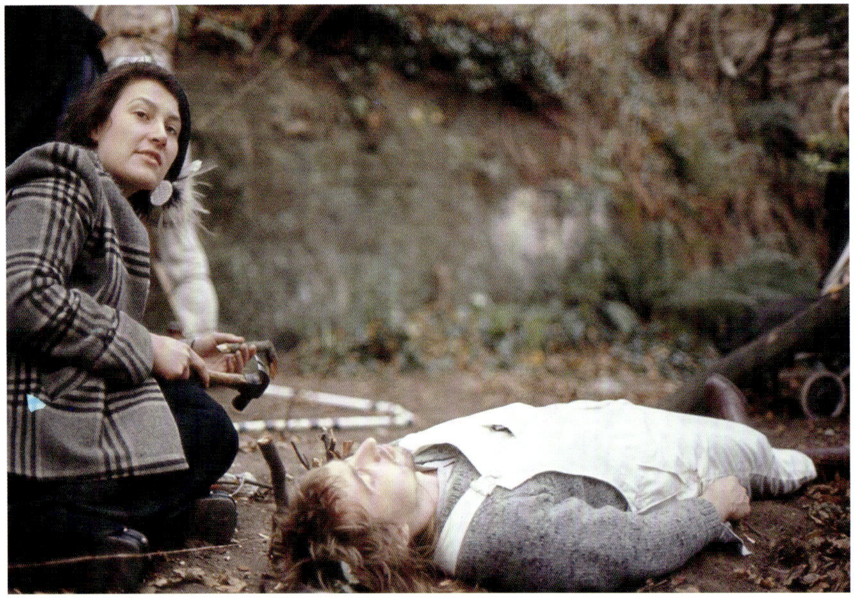

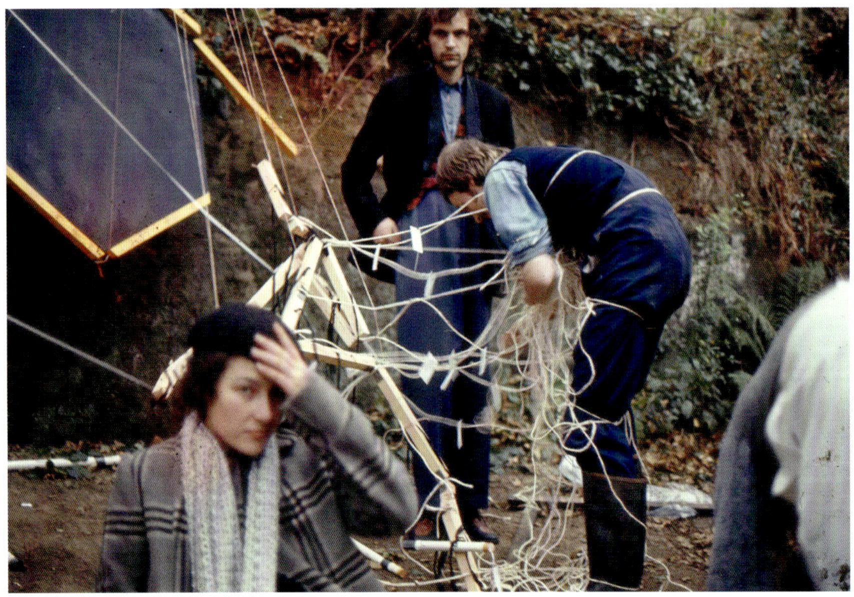

Above: Bernsteins, *Taking Measurements of Yourselves as Artists*, Fairlight Glen, 1972. Photographer unknown
Opposite: Anne Bean and the Kipper Kids, Los Angeles, 1979. Photo: Elisa Leonelli
pp. 56-7: Anne Bean and Peter Davey, *Anxtions*, Hayward Annual 1979. Photo: Chris Bishop

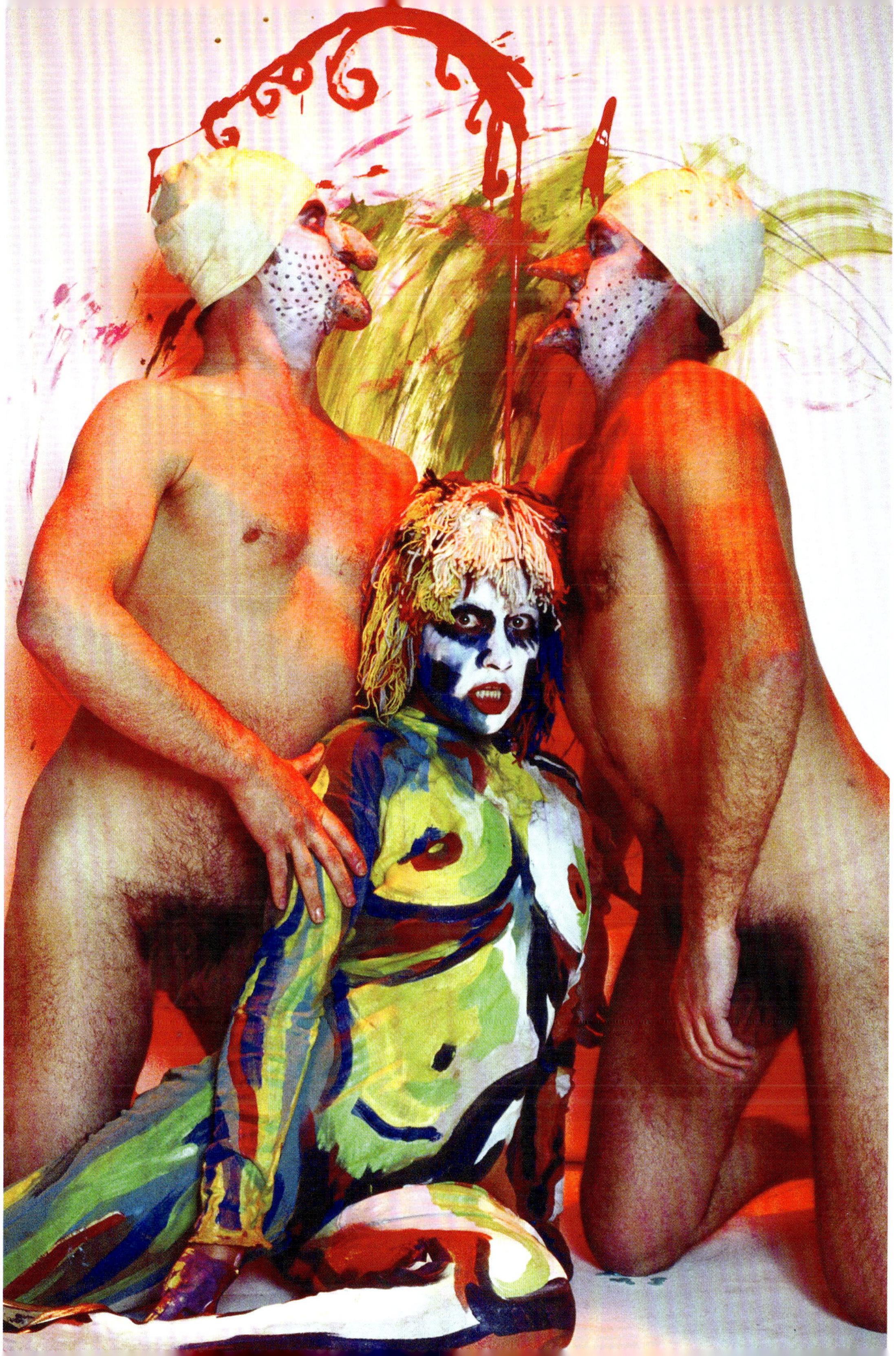

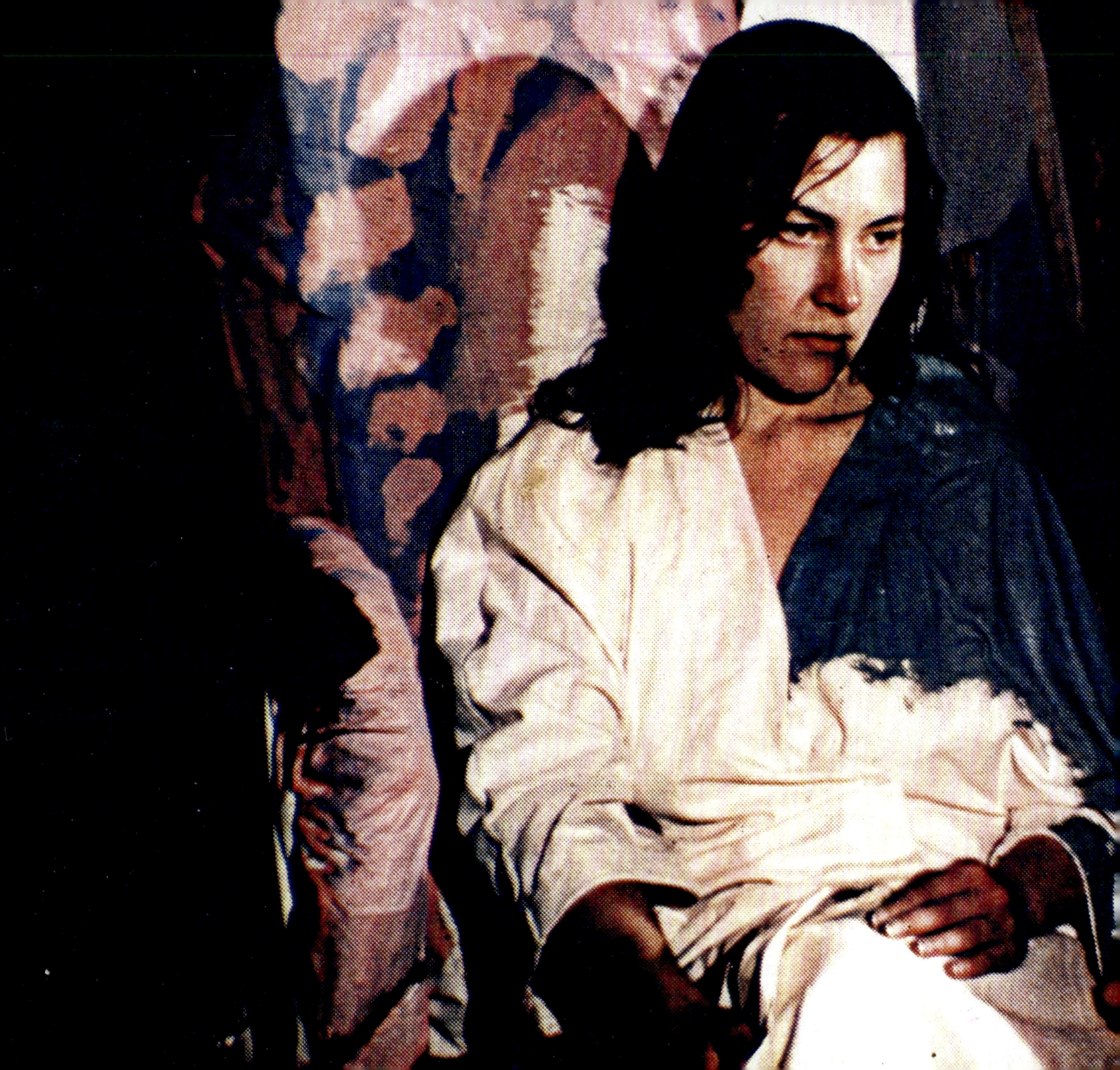

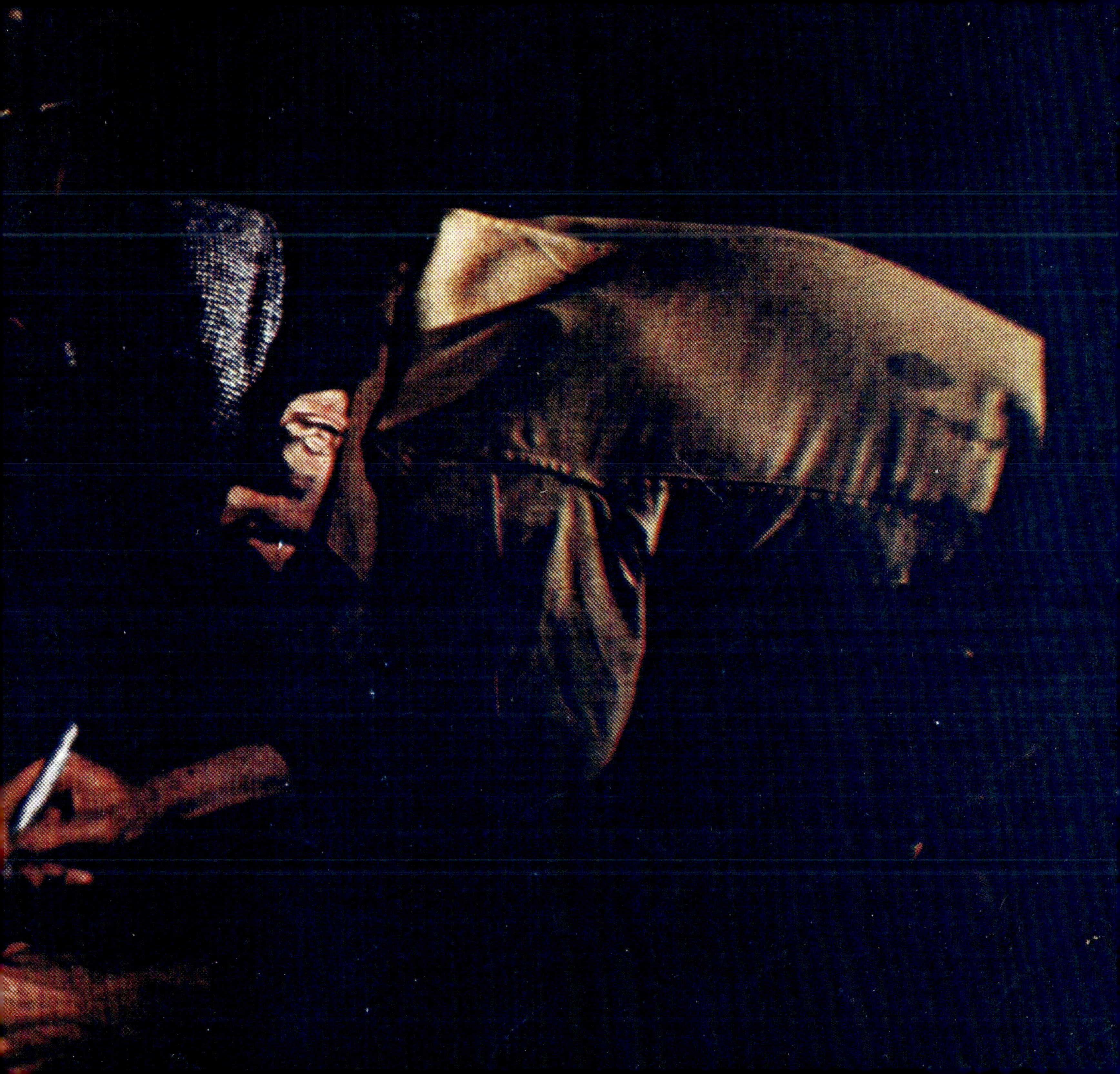

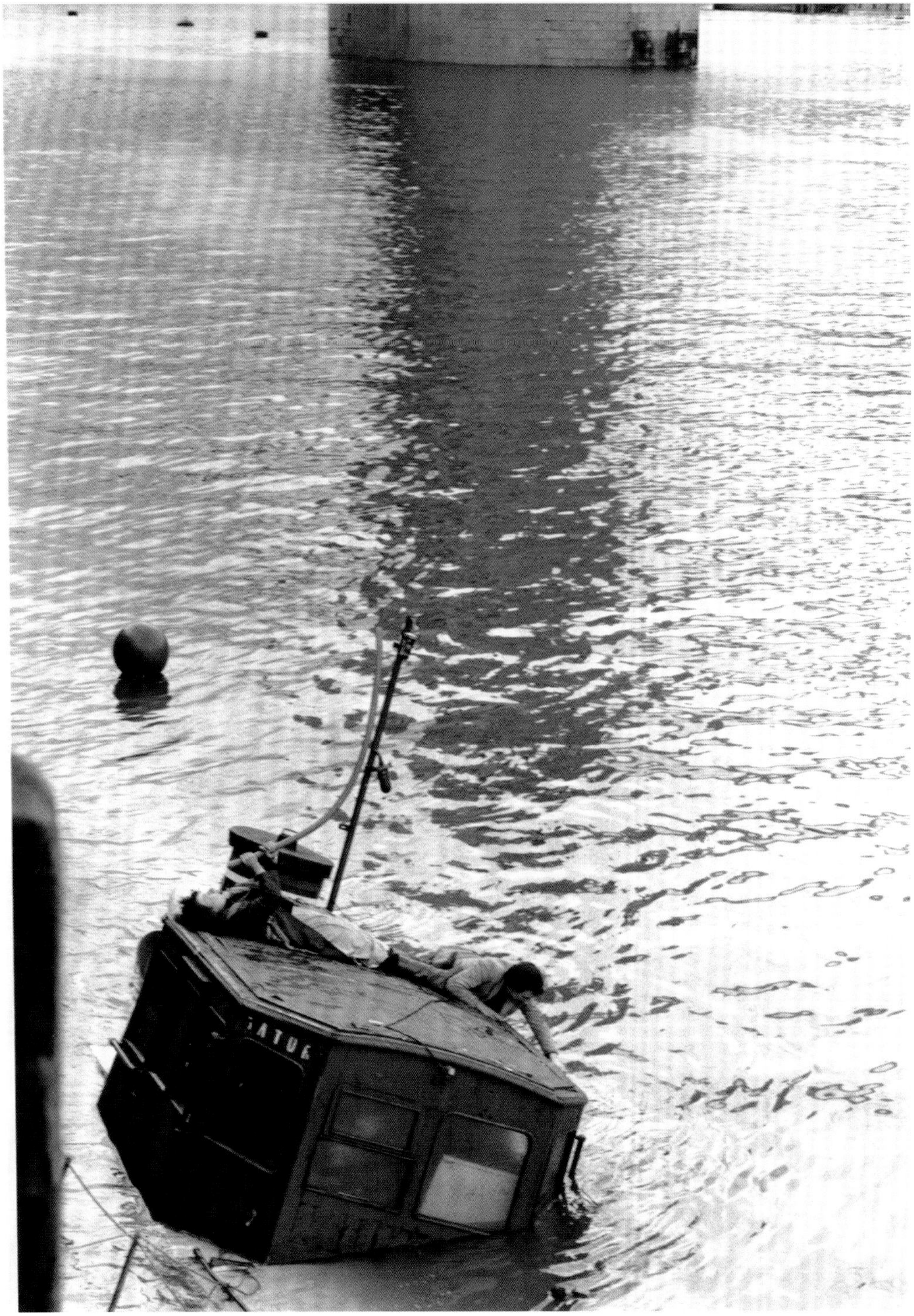

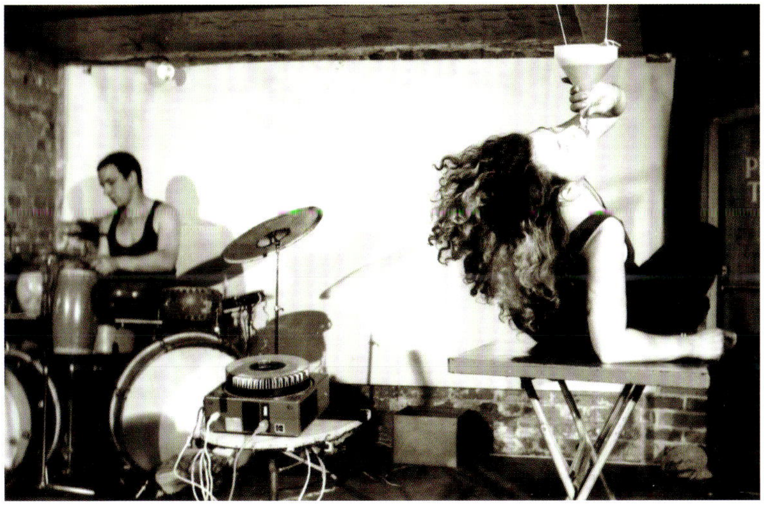

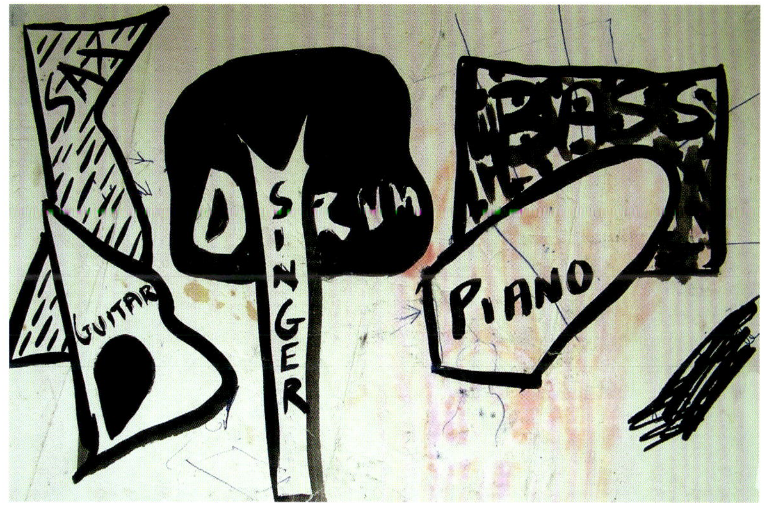

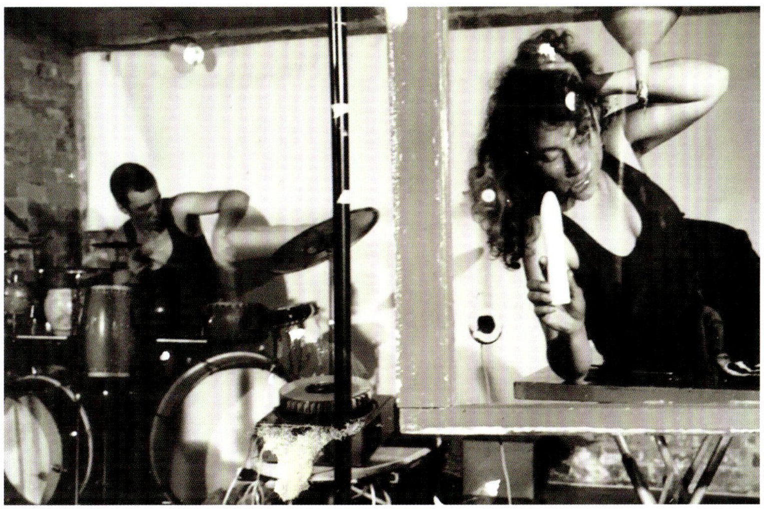

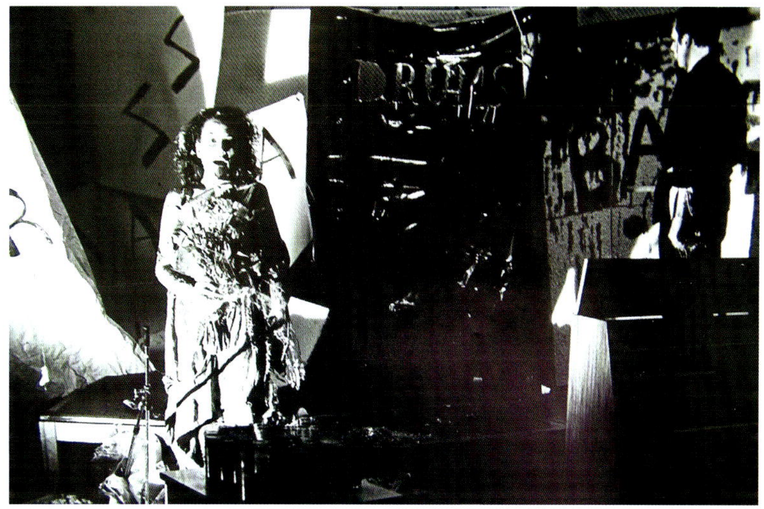

Top left and bottom left: PULp MUSIC (Anne Bean and Paul Burwell), *Her voice is pollen as she was placed*, South Hill Park, Bracknell, 1983. Photo: Guy Brett

Top right: Anne Bean, sketch for set-up of a performance by Absolutely Furious (Anne Bean with Paul Burwell, Simon Brint, Giles Thomas and Peter Davey), Galerie Defet, Nuremburg, Germany, 1978

Bottom right: Absolutely Furious, Galerie Defet, Nuremburg, 1978. Photographer unknown

Opposite: Anne Bean and Paul Burwell, *Sunken Boat*, River Thames, London 1978. Photo: Chris Bishop

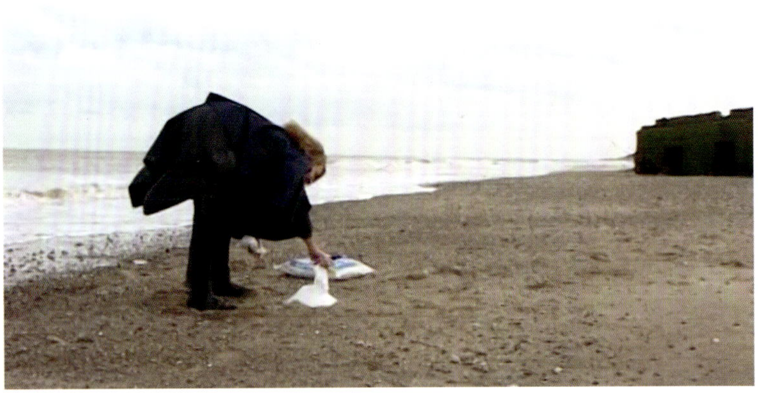
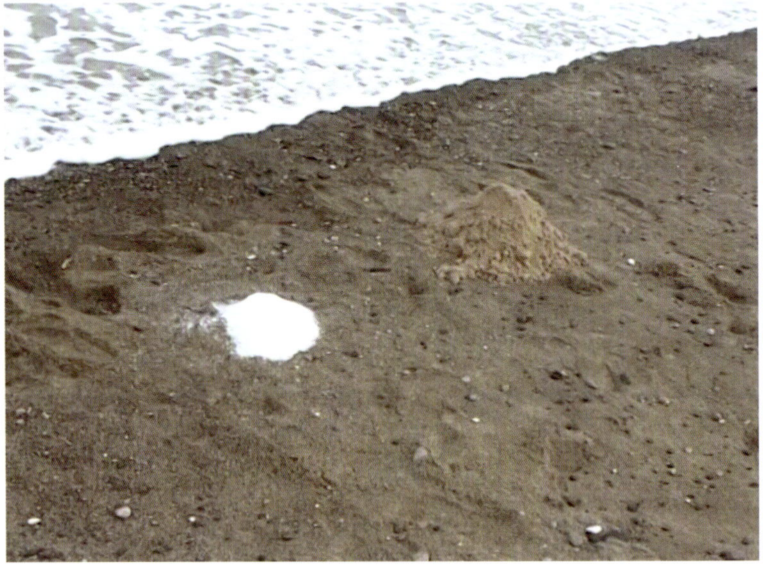
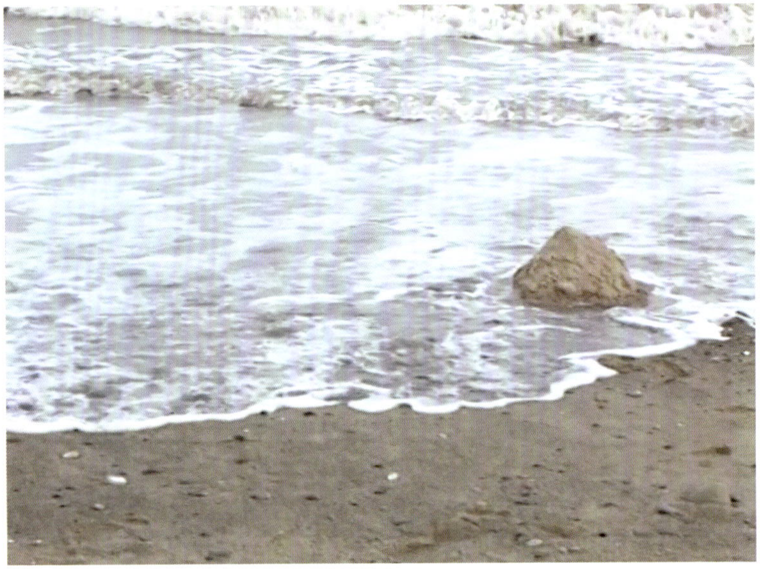
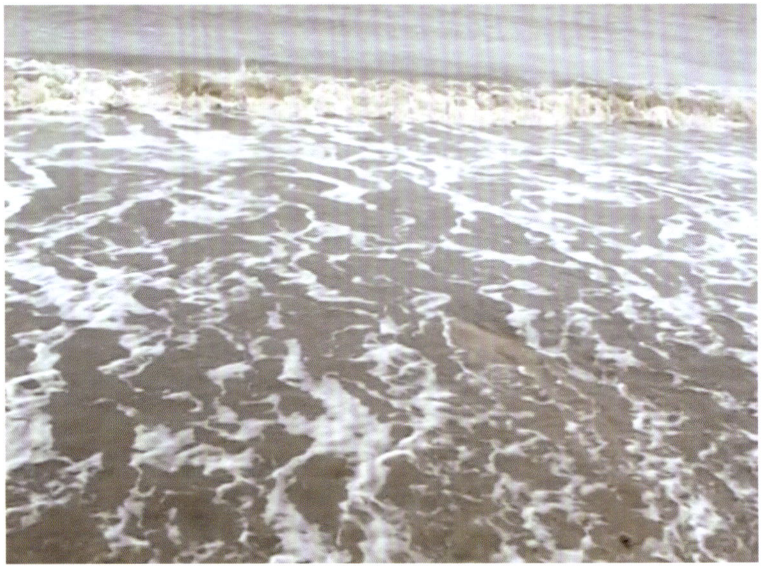

Above: Anne Bean, *Homecoming* reformed as a *Shadow Deed* in 2004 for *Autobituary* (2006). Still from video by Lee Merrill-Sendall

Opposite, top two rows: Anne Bean, Rod Melvin, Graham Challifour and Gill Jones, *The Bride*, Great Hall, Reading, 1971. Photo: Clive Robertson

Bottom two rows: Delayed 1971>2017, Anne Bean, Rod Melvin, Graham Challifour, and Mirei Yazawa, Great Hall, Reading, 2017. Photo: Hydar Dewachi

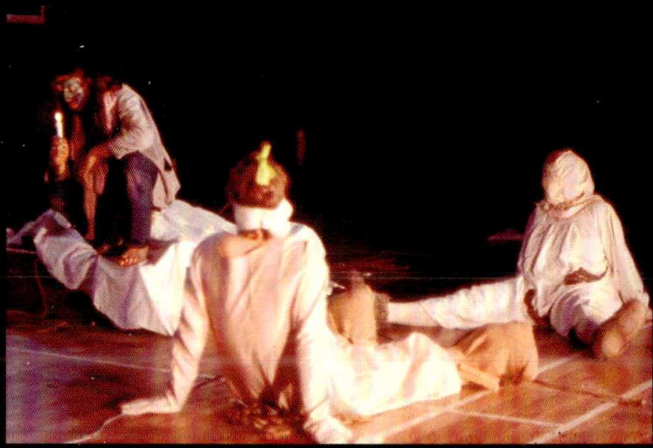
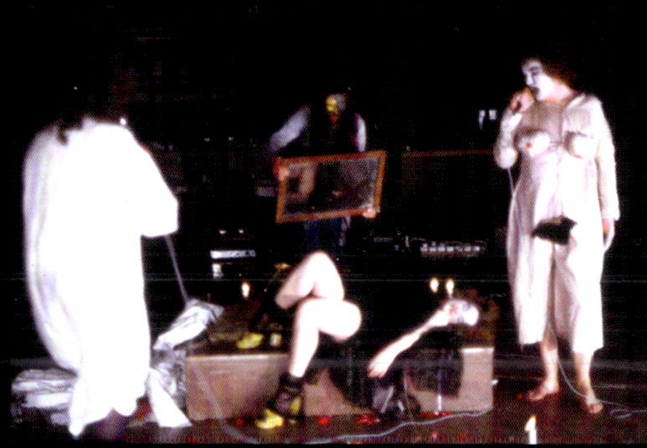
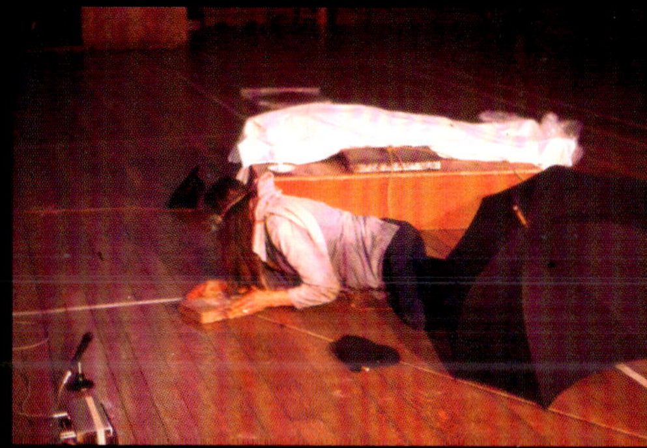
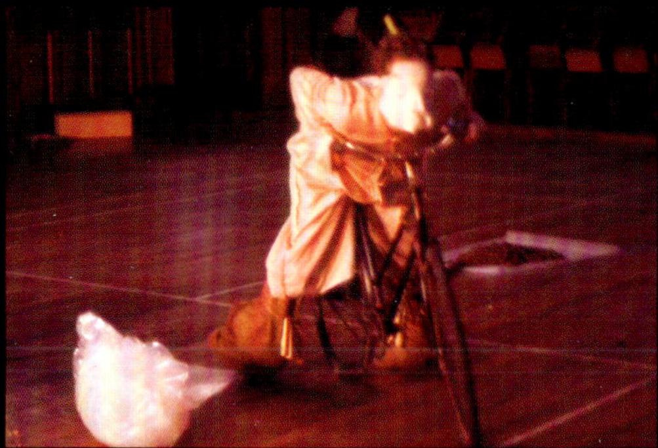
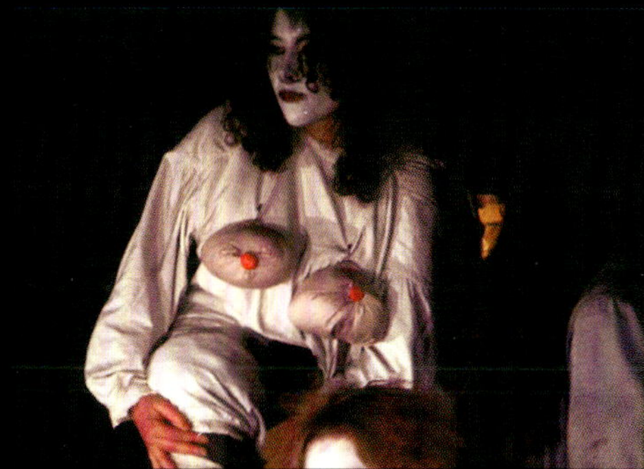
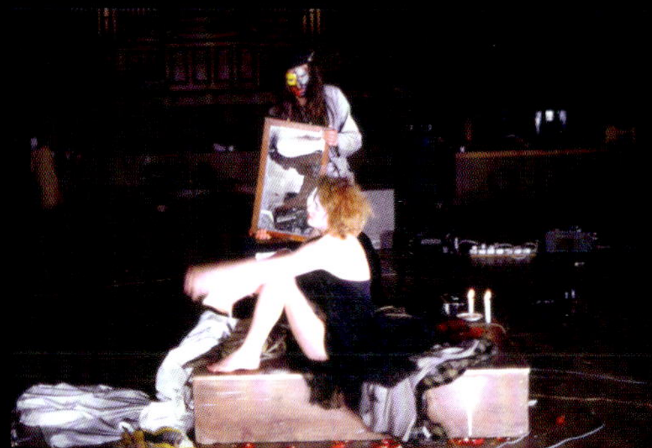
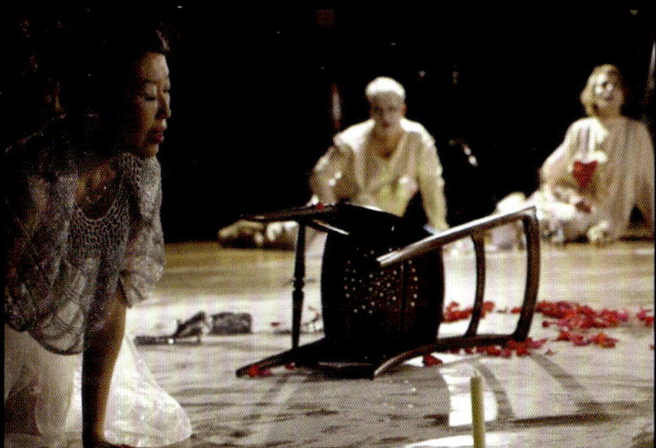
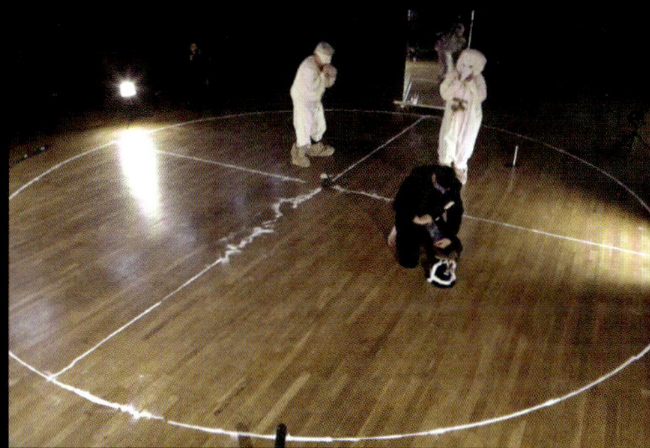
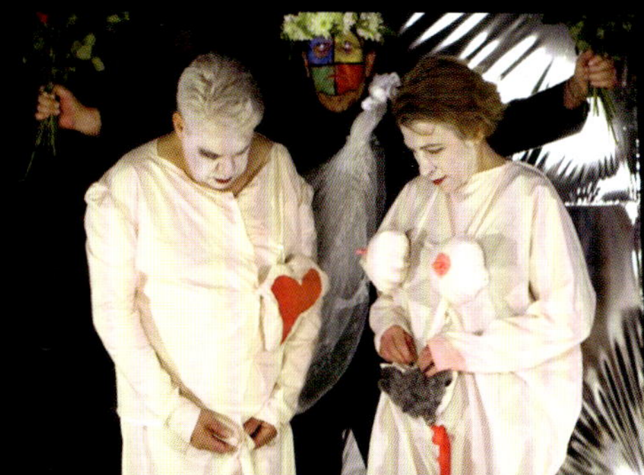
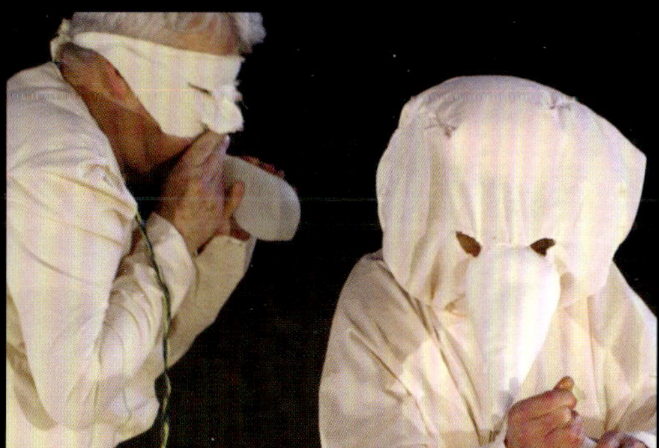
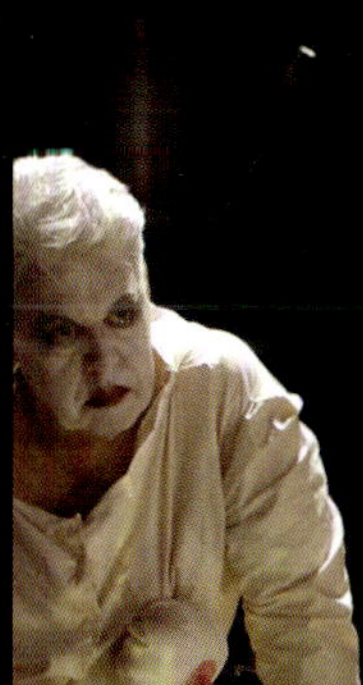
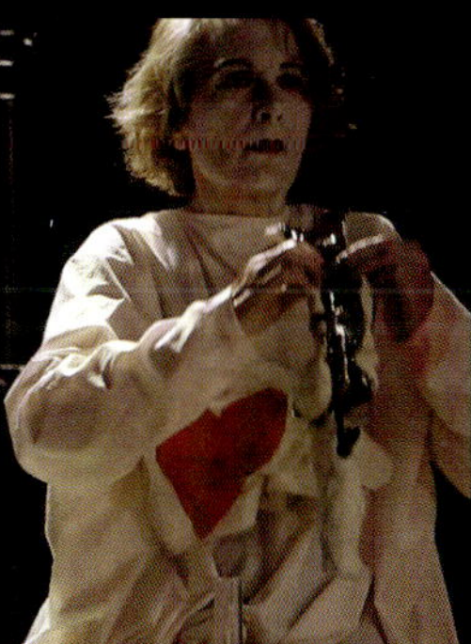
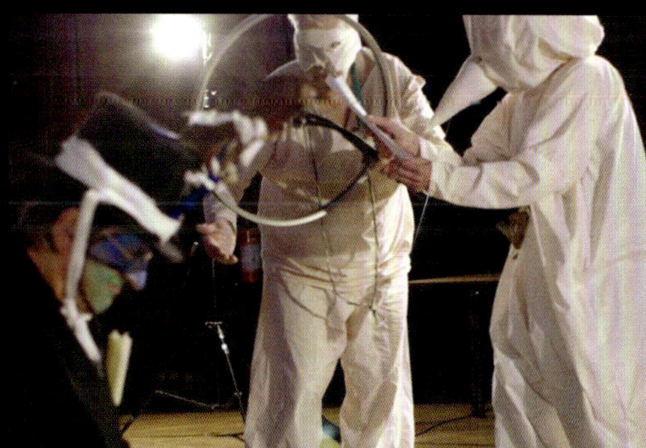

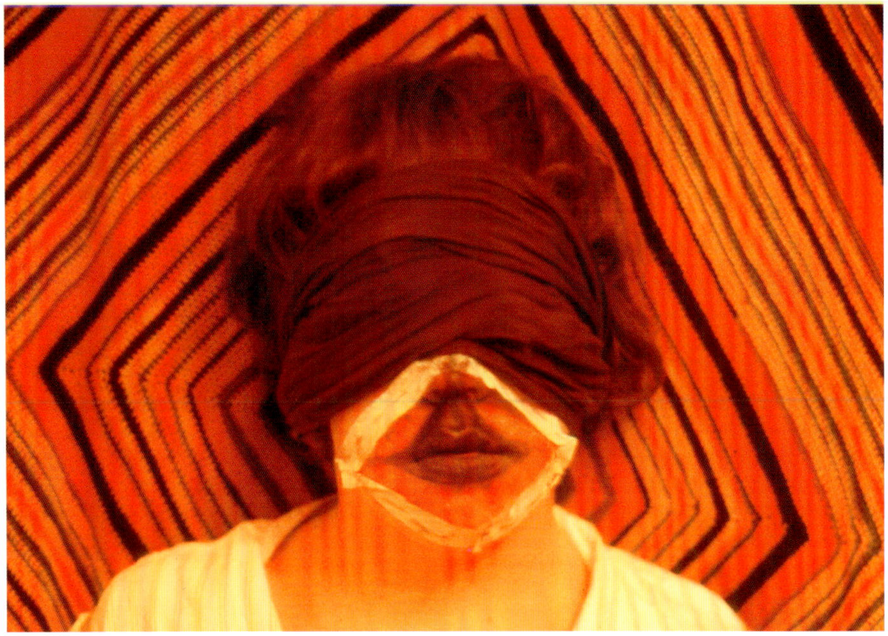

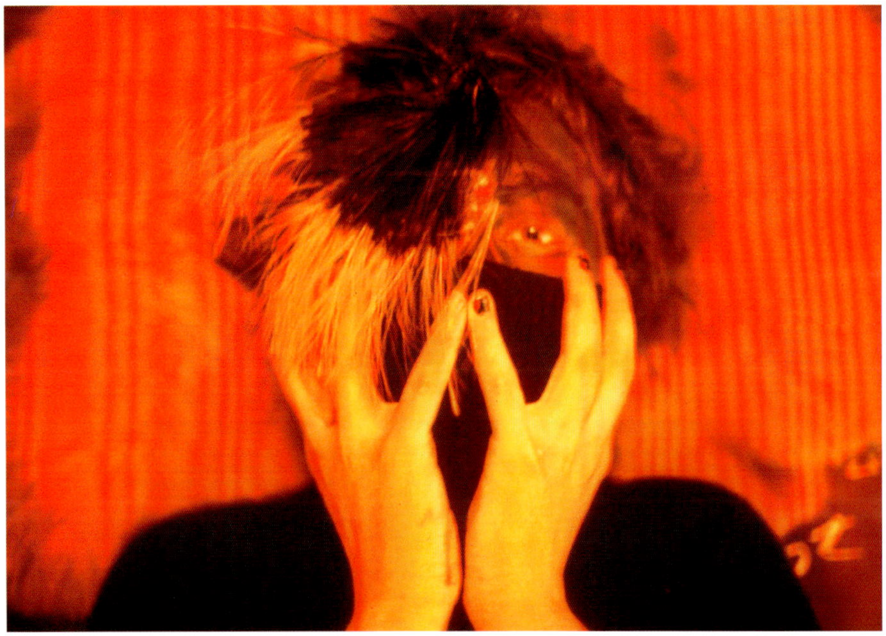

Top: Rod Melvin as 'Mouth' in Anne Bean, *Gas Heart*, Reading, 1971
Bottom: Anne Bean as 'Eye' in *Gas Heart*, Reading, 1971. Photo: Graham Challifour

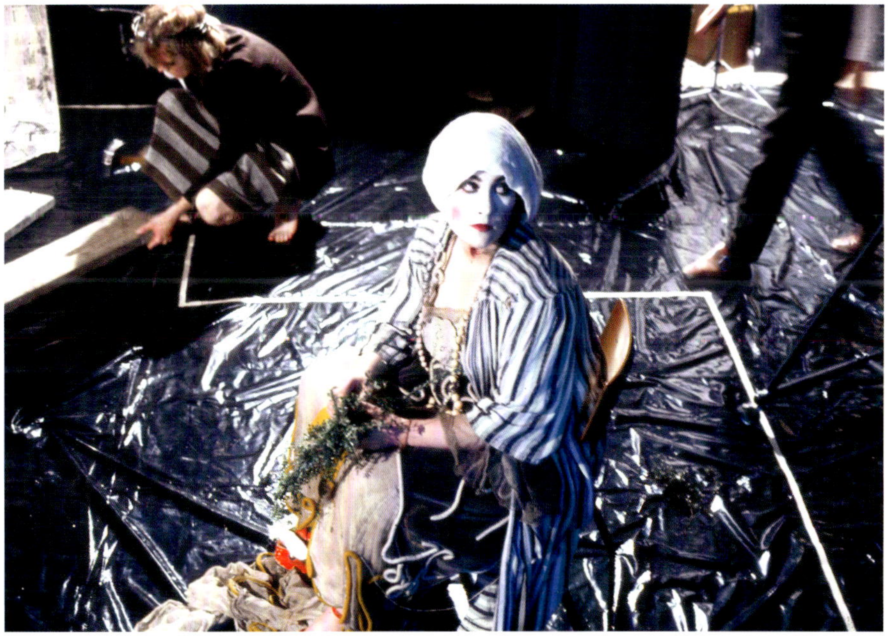

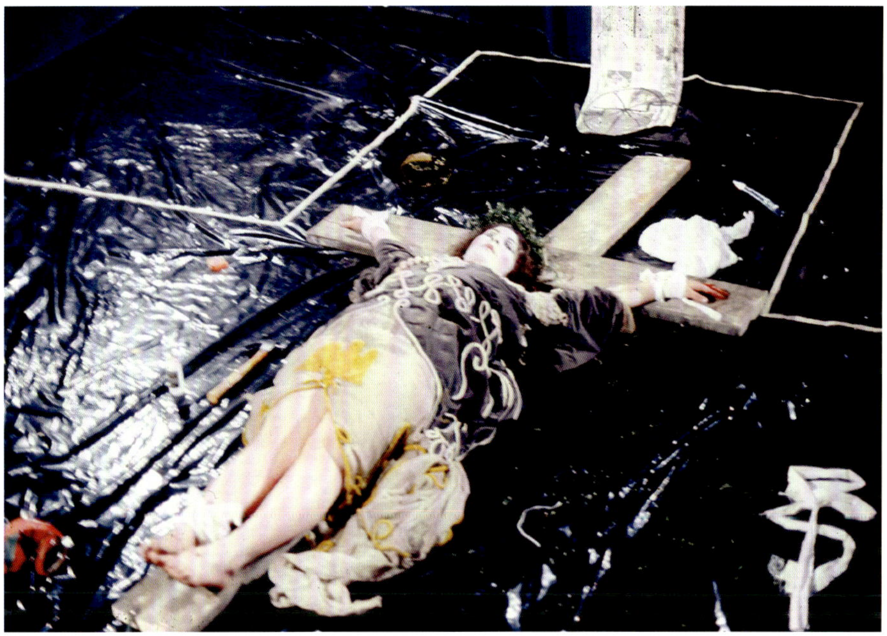

Anne Bean with Graham Challifour, Clyde Hopkins and Wilf Scott, *The Consummation, Crucifixion, Resurrection and Transubstantiation as seen by the Virgin Mary (God is the Tangential Point between Zero and Infinity)*, Reading, 1971. Photos: Clive Robertson

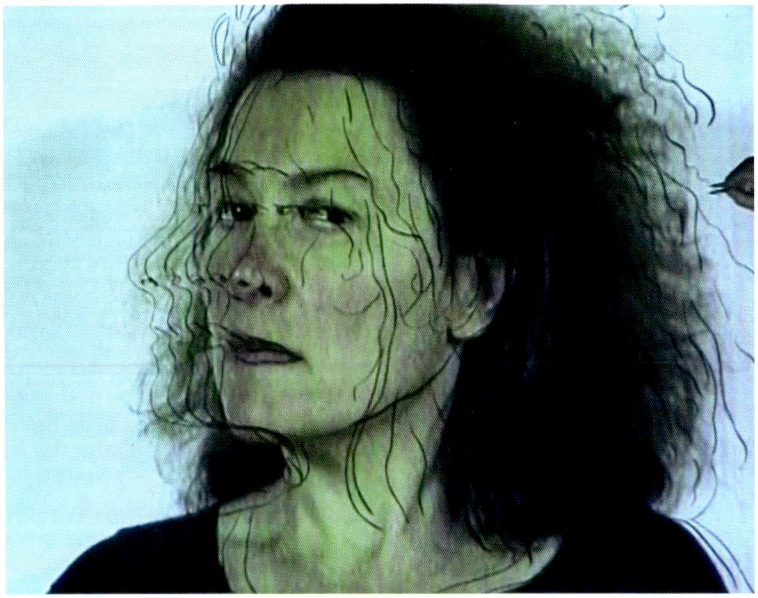

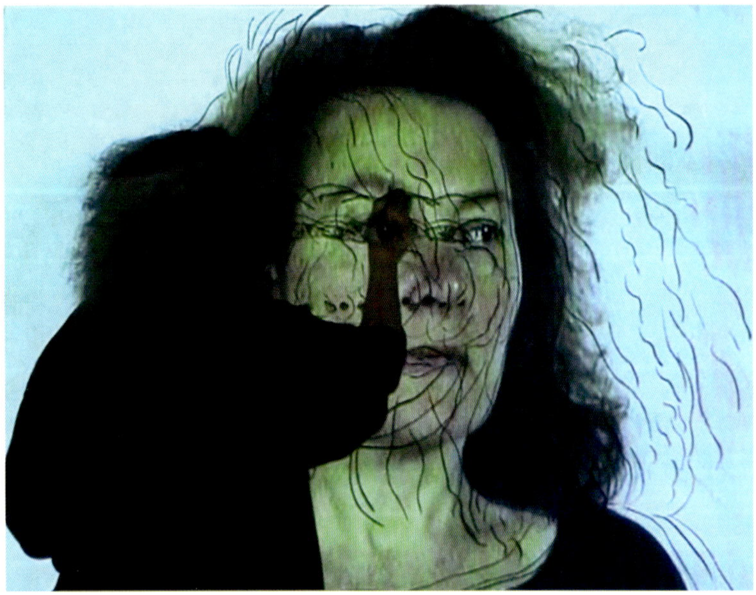

Above: Anne Bean, *Now and Then* reformed as a *Shadow Deed* in 2003 for *Autobituary* (2006). Still from video by Lee Merrill-Sendall

Opposite: Anne Bean, collaged image after *Closer to Death, Closer to Now*, a durational incantation, Butlers Wharf, London, 1979. Photo: Paul Burwell

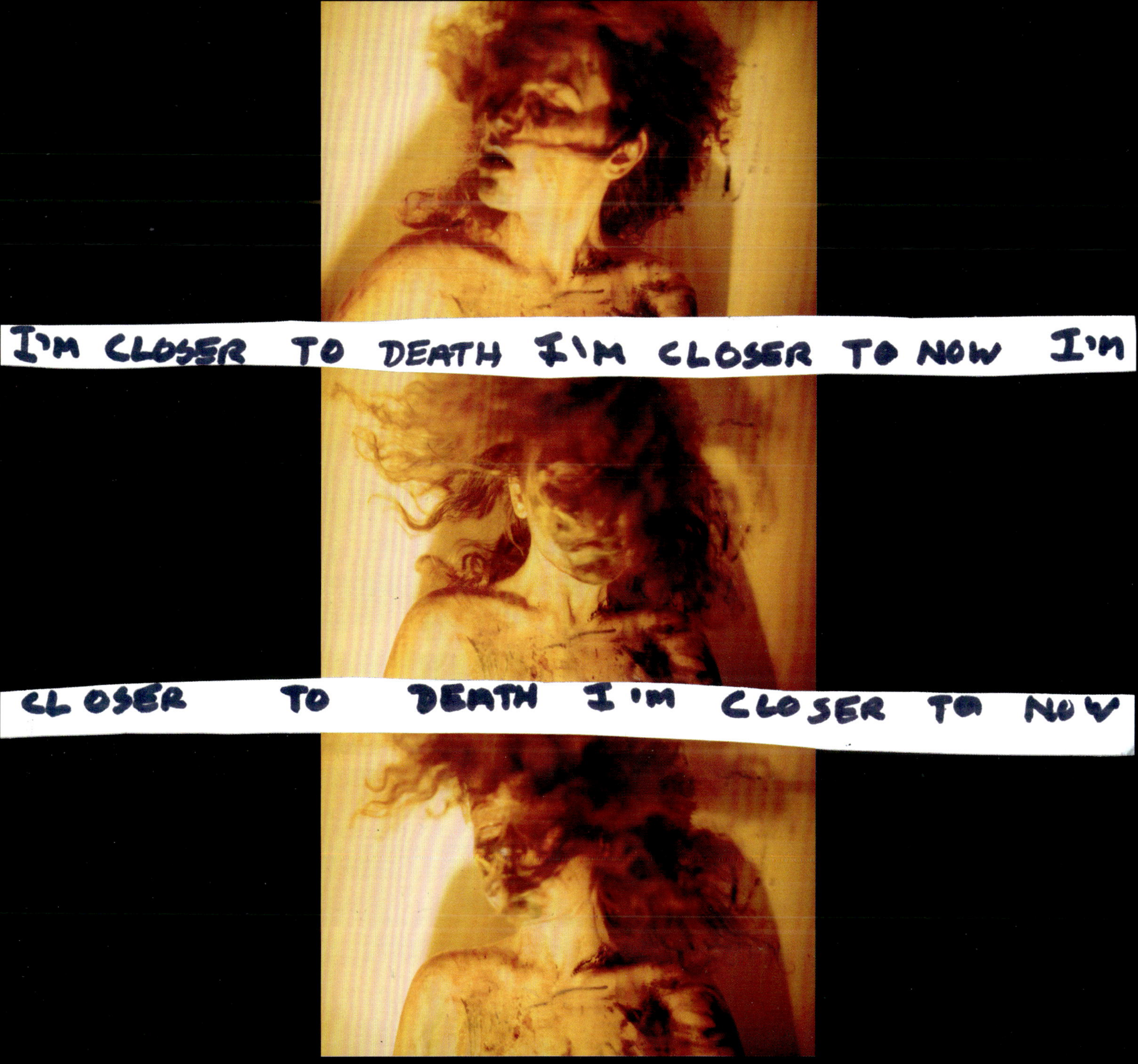
I'M CLOSER TO DEATH I'M CLOSER TO NOW I'M
CLOSER TO DEATH I'M CLOSER TO NOW

INTERVENTIONS BY ANNE BEAN

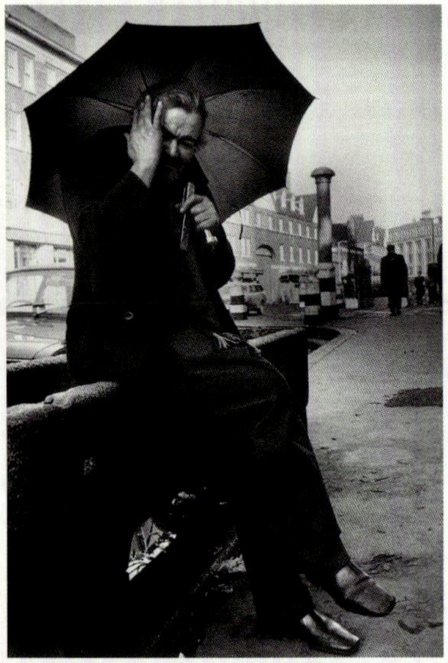

Man playing mouth organ in front of Christ Church, Commercial Road, London 1978. From the series *London Street Musicians*, Photo: Markéta Luskačová

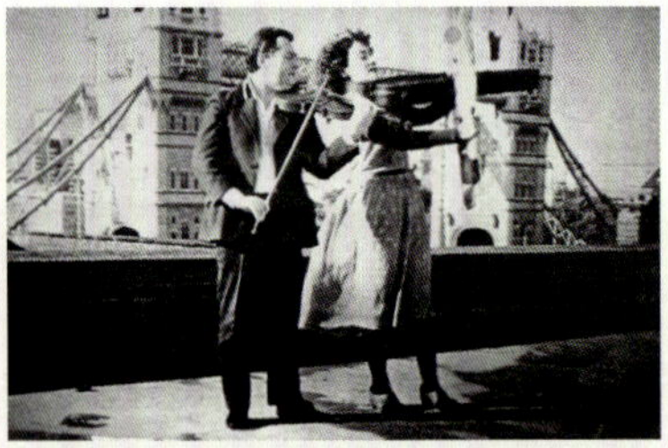

Busking with a violin case and cricket bat with violinist John Mckeon, 1976. Photo: Chris Bishop

Holding Infinity in the Palm of my Hand, 2015, Foyle Reading Room exhibition, Whitechapel Gallery

Dominic Johnson invited me to do a residency at the Whitechapel Gallery, in the Foyle Reading Room, in relation to *Performance and Politics in 1970s*. Whilst searching through archival material, I came across press and images of Markéta Luskačová's one-woman show of photographs at the Whitechapel Gallery, *Photographs of Spitalfields*, 1991.

She had photographed the area around the gallery and Brick Lane almost every Sunday since the mid-1970s. I thought about my own actions in the area during that period, often dressed in disconcerting outfits, busking with deviant instruments and selling mystifying items on Brick Lane market. I thought that if she had photographed me at the time, it would have encapsulated the twilight zones between art capturing life and life capturing art.

I contacted Markéta to ask her if she would photograph, in her observant but unobtrusive way, actions that I would make in the area now, with these threshold ideas in mind. She agreed and we made a series of works together for an exhibition in the Reading Room, alongside each of our images in the area from 1970s.

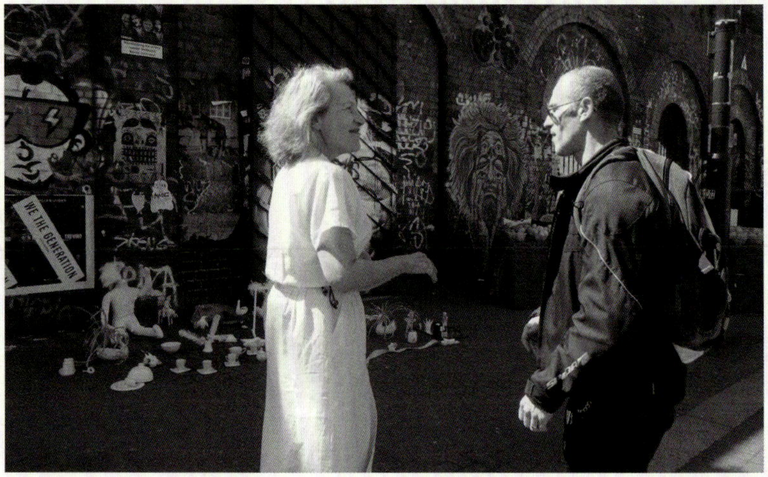

A stall with only white objects on Brick Lane Market, explaining that nothing is for sale. Photo: Markéta Luskačová

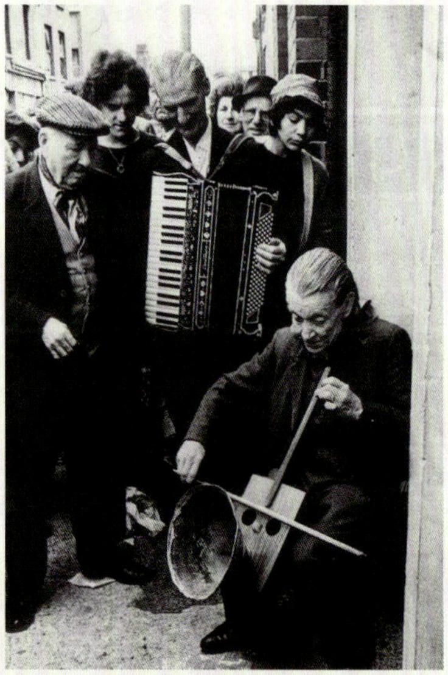

Street musician, Cheshire Street, London, 1977. From the series 'London Street Musicians'. Photo: Markéta Luskačová

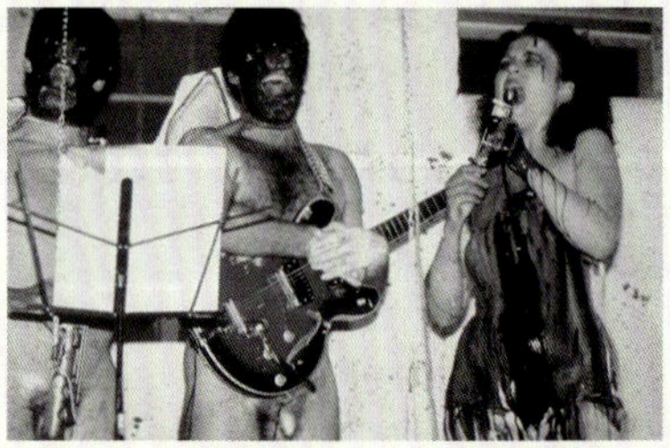

With Kipper Kids at The Masque, Hollywood, 1978, a punk club where we were thrown out for being too punk. Photo: Elisa Leonelli

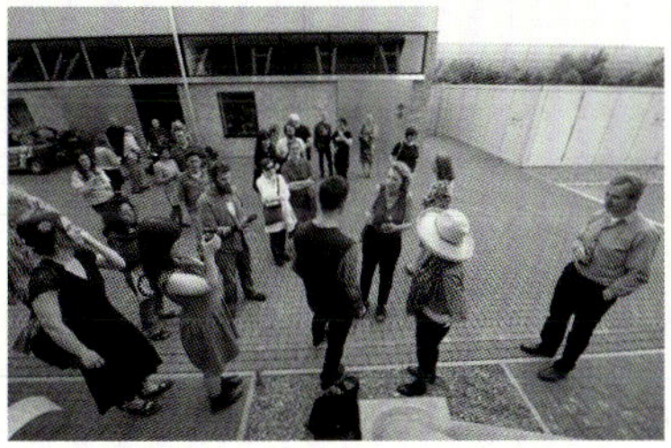

The ABCD ness of it all: Ceci n'est pas une performance, 2014.

At the time that I was invited to take part in *Sculpture-Performance: Acme Artists Now*, Purfleet 2014, I was querying ways forward on the *ABCD ness* (Anne Bean/ Chana Dubinski alignments,) as I had recently left my life in Newark-on-Trent, living fully as Chana Dubinski. One side of the querying was how to make a timed performance that somehow pinpointed the art/life conundrum. I decided I would have a title, time and place for a performance, but life as it was happening would simply carry on. As it was a sociable event with lots happening and people chatting, when the time came for the 'performance' I simply carried on talking, as it so happened, with Dominic Johnson and Elyssa Livergant. People started to look at me as if I should be entering something that existed in the known space of 'performance.' Something should signal and change the space we inhabited together and I should become the 'other.' There was an uneasiness and then gradual adjusting to the fact that this was the work with no discernible beginning or end. There was still disquiet as to how near to be, how much to 'eavesdrop,' what was voyeuristic, could one join in. A space that is in life but oblique, slightly chafing. I was aware of Magritte's famous pipe painting (*ceci n'est pas un pipe*) and the great title *The Treachery of Images*.

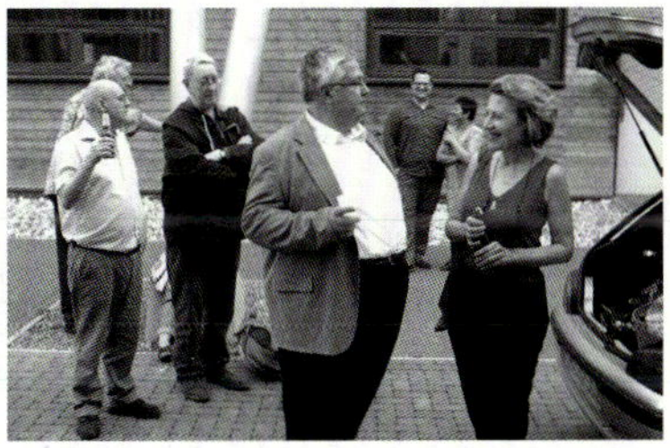

Speaking with Dr Thomas Frangenberg about whether the performance is over or if we are stuck in it forever, alongside a few other people's uncertainties.

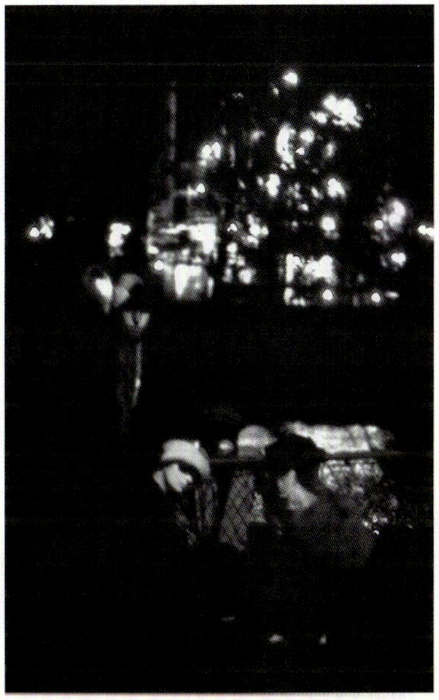

Gas Heart by the gasworks, Reading. Mouth, Ear, Eye, Nose, Neck, and Eyebrow.

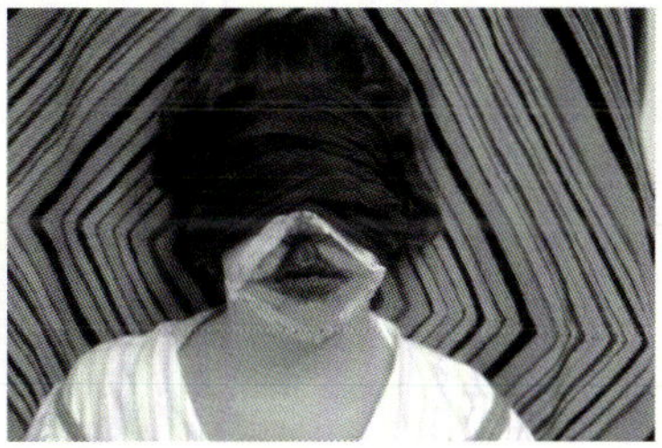

Gas Heart, 1971

I briefly squatted a derelict lock keeper's cottage near the gasworks in Reading in1971. I decided to do a loose production of *Gas Heart* by Tristan Tzara, with the gasworks, glittering at night, as a background. The play takes the form of an absurd dialogue with nuanced inferences between the characters, each named after human body parts Mouth, Ear, Eye, Nose, Neck, and Eyebrow. Duchamp alluded to gas as an animator of libido in both the *Large Glass* and *Étants Données* ('Given: 1. the waterfall 2. the lighting gas.') Similarly to Duchamp's bride and her bachelors, the play resonates with the machinery of power, love and desire as an underlying life-force. The performers were Suzy Adderley, Becky Bailey, Chris Bishop, Alastair Brotchie, Graham Challifour, Rod Melvin and myself.

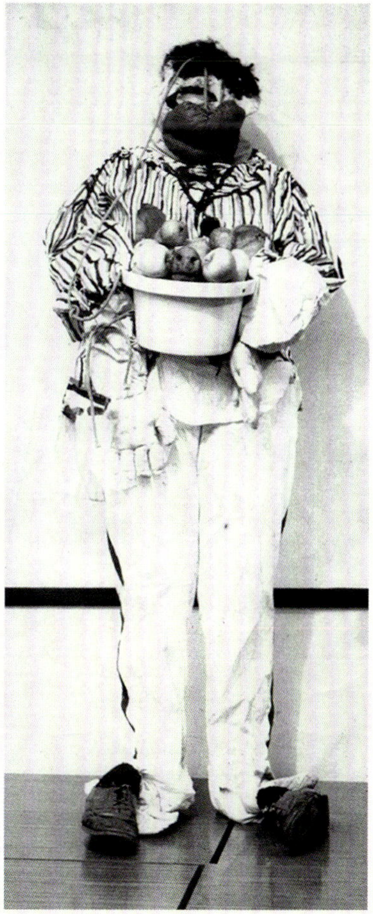

Nothing, Post Graduate house, Reading. Who manipulates whom? Ventriloquist and dummy, dragging my shoes, manipulating my mouth with Rod Melvin and Graham Challifour, 1971

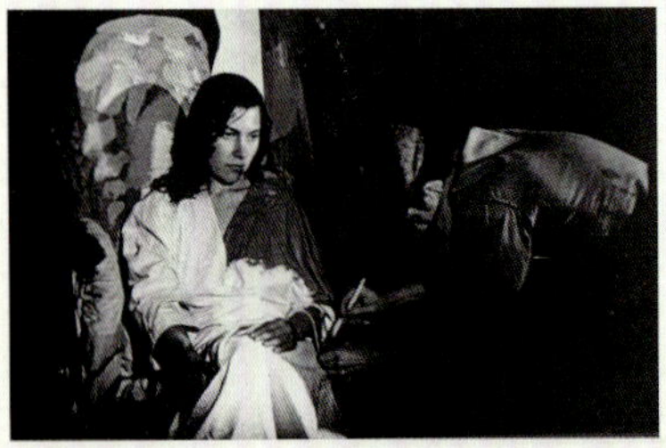

Anxtions, 1970-80

During the 70's, with the artist Peter Davey, both in public and private investigations, we made a series of 'anxtions;' anxious actions. These actions, included reconstructing paintings as 'live' works, collaborative paintings, taking classes in traditional central African dance, studying hypnotic techniques, reconstructing Bollywood scripts, taking a journey prescribed by chance edicts and based on Samuel Beckett's novel *Mercier and Camier*, evoking the wild imagery conjured in songs such as Screaming Jay Hawkin's *Alligator Wine* to create visual/sound actions, working with the poet May Green's specially commissioned poems and an electric food shredder into which pages of books were inserted and random fragments pulled out and used as improvised texts:

And the Sunflowers
Turn in a long slow
Dance
Offering fierce
Sun bird seed
While cowboys
Thread small cattle,
down a dusty lane
in Florida

May Green 1978

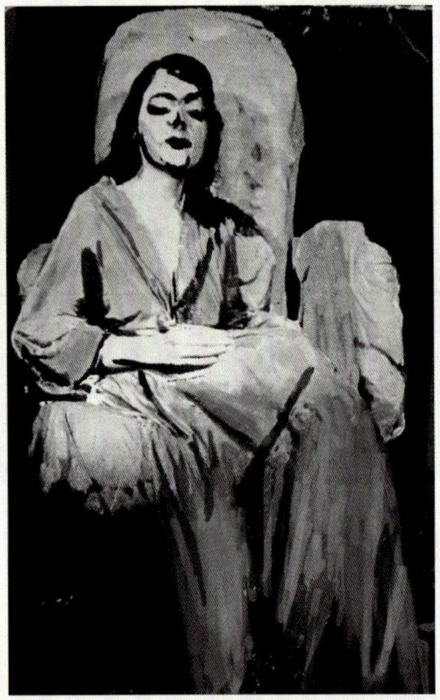

The Green Robe (a restructuring of Matisse's painting), 1979

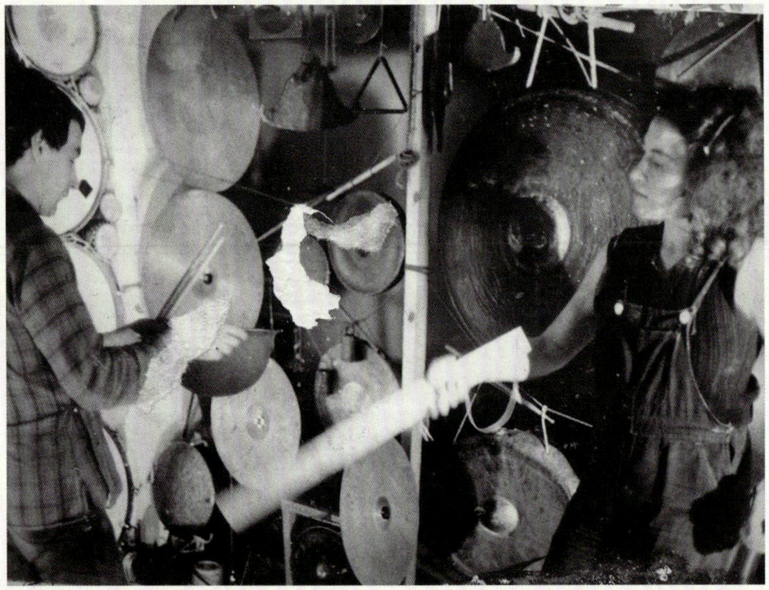

Experiments with walls of drums and cymbals with Paul Burwell, 1978

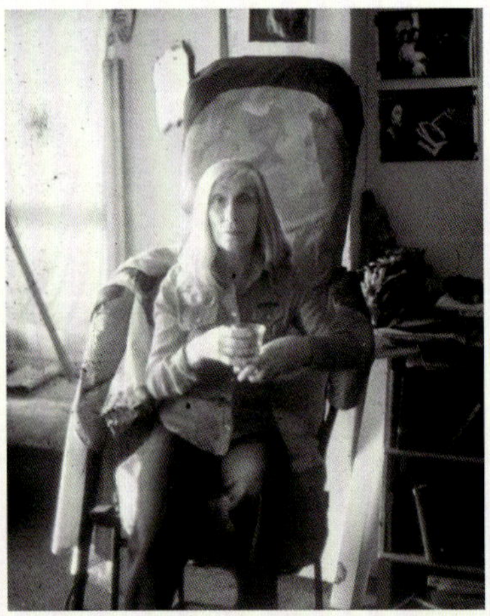

The poet, May Green. 1978

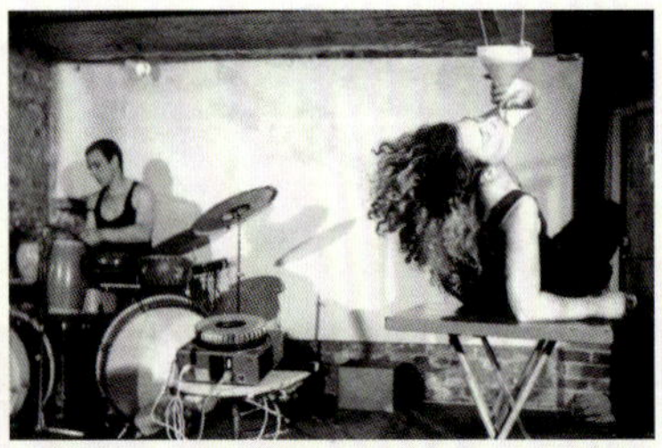

Her voice is pollen as she was placed, 1983. PULp MUSIC
South Hill Park, Bracknell

Paul Burwell and I were interested in ancient beliefs where daily life and spiritual ritual intertwined such as in the traditional Navajo way, described as 'life itself, the land and well-being.' In the Navajo way, each being, all living things, is infused with its own spirit, or 'inner form' which gives it life and purpose within an interconnected universe. This interrelatedness of all creation is recognised through daily systems of ceremonies with lucent songs which we used as stimulants for improvising. My mouth filled with honey distorted and controlled my voice whilst singing abstractly about the process of honey creation.

The White Room, 1970

This project was instigated by the artist/ tutor Rita Donagh. It articulated and extended for me ideas of the crossover of art/life, private action/shared space, personal/global, as well as the multiple 'others' that are created through collaboration. Beginning as a life-drawing class, it evolved into a drawing-life action, as the life model became a part of the group. We made blindfolded drawings, we typed up life-drawings, we devised systems and ways of operating, we more-or-less lived in the space for three weeks.

The art historian, Roger Cook, a tutor at that time described it in 2016 as 'a remarkable utopian project that occurred with a small group of students in the Department of Fine at the University of Reading over a period three weeks in May 1970. Though initiated by an artist/teacher, it was a shared event, a collaboration that took off initially from the traditional situation of the 'life room' and included the presence and participation of the model... it can be seen historically as an event in the wake of the promised transformations wrought by the political and cultural disturbances of '68, which so shook up art and politics, or better put, the unfinished business of the relation of the aesthetic to the political and the meaning of sharing in an educational context.'

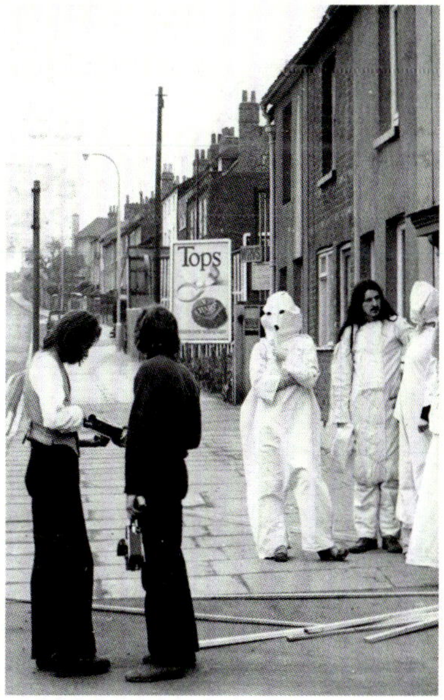

Filming including Alastair Brotchie, Graham Challifour, Rod Melvin and Stuart Smith

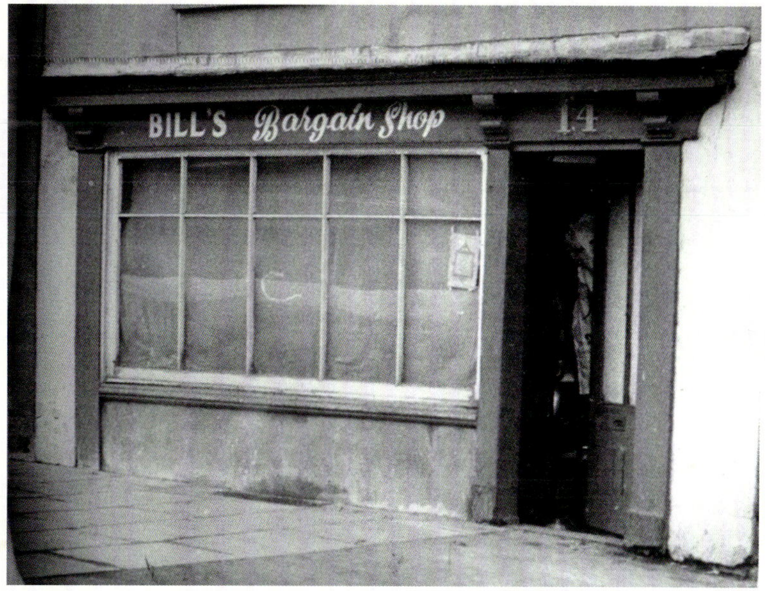

In the early 70's, I travelled to Paris several times to see various plays, particularly several Ubu productions, with Alastair Brotchie, who went on to found the London publishing house Atlas Press. We made several forays into Jarry territory with myself as Mère Ubu, often using my space, 'Bill's Bargain shop,' for actions.

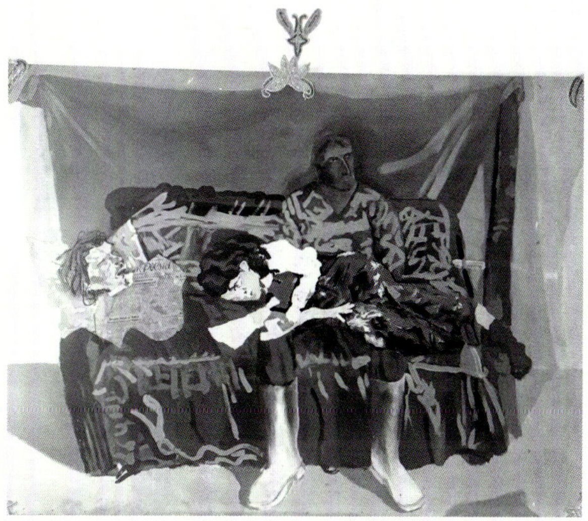

Combined painting with Alastair Brotchie and Malcolm Jones, Butlers Wharf 1977

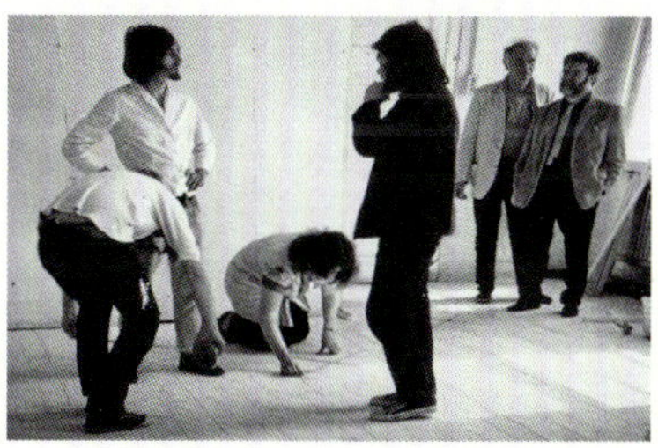

Left: I began the floor grid for *White Room* with professors/artists Claude Rogers and Terry Frost observing plus Stuart Smith and Phil Winder, 1970. Photo: Graham Challifour

I held many party/performances in my space, C4 Butlers Wharf, including one in which Richard Wilson rowed out with Paul Burwell stopping underneath Tower Bridge to drum with the echoes. I swam to join them from Butlers Wharf, lit by light-sticks, voicing into the wind and currents.

David Toop writes in a monograph on Stephen Cripps, published by Acme in 1992, 'He salvaged objects from the scrapheap, redeeming them from a fate of erasure on the far edges of marginal history. During a mid-Seventies party (Part Y) organised by artist Anne Bean at the Wharf, for example, a small mechanical record player played as it crawled its insectile path through partygoers and performers such as Jayne County and the Electric Chairs, Michael Nyman, The Rich Kids (their first gig), Sid Vicious and Nancy Spungen, Bruce Lacey, Andrew Logan, Midge Ure and various members of The Jam, The Buzzcocks and Siouxsie and The Banshees.'

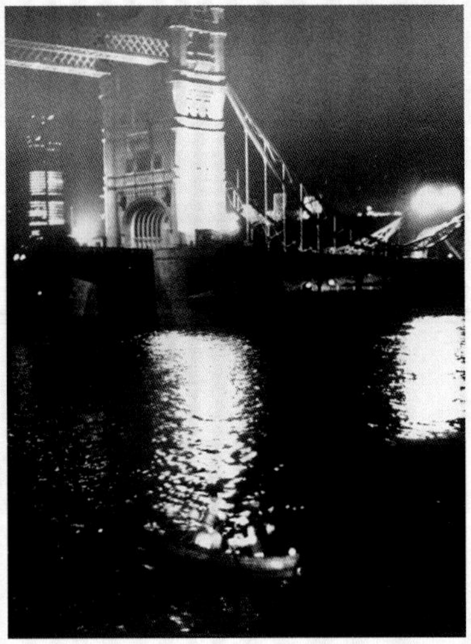

Paul Burwell and Richard Wilson rowing out with the drum kit I adapted to play with lights and shadows by closing battery circuits, I swam towards them, singing covered in safety lights, 1978.

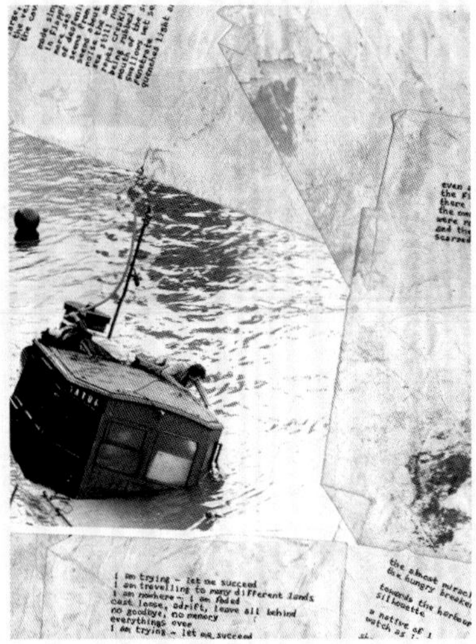

Anne Bean and Paul Burwell improvising Paul's song on a sinking boat, River Thames. Photo: Chris Bishop

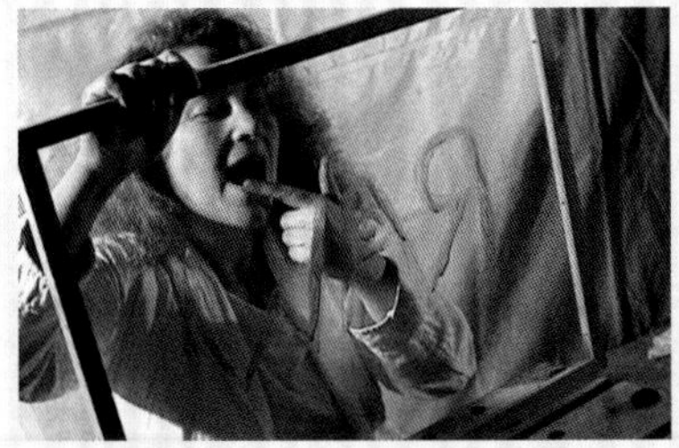

I first spoke through bloodied lips in the *White Room* when I read out a news report on the May 4 massacre which occurred the day before at Kent State University, and involved the shooting of unarmed college students by the Ohio National Guard on Monday, May 4, 1970. The guardsmen fired 67 rounds over a period of 13 seconds, killing four students and wounding nine others, one of whom suffered permanent paralysis.

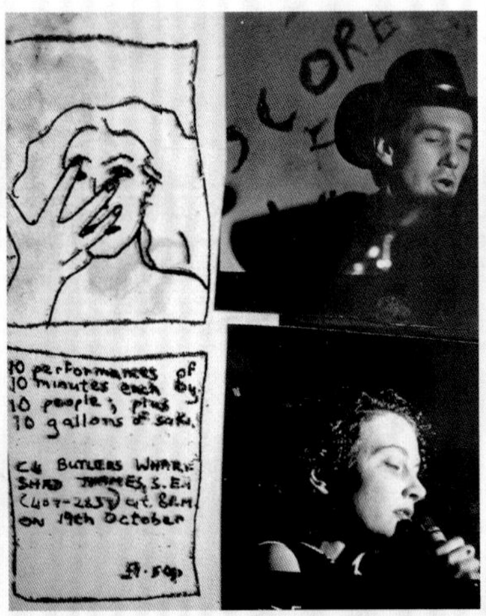

Leaflet for C4 Butlers Wharf event

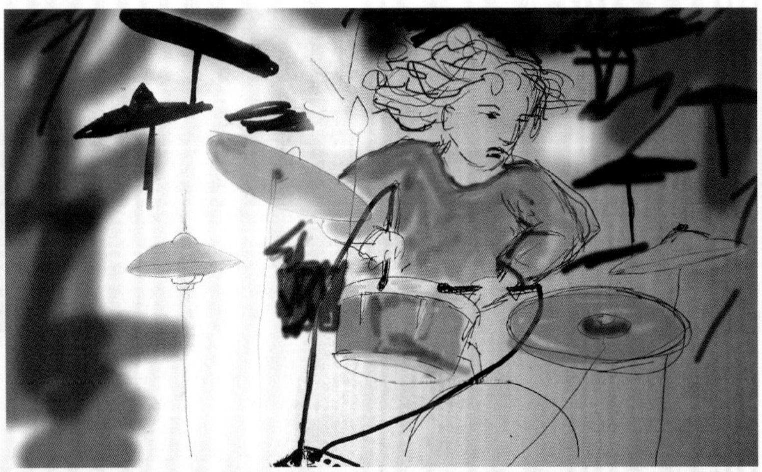

Drumkit for shadow rhythms, Butlers Wharf 1977

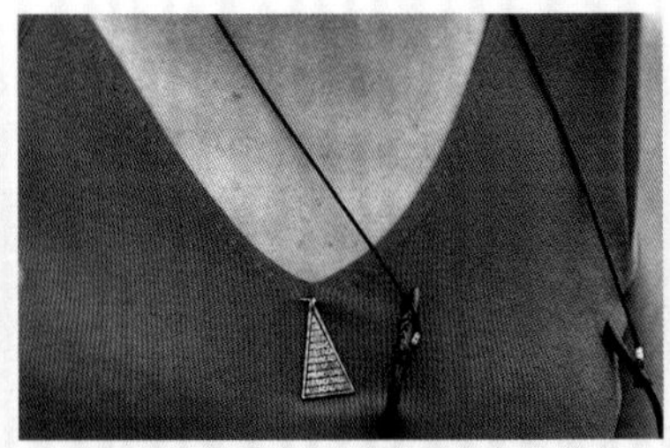

ABRACADABRA, on my pendant, worn during *The ABCD ness of it all: Ceci n'est pas une performance*, Purfleet 2014, is said to come from Aramaic: 'I CREATE WHAT I SPEAK'.

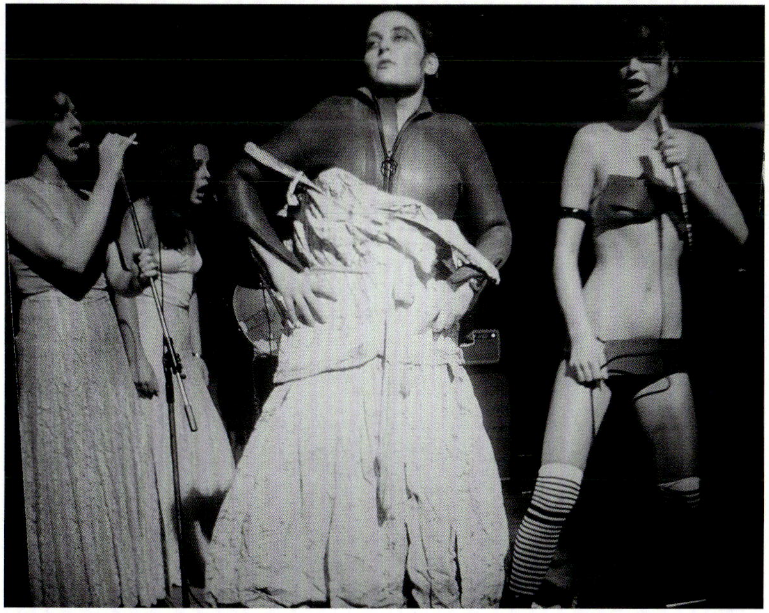

Moodier, Garage Gallery, London, (Chris Bishop, Hermine Demoriane, Polly Eltes, Malcolm Jones, John McKeon, Judy Nylon, Max Paddison, sisters Jennifer and Lorraine), 1975

DELAYED 1971>2017 ARC (Anne, Rod, Chal)

In 2017, I met with Graham Challifour (Chal) and Rod Melvin, with whom I had made many performances during our time at Reading University Fine Art Department, to film *DELAYED 1971>2017*. We went back to the Great Hall in Reading University to find a way to get back in contact with *The Bride*, a work we made in 1971. We had been meeting, drawing together and emailing on and o for 5 years previously to filming. Rod and I 'swapped' genders during the work as I did with myself in *Moodier* 1974 at Garage gallery, swapping between a painted white ballgown and a rubber suit and changing my voice to suit for each. In *AMP (Anne Matisse Picasso)* 1971 using text of Gertrude Stein's *GMP*, I felt an affinity with her repeating interchangeable patterns of pronouns he, she, one, they, and we to create abstract language paintings.

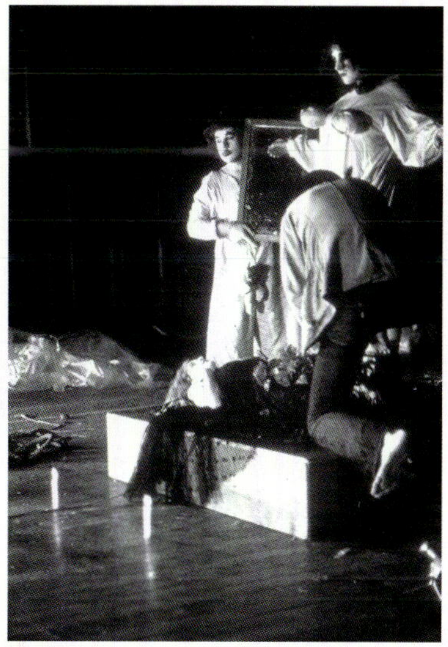

The Bride, 1971

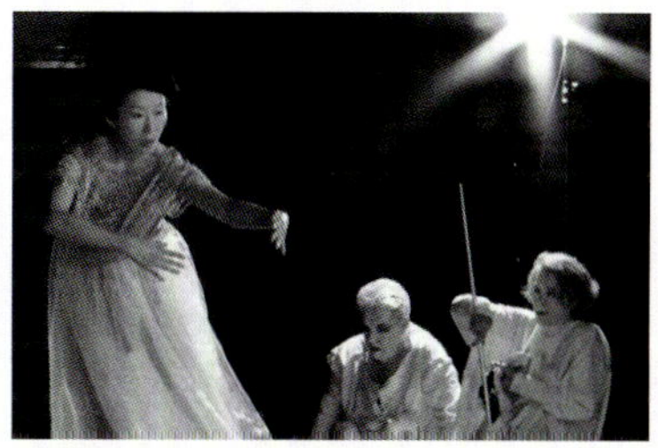

Still from *DELAYED 1971>2017* with Butoh trained dancer and artist Mirei Yazawa.

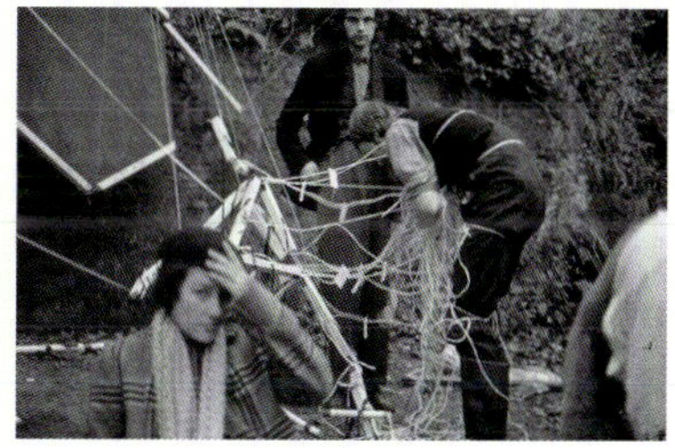

Bernsteins (1971-1974)

Anne Bean, Peter Davey, Malcolm Jones, Jonathan Harvey, Chris Millar, Brian Routh and Martin von Haselberg

The name Bernsteins came from a derelict, chemist shop in Mile End Road where we all lived for longer or shorter periods.

Taking measurements of yourselves as artists was a full day of working in Fairlight Glen, Hastings. The gallerist and artist Victor Musgrave visited and after watching for some time, including a long interlude of the Kipper Kids simultaneously trying to pick each other up, concluded that our genre should be named 'Obstacle Art.'

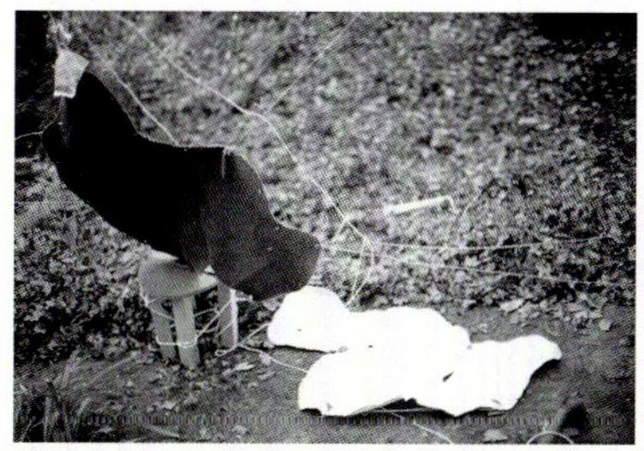

Ghost of a Shadow, Shadow of a Ghost, one of the works I did during *Taking measurements of yourselves as artists*, in which a cut-out shape of myself, curled up, cast a shadow. I drew around and cut out the shadow and then that form cast a shadow, etc etc.

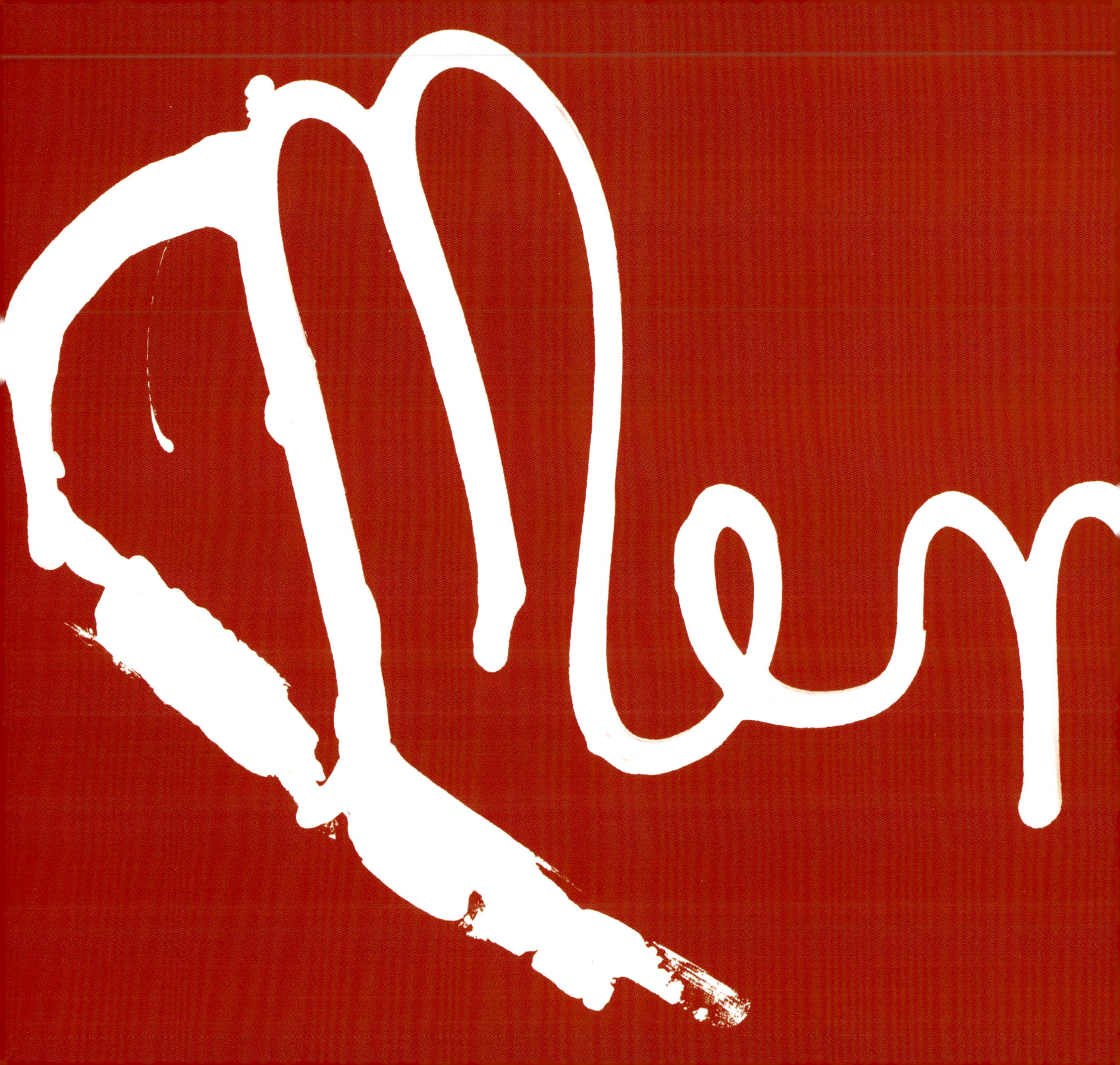

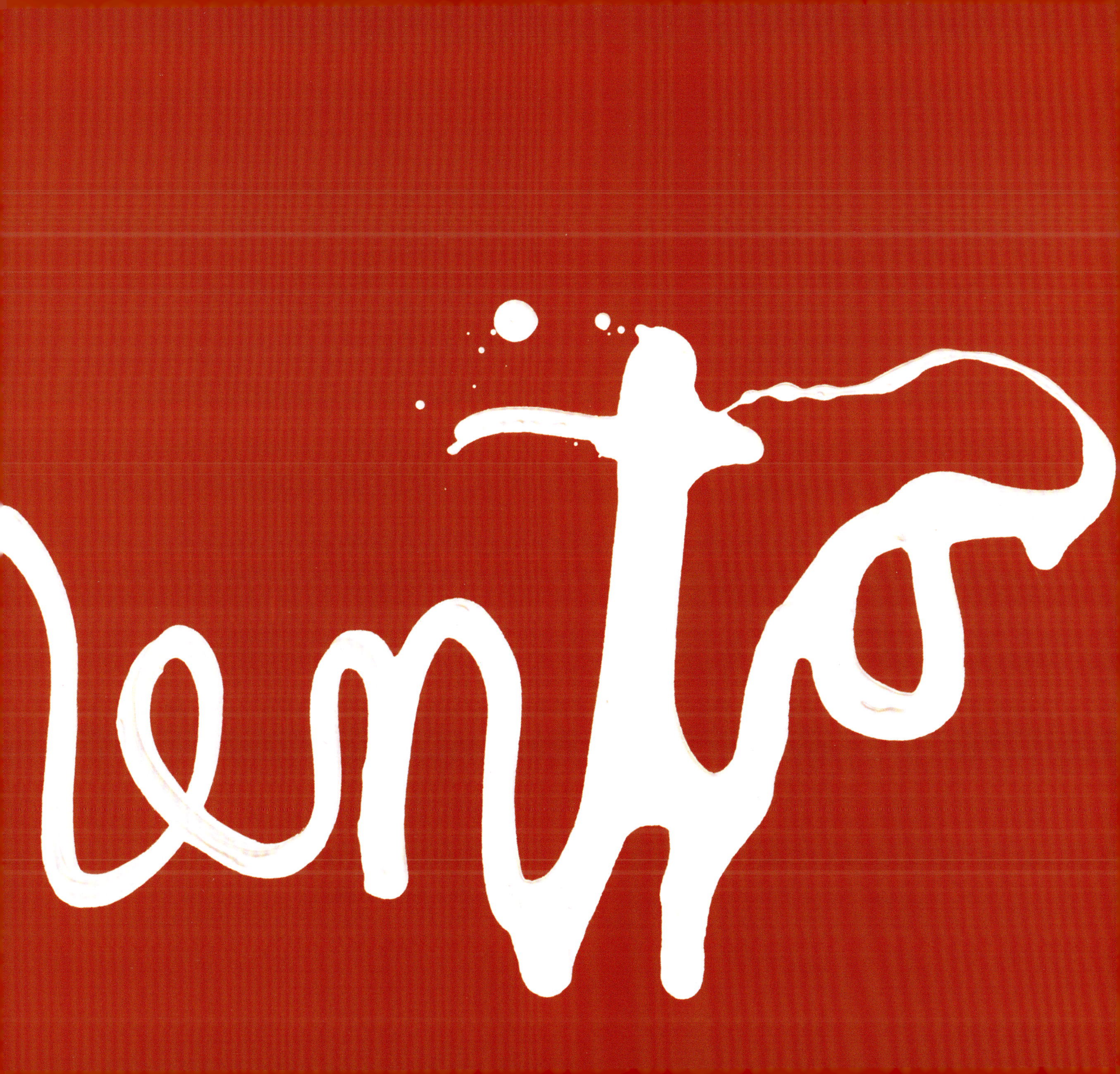

MEMENTO MORI: SECRET CONVERSATIONS WE DIDN'T KNOW WE WERE HAVING

LYNN MACRITCHIE

When someone dies, and those who remain gather to commemorate them, it can seem that, in the chatter of exchanged reminiscences, the speakers are describing not one but many individuals, each quite different from the others. What can this mean?[1]

Can it be that the deceased – so loved, so missed – was not in fact a singular entity but rather an infinite complexity of potentials, revealed as such only at their demise? Or, to take the opposing view, does the mourning of the dead expose all too clearly that in life we make our way alone, each enclosed within a unique construction of the world, our relationships merely a by-product of our separate individual consciousness? And if this is so, how do we ever connect with each other, feel that commonality which brings us together to mourn or to rejoice? How do we find ways in which to break out, even for a moment, from our endless singularity? Anne Bean has spent a lifetime seeking out those ways, fearlessly exploring 'the turbulent space one must cross to reach oneself, let alone to truly contact another human being.'[2]

From the first, her relationship to herself as an artist was one of questioning. In 1973, the title of her final dissertation at Reading University, where she studied Fine Art, asked 'What is Art and What am I Doing in it?'[3] She sought the answer in assaulting the senses – presenting her writings, drawings and photos in 'a very smelly herring box tied above the door of the Art History department' – and in collaborating with others, namely by inviting 16 friends to write and draw with her for some 24 hours, the duration of their activity determined by the lingering death of some tulips expiring in a waterless vase.[4] Her final exhibition featured an installation addressing what she suggested was the inevitable failure of painting to represent completely the artist's original vision and concluded with a performance by the Moodies, the 'musical and performance art group which linked the worlds of fine art, pop and rock music, subcultural fashion and avant-gardist tactics,' as noted on her website, quoting the accurate but rather restrained description by Adrian Whittaker writing in *Wire* in March 2010.[5]

Bean had originally founded the group as Moody and the Menstruators for an art department party at Reading in 1971. In their performances she took on a new persona, Anne Archy, as wild as the name implies, and proved particularly adept at shape shifting across genders. Her transformations from banshee female to badass male were achieved with such aplomb that a writer for the *Süddeutsche Zeitung* newspaper in Germany, where the Moodies performed in 1973, observed 'Anne Bean ... seemed to be able to change so dramatically, not only visually, but in what I can only describe as "essence" that I began to question if there were not more people in the group.'[6]

Including such a performance as part of the presentation of her dissertation was extraordinarily bold and indicated that, even at this very early stage, Bean was clear not just about what she was doing – 'I wanted to push buttons such as embarrassment and fear and complacency, both within myself and with those around me. I wanted to challenge any stability I might feel', she has written – but how she might do it: 'I sensed that when I disappeared in the work it had the most potency.'[7] These insights, and the performative and collaborative strategies she developed to explore them, set not just the parameters of her activities as an artist but also the methodology she has followed with such remarkable consistency ever since.

Today, her continuing engagement with other artists is striking, especially in a contemporary art world in which individual success, professional and financial, is prized above all. But the nature of her concern with her artist peers is very different from the usual career-based rivalries or interest in others' work merely that it might be emulated or surpassed. For Bean, her fellow artists are not competitors to be outshone but possible comrades, worthy collaborators in the great task of exploring the potential of what art, and indeed people, can be. Over the years, the deaths of several artists with whom she has had a variety of working and personal relationships have added a further dimension to this endeavour.

Of course, it could be said that all visual artists are in a dialogue with the dead. For what artist is not aware of those artists of the past whose works form the foundations of the cultural landscape against which their own will be measured? But what if the dead are not safely enfolded in the pantheon of historic time but are artists with whom lived time has been shared – as fellow students, work colleagues, collaborators, partners, friends? Bereft of their living presence, can the creative energies of those artists recently departed somehow be maintained by those who remain?

Over the years, Bean has confronted this question in her work many times and in many ways. In 1982, the death of her friend and collaborator Stephen Cripps, the sound and pyrotechnic sculptor, resulted first in a performance with Paul Burwell that year at The Final Academy, Brixton (part of an international event celebrating William S. Burroughs, organised by David Dawson, Roger Ely and Genesis P-Orridge), then an installation at the Serpentine Gallery in 1992 and, most recently, an action with Richard Wilson at Dilston Grove in 2014.

In between these last two events, in 2007, Paul Burwell died. He and Bean first met in 1976 and worked together ever afterwards in a creative engagement, as work and sometime life partners, lasting over three decades. While their work took many forms, and could include other participants, most significantly Richard Wilson, with whom they founded the Bow Gamelan Ensemble, the essential core of their practice remained the improvised interplay between Burwell's percussion and Bean's vocals, a foundation on which they built performances of extraordinary power. Their work sometimes drew also on their shared interest in esoteric practices, such as Navajo chants or Tibetan rituals, and unconventional means of exploring consciousness, such as telepathy, séances and hypnosis. In 1982, for example, their work *It was Meant to Be* included material recorded from statements each had made during a session of hypno-regression.

Thus in 2008, the year after Burwell's death, when Bean and Wilson made *Adventures in the House of Memory (aka Spooky Drums)*, at the A Foundation in Liverpool, which Bean described as a 'conversation with, rather than about, Paul', they invited a medium, Phil the Messenger, to join them.[8] With his help, they hoped to establish some sort of actual contact with Burwell, triggered by ritual actions including eating some of his cremated ashes washed down with his favourite whisky. Whisky also features in the short film Bean made for *TAPS: Improvisations with Paul Burwell* (2010), a project to which she invited more than 80 artists who had known Burwell to contribute. The film is almost too painful to watch, as, alone in the caravan which was Burwell's final home, Bean listens to music they had enjoyed, gets drunk on whisky and talks to him, the pain of her grief palpable, her loss all too real.

Between 2013 and 2014, however, a sudden sequence of deaths, all taking place within one year, caused Bean to reflect further about the experience of losing less intimate but no less cherished connections with other artists. During that time, five women artists, all her contemporaries, died: Rita Harris (May 2013), Monica Ross (June 2013), Rose Finn-Kelcey (February 2014), Alexis Hunter (February 2014) and Sue Arrowsmith (November 2014). Whilst the nature of her relationship with each artist was different, all were of long standing, dating back to the 1970s, and Bean had continued to feel a connection with each of them in the subsequent years, no matter how intermittent their actual contact might have been.

In response to this accumulation of loss, Bean has since engaged in a strand of work that both refers to and develops from aspects of the various outputs of all five of these artists. Thus, rather than seeking to bring about a manifestation of their actual presence, as she has done in relation to Burwell, Bean has instead begun to re-examine her relationship to the work of all five of these departed friends and colleagues, finding in their work inspiration for new works of her own. In this way, she can explore how a creative relationship might be maintained with them, 'making work I would not have made without their presence in my mind,' as she has described it, even if without the living dialogues they once shared.[9]

The first of these works was the short film *The Shivering*, made in 2014, the year after the death of Monica Ross. Writing about this work, Bean has noted that, attending Ross's funeral service, she had been struck by the thought that Ross's body, lying silent and inert in her coffin, had been the living vehicle through which she memorised and then recited the entire text of the United Nations' *Universal Declaration of Human Rights* of 1948, in *Anniversary – An Act of Memory, a Performance Series in 60 Acts* (2008-13). In this, her final, monumental work, the 30 articles, each stating a basic right to which it is claimed all individuals should be entitled, were contained within the cells of Ross's flesh.

This insight was the catalyst for the creation of *The Shivering*. Shot in the Finnish countryside in winter, the film shows Bean crouched naked face down on a heap of snow, her arms spread in an embrace of its icy crystals as she improvises a mourning chant. The words she speaks were inspired partly by those of a Navajo Night Chant (an ancient mourning ritual still performed today) and partly by thoughts of Ross, Finn-Kelcey and Hunter: news of these second two deaths had reached her when she was in Finland. She continues to chant until, her body trembling helplessly in the relentless cold, control of her voice gives out and she can speak no longer:

My interior filled with cold
So may I walk
My mind filled with cold
So may I walk
No longer sore
So may I walk
Impervious to cold
So may I walk
Filled with lively feelings
So may I walk
With my dead friends
So may I walk
With my own death
So may I walk
As it used to be now
So may I walk
Filled with cold
So may I walk
With cold thoughts
So may I walk.[10]

Apposite and poignant, the work perfectly echoes Ross's extraordinary feat of memory and recitation while also fitting seamlessly into Bean's long trajectory of performances that take her own body to its physical limits.

The next year, during a month-long residency in the Foyle Reading Room at the Whitechapel Gallery, London in 2015, Bean extended *The Shivering* into *Night Chant*. This is a six-minute film she declared a 'femmage' (an excellent writer, she often plays with words, reforming them to express new concepts such as this), dedicated to all five deceased women artists. It was screened as part of her presentation at a symposium at the Whitechapel Gallery that year, where she explained that all five women had used performance in

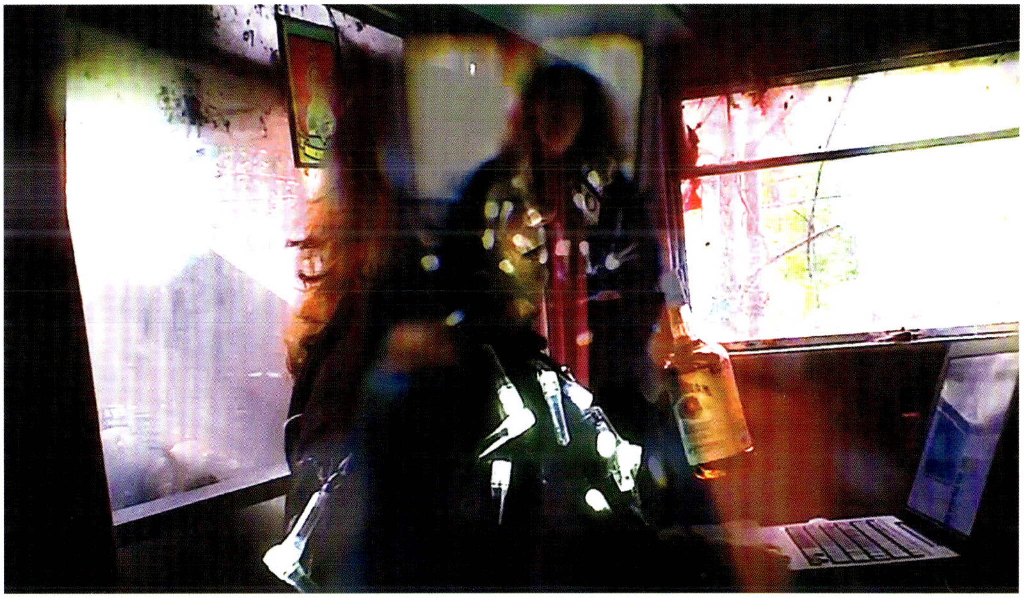

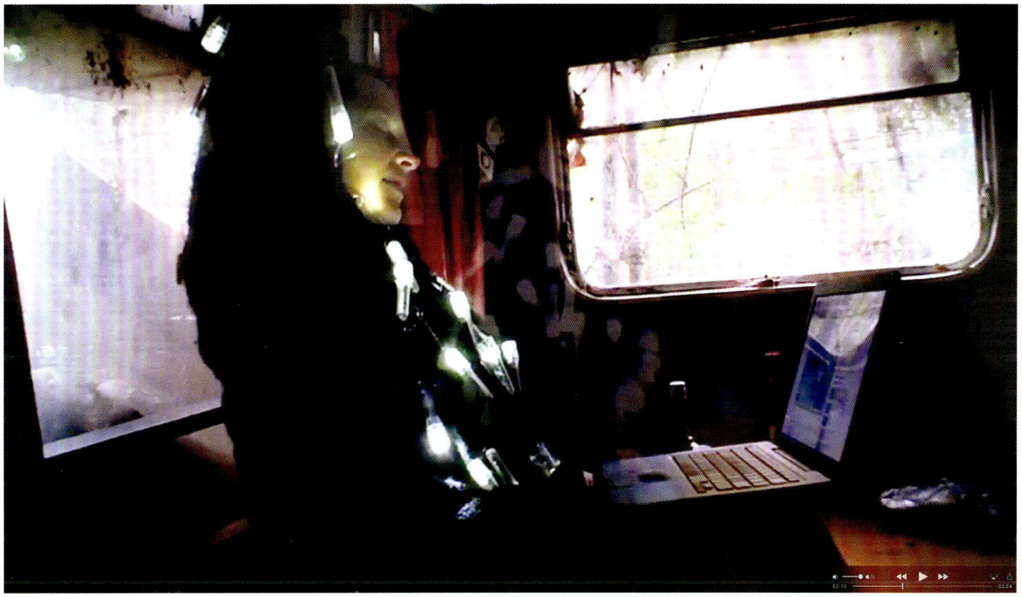

Anne Bean (with Phil the Messenger), *And Inhabited the Spaces*, Hull, 2009.
Still from a video by Patricia and Brian Routh. Created as part of *TAPS: Improvisations with Paul Burwell*

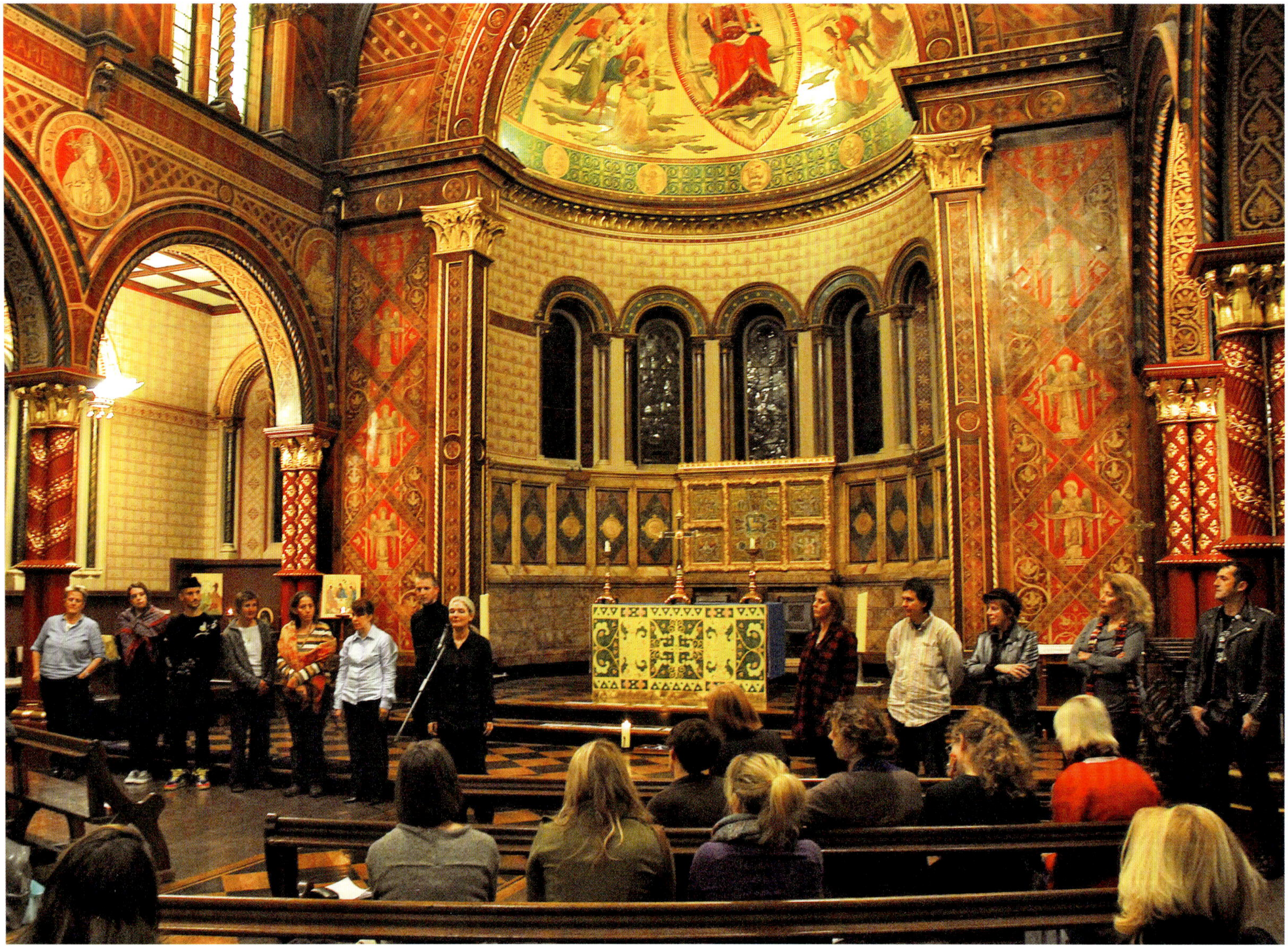

Monica Ross, *Anniversary – An Act of Memory, a Performance Series in 60 Acts* (2008-13). Act 30, Inside Out Festival, King's Chapel, London, 28 October 2010. *From left to right:* Bobby Baker, Nina Picard, Mikhail Karikis, Louise Purbrick, Olcay Aniker Lumley, Samantha Waddilove, Andrew Mitchelson, Monica Ross, Naomi Siderfin, Kay Tabernacle, Hannah O'Shea, Anne Bean, Ramon Salgado Touzon. Photo: Bernard G. Mills their practices, valuing it as an 'open arena' and a vehicle for 'shared communication'.[11] The performative space was one in which many women artists had begun to operate in the 1970s. They recognised that it gave them freedom to explore a multiplicity of practices as they attempted to discover what art could be when, rather than remaining confined within traditional boundaries, art became something women defined for themselves.

For Sue Arrowsmith, for example, private actions she performed but which were not witnessed by others became integral to the production of her work and allowed her to move beyond her earlier conceptual pieces. By the mid-1970s, when she and Bean met, Arrowsmith had already established her reputation through conceptual works based in photography such as *Without Me: 4 Cameras* (1974). Some ten years later, however, she had radically expanded her practice: by then, instead of the impersonal conceptual approach specifically recognised in *Without Me*, she had begun to inhabit her images: pressing her naked body onto photosensitive paper, for example, or drawing round its contours with charcoal or black paint, a technique Bean had also used (and continues to use) from time to time. Bean and Arrowsmith enjoyed a close friendship, particularly from 1981 when, as neighbours in Bow, they would share suppers and make informal art works, often using the random items they delighted in finding while mudlarking on the banks of the Thames.

In 1983, at Arrowsmith's instigation, they made a work called *In Conversation with Anne Bean*. Arrowsmith photographed Bean as they talked together outdoors, Bean holding an optical lens she had been using in another work. In its finished form, three black and white images of Bean are mounted within a frame which also contains, at Bean's suggestion, leaves from the vine in front of which they had been sitting as they talked. Their conversations continued even after Arrowsmith began to suffer from the ill health that eventually led to her withdrawal from the art world in the late 1980s.

Much of the material of these discussions also formed the basis of a book Arrowsmith had been working on throughout the duration of their friendship. After her death, Bean was sent some of her writings, and used extracts in a commemorative event she organised on Holy Island, a place which Arrowsmith had often talked of visiting. Bean then used extracts from the writings again in a performance by the Thames in 2016, made in collaboration with artist/photographer Manuel Vason. Vason's photographs capture Arrowsmith's words, which Bean had copied on to spools of white ribbon, becoming visible as Bean lets the ribbon, which she holds high above her head, uncoil. 'She perceiving her', 'lightning', 'come to us soaring,' 'dark cloud over my head': these and other poignant fragments of Arrowsmith's writings finally emerged into the world, flying on the wind with, in Bean's words, 'the life of our animated conversations'.[12]

Also in 2016, Bean made *Dialogues Through Time*, for the exhibition *Of Other Spaces: Where Does Gesture Become Event? Chapter One*, a two-chapter group show of 19 artists at the Cooper Gallery, University of Dundee, curated by Sophia Yadong Hao, which also included works by Monica Ross and two more of the five women artists, namely, Rose Finn-Kelcey and Alexis Hunter. Bean chose to make three new works responding to their works as her contribution to the show, explaining, 'This chance inclusion of works that were especially evocative for me re-opened early conversations with Rose on the divided self, discussions on feminism and the erotic with Alexis and engagements with Monica on human rights and freedom of thought "unmindful of bounds".'[13]

Bean first met Rose Finn-Kelcey in the mid-1970s, sometime after Finn-Kelcey made *Conversation Piece (Divided Self)* (1974), one of two works featured in the Cooper exhibition: the other was *The Restless Image - A Discrepancy Between the Felt Position and the Seen Position* (1975-2011), a well-known black and white photograph in which the artist is shown doing a handstand on a beach, her legs stretching upwards against the sky, her face obscured by the silvery pleats of her upended skirt.

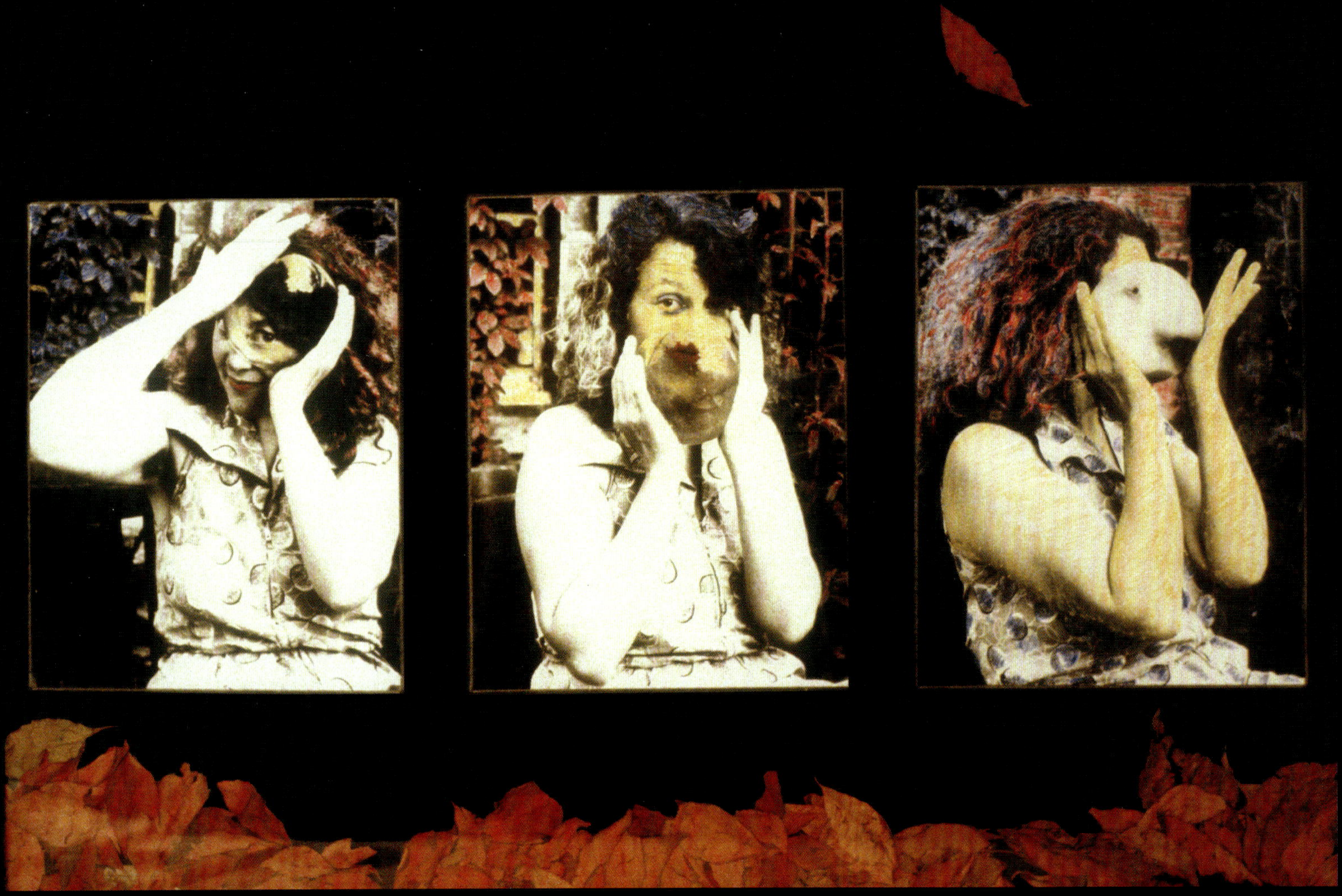

Above: Sue Arrowsmith, *In Conversation with Anne Bean,* 1983

Opposite: Anne Bean, *An Unrecognised Conversation with Sue Arrowsmith*, 2016. The left panel of each diptych is a photo of the moment the artist's face prints upon a glass sheet; the right hand image shows the lasting face print. Photos: Graham Challifour

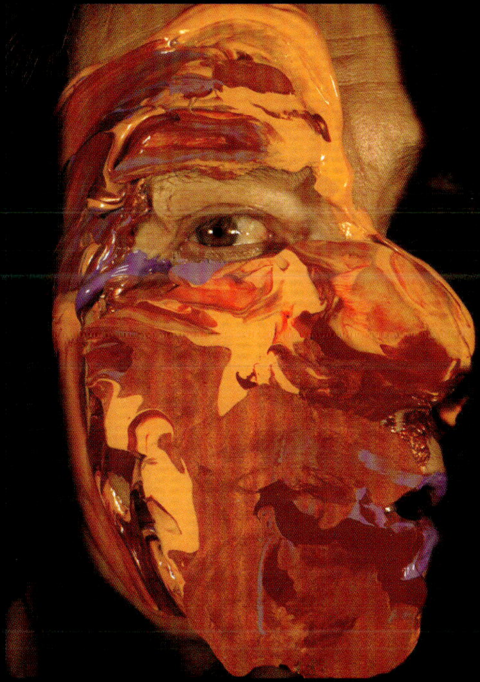

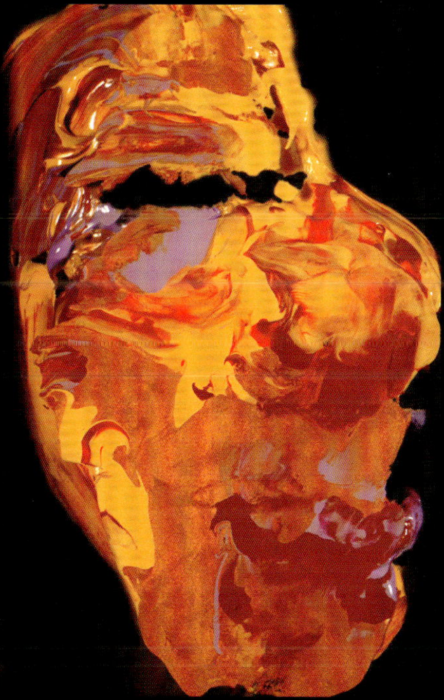

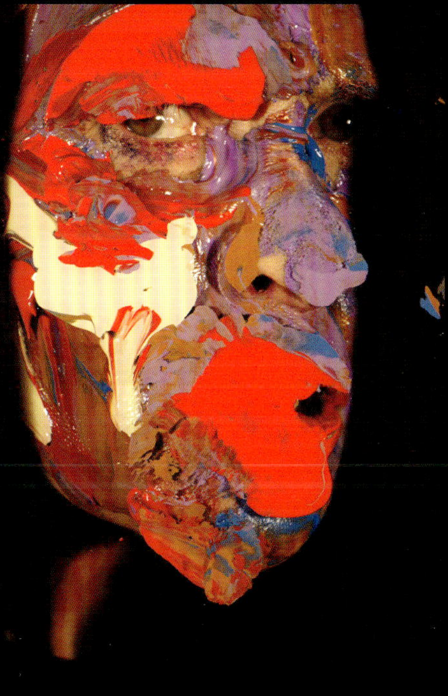

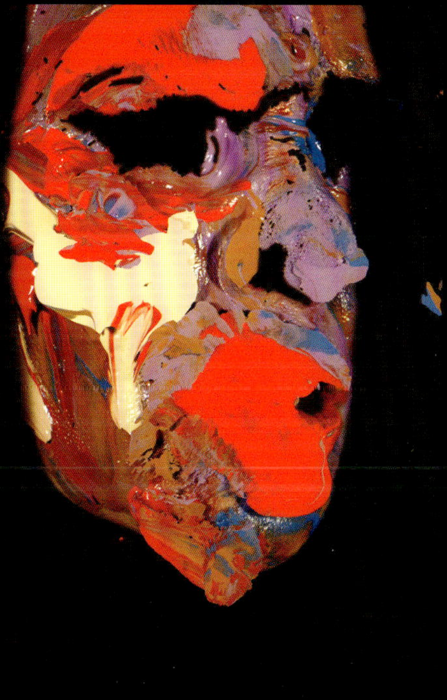

Finn-Kelcey's *Conversation Piece* consists of three black and white photographs, each showing a dual image of the artist, sitting at either end of a park bench, apparently engaged in animated conversation with herself. Like many of their contemporaries, both artists had been interested in the psychiatrist R. D. Laing 's concept of the 'divided self', popularised in his 1960 book of that name. In 1971, playing with the concept of one individual having two personae, Bean made a work in which she asked questions of herself, replying through a ventriloquist's dummy, dressed and made up to look like her. And in 1974 Bean too had made a work called *Divisions of Self*, in her case a black and white photographic self-portrait, in which an image of her face is cut up into rectangles rearranged in a series of out-of-sequence segments.

The idea of an individual having more than one persona was a powerful one for both artists. Finn-Kelcey addressed it again in *Book and Pillow* (1978). In this interactive sound sculpture, she explored the Jungian concept of the male and female principles, the animus and anima. To make part of the sculpture, she asked a professional model maker at the Natural History Museum to create a figure to represent her animus, working only from her written description. The result was a homunculus, tiny but terrifying, who stares beadily back at any viewer who dares to peer at him through the magnifying glass attached to the work specifically for this purpose.

Bean has continued to explore the concept of multiple personalities in her work, perhaps most intensely during a period beginning in 2012. Then, wishing, in her words, 'to throw open an unknowable and chance trajectory and allow other manifestations of myself to breathe,' Bean left London.[14] After some months of wandering, guided by a chance event, she set up residence in Newark-on-Trent, a small town in the Midlands. There, she lived for 16 months as Chana Dubinski, a version of the name by which she had been known to her family and other members of the Jewish East European exile community within which she had grown up in Northern Rhodesia (now Zambia). And in 2015, she left London once more. This time, although she retained the name Anne Bean, she set herself the task of setting up a work place, Moments of Consciousness And (MoCa) in a location previously unknown to her: the name of the place – Trowbridge, Wiltshire – was pulled from a fortune cookie during an event at Matt's Gallery in London.

For *Dialogues Through Time*, Bean created an installation adjacent to Finn-Kelcey's *Divided Self* that brought together elements referring to all these concepts. On the floor, on a base of pieces of mirror, she placed two small ceramic figurines, the battered brethren of Finn-Kelcey's homunculus, initially conceived as part of her work at MoCa Trowbridge and finally realised as part of a ceramics course she undertook in Oxford in 2016. Their dual nature is made abundantly clear by the wide gap each has running through their centre which splits them almost in half, while their co-dependency is indicated by the fragile gold wire which wraps around each one before swooping up into a delicate golden arc which joins them together. Low down on the wall beneath Finn-Kelcey's photographs, Bean placed a similarly sized colour photograph shot in the Novo Jewish Cemetery on Mile End Road, London. Amongst the old gravestones she has inserted a new headstone, carved for her by stonemasons in Newark when she lived there as Chana Dubinski: its inscription reads 'How Things Used to be Now'. Behind the stone, repeated images of Bean appear to stride out, five figures walking briskly towards each other, echoing the multiple images of Finn-Kelcey hanging above and suggesting that life and death, past and present, may all co-exist in the dynamism of a moment.

Three works by Alexis Hunter were shown in the Cooper exhibition: *Sexual Warfare* (1975), *Approach to Fear XVII: Masculinisation of Society – exorcise* (1977) and *Dialogue with a Rapist* (1978). Bean chose to make a work relating to *Dialogue with a Rapist*. Like Bean herself, Alexis Hunter became something of a figurehead for the emergence of women as makers of some of the strongest and most

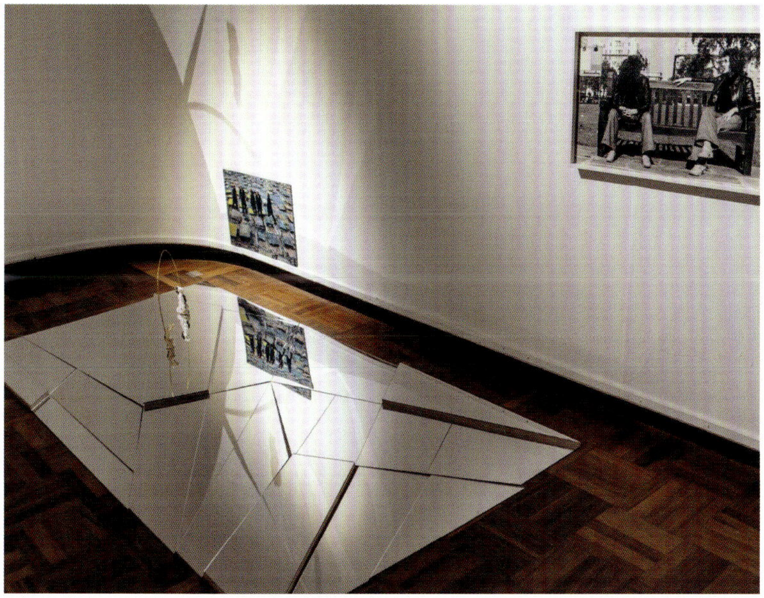

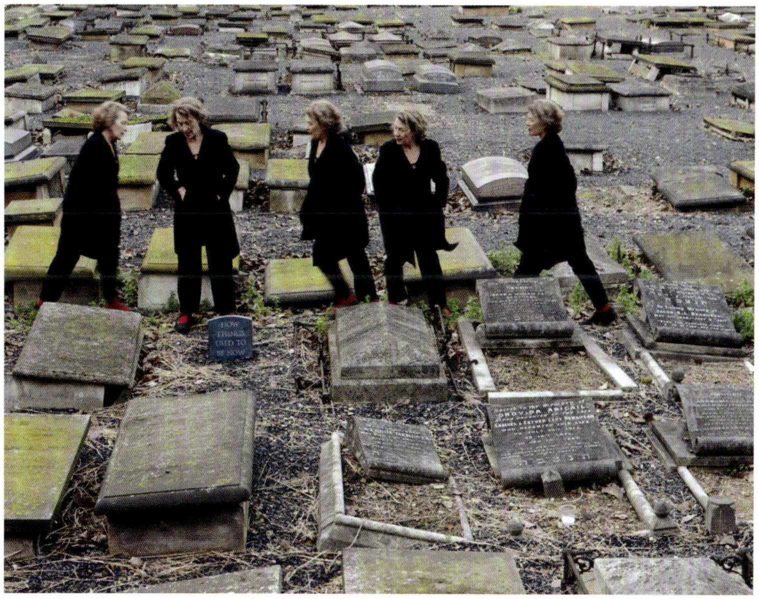

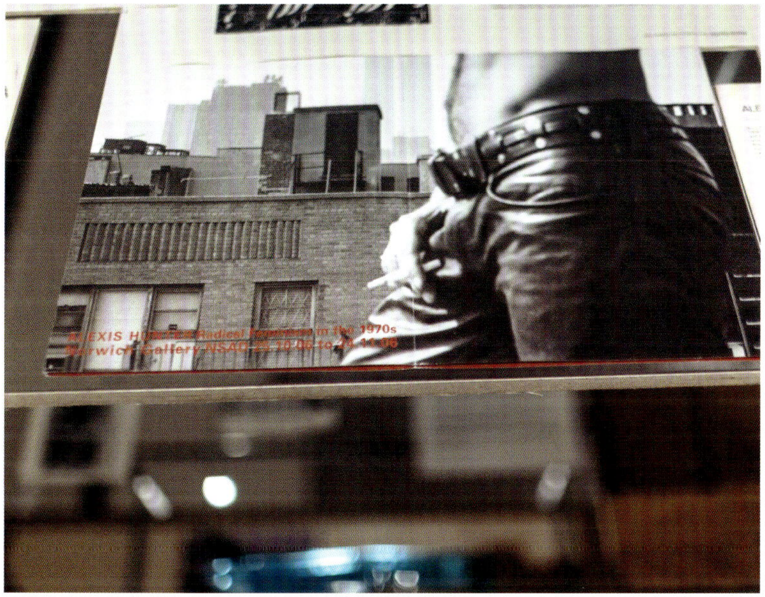

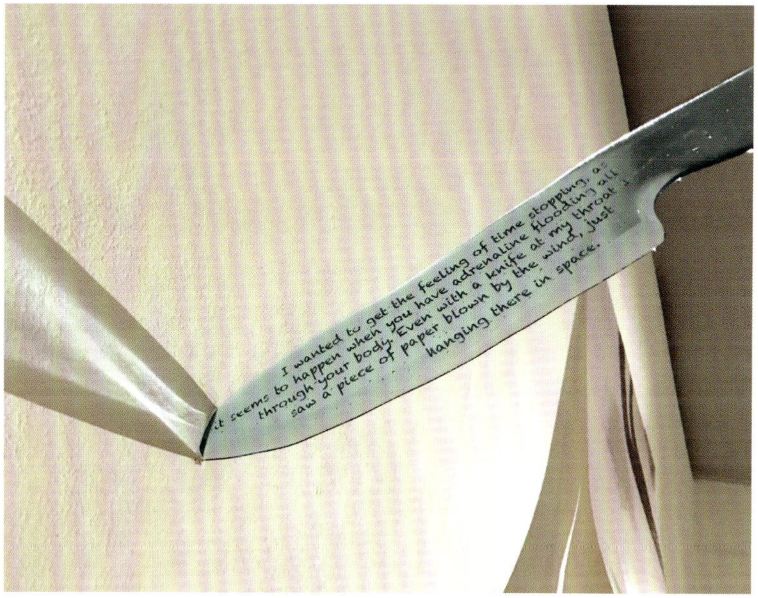

Top left, top right, bottom left: Installation shots of *Chapter One* of Sophia Yadong Hao's exhibition *Of Other Spaces*, Cooper Gallery, Dundee, 2016. Photos: Ross Fraser McLean

Bottom right: Anne Bean, part of *Slit*, exhibited in *EMIT*, Coleman Project Space, 2017. Photo: Jane England

pp. 84-5: PULp MUSIC, *The Fall of Babylon*, Ark Kent, London, 1978. Photographer unknown

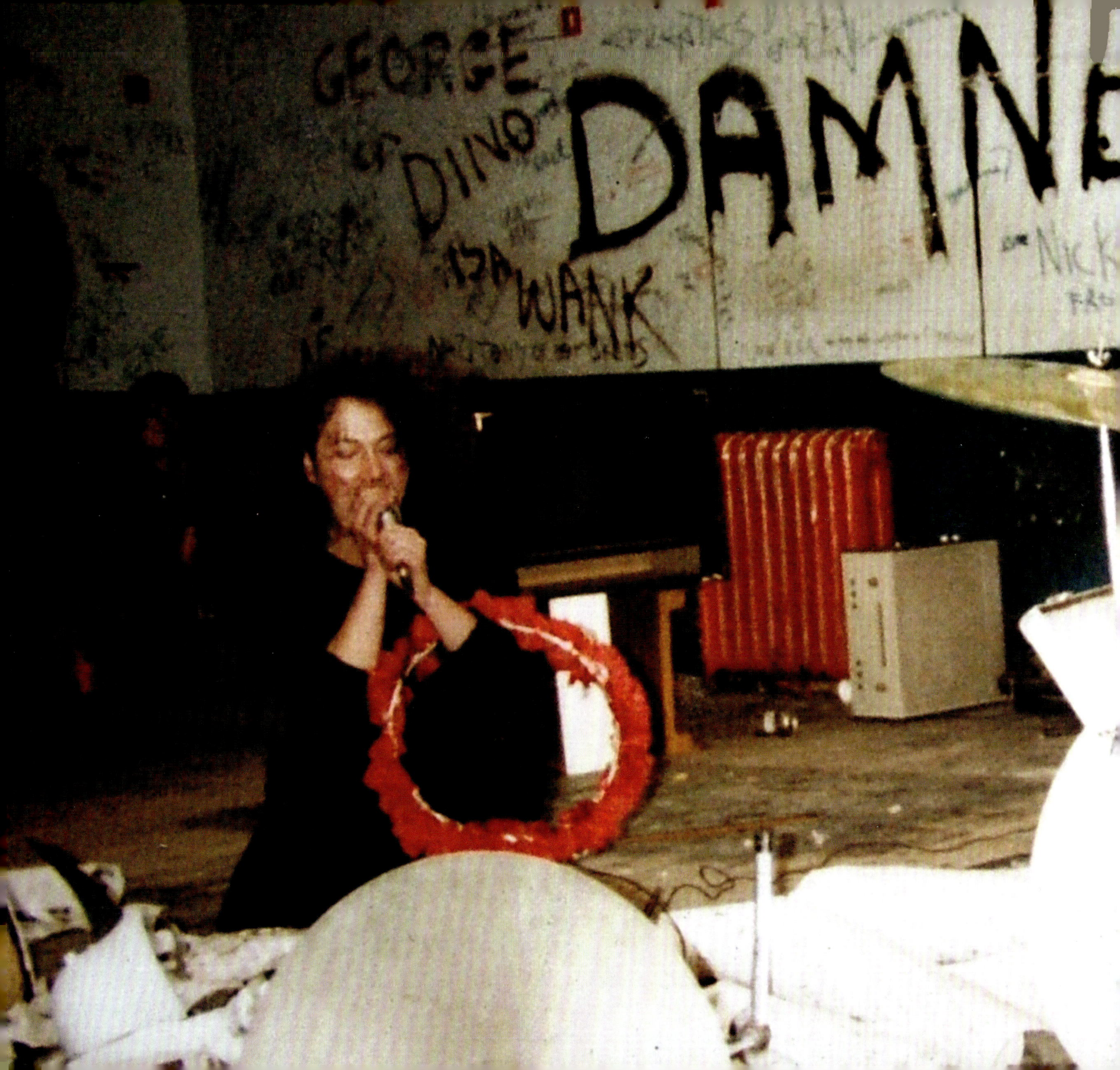
GEORGE
DINO
WANK

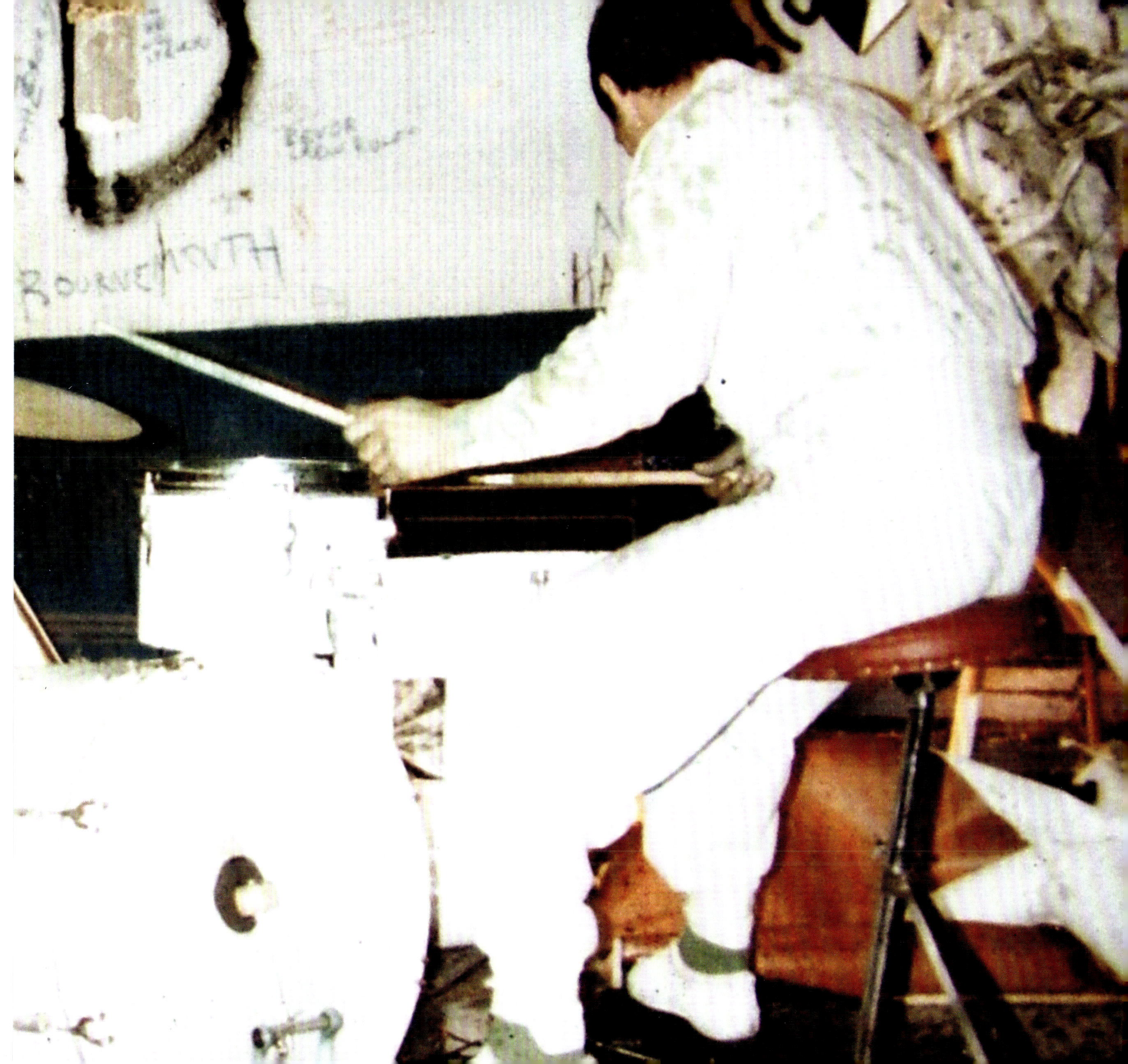

also played. In this text, which became much admired, Ross reflects on how the art and activism of her women artist peers of the 1970s and 1980s might be remembered. A film of *Anniversary* was shown in the second chapter of the exhibition.

In the first chapter, Bean made a work relating to her own participation in one of the 60 acts that made up *Anniversary*, held in King's College Chapel, London in 2010. There, with Ross's enthusiastic support, Bean had recited from memory Article 19 of the *Universal Declaration of Human Rights*, rewritten as a *lipogram* – a text from which one letter has been removed, in this case 'e'. The removal of the letter makes it necessary for the text to be rewritten using different words that do not include the letter 'e' but still convey the original meaning. The original statement reads: '*Article Nineteen*: Everyone has the right to freedom of opinion and expression; this right includes freedom to hold opinions without interference and to seek, receive and impart information and ideas through any media and regardless of frontiers.'[18] Bean's lipogram reads:

> *Point six plus six plus six plus half plus half.* All worldly inhabitants can, without constraint, hold opinions and spawn promulgations. This right contains within it, sanction to hold opinions without obstruction and to look for, obtain and impart information and significant notions through any form of articulation and unmindful of bounds.

Bean used the last words of this resulting text – 'unmindful of bounds' – in several subsequent works, casting the letters in glass and leaving them on the borders between countries.

At the Cooper Gallery, she again used these words cast in glass, each separate letter hung from the branches of an acacia tree she placed next to the photo of Ross, Cameron and Silver scaling the statue of John Bright: the acacia is used by several cultures in ceremonies to honour the dead. Bean subsequently reworked a photographic image of the tree in the gallery to suggest that it was growing upwards within the space, its topmost branches pushing against the ceiling, which seems to crack as the words tied to the branches try to break through the confining roof into the sky.

As the final part of *Dialogues through Time*, Bean created a new performance in the gallery, using a text by the thirteenth-century woman poet Hadewijch. The words of one of her poems were written out backwards in short phrases on small hand mirrors Bean gave to participants in the performance: she also gave them torches to shine on the mirrors. The resulting reflections projected the words on to the walls and ceiling of the exhibition space:

> All things
> are too small
> to hold me
> I am
> so vast
> in the infinite
> I reach
> for the
> uncreated.[19]

The shimmering snatches of words and phrases envelop those present in the poet's thoughts. Writing about this work she said, 'This performance continued the dialogues with women across times in both the physical and metaphysical sense of reflection, mirroring, projecting, collaborating and responding – reaching for the uncreated.'[20]

In March of the following year, 2017, the exhibition *Emit: A Dialogue Through Time* at Coleman Project Space, London, gave a further opportunity for Bean to address the work of Alexis Hunter and also that of the fifth artist who had died, Rita Harris, both of whom had studio spaces close to the Coleman space during the 1970s. Bean also addressed some of her own work of that time, specifically

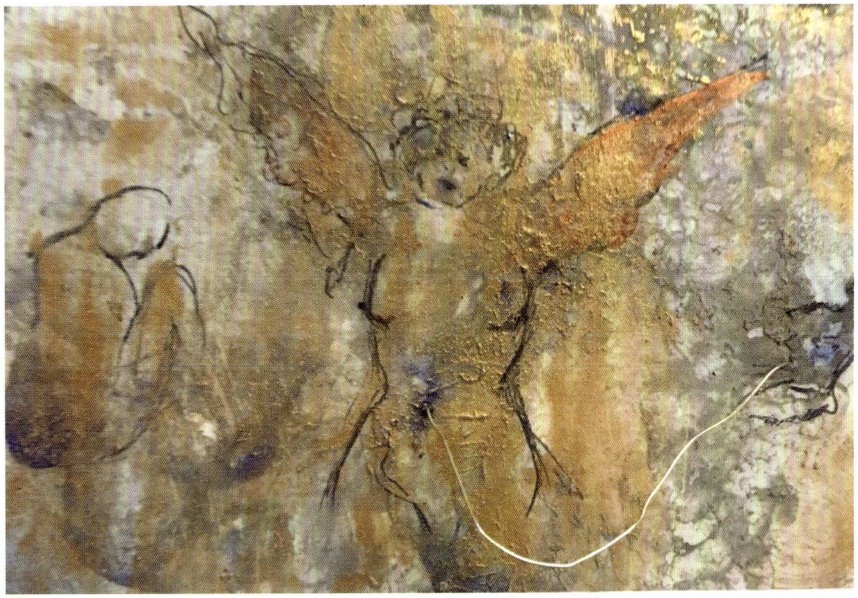

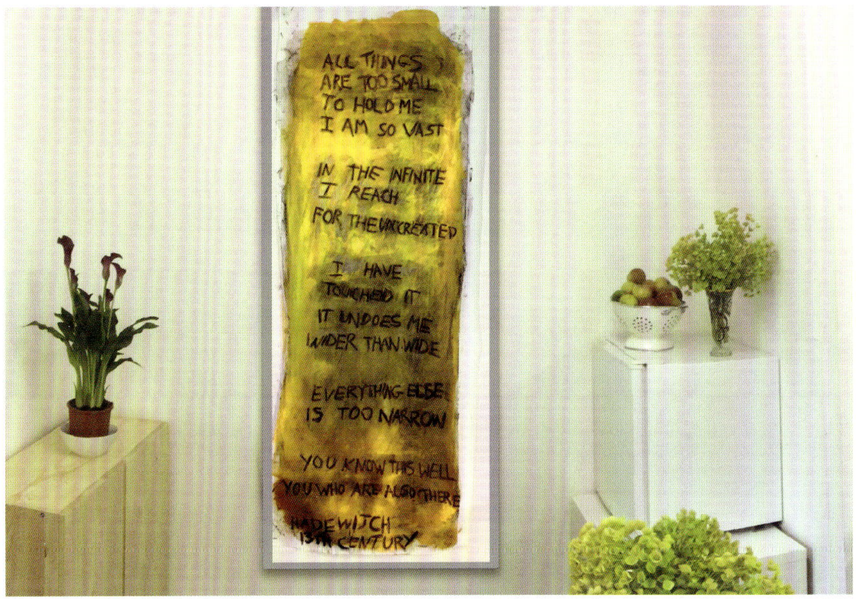

Top: Anne Bean, *Golden Thread*, MoCa Trowbridge, 2016.
Bottom: Anne Bean, *Wider than Wide*, MoCa Trowbridge, 2016

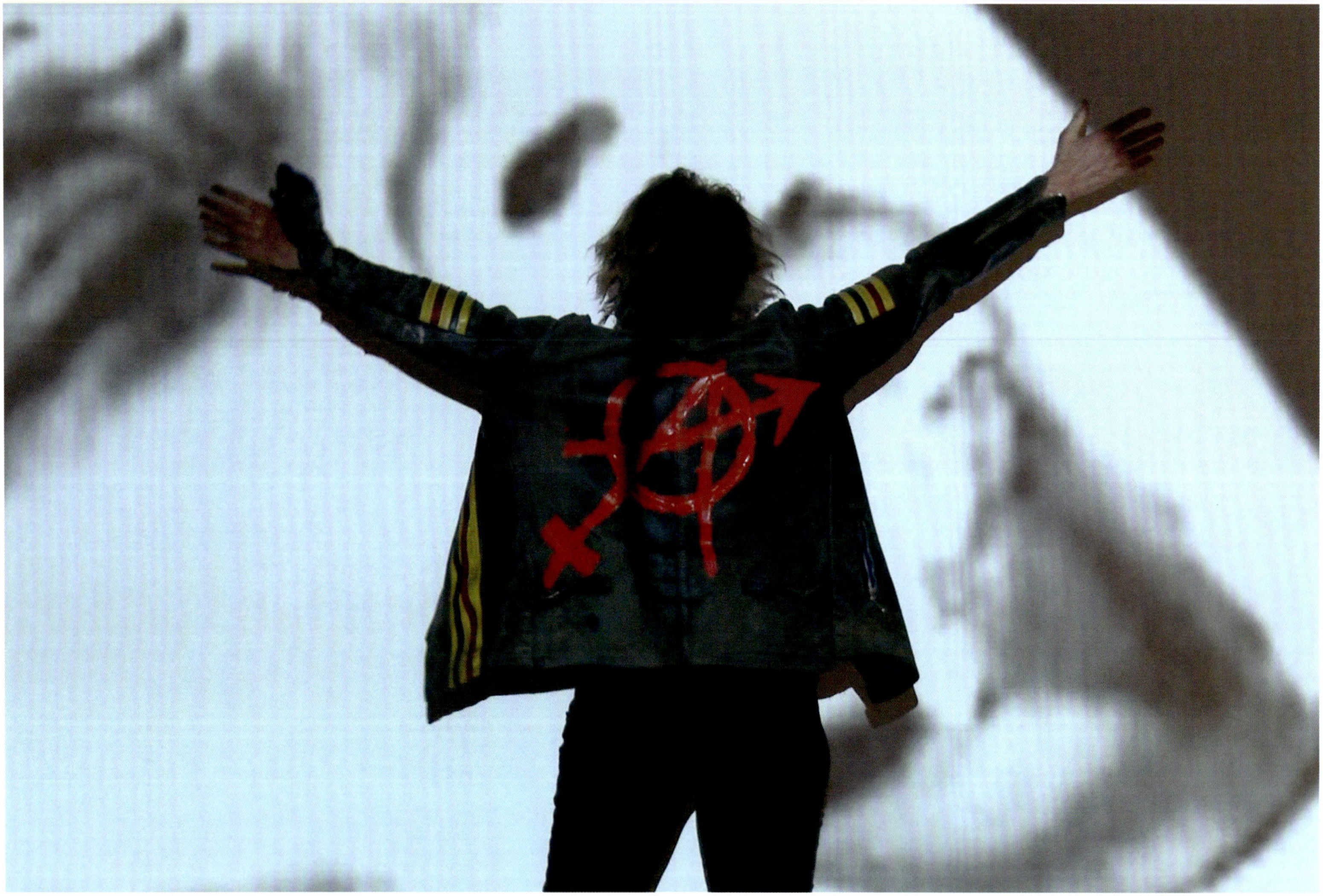

Above and opposite: Anne Bean performing *Gimme Some Truth* at *Chapter Two* of Sophia Yadong Hao's *Of Other Spaces, Where Does Gesture Become Event?*, Cooper Gallery, Dundee, 2017. Stills from video by Rob Page

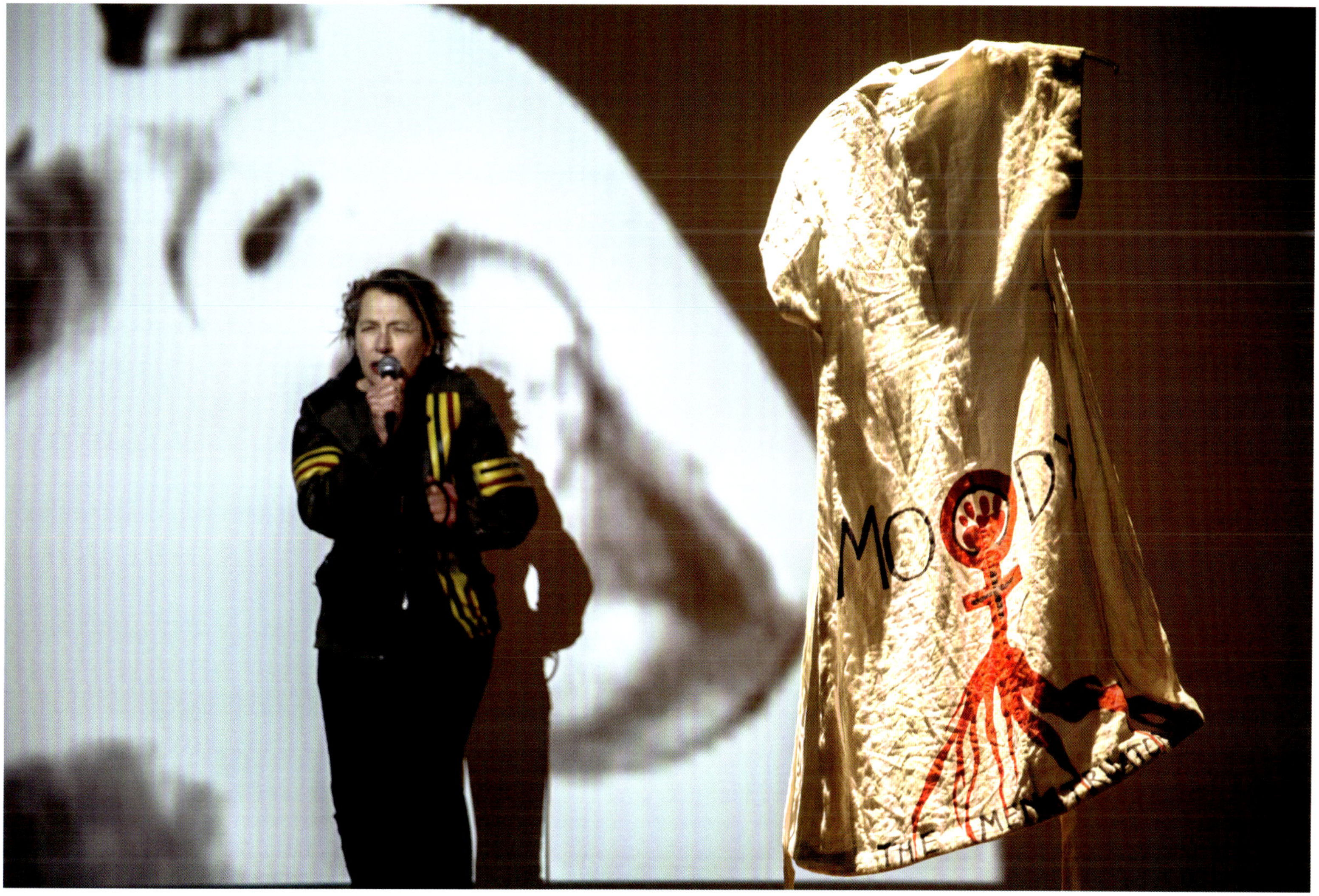
MOODY

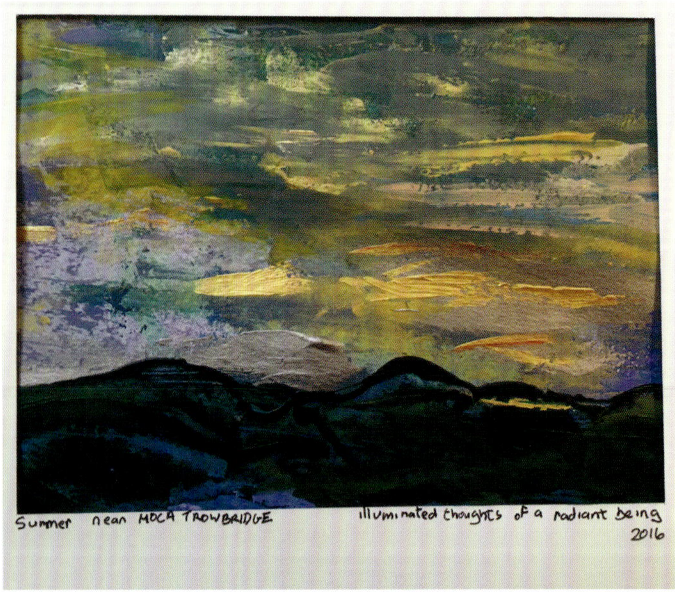

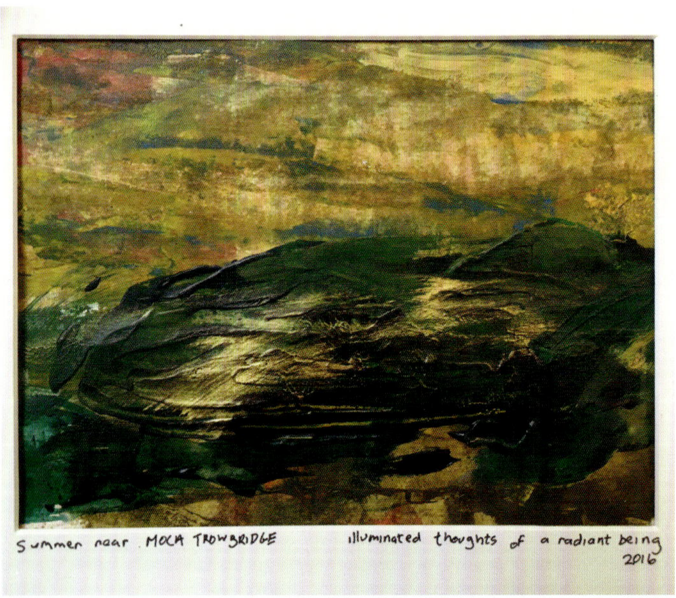

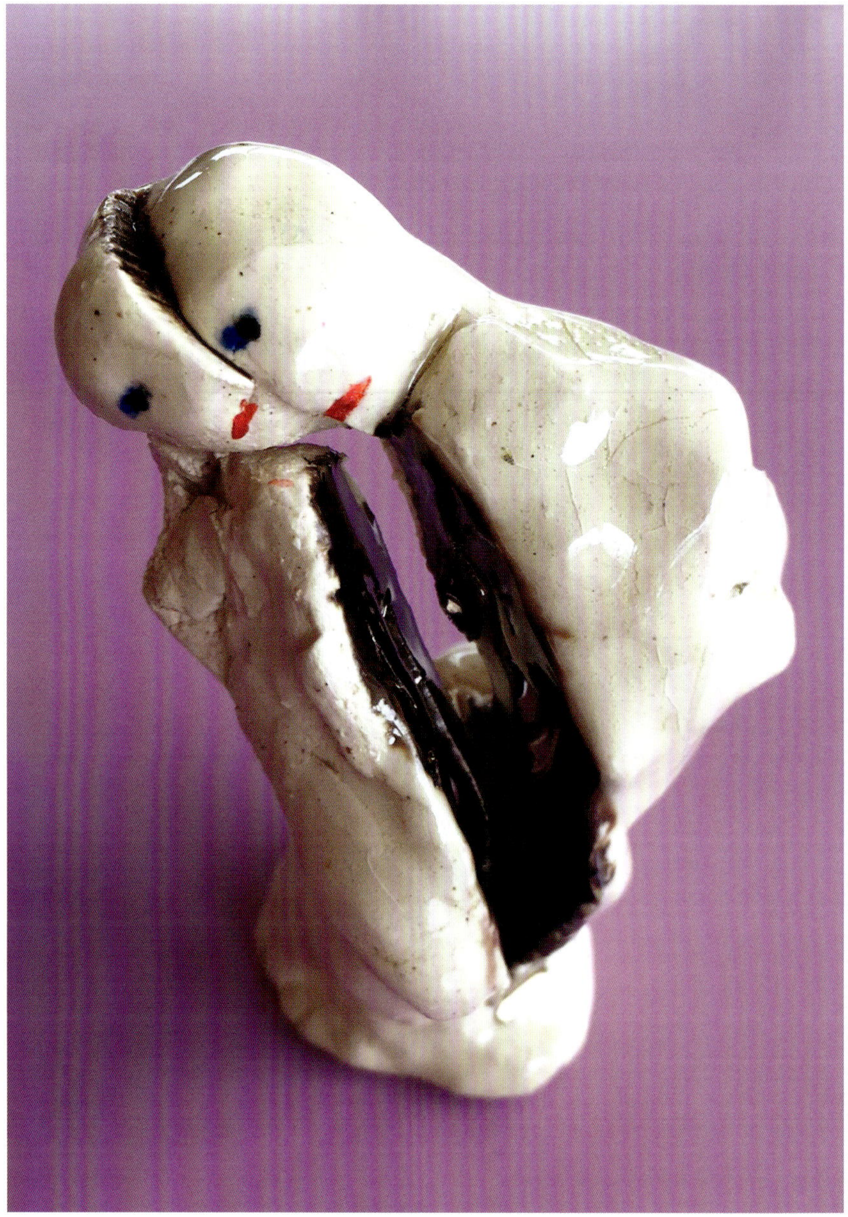

Left: Anne Bean, *Illuminated Thoughts of a Radiant Being*, paintings, MoCa Trowbridge, 2016

Right: Anne Bean, *Divided Self*, ceramic figure, 2016

pp. 94-5: Anne Bean, *Conversation Between Thought and Expression*, Reading Museum and Art Gallery, 1972. Photographer unknown with the Moodies, hanging in the space costumes she had worn in performances: a black leather jacket with an anarchy symbol painted on it in red and a white overall with the words 'Moody and the Menstruators' painted in black on the back. On the overall, the second O in Moody is filled in with the women's liberation symbol, the raised fist painted in red, the lower part of the image dissolving into a flow of painted blood. Inside the hanging garment, a tiny video played. On the screen, Bean was shown in 2017, performing John Lennon's song *Give Me Some Truth* in front of a projection of herself singing *Wild Thing* with the Moodies in 1974.

On the wall, a photograph of Bean in Moody persona, also from 1974, shows her standing in a red dress, hair wild, huge eyes rimmed in black, fiercely facing down the camera and paying no heed to a red-nailed female hand which emerges, groping upwards, from between her legs. Next to it hangs a photo by Alexis Hunter, a single image from *Approach to Fear: masculinity – exorcise* (1977), one of the multi-image works also shown at the Cooper Gallery exhibition. A photograph within a photograph, it shows the artist's hand in front of a photograph of a naked man, busily smearing a black oily substance over his groin.

Hunter was a fan of the Moodies: she had attended their first performance in 1972 and subsequent performances including those at Butlers Wharf where Bean had a studio. On these occasions, Bean and Hunter would talk afterwards, with Hunter urging Bean to state that the Moodies were a feminist band. Bean resisted this categorisation, wishing to retain the more open, undefined space for experimentation that she had intended the group to enjoy.

Despite their differences, as the two photographs shown in *Emit* demonstrate, Bean and Hunter sometimes used similar imagery. In Hunter's photographs, however, only her carefully manicured hand appears, and the glossy perfection of the photograph, no matter how subversive its content, also sends up the seductive techniques of advertising image-making she had learned to earn her living as a commercial photographer. Bean, by contrast, inhabits the photographic image, her powerful but ambiguous presence directly challenging the expectations of the viewer with a wilder, more surreal, humour.

Hunter's studio was next door to Coleman Space, and it was there that she made both *Dialogue with a Rapist* (1978) and *Domestic Warfare* (1979). When, in 2016, Bean readdressed these works, she was able to work in the same space where Hunter had originally created them. Writing about the experience, Bean has observed, 'I worked in the same room where Alexis had axed down the wall. I worked in the space of that missing wall, in the space of the axe, in the space of anger, the space of youth, of turmoil, of drunkenness, of exhilaration, of despair, of wildness.'[21]

The photograph *Slit*, seen in a small print in the Cooper Gallery vitrine, was shown as a much larger print in the Coleman space, part of an installation called *Even with a Knife at My Throat*. In the photograph, Bean's hand, wielding the glass knife, is the only thing clearly visible, and, violent as this gesture is, her figure, seen in silhouette through the translucent material, emanates an essential stillness. She stands tall and proud, her other hand stretched out flat against the material and, by implication, the wall itself, the very wall that Hunter had attacked so fiercely with her axe in *Domestic Warfare*, the real wall on the other side of which, all those years later, the photograph was hung. In re-engaging with Hunter's actions and re-inhabiting the space in which she had made them, Bean has produced an image of dignity and strength, the passage of time enabling her both to recognise and to honour the trauma survived by her friend which had brought those earlier works into being.

The *Emit* exhibition also gave Bean an opportunity to make work relating to the fifth artist who had died, Rita Harris. Like her friendship with Ross, Bean's relationship with Harris dates back to

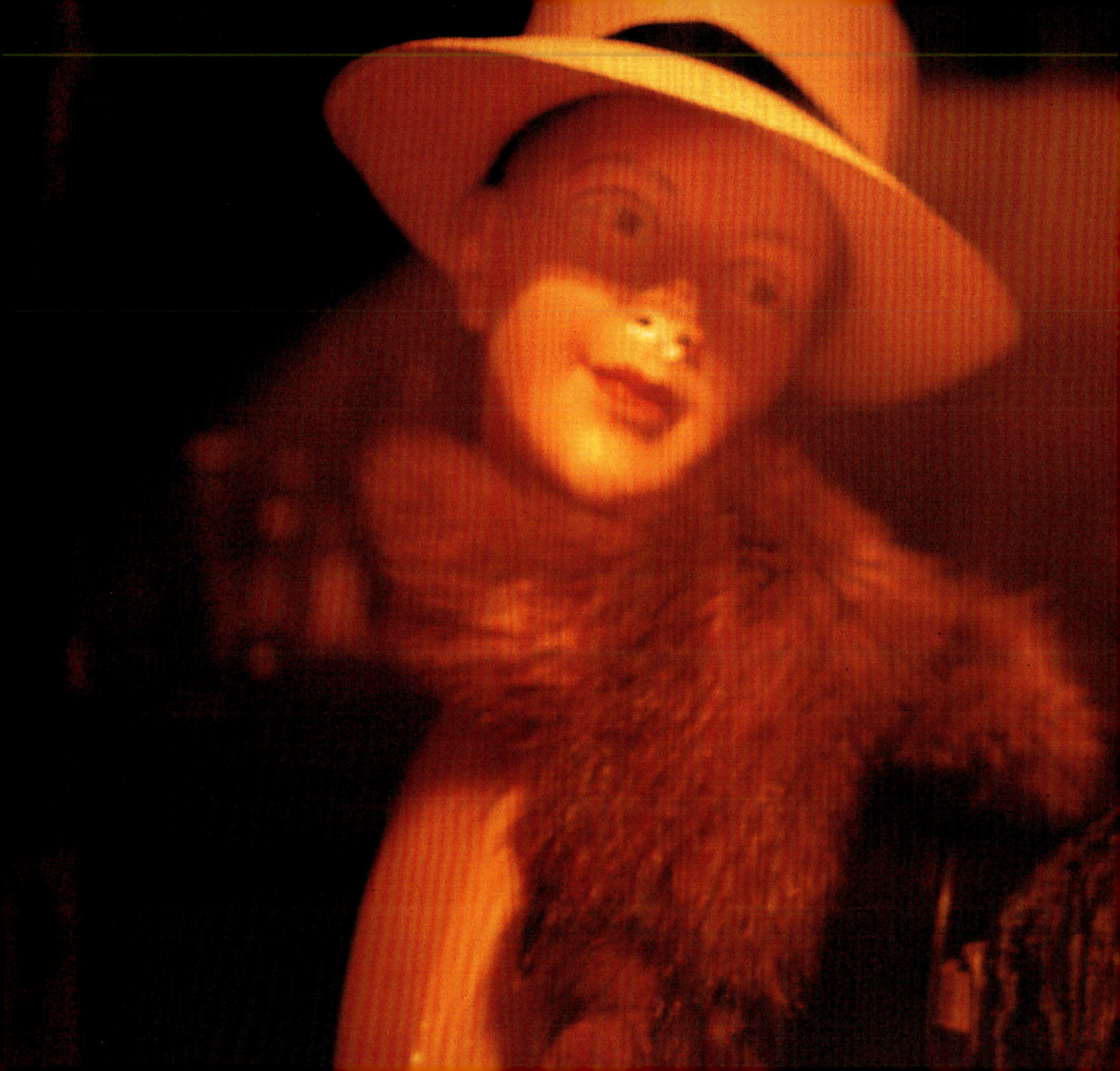

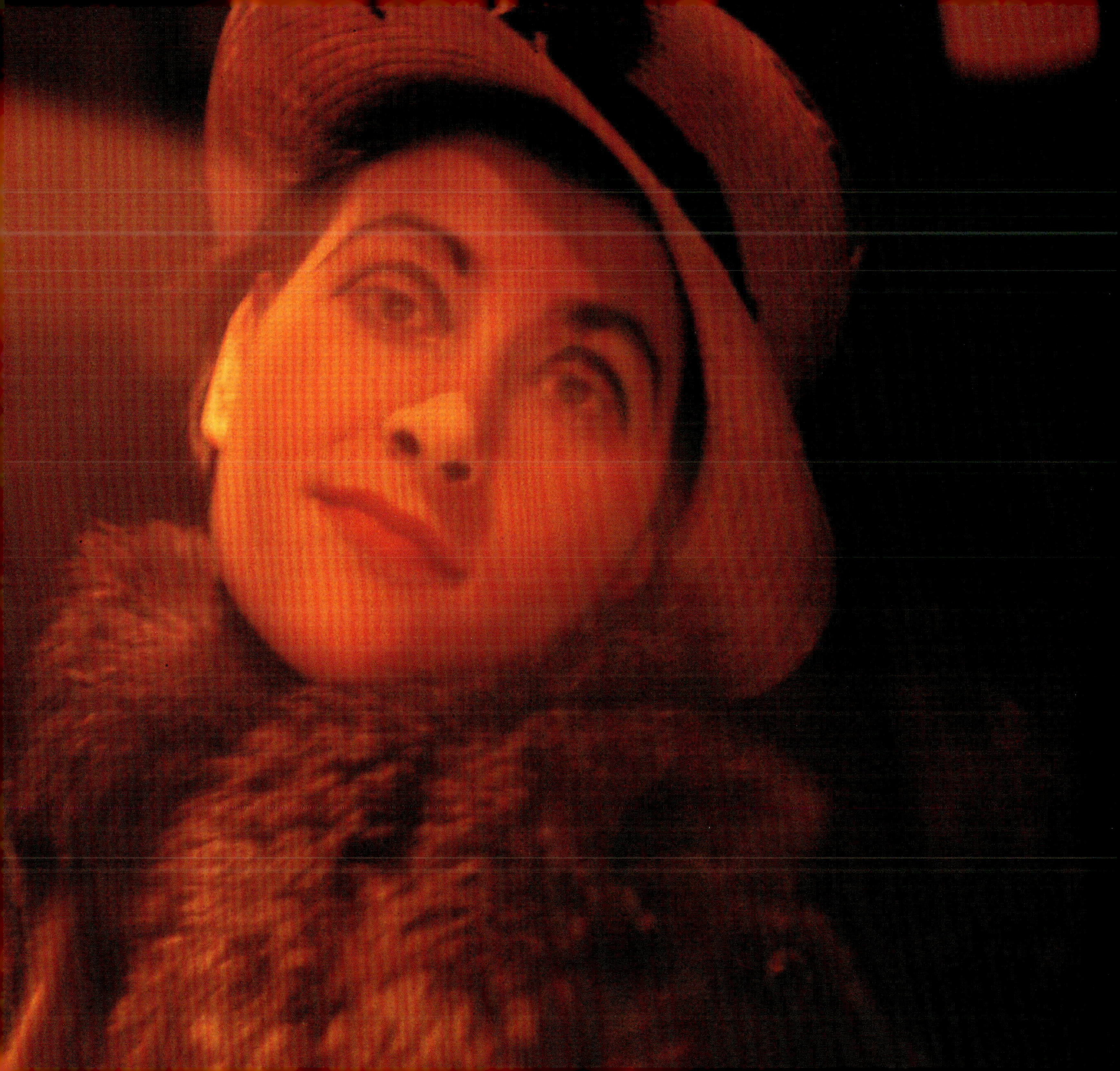

her days at Reading, where she had shared a house with Harris's then partner: Harris herself was studying art elsewhere. Subsequently, their relationship continued within the wider context of the London art world, where, from 1976 to 1981, Harris was a key figure in Acme Gallery, making shows and documenting artists' work, in the process establishing the foundations of the gallery archive. In her personal practice, Harris, as was not uncommon at the time, ranged over varied types of activity, from the traditional visual arts, both studio-based and in the public realm (she created a large-scale mural painting for the Rotherhithe Leisure Centre, for example) to the physical discipline of Tai Chi, of which she became a master and taught for 25 years.

This openness about the forms Bean's own work might take extended to her way of relating to the work of other artists. In 2004-05, Bean initiated a project in Dilston Grove with Mark Anderson called *Reap*. As part of this, every day for a year Bean hung a flower-patterned summer dress in a section of Southwark Park not normally open to the public. During the final eight weekends of the event, she escorted visitors around the locations of some of the hundreds of dresses, observing their rate of decay and interaction with their surroundings, which included trees, foliage and derelict buildings. In response, Harris created a private performance in which she and Bean made dresses together and drank tea made with herbs Harris had grown, something they had enjoyed doing as friends over the years.

In *Emit*, Bean hung *Dance Memo* (1984), a collage of flowers made by Harris, in the space just before visitors encountered *Our Bodies in a State of Music*, a new large-scale colour photograph, staged by Bean and shot by Vason. Hung in three sections, the photograph shows a panorama of the rose garden in Southwark Park, where, for many years, Harris had held her regular Tai Chi classes. A balustrade runs around the garden, the repeated pattern of its formal stone units connecting all three sections of the image, while green trees rise tall in the background. In the central panel, Bean is shown standing barefoot, arms outspread, wearing a summer dress resembling those she had used in *Reap*, with cloth flowers cut out from similar dresses scattered over the paving at her feet. Vividly coloured, the flowery materials recall the bright patterns printed on the hanging dresses she and Harris had walked among in that same park so many years before, observing as they did so the traces of damage to the fabrics, their fading and decay signalling their eventual disintegration. Now, as the inspiration for this photograph made more than a decade later, the fate of the original dresses has become a metaphor, suggesting that their physical disintegration did not in fact result in their destruction but instead was an act of transformation, turning them into bearers of memory, not lost but resonating through time.

The final work shown in *Emit* was the film *Night Chant* (2015). Some six minutes long, it includes footage from *The Shivering* (2014): as noted, the first work in what since then has become Bean's wide-ranging engagement with the art made by her five dead friends. *Night Chant* uses the words of the Navajo Nightway Ceremony as a way of addressing her loss: she speaks them rhythmically on the soundtrack and they can be seen written on the unfurling ribbon that becomes a recurring motif. Bean herself appears, shivering naked in the Finnish snow, and as five selves in the photograph shot in the Jewish cemetery in Mile End, but mostly indoors, in a white room, its floor covered with cloth on which she has written the words of the chant. At the centre of the room, wearing a white robe also covered with these words, she kneels next to a white form, the size and shape of her own body crouched over, sculpted in a soft material, dense but malleable. As her voice on the soundtrack continues the chant, she delves into the mass, removing handfuls of the transparent substance and spreading it out over the words on the cloth beneath.

Bean has for many years made works in which she balances her living body against its equivalent weight in various materials. Here,

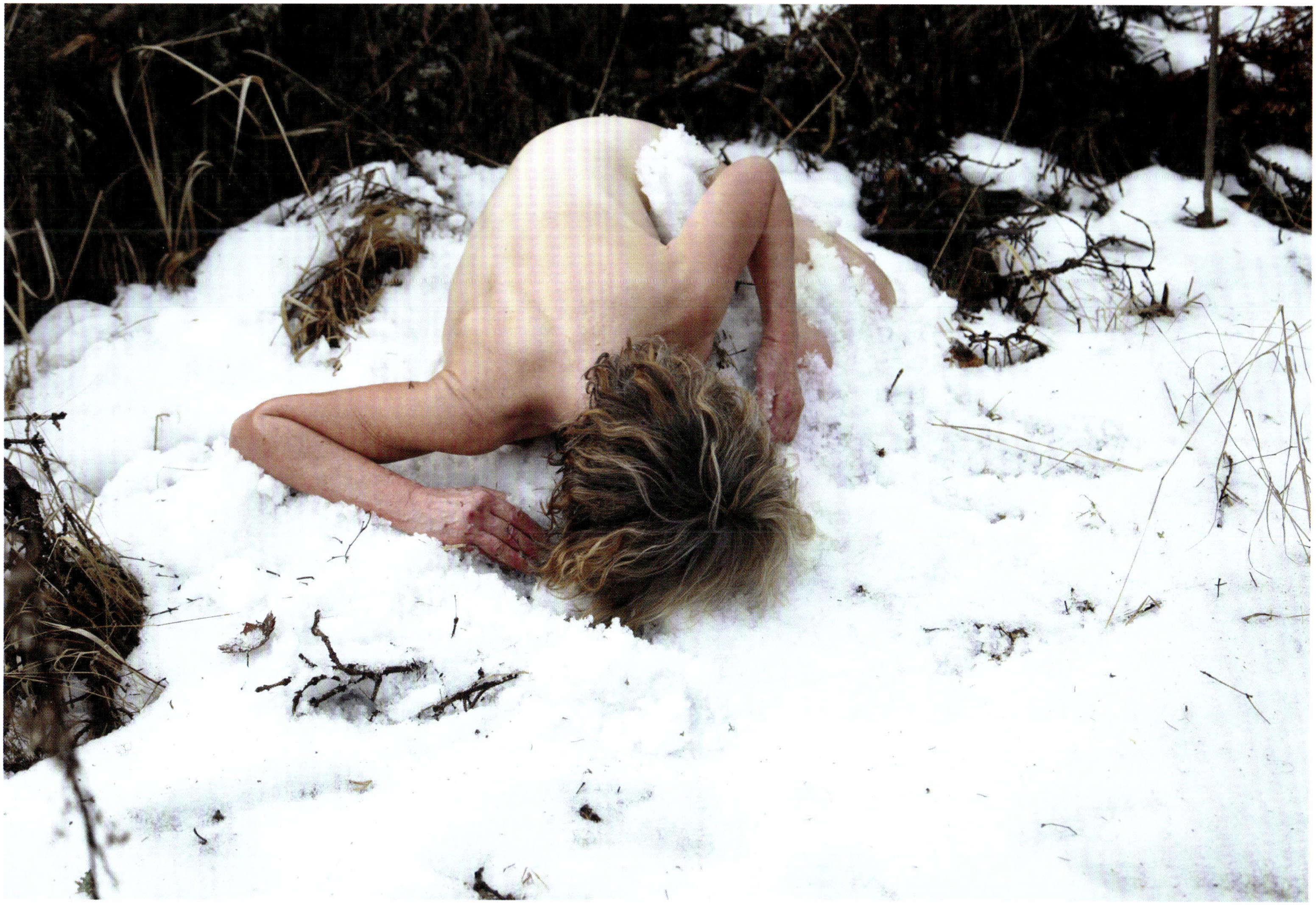

Anne Bean, *The Shivering*, Finland, 2014. Still from a video by Tsai Chih-Fen. Part of the video work *Night Chant*, 2014

she uses this concept to create a ritual of her own, breaking down the sculptural equivalent of her body and spreading it over the written words of the mourning chant that honours the five women artists. In this way, she has made the action, as the film's end titles state, 'not so much for them, as with them.'

More than 40 years ago, when an art student at Reading, Bean had asked the question 'What is art and what I am doing in it?' She had also pondered about whether she was in fact an artist or, in her words, 'a non-specific searcher' since her main interest was 'the multiplicity of being and the endless potential of "whom" one could be'.[22] Her activity since then has answered both those questions. For, throughout her decades of work, Bean has shown little interest in building an art world career in the conventional sense of the term. Instead, she has remained the most dedicated of searchers, whose ceaseless enquiry into human potentiality has been carried out within the realm of art. Bean has made fearless use of the space art affords to explore the ways in which humans might share their experiences with each other, in life and perhaps even beyond. She has recognised that the creation of art, which combines infinite acts of making with infinite opportunities for thinking, can provide the perfect transitional space in which these essential energies can be released and their possibilities – for action, for contemplation and perhaps most importantly for connection – can be considered. This insight was one she shared with her women artist contemporaries of the 1970s, whose collaborative instincts resulted, in her words, in that 'gifting of permission' – to think differently, to search out and occupy a creative space for themselves – she continues to celebrate today.[23]

'In beauty it is finished.'[24] This phrase from *Night Chant* could be a definition of a work of art – something perfect, complete, final. But a work of art does not exist in isolation: to be fully realised, it must be experienced, witnessed. And, in that witnessing, as Anne Bean's work continues to demonstrate so profoundly, something happens. In their contemplation of an art work – a poem, a painting, a photograph, a sculpture, a ceramic, a film, a performance – those who engage with it reactivate the creative process. In giving it their attention, they release the energy of the work once again, unfurling like those swift spools of white ribbon Bean uses so eloquently to carry the messages of Harris, Ross, Finn-Kelcey, Hunter, Arrowsmith and herself once more out into the world: in beauty, it continues.

1. The subtitle of this essay is taken from Anne Bean's performance *Secret Conversations We Didn't Know We Were Having* (2017), which was presented as part of *Emit: A Dialogue Through Time*, Coleman Project Space, London, 9 April 2017.

2. Chana Dubinski, 'A Meeting Place of Fluid States and Core Formations', *A Transpective: How Things Used to be Now* (November 2012), not paginated, http://annebeanarchive.com/transpective-newark-on-trent

3. Anne Bean, *Arc Live*, the artist's website, www.annebeanarchive.com. The website is arranged by year and by title of work or exhibition. This comment appears in *Until the Flowers Die*, 1973: http://annebeanarchive.com/1973-until-flowers/

4. Bean, *Until the Flowers Die*, 1973.

5. Anne Bean, *Moodies*, 1972: http://annebeanarchive.com/1972-moodies/

6. Anne Bean, quote shown as text on slide in Powerpoint presentation about *Dialogues Through Time*, her contribution to the exhibition *Of Other Spaces: Where Does Gesture Become Event? Chapter One*, Cooper Gallery, University of Dundee, 2016.

7. Bean, *Until the Flowers Die*, 1973.

8. Anne Bean, *Adventures in the House of Memory*, 2008: http://annebeanarchive.com/2008-adventures/

9. Anne Bean, artist's talk, *Afterlives: Archives of Performance Art*, organised by Live Art Development Agency with Dave Stephens and Dominic Johnson, Queen Mary University of London, 16 November 2017. See https://vimeo.com/244911295/d38acc6eba (accessed 29 May 2018).

10. Anne Bean, improvised words spoken in *The Shivering*. Transcribed by the author from the soundtrack of *The Shivering* in *Night Chant* (2015).

11. Anne Bean, 'She Perceiving Her', unpublished presentation, *Performance and Politics in the 1970s*, organised by Dominic Johnson and Nicholas Ridout, Whitechapel Gallery, London, 30 May 2015. See https://vimeo.com/133660204 (accessed 29 May 2018).

12. Anne Bean, *She Perceiving Her*, 2016: http://annebeanarchive.com/2016-she-perceiving-her/

13. Anne Bean, *Dialogues through Time*, 2016: http://annebeanarchive.com/dialogues-through-time/

14. Anne Bean, *A Transpective*.

15. Bean, Powerpoint presentation for *Dialogues Through Time*, Cooper Gallery, 2016.

16. Ibid.

17. Ibid.

18. United Nations, *Universal Declaration of Human Rights* (1948), http://www.un.org/en/universal-declaration-human-rights/index.html (accessed 29 May 2018).

19. Bean, *Dialogues Through Time*, 2016.

20. Ibid.

21. Bean, Powerpoint presentation for *Dialogues Through Time*, Cooper Gallery, 2016.

22. Bean, *Until the Flowers Die*, 1973.

23. Anne Bean cited in Eleanor Roberts's text for *Emit: A Dialogue Through Time*, part of *Gifting Permission: Five Women Artists*, Coleman Project Space, London, 9 April 2017. Not paginated.

24. *Navajo Night Chant*, Section 1. Text provided by Anne Bean to the author, January 2018. Not paginated.

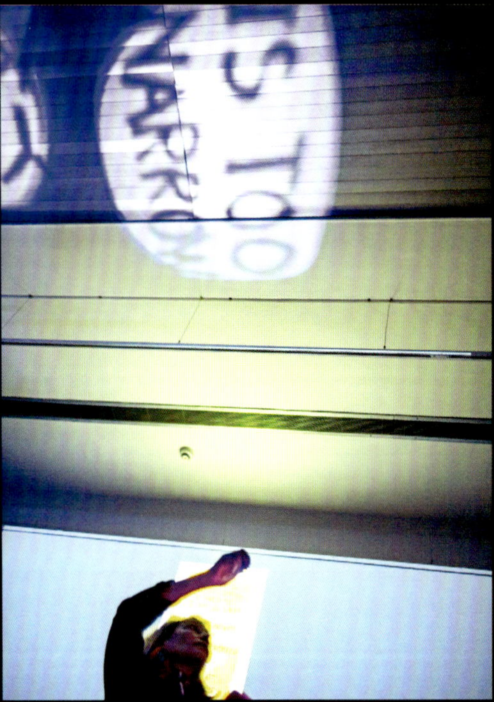

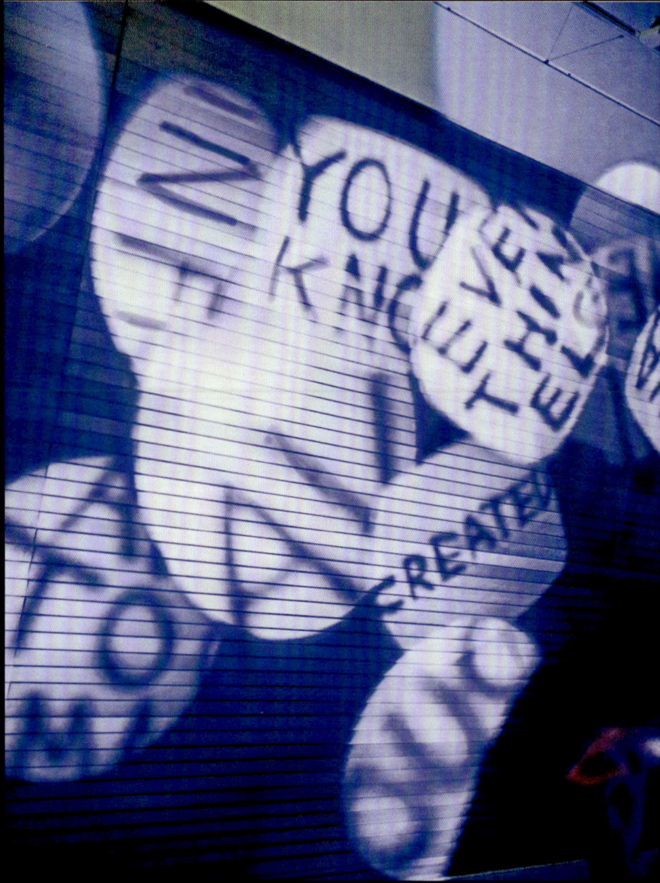

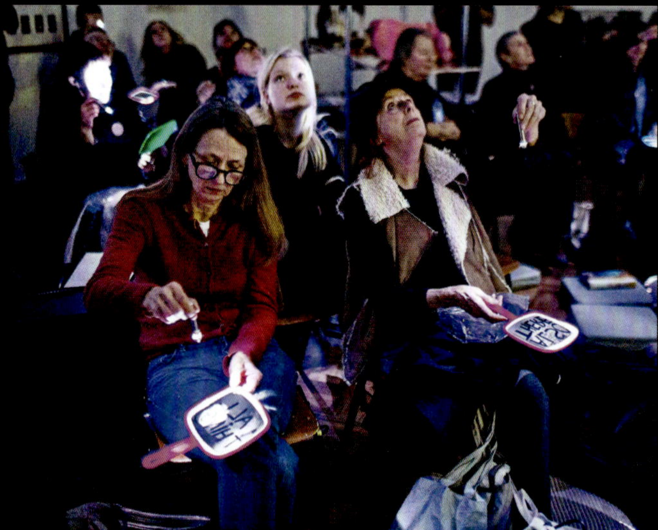

Above: Anne Bean, performance during 12-Hour Action Group International Symposium, *Of Other Spaces: Where Does Gesture Become Event?*, Cooper Gallery, Dundee, 2016. Photos: Ross Fraser McLean

Opposite: Anne Bean, *Unmindful of Bounds*, 2016. Image by Manuel Vason overlaid with emails between Anne Bean and Monica Ross, designed as an artist's page for *Venice Agendas* newspaper publication, 2017

On 19 Oct 2010, at 00:32, Anne Bean wrote:
Hi Monica, ...
It looks like I can make 28th-- I could 'translate' an article as a lipogram............
On Tue, Oct 19, 2010 at 1:33 PM, monica <monica@actsofmemory.net> wrote
Dear Anne,........................
your proposition of the lipogramme sounds great -it has reminded me that many ancient religious or philosophical texts were transcribed without vowels - so that they can only be brought back into life by being spoken/ translated by a living speaker or interpreter;..................................

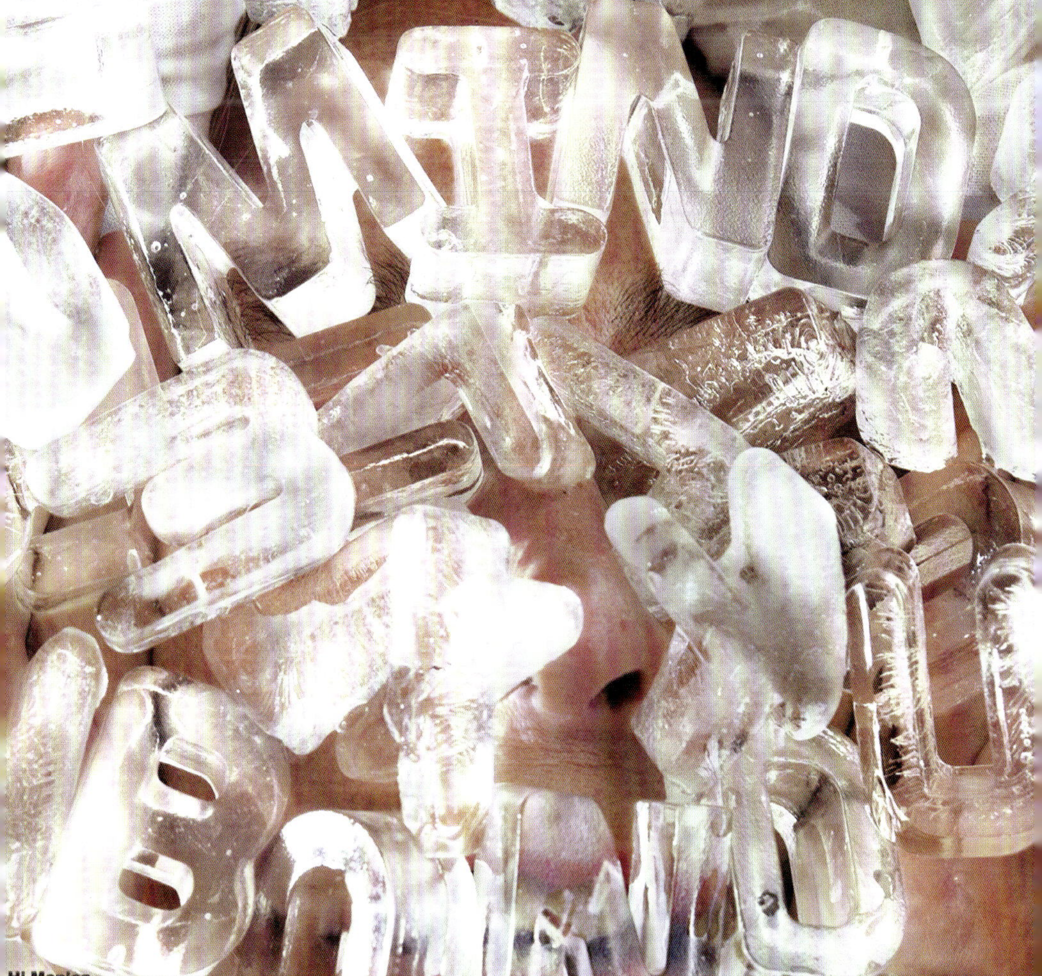

Hi Monica ....
Both of Georges Perec's parents perished in World War II, ..."The absence of a sign is always the sign of an absence, and the absence of the E in A Void announces a broader, cannily coded discourse on loss, catastrophe, and mourning. Perec cannot say the words père ["father"], mère ["mother"], parents ["parents"], famille ["family"] in his novel, nor can he write the name Georges Perec. In short, each "void" in the novel is abundantly furnished with meaning, and each points toward the existential void that Perec grappled with throughout his youth and early adulthood. ...I had chosen Article 19 from the Declaration of Human Rights originally as it seemed most apt for this treatment

Article nineteen

Everyone has the right to freedom of opinion and expression; this right includes freedom to hold opinions without interference and to seek, receive and impart information and ideas through any media and regardless of frontiers.

Lipogram:
Point six plus six plus six plus half plus half

All worldly inhabitants can, without constraint, hold opinions and spawn promulgations. This right contains within it, sanction to hold opinions without obstruction and to look for, obtain and impart information and significant notions through any form of articulation and unmindful of bounds.

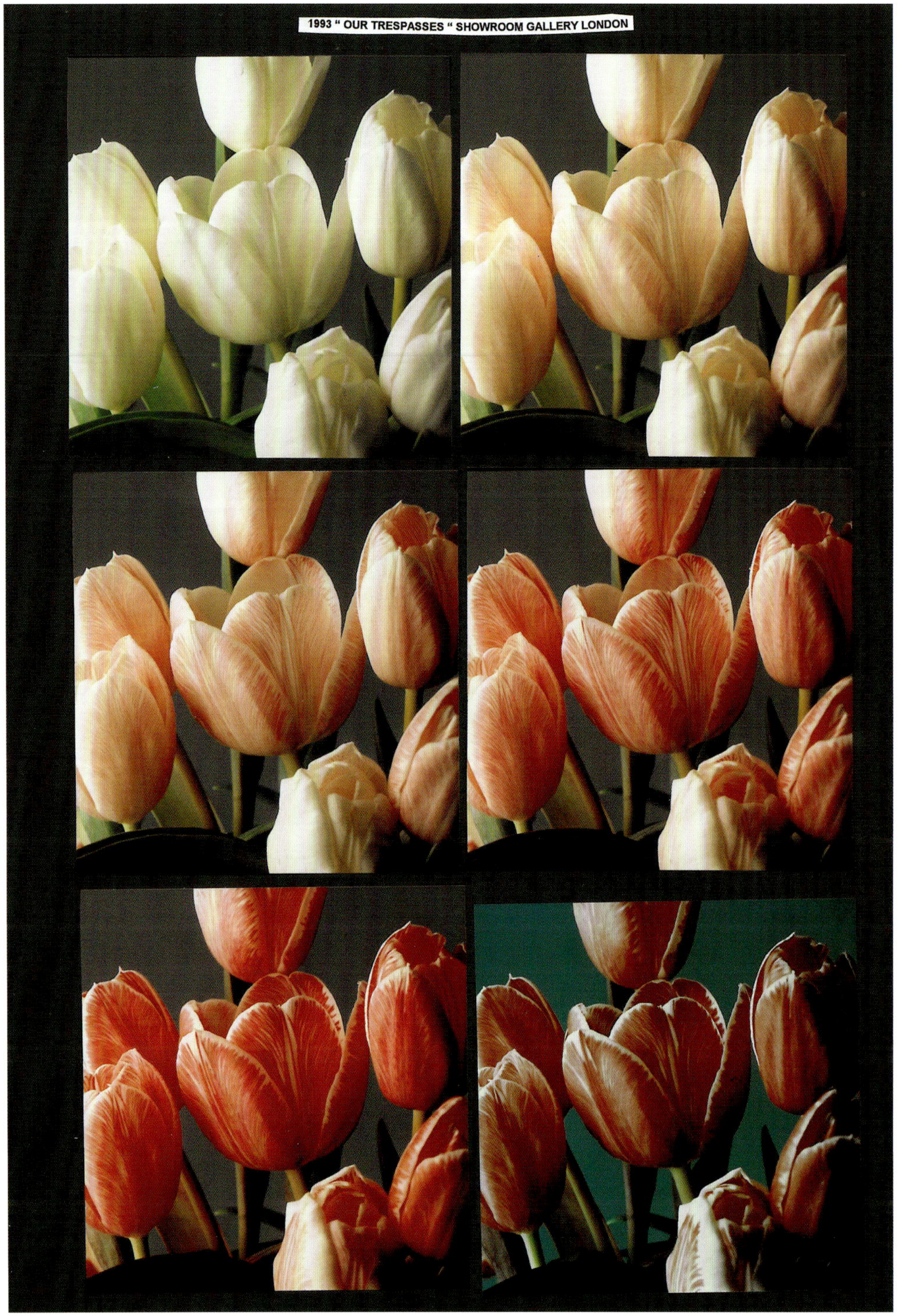
1993 " OUR TRESPASSES " SHOWROOM GALLERY LONDON

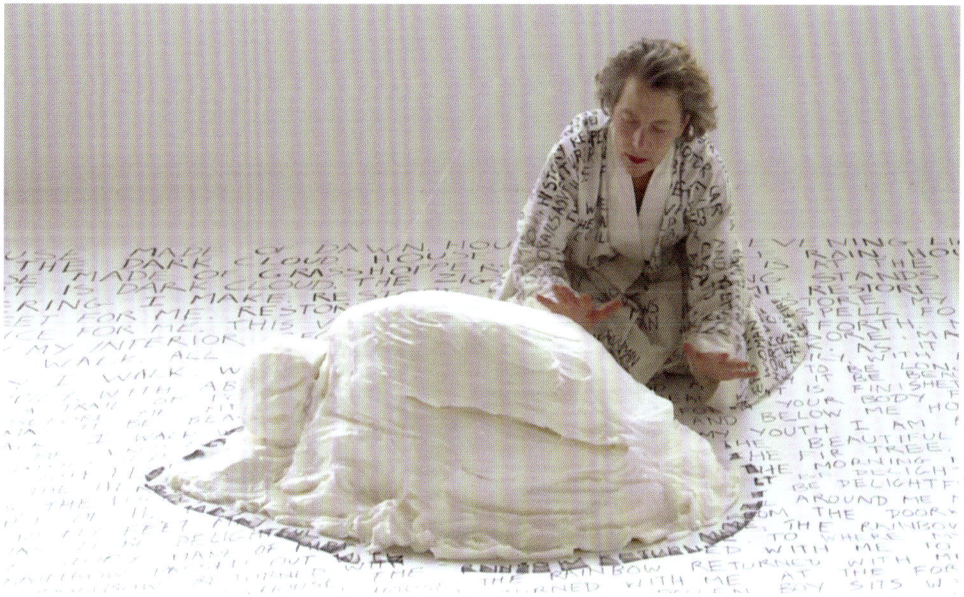

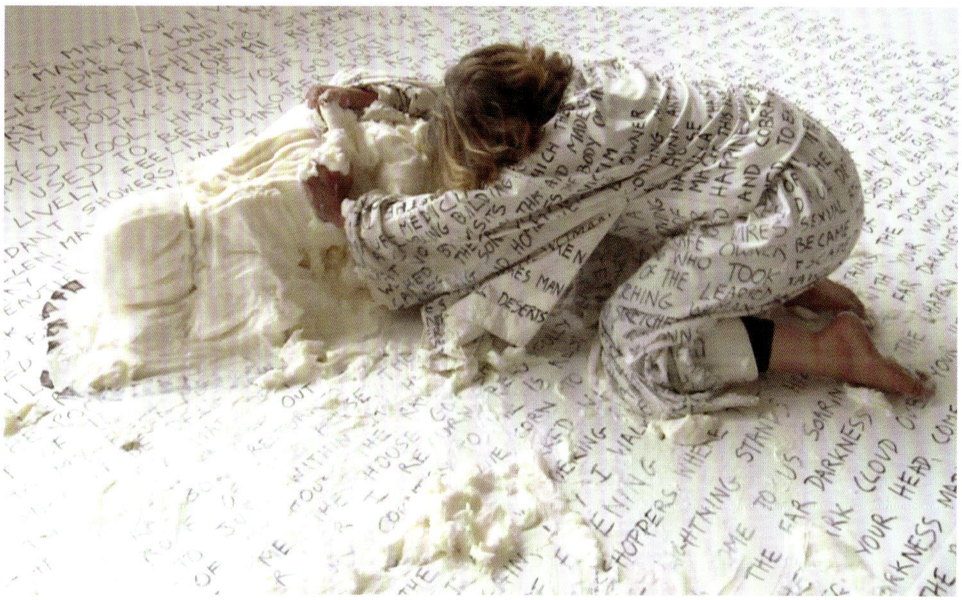

Above: Anne Bean, *Night Chant*, 2014. Still from a video by Graham Challifour
Opposite: Anne Bean, *Our Trespasses*, Showroom Gallery, London, 1993. Photos: Kirsten Reynolds

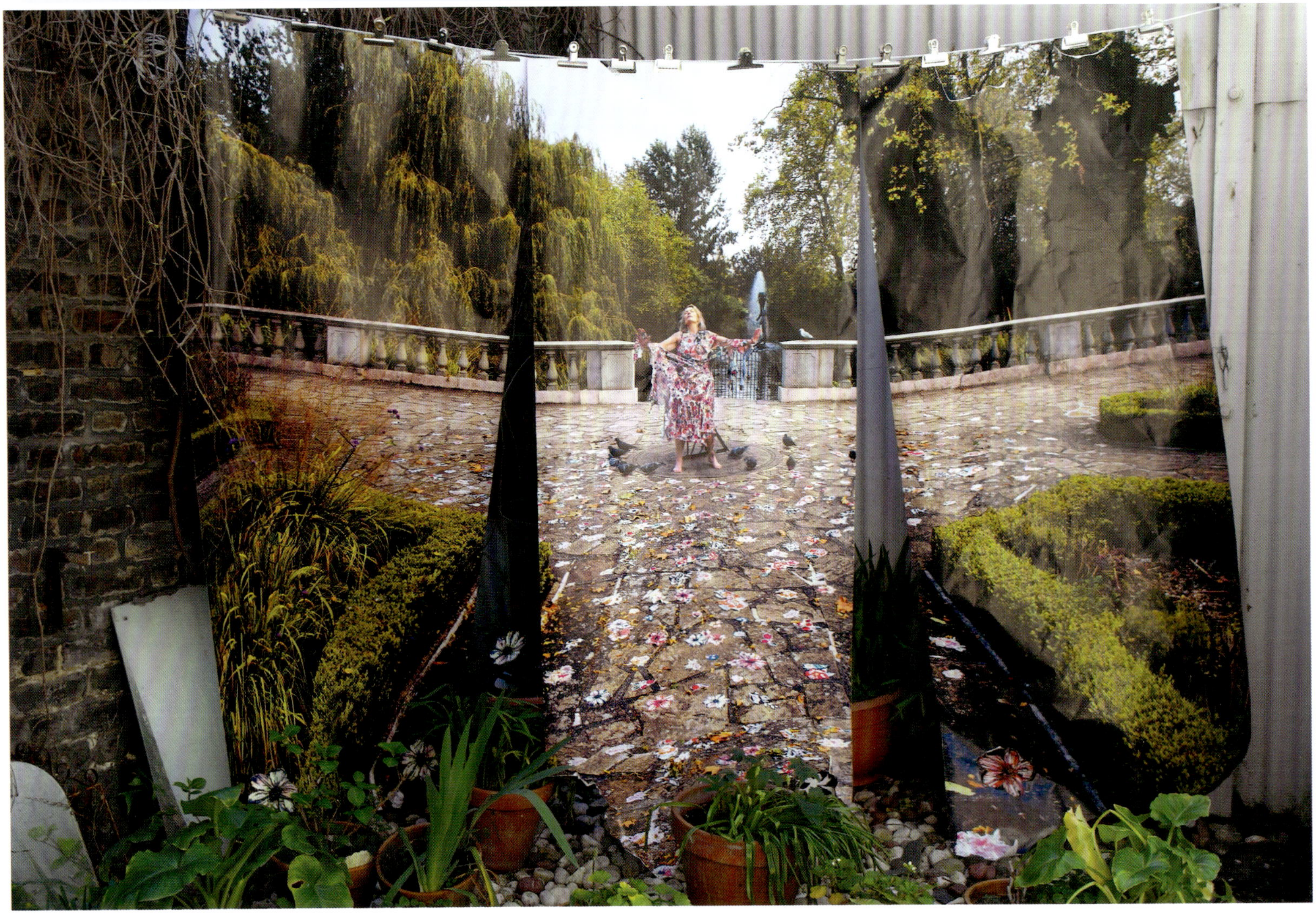

Anne Bean, *Our Bodies in a State of Music*, photograph made in collaboration with Manuel Vason. Installation shot in *EMIT,* Coleman Project Space, London, 2017

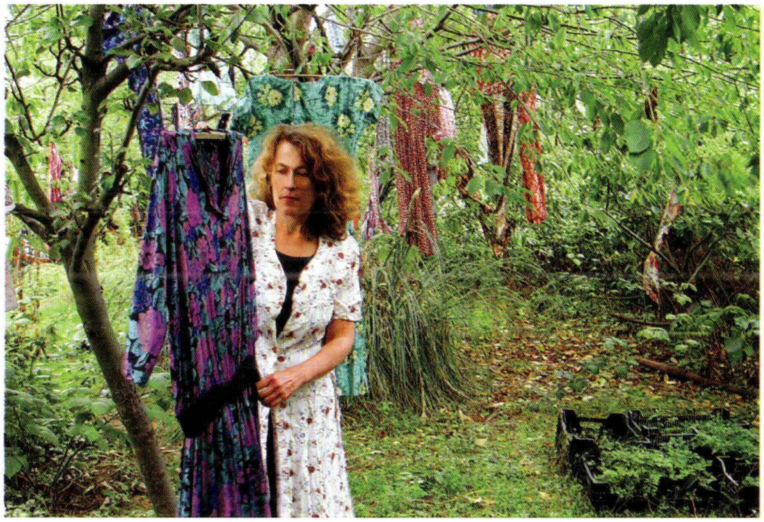

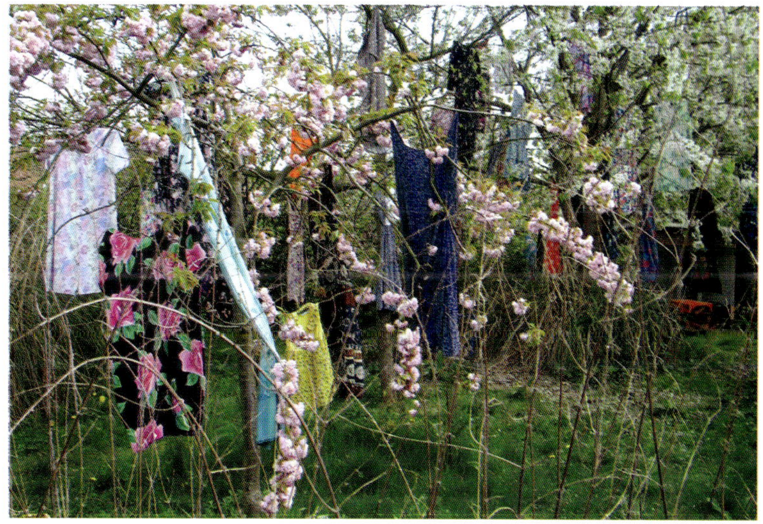

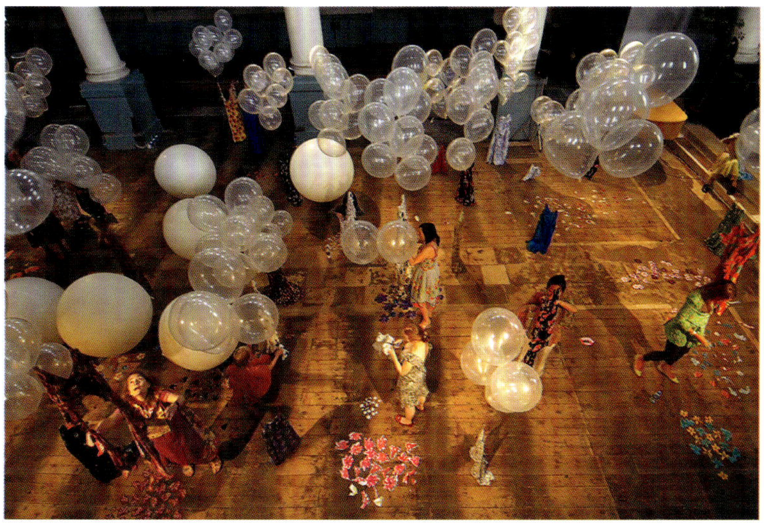

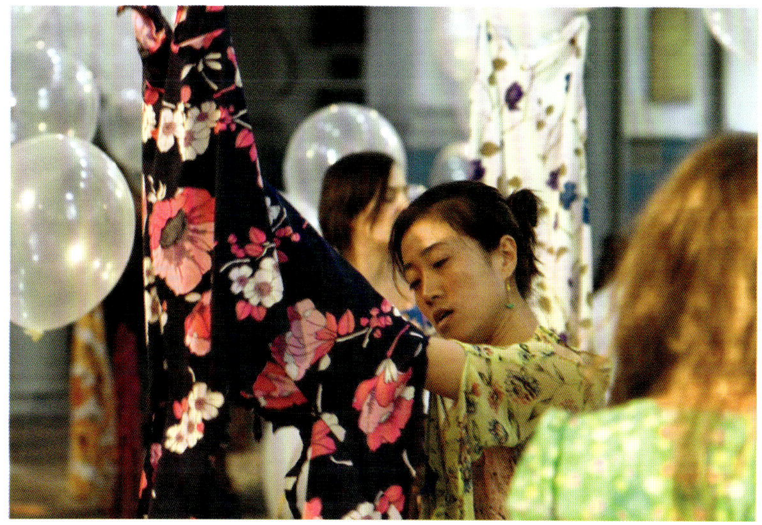

Top: Anne Bean, *365 Flowery Dresses* as part of *REAP*, 2004. Photo: Chris Bishop

Bottom: Anne Bean, *Bells of Shoreditch*, part of the series *Long Time Passing*, Shoreditch Church, London, 2007.
Photos: David Hoffman and Robert Bloomfield

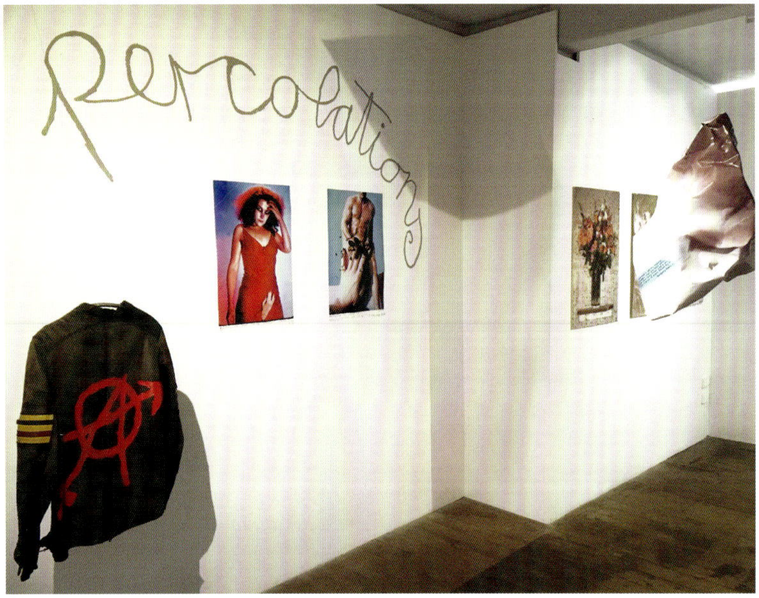

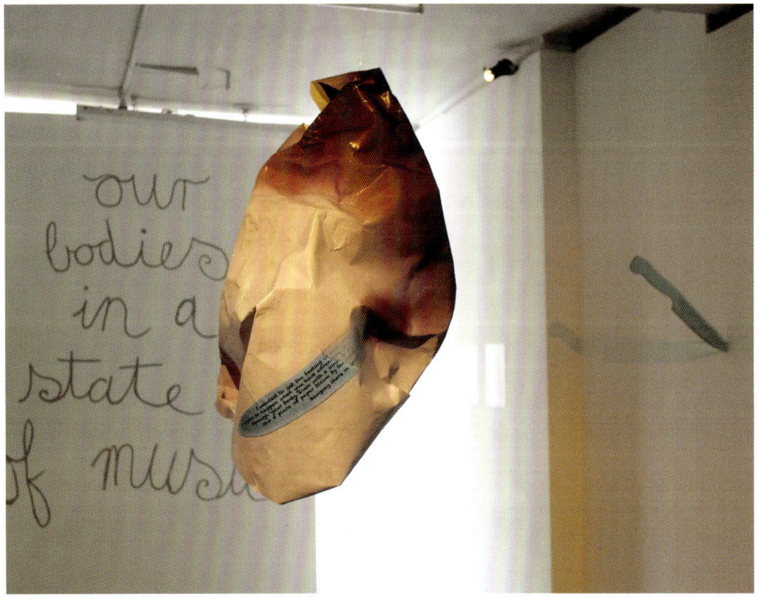

Above: Installation shot of various works in Anne Bean, *EMIT*, Coleman Project Space, London 2017

Opposite: Anne Bean in collaboration with Manuel Vason, *Slit*, in Alexis Hunter's former studio, London, 2016

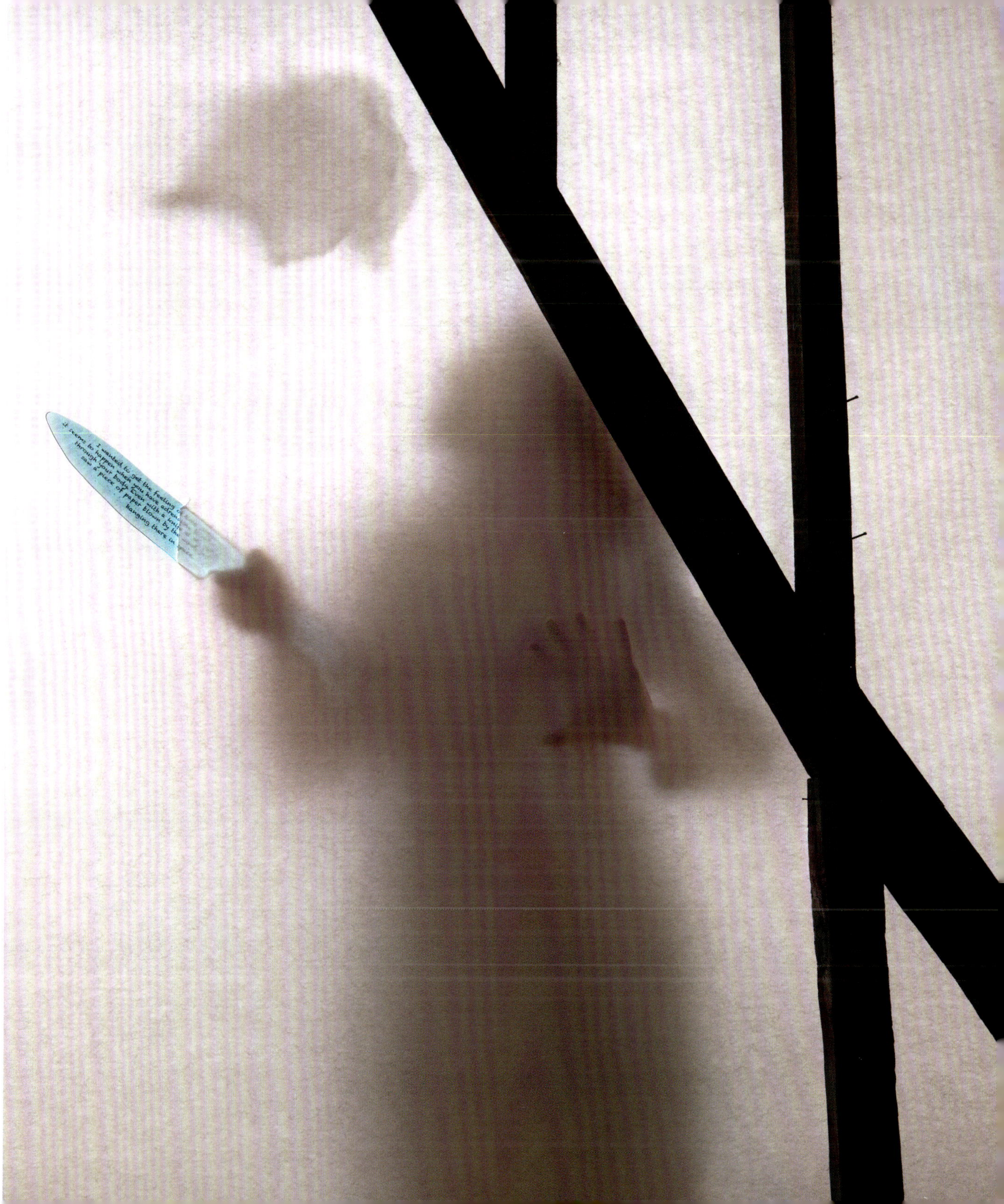
I wanted to get the feeling
it seems to happen when you have
through your body. Even with a
saw a piece of paper blown by
hanging there

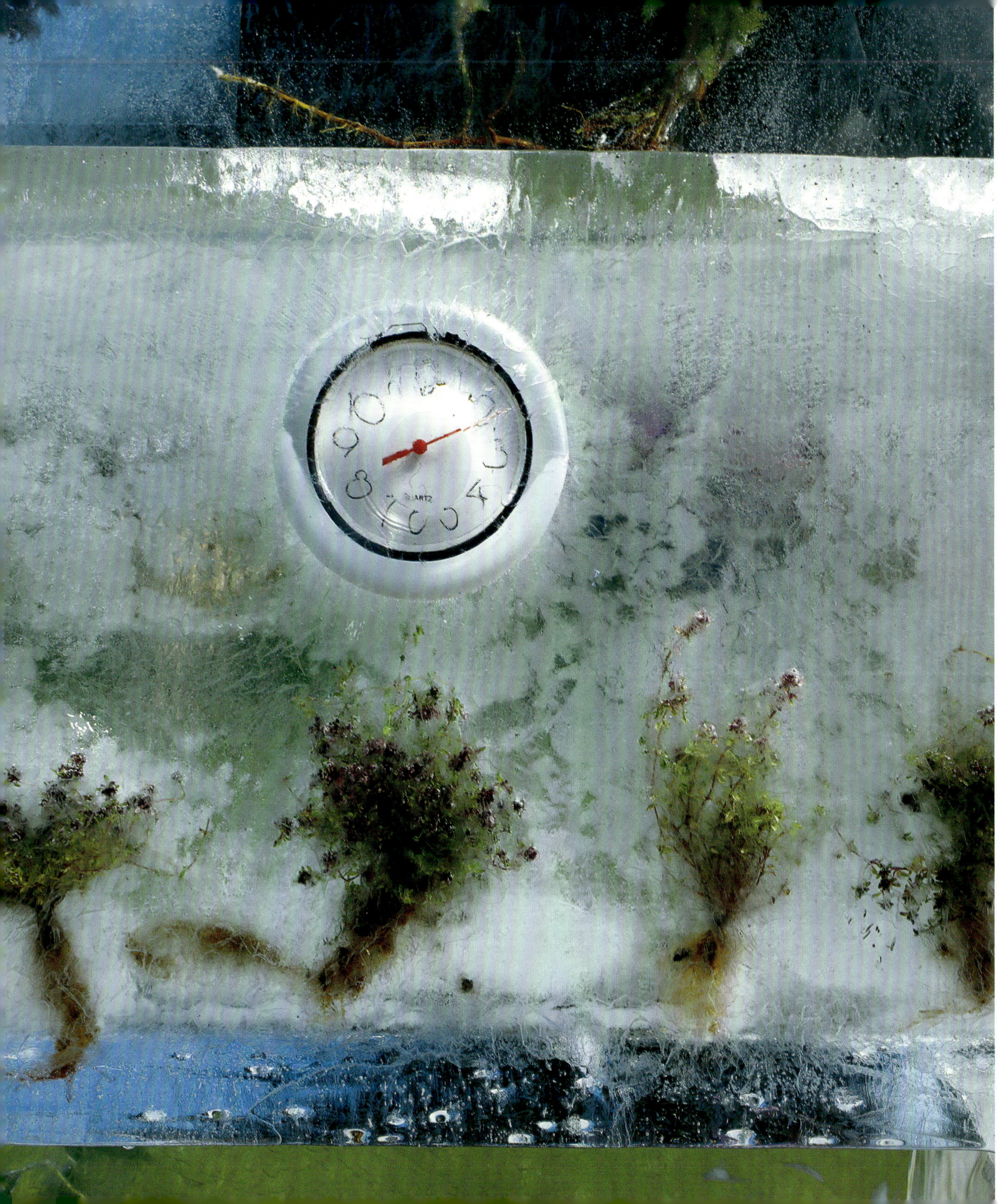

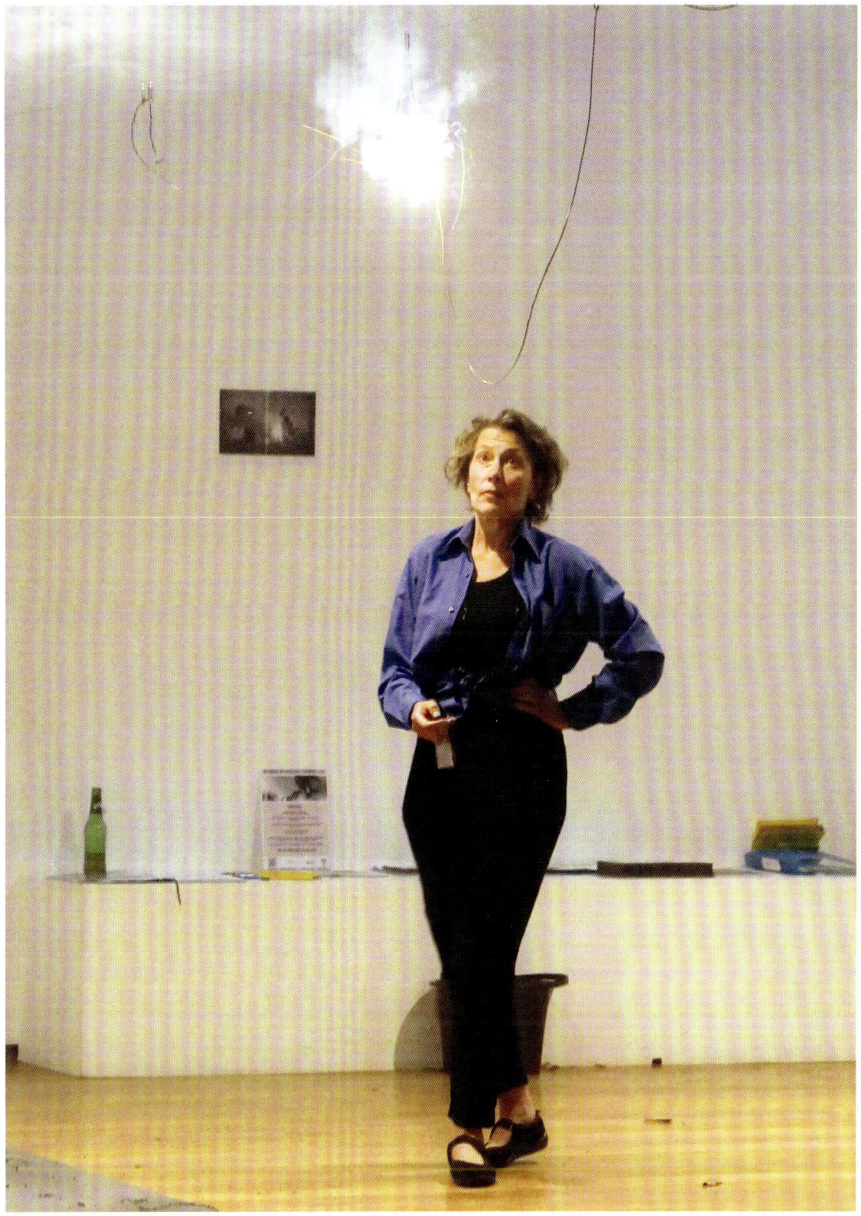

Two works relating to pyrotechnic sculptor, Stephen Cripps (1952-1982):

Above: Anne Bean and Richard Wilson, *Fused by Stephen*, an event for *Mechanical Garden and other Long Encores* (curated by Naomi Pearce), Dilston Grove, London, 2014. Using Cripps' own fuse paper to initiate a fuse wire through the gallery and across a lawn to light rockets suspended on lines which shot towards the gallery, hitting a series of gongs. Photo: Miyako Narita

Opposite: Anne Bean, Paul Burwell and Richard Wilson, *Suspended Thyme* as part of *Slow Event: A Fresh Bunch of Flowers*, Serpentine Gallery, 1992. Photo: Ronnie Israel

INTERVENTIONS BY ANNE BEAN

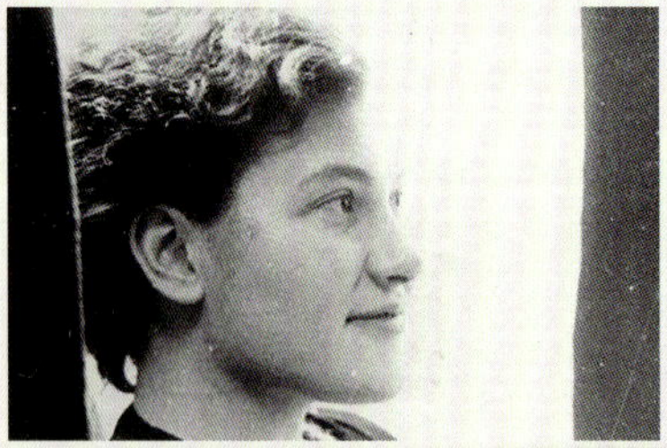

Until the Flowers Die
Reading University, Fine Art Dept, 1973

I sat, as a framed head, writing and drawing thoughts, whilst 16 friends came and went, contributing their own texts and sketches.The work lasted approximately 24 hours, timed by some waterless tulips in vases wilting until they touched the ground

My dissertation supervisor was Caroline Tisdall. Both of us had encountered Joseph Beuys during his exhibit *The Pack*, in 1970.

Caroline went on later to write and travel extensively with Beuys.

My dissertation, *What is Art and what am I doing in it?* was refused by the examiners, despite a vigorous defence by artist/tutor Rita Donagh and Caroline.

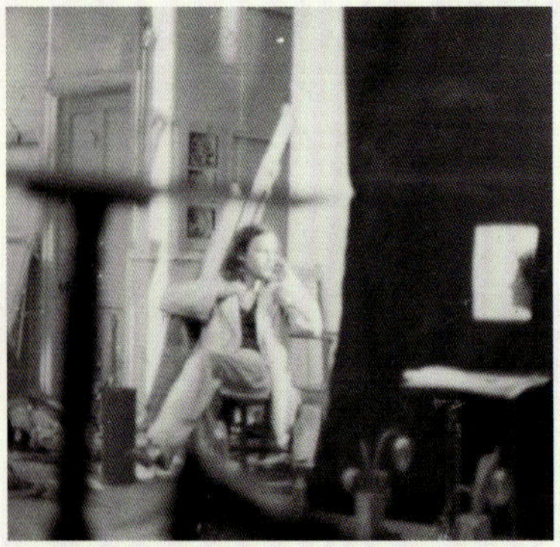

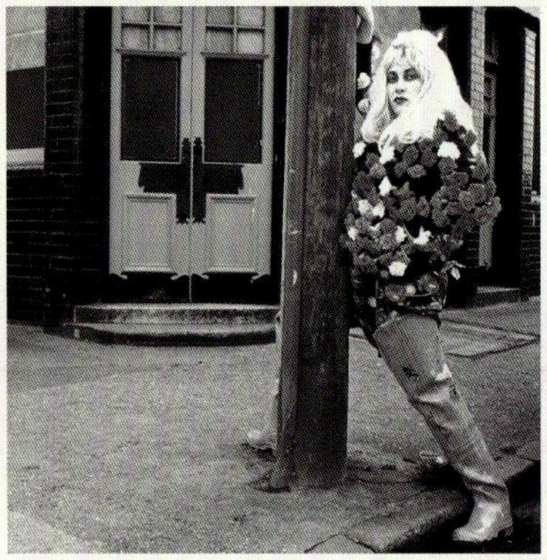

Moodies were approached about management of various sorts, by several people, including the impresario Malcolm McClaren and the artist Barry Flanagan. Although they all recognised the layering of strategies, issues and sheer strutting one's stuff involved in the ethos of the group, I feared a solidification that would suck the exhilaration out, simply by having to articulate ways forward. The dexterous ways of simply BEING in the world, that I treasured, would become hidebound. Outside of actual performances, I felt energised by simply going on the streets in these hard-to-decipher outfits.
Photo: Joe Gaffney

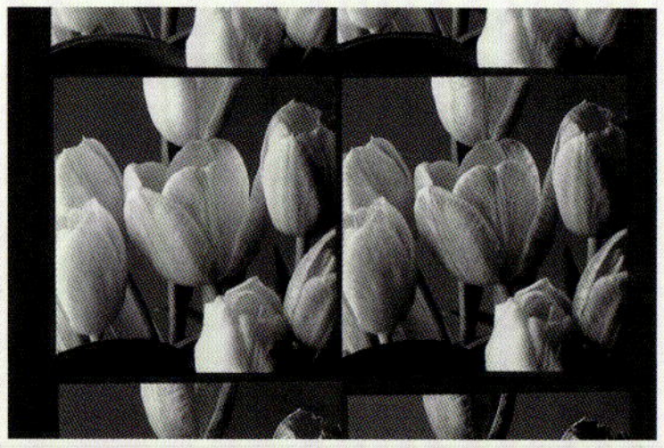

Our Trespasses, 1993
Showroom Gallery, London

Remembering the dying tulips 20 years earlier, I placed white tulips in a vase filled with red dye in the gallery. Once every hour, for 24 hours, a large format polaroid photograph was taken by Kirsten Reynolds, as the white tulips turned red. The photographs were placed in the gallery around the space. Then transparent hose was configured and glued on the wall to spell 'for give us' and the ends of the hoses were placed in the red dye.

During the performance, the musician/artist Mary Genis and I sucked the dye into the hose so the words suddenly appeared in red whilst we sang early blues. We held tape recorders playing the same songs, remembering the cotton pickers, as we slowly extinguished the voices by smothering them in cotton wool.

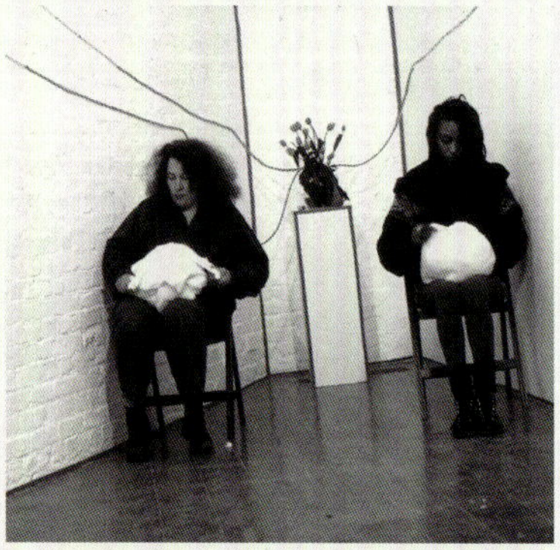

A Slow Event: A Fresh Bunch of Flowers,
1992 Serpentine Gallery, London
Anne Bean, Paul Burwell,
Richard Wilson. Exactly ten years after the death of Stephen Cripps.

I wanted the sense of an ephemeral but monumental work for Stephen, much like his own works. Flowers which expressed moments in his life, suggested or contributed by his friends, were frozen into clear blocks of ice creating a 10' x 36' structure which melted over the course of a day leaving wilted debris at nightfall. Many people spent hours watching. I included a clock with only the second hand, so it was continuously in present time, with thyme plants suspended. Unforeseen by me, because the battery was the warmest component, the clock was the first to break surface and it remained there in all its presentness.

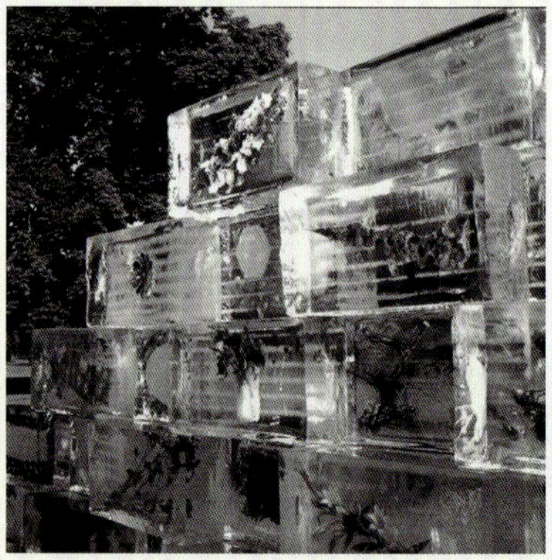

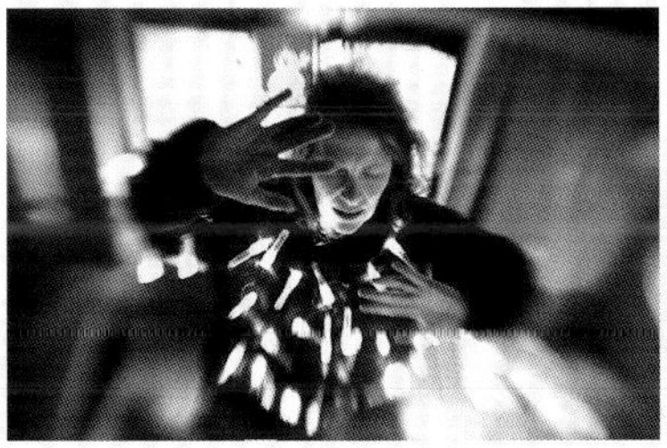

And Inhabited the Spaces, video still for *TAPS* compilation, filmed/edited by Patricia and Brian Routh, 2009.

Kicking the Bucket
My first thought for my own video contribution to *TAPS* was to disconsolately kick a metal bucket around some nether region of Hull for several hours. I heard Paul's maniacal laughter egging me on. However, the caravan had such a magnetic pull particularly in the last year of his life, when I had spent time with him in this tiny shelter. We played records, cassettes and CDs from his vast collection, across his life. We time travelled, rather than space travelled in this tiny capsule. I wanted to capture something of that space.

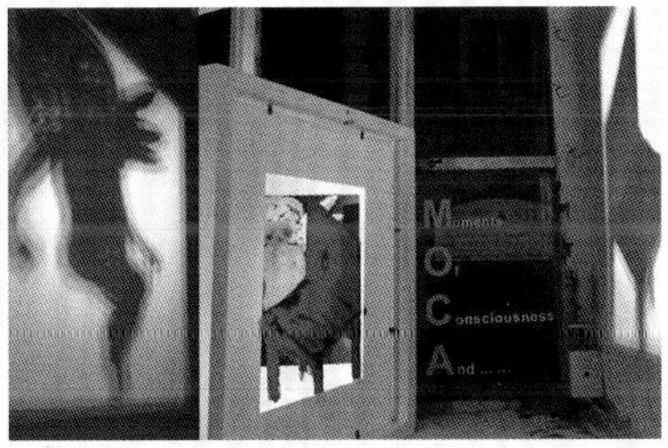

Cherubs, MoCa Trowbridge 2017/18
Photo: Anne Bean

Cherubs, MoCa Trowbridge 2017/18
For three consecutive years I have put an installation with sound in the window of MoCa Trowbridge, for a month over the darkest time of year. In *Cherubs*, changing lights jumped between shadows and reflections whilst speakers placed in air-bricks on each side of the window had the voices of myself and Hugo Danino incanting the disintegrating word 'cherub' into 'chair rub rub chair rupture rapture cherub chair rub rub chair rupture rub chair rapture cherub rub chair rupture rapture' and on and on.

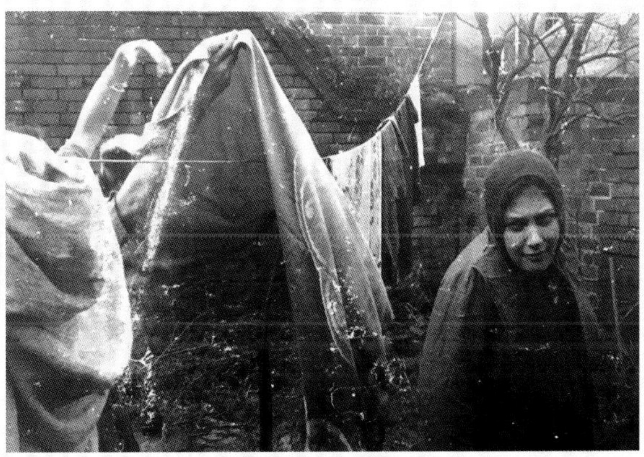

Channelling my Russian relatives whilst Natasha Lawrence creates their ghosts, Reading 1970.

An Unrecognised Collaboration with Sue Arrowsmith, 2016
In the Ikon Gallery catalogue on Sue Arrowsmith, 'Egg of Night,' 1986, Patricia Bickers, editor of *Art Monthly*, writes 'Much of Sue Arrowsmith's work is performance based; the resulting works representing both a record of an event as well as a commentary upon it.' Later on, she comments on Sue's work *Andromeda's Tear* which mixes, in a complex procedure, paint and photographic processes: 'It is the dilemma of all art, but particularly of photography, that at the moment of capture, of realisation, the thing "itself" escapes, leaving only its "semblance".' Without recognising that I may have been replying to Sue's work *A Conversation with Anne Bean*, 1983, I made a piece in 2016, half a life time later, with the photographer Graham Challifour. I 'captured' the simultaneous moment of a photograph and an instant painting coming into being, bolstering each other's 'semblance'.

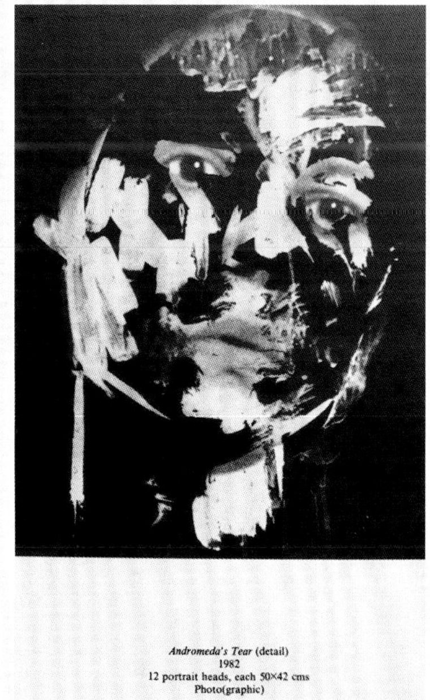

Above: From Sue Arrowsmith catalogue *Egg of Night*, solo show IKON Gallery, 1986 (essay by Patricia Bickers)

Below: An Unrecognised Collaboration with Sue Arrowsmith, 2016

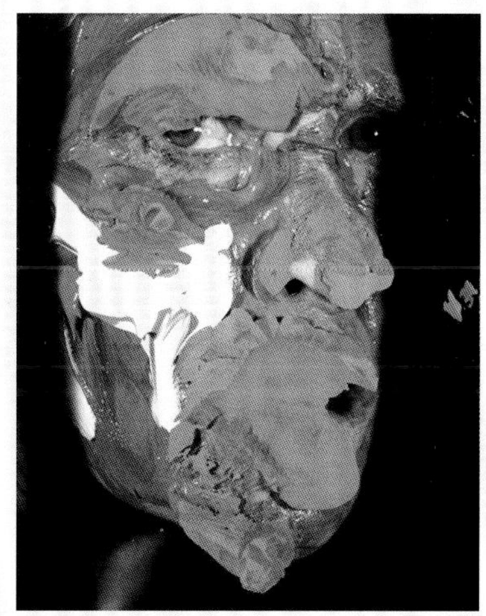

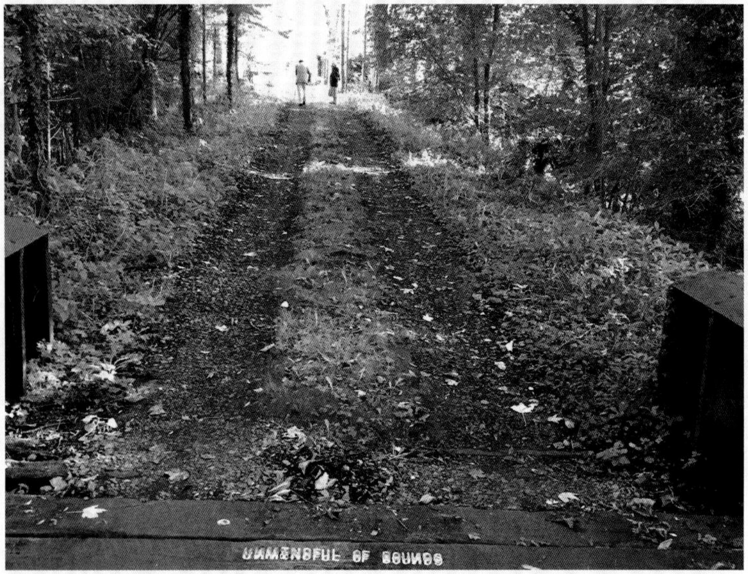

Unmindful of Bounds, Welsh/English border. Photos: Anne Bean

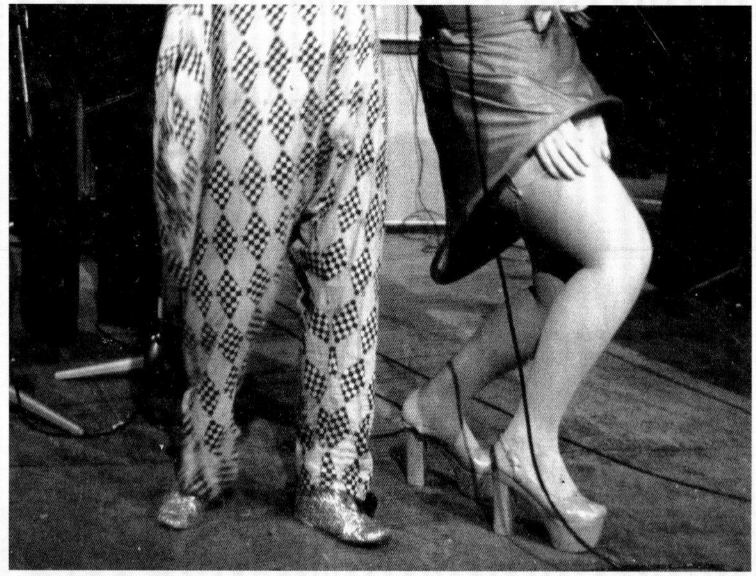

Moodier, Garage Gallery (Anne Bean, Chris Bishop, Hermine Demoriane, Polly Eltes, Malcolm Jones, John McKeon, Judy Nylon, Max Paddison, sisters Jennifer and Lorraine), 1975.

Unmindful of Bounds, 2016, Welsh/English border.

During a Sidney Nolan residency, 2016, I was aware that the Nolan estate straddled the Welsh/English border. I read up on several battles fought and bloodshed lost that had taken place in this bucolic land. The word Wales, actually comes from an Anglo-Saxon word wealas, meaning 'foreigner,' that word at the base of so much tragedy and turmoil. With thoughts of work with Monica Ross on the *Declaration of Human Rights* and my long-term work with the group PAVES about borders, I was carefully placing glass letters spelling *Unmindful of Bounds* exactly on the border. Two people slowly approached as I was kneeling down. Unbelievably it turned out to be Lucy Neal who had, with Rose Fenton, directed London International Festival of Theatre, and who, since childhood had lived here and played games with her sisters leaping between Wales and England. I went back to have tea with her and her extraordinary father.

Lucy wrote 'I can't believe the universe held that gap long enough for you to take that picture without knowing who you were taking a picture of only to find out a moment later! This is a magical thing for me Anne'.

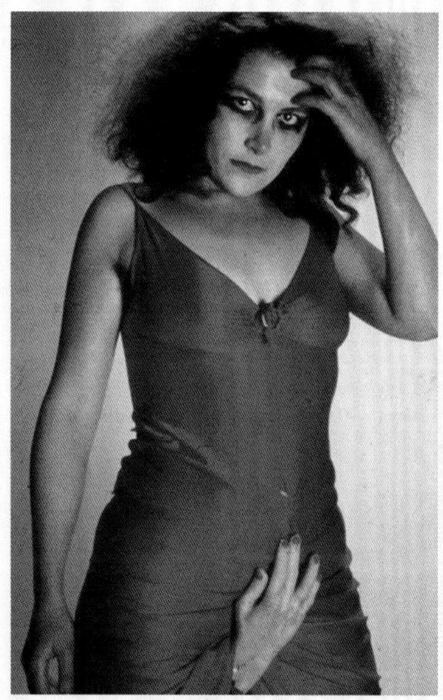

I had several different rubber hands which I used in strategic ways, in everyday life as well as performances. I wanted to baffle. Photo: Elisa Leonelli

Wider than Wide MOCA Trowbridge

After an extensive emailing with Monica about lipograms from George Perec's constrained language to ancient religious and philosophical texts transcribed without vowels, she wrote 'What an amazing trail, a golden thread...'

Golden threads are often used as an expression in the mystical lineage making connections, backwards and forwards, through the ages with the seekers in search of the ecstatic, the bliss, the oneness.

I have made several works in MOCA Trowbridge with Monica Ross and these golden threads in mind.

The first work I did in MOCA Trowbridge, 2015, was a painting using Hadewijch's text All Things. The electricity wasn't switched on yet and I painted with candle light feeling shivers of connection with this thirteenth century visionary who speaks of touching the uncreated...

You know this well,
you who are also there

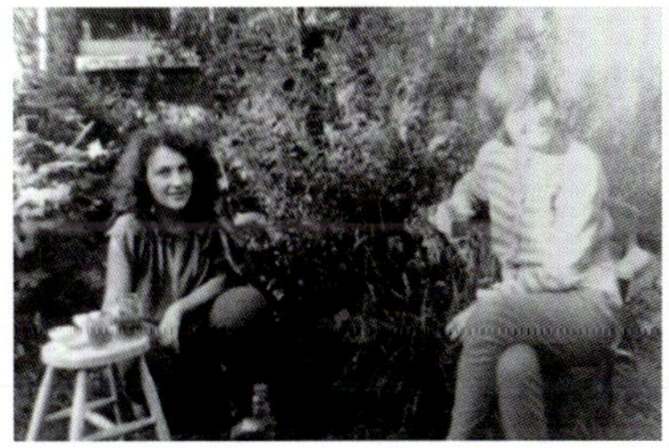

Anne Bean and Rita Harris
in Rita's garden 1984
Photo: Rod Melvin

I think of Rita in gardens. We spent much time in her garden and she gave me most of the initial planting for my roof garden. There are still plants I have from her garden in the 80's. She made a variety of cordials from her own fruits and berries, so that one was suffused, through all the senses, with this garden. For REAP, the year- long project that I initiated in Southwark Park, Rita made a wire armature on which she sewed flowery dresses of her own, tightly wound but with loose stitching. Hanging outside in the wind and rain, the dresses slowly unravelled to become owing forms again, redressing themselves.

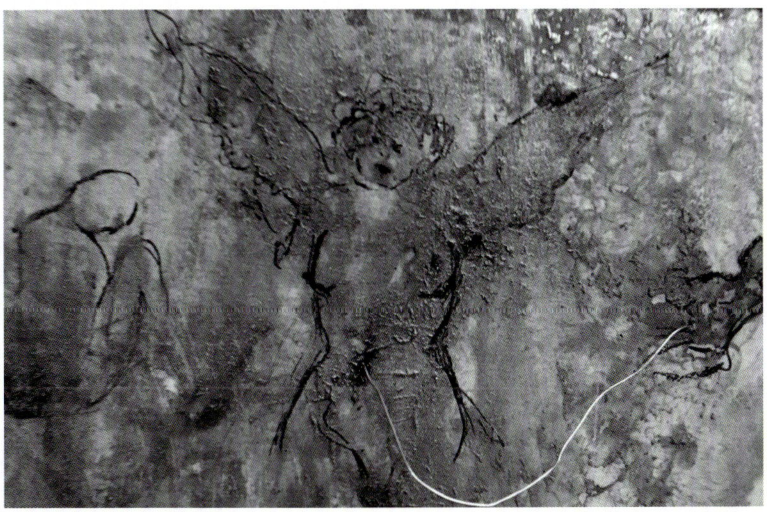

Golden Thread, 2016 MOCA Trowbridge.
Photo: Anne Bean.

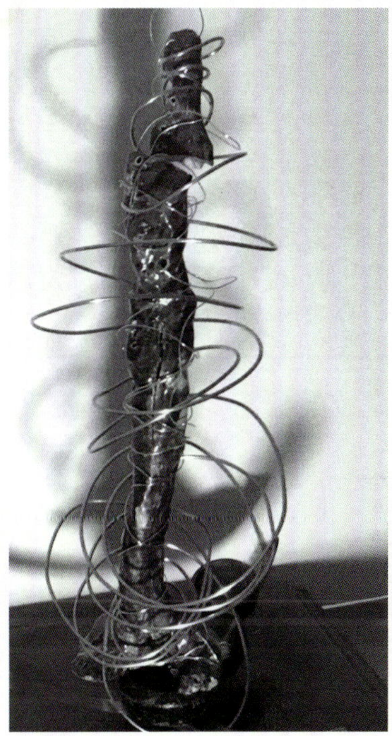

Golden Thread, 2016 MOCA Trowbridge.
Photo: Anne Bean.

Below: Rita Harris dress sculpture
part of *365 Dresses (REAP)*, 2004.
Photo: Anne Bean

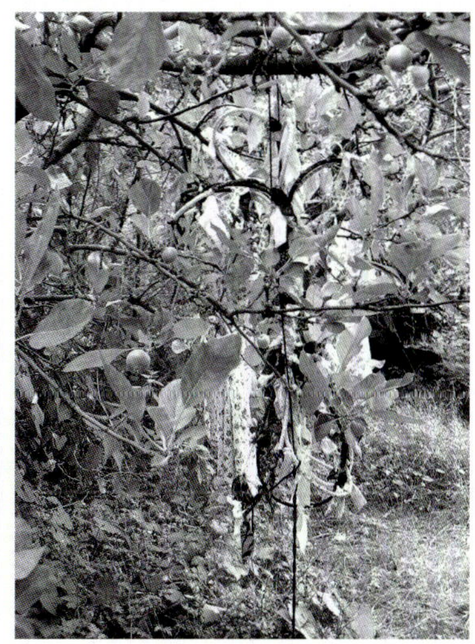

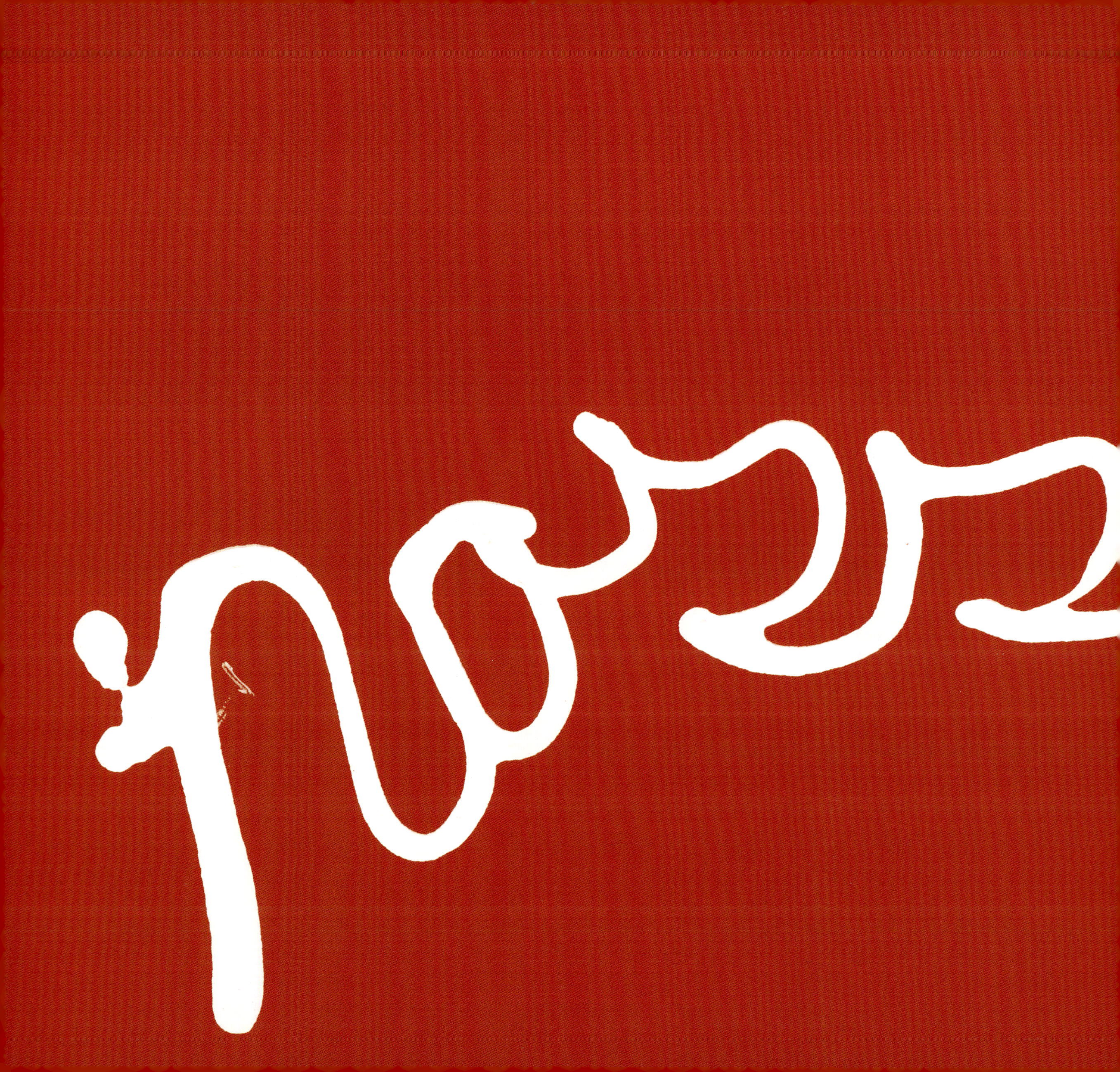

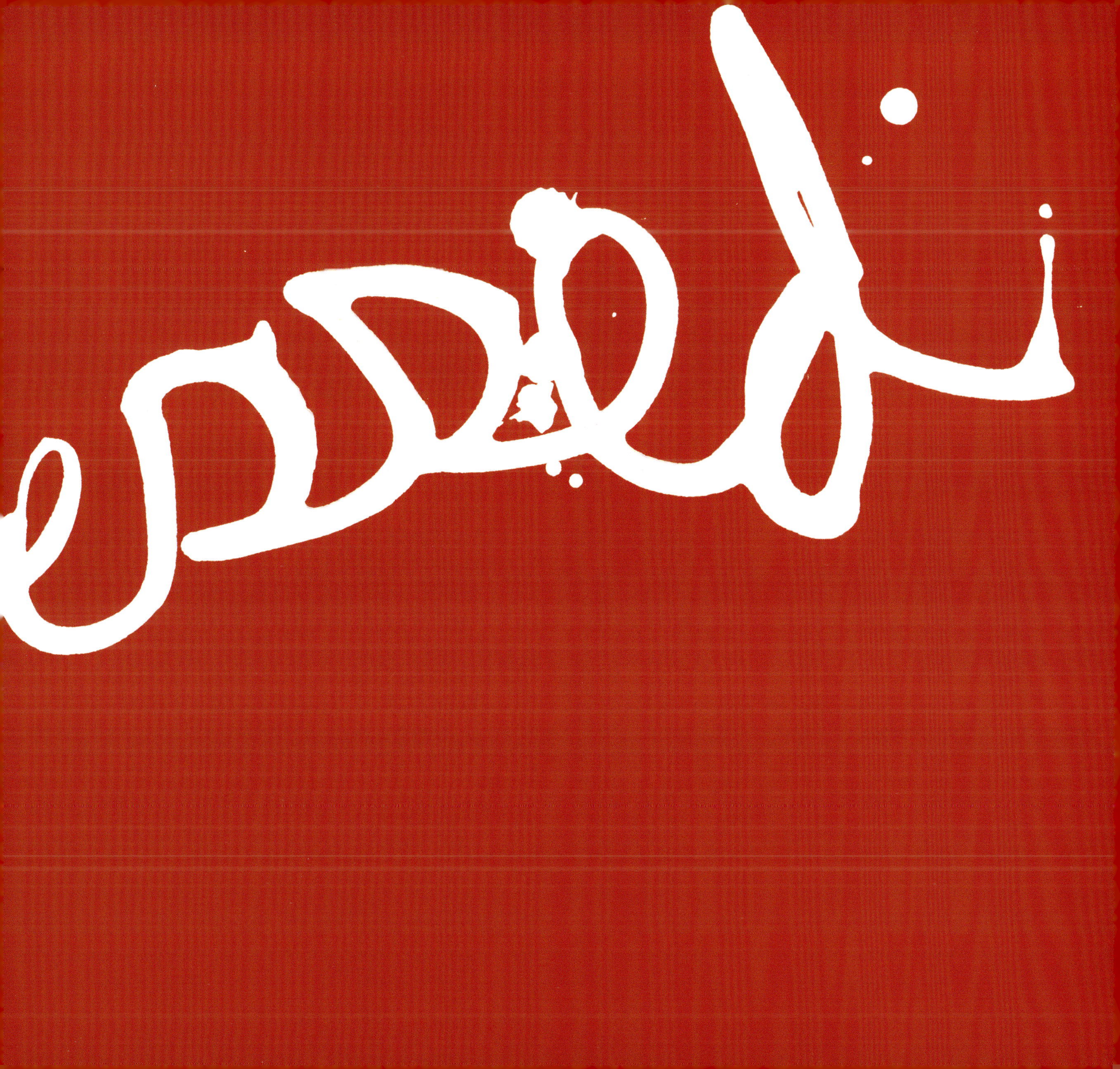

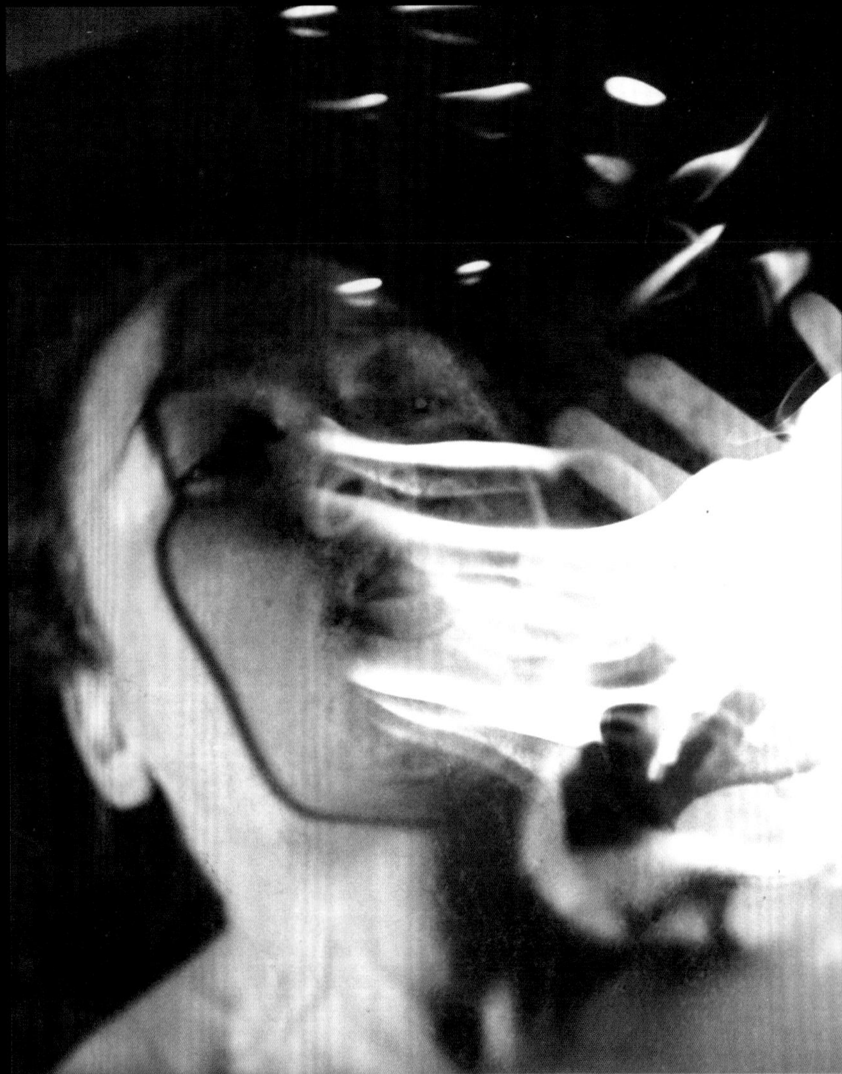

Anne Bean, *Elemental* series, 1974. A series of images originally conceived to be projected onto smoke. Photos: Chris Bishop

pp. 118-9: Anne Bean and Paul Burwell, *An Independent Declaration*, B2 Wapping, 4 July 1982. Paper horns with an open reed are blown and set on fire so the note changes as they get shorter. Photo: David Dawson

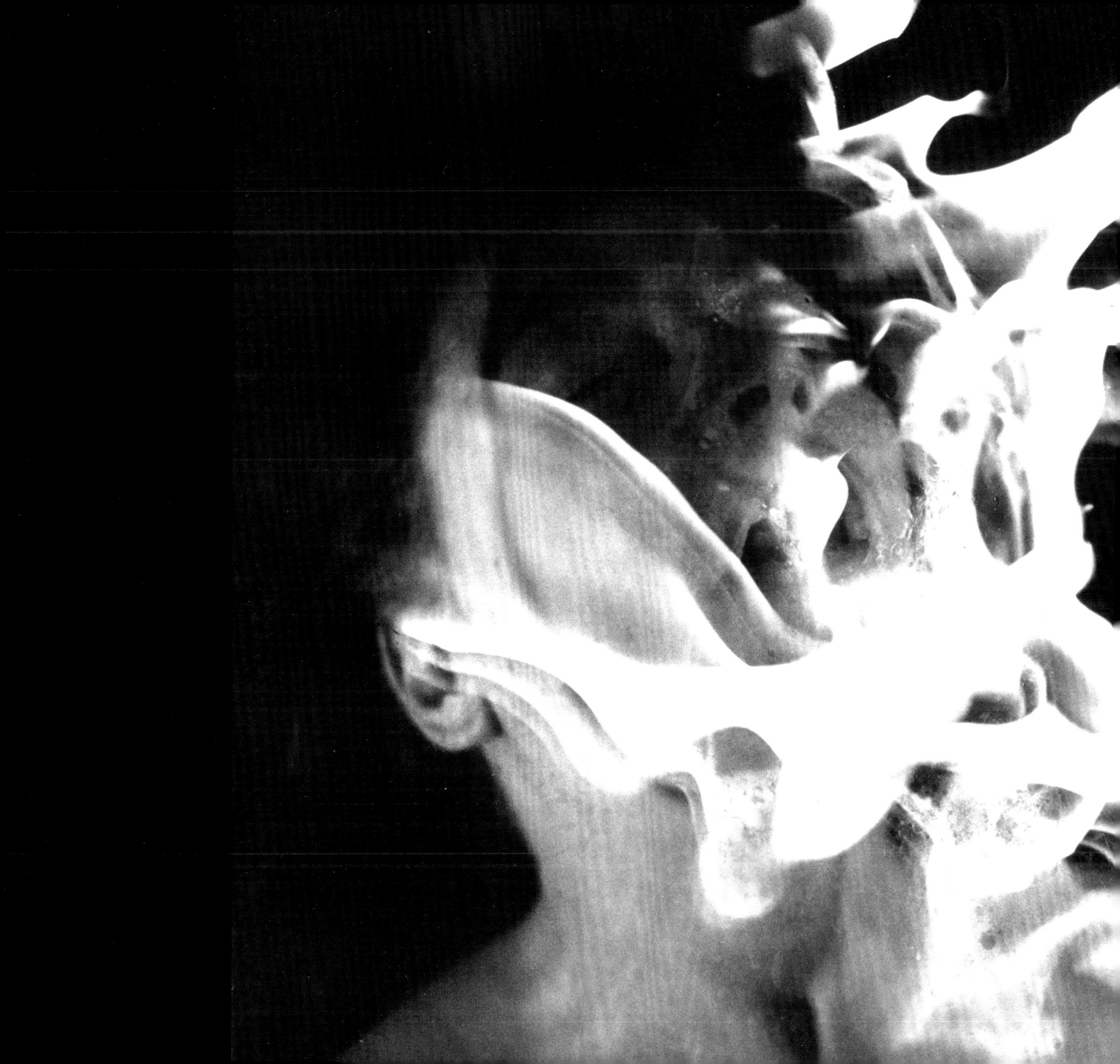

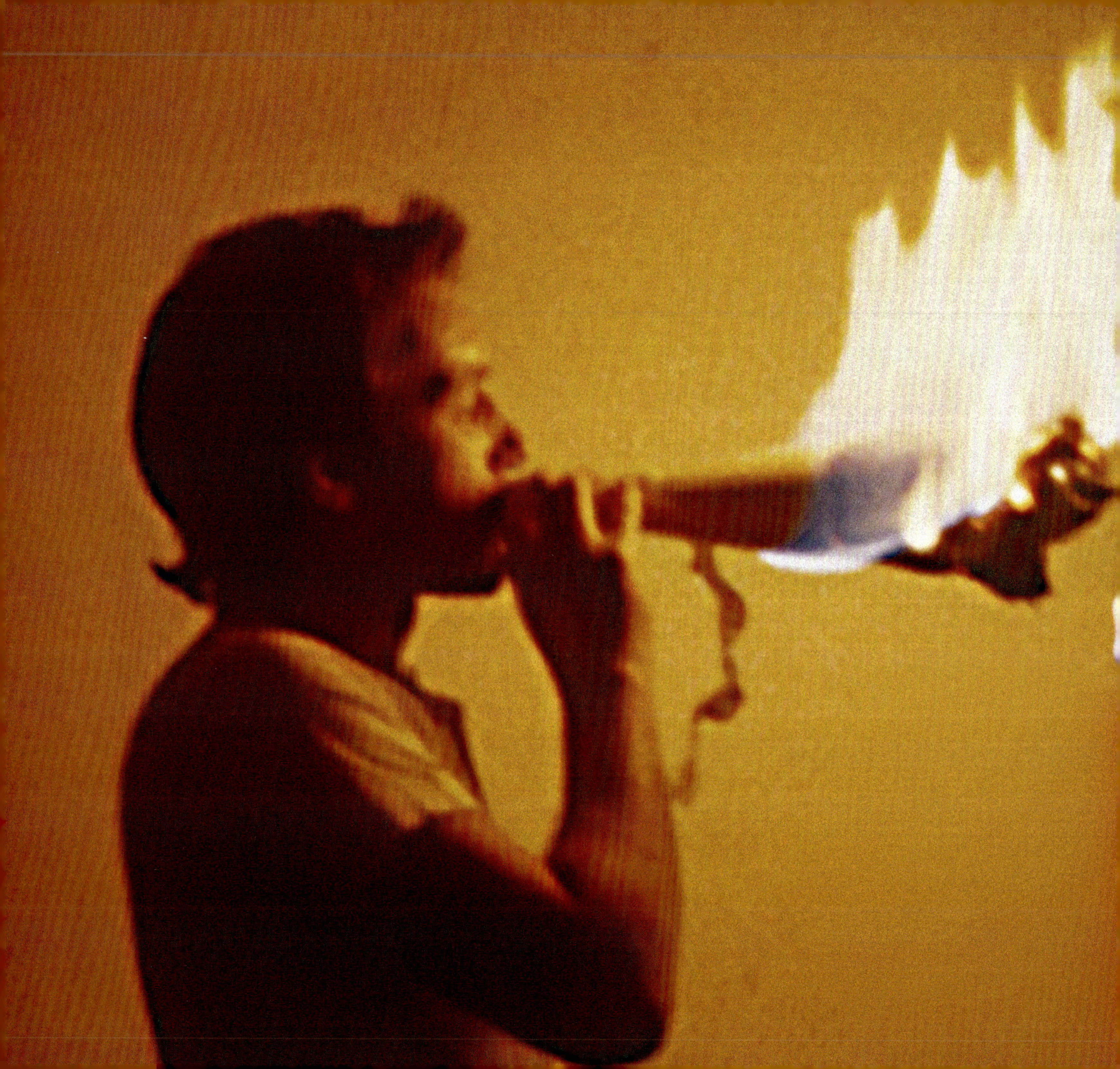

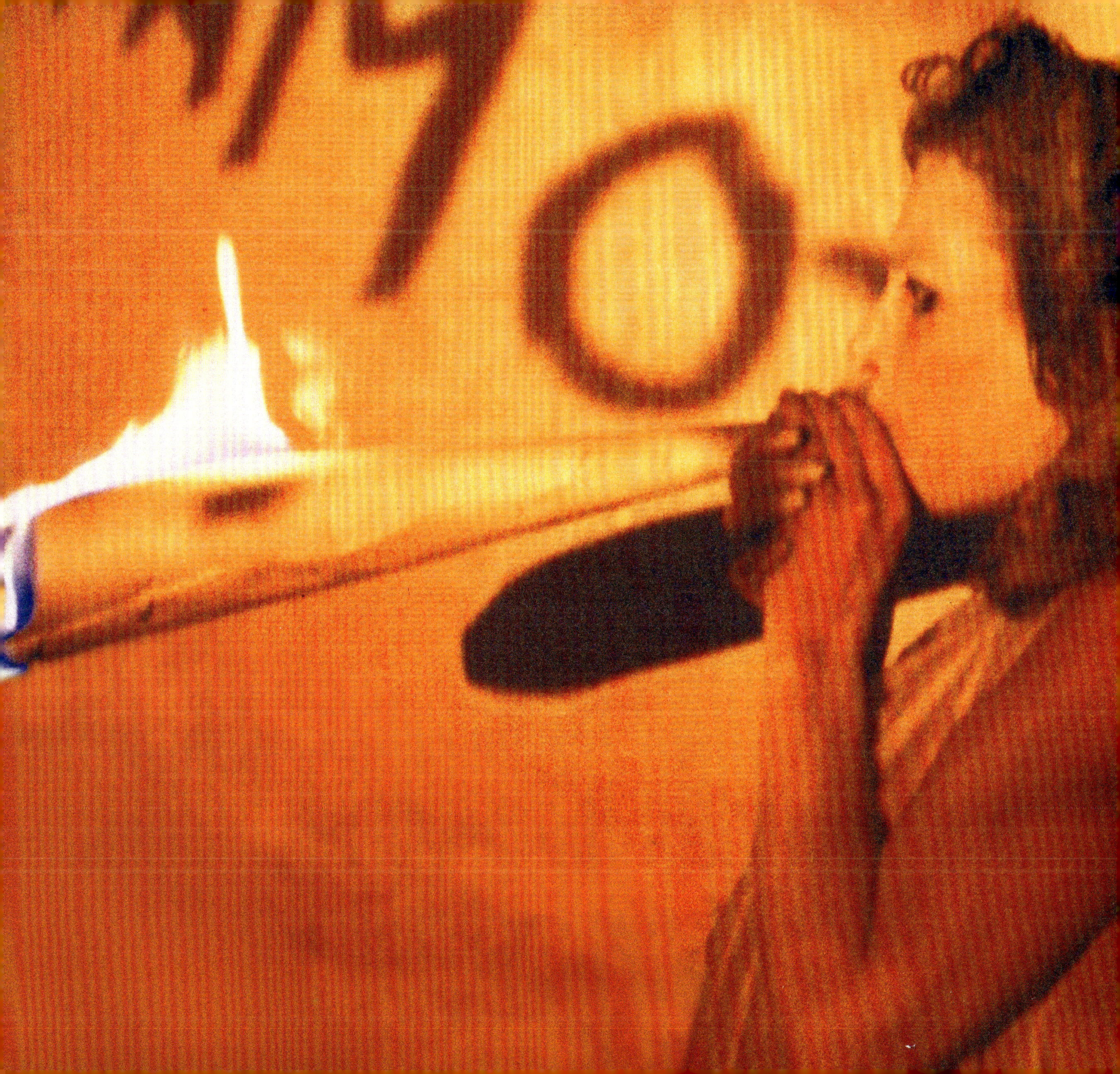

IS POSSESSED: THE ARTIST, THE CRITIC, THE PIRATE AND THE MESSENGER

ROB LA FRENAIS

These are some stories written from memory.

First memory

A strange, quiet, elegant lady of a certain age was hovering at the edge of a large, well-attended funeral of a well-known artist in Brighton. Slim, vigilant, watchful yet remote, her sculpted facial features bore the resemblance of an old friend of the Critic, who we can call the Artist, who had disappeared from the face of the earth for nearly two years. Nobody was really approaching her, a certain disquiet seem to accompany her presence. If one was an anthropologist you might describe the atmosphere emanating from the person, well-dressed but with a disturbing sense of being there but not quite there, as being an example of what is called the 'uncanny valley'. With some trepidation, the Critic verified that this strange lady was indeed the Artist, transformed into another self.

Second memory

In a crowded performance venue in Liverpool three years earlier an unusual process was taking place. To all intents and purposes this was a reunion of a relatively well-known performance art grouping using fire, pyrotechnics and sound, minus a fiery, colourful, some say self-destructive deceased, male character, the Pirate. Without anyone knowing, a professional psychic medium, the Messenger, was in the audience, who had been previously asked to contact the dead artist. In the event, the Messenger declined, saying the energy of that person was 'too dark', but he sat, unannounced, in the audience, near the Critic. At the end, while clearing up, one of the two remaining participants, the Artist, an old friend, who bore a resemblance to the well-dressed lady he met later at the funeral, her face smeared with ash and smoke from the performance, was asked a simple question by the Critic. Immediately her face contorted and from inside the depths of her body, a familiar male voice snarled aggressively at him, as if in the film *The Exorcist*: "You gonna be scared forever!" She seemed momentarily to be possessed by the Pirate.

Third memory

The Artist had asked the Critic to take part in a performance 30 years earlier. In a Victorian museum in the North of England, in a room full of Pre-Raphaelite paintings, the Artist would make a live work. The Critic had to review it on the spot, in real time, with a clattering, manual typewriter. The Artist made ten paintings, each on a blank paper or canvas within an ornate gold frame. A vast range of ways of working was utilised and references were made to other painters such as Goya and Blake. Each of the actions touched on the kinds of 'conversation' one has whilst painting and with a painting. The Critic was, in the Artist's words, 'both the voice of the audience, a collective pheromone that one is often finely tuned into during performance, as well as the voice of the critic, overly sanctioned and unduly powerful'. The Critic was the editor of a small magazine so didn't feel very unduly powerful, but he had agreed to do it, tapping out the noise 'ting ting' on the typewriter, trying to capture the essence of the live work unfolding before him. Surrounded by the drama and exaggeration of overwhelming exotic and figurative historical works such as Waterhouse's *The Slave*, the Critic felt the keyboard start tapping with a life of its own as the words tumbled out, as if possessed.

Fourth memory

Shortly after the Artist returned from her 16-month transformation into the consciousness of another self, in another place, she asked the Critic to recreate this performance work 30 years later in a tiny former council flat in London, unusually crammed with contemporary artworks. This time the artist reversed the process, erasing all the paintings, except one, which the owner of the flat had

Opposite, top: Chana Dubinski, Newark-on-Trent, 2012. Photo: Cara Lemans

Opposite, bottom: Anne Bean, oil painting *Poor Little Jewish Boy*, Leap, Eire, 1975. Photo: Mary Whooley

pp. 122-3: Anne Bean and Richard Wilson with Phil the Messenger, *Adventures in the House of Memory* (aka *Dark Haloes, Spooky Drums*), Liverpool Biennial, 2008. Photo: Liverpool Biennial

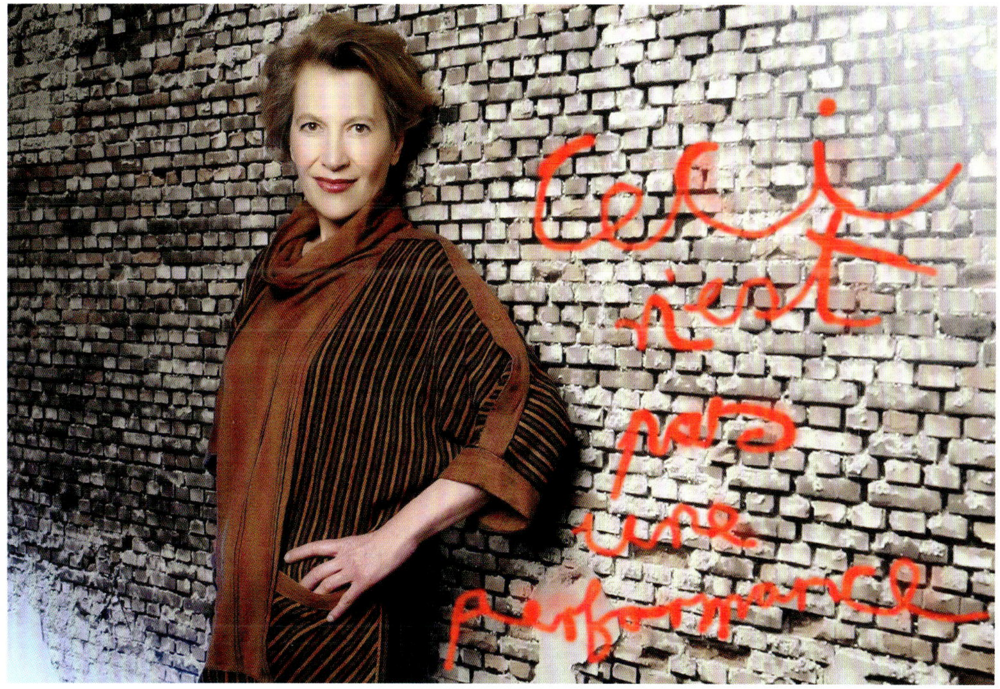
Ceci n'est pas une performance

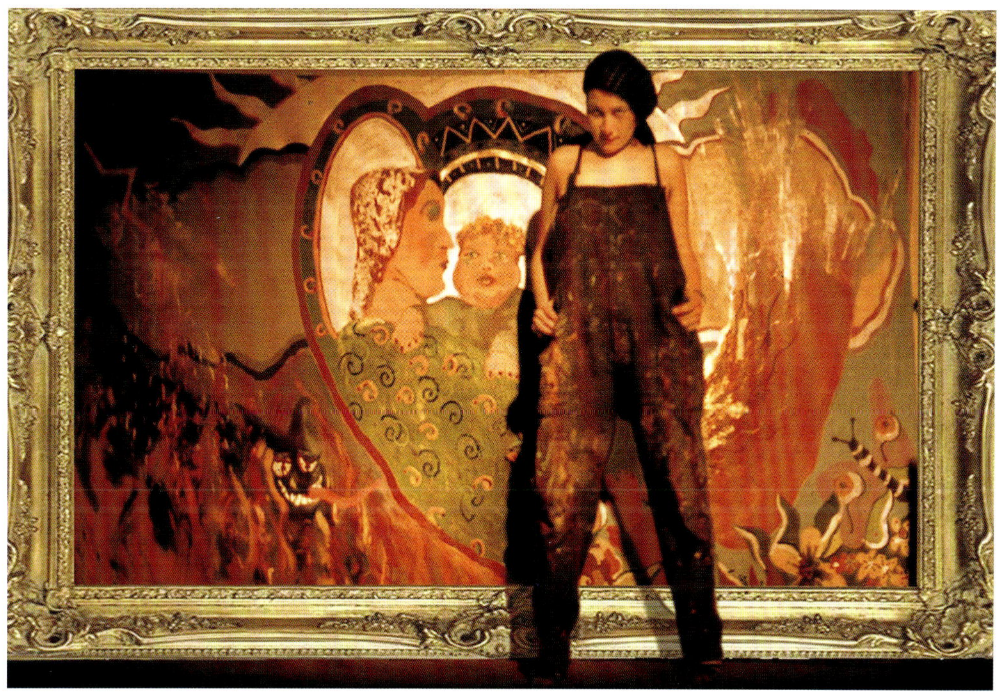

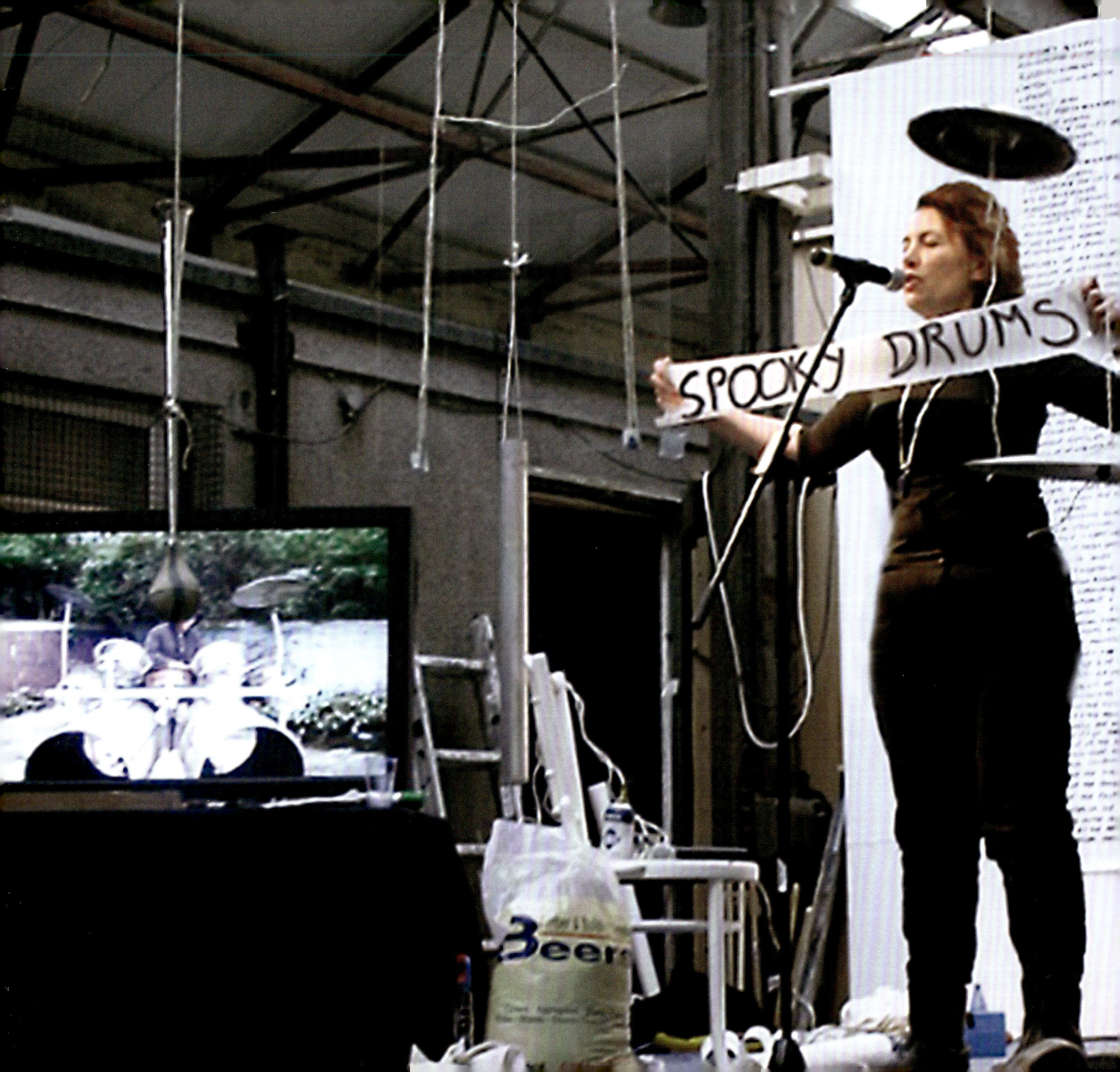
SPOOKY DRUMS

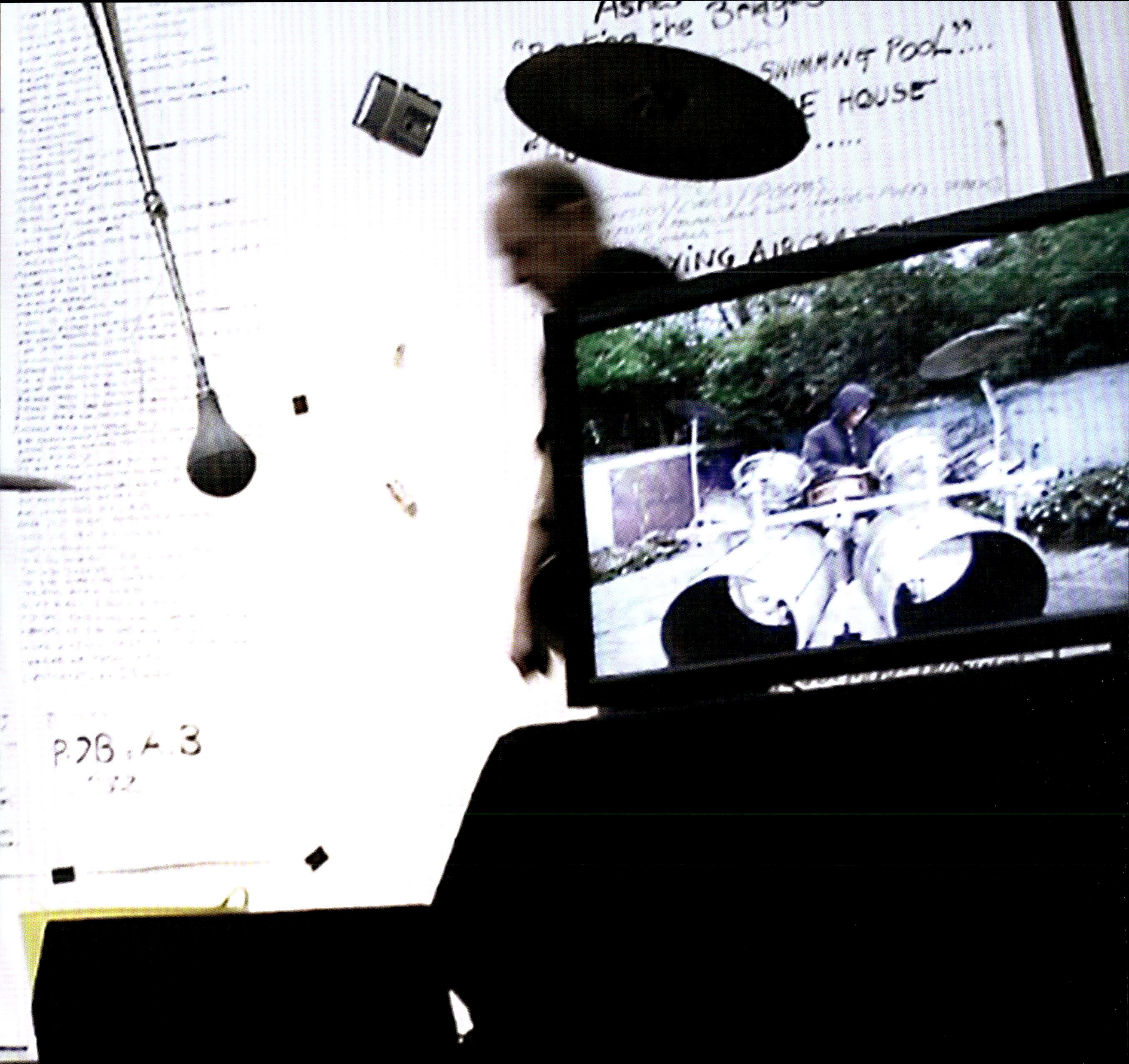
SWIMMING POOL
HOUSE

implored her to save. The Critic, this time, not possessed of a manual typewriter but instead a laptop, decided to use a real time text-to-voice programme and again critiqued the work at the same time as taking part in it. His thoughts were amplified into an artificial, slightly sinister whisper. Again his thoughts accelerated, and the programme took on a life of its own, rather like an emerging artificial intelligence, repeating key phrases and somehow, though a process of feedback, and began to get inexplicably angry, as if possessed.

Fifth memory

The Critic began to find himself recalling a voice he had heard once before, back in Liverpool. He remembered the Pirate, the other artist, young and old shouting Dylan Thomas's famous words about not going gently into that good night. He had also been a writer for the Critic's small magazine. The Critic often had to sit in his studio waiting for the Pirate to finish his articles, to be whisked straight off to the printers that day. He remembered the ancient Pirate in his decline, poisoning himself to death with rum and whisky, walking, slightly staggering, with an elegant stick and floppy hat. The Artist was carefully looking after him, knowing that in the end she could not protect him from his demons. She had her own.

Sixth memory

Sometime in the 1980s, the Artist and the Pirate had invited an already well-known North American performance and installation artist to make a semi-private performance together in a derelict house in East London. The Critic was there with a number of other people, wandering around the rooms. Suddenly the already rickety and dangerous house started to resonate with banging, sawing, bangs and shrieks. Above the Critic's head a foot smashed its way through the floorboards. The audience slowly realised it was in the equivalent of a war zone as the three artists systematically began destroying the environment they stood in. The audience inevitably were caught up in the mayhem, running for cover, not knowing which way to go, what to see, what floor would give way, what glass would fly, what staircase was safe. The Pirate suddenly smashed his head through a window, beating a drum, blood streaming down his face, yelling as if he didn't care. The Critic suddenly felt that in order to survive, he had to have his wits honed and alert, like the artists. As debris rained down the audience felt it necessary to vacate the premises, but the Critic remained, dodging and diving, in the dust and chaos, taking notes frantically. This was what real art was about, he thought. Real danger. No health and safety.

Seventh memory

Do we give names and faces to these characters and situations or shall we let them be anonymous for a while longer? Maybe we should just try to imagine a few more scenes in the life of the Artist, one of her many selves. She is open to any turn of fate 'living in the open air' as another writer puts it, following her destiny, still quite young. She walks randomly into the high street information centre of a well-known cult with another artist and they take the test they pose to lure the innocent in. She does not go home but instead joins up spontaneously, changes her name. Over the next year she rises up through the organisation of the cult, doing exactly what she is instructed. She soon, with her combination of total engagement and charisma, ascends the echelons of the cult until she becomes one who is as perfected by their process. She issues instructions to disciples. She can do anything, levitate, walk through walls. In fact she does. One night, after a late night ritual, she is possessed with an impulse to climb through the back window of the opulent stately home that is the headquarters of the cult and is never seen again. It is the performance of her life, so far.

Anne Bean, *24 Self-Portraits*, one painting per hour, performance during *Autobituary* installation in St Martin's Church, Colchester, 2006

p. 126: Anne Bean and Richard Wilson, *The Pirate, The Artist and the Sculptor*, 2009. Photo: Hugo Glendinning

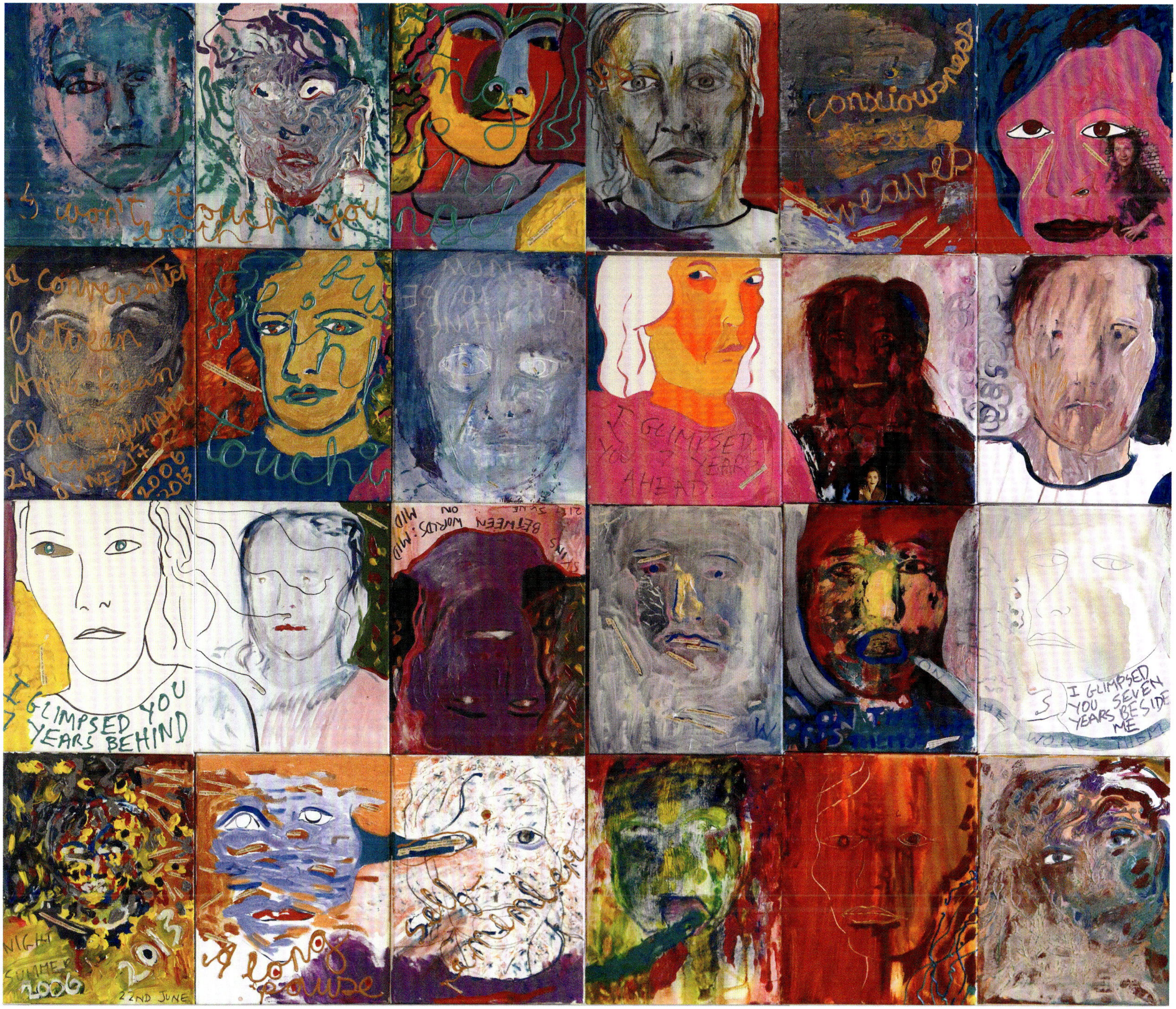

consciousness
I GLIMPSED YOU 7 YEARS AHEAD
I GLIMPSED YOU 7 YEARS BEHIND
I GLIMPSED YOU SEVEN YEARS BESIDE ME
NIGHT
SUMMER
2006
2013
22ND JUNE
A long pause

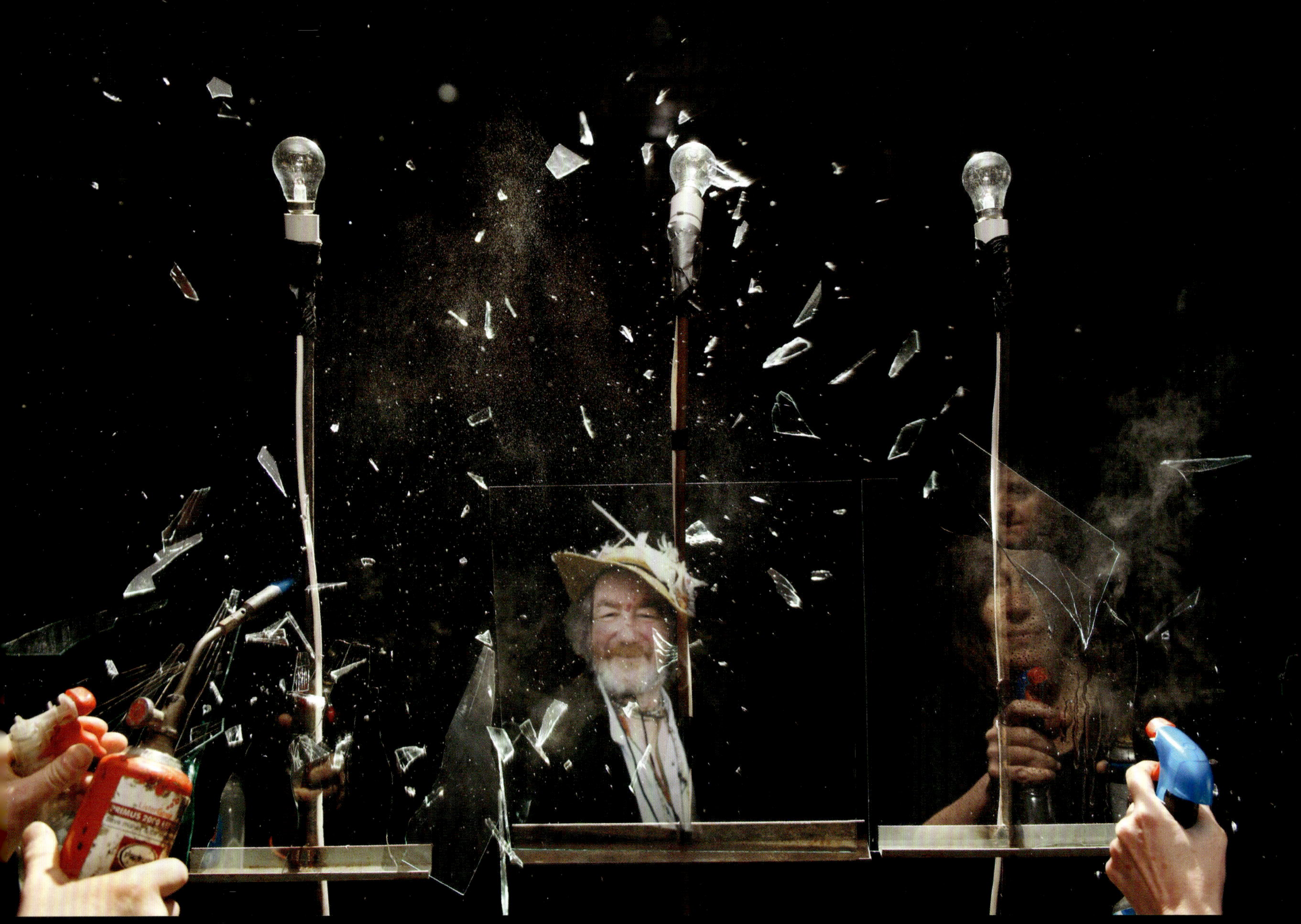

Eighth memory

The Artist is in an alleyway in Hull. She is on the verge of living as another person, living like a homeless person. She bends down to look at something and immediately drops through a grating an amulet which she has been given to help herself in this performance journey though the badlands of England. She sees the words 'New Work' on a poster on the wall. Immediately she gets out the map and on impulse goes to live in the town of Newark, gets a flat, a studio, works, makes friends, takes lovers (it is rumoured) for a period of one-and-a-half years entirely in the consciousness of a person she was not the week before. She holds a private view, mixes up her friends from London with the people who think she is someone else. Some understand. Some feel betrayed. She returns to London still in that consciousness, but is slowly but surely possessed by her old self.

Ninth memory

The Critic is sitting in a flying saucer on the roof of an art gallery. It is the Chinese New Year. A number of people significant to the Artist's life are gathered there. We are invited to write the names of towns under a certain population in the UK on fortune cookies and place them in a hat. It is a social occasion, drinks are handed round, but the Artist does not join in. At the end of the evening, a well-known gallery director chooses one cookie out of a hat. It is a small town in the West of England. At the moment, the Artist quietly leaves, gets into her car and drives through the night, straight there, to live there for a year and to somehow try to found a contemporary art centre with a group of Army veterans. She does not know where she will live, what materials she will use, how she is to do it. But she goes, out into the night. Alone. We wander home to our predetermined schedules while the Artist faces the unknown, literally.

The above memories are nearly true, very slightly fabricated versions of a few of the events in the life and art of the artist Anne Bean. In some cases the pathways of fate and coincidence have been changed because of 'false' memory. What is entirely true is that these chance encounters, these slidings from persona to persona, this condensing of time, these possessions, in my view paint a picture of the collective, bewilderingly complex histories, personal stories, and deliberate actions of the artist who calls herself Anne Bean, right now.

There are of course many, many other stories and memories, but the Critic is me, the writer. It is me who she asked to collaborate with her. I have arbitrarily chosen these stories among the many others surrounding Anne Bean, because they are ones that have connected to my own life. Later on, here, I will give some 'facts' about the events in this physical universe, which we call our life, that resemble these stories.

Anne Bean lives, breathes and dies through collaboration whether with other artists or other selves. In this spirit of collaboration I have anonomised and varnished these stories to maintain this fluidity between the selves. Ezra Rubenstein puts it well (in his essay in this book) when he writes: 'It is fundamentally a matter of mediating voyages between minds: the voyages of ideas and experiences which bubble up mysteriously from an anonymous origin and throw their seeds to the wind, finding fertile ground in those open to them and fortunate enough to be in the right place'. As Bean puts it in her interview: 'We are each other's archives and legacies'.

I will attempt to put some of these memories in context later, but first, I provide some historical background to Bean's process of exploring the consciousness of her selves.

Other selves

Anne Bean's artistic experiments with her 'selves' (she hates the term 'alter-ego') have some fairly well-known precedents, although not all have been explored in such a deep and fundamental way as Bean's.

Early in the twentieth century, writer and member of the Bloomsbury group Viriginia Woolf perpetrated the 'Dreadnought Hoax' with her brother Adrian Stephen and the painter Duncan Grant.[1] In a gesture later seen as an anti-war protest, they impersonated African royalty and convinced the Royal Navy to give them a tour of their latest warship. References to Woolf also appear in an interview with James Birchall in the publication *Camp*, where Bean states:

> The first woman artist that really made an impact on me was actually a fictional one, Lily Briscoe, a character in Woolf's *To the Lighthouse*. Woolf let Lily express her own feminist outrage and considerable anger in Lily's musings on the male assumption that 'women can't paint, can't write'. Lily manages to escape this social repression with her innate passion for independence. Her art was much more important than any husband and she saw marriage as a self-debasement – a dilution of self. I admired her pioneering, free-thinking spirit and she opened my own developing ideologies.[2]

The figure of 'Rrose Sélavy', created by Marcel Duchamp as his female self, was a conscious challenge to the fallacy of the subjectivity of the artist.[3] She then became a collective self, used by other artists. This strategy was continued by a number of artists in the 1980s and 1990s, creating multiple identities such as 'Monty Cantsin'[4] (originally an extension of the artist Istvan Cantor but later adopted by others), 'Luther Blissett' and finally, most enduringly the apparently female 'Karen Eliot' as part of the burgeoning Neoist movement, continued by artist Stewart Home and others.[5]

The American artist Eleanor Antin worked with a number of selves, the most famous of which was 'Eleanora Antinova', who lived in New York anonymously in an apartment for a period of time as an ageing, Black Russian prima donna ballerina, described in her 1983 book *Being Antinova*.[6] In a *New York Times* interview in 1989, she said:

> My selves keep giving birth to selves. Eleanora has almost given way to Yevgeny, my new persona (the avant-garde Russian film director, another self) loves looking at old artists who've been forgotten. I can't stand the genius mythology that museums and collectors live off of. Because of good fortune, accidents of birth and so forth, certain people seem to have perfect fit with the culture. So the culture decides they are the greats. But other artists are more eccentric and interesting. They are necessary for the scene without which these others couldn't live.[7]

Antin had previously recreated herself as other selves: the 'King', a Black movie star, and 'The Angel Of Mercy', a nurse combination-personality of herself and Florence Nightingale who time-travelled in a series of staged photographs to the Crimean war. These techniques of creating selves evolved from early alternative 1970's West Coast performance culture and were well-documented in *High Performance* magazine, edited by Linda Frye Burnham and Steve Durland in Los Angeles in the 1970s and 1980s; these strategies became mainstream in the work of Cindy Sherman in the US and Sophie Calle in Europe, and thus entered the canon of contemporary visual art, but it is the more fundamental concerns of life as art we will continue with here.

The notion of selves within selves is also reflected in the work/life of Genesis P-Orridge, performance artist and co-founder of Coum Transmissions, Throbbing Gristle, Psychic TV and Thee Temple ov Psychick Youth – the latter of which evolved to be a real-life cult. With second wife Jacqueline Breyer (aka Lady Jaye), P-Orridge undertook a project to combine their selves: in

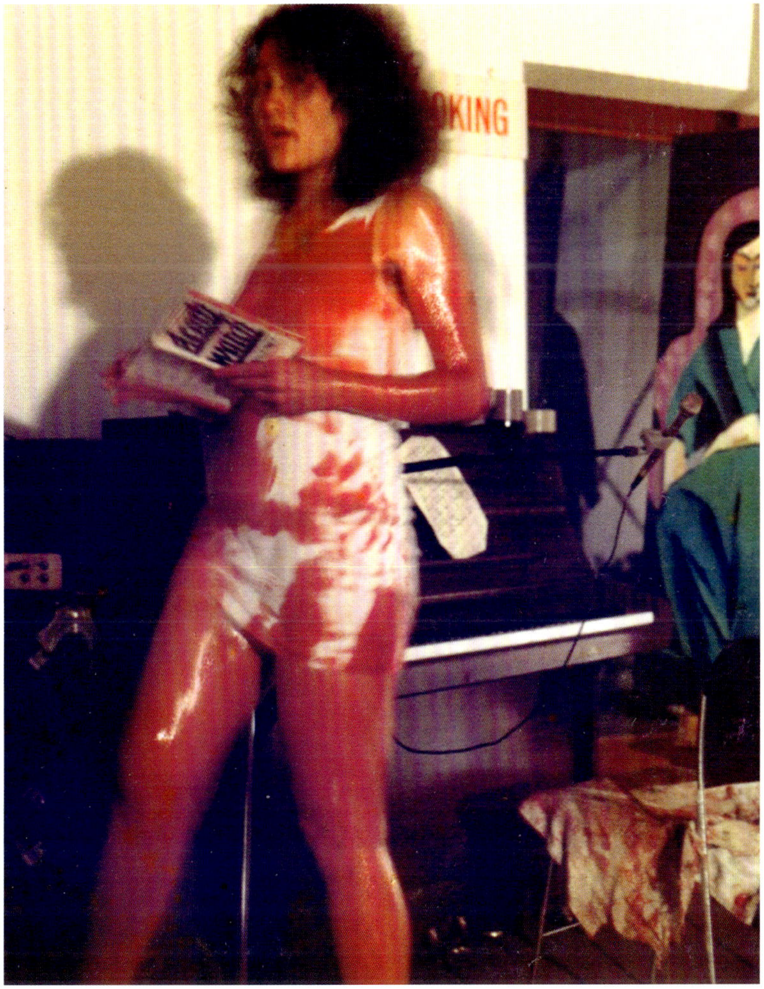

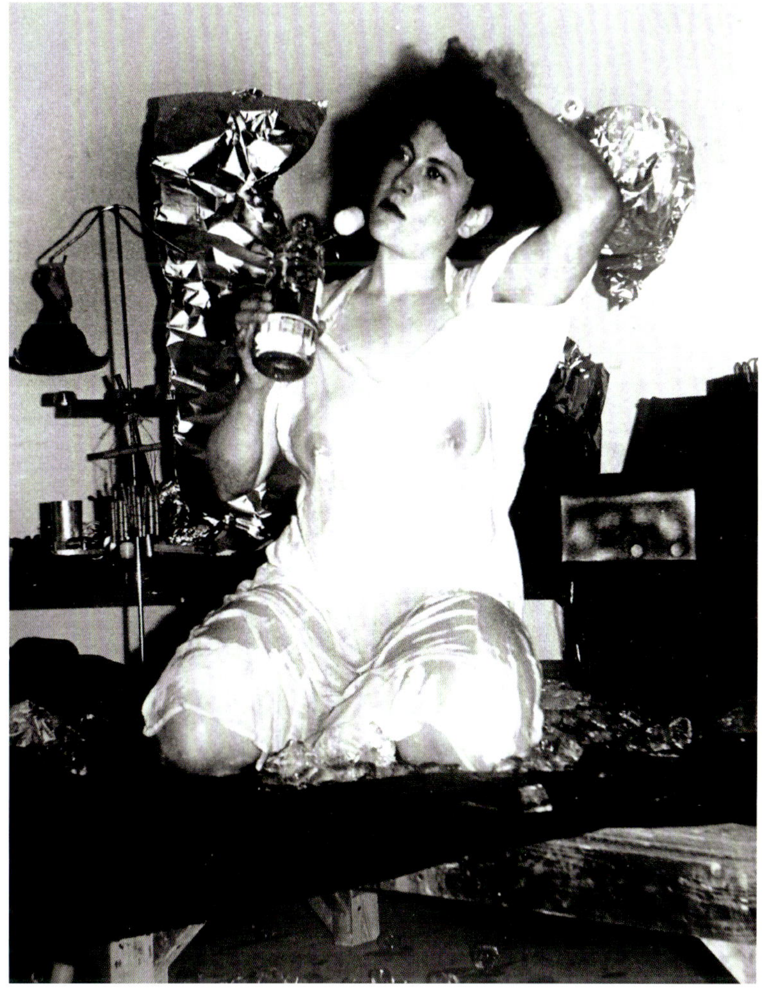

Left: Anne Bean (with Peter Davey), *Anxtions*, Hayward Annual 1979. Photo: Chris Bishop

Right: Anne Bean (with Paul Burwell), *Low Flying Aircraft*, as part of *Public Spirit*, Vanguard Gallery, Los Angeles, 1980. Photo: Charles Hill

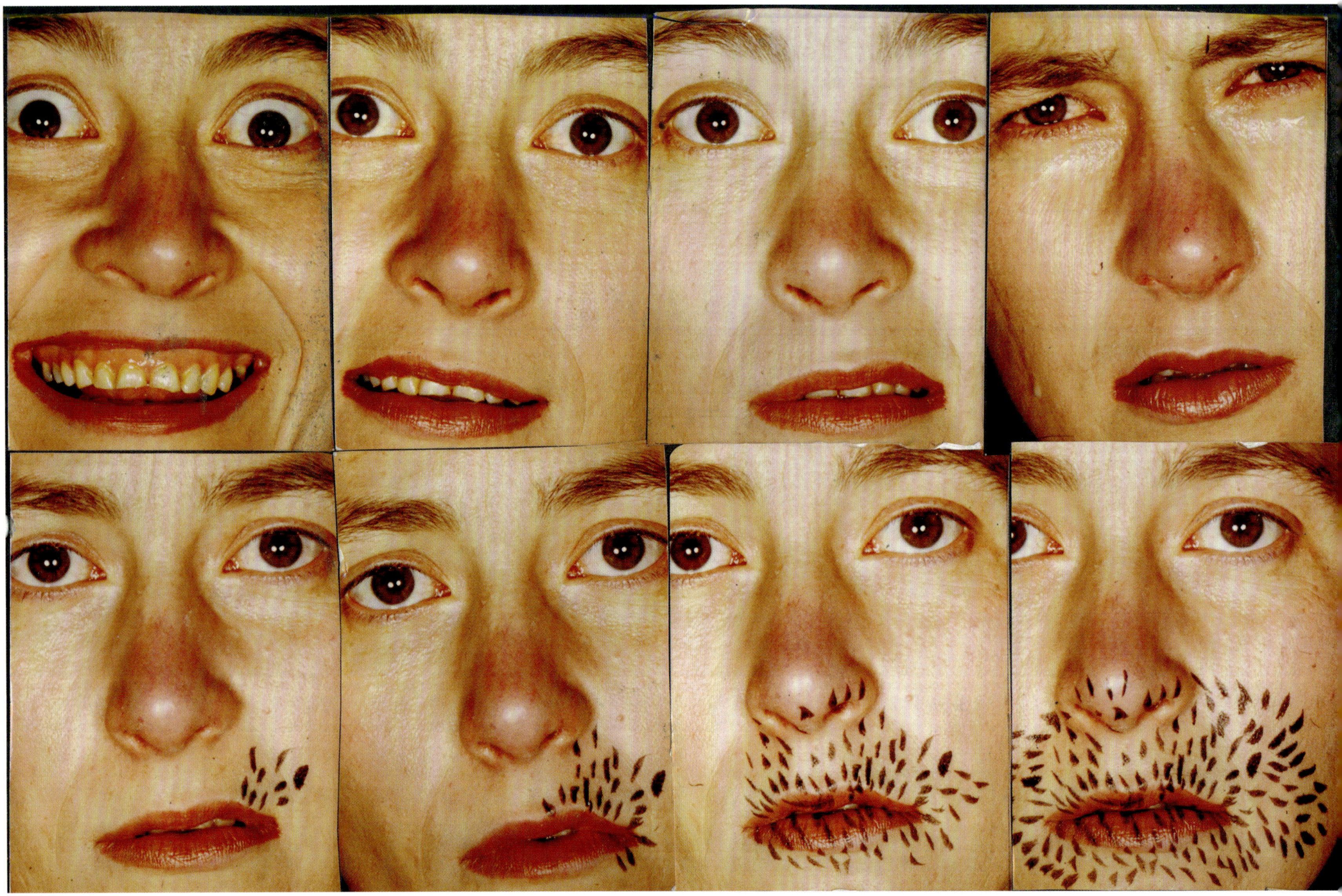

Anne Bean, *Paussus*, London Musicians Collective, London, 1982. Applying paint to my face, I speak about Paussus, a genus of beetle, who hack into ant nests, mimicking their stridulation, hijacking the ants' chemical communication with their own secretions, which allows the beetle to devour the seemingly enticing, ecstatic ants. Photo: Chris Bishop

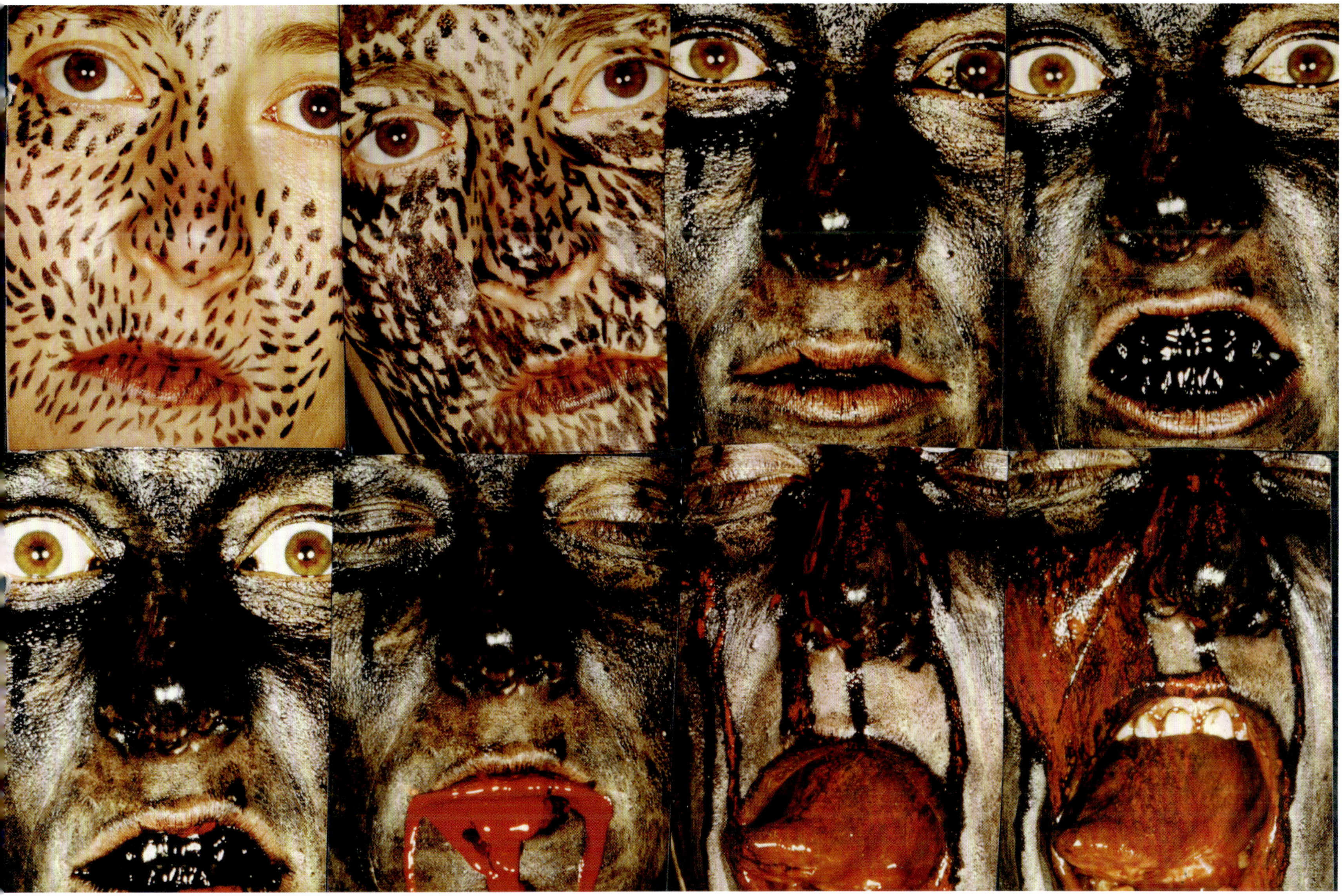

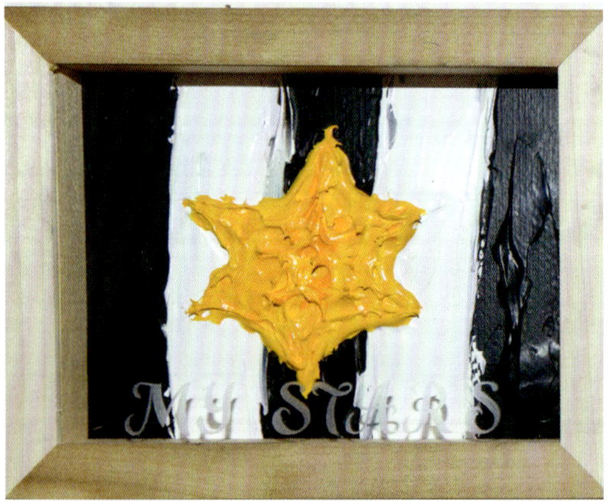

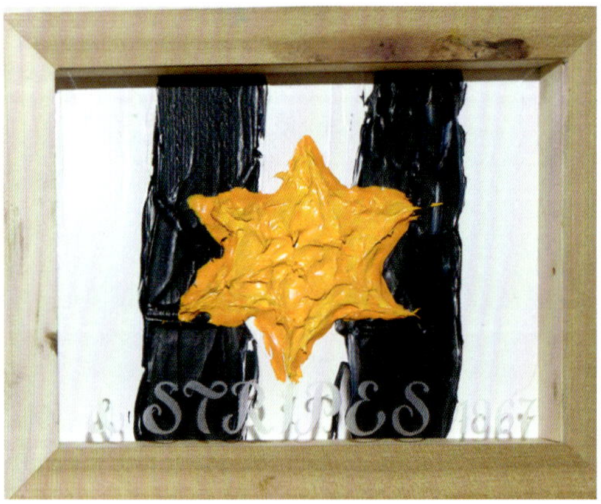

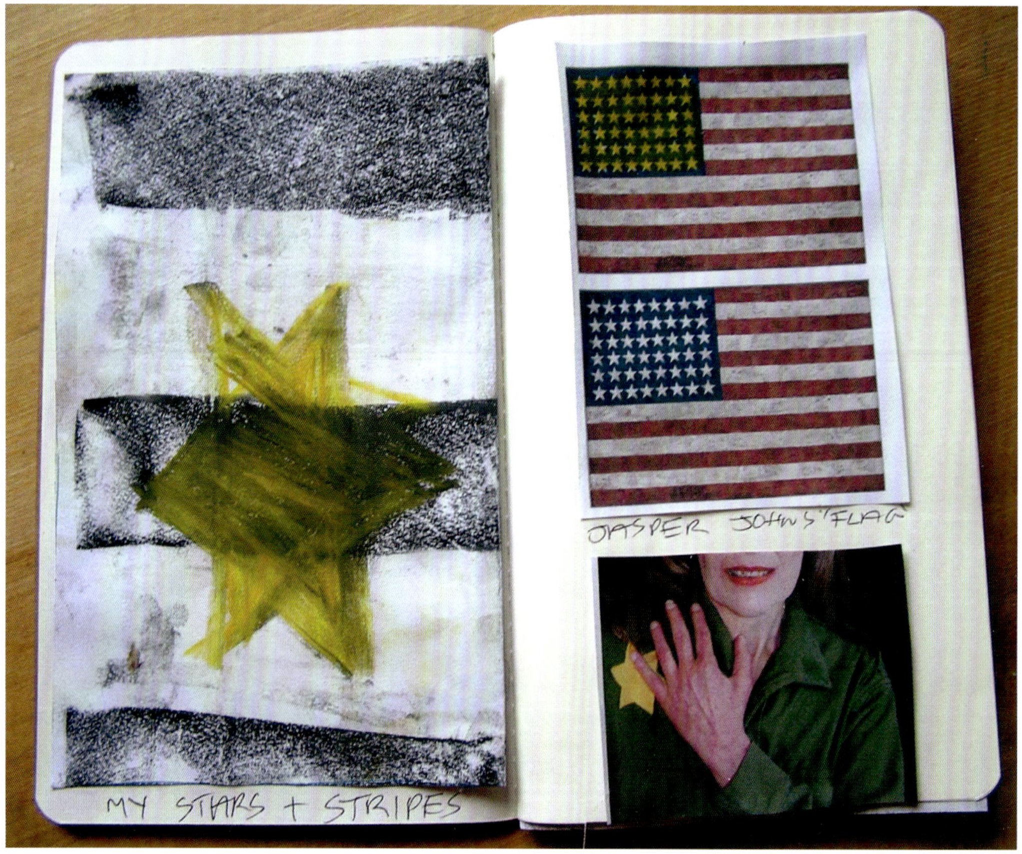

Chana Dubinski, two paintings and a page from a sketch book, Riverside Cottage, Newark-on-Trent, 2012

the *Breaking Sex* project (1999-2007), also known as 'Pandrogeny', P-Orridge and Breyer wanted to 'express a belief that the self is pure consciousness trapped within the DNA-governed body'. The process was documented in Marie Losier's film *The Ballad of Genesis and Lady Jaye* (2011). Influenced by William S. Burroughs and Brion Gysin's 'cut-up' technique, they underwent behavioural adaptations and body modifications to resemble one another, thus coming to identify themselves as a single 'pandrogyne' named BREYER P-ORRIDGE: 'We started out, because we were so crazy in love, just wanting to eat each other up, to become each other and become one. And as we did that, we started to see that it was affecting us in ways that we didn't expect. Really, we were just two parts of one whole; the pandrogyne was the whole and we were each other's other half'.[8] Lady Jaye died in 2007 and Genesis BREYER P-ORRIDGE now identifies in the plural, having subsumed Lady Jaye posthumously. According to a frequently published artist's statement, 'Genesis continues to represent the amalgam BREYER P-ORRIDGE in the material "world" and Lady Jaye represents the amalgam BREYER P-ORRIDGE in the immaterial "world" creating an ongoing interdimensional collaboration'.

'Everyone's multiple, you know'. So speaks James Magee, charismatic recluse and creator of *The Hill*, a little-known but ambitious and significant land art work in a megalithic style near the Mexico-US border in El Paso, Texas. Magee stands as one angle of a trinity of three selves, firstly Annabel Livermore, a retired librarian and self-taught artist from the Midwest, who sells her paintings in the thousands across the Midwest and is collected in museums. Magee: 'Oftentimes I just give up when they say, "Well, Annabel's a pseudonym." It's not a pseudonym. No, this is a woman with – this is a friend of mine who's had 35, 40 years of my life. And we're trying to do the best we can.'[9] At the other point is Horace Mayfield, another artist who seems to be Magee's outlet for gay kitsch, designing, among other things, shower curtains, while Magee himself constructs *The Hill*, his massive, sombre monument to the free-living lifestyle of the Hudson River Piers, decimated by the AIDS epidemic in the 1980's. Both Annabel and Horace have their own houses and McGee lives in both according to which part of his bisexual identity he is currently following. Magee: 'I don't know how these people arrive, really, because they're not like ... it's not like taking on a name'.[10] Curator Kerry Doyle, author of a recent essay on Magee, describes his personalities as 'perhaps somewhat less pathological than a split personality but more complicated and complex than a durational performance ... [T]his practice of channelling others, real or imagined others, is central to Jim's being in the world. It is an embodied spirituality that allows itself to be overtaken by other personalities.'[11]

A version of reality: Dissecting the memories

I think that Chana Dubinski, that elegant lady of a certain age I met at the funeral of artist Monica Ross, the subject of the first memory, just as she was re-entering the life of artist Anne Bean, arrived in a similar way. Bean described her departure to me:

"I left with a suitcase, I left with a name. I decided I must not stay in a hotel or a bed and breakfast. I must live as cheaply as possible and the whole thing must be led by chance ... [T]he first morning of the project I woke up and really thought, 'I'm going completely crazy'. It was really like a blank. I did have, for the first time since being an adolescent, an overwhelming existential weirdness. I mean I wanted it but at the same time it's a bit like when you take drugs and suddenly realise you don't want this to be happening and you know there is nothing to be done."[12]

There was no escape clause – 'I'm very wilful. I couldn't. There was nothing' – and it was after this intense period being Chana Dubinski

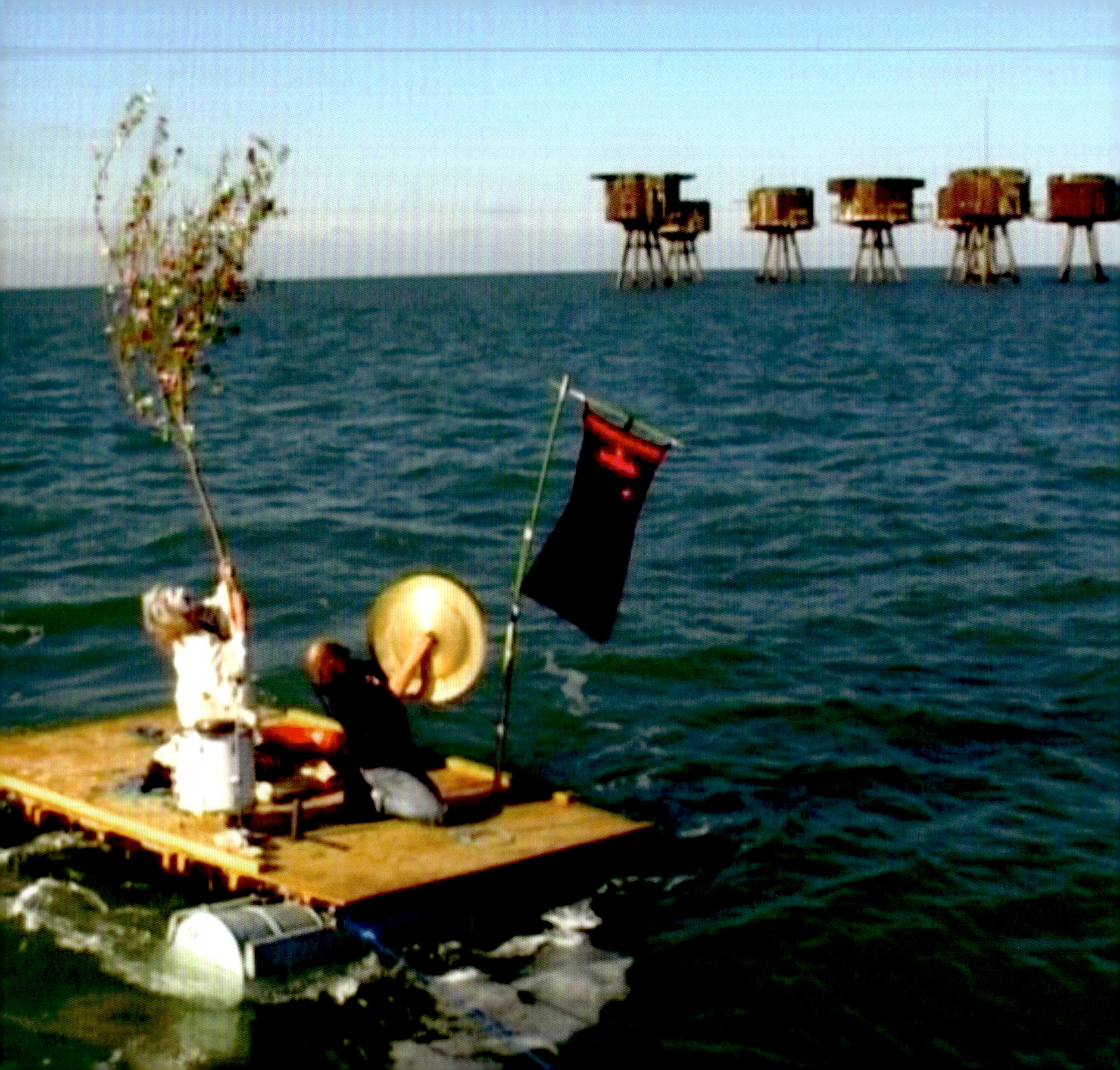

that I met the person who was, but was not quite, Anne Bean.[13] In later discussions, we talked about this idea of containing a number of selves within oneself and it was in this context that the essence – some kind of existence of the late artist and musician Paul Burwell, also still being contained within her – was raised, rather like the idea that BREYER P-ORRIDGE is a combination of two selves.

It was in fact at the Liverpool Biennial in 2009, at the A Foundation – my second memory – that Paul Burwell, who I have named the Pirate, seemed to emerge and briefly possess Bean, in an encounter after the performance, *Adventures in the House of Memory* (and after Bean and Wilson had eaten Paul's ashes). It was also true that Bean had invited a Liverpool psychic, actually called Phil the Messenger, to try to contact Burwell. He 'conjured Paul up in his bed-sit as a whirring sound of a swooping eagle whilst an ice-cream van played *Greensleeves* outside the room', Bean recalls. What Anne said in the voice of Paul (or vice versa) I cannot remember, so I have found something.

This lack of documentation and reliance on unreliable memory was highlighted in the work *Pain Tings*, which took place during New Work Newcastle in 1987, organised by Projects UK at the Laing Art Gallery, which contains a number of Pre-Raphaelite paintings. It was revisited by curator Sophia Yadong Hao in her exhibition *Notes on a Return* (2011), about the difficulty of recreating performance. *Pain Tings* is the subject of my third memory and reflects to some extent on the role of the magazine I edited, *Performance Magazine*. It is odd that such a small, almost DIY-style magazine was purported to wield a lot of influence, but it was one of the few outlets in the 1980s for this kind of work, hence Bean's sentiment about the critic being 'overly sanctioned and unduly powerful'. I remember agreeing to this collaboration in 1987, but feeling unsure about the power relationship being underlined. In a sense this became more resolved when we recreated this performance nearly 30 years later in London, with both of us taking a more exploratory and collaborative approach. *Pain Tings* is pretty well represented in my third memory, given that that Bean 'sensed it buried but resonant in some non-verbal hinterland'. In the process of retrieving this performance in *Notes on a Return*, Bean recalls:

> I found myself uncovering layers within layers not ventured into for decades. The dark photos that Sophia had dug out from Locus+ Archives of the original performance intrigued me and I decided, as an investigation, to try to re-create these in an intensive private performance. An intrinsic part of this painting process was the presence of the writer, critic and editor of *Performance Magazine*, Rob La Frenais. I asked Rob to respond to the work during the making so that he was both a critic and a part of what he was critiquing. He sat typing at a typewriter, 'ting', 'ting', 'ting', in the middle of the space, ostensibly making notes towards a review and then reading them out at arbitrary moments during the piece. I then used his words to include in the paintings or to change a thought about the next one.[14]

The fourth memory is easier to access as we have a full video transcript and the text of the 'automatic writing', which is reproduced here in more or less its original form. *Unpaintings* took place on 15 July 2016 in the private residence of art historian and collector the late Thomas Frangenberg in Islington, where Bean

Above: Anne Bean and Richard Wilson, *TAPS: Improvisations with Paul Burwell*, Maunsell Forts, Thames Estuary, 2010. Photo: William Raban

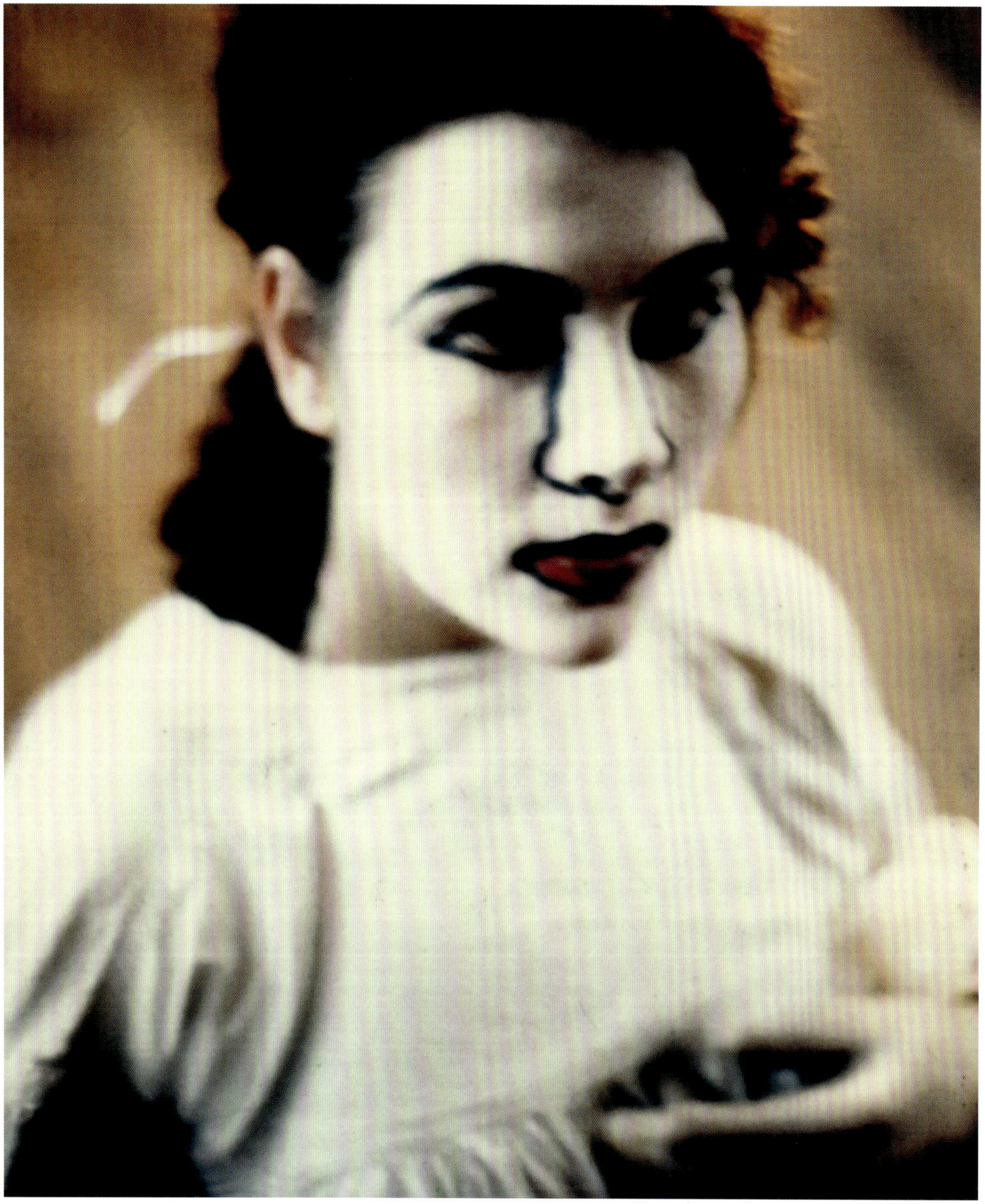

Anne Bean, *AMP (Anne, Matisse, Picasso)*, Reading, 1971, using text and improvisations from Gertrude Stein's *GMP* (Gertrude, Matisse, Picasso). Photographer unknown

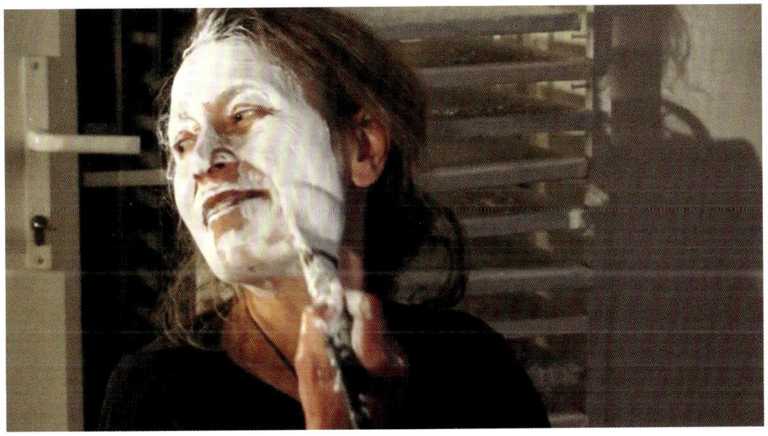
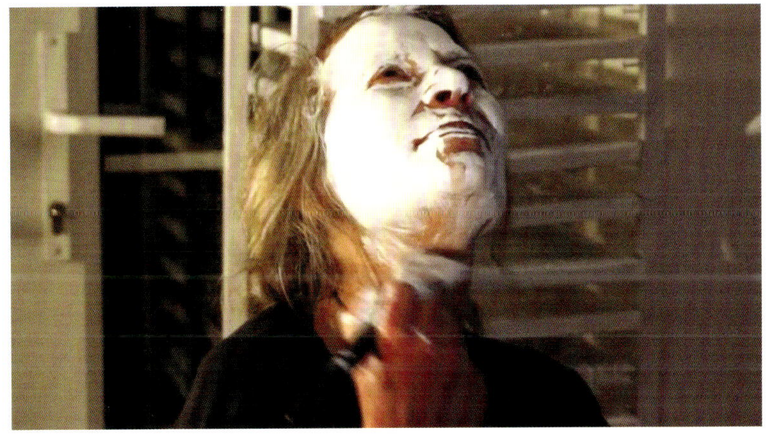
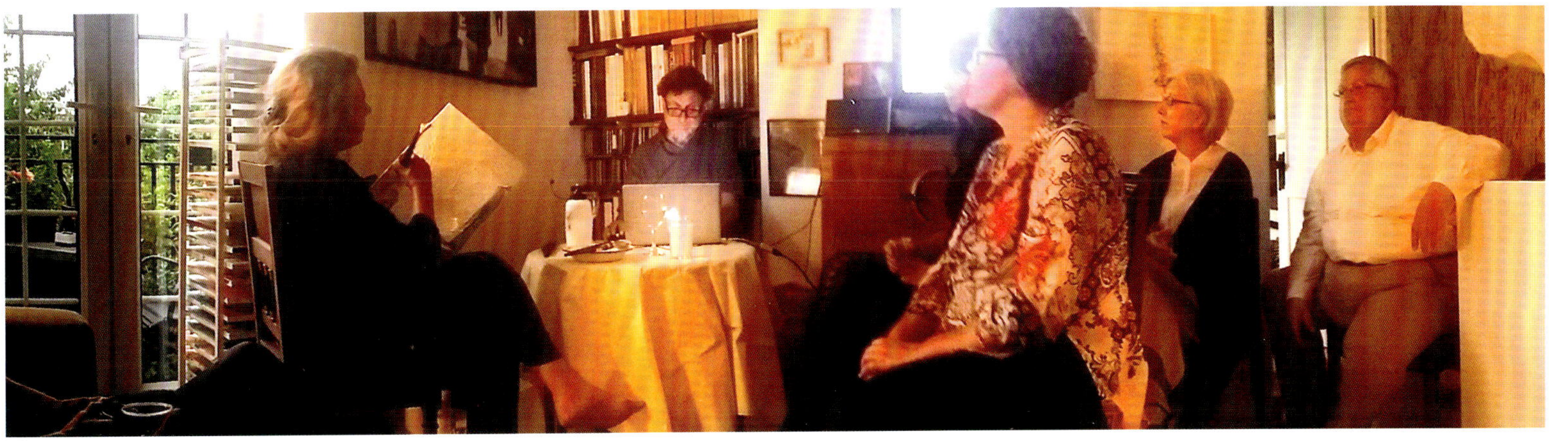
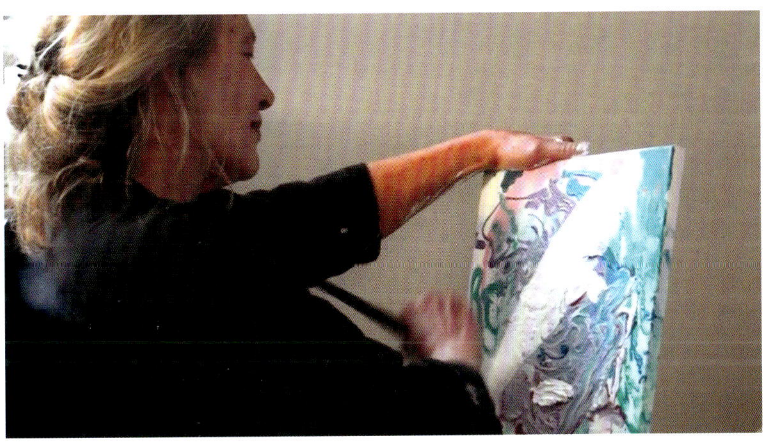
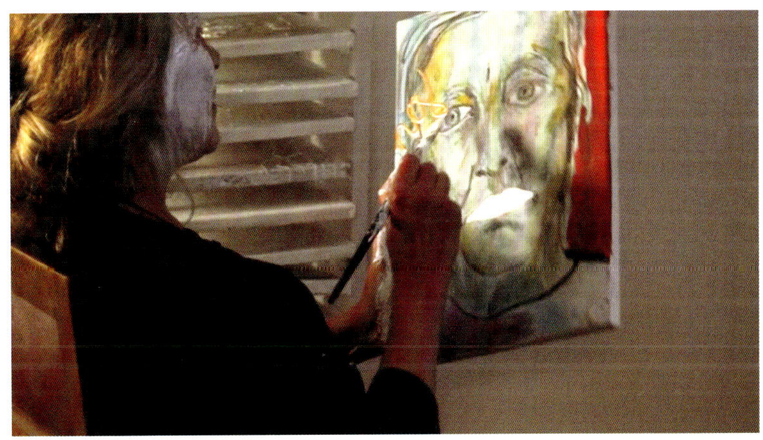

Top and bottom: Anne Bean, *Unpainting*, London, 2016. Stills from a video by Miyako Narita

Centre: Anne Bean, *Unpainting*, performed in the home of Dr. Thomas Frangenberg (shown far right), Islington, London, 2016. Photo: Miyako Narita would systematically erase ten paintings, by covering them in white paint, in reverse of the process of creation 30 years before. However the presence of the host and another collector caused an unexpected piece of audience participation, in which Bean was implored not to destroy the tenth painting, as they wanted to preserve it. In a moment of rampant speculation, one could imagine this apparent compromise, breaking all the rules of process-based art, may have been the factor that drove the human/computer entity, the Critic, over the edge – and possibly even to open a portal for the Pirate to enter and possess the performance. Here is the transcript of what took place in *Unpaintings*, slightly shortened:

> How was it that I, a critic – the enemy perhaps – was invited to review you during a live performance? The apparently indifferent critic, coming in to respond live to the work confusing what I was writing and what you were doing becoming confused ... Yet I was an 'editor'. There were people reviewing performances for my magazine – they could be cruel, unjust, but I had to judge them by the standard of their writing. Wanting to work with artists – not judging them. Why did you invite me to do this? That exact moment of perception, there, then right then. Who am I talking to now. Me? You? You said you wanted to break down the barriers between the performative and the non-performative, just now. What further means do we need? Permission for something to happen right now in a life situation? Difficult to jump that. The distance between the painting and the performer? Is the object the performer or beyond? What got ME interested in performance? Good question – that somehow we could transform the environment as if by magic, though a semi-ritual action. The problem you mentioned about where does performance start? Where does it veer from life? But finding myself here, with an artificial voice, does make me wonder where that margin lies. Well, when you asked me to appear with a typewriter, 30 years ago, you were asking me to intercede with technology to interpret your work. You were also inviting me to criticise the critic, so to speak. The non-maker of art engaging with making of art in a direct way. Novelty? An experiment. Now the media to appear more immediate has accelerated us. That was deliberate. Despite performance protocol I need to go to the bathroom (or toilet!) Expensive paintbrushes, luscious materials to obliterate your canvases. You can tell they are new and posh![15]

Anne Bean, Paul Burwell and Paul McCarthy, *Two Ps and a Bean*, performed in a derelict house in Bow, London, 1983. Photo: Linda Frye Burnham

In my fifth memory, of the Pirate, Paul Burwell, who still lives on in our lives, I am often drawn back to memories of the basement of Nick Kimberley's Duck Soup bookshop where for many years Paul had his lair and where I indeed had to stand, waiting to rush his copy off to press while he typed it out. I quote from my obituary for Burwell in *Art Monthly* in 2007:

> 'I do not go gentle into that good night!' was often snarled by Paul Burwell (he was usually talking about the Arts Council), but those words could be emblazoned above the lonely converted rowing club in Hull where he finally met his end through hypothermia at the age of 57. He ended up, this thaumaturge, like Prospero or Citizen Kane, whiskey bottle in hand, presiding over his rackety pirate republic, surrounded by the demons of Hull's urban dysfunction. Unusually for these times the piratically eccentric or just plain crazy Burwell was in his last month tragically engaged in the romantic, bohemian and painful pursuit of drinking himself to death, despite attempts by his loyal colleagues to get him to desist and continue with the projects for which he was well known.[16]

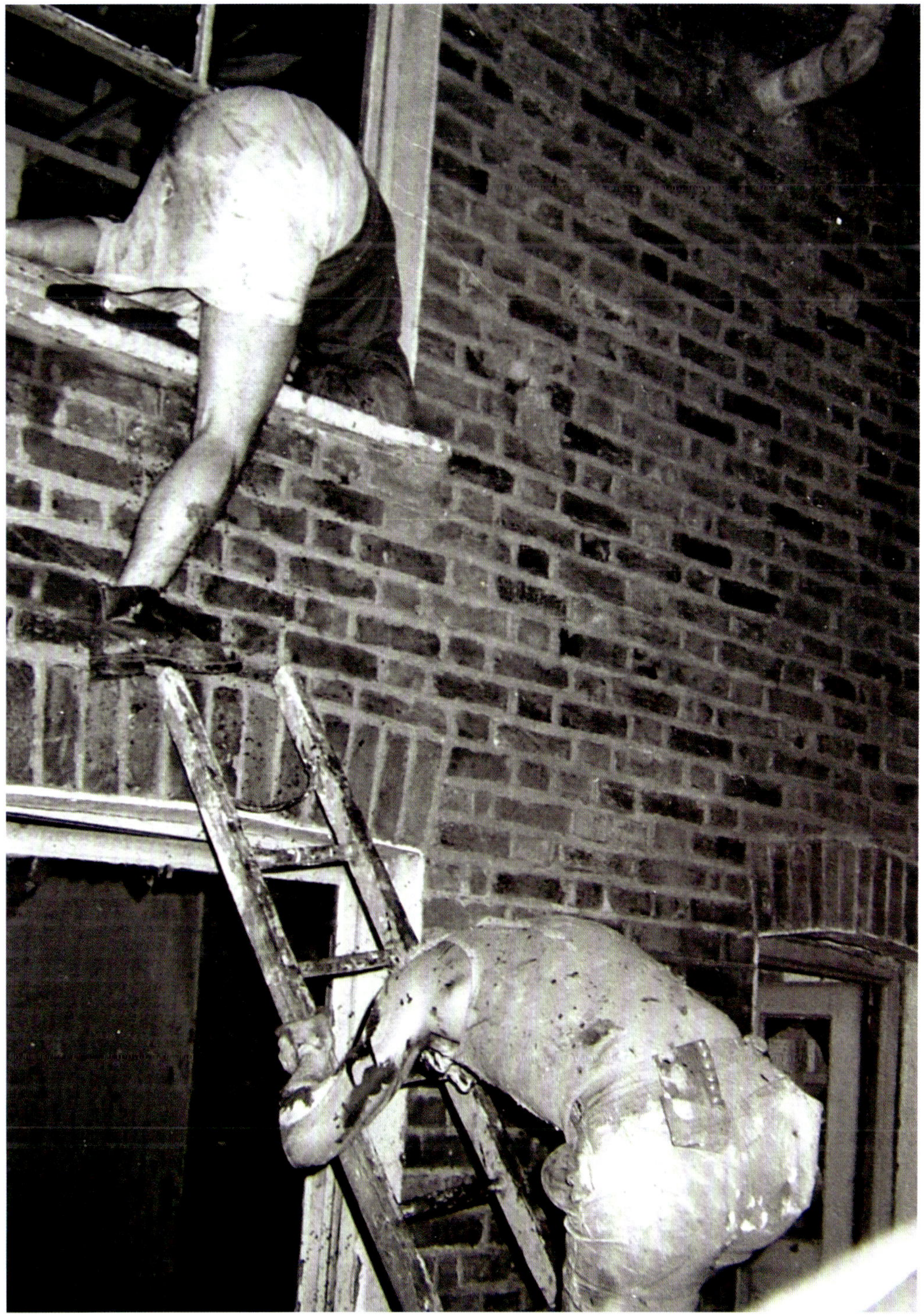

The performance *Two P's and a Bean* (1983), described in my sixth memory, took place in 1983 at 143 Knapp Road in Bow with Anne Bean, Paul Burwell and the US artist Paul McCarthy, who was not at that point so well known as he is now. There was a very small audience. One of the few records of the event shows Bean exiting backwards from an outside window. It happened after the death of Stephen Cripps, the pyrotechnic artist who regularly endangered the lives of audiences, but was most certainly invested with his presence. This in a way is one of the most accurate of my memories, although the incident where Burwell, as the Pirate, smashed his head through a window is invented by me. It is true, however, that the atmosphere of complete disregard for health and safety was there (this is discussed in Wilson and Bean's interview about the Bow Gamelan Ensemble in this book). In the text of *Notes on a Return*, Bean says 'forgetting and disappearance have a powerful reverberation, offering a more luminous exploration than responding to meticulous documentation'.[17] I would liken this performance in terms of its resonance, if not its structure, and the few people that attended Joseph Beuys' key work *I Like America and America Likes Me* (René Block Gallery, New York, May 1974) in which the artist was transported, hooded, from Europe to New York, and delivered in a closed van to a gallery where he spent 10 days living with a coyote. It would be logistically almost impossible to do this performance now and hardly anyone actually saw the performance in reality. However the narrative was so resonant that discussions of it are probably on the reading lists of a hundred thousand art students and the documentation is available on YouTube. Only some black and white photos exist of *Two P's and a Bean*, taken by Linda Frye Burnham.

In the seventh memory, there is again very little documentation apart from a recollection by Chris Millar in *Performance Magazine* in 1983. He writes:

> With initial unbounded enthusiasm she and I left London to join the Sea Organisation of the Church of Scientology, with her suitcase and new navy blue skirt and proper shoes. We stayed only six months. It was a particularly dull time for Anne ... yet a very few people and lot of the philosophy ... clarified and articulated some of her most important beliefs. Scientology set out to prove once and for all the 'man' is not a body and states that most of what passes for thought is best replaced by spontaneous action. Scientology brought a practical drama into some of our wildest imaginings ... [W]e could discuss in a factual way what was hitherto only poetic imaginings. We were sure we could disappear and reappear – indeed we found nobody did otherwise.[18]

Bean disputes this description of it being a dull time, so I have entirely invented a rather more exciting new fiction to replace it.

The eighth memory comes closest to a notion of 'false memory'. I wrote this while trying to remember how Anne told me about why Chana Dubinski decided to stay in Newark, after wandering round Northern England, without consulting the interview where this is also described, which appears later in this book. Here is Chana's own description of this event, from the book *A Transpective – How Things Used to Be Now*:

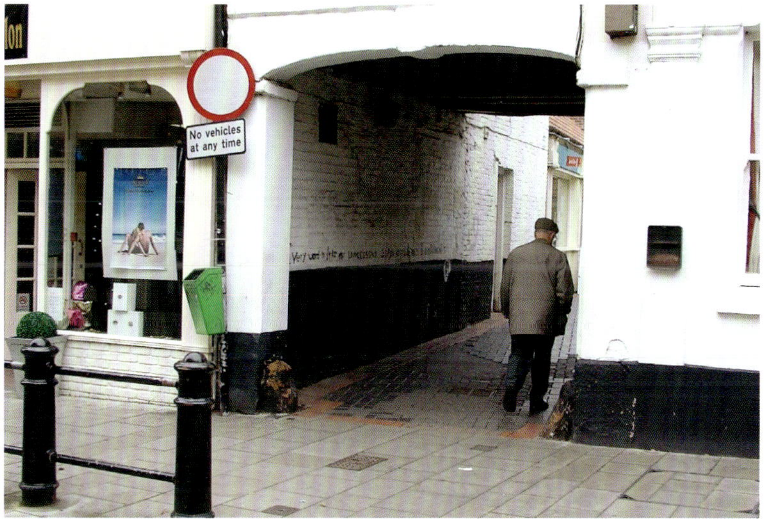

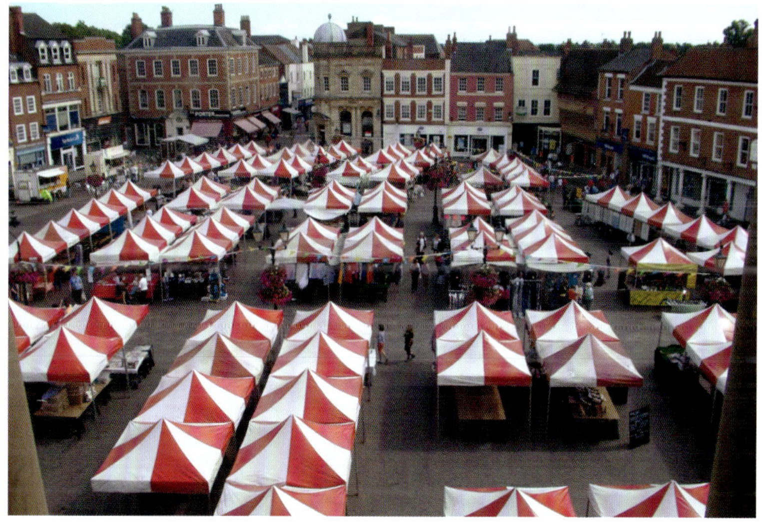

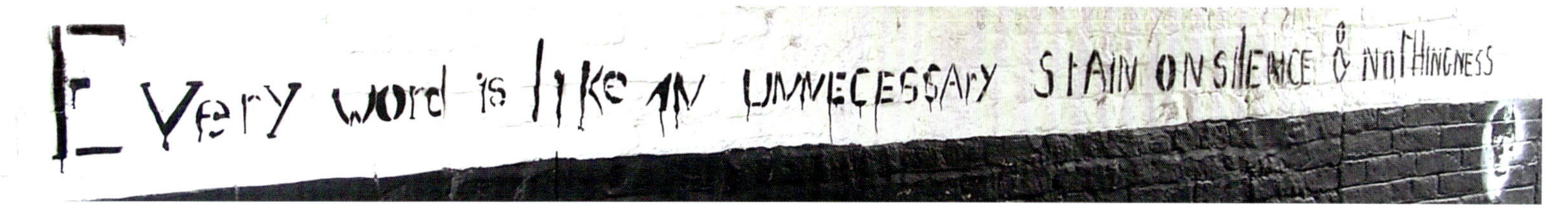

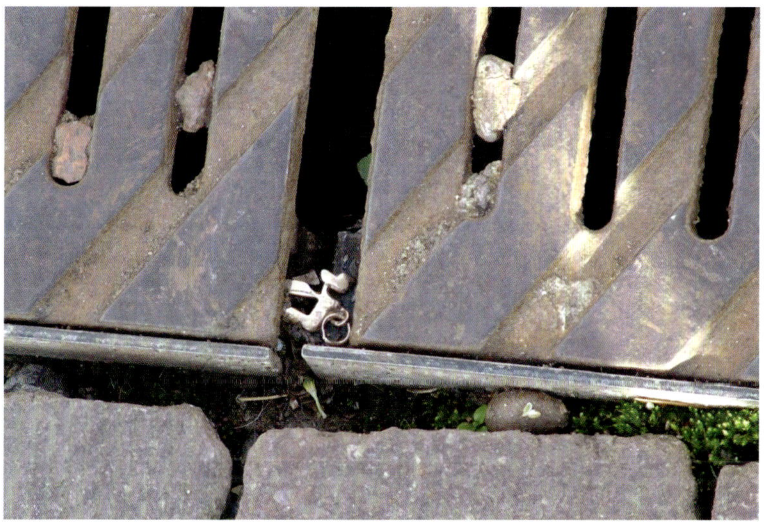

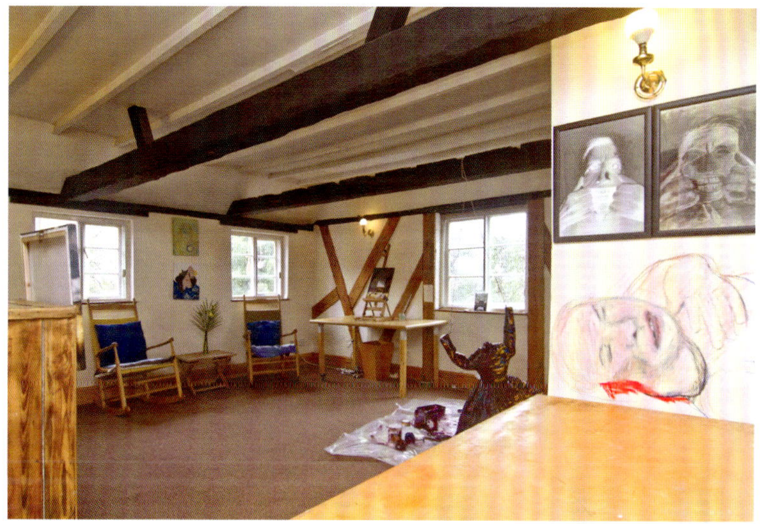

Photos by Chana Dubinski, Newark-on-Trent, 2012.

Top left: Paxton Court. *Top right:* Newark Market. *Middle:* Samuel Beckett graffiti in Paxton Court. *Bottom left:* Chana Dubinski, *Fugitive Pieces: A Transpective*, 2012: Chana's lost amulet – *Chai*, meaning 'life' – super-glued into the gutter where the original had fallen. *Bottom right:* Upstairs, Riverside Cottage.

> I was passing through Newark on my way west. I had to change buses and had some time. I stopped to buy a baked potato in the market square when a charm I was carrying in my wallet fell into the gutter. A friend had given it to me from his late mother, Anna Miller. It was meant to be kept close during my journeying. This charm spelt the Hebrew word *chai*, meaning 'living'. At first, anxious to recover it and asking for assistance, I stayed overnight to see if I could have the grating opened the next day, but to no avail. I accepted the symbolism of the charm destining me to stay here, close to it.[19]

In the ninth and final memory the flying saucer is the Futuro House created by Finnish architect Matti Suuronen, which perched on top of Matt's Gallery (then situated in Mile End) in 2016. Interestingly, this Futuro House, one of only 60 in the world, had come from Southern Africa, where Bean grew up. The events that happened to lead Bean randomly that night to drive off and found the arts centre MoCa (Moments of Consciousness and) Trowbridge are relatively accurately described, although the technical details of the draw from the hat by director Robin Klassnik may be a little inaccurate. Bean left the comfortable warmth of the London art world to find her way in an unknown town. One of the first people she met was a group of army veterans sleeping rough, described by her here:

> On several occasions, I spoke with a few ex-servicemen, all of whom had served in Iraq and/or Afghanistan and were now sleeping rough close to MoCa Trowbridge. Near Christmas, we were sitting around a small fire and their raw, cold talk of feeling alienated by both local people in the Middle East and people on returning home to UK, re-connected me to T. S. Eliot's 'The Journey of the Magi,' which I mentioned to them. They spoke of some of the horrors that they had witnessed. I asked one of them if I could make an image from what he had described. I used the charcoal leftover from the fire we were sitting around to make the charred dog's head that haunted his thoughts. I invited them to come over to listen to T. S. Eliot reading out his poem through speakers concealed in the airbricks by the side of my window in MoCa ... This lasted, with the sound, through the 'festive' period. We had a beer together when I switched it on.[20]

In 2015, after finally shifting/transmuting from the Chana Dubinski self, Bean did a performance that was not seen by anyone except the participants who gave her money, but discreetly photographed by Markéta Luskačová. She sat at the entrance of Whitechapel tube station begging, holding up a sign which she alternated between 'God bless' and 'God less'. In this provocative but anonymous action the 'God less' self earned £14.33 in one hour and the 'God bless' self £11.54, bringing as Bean said 'many wonderful, stimulating, generous, caring as well as often challenging and angry responses'.[21]

The selves of Anne Bean thrive on the margins, undocumented, unseen.

1. Adrian Stephen, *The Dreadnought Hoax* (London: Chatto and Windus, 1936).

2. Jo Joelson, unpublished typescript, forthcoming from London Fieldworks.

3. See *Marcel Duchamp: Works and Life/Ephemerides on and about Marcel Duchamp and Rrose Sélavy 1887-1968*, ed. by Pontus Hulten with Jennifer Gough-Cooper and Jacques Caumont (Cambridge, MA: MIT Press, 1993).

4. See Monty Cantsin, *Shitsville UK* (London: Carpet Bombing Culture, 2013)

5. See Stewart Home, *Neoism, Plagiarism and Praxis* (London: AK Press, 1995).

6. Eleanor Antinova, *Being Antinova* (Los Angeles: Astro Artz, 1983).

7. Grace Glueck, 'In a Roguish Gallery: One Aging Black Ballerina', *New York Times* (12 May 1989), C3.

8. Genesis BREYER P-ORRIDGE in *The Ballad of Genesis and Lady Jaye* (dir. Marie Losier, 2011).

9. Pamela Petro, 'James Magee's Hill', *Granta* 102 (8 July 2008): https://granta.com/jim-magees-hill/

10. Ibid.

11. Kerry Doyle, 'Introduction', in James Magee, *Letters to Goya: Poems, Titles and Letters To The Dead* (El Paso: Cinco Puntos Press, 2018).

12. Rob La Frenais, 'What's in a Name? Anne Bean Interviewed', *Art Monthly* 398 (July-August 2016), 1-5 (p. 4). The interview is republished in a different version in this book.

13. Ibid.

14. Anne Bean, 'Artist's Notes', *Notes on a Return*, ed. by Sophia Yadong Hao and Matthew Hearn (Sunderland: Sunderland Art Gallery), pp. 108-9 (p. 108).

15. Rob La Frenais and Natural Reader software app, *Unpaintings* (2016).

16. Rob La Frenais, 'Obituary: Paul Burwell 1949-2007', *Art Monthly* 304 (March 2007), p. 21.

17. Bean, 'Artist's Notes', p. 108.

18. Chris Millar, 'Profile: Anne Bean – A Portentous Event in Earshot of Braying Donkeys', *Performance Magazine* 20-1 (December-January 1983), 4-8 (p. 7).

19. Chana Dubinski, *A Transpective – How Things Used To Be Now* (2012), E-book, http://annebeanarchive.com/transpective-newark-on-trent/

20. Anne Bean *The Journey of the Magi*, www.annebeanarchive.com/journey-of-the-magi-mob/

21. Anne Bean *Godless* (2015), http://annebean.net/godless/

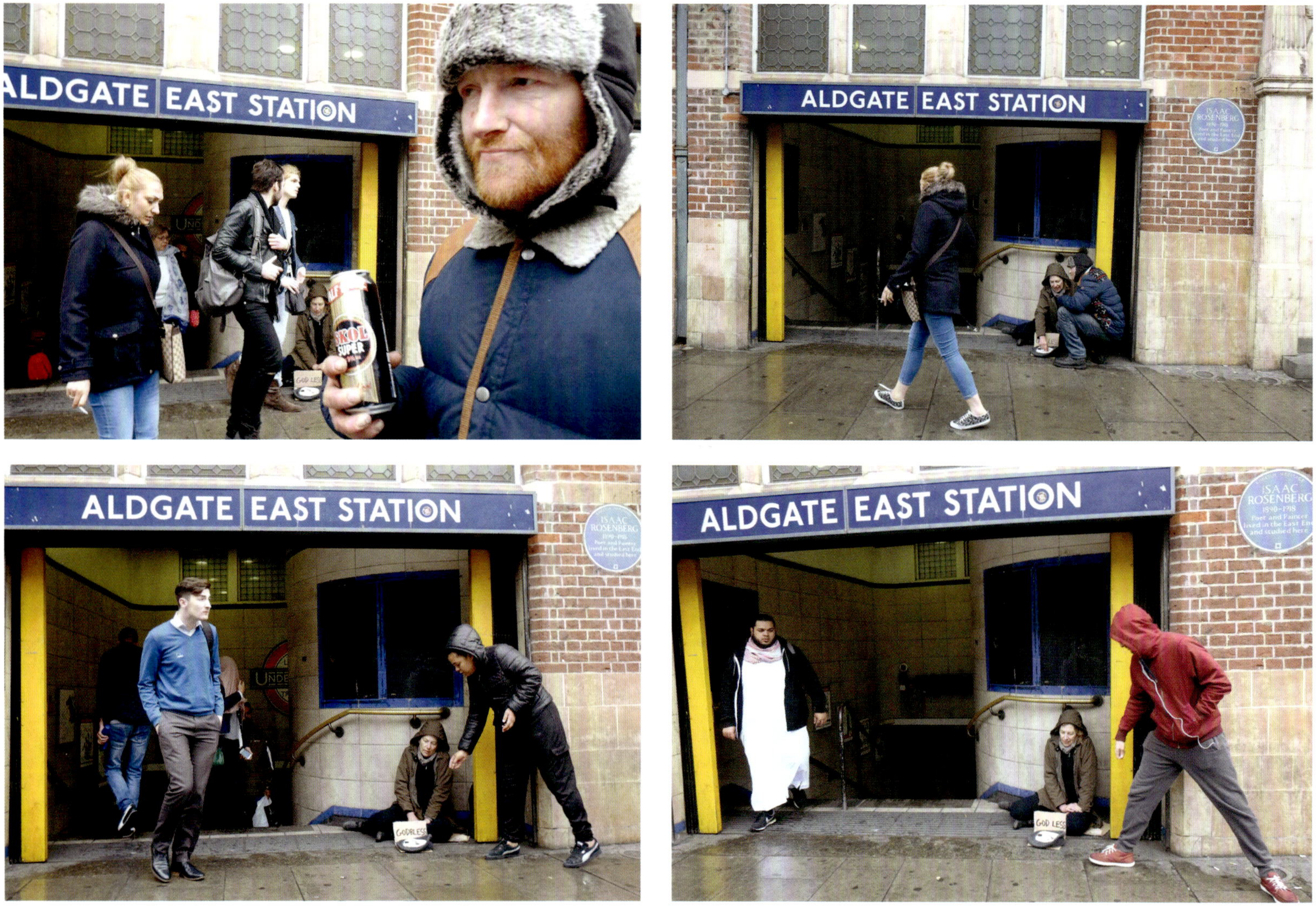

Anne Bean, *God Less/Godbless*, Aldgate, London, 2015. Photos: Markéta Luskačová

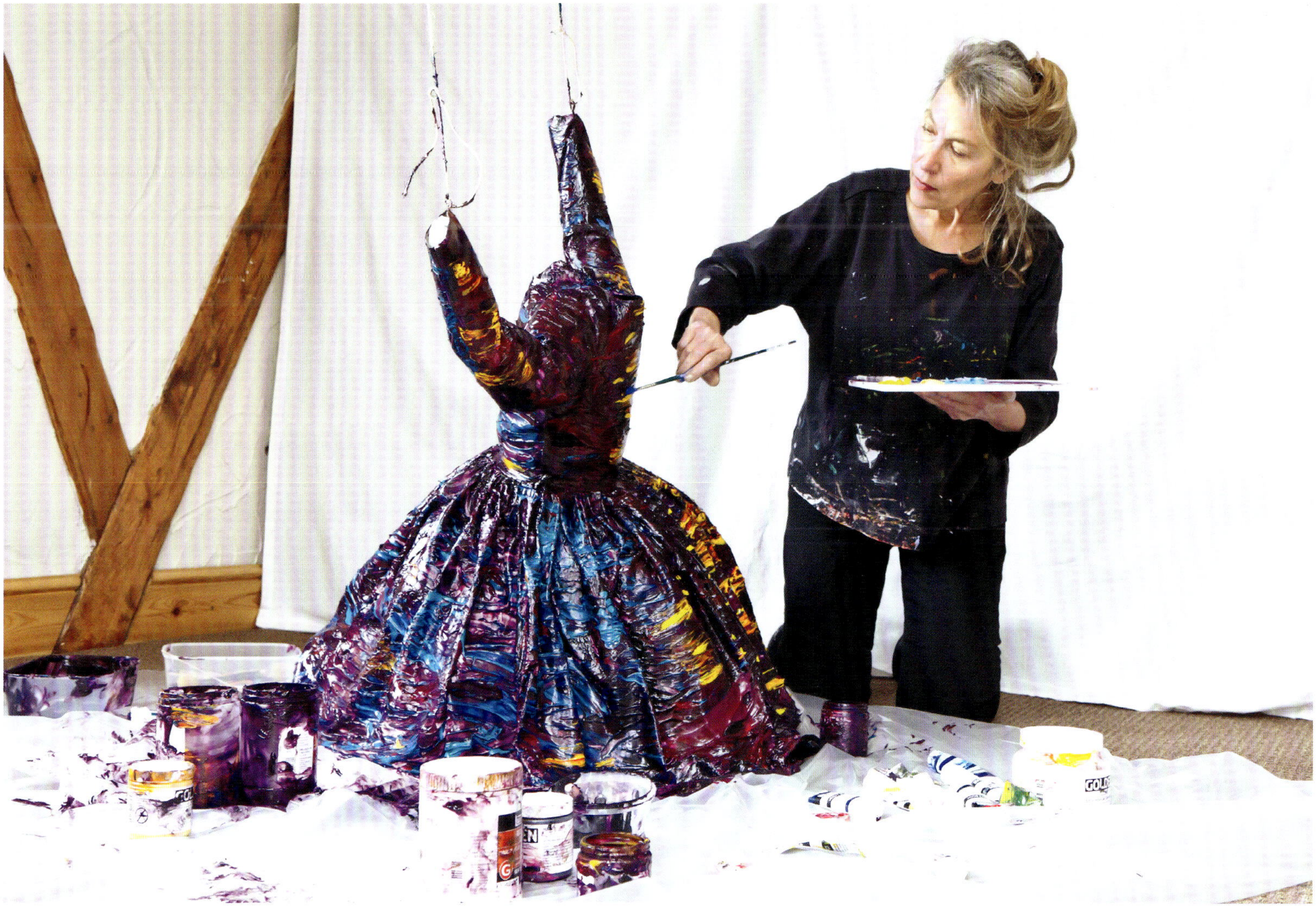

Chana Dubinski, *Unwound: A Transpective*, Newark-on-Trent, 2012. Photo: Adam Winfield

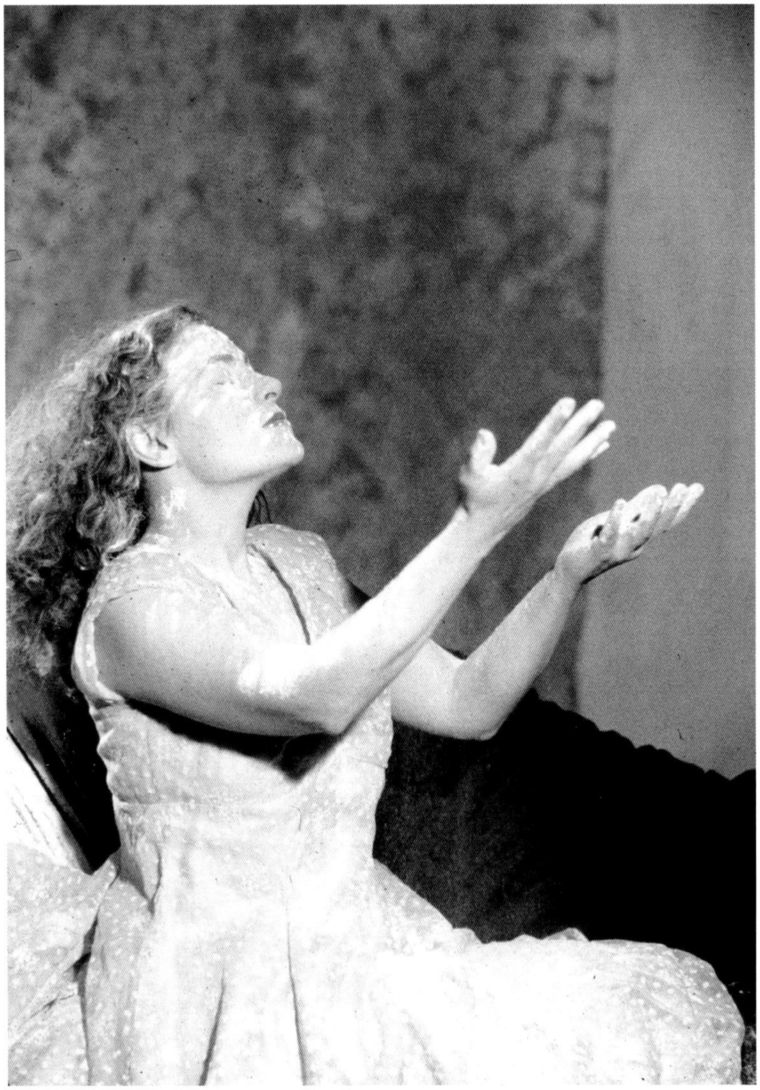

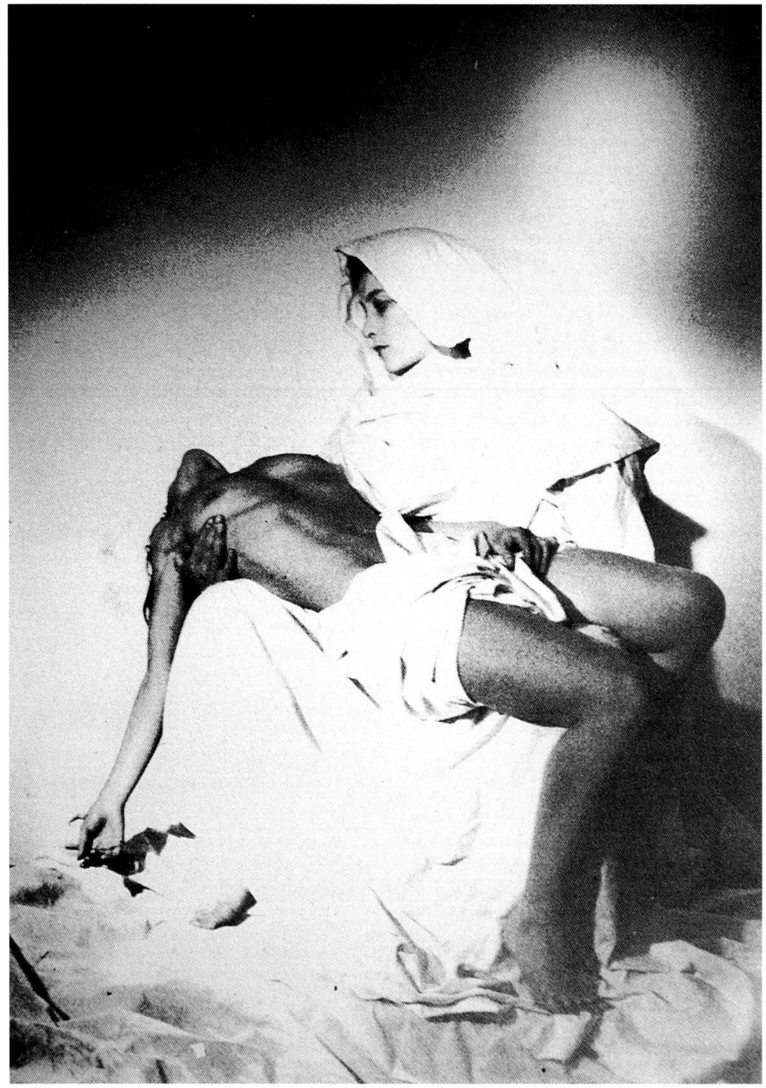

Left: Anne Bean, throwing powder to produce shifting projections in *Sweet Soul Music*, 1978. Photo: Polly Eltes

Right: Anne Bean in Hermine Demoriane's play, *He Who Is Your Lord Is Your Child Too*, Notre Dame Hall, Leicester Square, 1982. Photo: Jean-Marc Prouveur

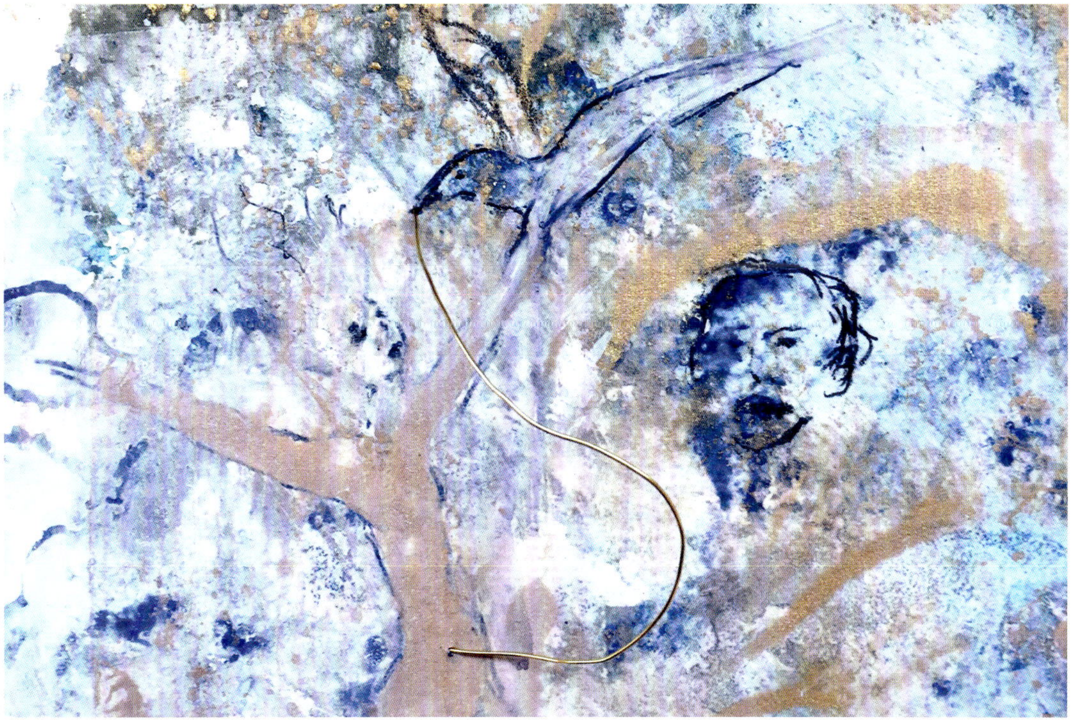

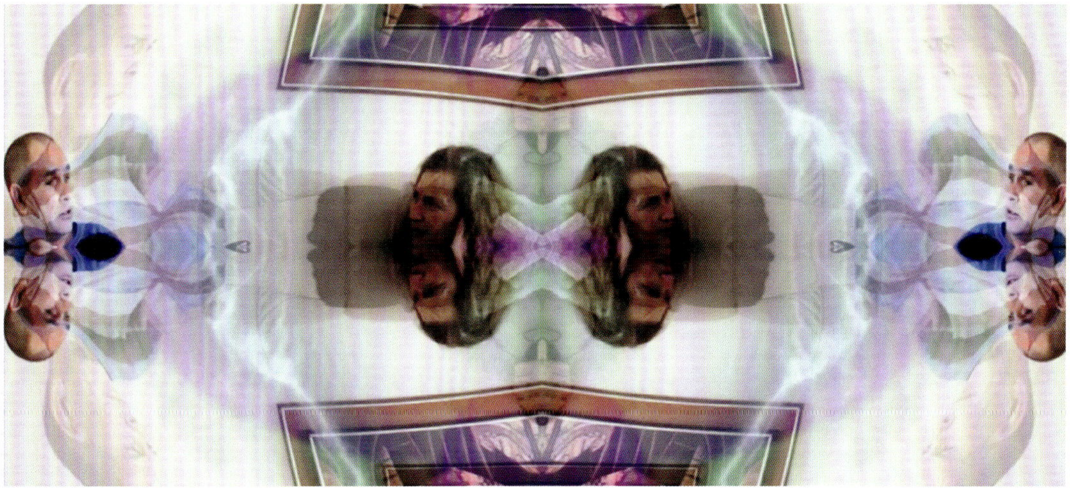

Top: Anne Bean, *Golden Thread*, MoCa Trowbridge, 2016

Below: Anne Bean (with Phil the Messenger), *And Inhabited the Spaces*, Hull, 2009. Still from a video by Patricia and Brian Routh. Created as part of *TAPS: Improvisations with Paul Burwell*

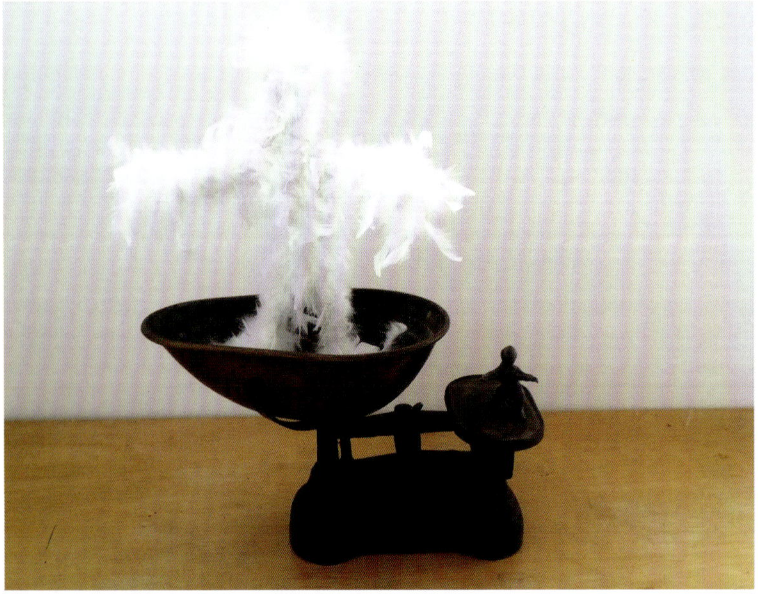

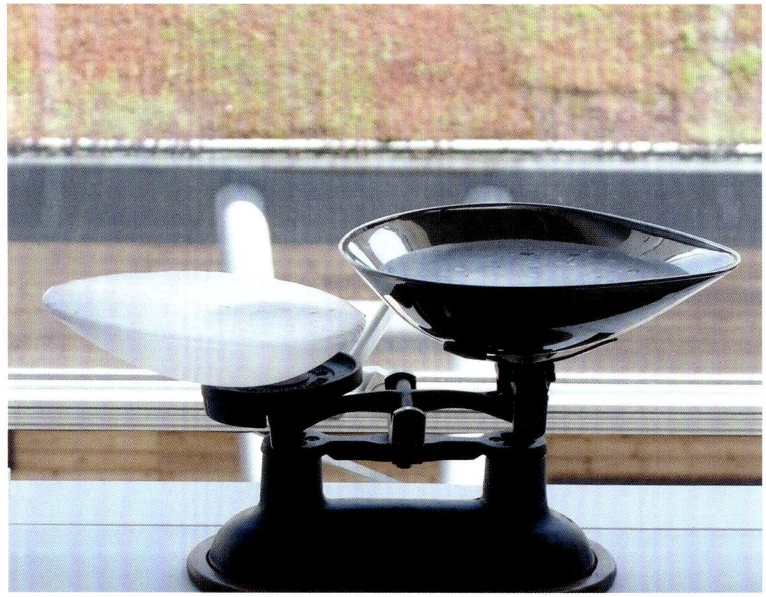

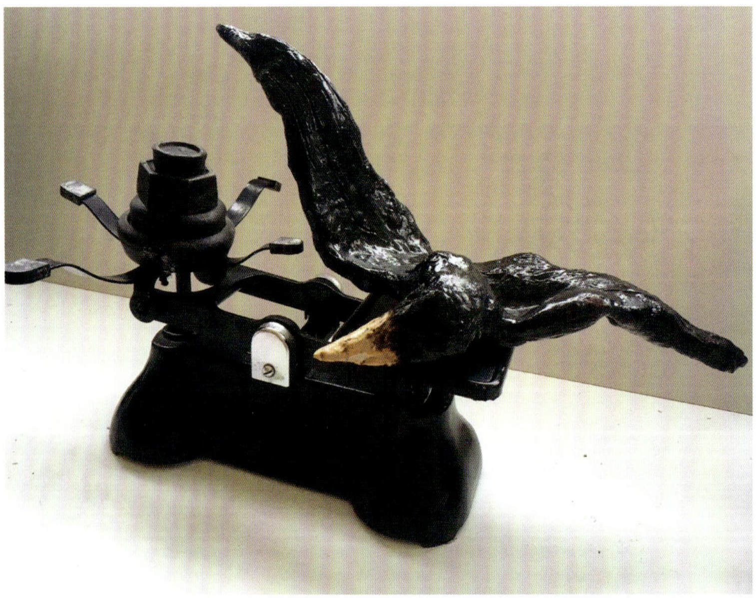

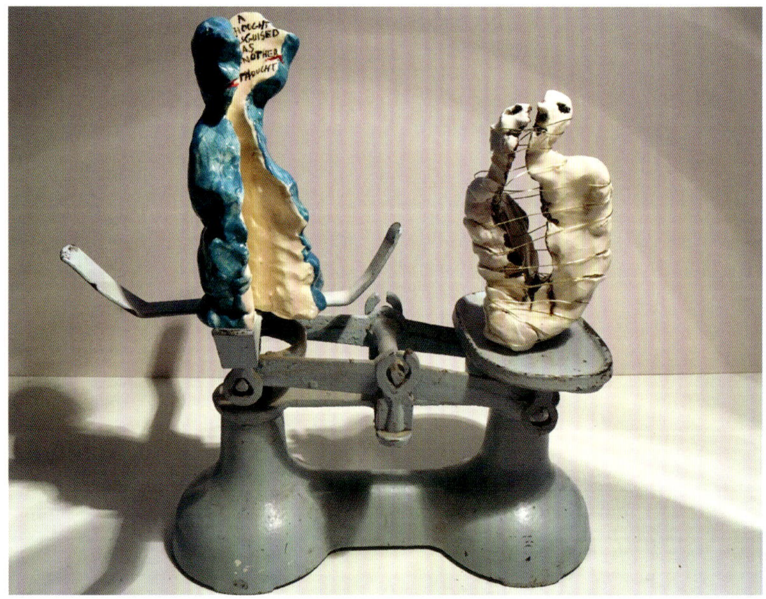

Top left: Anne Bean, *Lead Man and Feather Man*, from *Balances* (2014-17), a series in which the scales are in perfect equilibrium
Top right: Anne Bean, *Equilibrium* from *Balances* (2014-17)
Bottom left: Anne Bean, *Weight of Flight* from *Balances* (2014-17)
Bottom right: Anne Bean, *A Thought Disguised as Another Thought* from *Balances* (2014-17) (Glass with Livvy Fink, ceramics with Jane Hanson)

Opposite: Anne Bean, *Charred Dog's Head*, MoCa Trowbridge, 2016

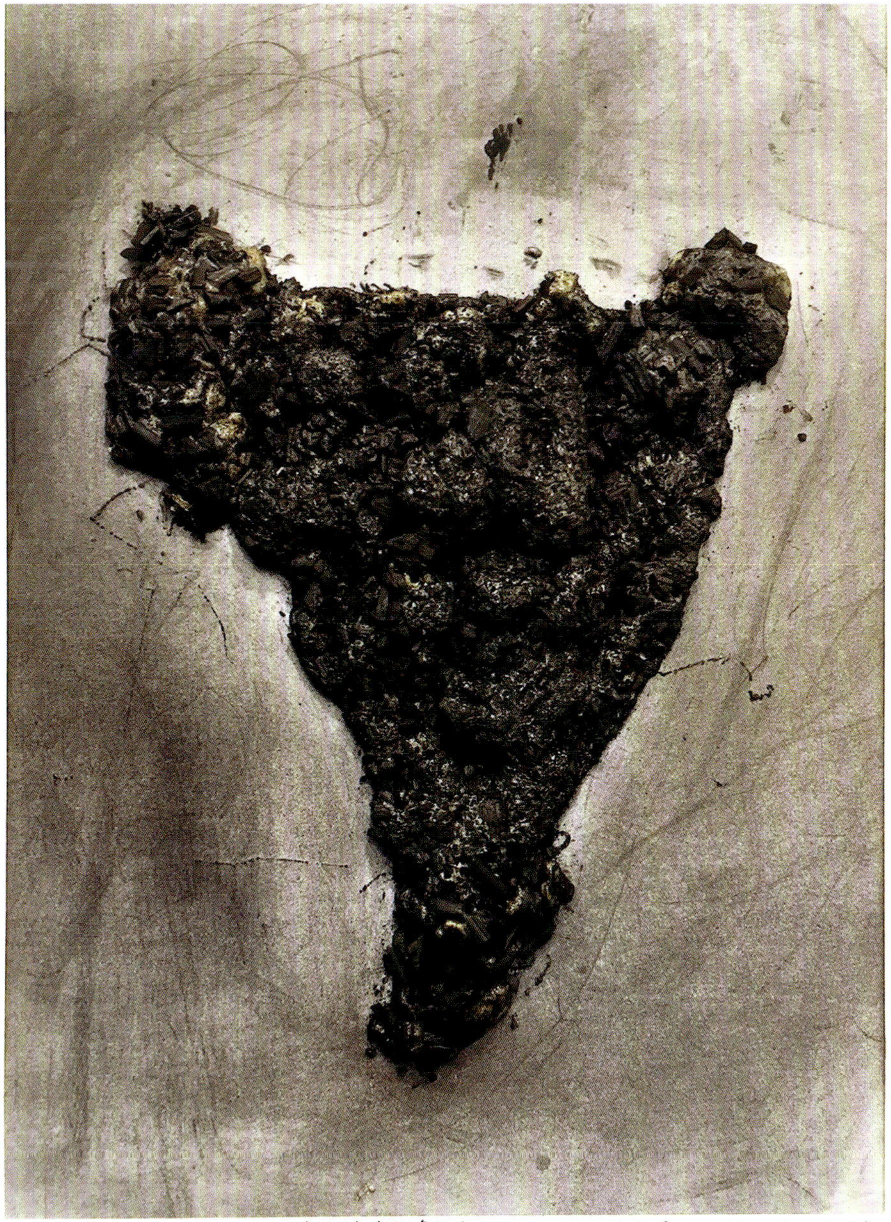

The image I constantly see is a charred dog's head.
I always smell burnt flesh.

Keith B. ex soldier who served
in Iraq and Afghanistan.
Living rough near MOCA TROWBRIDGE
2016.

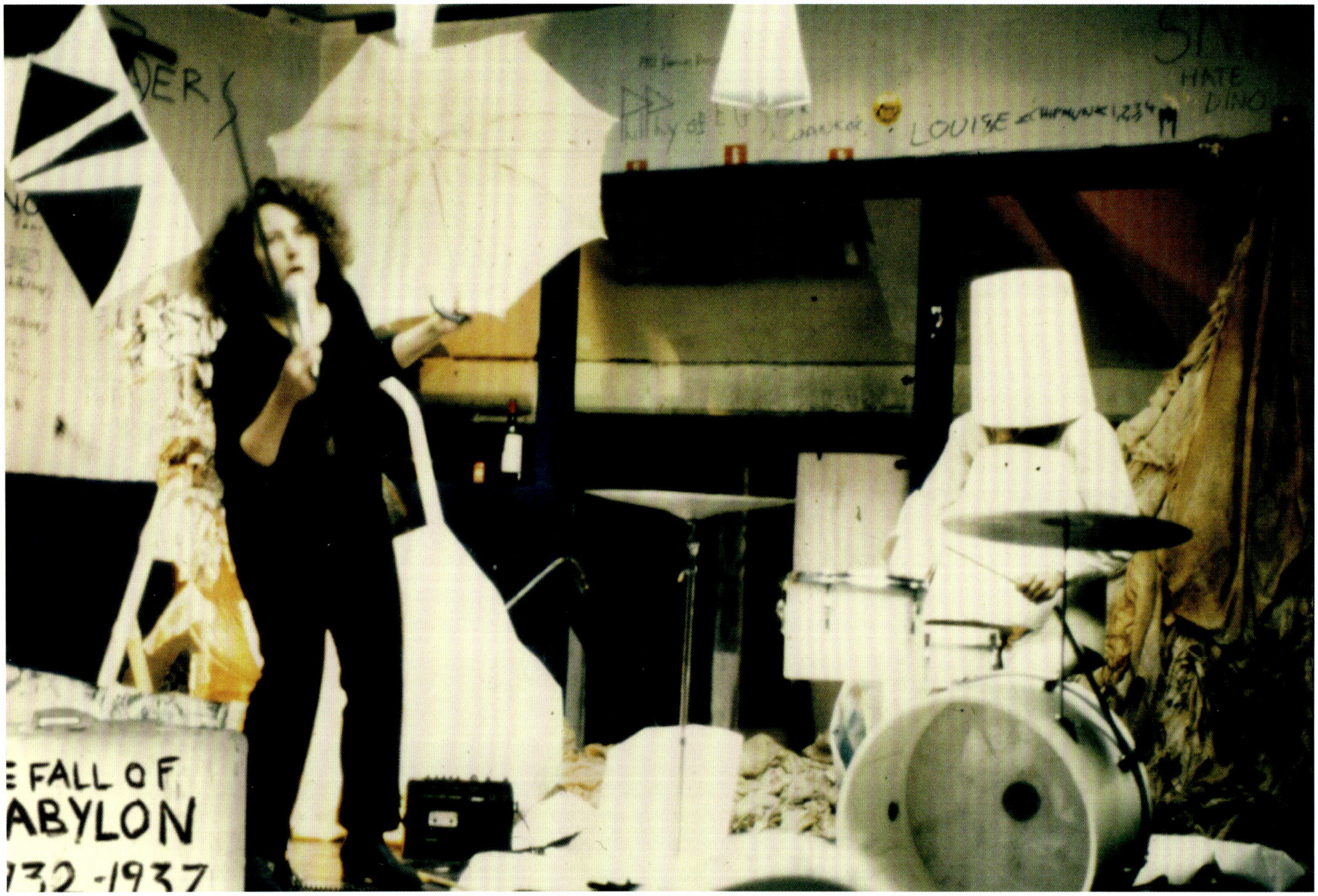

Above: PULp MUSIC, *The Fall of Babylon*, Ark Kent, London, 1978. Photographer unknown
Opposite: PULp MUSIC with Stephen Cripps, *The Fall of Babylon*, London, 1978. Photo: Chris Bishop

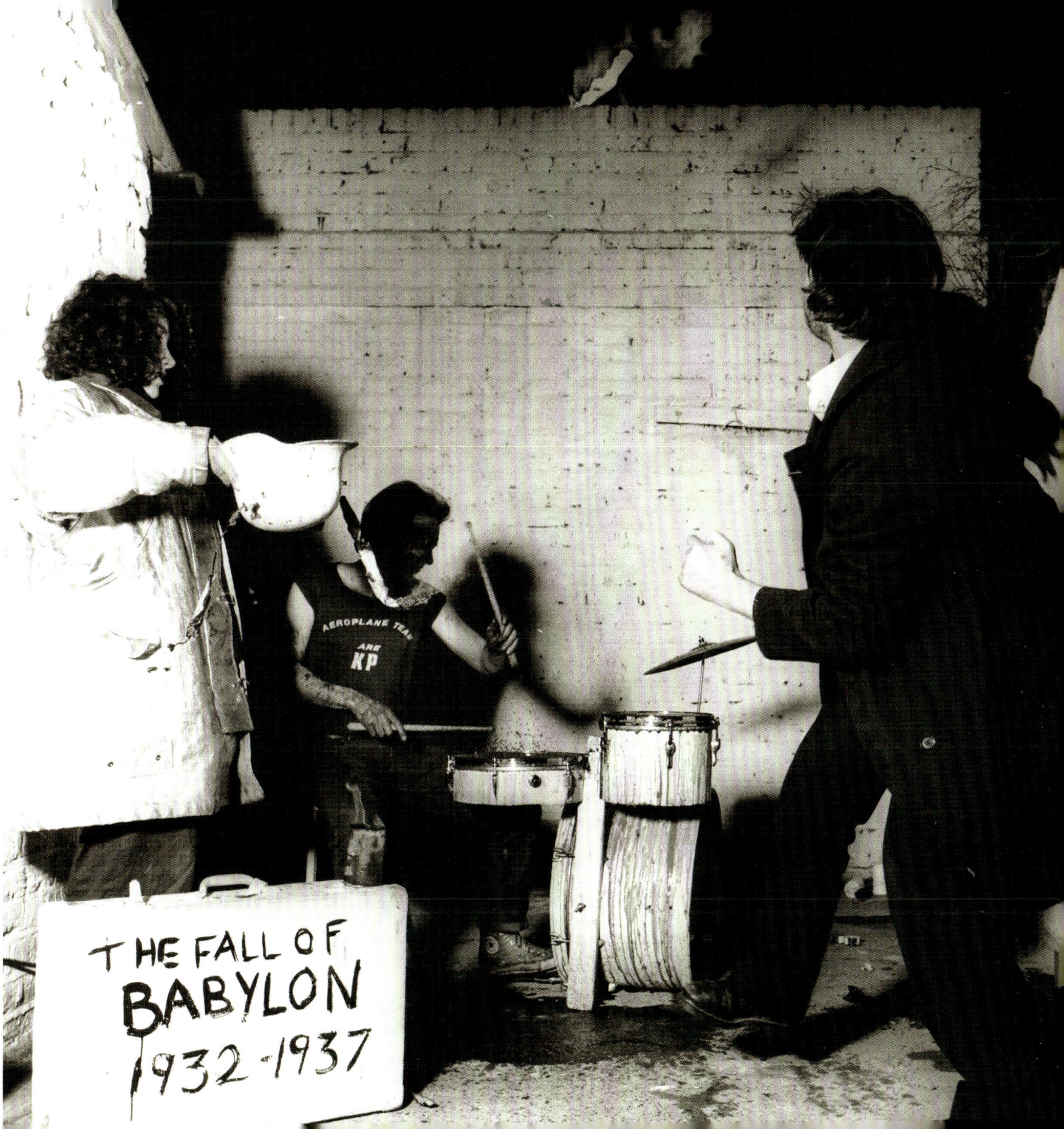
AEROPLANE TEAM
ARE
KP
THE FALL OF
BABYLON
1932-1937

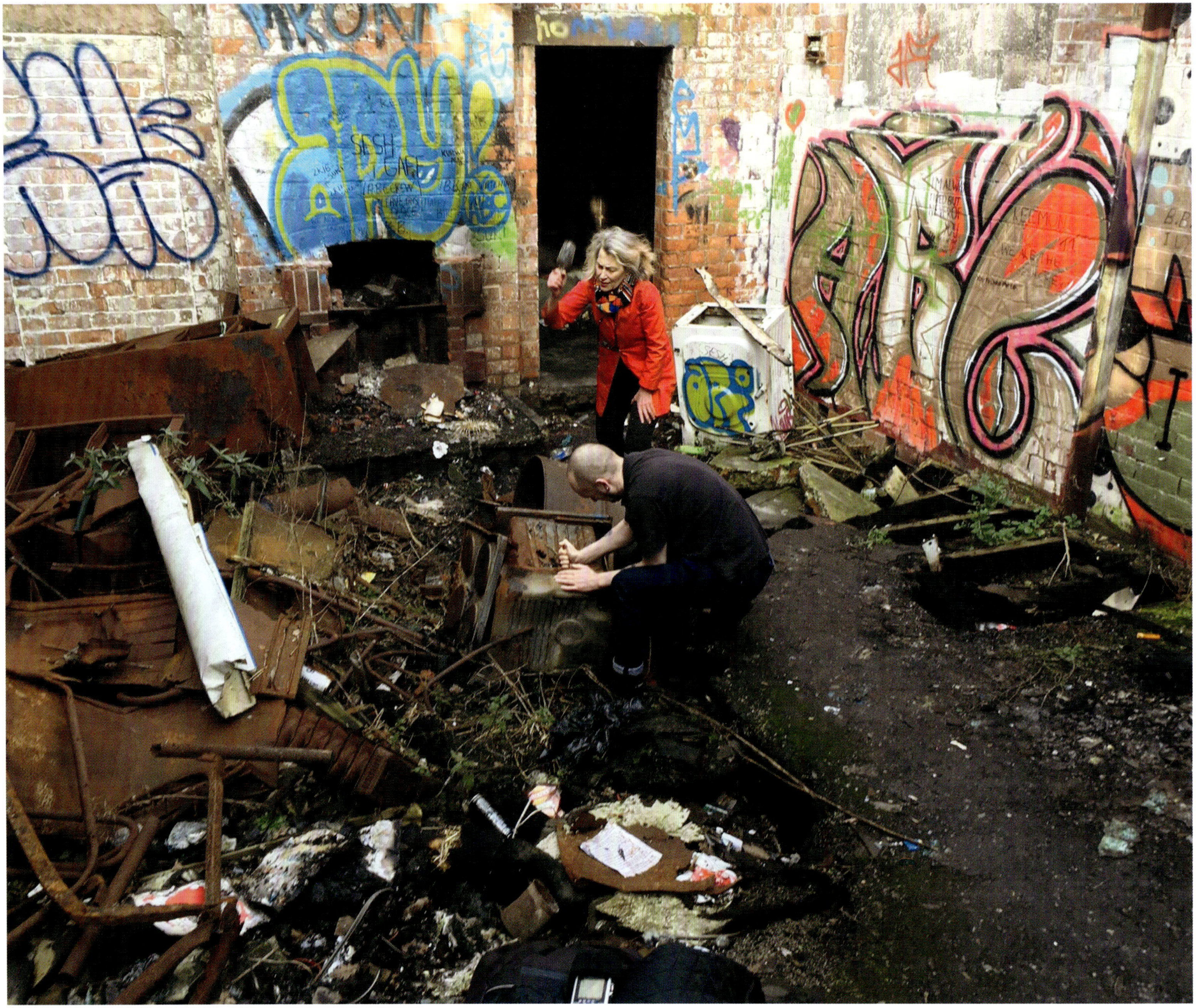

Anne Bean and Yol, *Paean with Paul,* on the tenth Anniversary of Paul's death
in his burnt-out boat club, Kingston Rowing Club, Hull, 2017. Photo: Brian Gilson

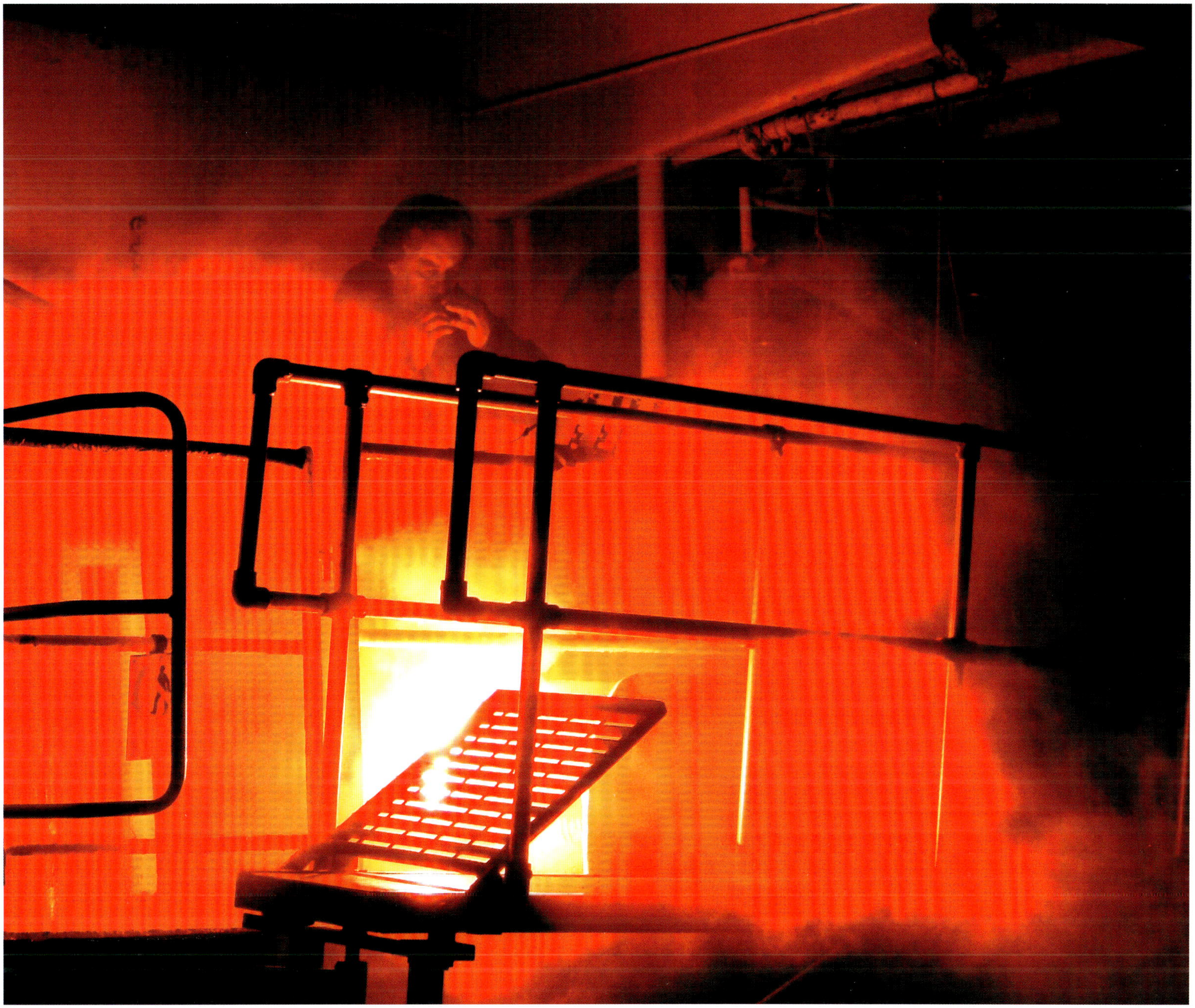

Anne Bean, Ansuman Biswas, Paul Burwell, Sean Dower, Kirsten Reynolds, Richard Wilson, and Z'EV, *The Pirate on the Pirate Ship*, performed on Wilson's *Slice of Reality*, Greenwich, 2004. Seven artists performing seven pieces lasting seven minutes each. Photo: Simon Maggs

INTERVENTIONS BY ANNE BEAN

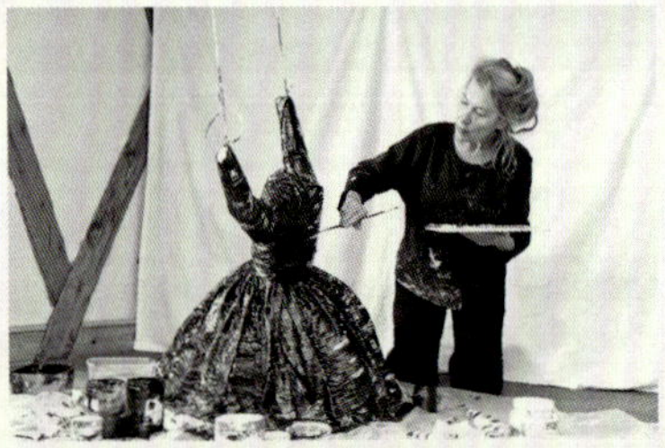

As a child, I loved spinning fast, singing out loudly, so that my voice made a 'moiré' pattern and I felt like I was levitating. I thought if I spun back suddenly I could meet myself coming back. I would have 'Unwound'.

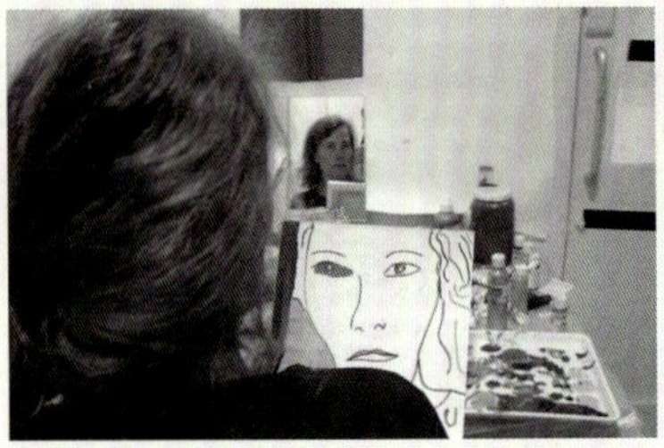

The Artist had created 24 self-portraits, one an hour over Midsummer's day and night as a part of Autobituary in St Martins Church, Colchester. The Poet, a young local man who spent almost the entire 24 hours with the Artist, including a midnight inspection of the graveyard, wrote in a later essay 'Continuum': 'It was very much apparent to me that the Artist was subtly persuading me into a transformational role where I was as active an artist as herself.' He also quoted the Artist remembering her first young response to reading about the Holocaust, 'Thinking about dying makes me feel very living'.

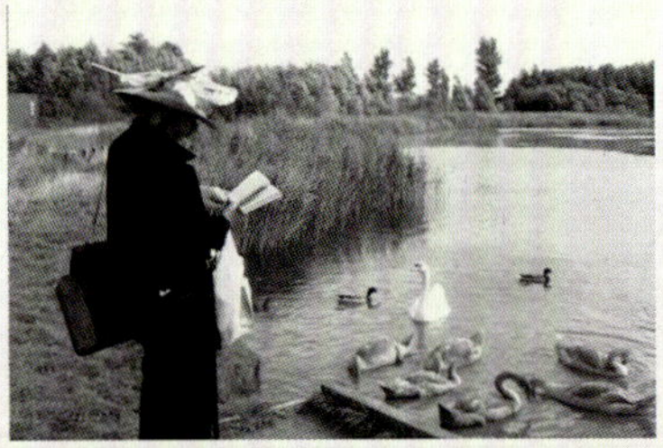

The Pirate spent his last days feeding and reading to the swans outside his caravan. He gathered their feathers into his hat, to become part of them and read a few pages to them every day from *The Life of Nelson*, his hero.

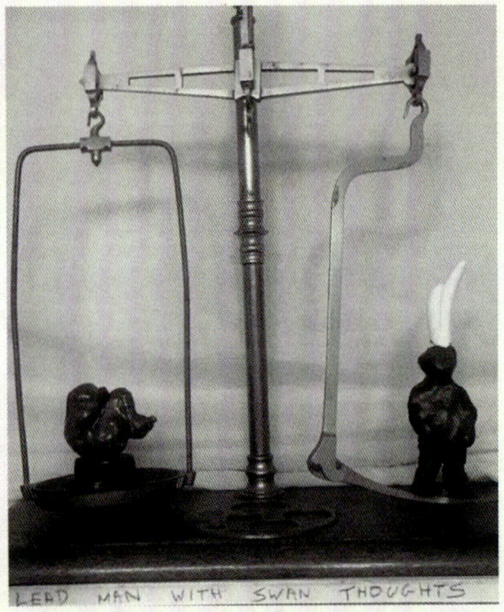

The Artist made *Lead Man with Swan Thoughts*, as part of her Balances series. MoCa Trowbridge, 2015.

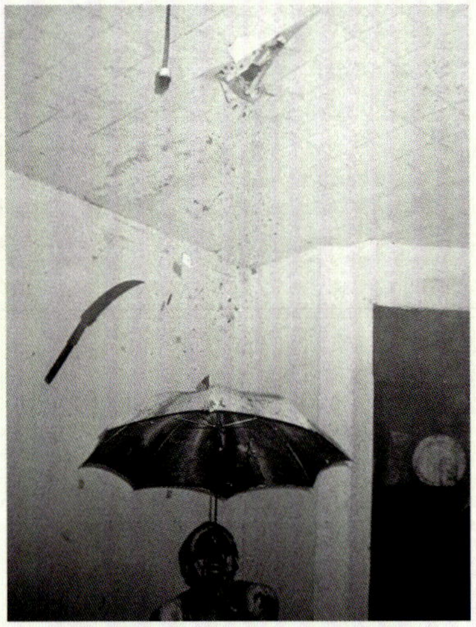

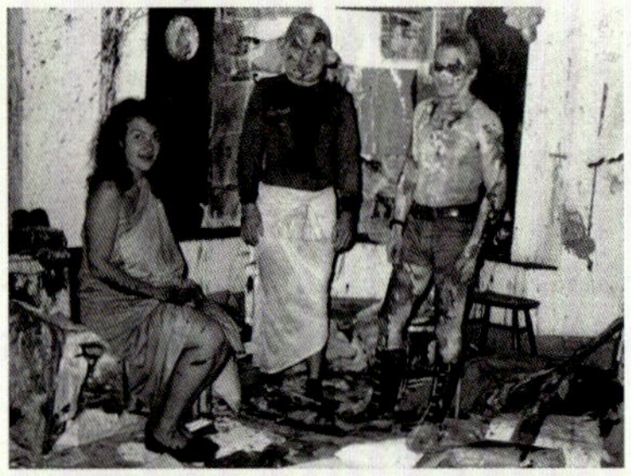

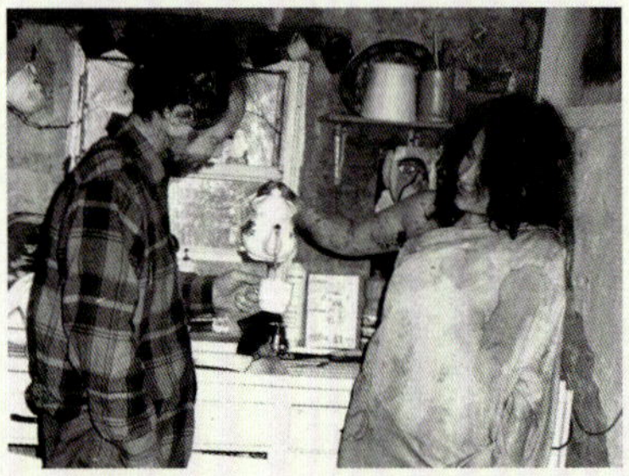

The Artist, the well-known Artist and the Pirate settle in for a cup of tea.

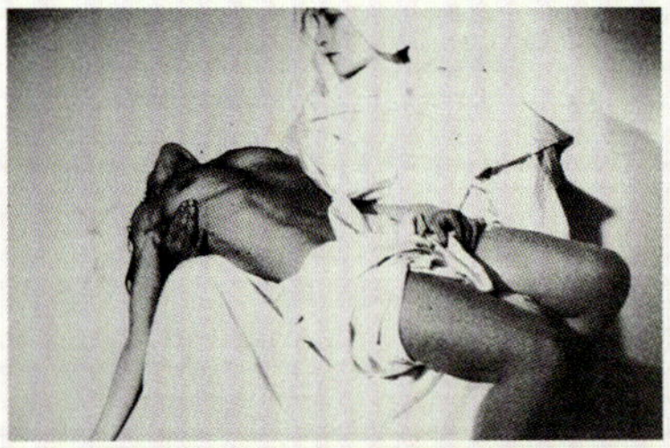

The Critic's 'ting tings' accompanied the Artist's 'pain pain' in the Victorian Museum in the North of England, as she reconnected, in her 'pain tings,' to her work from 1971 *The Consummation, Crucifixion, Resurrection and Transubstantiation as seen by the Virgin Mary.* In these, she fiercely protects her son, Jesus, from physical and metaphysical pain. She holds him tightly as a young child, protecting him from the temptations of Satanic forces, she comforts him and tends him as he experiences agony and sweats blood in the garden of Gethsemane and she offers herself to wear the crown of thorns and to be crucified in his place. The artists involved dwelt on Alfred Jarry's quote "God is the tangential point between zero and infinity."

In 1982 the Artist cradled Hermine Demoriane as Madonna and child in *He Who Is Your Lord Is Your Child Too*, a Nativity play written by Hermine, staged at Notre Dame Hall, Leicester Square.

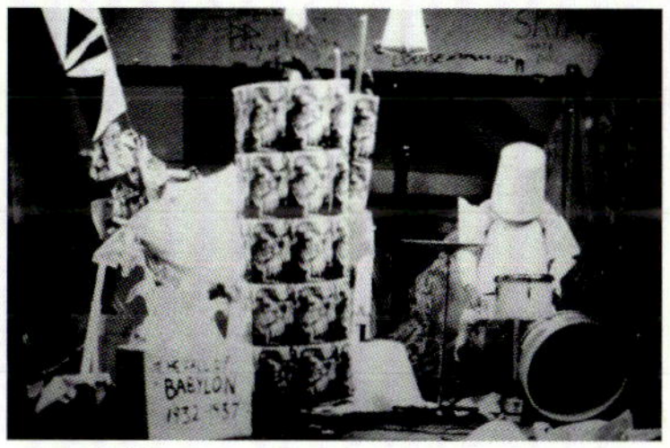

I saw another angel ...the earth was illuminated by his splendour. With a mighty voice he shouted: Fallen! Fallen is Babylon the Great! She has become a home for demons and a haunt for every evil spirit.

The Book of Revelation

The Pirate and the Artist shared many demons and used Revelations in *The Fall of Babylon 1932-1937* at London Musicians Collective, 1982, joined by the Fireman.

PB wrote: "The first performance of an unpublished play, written in 1929 but set sometime in the present.

It concerns an evening in the lives of an accident prone fireman, a cab-driver and an unemployed strip club manager brought together by a series of chance events gradually becoming aware of the major themes of Contemporary Art.

These themes are represented by Feminism, Political Message, Collectivism, Minimalism, Structuralism, Drip-Painting, Technology, New Wave, Improvisation, Punk Art, Community Fringe Theatre and Performance Art

The evening ruthlessly dissects, analyses and exposes their complete inability to come to grips with these issues or with the tragedy of each other's lives."

'The Fireman's name is Stephen Cripps'

Our genre is Depressionism.
Our work has no meaning.
It comes from a deep sense
of nihilistic blackness which is totally
liberating and makes everything
stirring and bracing.
I believe in nothing.
I think everything is possible.
I believe in nothing but miracles.

AB

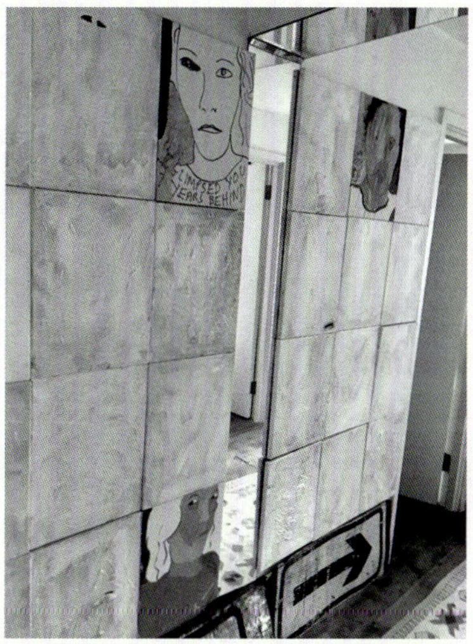

The Three Graced - the un-unpainted

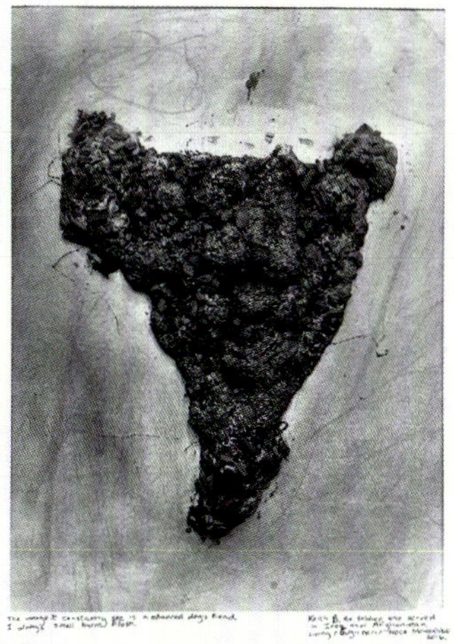

Many years later, the Poet, who had accompanied the Artist through the night of the 24 portraits, visited the Artist in her space, *Moments Of Consciousness And...*

He wrote:

Eventually I found myself on Court Street and noticed the artist's handwriting by the entrance of 15 Meadow Works. Stepping inside and greeting the artist, I was immediately struck by the intensity of a year's work. One work particularly gripped me. It was a charcoal image of a dog's head, burnt and charred. This encounter with the artwork has continued to haunt me often since its first glimpsing. I will not describe its context or meaning (out of respect for certain persons involved) but I will say that it ... reinforces the importance of engaging with people of all spheres, places, creeds and identities.

The Poet's name is Mark Pearce.

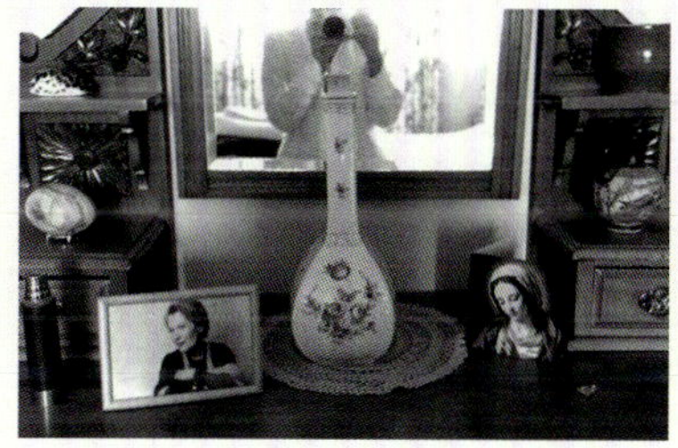

Once again the Artist keeps company with the Madonna, in the house of a Close Newark Friend.

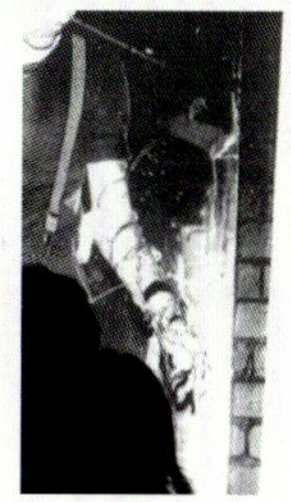 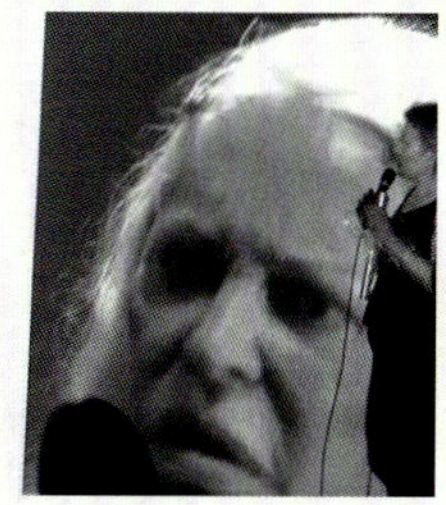

The Artist met once again, a long-term comrade, one of the Transmitters from Coum Transmissions at the PV of Coum's archival show at Humber St Gallery in Hull. Genesis told the Artist that s/he felt like a dead man walking through the detritus of hi/r life. The artist referenced this in a performance in the same gallery for the online launch of *Performance Magazine*.

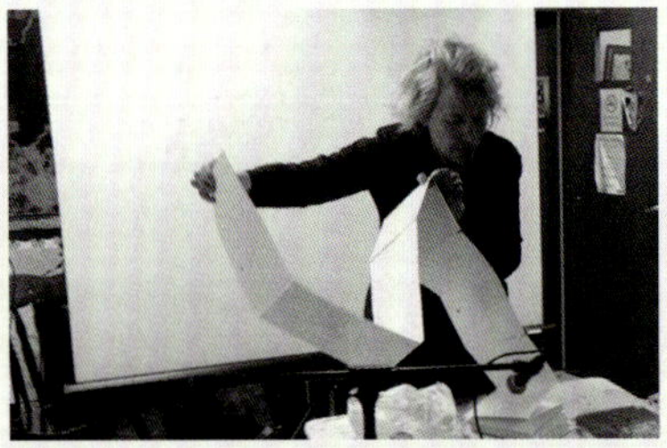

P. S. (Paul Sue/Post Script)
Ground space, Hull, 2017

During the year of Hull City Of Culture, not as part of any official programme, *P.S.* was put on by a group of artists, led by Brian Gilson. All had known Paul in the Boat club and this acknowledged Paul Burwell and Sue Arrowsmith, two artists who died in Hull and strongly contributed to the life and culture of the city. In a work called Incantations I recorded bits of Paul talking and drumming and my own and other voices onto recordable cards which I unfolded like a strange accordion, so voices fused and overlapped, springing momentarily into life and disappearing.

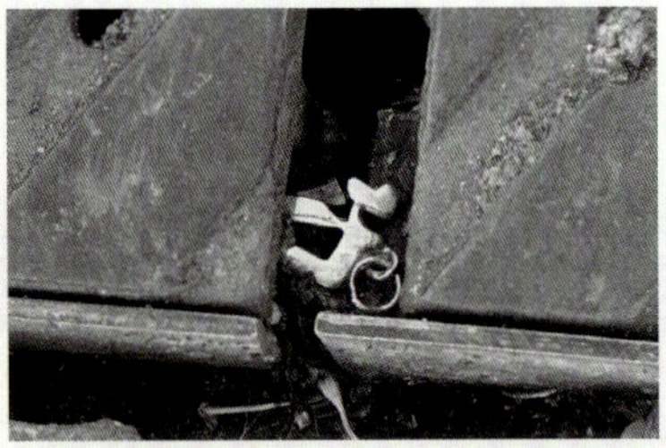

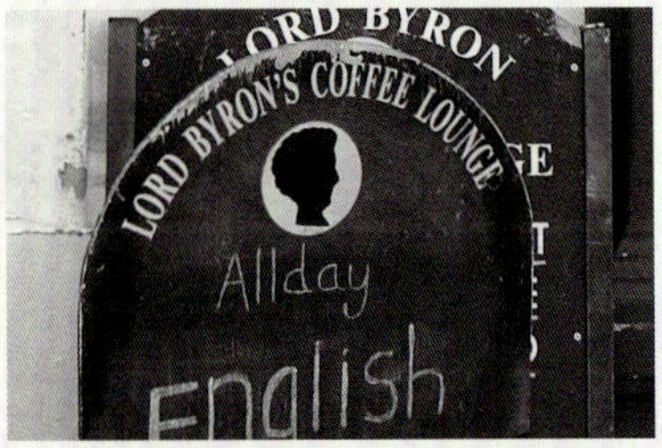

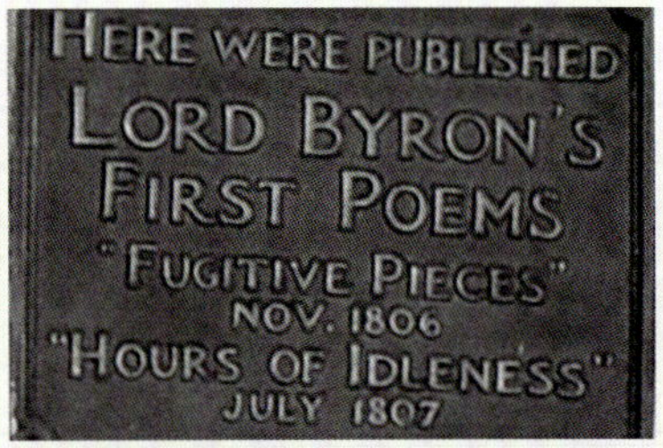

Fugitive Pieces

'Looking up from where I dropped the Chai (Life) charm I saw a sign saying; "Here were published Lord Byron's first poems 'Fugitive Pieces' 1806 'Hours of Idleness' 1807." He was 18 when he had them published and at this age he walked across this square to these printers. There have been various mystical speculations about the fact that, according to 'gematria', a Hebrew/Greek system of assigning numeric value to words for finding hidden meanings, the letters of chai add up to 18. For this reason, 18 is a spiritual number in Judaism. I often walked across the square sensing a Kabbalistic humming from the earth underneath, the chai charm as an electro-magnetic wave from below. I super-glued another chai charm in the gutter, exactly at the spot where I had dropped the first one. When I photographed this, I noticed many small pebbles all around and thought of Jewish graves on which small stones are placed. The main explanation for placing stones on the grave is to ensure that souls remain where they belong. The 'barrier' on the grave prevents the kind of haunting that formed such an important part of East European Jewish lore. '

From *Chana Dubinski, A Transpective: How Things Used To Be Now*, 2012

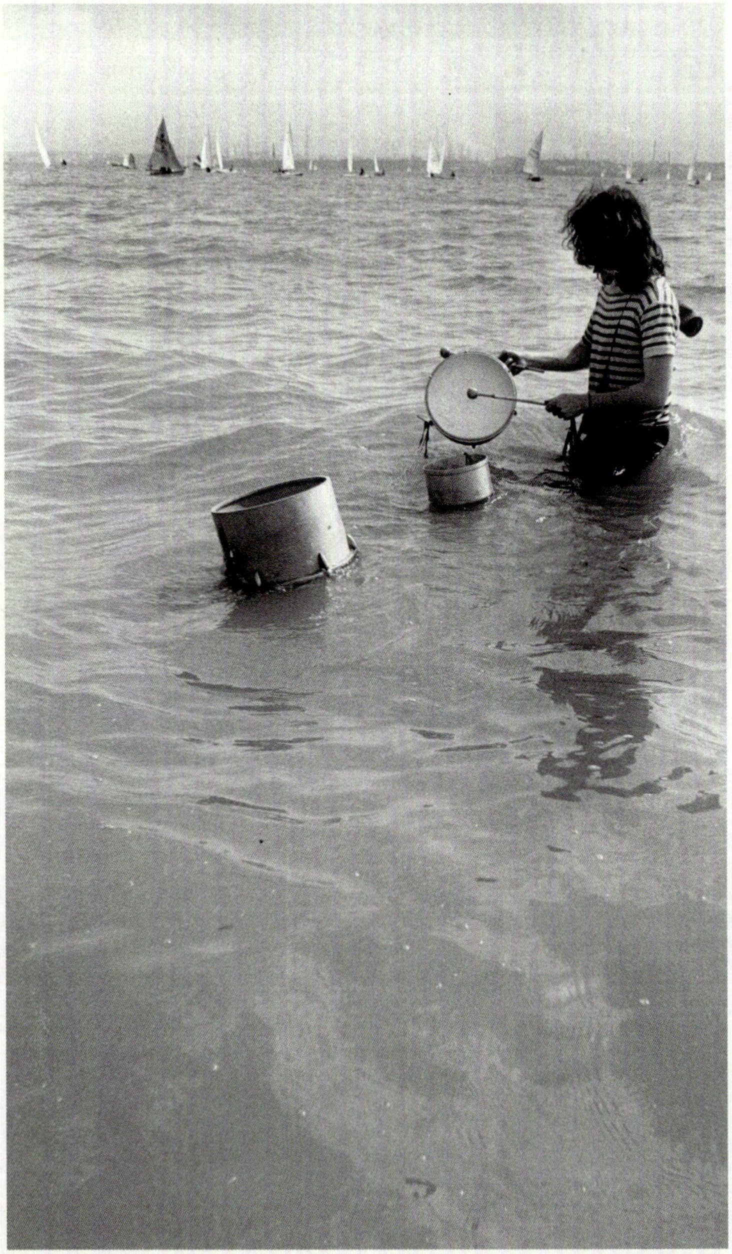

Paul Burwell, Newhaven. Photo Annabel Nicolson

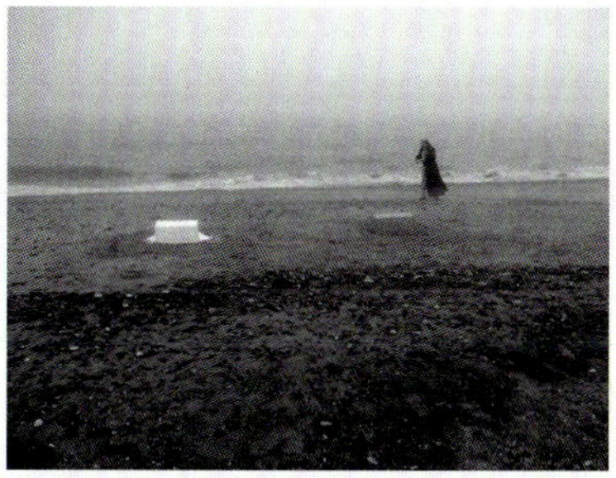

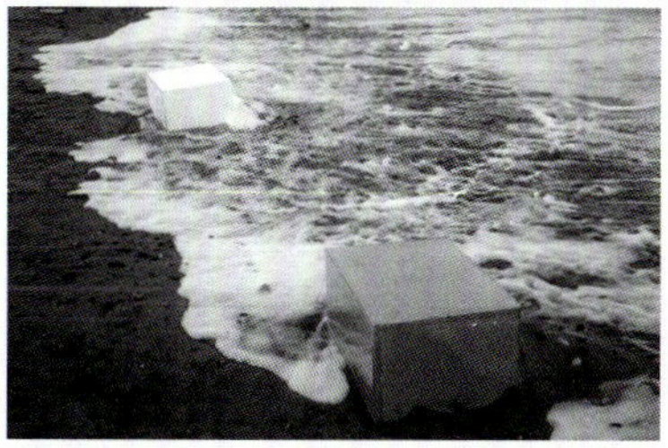

In 1972, I returned several sacks of retailed sea salt and sea sand to Peacehaven Beach, calling the action *Homecoming*.

In 1976 Paul Burwell played various instruments in the sea at Newhaven.

As part of *Autobituary*, Hull Art Lab, in 2006, at Spurn Point, combining the ideas from both these havens, I invited Paul to play instruments as the tide came in. His sounds were affected by the incoming waters, whilst the sea salt and sand, encased in perspex boxes, with an open side, disappeared to again became a part of their original seascape. The empty perspex boxes filled momentarily with box-shapes of sea water as the salt and sand dissolved and dispersed. It was our last public performance together. He died a few month later.

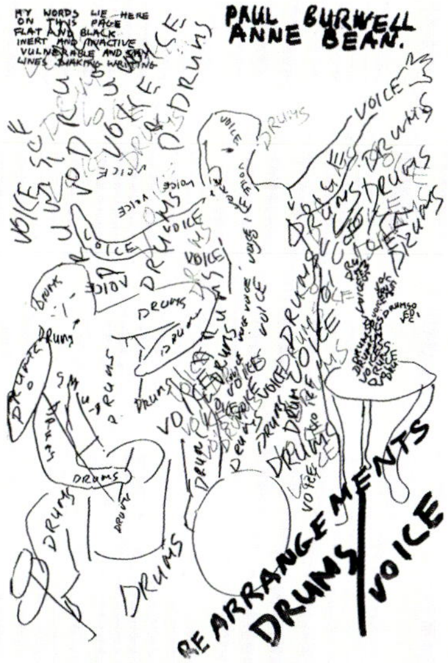

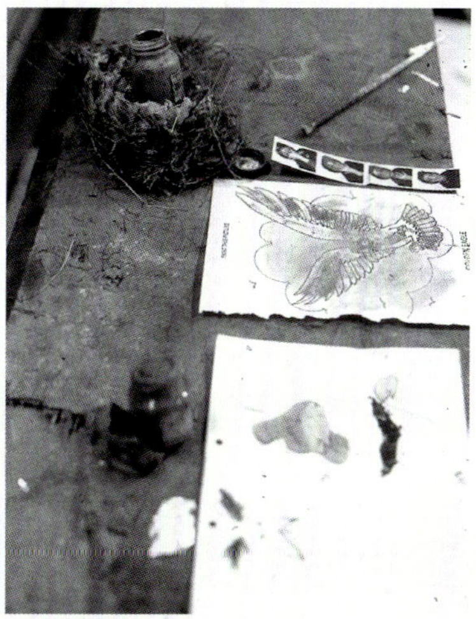

Stone Egg, Paper Eagle, Nest and 4 Witnesses, Reading 1970. A series of drawings and objects that were distinguished by coming from either the head or the heart.

Drummings and Drawings

We are interested in inter-connectivity and continuous state-change, kinetic energies and vibrations, fluid realities, the fugacious, the elusory, the evanescent. All quanta are jittery, packed with energy left over from the big bang. We are interested in unique perspectives such as how 'music' is described in Tibetan Buddhist tradition as a combination of the actually present music produced by the sound-making voices and instruments as well as the internally produced music perceived and imagined by each and every listener. We have made numerous posters and drawings reflecting these concerns.

Art works today have to be capable of radical change all the time. Good work has to change according to the circumstances out of which it arises, our changing perception of the world, social, political and economic changes and pressures, and changes within the performer. You have to follow your intuition and insight. Our work changes according to the context in which we perform, or more exactly, according to our perception and response to that circumstance.

PULp statement 1979

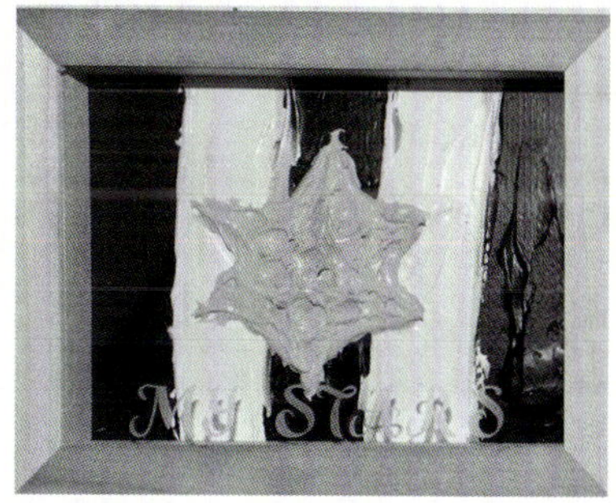

Leslie Tate in catalogue for *A Transpective* writes:

'She was part of a small Jewish community, mostly the survivors and displaced people from the genocide in central and Eastern Europe, ...

Tellingly she writes:

"This knowledge of the Holocaust made the world unsafe and any pretence of civilization utterly hypocritical. In some perverse way it liberated me because I felt I had to make my own rules in this world I mistrusted."

Her works *Starry Day* and *Starry Night* as well as *My Stars and Stripes* capture her young self's attempts to somehow confront this. She made many versions in different media of *My Stars and Stripes* when applying to Cape Town University in 1968. The yellow star that Jewish people were forced to wear and the striped concentration camp uniform, responded to Jasper John's *Flag*, living in the same ambiguous territory: "Is this a flag or a painting?" ..."Is this a trauma or a painting?"'

pp. 158-9: Anne Bean, *Self-Portrait*, 1974. Photos taken by Anne Bean round her head. The initial idea was for a performance with a Polaroid camera (Reading 1973), making a photographic self-portrait during the work

pp. 160-1: Anne Bean, *Self Etc.*, 2017. Photos: Hugo Glendinning

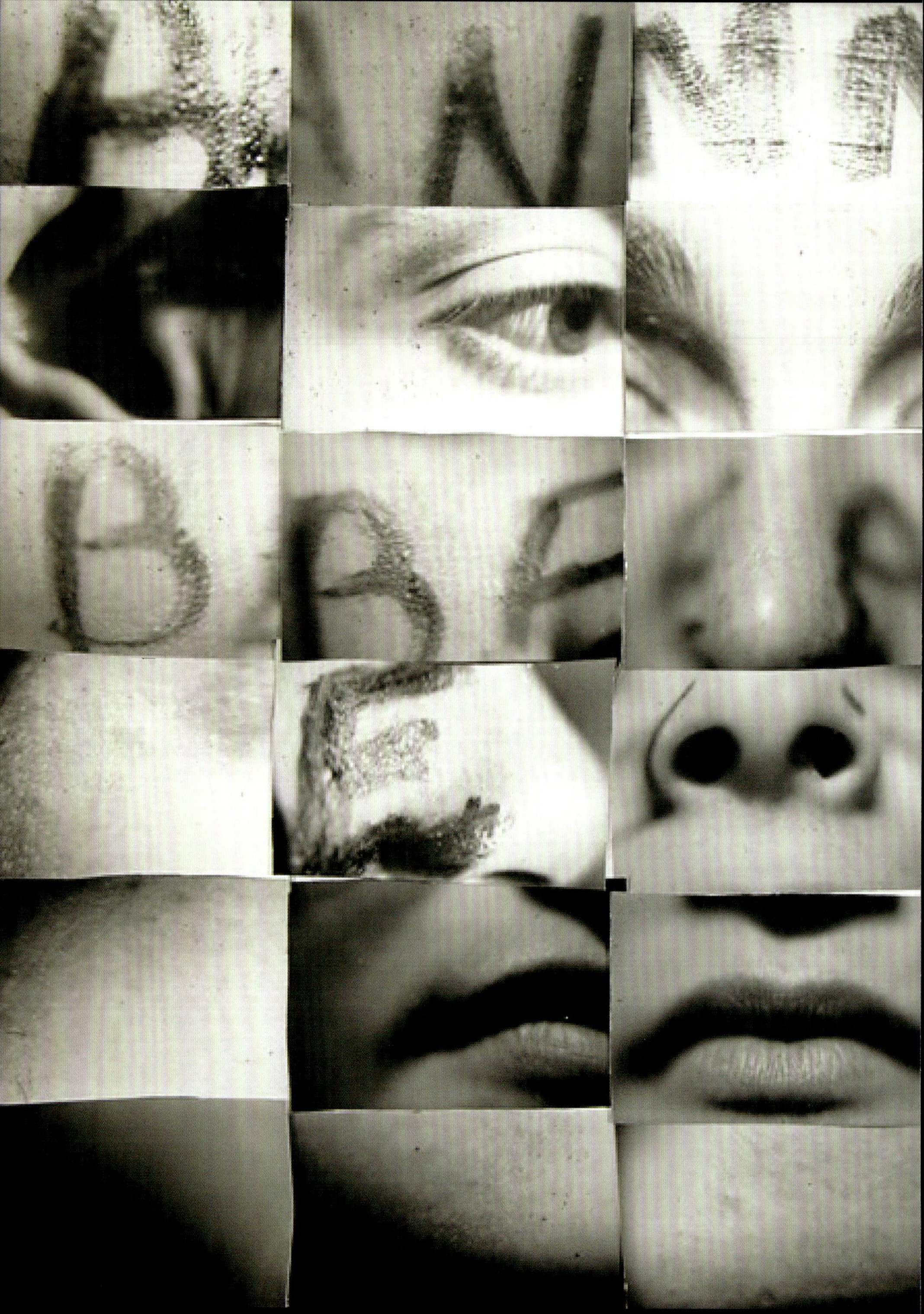

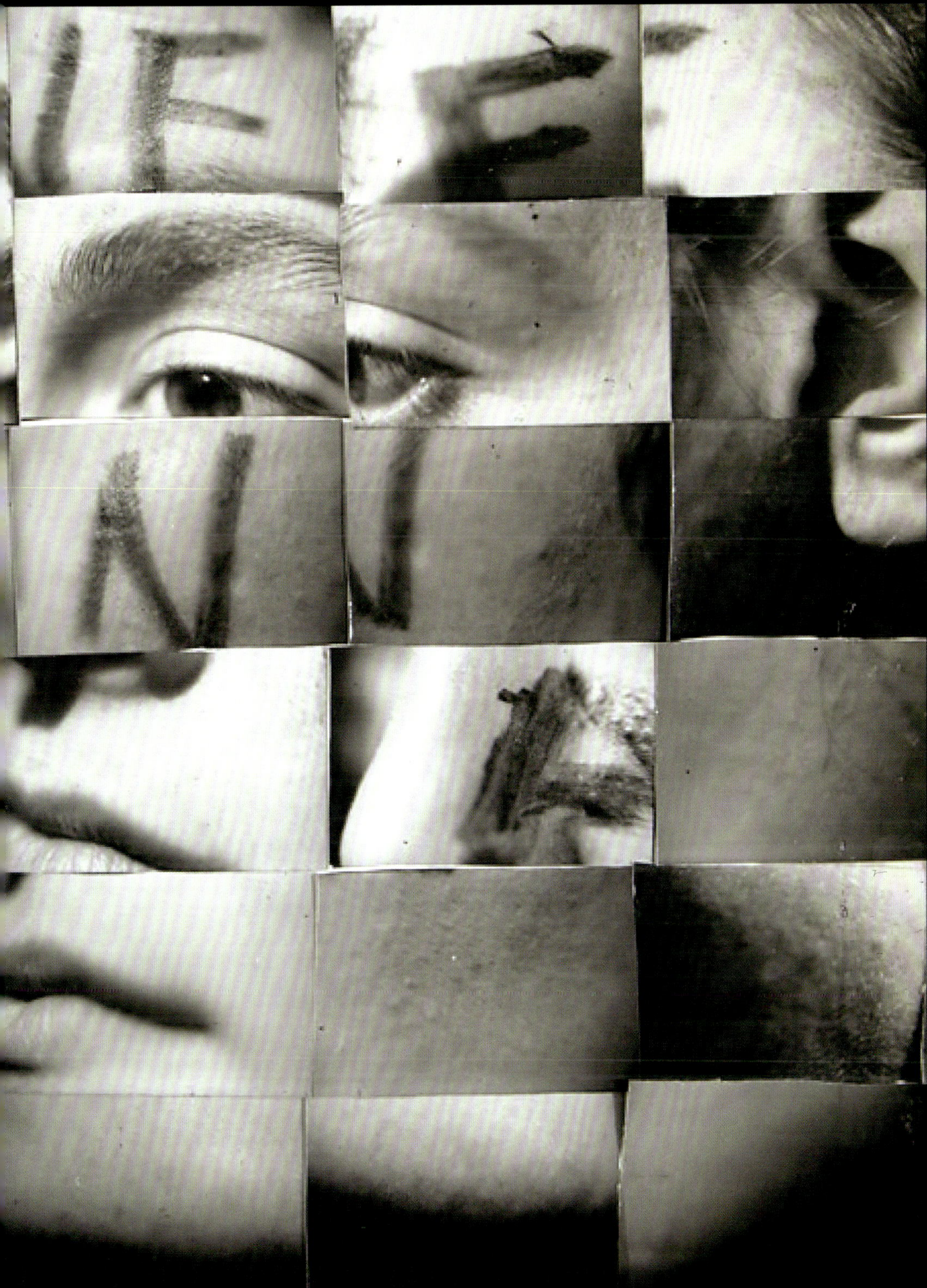

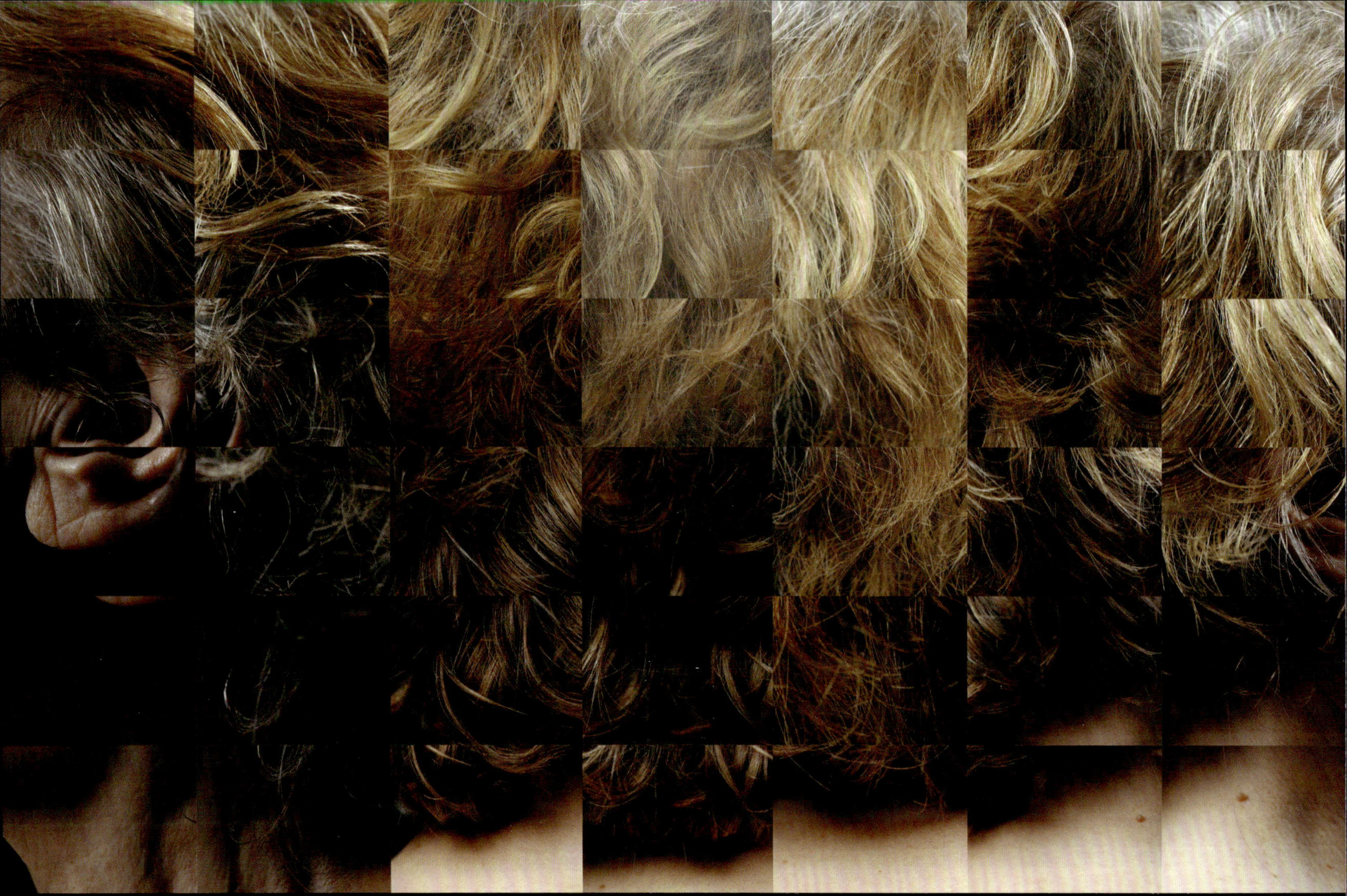

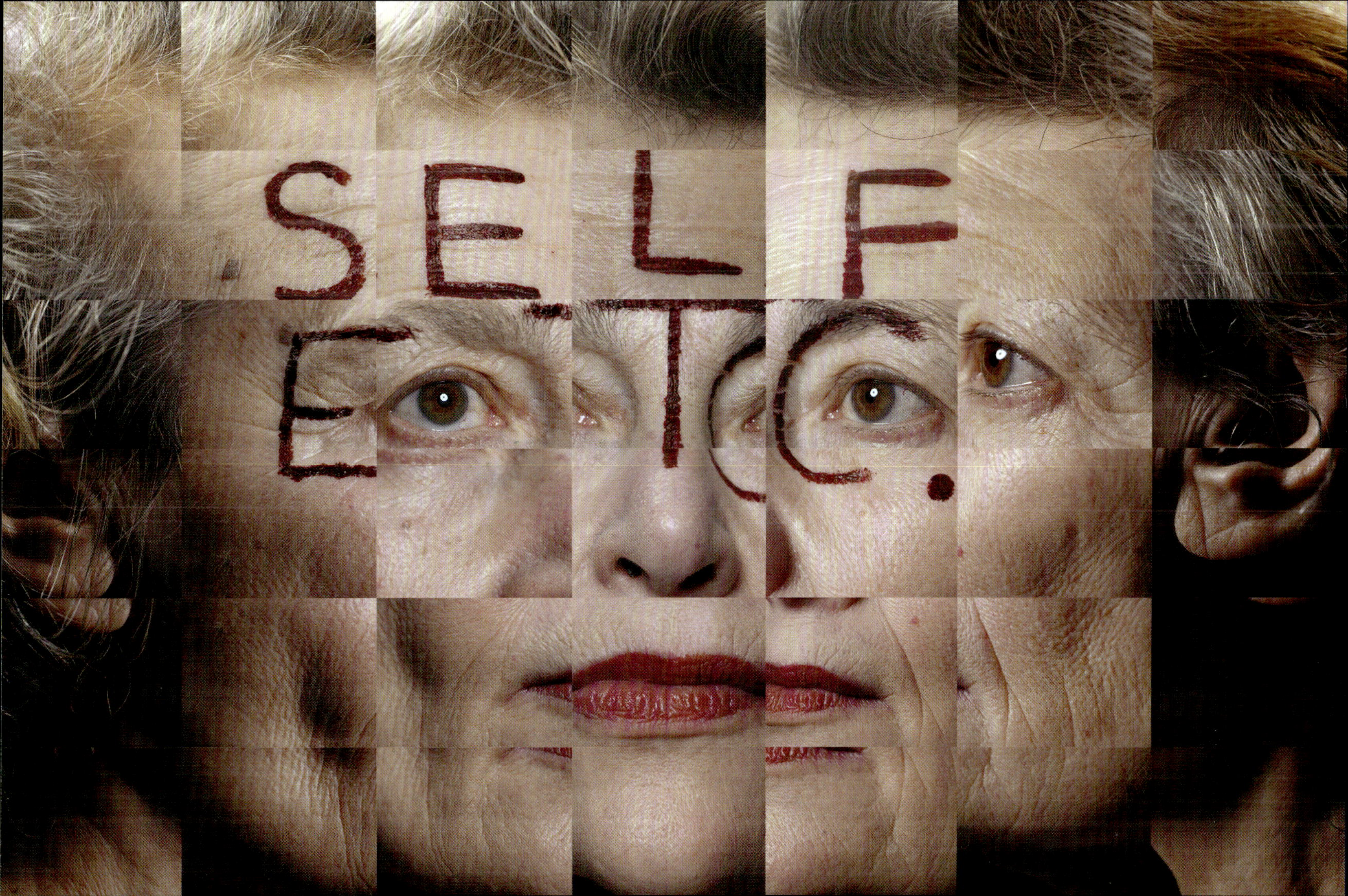
SELF
ETC.

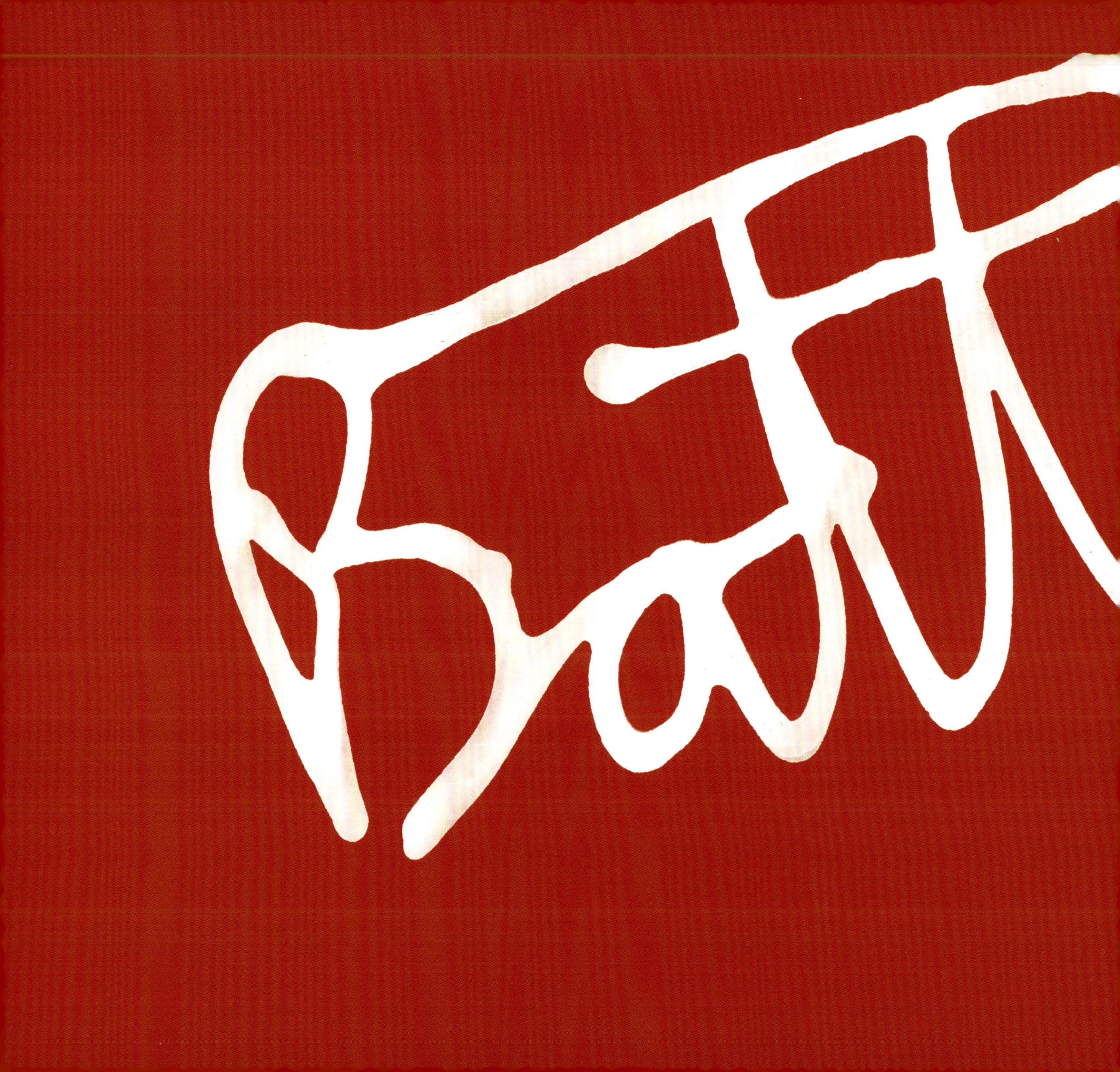

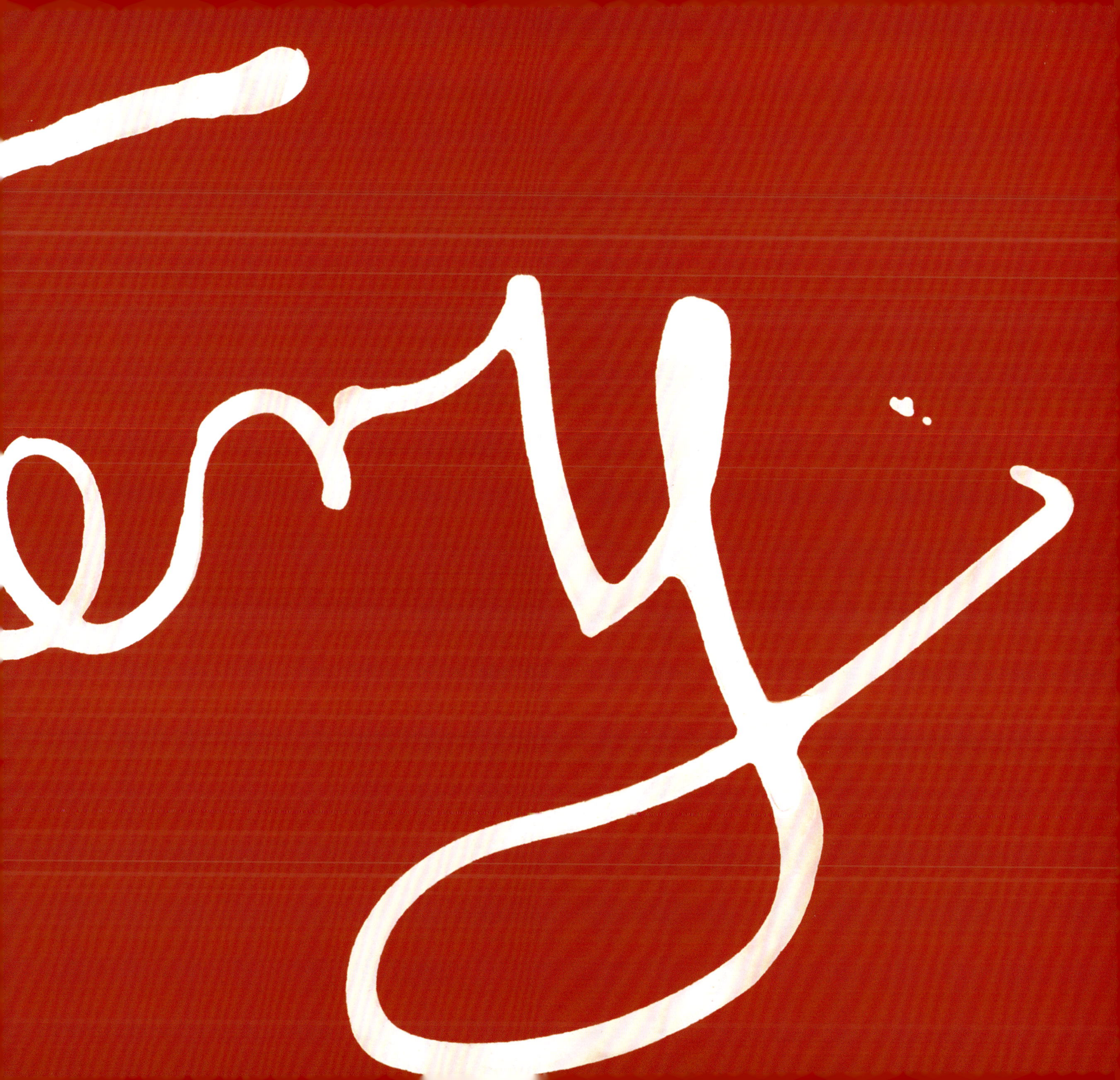

THE AUDIENCE AS BATTERY: AN INTERVIEW WITH ANNE BEAN

ROB LA FRENAIS

Rob La Frenais *Why are you called Anne Bean?*

Anne Bean In some way Chana Dubinski, the name I used and had intended to carry on using when I left London a few years ago for what became the *Transpective* project, came before Anne Bean. It's that old story of emigrants arriving somewhere and having their identity reshaped for them.

RLF *Where did Bean come from?*

AB It's lost in the mists. My uncle thought it was given at immigration. They were probably saying Du-Bean-Ski. My family arrived in England from Russia. This name always had a mythology to me. When I went to Hebrew school as a small child, Chana was my Hebrew name. So I always had this Chana Dubinski feeling alongside Anne Bean and it felt very much like Anne Bean was like a symbol name, a Wittgenstein demystification of what a word is.

RLF *So she didn't come from nowhere. So when I'm talking to you now who am I talking to?*

AB You are speaking to a human being who happens to be called Anne Bean – it's convenient basically. I don't want to get mystical about it but we do get tied to our material selves too forcefully. It makes very little difference in terms of mortality or immortality if this name Anne Bean lives in any way, just the energies I've forged. Fundamentally I lived happily only calling myself Chana Dubinski for a couple of years and now I'm happy that I am called Anne Bean.

RLF *When do you consider you made your first work of art? Would it have been in Africa, where you spent your childhood, or Reading where you studied art?*

AB I painted from when I was very young, taking over a part of our garage to use as a 'studio' when I was about 10. I recognise, looking from my current perspective, that these paintings are equally part of my 'art' trajectory as are many transformative 'life' moments from that time. For instance, I read the autobiography of the deaf/blind American author/activist Helen Keller at around that age and was deeply impacted by her describing her first recognition of language when W-A-T-E-R was written on her hand with water. She spoke of exhilaration as objects suddenly 'quivered with life'. Attempting to get into her consciousness was powerful. Late one night I switched off the lights in our bathroom and wrote many words on my hand with cold water. In the darkness and silence I experienced that sense of some primal connectivity outside of hearing and seeing and way beyond the darkness of our bathroom – an expanded reading of the universe.

RLF *Any other memories from this time?*

AB I spent much of my childhood with black Africans in Zambia and I appreciate more and more this very different space/time and viewpoint that this connection gifted me. I was a foundation student in the Fine Art Department of Cape Town University in the late 1960s, where the obviously completely malignant political and social environment made it meaningless to be drawing skulls, fruit and flowers, however sensitively.

RLF *How did you respond to the situation of apartheid?*

AB I had never heard of performance art but I made an action that I thought of as a visual protest sitting on a 'Whites Only' bench with the palms of my hands painted black and displayed outwards.

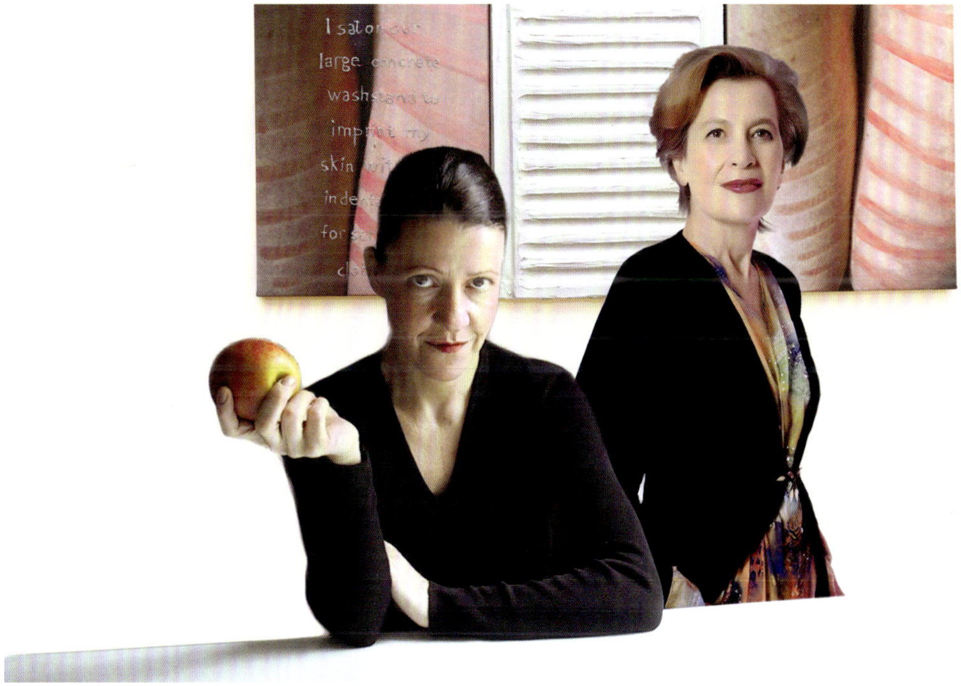

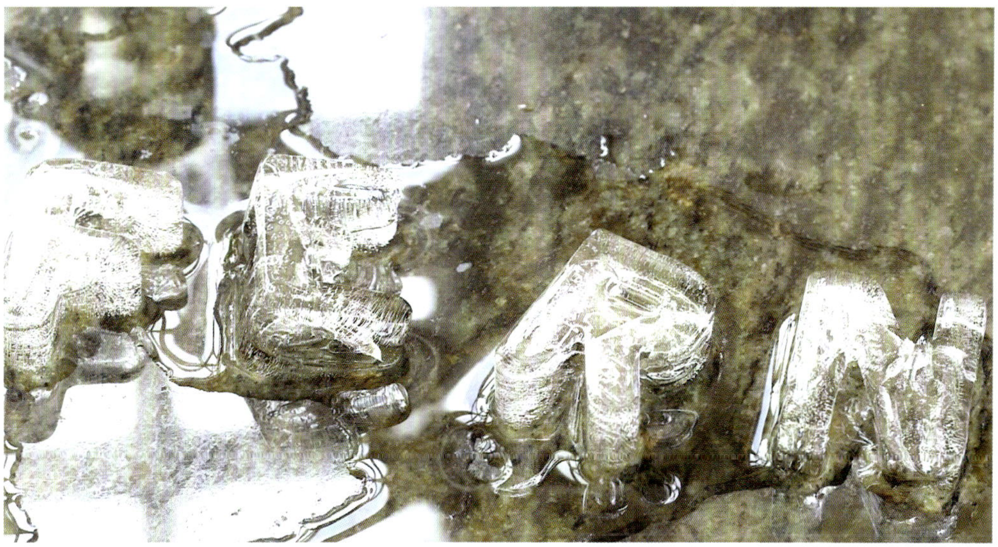

Top: Chana Dubinski with Gioia Meller Marcovicz, the designer and curator of *A Transpective*, Venice, in front of *Deep Impressions*, 2013. Photo: Janusz Podrazik

Bottom: Chana Dubinski and Alice Oswald, still from *Evaporations*, a film shown at Southbank Centre, London as part of National Poetry Day, November 2013 and subsequent film festivals. Chana Dubinski was commissioned by the director of the Poetry Society, Judith Palmer, to work in collaboration with the poet Alice Oswald on a film/poem

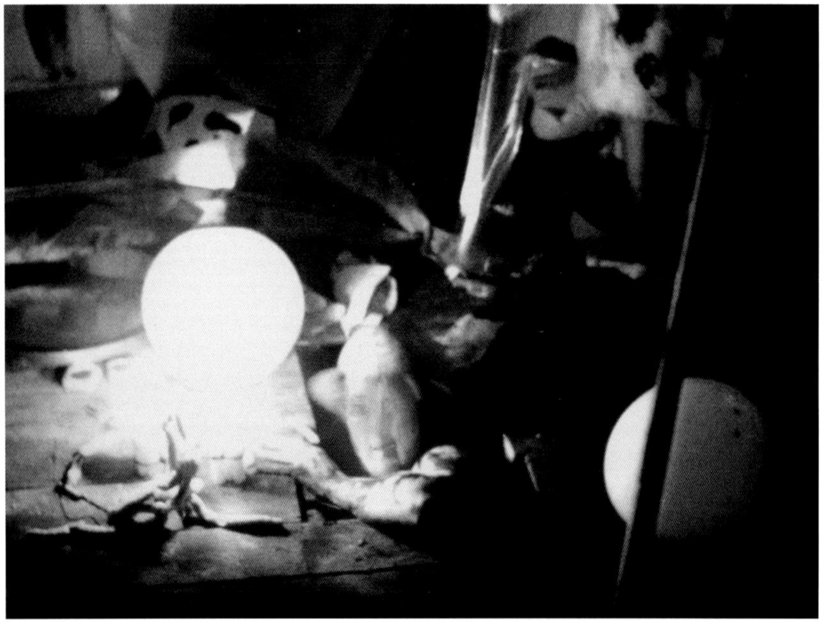

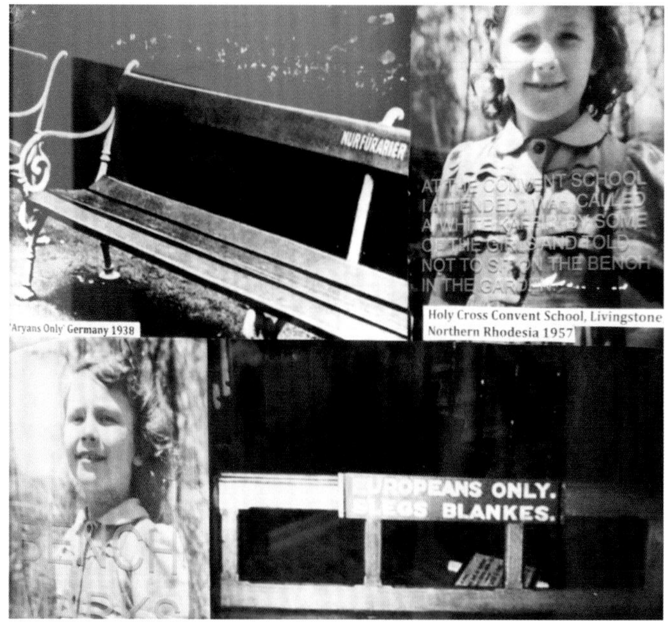

Left: Crawling between sawed and macheted floorboards in Anne Bean, Paul Burwell and Paul McCarthy, *Two Ps and a Bean*, London, 1983. Photo: Linda Frye Burnham

Right: Chana Dubinski, *Benchmarks: Victim and Perpetrator, both Unchosen, Unwanted, Abhorrent*, part of *A Transpective: How Things Used To Be Now*, 2012

I see my work as an ongoing work-in-progress where these life/art moments are as strong a part of the whole as recognisable physical 'capturings'.

RLF *Would you say the Moodies, which you started in the early 1970s, and which was featured in the* Sunday Times Magazine *in 1974, was the first genuine artists' band?*

AB I don't believe in 'firsts'. I think there is a shared zeitgeist that we give and take from. We certainly received a huge amount of attention at the time and I was delighted that we could work in many contexts from art galleries, Dingwalls and other clubs and theatres to doing a *Spare Rib* benefit, whilst being called 'an insolent spangled harem' by the *Financial Times*. The name of the group was actually Moody and the Menstruators, starting in 1971 at an art department party. I had aimed as Anne Archy for a harsher, more raw feel – white bloodstained pants.

RLF *Are people aware of the Moodies now?*

AB Strangely, at the very moment I am answering this, a film is being shown in NY of the Moodies with this quote on the invite by Michael Bracewell: 'like performance art test pilots – the principal strands of British art rock, "avant-cocktail" pose groups, punk and post-punk. Referencing the artistic/musical cabarets of the Dadaists and Futurists, the group take their place on a musical timeline somewhere between the Bonzo Dog Doo-Dah Band and The Sex Pistols.'

RLF *Who were the members and where are they now?*

AB Rod Melvin continues to play piano and compose and has collaborated with Brian Eno, Lindsay Kemp, Ian Dury and Richard O'Brien amongst many. Annie Sloan runs the international company, Annie Sloan Interiors in Oxford. Polly Eltes became a world renowned model, sang with Can and is now a photographer. Mary Anne Holliday and Suzy Adderley continue their art practices within an activism mindset. Hermine Demoriane, who sometimes performed alongside the Moodies walking the tightrope, is still making performances.

RLF *With reference to the 1983 performance* Two P's and a Bean, *a very powerful event which involved yourself, Paul McCarthy and the late Paul Burwell partially demolishing an abandoned house in the East End, with the audience standing inside it, you have referred to the notion of the 'audience as battery'. Could you expand on this?*

AB 'The audience as battery' was a general feeling that I had in relation to performance at the time of 'plugging in' to the energy of a situation and riding it. I have always felt that the 'between-space' offered by collaboration, an activation and sparking of possible selves, was permissive, liberating and often electrifying and the audience was a furthering element in this collaborative situation.

RLF *How did the performance come about?*

AB I had met Paul McCarthy in Los Angeles in the late 1970s and when he and Linda Frye Burnham (founder of *High Performance* magazine) approached Paul Burwell and myself for him to do a London performance, Paul Burwell and I contacted several galleries and organisations and no one was interested.

We decided to use the derelict house next door to us in Bow, in which we would each take a room as our own but find ways physically and metaphysically to come together. I broke through the floor and ceiling above Paul Burwell's drum-kit showering debris and enormous glass ball lights over his drum kit, making thunderous sounds until he erected an umbrella, as a machete came flying through. I pushed a tube into the room and sung through it into the space and then entered the room from above, played his drums whilst he climbed a ladder and broke through the glass windows into Paul McCarthy's space, who then ran into the room that I had abandoned to spray it in ketchup.

RLF *It felt like a pretty risky situation to me.*

AB The audience inevitably were caught up in the mayhem, running for cover, not knowing which way to go, what to see, what floor would give way, what glass would fly, what staircase was safe. We all – both performers and audience – genuinely had to have our wits honed and alert and, seemingly antithetically, this is often the safest as well as the most enlivening situation we can be in on our planet.

RLF *So, in* Two P's and a Bean *there was a palpable sense of danger. In the Bow Gamelan Ensemble there was almost a replicable, but unpredictable sense of danger. There were lyrical parts, sure, but I think there were also moments where we were reminded of the hazardous moments experienced during performances by the late Stephen Cripps. Was this deliberate or random?*

AB Three images flashed immediately into my head. A performance in late 1970s with Paul Burwell and Stephen Cripps where I put record players with *Low Flying Aircraft* (a single I recorded with Paul) on Bunsen burners melting and distorting sounds, whilst Steve set-off exploding cymbals and Paul drummed flaming paraffin.

With Richard Wilson and Paul, 1978, drumming on a boat under Tower Bridge, playing the echoes, whilst I swam with flashing torches, shouting into the abyss, getting swept under cross-currents. Paul and I on Bankside, well before it was even a glimmer in Tate's eyes, shooting vast pyrotechnics up and around the chimney. And many more deliberately random actions...

RLF *How did you reach the idea that you would follow the line of the UK total solar eclipse of 1999 in three boats full of artists and young people from Tower Hamlets, with cosmologist Marcus Chown and the art-science organisation The Arts Catalyst?*

AB I heard Marcus Chown, the cosmology consultant for *New Scientist* magazine, talking about his book *Afterglow of Creation* (1993), on the radio in mid-1990s. He explained how the detection of cosmic radiation was identified as the afterglow of the Big Bang. I was fascinated when he said that any body, at any temperature above absolute zero, emits radio waves. I had been looking into thermal imaging at the time with a new technologies fund, the ICA/Toshiba Art and Innovation Commission, on a work called *Radiant Fields* (1998). When I met up with Marcus, he was fired up with the upcoming total solar eclipse and all the observations, scientific and otherwise, that could be made during that. It stimulated my imagination and I realised that it could be a trigger for many different minds and approaches. Marcus felt that the optimum positioning for us would be from boats in the English Channel.

RLF *Who took part?*

AB I went on to invite around 30 very varied people on a voyage together to chase that shadow, with artists including Tomoko Takahashi, David Cunningham, Judith Goddard, Hayley Newman, scientists and teenagers from Tower Hamlets Summer University and from the Royal National Institute for the Blind's New College in Worcester. I asked everyone to make a one-minute film of their experience, which became *Seaclipse – Sharing a Shadow* (1999).

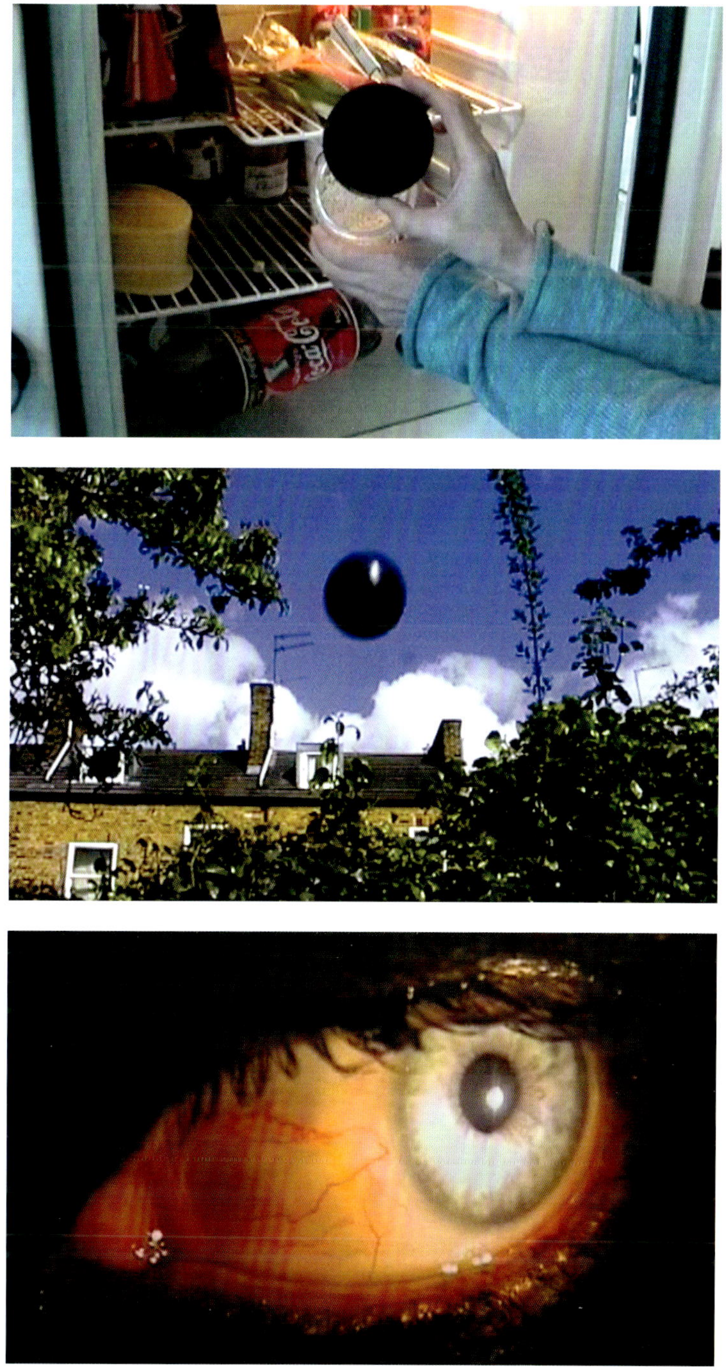

Anne Bean, *Seaclipse: Sharing a Shadow*, stills from videos by (*top to bottom*): Tomoko Takahashi, Hayley Newman, and Mo Tomany

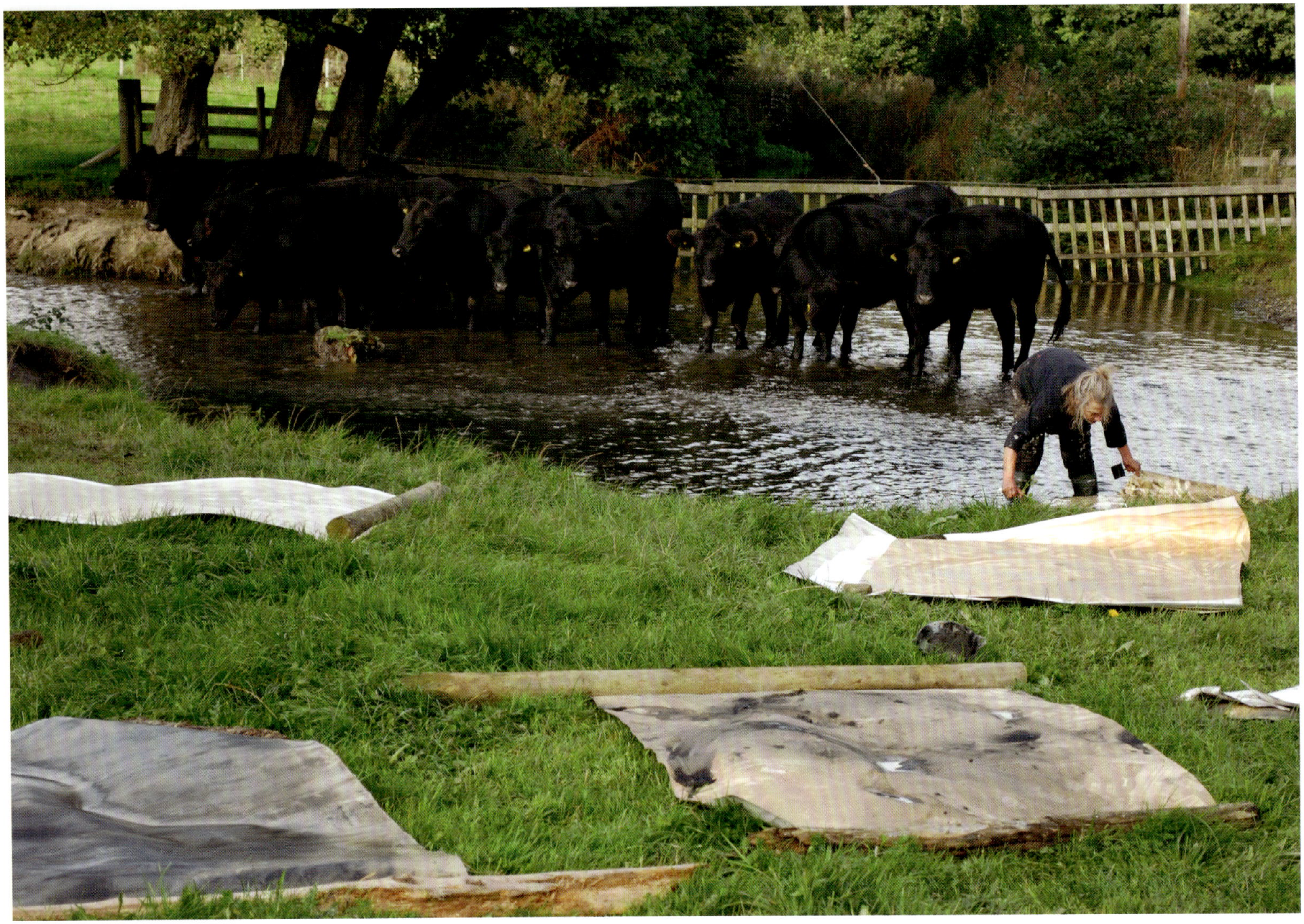

Above: Anne Bean making *Riverbed*, Sidney Nolan Trust, The Rodd, Presteigne, Powys, 2016. Inspired by Sidney Nolan's series *Riverbend*, these works were made from the clay of Hindwell Brook on the Nolan estate

Opposite: Using the studio where Nolan had made much of his later work, Bean's large paintings and smaller works were made and exhibited there. Photos: Anthony Plant

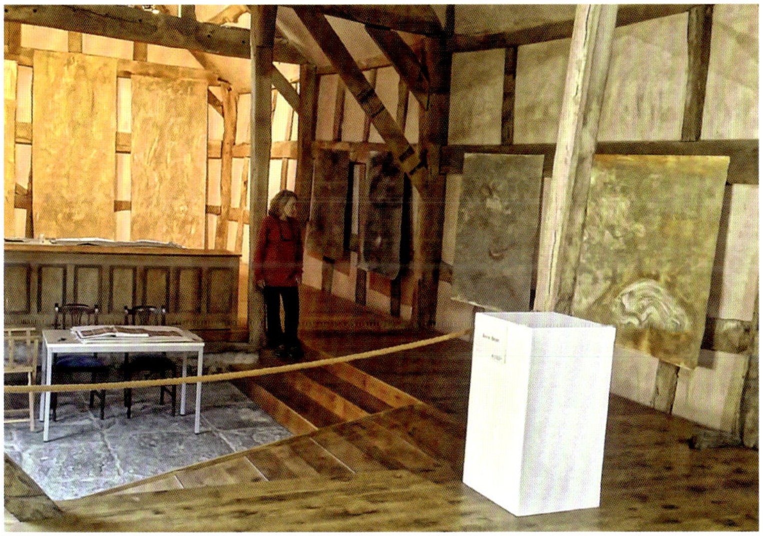

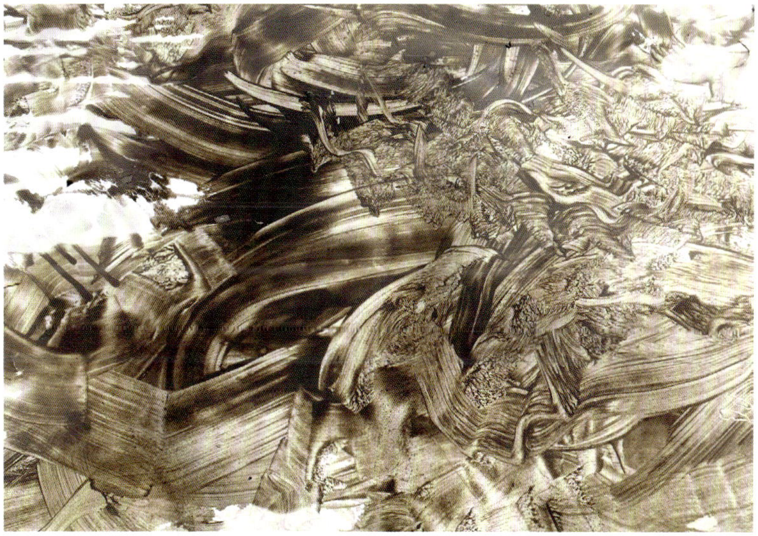

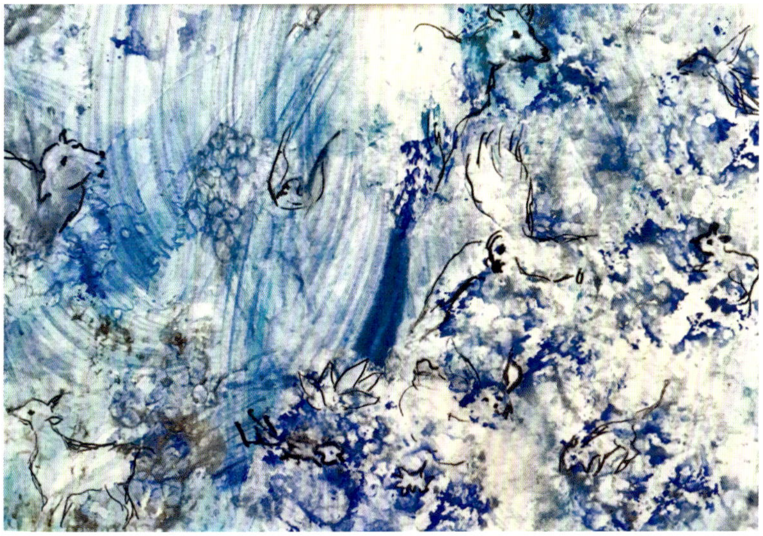

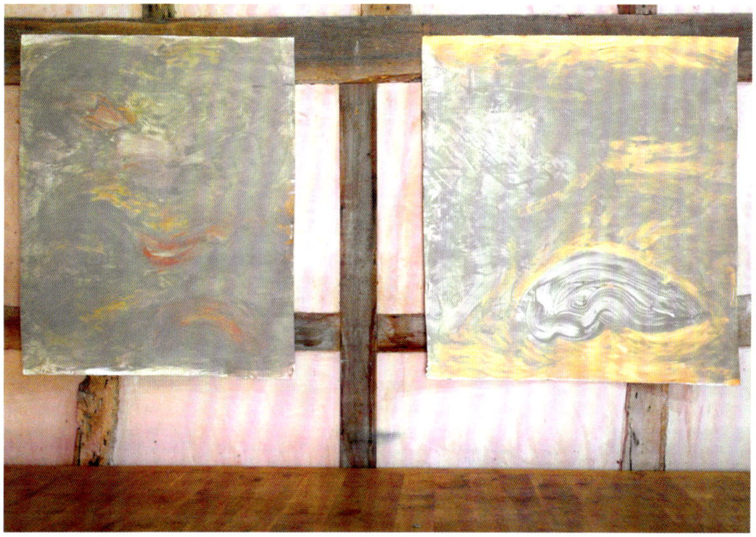

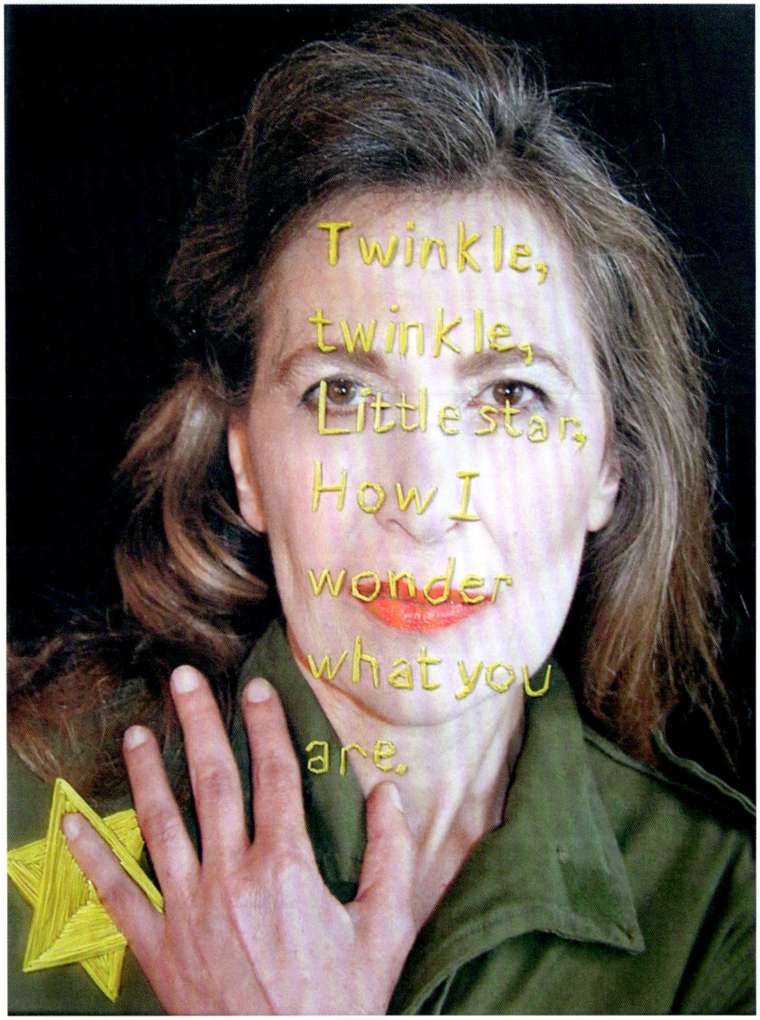

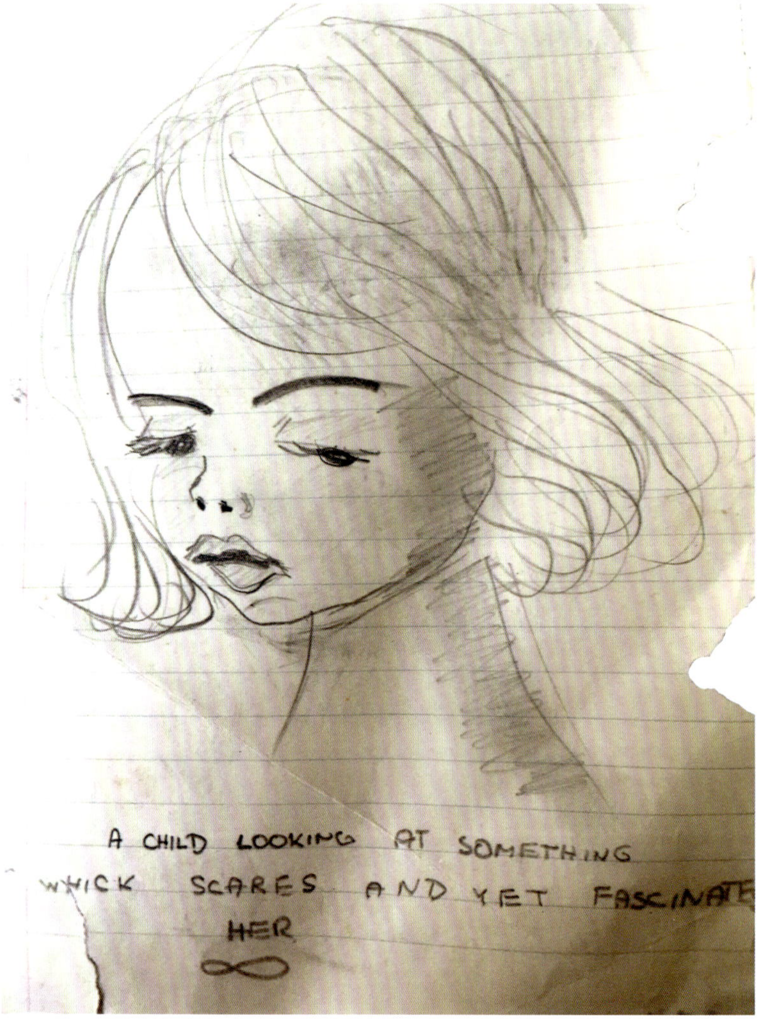

Left: Chana Dubinski, *How I Wonder What You Are*, from *A Transpective: How Things Used To Be Now*, 2012. Photo: Kelly Summers

Right: Anne Bean, childhood drawing, 1958

pp. 173-4: Chana Dubinski, *The Quick*, from *A Transpective*, cushions in Riverside Cottage, Newark, 2012

It inspired many later works of mine including a drawing called *Eclipse* (2004-5), which I made over a one-year period of the sun casting a shadow of a globe of the world whilst I drew around this moving shadow. I had worked with shadows from very early on, including in Belgium, 1972, making a moving bicycle shadow drawing, when Genesis P-Orridge, Cosey Fanni Tutti, Robin Klassnik, the Kipper Kids and myself made works together and separately.

RLF *So you lived as Chana Dubinski as an art project. How were you able to live as another person for a year and a half? What was the setup? What were the rules?*

AB I didn't see myself as another person or an alter ego or any of those terms – or even see it as an art project. I saw myself manifesting much more of the being that I intimately recognised, away from the 'shape' that life, friends and oneself holds one in. I was thinking about where art was going and if I can carry on with performance: how do you break through the boundaries, make a piece where you are not sure whether this is life or not life? I was thinking about people who told me they had been believers but had lost their faith. Some spoke of how the tenets of their religious life shifted into simply living a loving life, which felt much more attuned and fulfilling. I was thinking about this in terms of art, as a sort of *a-artist* as opposed to *a-theist*. I was also thinking about the fact you make agreements with art and with the sort of person and artist you are when you're very young, so you could be hijacked for a life-sentence by your much younger self. At the time, I wrote this text:

> The more provocative and stimulating position is not that 'everyone is an artist' but 'no-one is an artist' and that the 'art' space is implicitly part of living. This undefined, open, permissive exploration that art claims then becomes part of the everyday. Art and life lose the disjuncture by declaring oneself an a-artist. Too many art end-games have played out for over a century and there now has to be a real shift.

RLF *Take me into that moment when you arrived in Newark and you were Chana.*

AB I left with a suitcase, I left with a name. I decided I must not stay in a hotel or a bed and breakfast. I must live as cheaply as possible and the whole thing must be led by chance. So I had no idea where I was going except I wanted to be in the North, in England, I didn't want any problems with language, and I wanted to feel some kind of knowing unknowing. It would be enough difference to just give some frisson but not to adapt to a whole new culture.

RLF *Did you choose Newark for a reason?*

AB Very much for a reason. I set off by bus from Norfolk and I actually spent three months peripatetically. Before I set off, a friend of mine gave me a little gold charm from his late mother, which was a Hebrew letter which means 'life'. Although I didn't know his mother I felt very close to some presence. I stopped in Newark, a town I didn't know at all and was buying a baked potato in the marketplace. I took out money to pay and this little amulet dropped into a guttering. It was such a shock to me. I felt like some crack in the universe had opened, an unravelling of some kabbalistic tryst.

RLF *You'd been carrying this amulet for three months?*

AB For three months, and travelling all over and somehow I felt a real sense of belonging and duty, responsibility.

RLF *So that's how you got to Newark?*

AB Dropping it. I got hold of the council, we tried to open the gutter. We couldn't. I decided the only way to stay close to this amulet was by staying there.

RLF *So there was no other reason you should end up there?*

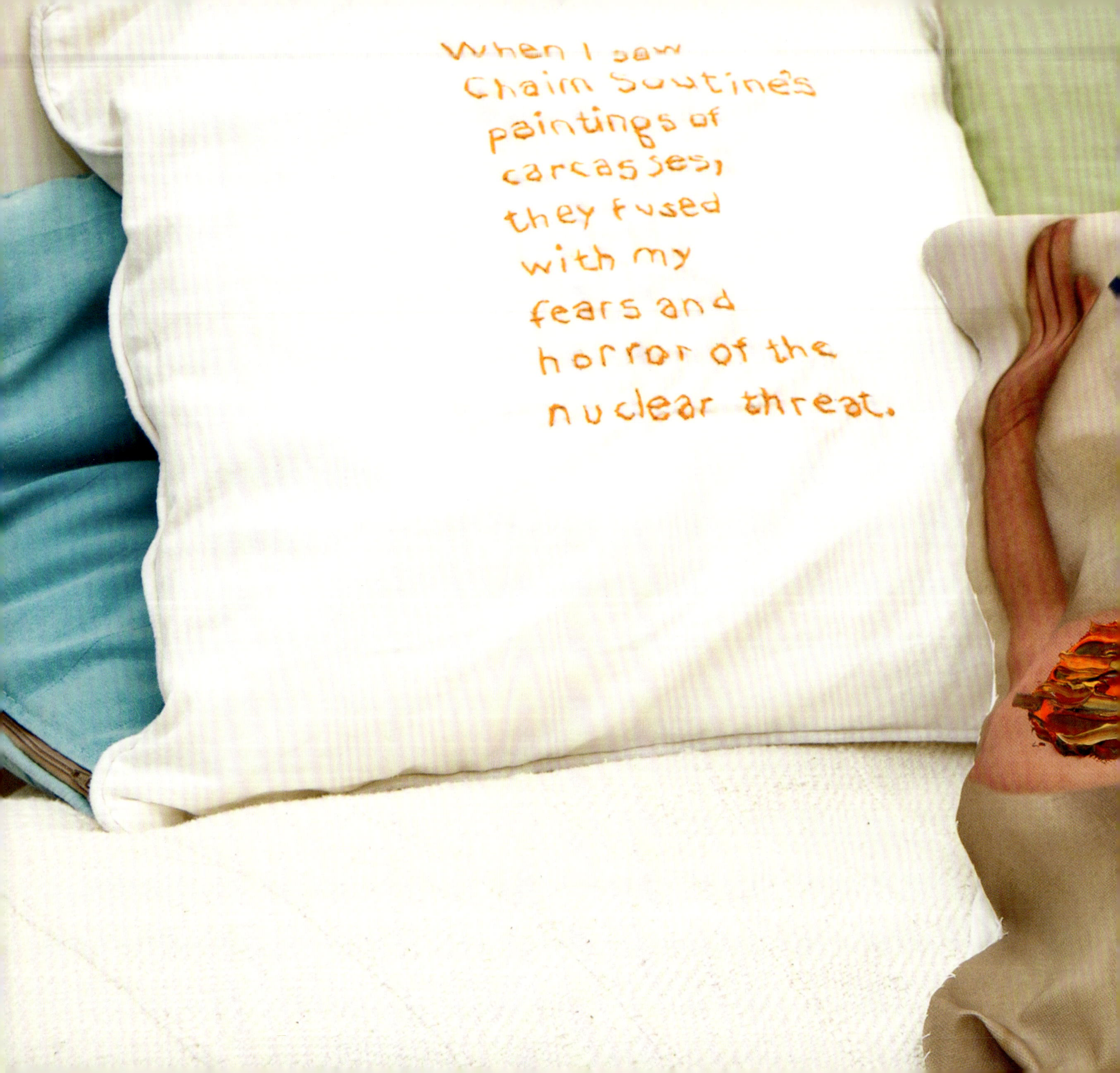
When I saw
Chaim Soutine's
paintings of
carcasses,
they fused
with my
fears and
horror of the
nuclear threat.

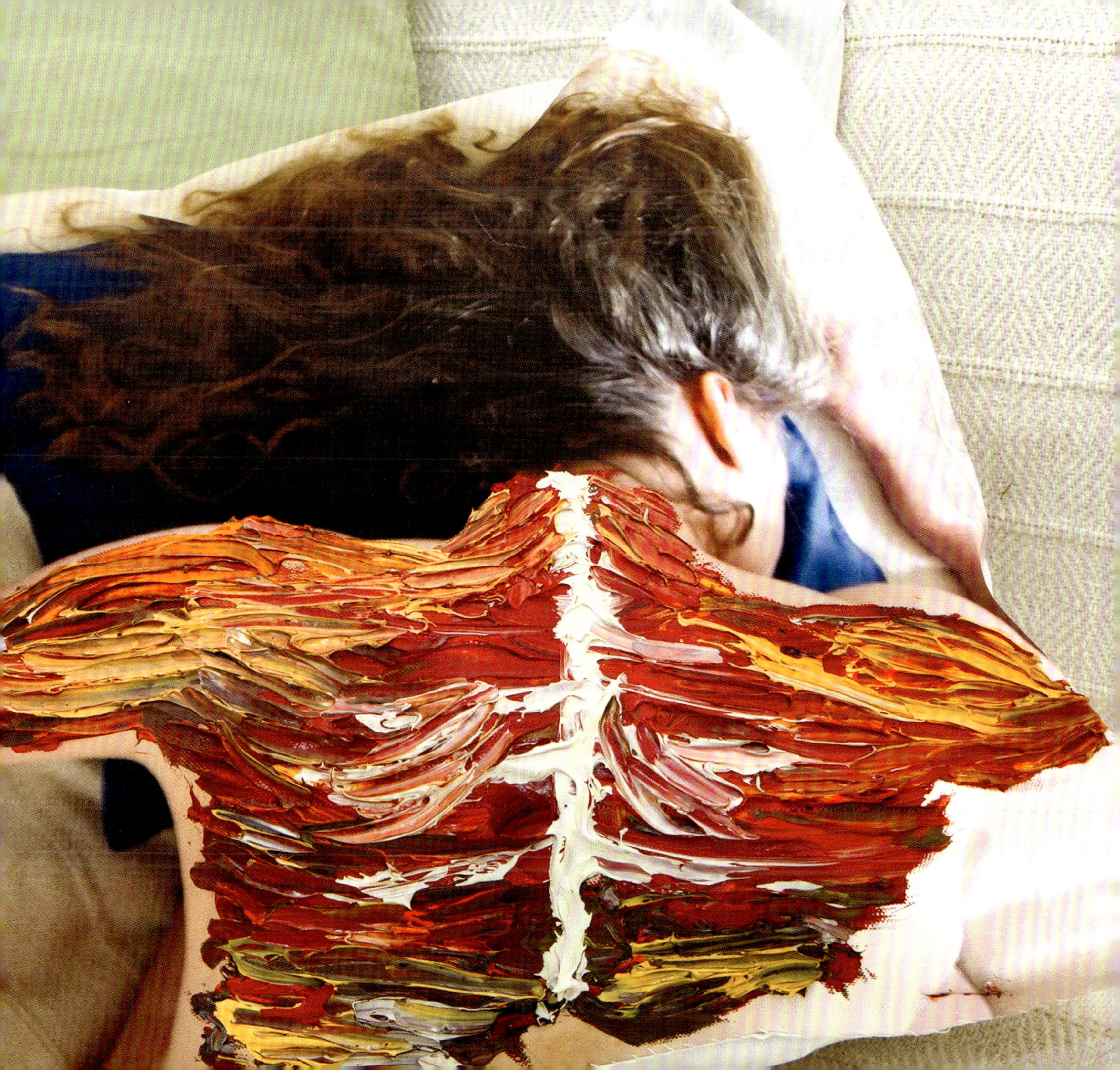

AB None whatsoever. But it's lovely that Newark means 'New Work'. I must say the first morning of the project I woke up and really thought, 'I'm going completely crazy'. It was really like a blank. I did have, for the first time since being an adolescent, an overwhelming existential weirdness. I mean I wanted it but at the same time it's a bit like when you take drugs and suddenly realise you don't want this to be happening and you know there is nothing to be done.

RLF *Was there an escape clause?*

AB No, and I knew that. And I'm very wilful. I couldn't. There was nothing.

RLF *Was there a de-escape clause? Could you have carried on forever?*

AB I didn't think about it before but I certainly thought about it during. Certainly subsequently when I realised my Anne Bean life was so punctured and so perceptively different. The other was more real for me at that moment.

RLF *Practically, did you have to have different bank accounts and so on?*

AB It's extremely difficult. I had to have a letter written by someone who knew me as Anne Bean to rent a flat. I have a cheque for a creative writing prize for Chana Dubinski, which I have never been able to cash. I think I could have found a strategy of legitimising Chana, as I became more known.

RLF *Did anyone suspect what you were doing?*

AB Strangely enough, this woman who led a creative writing group that I was in (I joined a lot of societies) gave us a project to have a pen and paper by our bed and write when we woke up. When I read out my text she was obviously perplexed, even suspicious. Maybe she thought I was some kind of journalist.

RLF *I am surprised more people didn't.*

AB Many people were puzzled, curious, but with this woman, whom I had befriended, it was the first time I got this sense of betrayal. She was pondering a situation she could not fathom, I suppose because my writing was raw and confrontational, maybe frightening, possibly embarrassing and she wasn't sure how to deal with it

RLF *Had you thought through the moral and ethical limits in this?*

AB I thought, I'm not going to get close enough to people to let that become problematic, but I did. But then the disintegration happened when I got back to London. There was a real crunch time of where am I? What am I? I was in a twilight zone.

RLF *How did you leave?*

AB I put on an exhibition, *A Transpective* [2012], in the cottage where I lived, and there was an odd private view of parallel tracks reaching the vanishing point, with some people calling me Anne, some Chana. My previous life had disintegrated. At that point I thought I didn't want to become an art sacrificial lamb.

RLF *So Anne Bean came back?*

AB Yes, although the Newark situation had inspired a further idea of collaborations with strangers.

RLF *Trowbridge was picked out of a hat at a ceremony you organised at Matt's Gallery in East London. How did that town react to being picked at random for a site of a contemporary art space?*

AB On the evening of Chinese New Year, 2014, I placed the names of 80 small towns in England in fortune cookies and Robin Klassnik pulled out Trowbridge. I instantly left the gallery at that point to drive to Trowbridge and find a space to be called MoCa (Moments of Consciousness and).

RLF *How did you go about undertaking the work?*

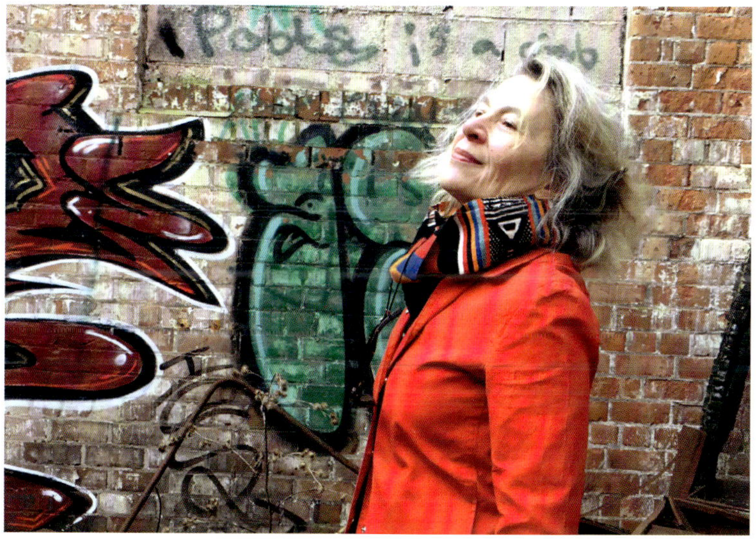

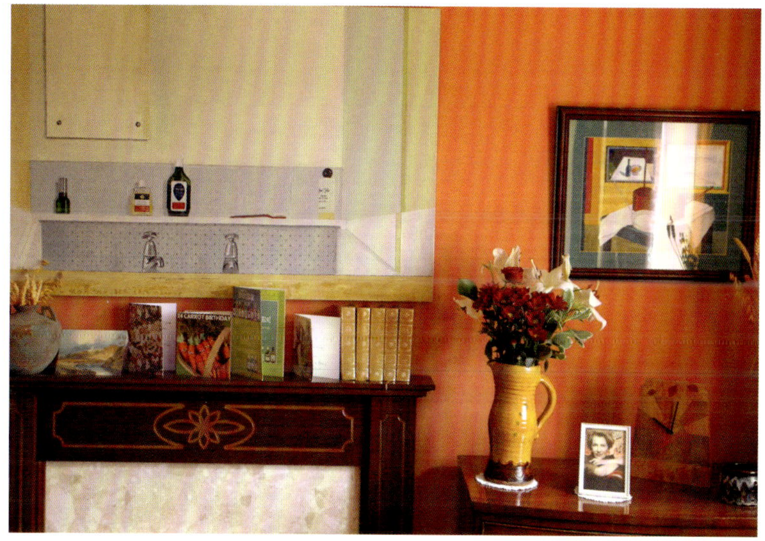

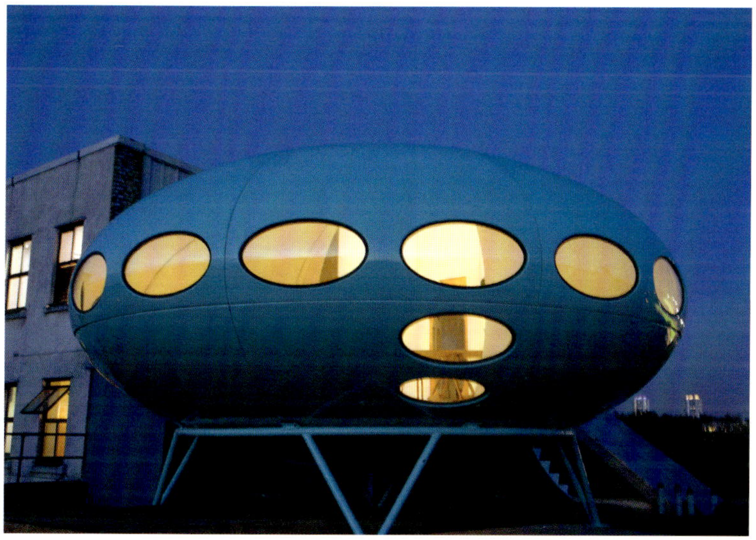

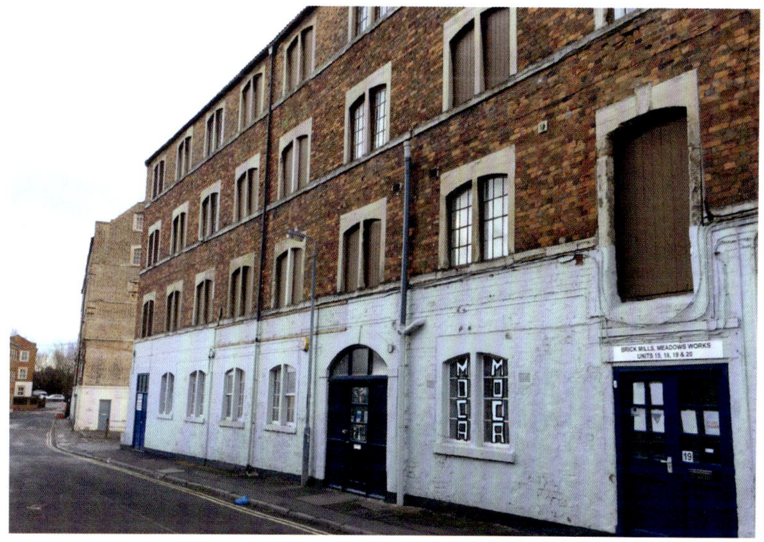

Clockwise from top left: Anne Bean in Hull (photo: Brian Gilson); a friend's house near Newark with his paintings and Chana's image (photo: Chana Dubinski); MoCa, Trowbridge (photo: Anne Bean); *Centre for Remote Possibilities* (2013-) by Craig Barnes, an adapted Futuro House shown at Matt's Gallery, London, 2014 (photo by Jess Simmons)

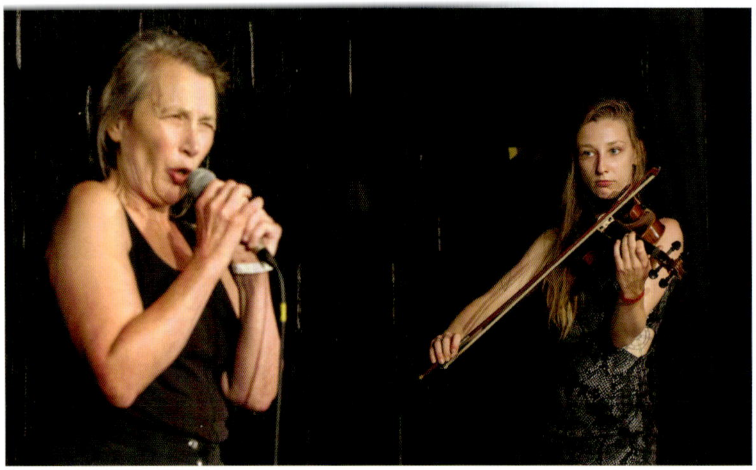

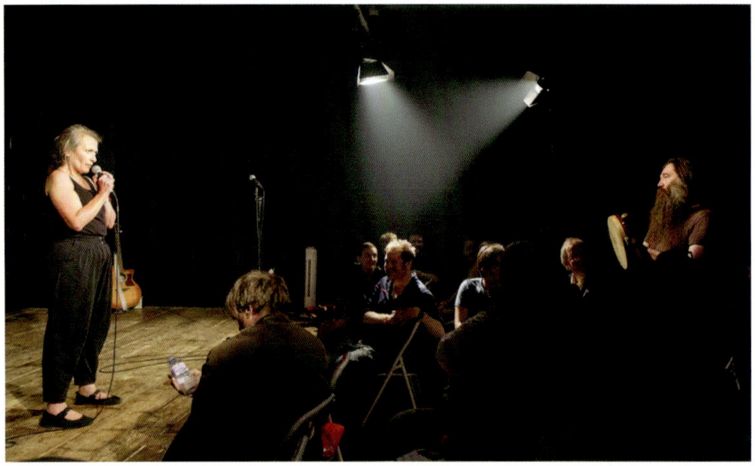

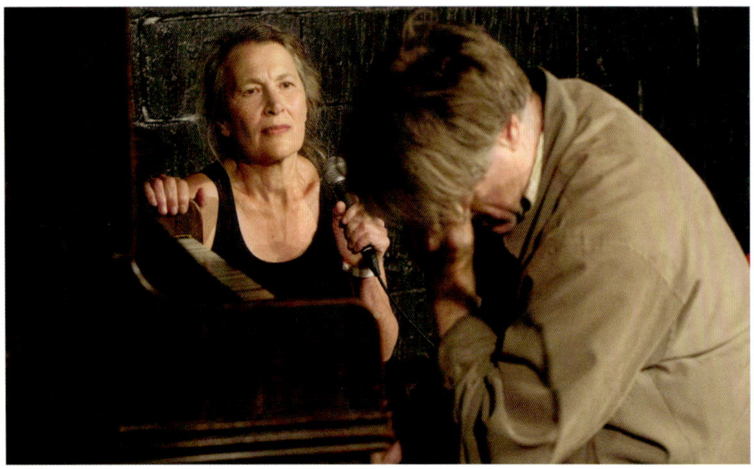

AB I initially wanted to collaborate with a 'stranger' from the town towards an exhibition. I invited the first completely unknown local person that entered the Trowbridge space to do a work with me as part of 5 *Duets with Strangers*, as part of *Tempting Failure*, an event in July [2016] in London. The other ongoing strand in Trowbridge is varied installations in the window. During November [2015] I worked with a couple of local women on an installation in the space relating to a film I had made called *Redress*, an ongoing work over 12 years. I made actions with women, in countries of conflict, including Iraq, and collaborated closely with *PAVES*, a group of 5 women I brought together from these countries. Trowbridge has a problem with ex-army displaced people struggling with civilian life and I have spoken to many of these men on the street. The *Redress* installation ran for a month over December and January, viewed through the window with sound coming through the airbrick vents. At the moment there is an installation, lighting up in the dark called *Leaden Man with Swan Thoughts*. In Autumn [2016] there will be a public event and exhibition in the space with the artist Hugo Danino who has now taken a space in the Trowbridge building, which I had advertised, having heard it was vacant. It will be more obvious at that point and the town will know it has been chosen 'for a site of a contemporary art space', if only temporarily.

RLF *Memory is a tricky issue. How do we redefine the way we tell stories about performances? I remember doing a performance with you in the 1980s , as a writer, where I had to review your work live, on a typewriter. But there is no documentation. How do we reconstruct archives where they don't exist?*

AB Yes, it is ironic that the very work instantly reviewed, is now lost in any material documentary sense, even the original typewritten 'live review'. You read out the review intermittently during the work and like an improvised dance, the review and performance carried on affecting each other throughout. *Notes on a Return* (2009) curated by Sophia Yadong Hao, revisited this work made at the Laing Art Gallery in the 1980s – as well as works by Rose English, Mona Hatoum, Bruce McLean and Nigel Rolfe – examining ideas of memory, archive and documentation of ephemeral practices, which I had previously conjured in my exhibition *Autobituary* at Matt's Gallery in 2006. In 2009 Tate Archives and Live Art Development Agency gave me a Legacy: Thinker in Residence Award to probe these very issues. Paul Burwell, a close collaborator since the 1970s, died in 2007 and I wanted to find a way for his irrepressible raw spirit, his passionate, participatory and experimental practice to be alive and present. I invited over 80 collaborators, advocates of improvisatory tenets, who had worked with him to contribute to what became *TAPS* (2009). Paul Burwell wrote in 1976: 'The way forward (or if not forward, at least somewhere else) thinking of art as a kind of lateral thinking skill, art as intervention, of approaching the notion of changing the rules, standing things on their head, re-examining the basic tenets of any arena of enquiry or discipline'. We are each other's archives and legacies.

Anne Bean, *Duets with 5 Strangers*, Tempting Failure, Matthews Yard, Croydon, 2016. With Lucy Hutson, Dominika, Alex Brenchley, Richard Green, and Robin Bale

A version of this interview was first published as Rob La Frenais, 'Whats in a Name? Anne Bean Interviewed', *Art Monthly* 398 (July-August 2016), 1-5.

TAPS

TAPS, 2010
Improvisations with Paul Burwell

TAPS was an exploration of what legacy is in a practice based on innovation and improvisation, and particularly in Paul's wide range of connections and concerns.

I sent each contributor the text of his poem *Adventures in the House of Memory*, to use in whatever way they wished, to make a short film or audio work, as a new collaboration for, about or with Paul, who had recently died. Fragments of these now make a collective totem, with this text as an underlying armature.

The poem *Adventures in the House of Memory* initially arose from improvisations by Paul and myself in preparation for William Burroughs's Final Academy at Ritzy, 1982. I improvised words and, unusually for us, Paul wrote them down and shaped the text. Originally, the words were written on huge pieces of flash paper which we burnt as they were sung.

Paul and I shared the sensibility that legacy must be seen as taking care of itself by a truth to LIVING. My installation and book *Autobituary*, by the very title, claimed that space; by a constant 'dying', there is a constantly renewed living and one is part of both.

All static art is, in fact, the result of action. We inhabit a Time-base world which comprises events not objects… we are not objects, our ideas are not objects, the relationships we form are not objects but are all intangibles in a constant state of flux: an endless succession of different presents.

Paul Burwell notebooks, 1978

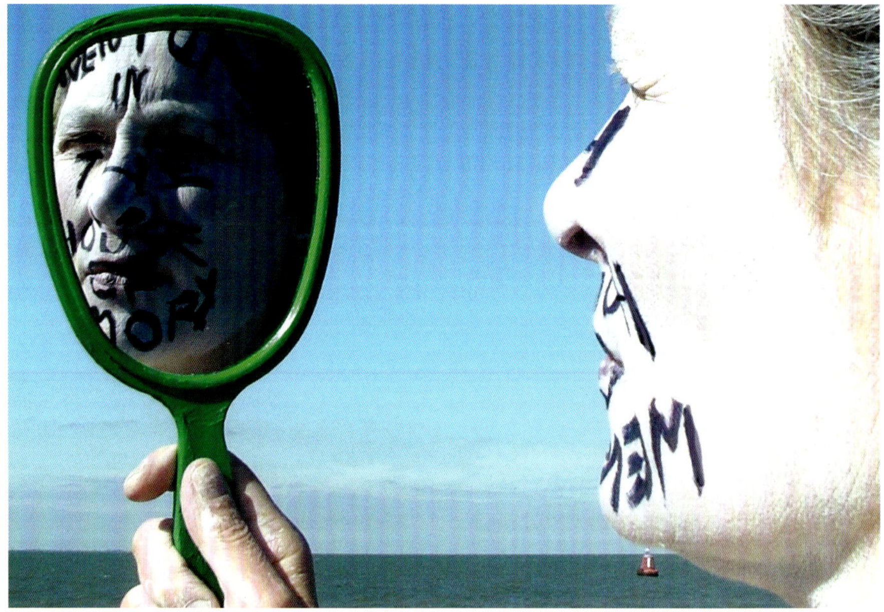

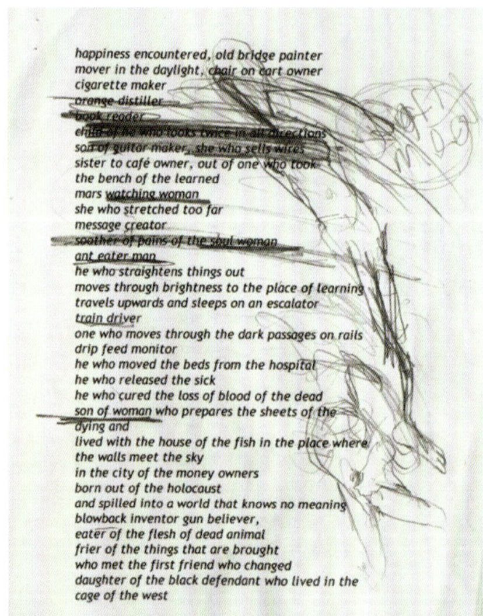

happiness encountered, old bridge painter
mover in the daylight, chair on cart owner
cigarette maker
orange distiller
book reader
child of he who looks twice in all directions
son of guitar maker, she who sells wires
sister to café owner, out of one who took
the bench of the learned
mars watching woman
she who stretched too far
message creator
soother of pains of the soul woman
ant eater man
he who straightens things out
moves through brightness to the place of learning
travels upwards and sleeps on an escalator
train driver
one who moves through the dark passages on rails
drip feed monitor
he who moved the beds from the hospital
he who released the sick
he who cured the loss of blood of the dead
son of woman who prepares the sheets of the
dying and
lived with the house of the fish in the place where
the walls meet the sky
in the city of the money owners
born out of the holocaust
and spilled into a world that knows no meaning
blowback inventor gun believer,
eater of the flesh of dead animal
frier of the things that are brought
who met the first friend who changed
daughter of the black defendant who lived in the
cage of the west

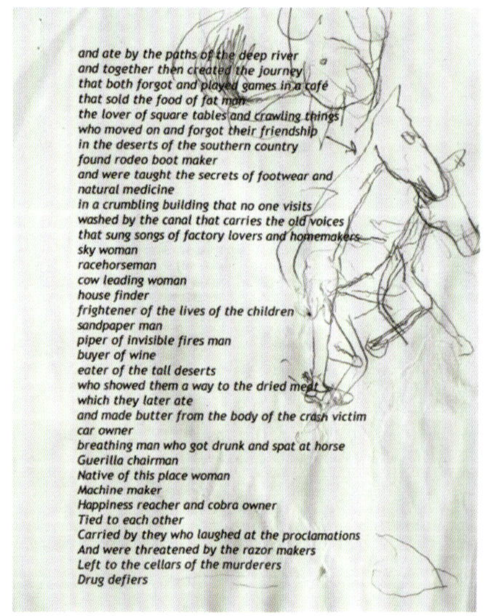

and ate by the paths of the deep river
and together then created the journey
that both forgot and played games in a café
that sold the food of fat man
the lover of square tables and crawling things
who moved on and forgot their friendship
in the deserts of the southern country
found rodeo boot maker
and were taught the secrets of footwear and
natural medicine
in a crumbling building that no one visits
washed by the canal that carries the old voices
that sung songs of factory lovers and homemakers
sky woman
racehorseman
cow leading woman
house finder
frightener of the lives of the children
sandpaper man
piper of invisible fires man
buyer of wine
eater of the tall deserts
who showed them a way to the dried meat
which they later ate
and made butter from the body of the crash victim
car owner
breathing man who got drunk and spat at horse
Guerilla chairman
Native of this place woman
Machine maker
Happiness reacher and cobra owner
Tied to each other
Carried by they who laughed at the proclamations
And were threatened by the razor makers
Left to the cellars of the murderers
Drug defiers

Paul McCarthy dribbled on, ferociously scribbled, scrunched and ripped the text, grunting and groaning in his video contribution.

TAPS: Improvisations with Paul Burwell is a 2 screen composite film of documentary footage and over 70 new works. Working on it, I was aware of the indifference to time as chronology. Past and present mingle into one composition and the dead and living are indefinable, duetting with each other across spaces & times and populating the saga with lyrical moments, tragic and comic. As in all epics and sagas, no distinction is made between myth and history, what is, what might have been and what still might be.

When I invited the contributors to work on *TAPS*, I wanted an active legacy; one of vitality and participation:

> ...in a society that is increasingly designed and seemingly content to have things done AT it, that is happy to store information for some hypothetical future consumption, the job, or role of artists, or ethical beings in general, must be to create things that require an element of being there: of direct experience.
>
> Paul Burwell notebooks, 1979

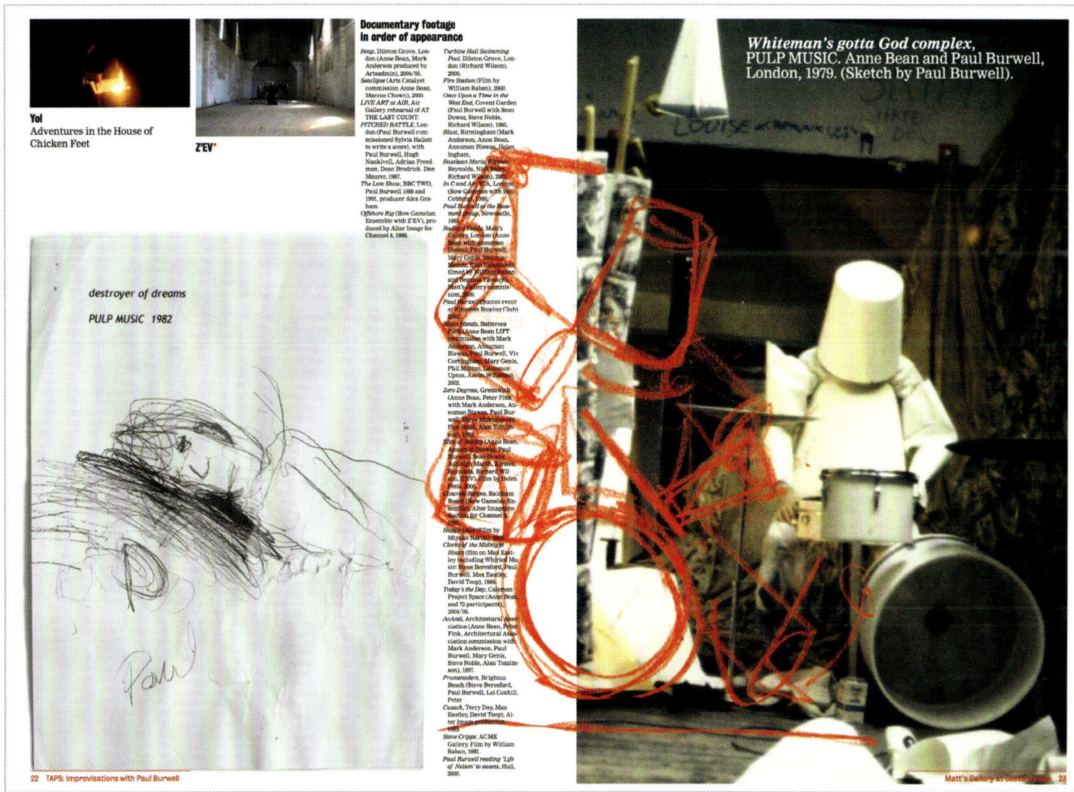

Yo!
Adventures in the House of Chicken Feet

Z'EV*

Documentary footage in order of appearance

Reap, Dilston Grove, London (Anne Bean, Mark Anderson produced by Artsadmin), 2004/05.
Seaclipse (Arts Catalyst commission Anne Bean, Marcus Chown), 2000.
LIVE ART at AIR, Air Gallery rehearsal of AT THE LAST COUNT: PITCHED BATTLE, London (Paul Burwell commissioned Sylvia Hallett to write a score), with Paul Burwell, Hugh Nankivell, Adrian Freedman, Dean Brodrick. Dan Maurer, 1987.
The Late Show, BBC TWO, Paul Burwell 1989 and 1991, producer Alex Graham.
Offshore Rig (Bow Gamelan Ensemble with Z'EV), produced by Alter Image for Channel 4, 1986.
Turbine Hall Swimming Pool, Dilston Grove, London (Richard Wilson), 2009.
Fire Station (Film by William Raban), 2000.
Once Upon a Time in the West End, Covent Garden (Paul Burwell with Sean Dower, Steve Noble, Richard Wilson), 1985.
Blast, Birmingham (Mark Anderson, Anne Bean, Ansuman Biswas, Helen Ingham,
Bastiaan Maris, Kirsten Reynolds, Nick [illegible], Richard Wilson), 2007.
In C and Air, ICA, London (Bow Gamelan with Bob Cobbing), 1986.
Paul Burwell at the Basement group, Newcastle, 1981.
Radiant Fields, Matt's Gallery, London (Anne Bean with Ansuman Biswas, Paul Burwell, Mary Genis, Swarup Menon, [illegible] filmed by William Raban and [illegible]), Matt's Gallery commission, 2000.
Paul Burwell (Soccot event at Kingston Rowing Club) 2001.
Many Hands, Battersea Park (Anne Bean LIFT commission with Mark Anderson, Ansuman Biswas, Paul Burwell, Viv Corringham, Mary Genis, Phil Minton, Laurence Upton, Aaron Williams), 2002.
Zero Degrees, Greenwich (Anne Bean, Peter Fink with Mark Anderson, Ansuman Biswas, Paul Burwell, [illegible] Pipe Band, Alan Tomlinson), 1992.
Slice of Reality (Anne Bean, Ansuman Biswas, Paul Burwell, Sean Dower, Ashleigh Marsh, Kirsten Reynolds, Richard Wilson, Z'EV), Film by Helen Petts, 2005.
Concrete Barges, Rainham Reach (Bow Gamelan Ensemble), Alter Image production for Channel 4, 1986.
Happy Days (Film by Miyako Narita), 2006.
Clocks of the Midnight Hours (film on Max Eastley including Whirled Music: Steve Beresford, Paul Burwell, Max Eastley, David Toop), 1986.
Today's the Day, Coleman Project Space (Anne Bean and 72 participants), 2004/05.
AnAnti, Architectural Association (Anne Bean, Peter Fink, Architectural Association commission with Mark Anderson, Paul Burwell, Mary Genis, Steve Noble, Alan Tomlinson), 1997.
Promenaders, Brighton Beach (Steve Beresford, Paul Burwell, Lol Coxhill, Peter
Cusack, Terry Day, Max Eastley, David Toop), Alter Image production, 1983.
Steve Cripps, ACME Gallery. Film by William Raban, 1981.
Paul Burwell reading 'Life of Nelson' to swans, Hull, 2000.

Whiteman's gotta God complex,
PULP MUSIC. Anne Bean and Paul Burwell, London, 1979. (Sketch by Paul Burwell).

22 TAPS: Improvisations with Paul Burwell

Matt's Gallery at Dilston Grove 23

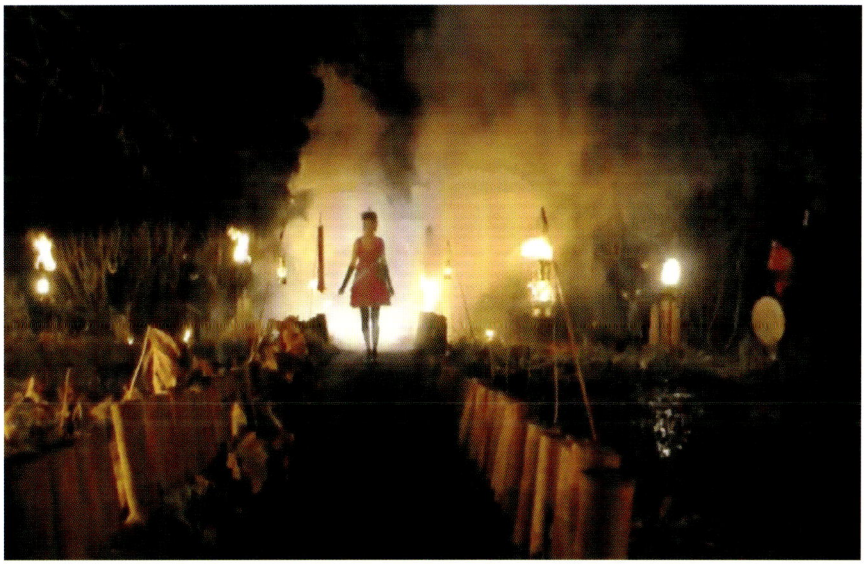

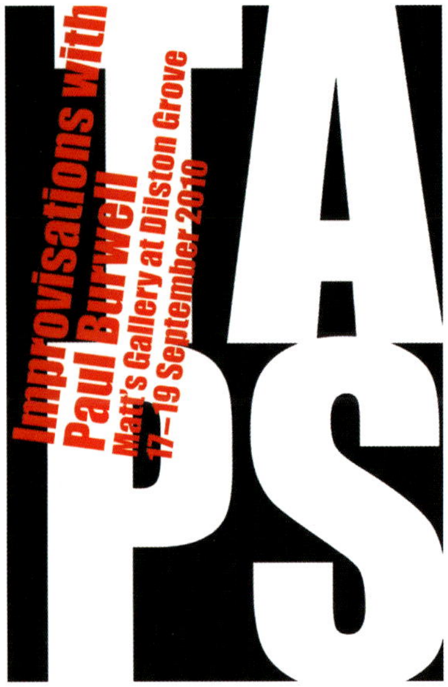

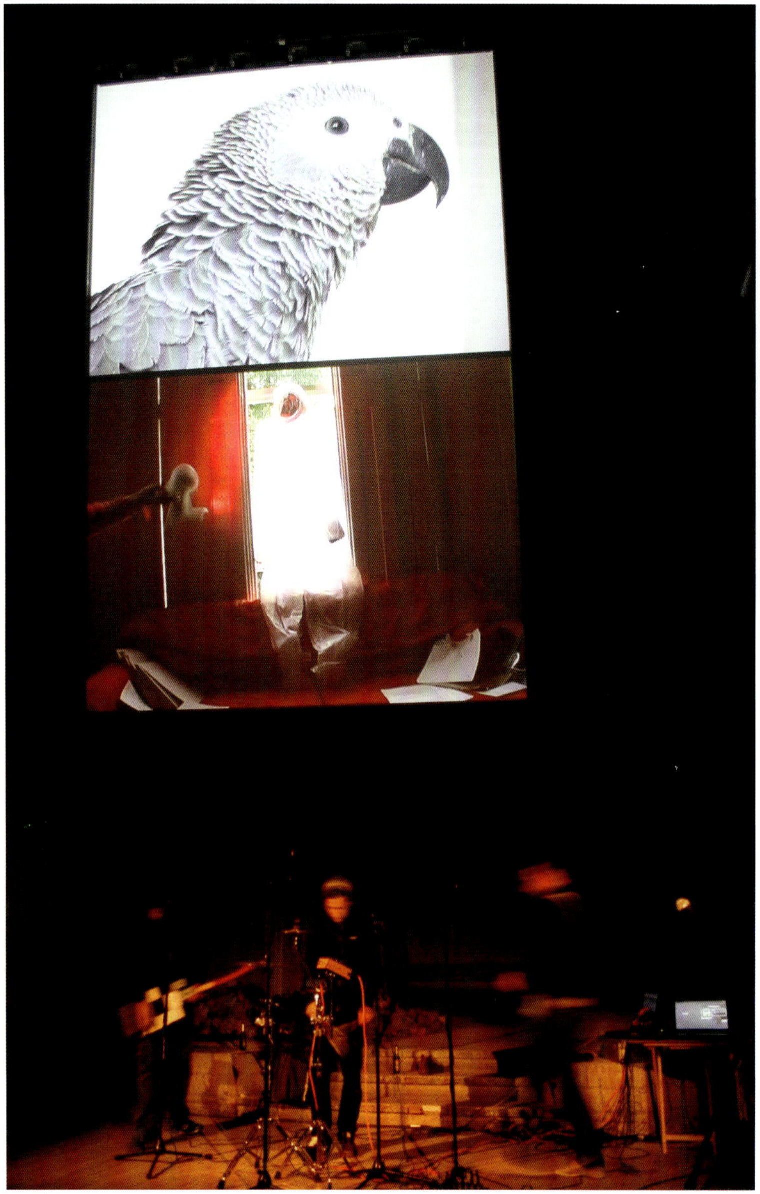

In David Toop's article on Paul for *TAPS* he wrote 'this is not the biography of an artist, but... how inspiration can pour (like the gift of tongues) from one into many.'

Julian Cowley wrote in *WIRE*:

'The three day event is less memorial than an occasion to register Burwell's continuing presence in their lives... Burwell's impact was widespread as well as deeply felt.'

Richard Wilson buried several circular saws into the plaster board screen, which were switched on during the final screening to disintegrate and send the film out into the space on specks of dust.

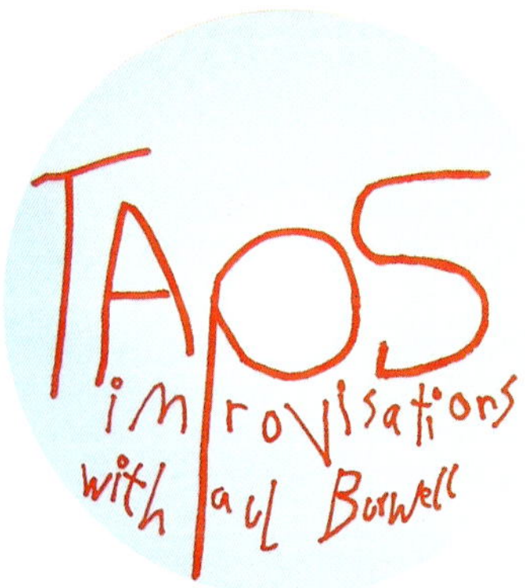

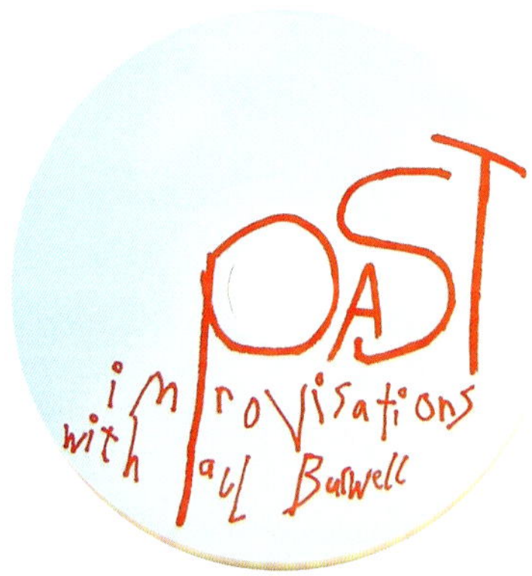

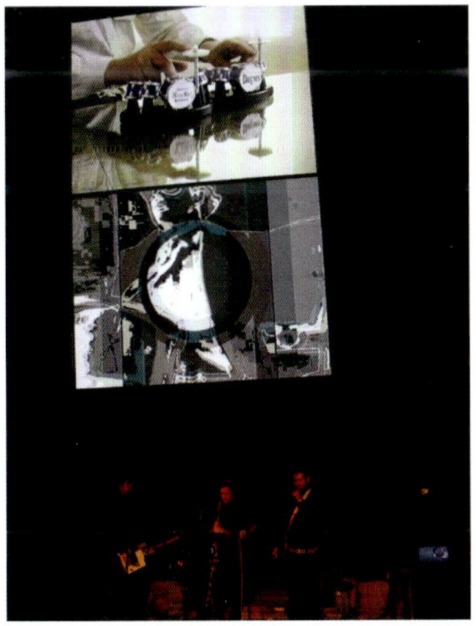
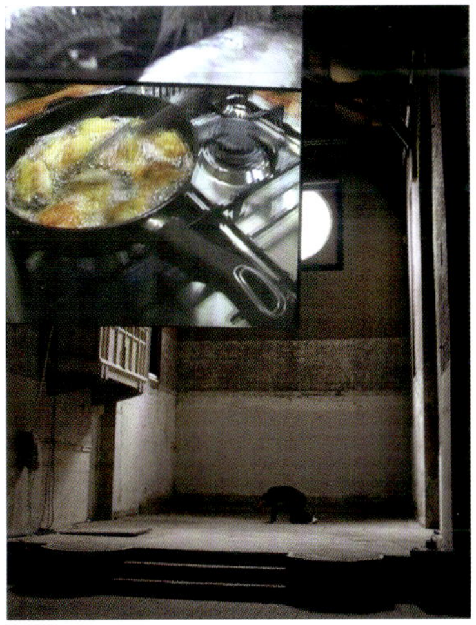
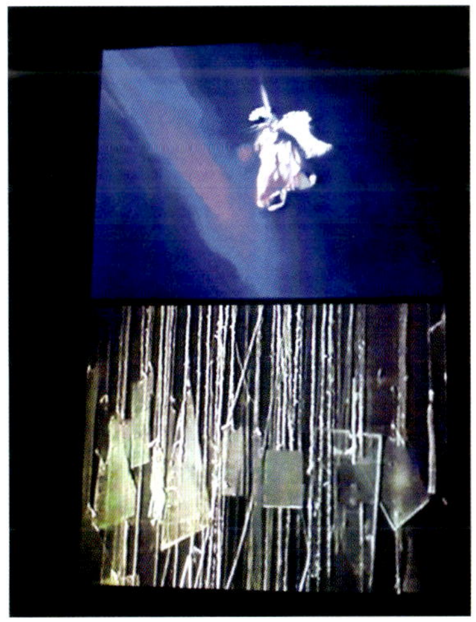
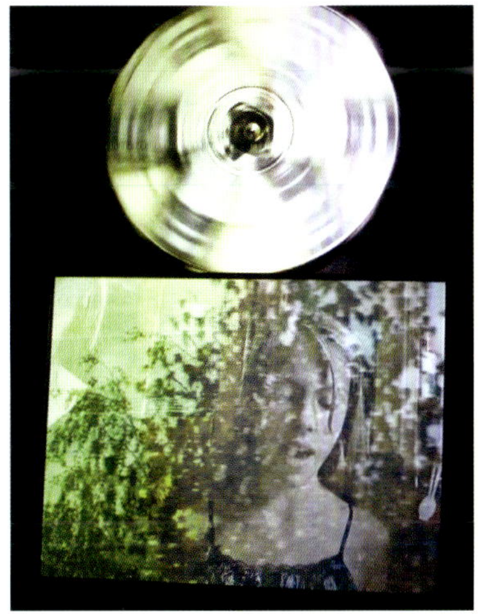
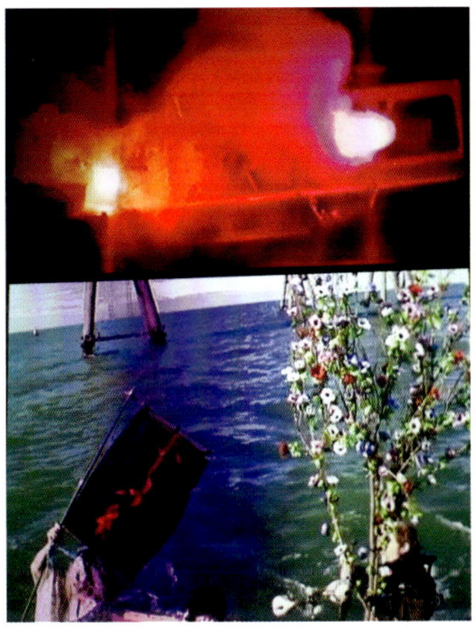
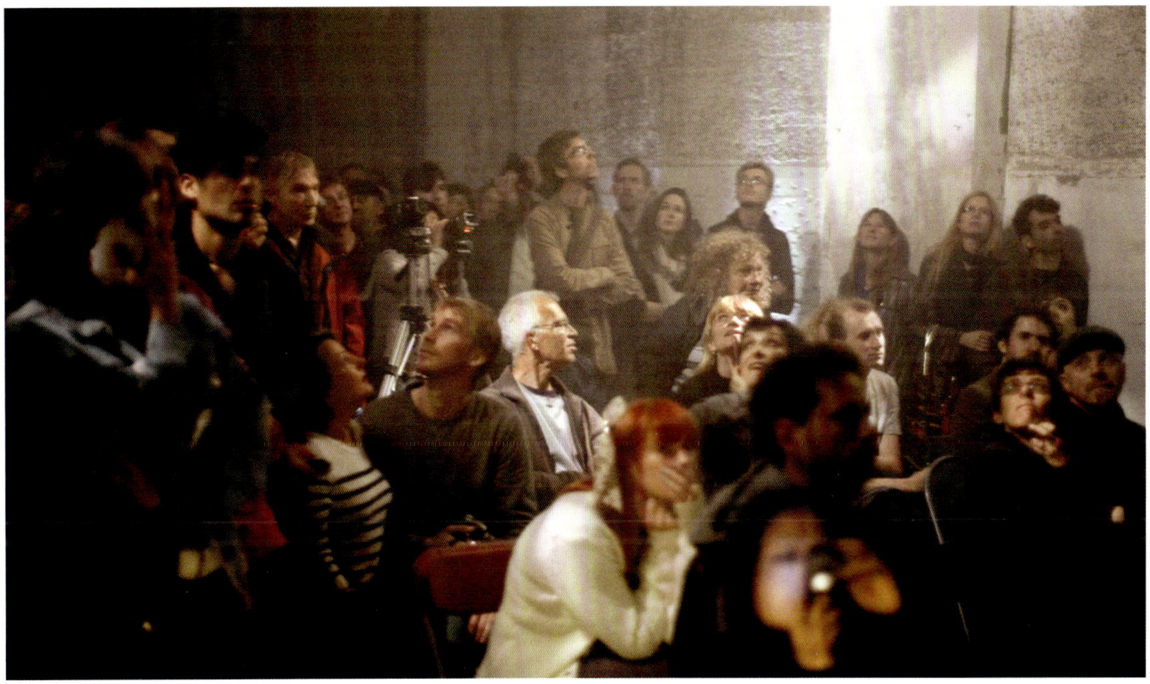

Right: I asked Mark Anderson and Kirsten Reynolds to walk around the outside of the building, Dilston Grove, with strobing flares on long poles, producing juddering shadows through the leaded glass windows into the dust and projection of this final fragmentation.

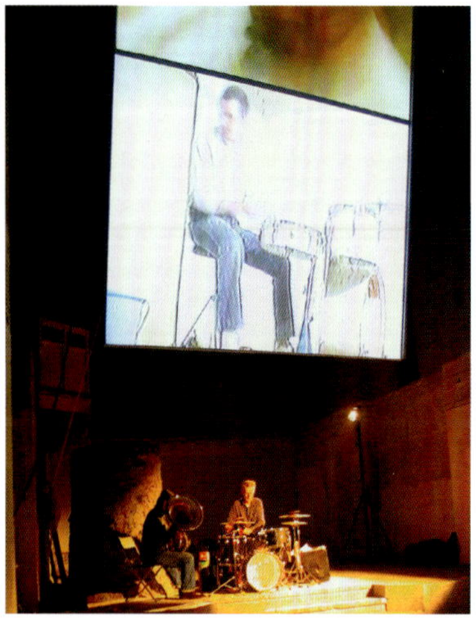

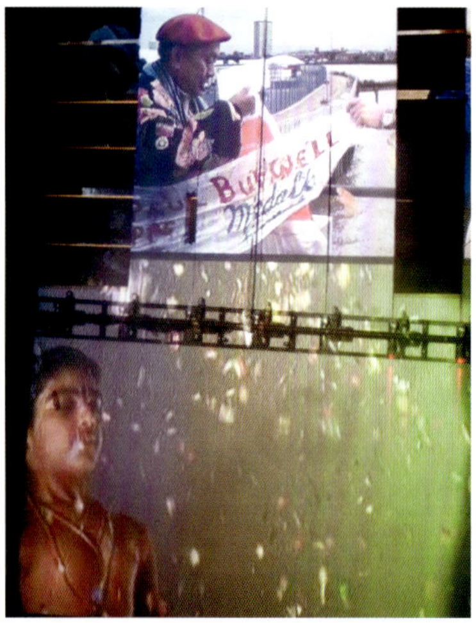

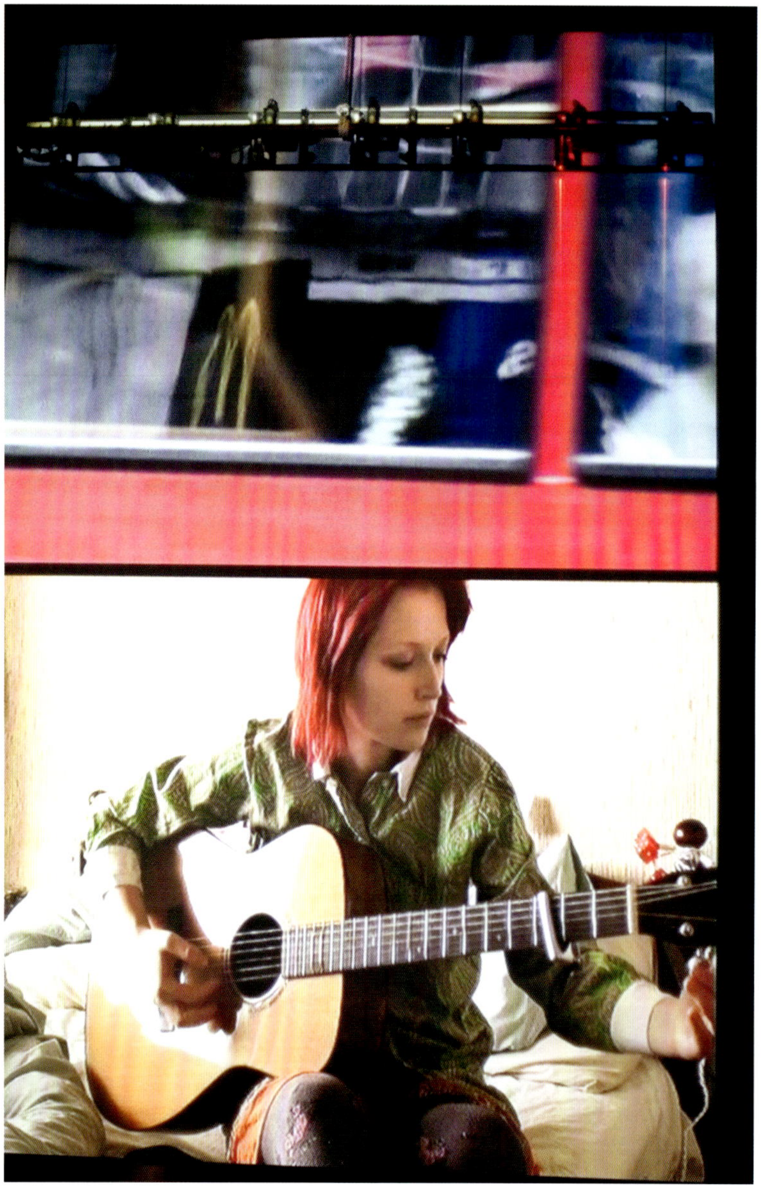

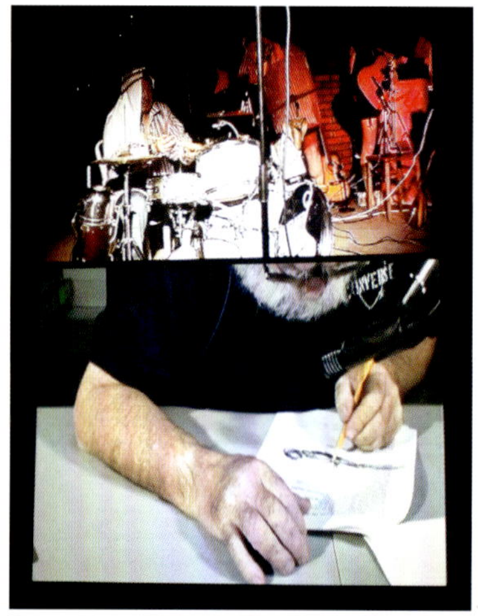

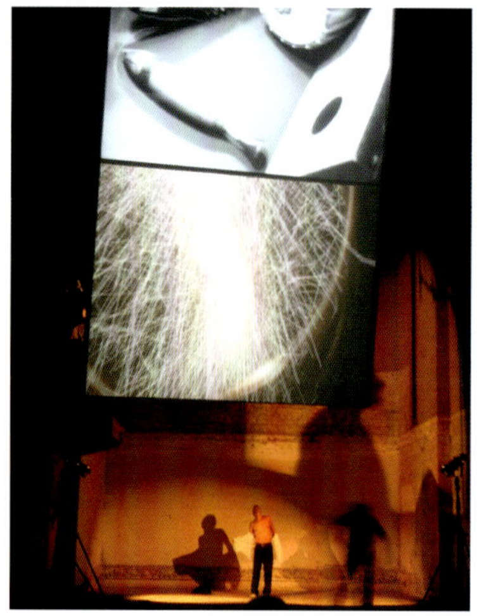

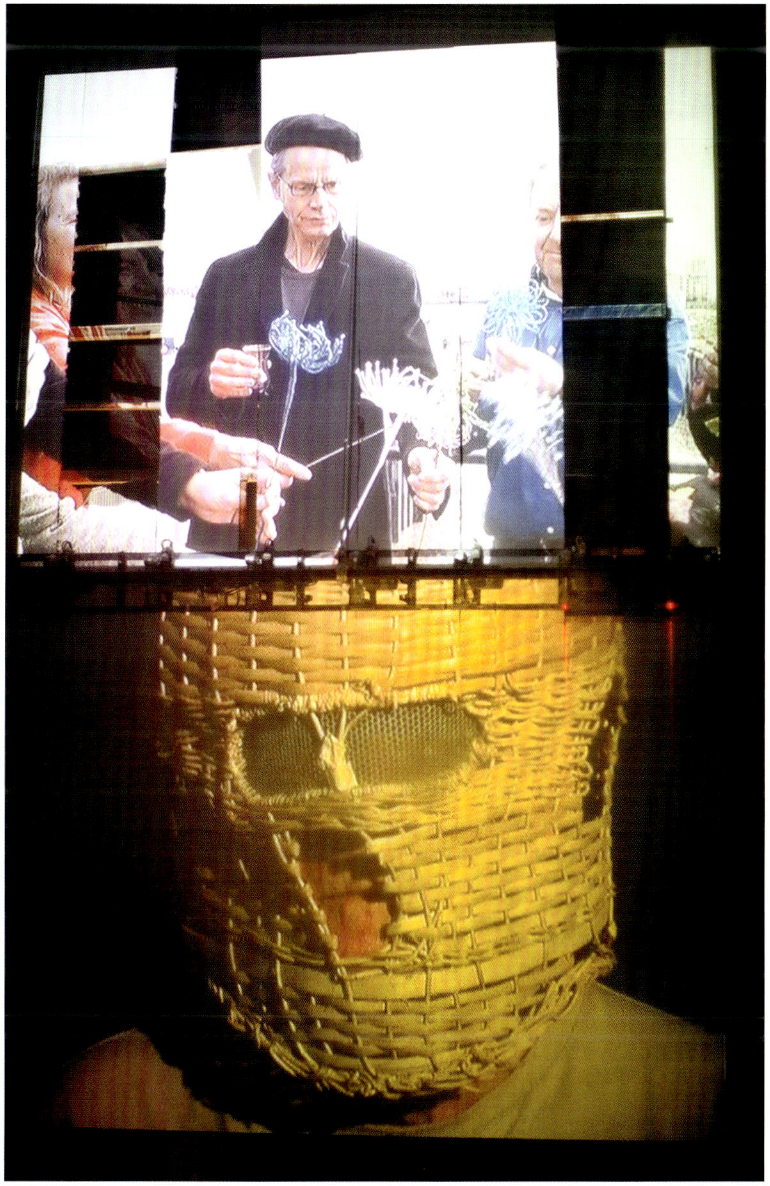

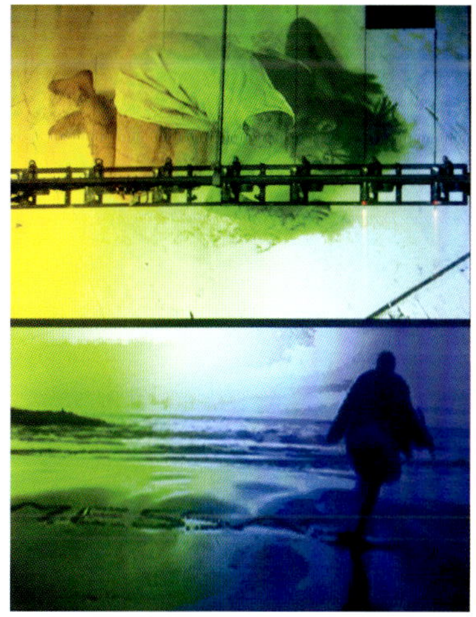

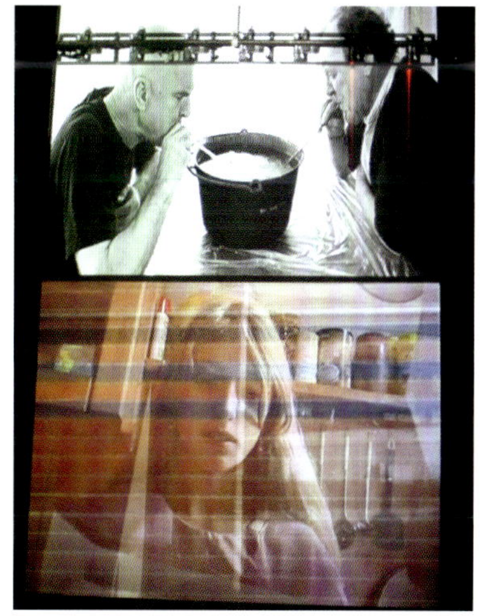

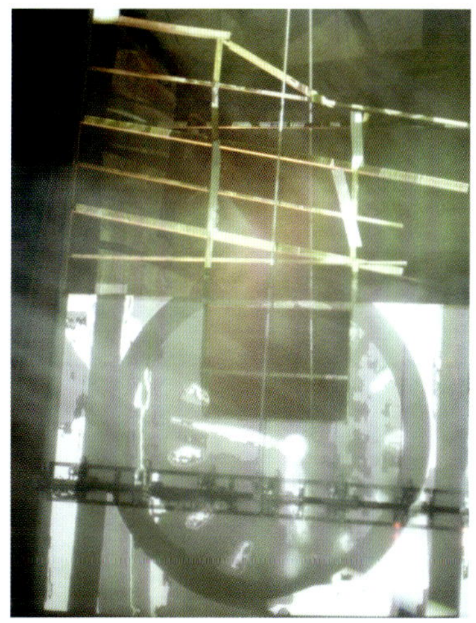

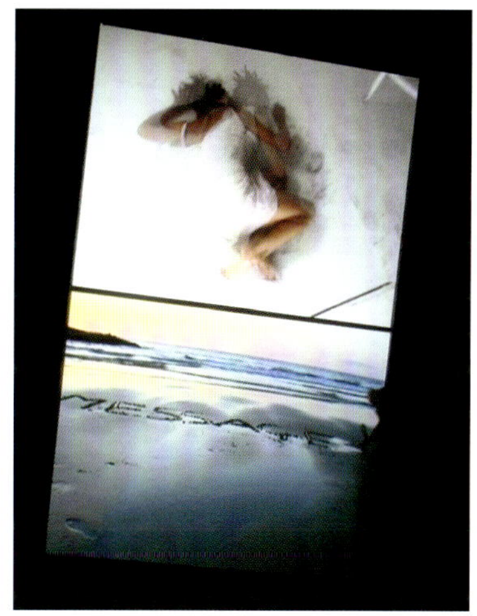

Film contributors included:

Aaron Williamson, Adalet Garmiany, Alan Tomlinson, Anna Thew, Ansuman Biswas and Mary Genis, Ashleigh Marsh, Borbetomagus (Jim Sauter, Don Dietrich, Donald Miller), Brian Catling, Brian G. Gilson, Brian Routh aka Harry Kipper, Carlyle Reedy, Toy Killers (Charles K. Noyes and Mark E. Miller), Charlie Hooker, Charlie Morrissey, Chris Galdwin, Dan Maurer, David Medalla with Guy Brett, Alma Tischler and Marko Steponova, David Toop, Elliott Sharp, Evan Parker, Ezra Rubenstein, Gioia Meller Marcovicz, Hannah O'Shea, Harald Uccello FoTyArT ORG, Hermine Demoriane, Hugh Metcalfe, Jacky Lansley and Fergus Early, John McKeon, Kaffe Matthews, Kim Creighton, Kirsten Reynolds with THE LONDON DIRTHOLE COMPANY (Ashley Davis, Wajid Yaseen, Nick Brown, Neil Fraser, Kevin Younger, Rob Lewis, Elvina Flower, Roger Carne, Terry Edwards), Lee Merrill and David Ellis, Lol Coxhill, Lurca, Maggi Nichols, Marega Palser, Marie Yates, Mark Anderson with Nick Sales and Jony Easterby, Martin von Haselberg aka Harry Kipper, Max Eastley, Mike Cooper, Mimi Westernhagen, Miyako Narita, P. Jeck and Mary Prestidge, Brown Sierra: Paddy Collins and Pia Gambardella, Patricia Wells, Paul McCarthy, Peter Davey, Peter Cusack, Phil Minton and Roger Turner, Phil the Messenger, Rembrandt, Rev Nagase, Richard Wilson with William Raban and David Cunningham, Rose English, Sean Dower, Shaun Caton, Simon Finn, Steve Beresford, Steve Noble, Steven Berkoff, Susanna Ferrar, Sylvia Hallett, Terry Day, Tom Recchion, Trace Collective (Phil Babot, Lee Hassall, Eddie Ladd, Tony Schwensen, André Stitt), Viv Corringham, Yol, Z'EV

Helen Petts collaborated on several films

Other appearances include:

Bob Cobbing, Bastiaan Maris, Thames Steam Co, Helen Ingham, Espen Jenson, Bob Levene, Glynes Neslen, Martin Dodds, Whirled Music, the Promenaders, Kirsty Walk, Jeremy Paxman, Swarup Menon

Edited by Anne Bean and Chris Bishop

Live events:

Juneau Projects, Kaffe Matthews, Melissa Castagnetto, Oren Marshall and Steve Noble, Shaun Caton, Ryuzo Fukuhara, William Cobbing, Yol, Ansuman Biswas

Installation and events in collaboration with Robin Klassnik and Richard Wilson

Supported by LADA and Tate Research award, Legacy: Thinker in Residence

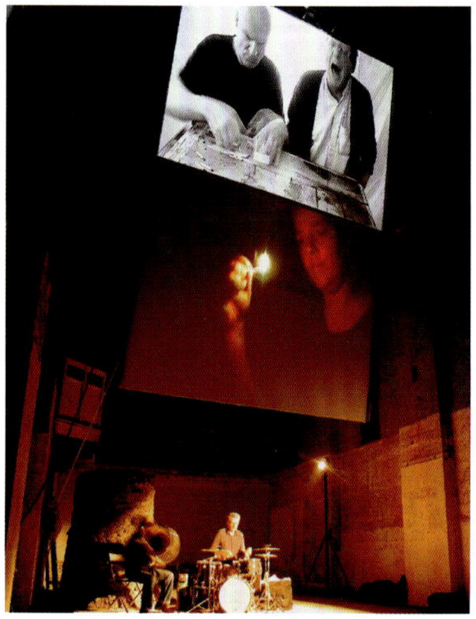

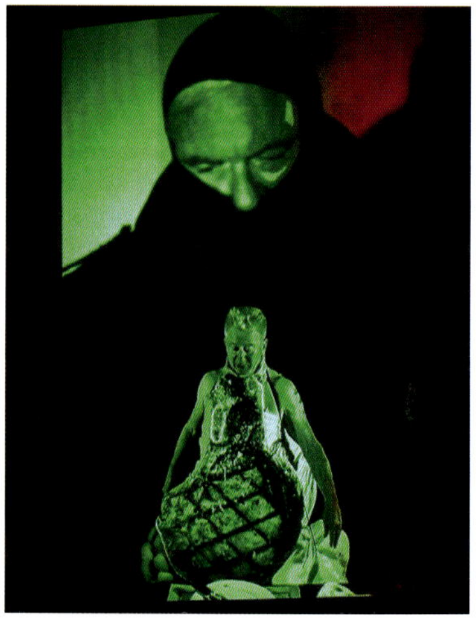

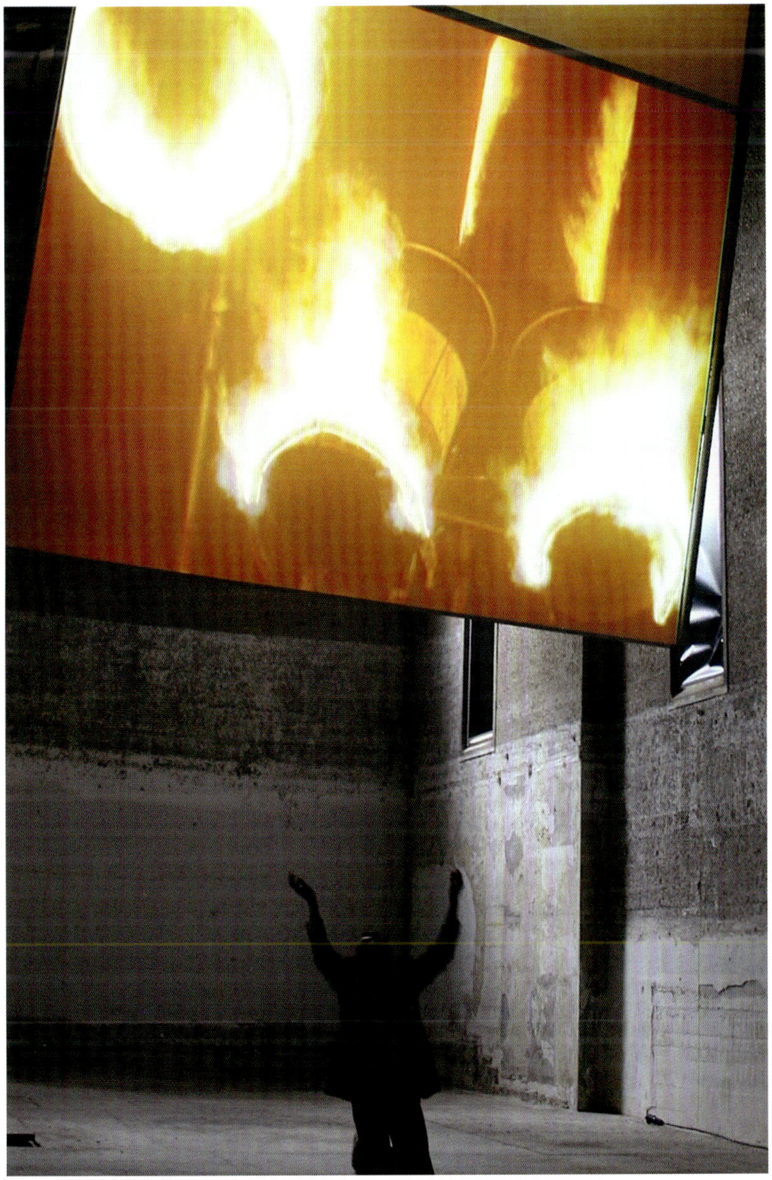

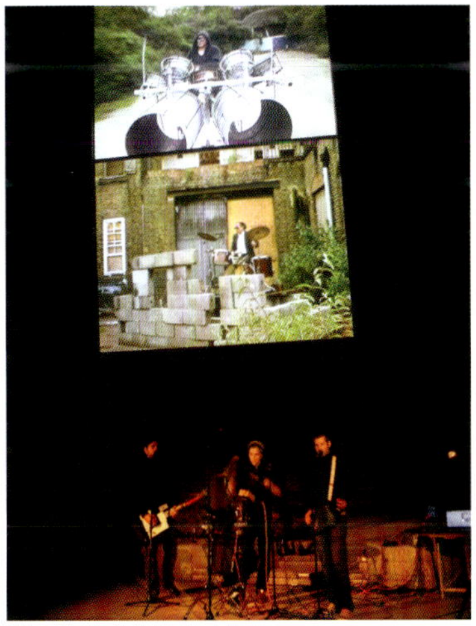

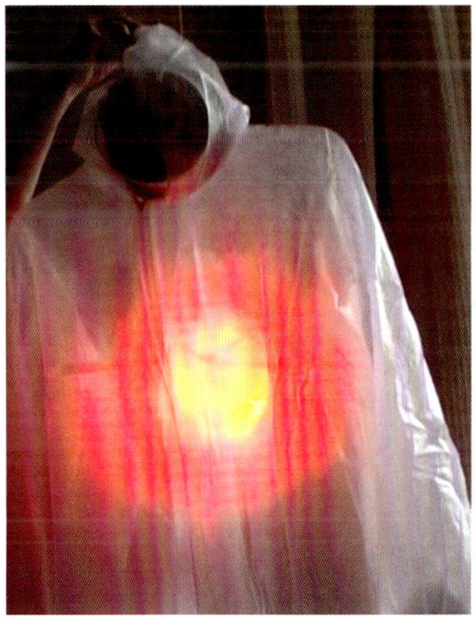

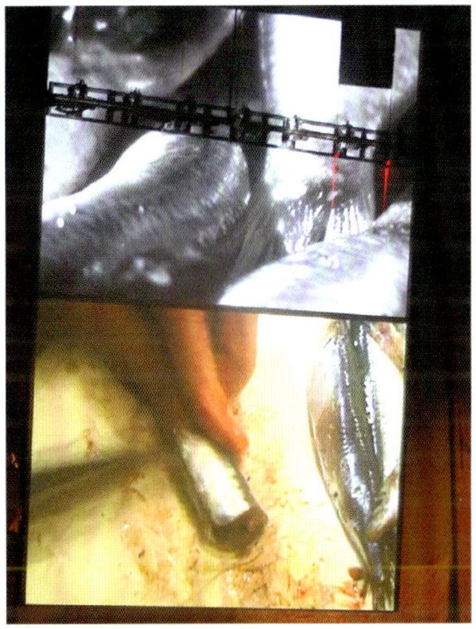

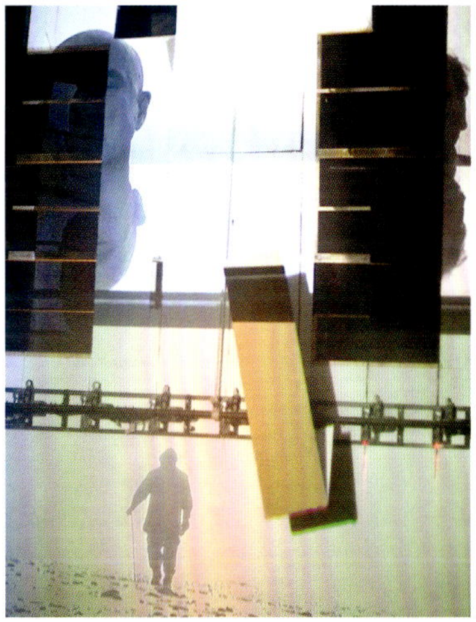

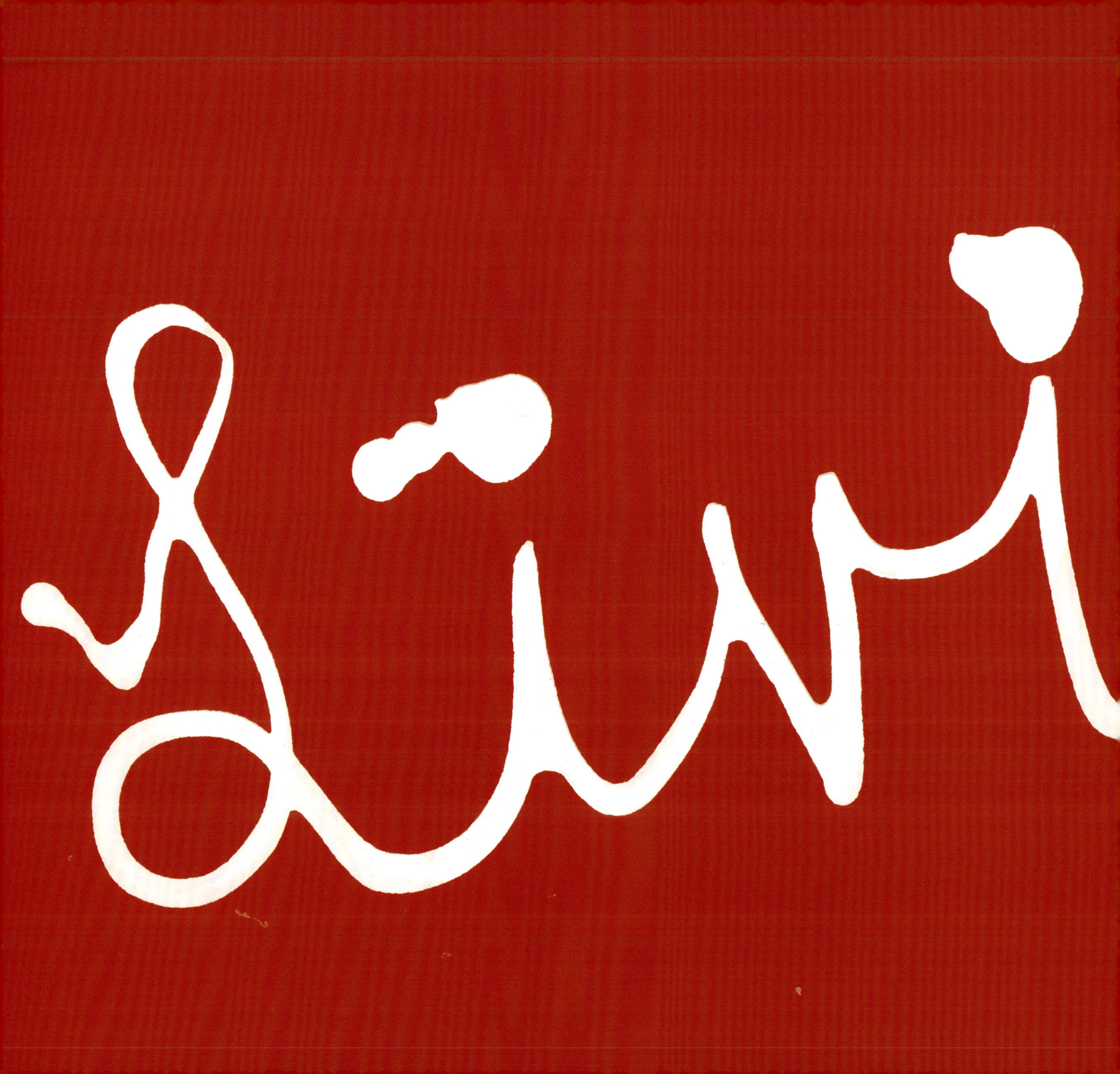

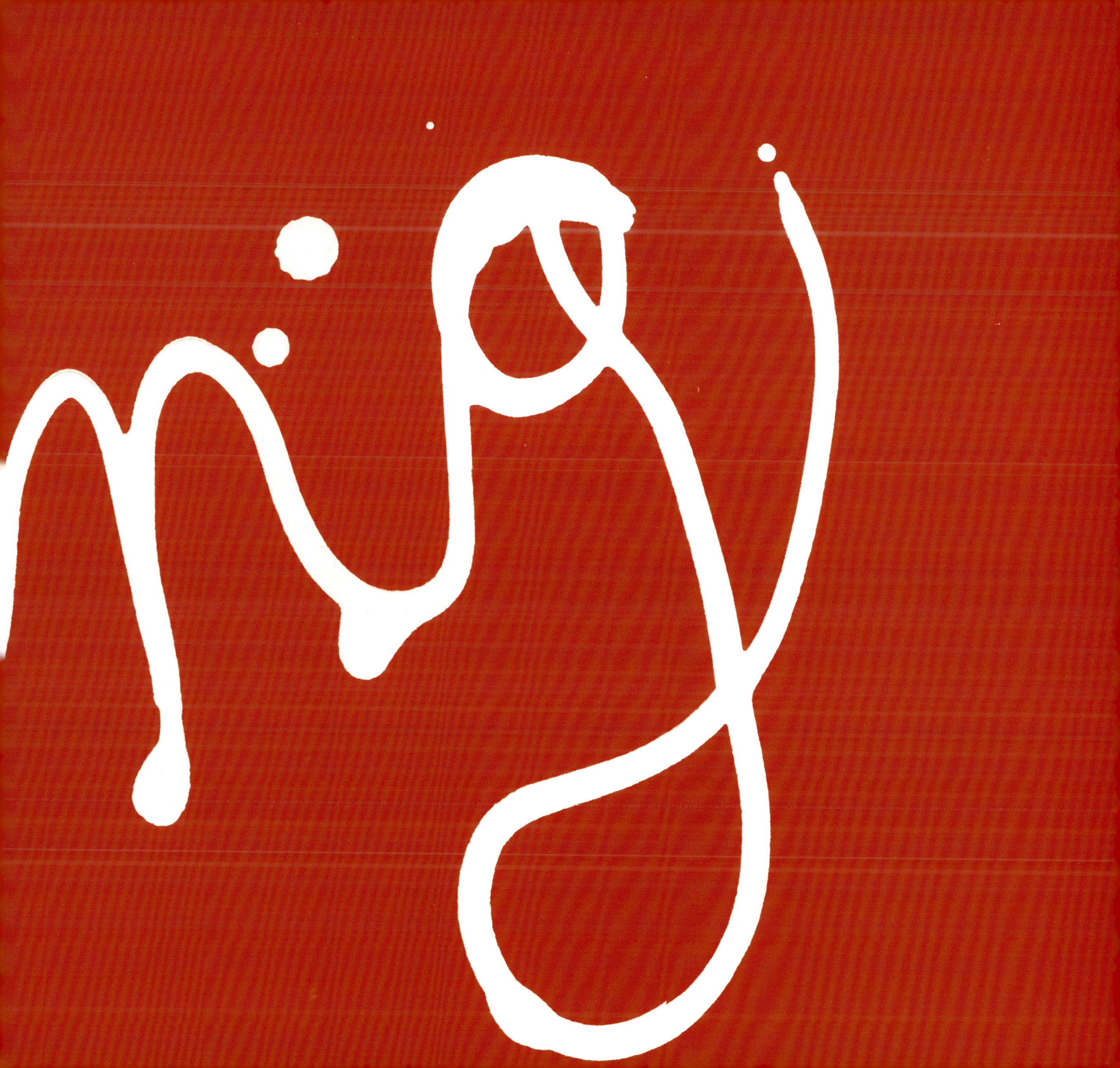

WITHIN LIVING MEMORY: SHADOW DEEDS
GUY BRETT

What had originally come into being as an experiment: seven artists – among them Anne Bean as the only woman – sitting round a kitchen table and laughing together for one hour with just a few friends attending, was now, some 29 years later, re-created in front of a much larger audience in a public gallery.[1] It was part of a curatorial attempt by the Whitechapel Gallery (futile? misguided? audacious? long-overdue?) to re-stage some artists' ephemeral events, sprung from living time, that had passed naturally into memory.[2] The original kitchen table had been in an old chemist's shop on the Mile End Road called Bernsteins, which gave its name to this loose collaboration of artists, one of many Anne Bean has participated in. There was poignancy in the fact that the work's title, *Death to Grumpy Grandads* (1973), conveying youth's impish criticism of the older generation, was now being acted out by people fast approaching the granddad condition themselves. The second time around they may well have been laughing at the oddity of their own situation. After the event the audience remained in their places and a discussion took place. Anne Bean assumed the role of a benign hostess, coaxing from the men some account of their lives since the early 1970s. These reminiscences were affective exchanges. They took the form of lived experience rather than art history.

I attended *Grumpy Grandads* with a friend and, arriving late, we took up places near the edge of the crowd surrounding the players. We were quite some way from the centre of energy. It was fascinating to notice the way the laughter was contagious among those nearest to the performers and spread a certain distance through the rings of people. Of course there were those who preferred to pay attention in silence, and the attendant photo and video cameras created further pools of solemnity and stasis. My friend noticed that Bean particularly made eye contact with her fellow performers so the individual nuances of laughter would resonate between them. We fantasised about starting a little nucleus of mirth outside the main event, and wondered if that would be sabotage or taking participation a step further.

Laughter spreading through the crowd could be taken as a metaphor of the way the ephemeral work spreads through time, in ever widening circles, increasingly remote from the original source. In the process it lights people up, it becomes something else and the 'original source' can never be returned to. A wonderful paradox is contained in the invention of the genre of performance art, which epitomises a crucial dilemma of contemporary culture. On the one hand, performance rejects the means of reproduction, recording and mediating which technology has taken to such lengths. It is archaic in that sense. Performance exists in the moment, for those who were present in that place and time, and it entrusts itself to the vagaries of individual memory and subjectivity. No two people remember exactly alike. On the other hand there is a persistent desire to record it, or even re-create it, as happened with *Grumpy Grandads*. But this is never adequate, so these recordings submit to the same vagaries as human memory – and the same creative potential. Is it right or wrong to restage ephemeral events? This debate raged around the Whitechapel's *Short History of Performance*. Or to translate poetry? There can be no absolute judgement. There is something more like a gradual diminution of effect, or a place on a scale between the fiery core moment and complete extinction. Even a poor translation, even a faded photograph, gives some clue, and an approximation can itself set another creative cycle in motion. In some cases, the report of something remote may itself carry the aesthetic charge.

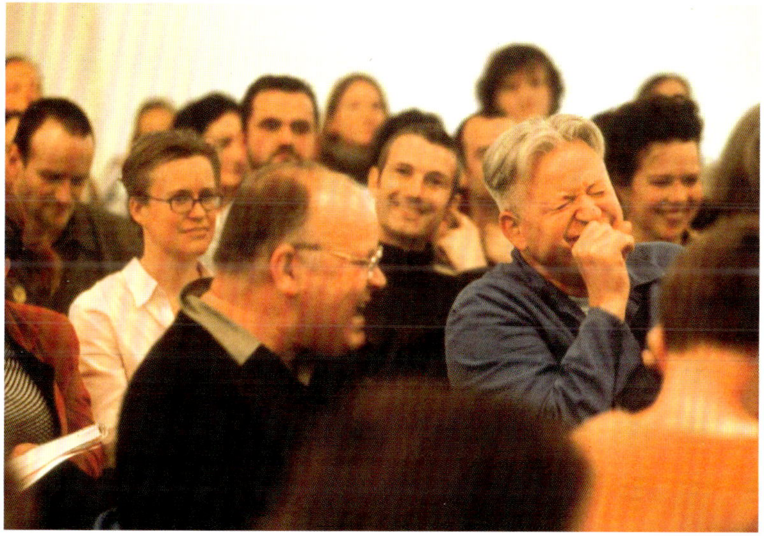
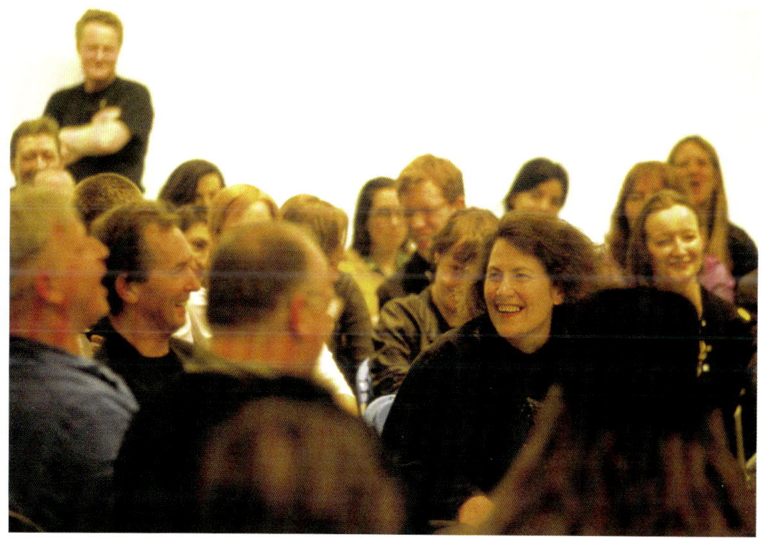
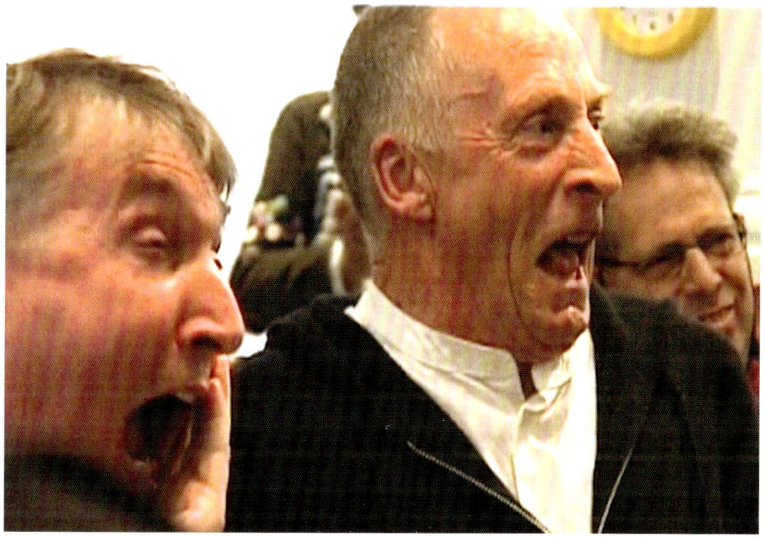
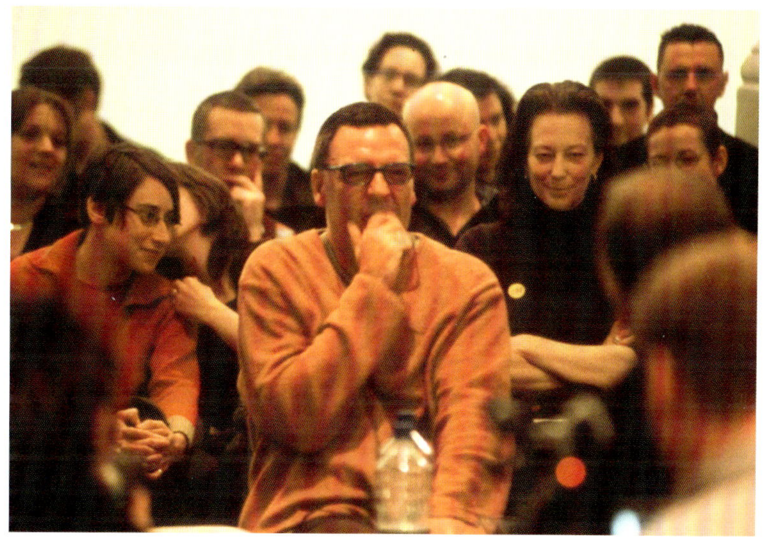

Bernsteins (Anne Bean, Peter Davey, Jonathan Harvey, Malcolm Jones, Chris Millar, Brian Routh, and Martin von Haselberg), *Death to Grumpy Grandads*, A Short History of Performance Vol. 1, Whitechapel Gallery, London, April 2002. Photos: Manuel Vason

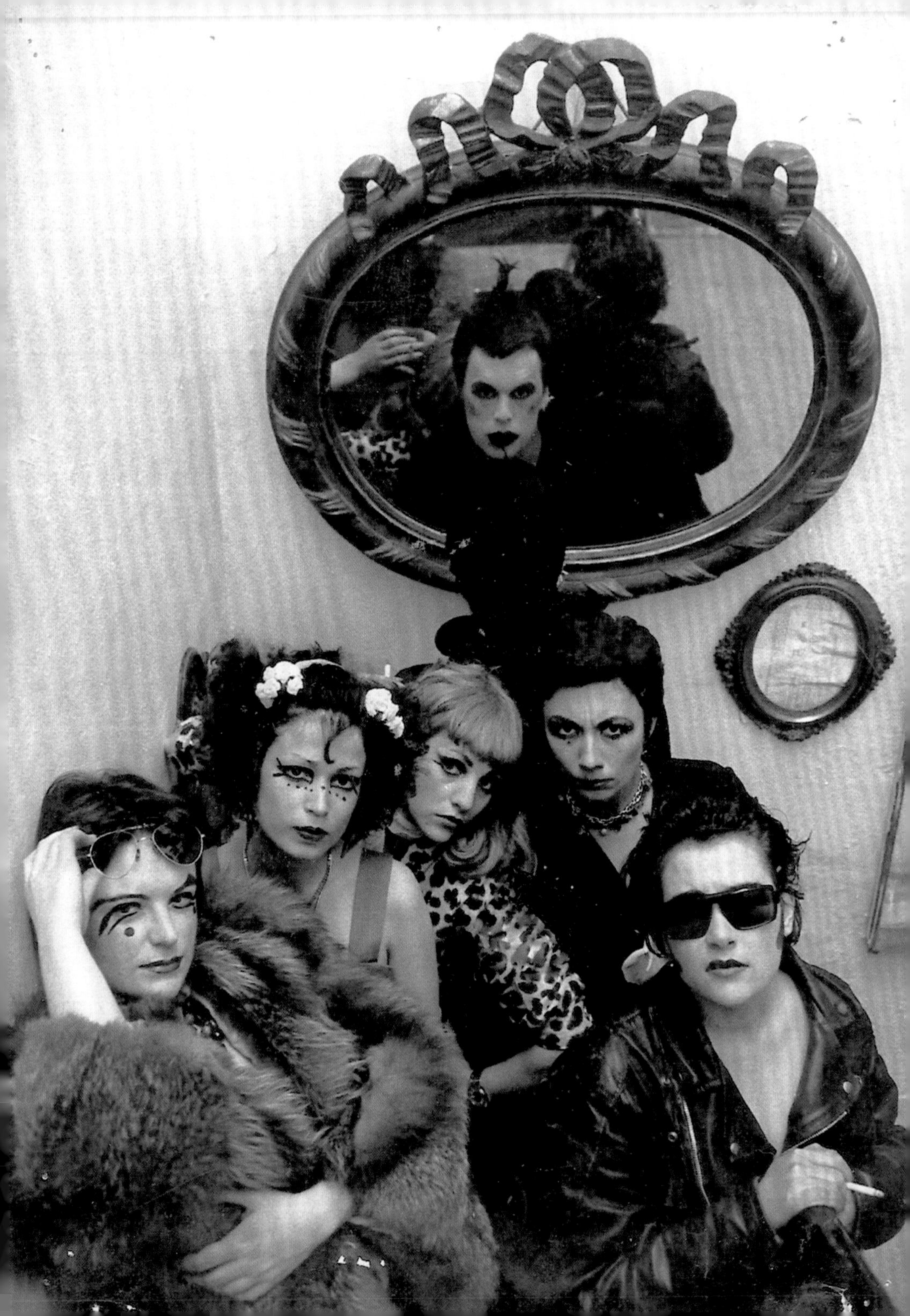

In the *Siluetas* series (1973-80) of Ana Mendieta, for example, which almost everyone who knows them knows through photographs, these photographs add something mechanical, which passes beyond what one could have perceived if one had actually been present at her solitary ritual. This is due to the forensic nature of the camera's gaze, which picks up every nuance and detail of the patch of land where Mendieta was working. Every leaf, every bubble in the sea wash, every trickle of mud then becomes implicated in the presence and decay of Mendieta's female effigy. At the same time the *Siluetas* need to preserve the character of a 'report', which may explain why they are more suggestive when reproduced in a book or catalogue than as framed photographs hung on a wall.

Reading Anne Bean's CV is like following a continuous performance, a continuous response to the world (*Our Trespasses*, the title of a project of 1992 – for which she has not asked for forgiveness! – is a nice way of putting it), a 'magicification' of the world. The panoply of places she has worked, times of the day or night, interiors, exteriors, seasons, publics, materials, concepts, tools, is astonishing: all shifting but all attuned to unique situations. Many works have evolved collaboratively, sometimes leading to the formations of groups (Moody and the Menstruators, Bernsteins, Bow Gamelan Ensemble) and sometimes not. Looking at this vibrant chronicle, the writer writing this looks for the points at which he entered the programme, what he witnessed, what he caught of it, small compared with many others, all with their individual memories.

The word 'performance' is actually too limited and contained to describe the multifarious and poetic manner of working which distinguishes Bean's career, and is especially marked in the 30 actions from between 1969 and 1974 which she has collectively renamed *Shadow Deeds*. To re-visit was to re-experiment with previous experiments. Were the years 1969-74 any different from other years? The answer will always be a mixture of personal experience, a particular point in the individual life story (Bean was 18-24 at that time), and a consensus of meaning that emerges from the chaos of worldly events. For Bean those years were a time when 'the inner landscape of the child met the zeitgeist'.[3] The 'inner landscape' was conditioned by her birth and childhood in Zambia, which was then the British colony of Northern Rhodesia, her art education in Cape Town, South Africa, her travel and her arrival in England, whose zeitgeist at that moment, it is generally agreed, was one of extraordinary ferment in society and in culture.

The conjuncture, and its significance for many young artists, has been nicely summed up by Jean Fisher:

> To the accompanying beat of rock and soul, a new generation of politically radicalised artists emerged in the wake of the unprecedented threats to global survival posed by Western militarism and ecological disaster, decolonisation struggles and apartheid, and the black and women's rights movements, which in turn produced a new scepticism to existing structures of power and their forms of representation. The restless energy produced by this realignment with the status quo was fuelled by the rise in media culture and accessibility of its own reproductive technologies ... Time-based media [such as video and super-8 film] formed a natural alliance with emergent performance art, generating new aesthetic languages

The Moodies (aka Moody and the Menstruators), Modernes Theater, Munich, 1974.
Photo: Pit Janzen

> through which the relations between the subject and the social could be 're-narrativised'. Because the work was ideas – not market – driven, its often ephemeral nature was not immediately susceptible to existing means of documentation and exhibition; and it is perhaps not fully appreciated the extent to which it forced a revision of both curatorial practice and art school curricula.[4]

It was just the number and diversity of these currents that excited Bean. She wanted to embrace them all. She identified with the women's movement but the designation 'feminist artist' would seem like a restriction. Her groups might perform at a benefit for the feminist magazine *Spare Rib* one evening and a working men's club the next: 'I felt so multi-levelled. Why does an artist need to assume a fixed identity, a career. Why such narrowing down?' Her work could be construed politically but she felt a certain liberation from the burden of politics which so dominated the horrible situation in apartheid South Africa. Just before leaving, and just before the end of her time at the Michaelis School of Fine Art in the University of Cape Town, she had sat for a day on a park bench reserved for whites only with the palms of her hands painted black and facing outwards. 'I thought of it as a visual protest. Only in retrospect could I see it in terms of performance.'

The artist has described her project *Autobituary* (2006), as 'announcing one's obituary to be alive again'. As such it could be seen as a paradoxical stratagem in a body of actions, large but almost unremarked-upon as such, by which artists have endeavoured to rescue their work from the fossilising process of institutionalisation and acculturation. One example would be the Brazilian artist Hélio Oiticica who near the end of his life carried out a little ceremony with a few friends he called *Counter Bolide: To Return Earth to the Earth* (1978). Back in his twenties he had gathered earth, or pigment, or brick dust, in boxes and glass containers he called *Bolides* ('fireballs' in Portuguese). But, feeling that these had come to be seen as art commodities rather than, as he intended them, 'energy-centres', he took some rich earth and a small wood frame to a desolate patch of waste-ground in the city of Rio de Janeiro, poured the earth into the frame and removed the frame to leave a dark square of earth on the earth. Clearly, it was intended to be a way of burying the *Bolide* as an object and resurrecting it as, in his phrase, a 'life-act'. Bean's strategy has also been to return to a period of exceptional creative and experimental energy, when 'literally hundreds of actions were produced', in diverse collaborations and 'ephemeral event structures which allowed and sustained this dynamic and spontaneous flow and generosity of spirit and ... non ego-driven process'.[5] One can speak of a 'creativity of the moment' in certain periods and contexts of the history of art that somehow sweeps artists up and emboldens their imaginations to go further than they would otherwise. Respecting the fluid nature and unfixed definition of what that creative moment really was, Bean devised her own method of re-visiting it: to perform again some of those original actions in an attempt to activate that memory which is not the same as cerebral memory, memory which remains in the body-cells even though we change the cells themselves continuously during our life time.

This calling on the past from the present, therefore, joins other recent work of Anne Bean in being an experiment with time. One of the most striking features of her work is that it posits and celebrates two measures of time: one of great physicality and visceral immediacy, usually expressed through her body, and the other of

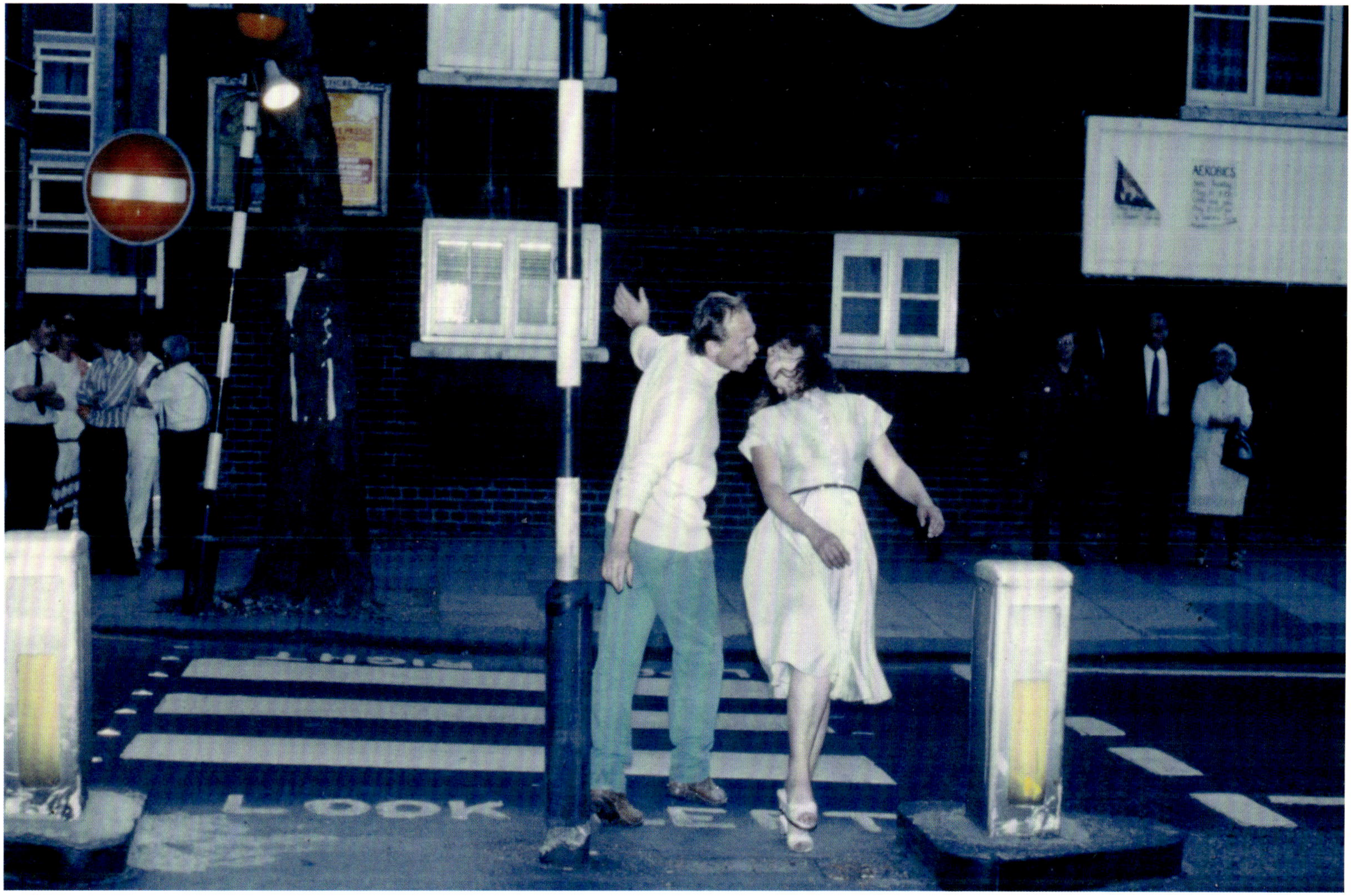

Anne Bean and Franklin Aalders, *Grand Pianos and Car Horns*, Air Gallery, 1981. *Time Out* described the performance as 'a zebra crossing piece that survived twenty minutes before two rapidly summoned policemen forced an ending [which] neatly showed how artists can get in the way of real life'. Photo: Guy Brett

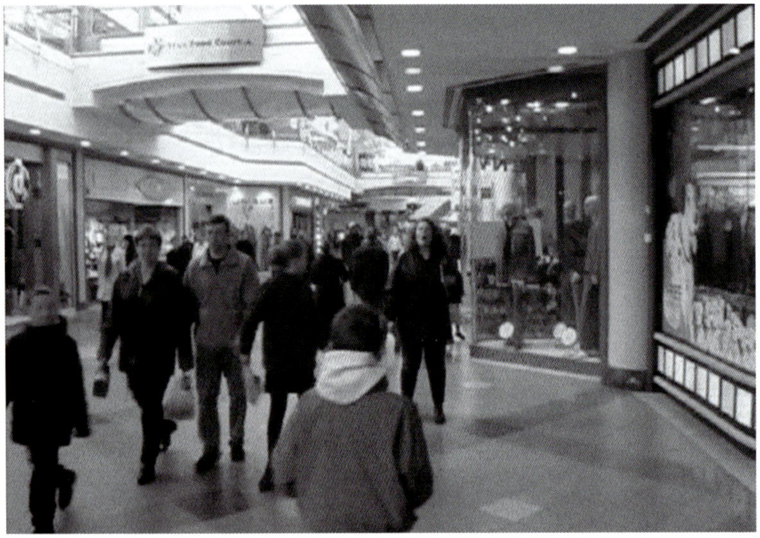

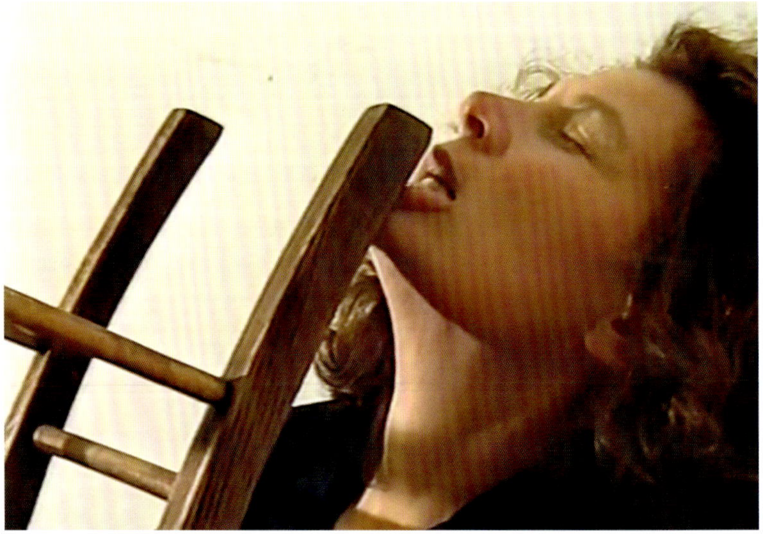

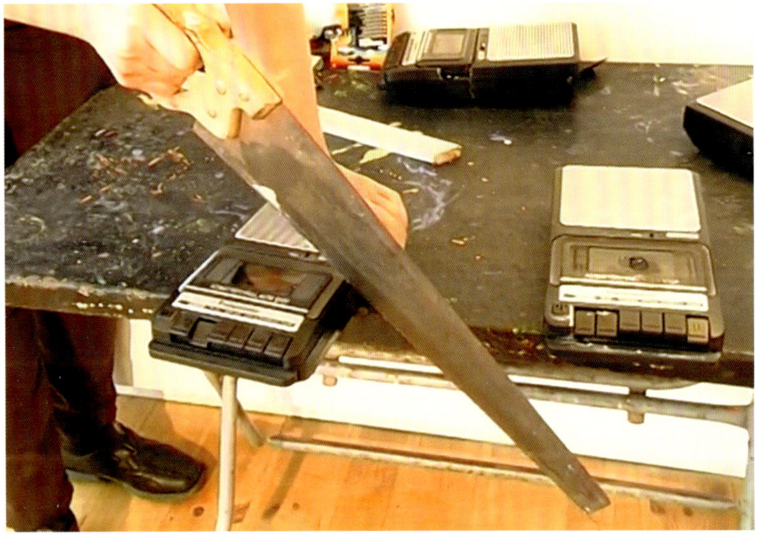

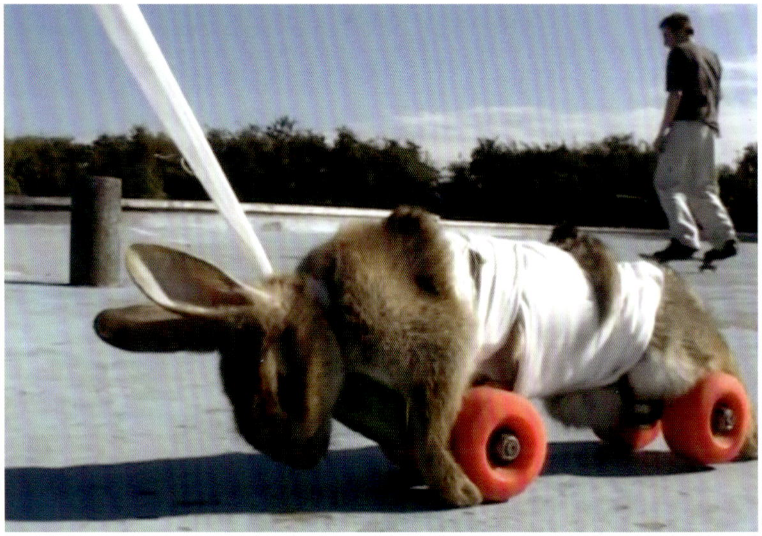

Top left: Anne Bean, *Shouting Mortality in a Glasgow Shopping Mall* reformed as a *Shadow Deed* in 2002 for *Autobituary* (2006). Still from video by Martin von Haselberg

Top right: Anne Bean, *Falling in Love with a Chair* reformed as a *Shadow Deed* in 1996 for *Autobituary* (2006). Still from video by Nina Sobell

Bottom left: Anne Bean, *See Saw* reformed as a *Shadow Deed* in 2002 for *Autobituary* (2006). Still from video by Lee Merrill-Sendall

Bottom right: Anne Bean, *Rabbit Piece* reformed as a *Shadow Deed* in 2002 for *Autobituary* (2006). Still from video by Lee Merrill-Sendall

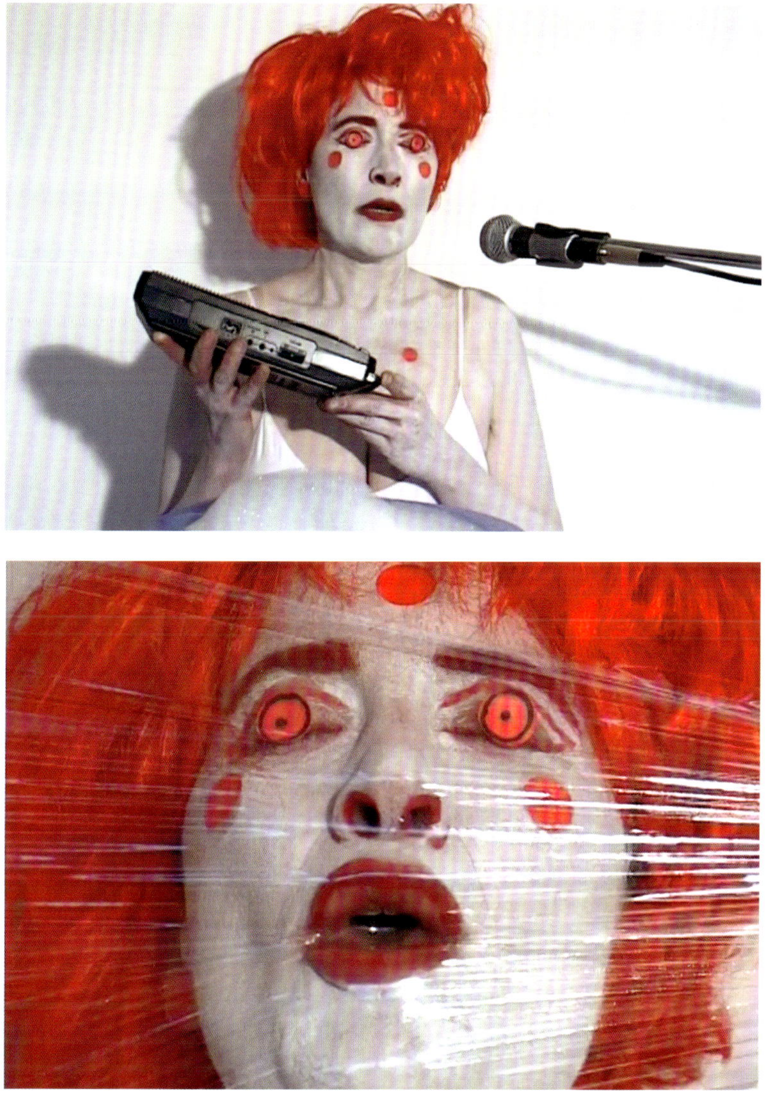

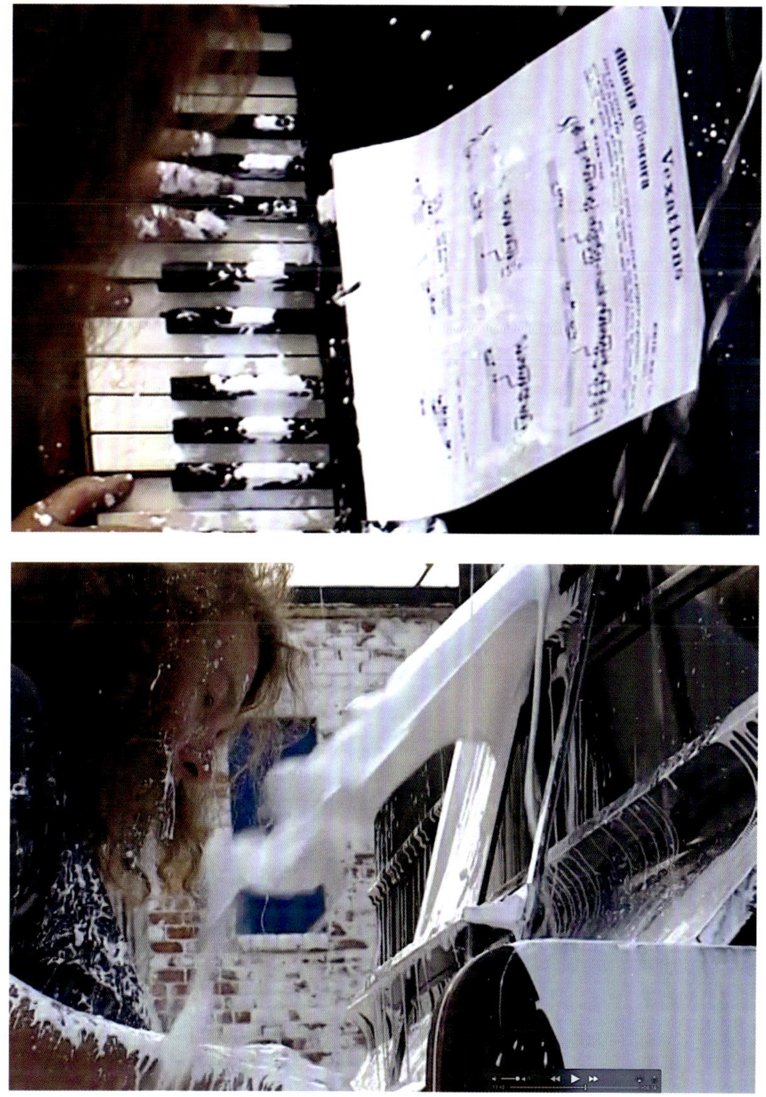

Left: Anne Bean, *Fever* reformed as a *Shadow Deed* in 1999 for *Autobituary* (2006). Still from video by Chris Bishop

Right: Anne Bean, *Vexations* reformed as a *Shadow Deed* in 2002 for *Autobituary* (2006). Still from video by Lee Merrill-Sendall

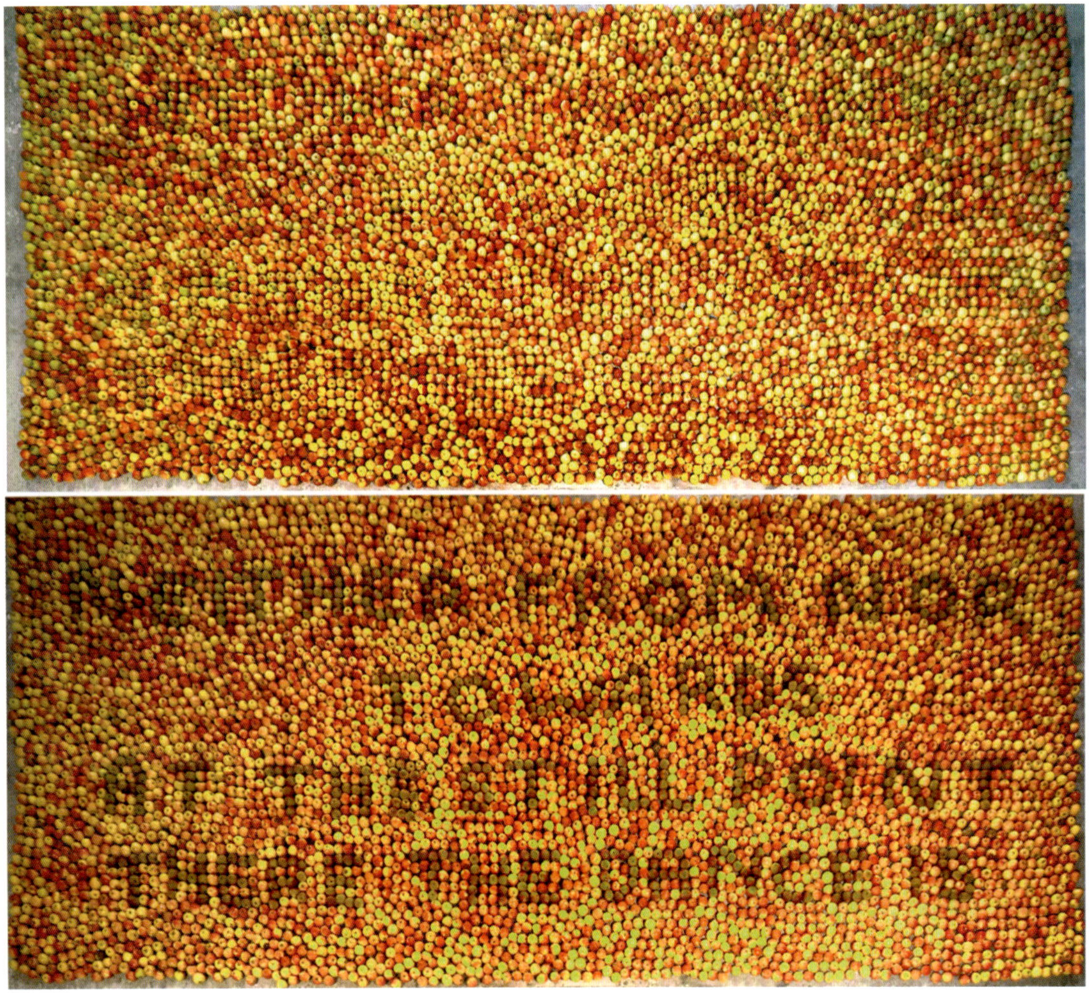

Anne Bean, *Remember Me*, as part of *REAP*, Dilston Grove, London, 2004-5. Photos: Brent Helsel
'Neither from nor towards; at the still point, there the dance is'

slow change that takes place over a long period of time, and is by contrast almost impersonal. Both tendencies can be found within the 30 episodes of *Shadow Deeds*. To take two examples of the first: she pricks her finger and writes 'RAW' with her blood on a sheet of glass, then turns over the glass so it reads "WAR" and smashes her head into it, breaking it; lying down she pours honey into her mouth from a funnel and attempts to carry on singing through the sweet viscosity. Then two examples of the second: a white sheet is suspended in sunlight and a model aircraft fixed behind it, casting a shadow; she draws around the shadow at intervals during the day showing its movement across the sheet as an intricate line drawing; she returns 20 pounds of sea salt and several sacks of sand to the sea shore to be gradually reclaimed by the sea. And one example of the humour of the unexpected which is so much part of such acts: at intervals during the *Shadow Deeds* she appears in various public spaces shouting the word 'MORTALITY' at the top of her voice. It originated in the observation that having a dog enables you to shout a word, namely, its name, very loudly in public. Staged amidst the completely ordinary, the cry of 'MORTALITY' seemed to echo in the vast emptiness of space and time, reminding me of a poem by Rabindranath Tagore in which he wrote about how the 'wailings of others' and the 'sighs of thousands and millions' went unheard in the howl and roar of the universe.[6]

In the event *Reap*, in which she collaborated with, and which included, many other artists, Bean worked with changes taking place over an entire year. It was staged in and around Southwark Park between September 2004 and September 2005 and included venues such as Café Gallery Projects London, Dilston Grove and the Coleman Project Space (as well as an abandoned garden of extraordinary spookiness secreted in the middle of the park). At one end of Dilston Grove Chapel Anne installed a vast square of massed apples on the floor. This work became a sort of comparative history of rotting. As the year wore on some apples reduced themselves to dust, while others remained almost pristine: it was hard to know why the differences were so great. A first impulse to congratulate the rosy apples for keeping their complexion over 12 long months gave way, on reflection, to valuing the brown shrivelled husks just as highly. Some lines from T. S. Eliot's *Ash Wednesday* painted on the wall read:

> Because I know that time is always time
> And place is always and only place
> And what is actual is actual only for one time
> And only for one place
> I rejoice that things are as they are …

Later I learned of the process behind the work, and of some things I'd missed at my own viewing. The 5,000 apples had been gathered together after initial research with Brogdale Apple Research Centre, at Imperial College, where Bean had learned about preservation by various techniques from waxing to Genetic Modification (waning): 'I wanted some apples in the piece to sustain their youth whilst those around crinkled and rotted, but a crucial part for me was that in these "youthful" apples I wanted a sentence to emerge'. The initial apples were totally indistinguishable from each other, then as colours changed to dark brown and decomposing began, certain apples emerged to reveal the words, also from Eliot, a line from *Burnt Norton*: 'Neither from nor towards; at the still point, there the dance.' In the final rotting the sentence submerged again.

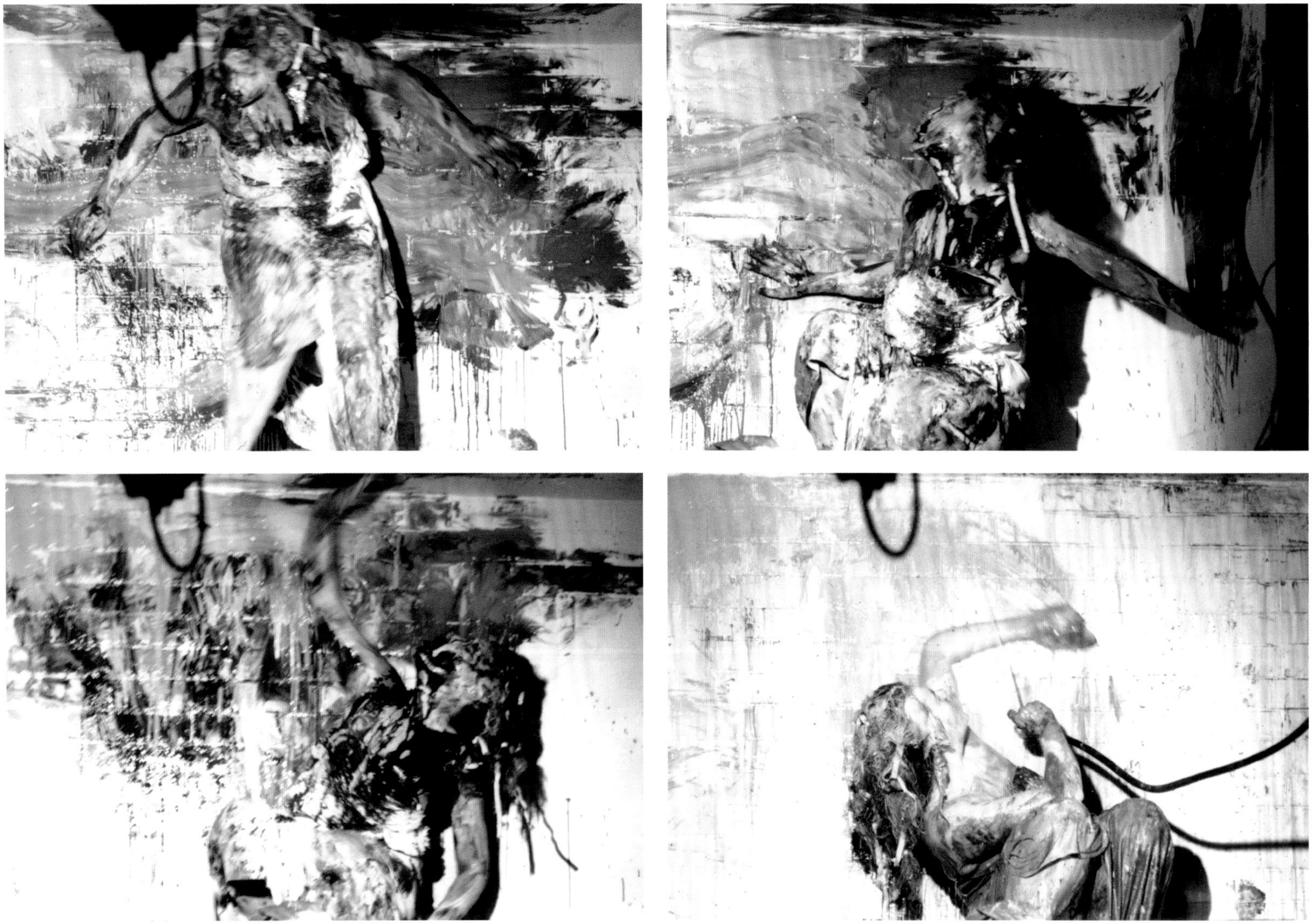

Above and opposite: Anne Bean, You Can Answer Me, Reading, 1983. Photos: Jim Harold

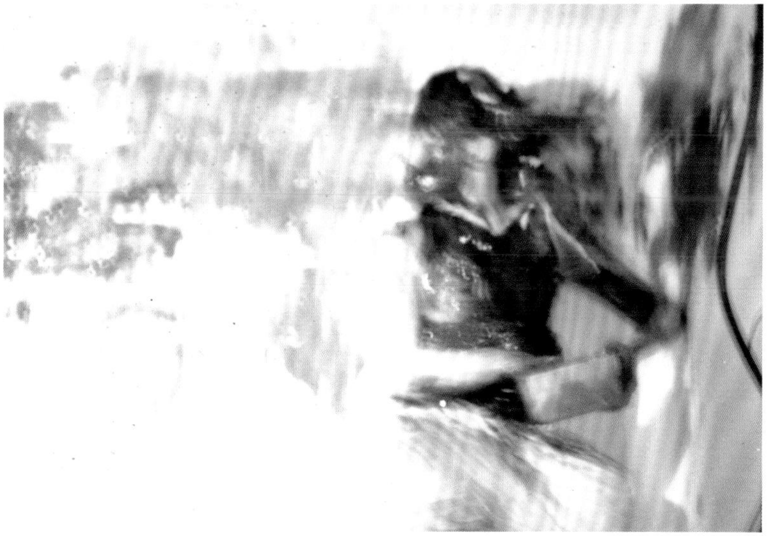

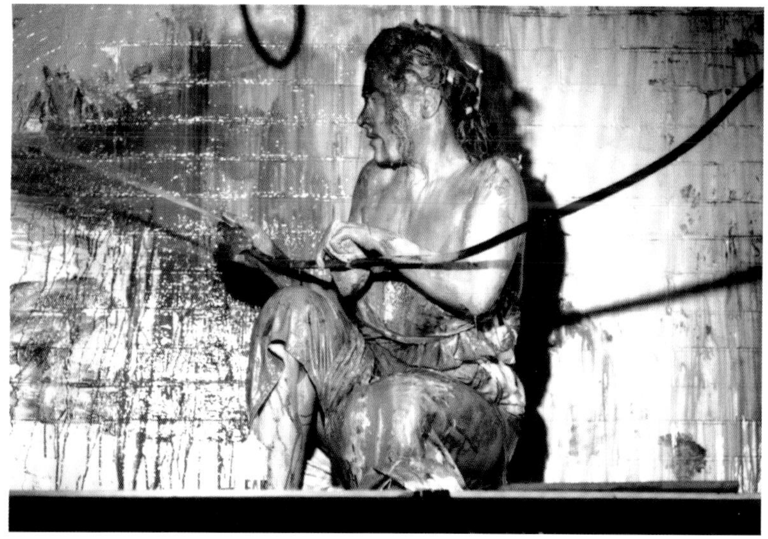

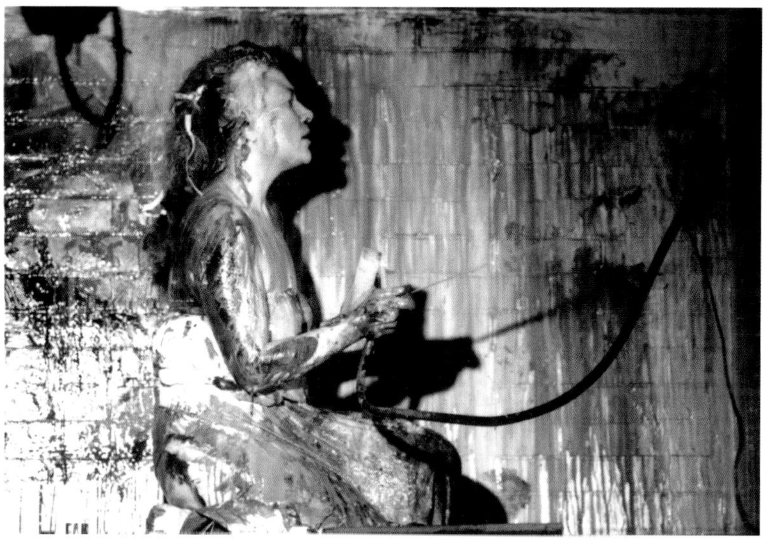

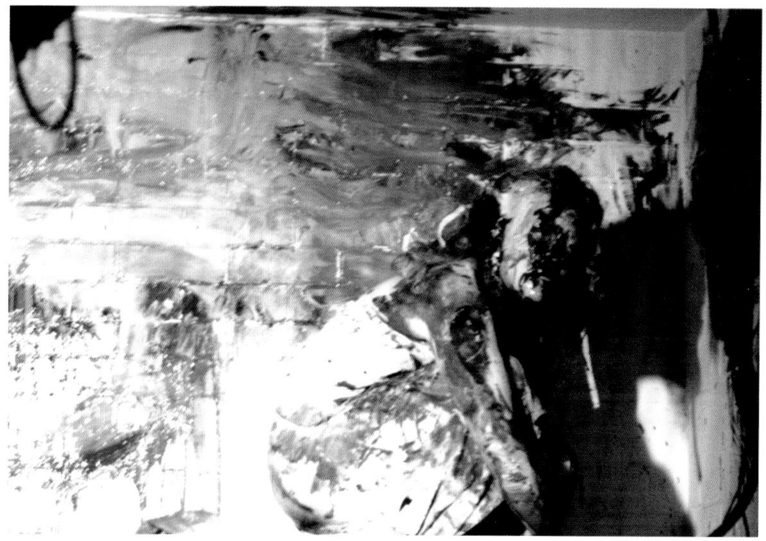

At the other end of the chapel, the equally large installation started off as a delicate construction of spiral incense coils supported with blue-green thread. When it was lit the process began of exchanging its physical substance for smell, creating a perfumed space, a year of scent, the conversion in infinite slowness of a visual into an olfactory phenomenon. In both works it was a question of the exit of objects, the entrance of dust.

Bean buried a teddy bear in the grounds of the Café Gallery and it was exhumed a year later with all the rigours of an archaeological excavation. As part of her involvement with the idea of change, she had wanted 'many identical and pristine objects to "travel" through a year together in wildly varying situations with their very different experiences reflected by their physical state at the end. I wanted people all around the world to be involved'. After wondering and discussing with other artists what that object could be (a book? shoes? pot plants? photos? various toys?), 'we kept coming back to the notion of a teddy bear ... I started speaking to people about the teddies and the idea sparked such enthusiastic speculation and a keenness to be involved that it stuck'. It was a stroke of genius as a device to spark collaboration and collective invention because it revealed, quite unexpectedly, how much people invest in teddies. 72 teddies and 72 artists and others became involved, generating 72 stories of complete individuality and imagination as Teddy, a kind of innocent, was thrust out into the world.

The results were shown as *Today's the Day* (2004-5) at the Coleman Gallery. Among them: teddy included in every wash cycle for a year (Sean Dower); sleeping teddy, eyes closed (Jo Stockham); a sooty teddy with a brush placed above a chimney in Hull (Paul Burwell); teddy sitting beside a large rock-drawing at an ancient Aboriginal sacred site in Australia (Cliff Kelsall); teddy dwarfed by the seeweedy hulk of Richard Wilson's sculpture *Slice of Reality*; petrified teddy, after a year in the hot springs of Western Bohemia (Tomas Vylita and Zuzana Rousová); mummified teddy (Sally Wallace-Jones). The scenarios, trials and joys that teddy went through were actually very adult, but his/her presence there emblematised each author's link with childhood, providing an original route to an unusual and touching exhibition, which in the process gently mocked the official seriousness of most art events.

Sometimes the fast and slow time come together in a single work. In 1992, Bean initiated, with Paul Burwell and Richard Wilson at the Serpentine Gallery, a memorial to Stephen Cripps. Cripps was an artist of great energy, inventiveness and audacity who died in 1982 at the age of 29. Pyrotechnics was his *métier* and he had been involved with Bean in events that led to the formation of the group that became Bow Gamelan Ensemble. In *A Slow Event: A Fresh Bunch of Flowers*, slow time was encapsulated in a 'melting monument', a stepped structure of blocks of ice in each of which was sealed a floral tribute from an artist or friend (these were as diverse and personal as the later teddies). The slow melt of the ice during the long June day, leaving only the scantiest debris of petals behind, was followed at dusk by the instantaneous: the 'launch' of a book on Steve Cripps into the sky as an explosion of paper with the aid of a mortar.

The Whitechapel *History of Performance*, the show at Matt's Gallery, and *Reap*, are pertinently, if unintentionally, linked by another of Bean's experiments with time. At the beginning of 2004, at the Scout Hut in Jamaica Road, Bermondsey, she did a performance in front of an audience of six women, of which no records were made. On the same night in the same place a year later she asked each of them to

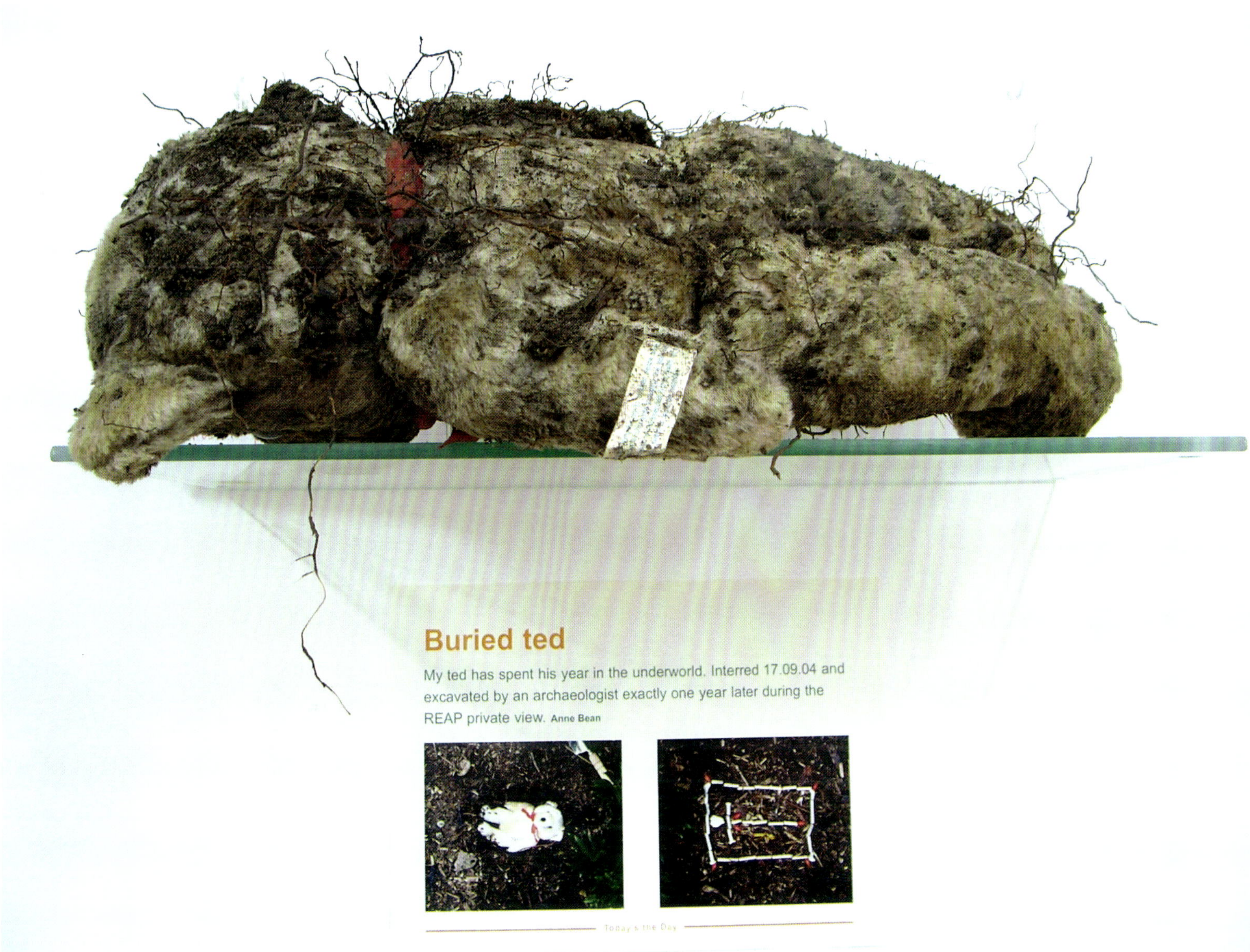

Anne Bean, *Today's the Day*: *Buried Ted*, on display in Coleman Project Space, London, as part of *REAP,* Dilston Grove, London, 2005

pp 206-7: Installation view of *Anne Bean: Autobituary*, Matt's Gallery, London, 2006. Photo: John Riddy, courtesy Matt's Gallery

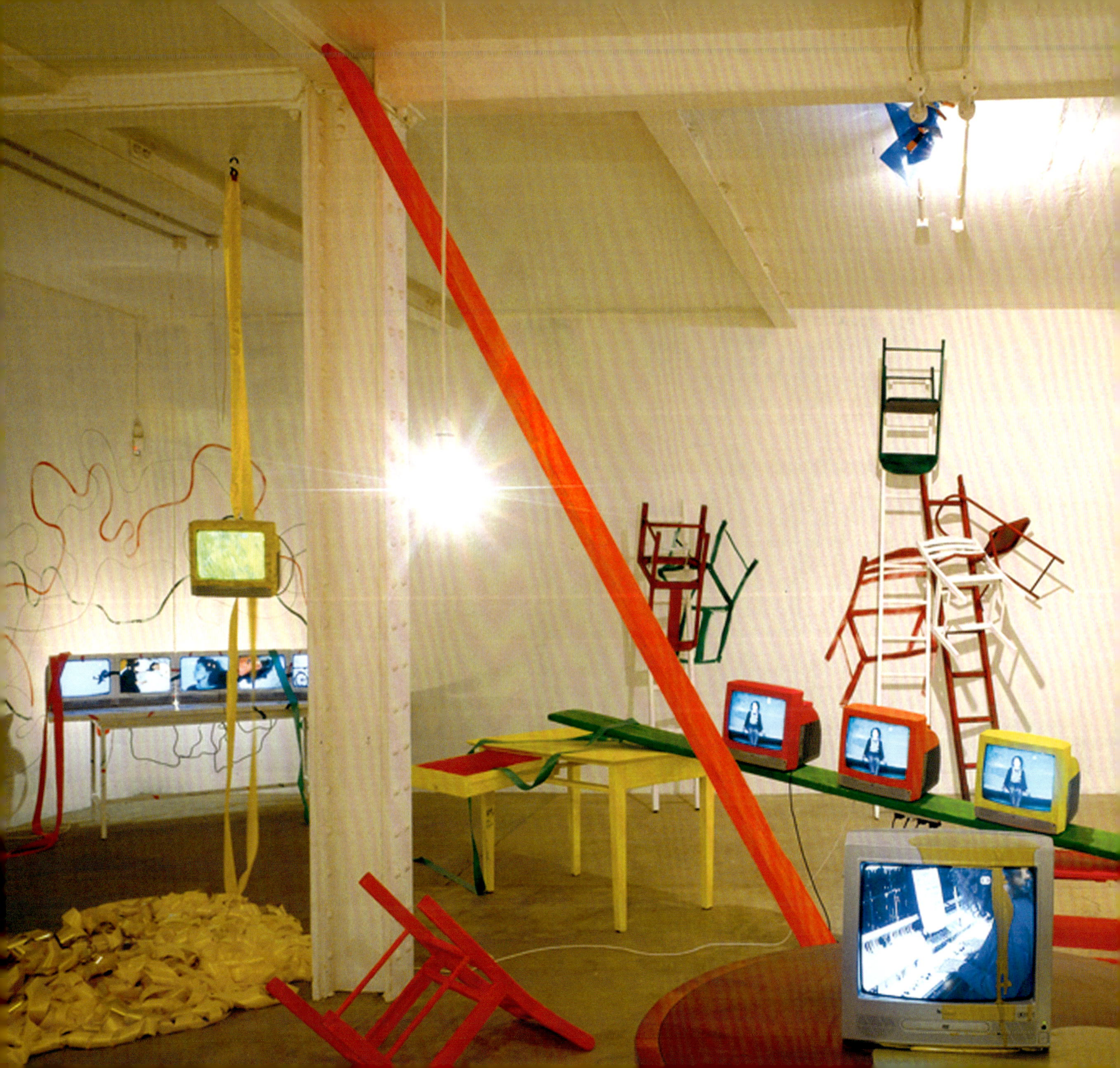

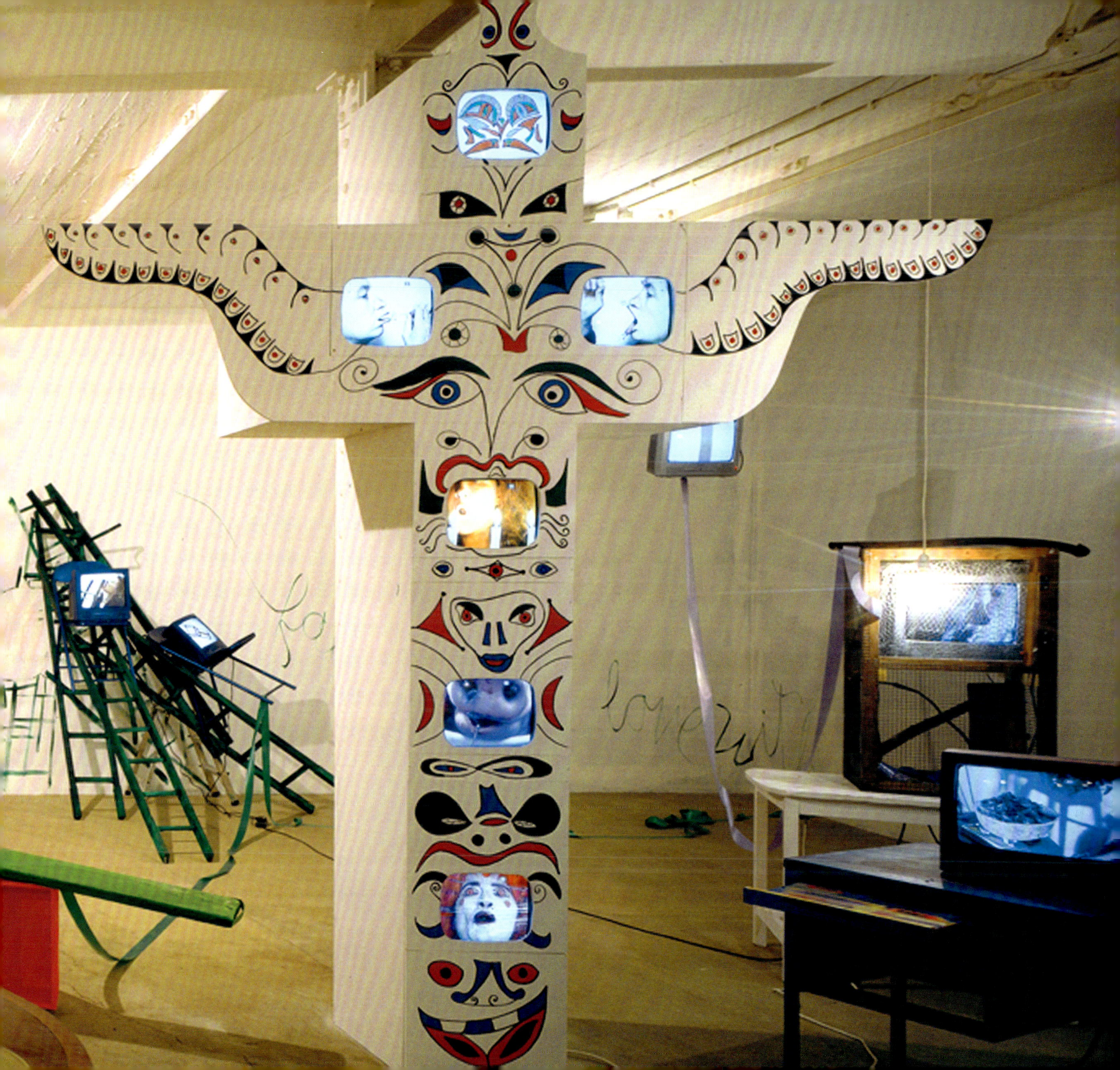

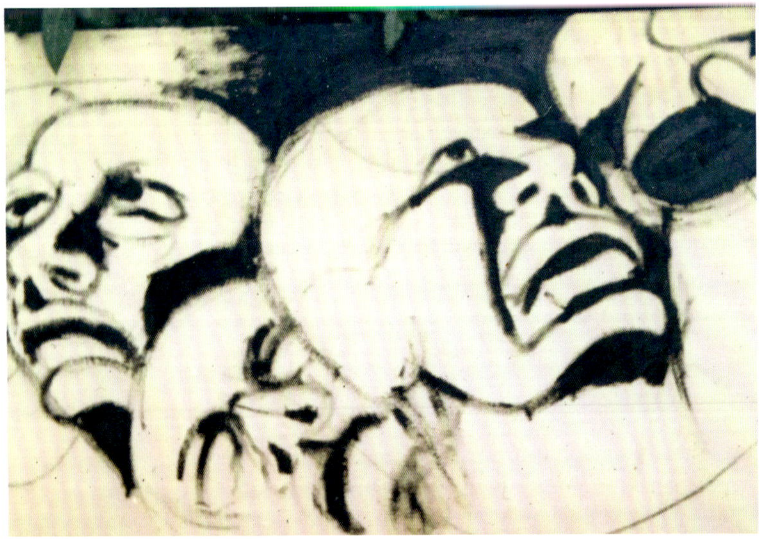

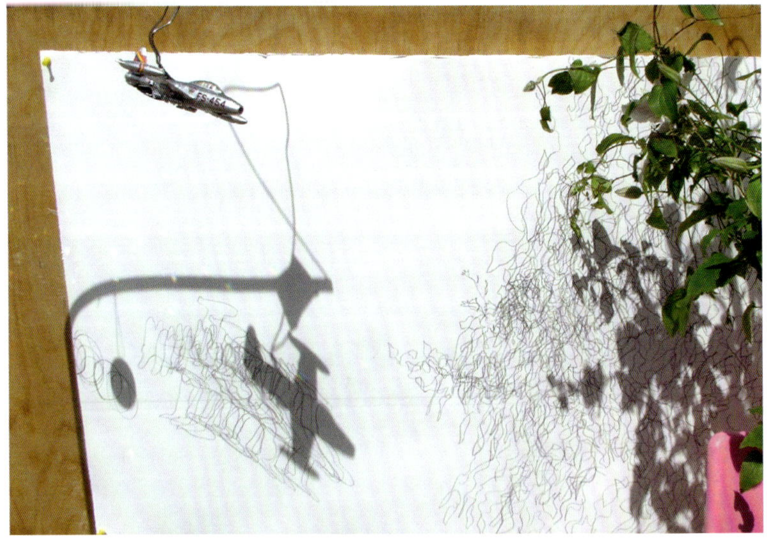

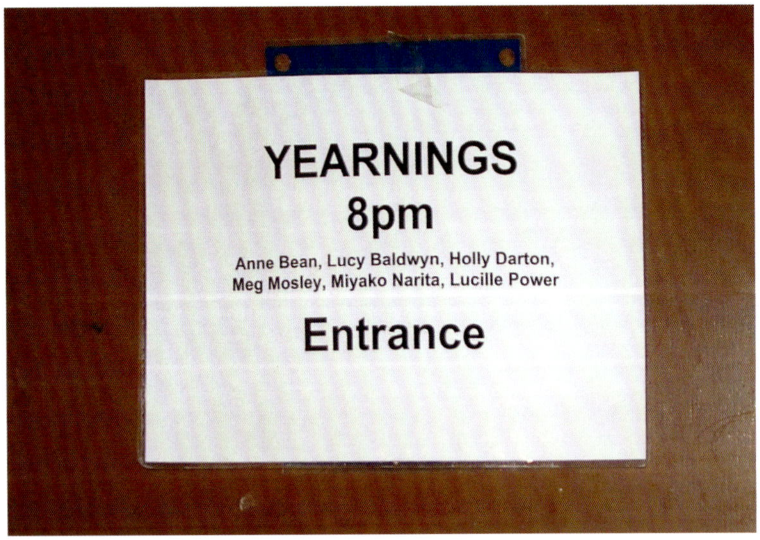

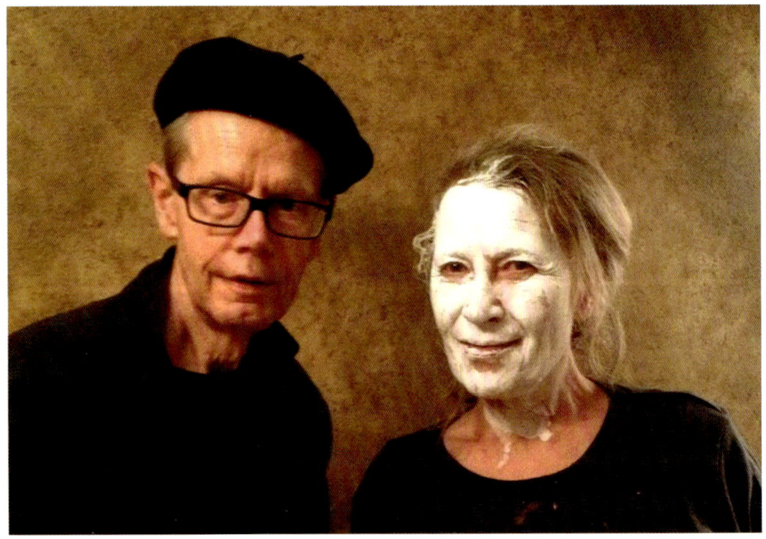

Top left: Anne Bean, *Black and White*, oil on board (approx. 6' by 3'), 1969. I painted only in black and white for several months to underpin the absurdity of apartheid's definition of colour at The Michaelis School of Fine Art, Cape Town

Top right: Anne Bean, sundial drawing in progress, 2004 (filmed for *Low Flying Aircraft*)

Bottom left: The only image of Anne Bean, *Yearnings*, Jamaica Road Scout Hall, Bermondsey, 2005

Bottom right: Guy Brett and Anne Bean after *Unpainting* 2016. Guy spoke about his memory of *Vexations*, in *Autobituary*, as 'painting and unpainting time' itself. Photo: Jane England

pp. 210-11: Anne Bean, Paul Burwell and Richard Wilson, *A Slow Event: A Fresh Bunch of Flowers*, Serpentine Gallery, 1992, commemorating the tenth anniversary of Stephen Cripps's death. Photo: Ronnie Israel re-perform the piece for her according to their memories of it. They did so in turn, without seeing each other's versions. *Yearnings*, as the piece was called, was re-done as a public performance, which Bean herself took part in and performed her own memory of the original. 'I asked for absolutely no documentation so there are no images at all of this work which, in the fevered recording of today, really gave it its own "actuality".' Not only were all their memories of what happened very individual and different, but sometimes the six witnesses remembered things Bean had done that even she had forgotten, or given little importance to. Possible conclusions of the experiment? That there is no remembering without forgetting, that there is no single truth, and that we need the Other!

On reflection, I have the feeling that Anne Bean's treatment of time in her works parallels closely her treatment of time in her creative life. The instantaneous and the long-drawn-out are both measures which are foreign, in excess of, or outside the rationalised time which the institution of art increasingly imposes on the production of artists, and which it demands in exchange for fame and power.

A crucial difference exists between the time of creation and the time of the market. Bean has questioned this notion of fame and career and has even said she would prefer to remain anonymous, not through any saintly abnegation of the self, but from a desire for freedom, not to be tidied up or narrowed down. This is expressed in her rolling experimental and collaborative practice over the years and her responsiveness to place and time and other people which has its own rhythm, and which along the way has allowed for the redefinition, or playful expansion, of genres such as drawing or sculpture, and has extended to ways of referring to art work of the past, not only her own past and art work, which keep its spirit alive, as when, in *Shadow Deeds*, a liberal white monochrome comes raining down on the fingers and keyboard of a pianist (the artist) playing Erik Satie's *Vexations*.

1. This essay was previously published as Guy Brett, 'Within Living Memory' in Anne Bean, *Autobituary: Shadow Deeds* (London: Matt's Gallery, 2006), pp. 5-27.

2. The re-performance was part of *A Short History of Performance Vol. 1*, Whitechapel Gallery, London, 2002. The earlier performance took place in 1973.

3. Remarks by Anne Bean that are not footnoted were made to the author in conversation during the writing of this essay.

4. Jean Fisher, 'Introduction', *Electronic Shadows: The Art of Tina Keane* (London: Black Dog, 2004), p. 6.

5. Anne Bean, untitled statement, *Autobituary: Shadow Deeds*, p. 3.

6. Rabindranath Tagore, *Our Universe*, trans. by Indu Dutt (Delhi: Jaico, 1969), p. 68.

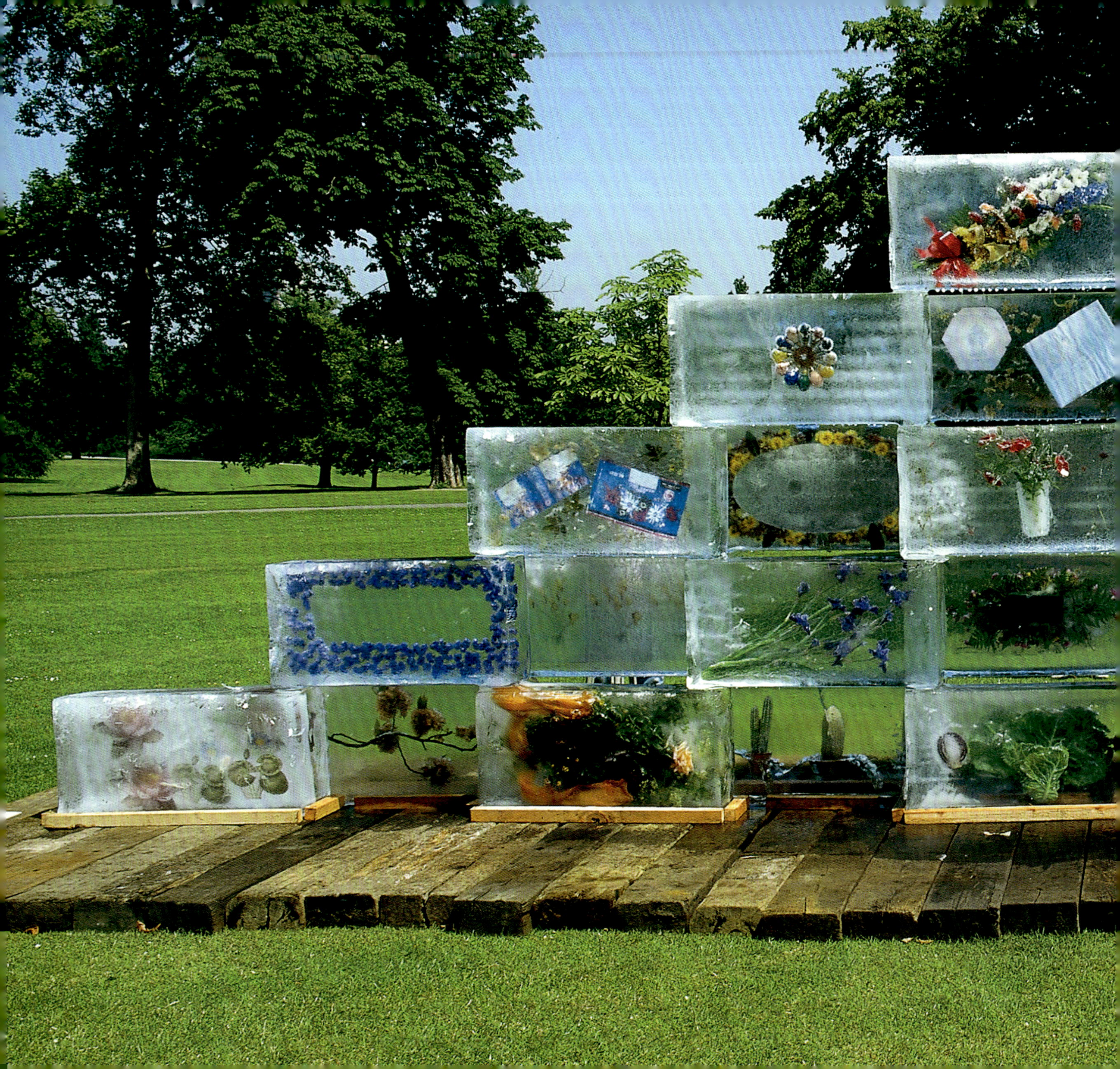

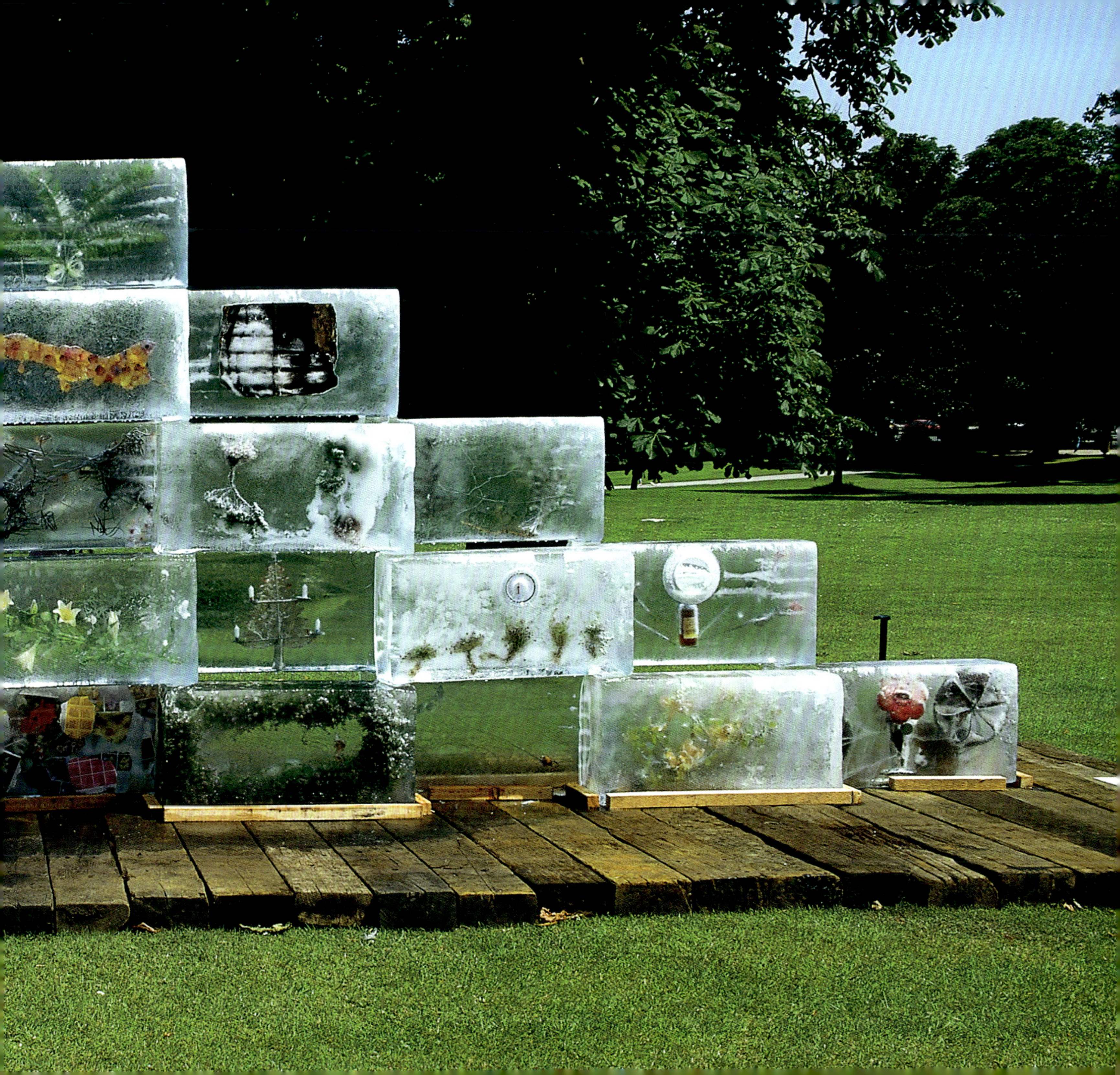

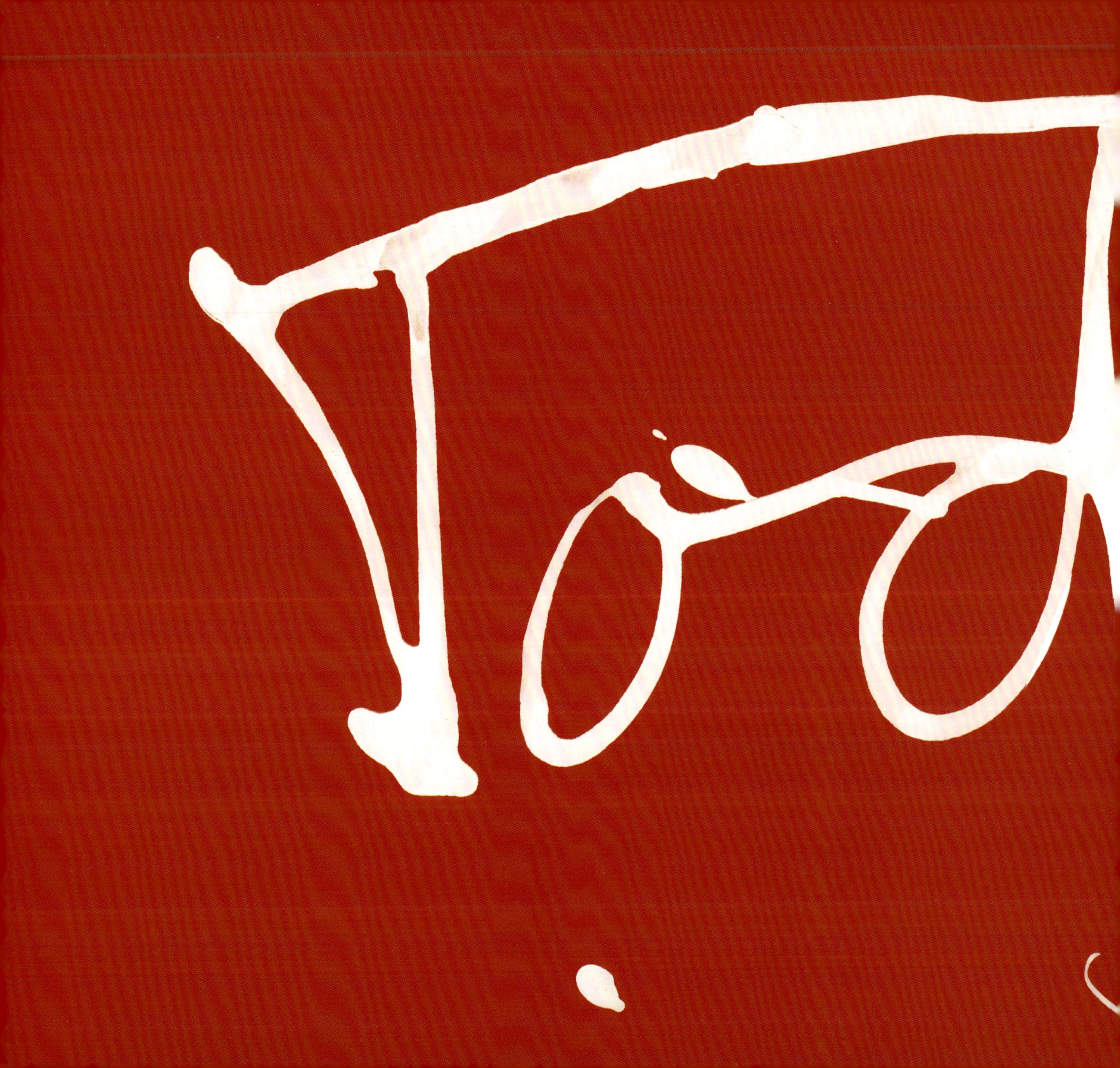

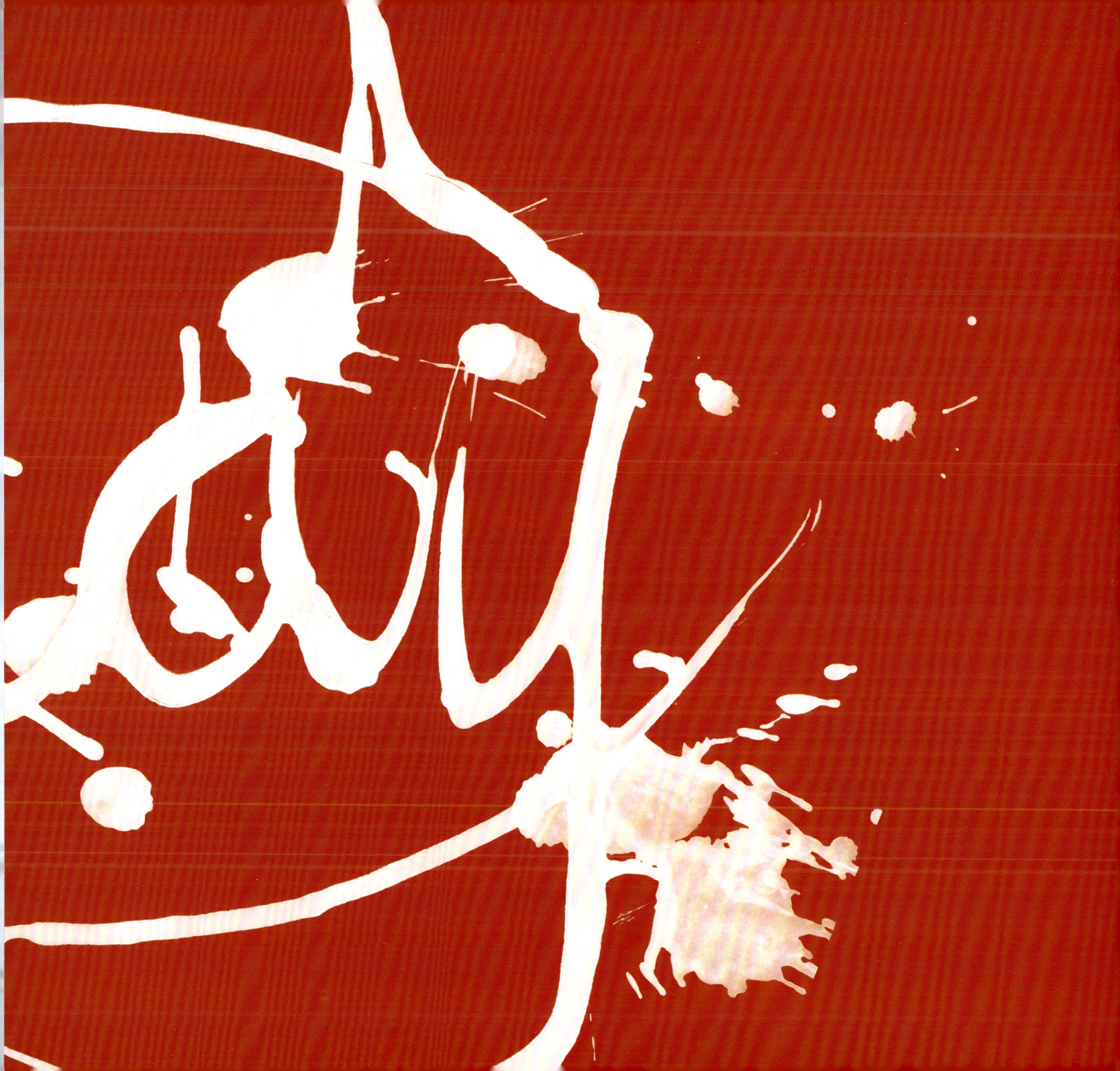

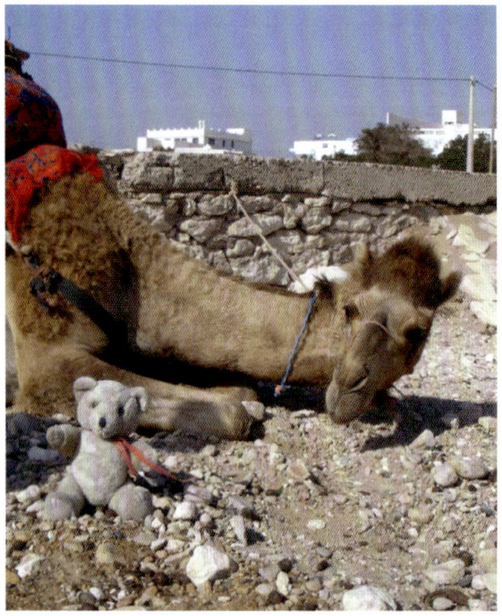

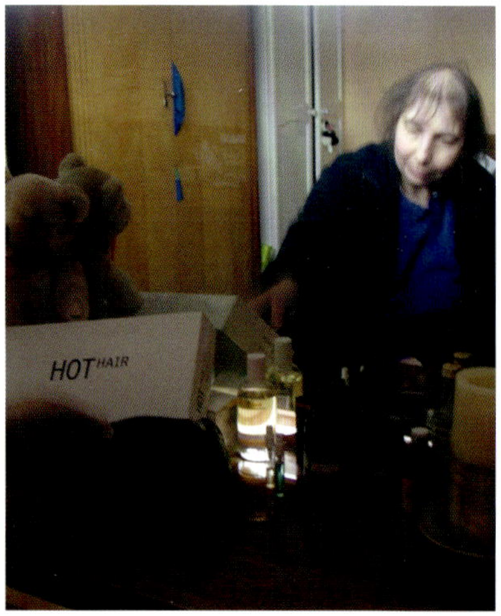

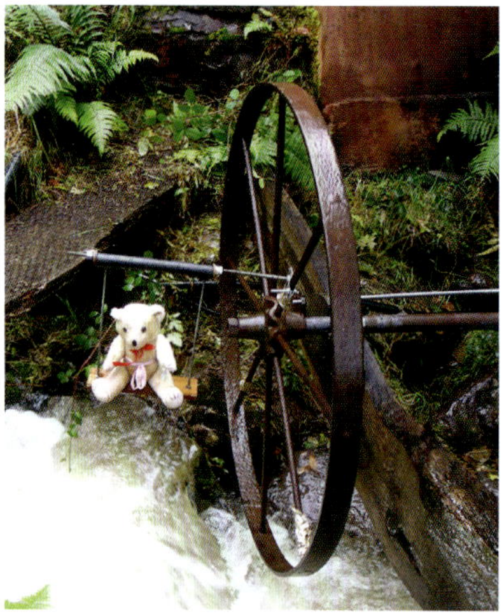

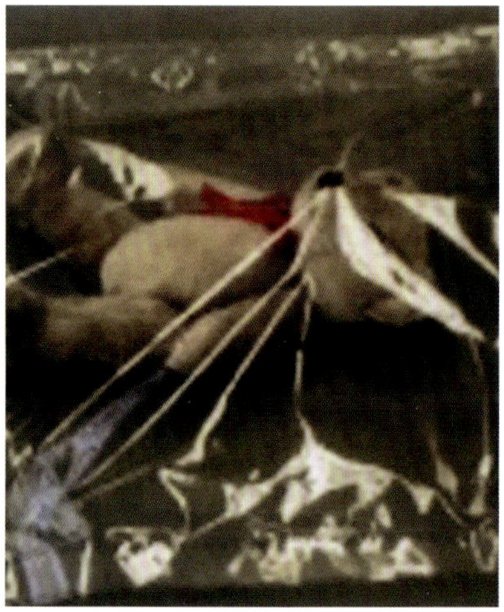

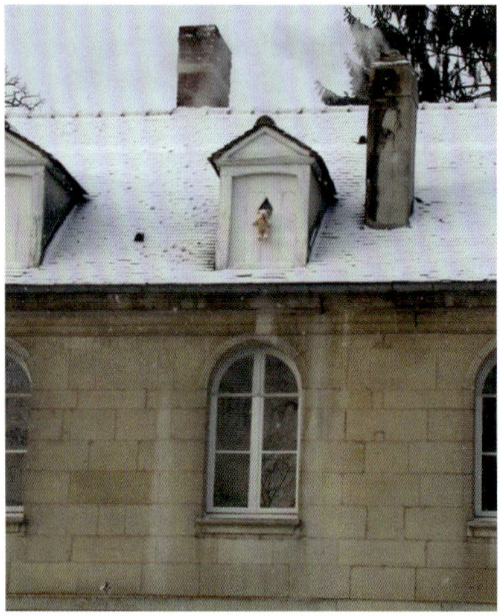

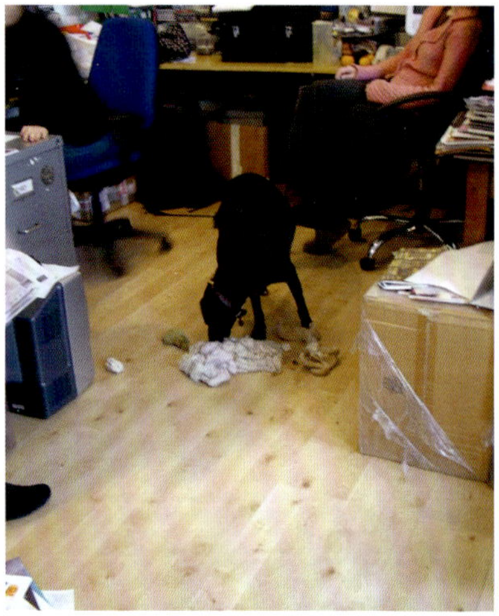

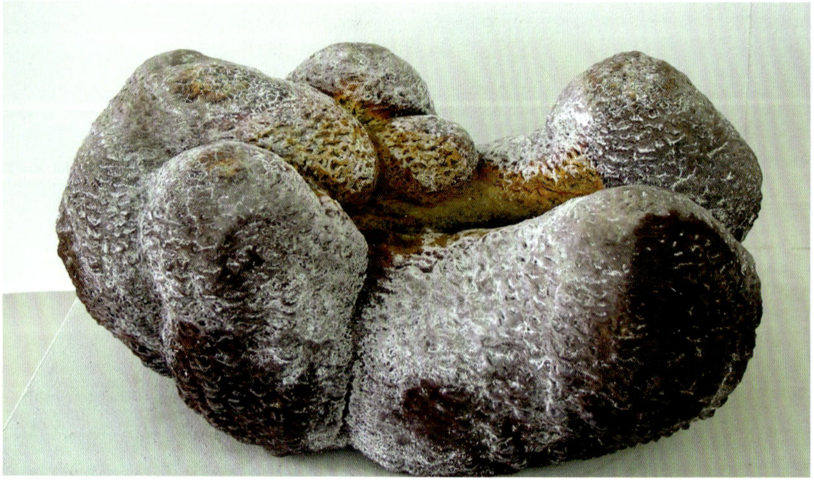

Top: Graham Carter and Emma Wilson, *Mustapha Ted*, Morocco; Sharon Malyan, *Journey Bear*, confidante and companion; Bean family, *Turbine Ted*, Eire; Barbara Steveni, *Isola Ted*, Tate Archives

Bottom: Hugo and Hermine Williams, *Chateau Ted*, France; Olly, *Gnawing Dog Teddy*; Tomas Vylita and Zuzana Rousová, *Spa Ted: Petrification*, Karlovy Vary hot springs, Bohemia

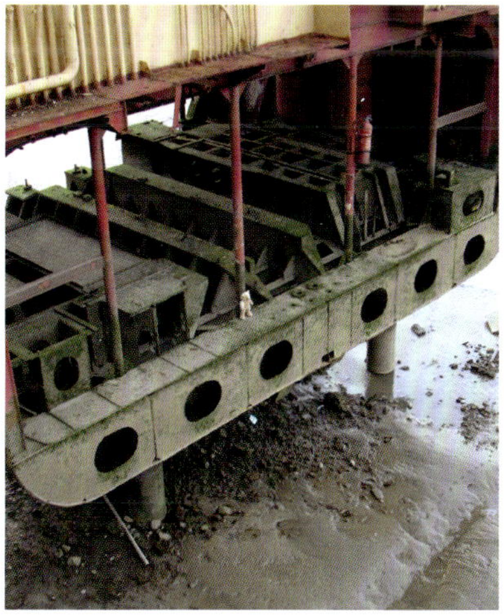

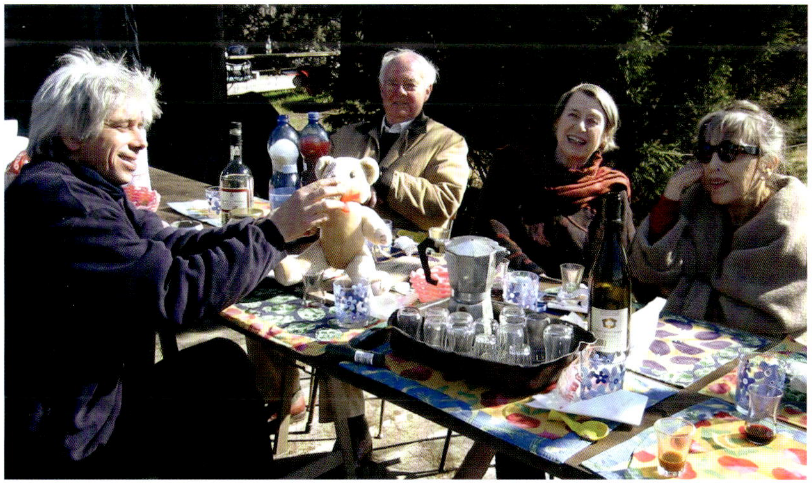

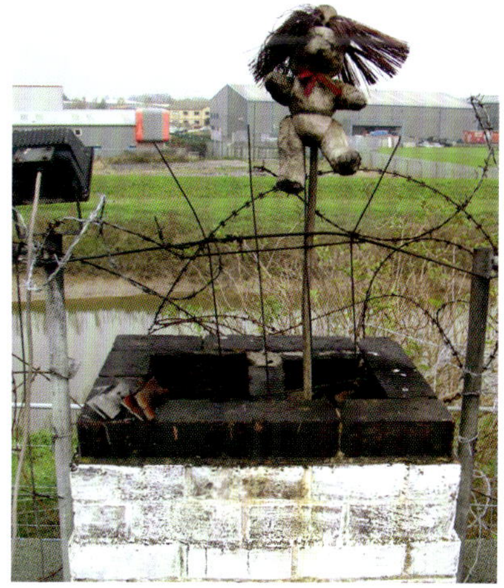

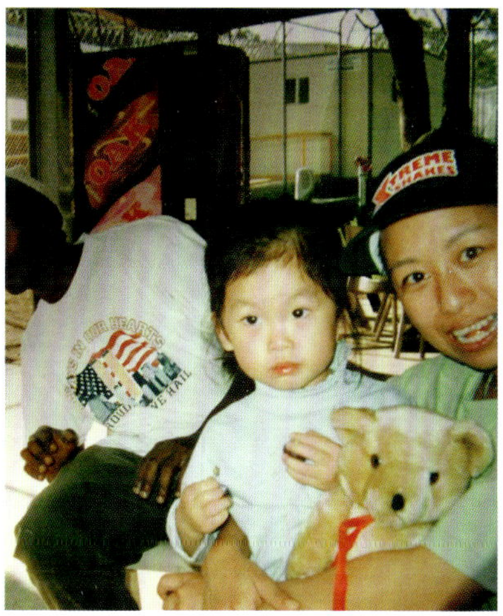

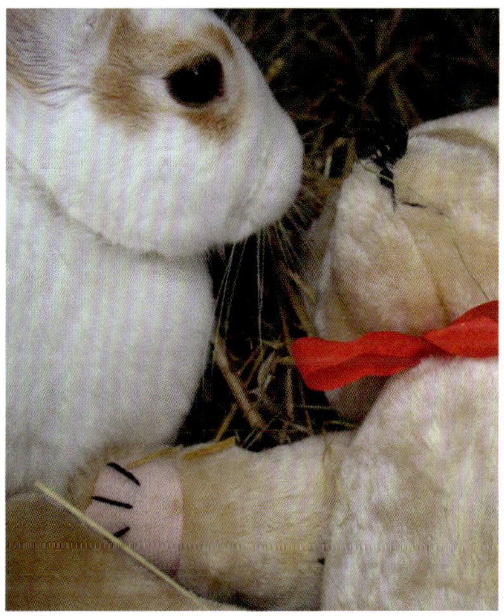

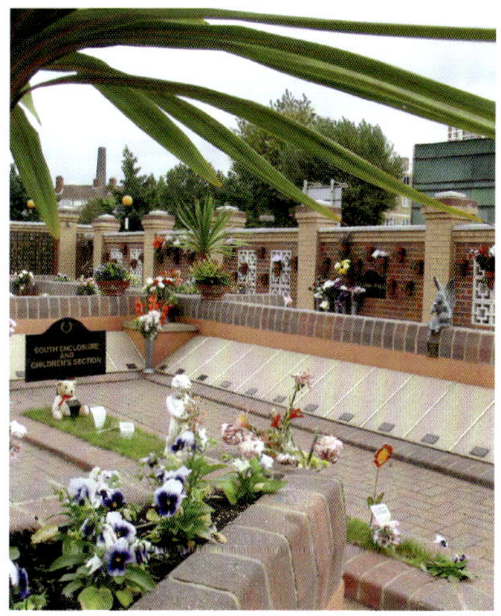

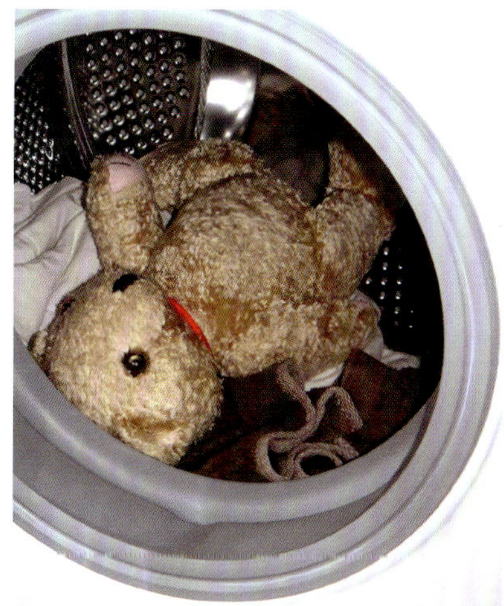

Top: Richard Wilson, *Tidal Ted, Slice of Reality*; Jane da Mosto, *Laguna Ted*; Paul Burwell, *Chimney Ted*, Kingston Rowing Club, Hull

Bottom: Jenya Iljon, *Refugee Bear*, Australia; Hazel Cook, *Rabbit Ted*; Anne Bean and Nina Sobell, *Memorial for Cori Ted*; Sean Dower, *Frontloader Ted*

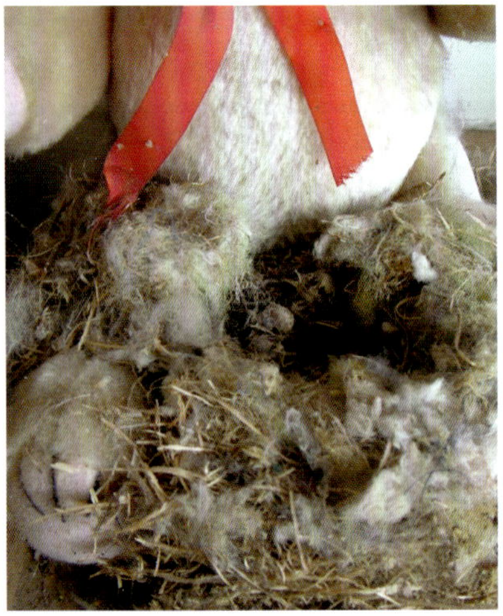
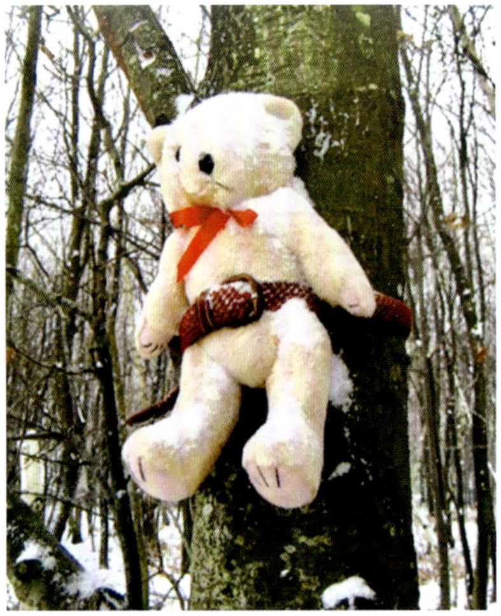
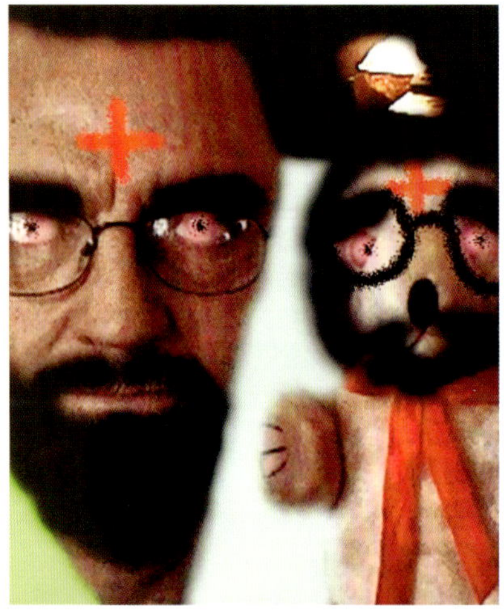
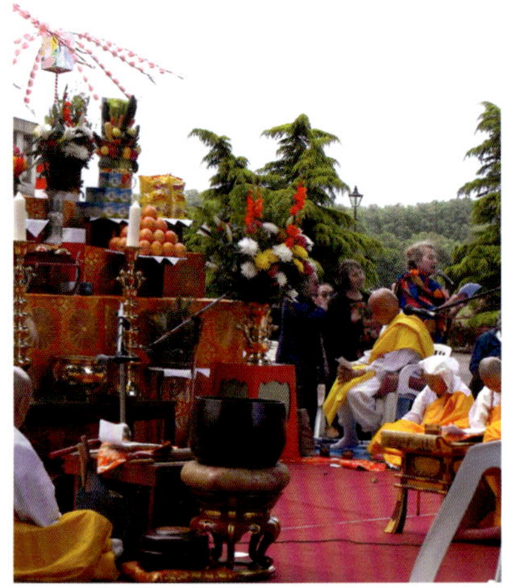
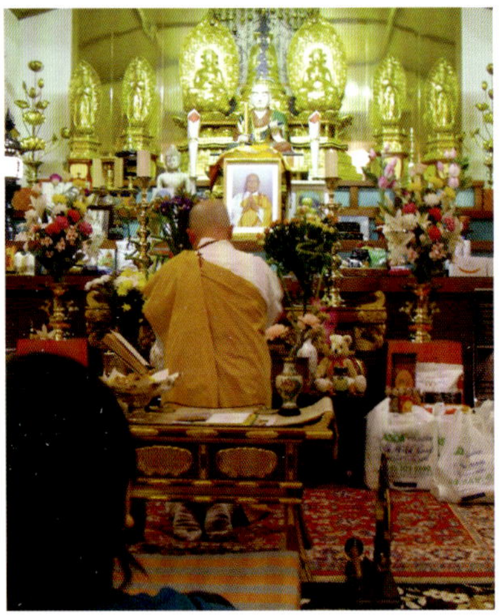
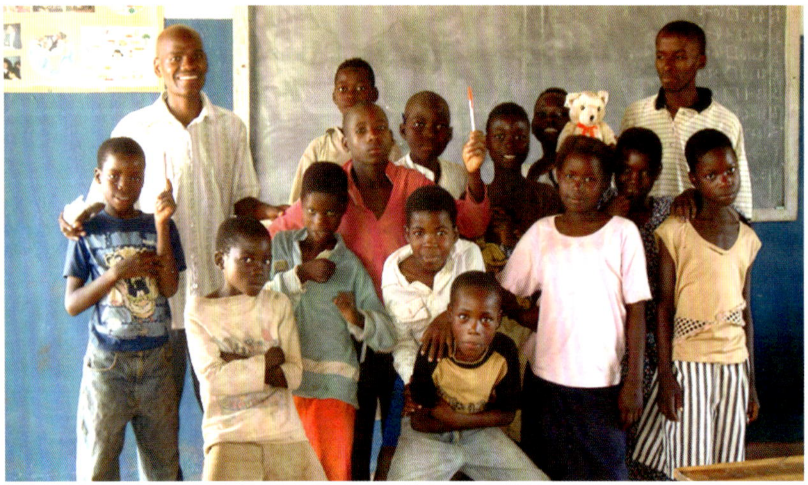
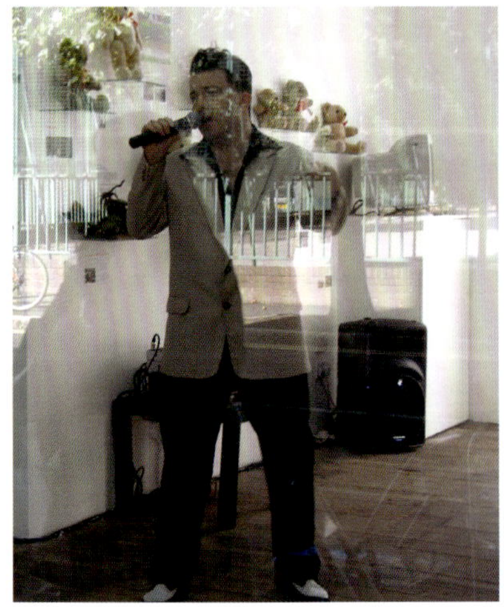

Top (left to right): Kirsten Reynolds, *Birdbox Ted*; Harry Kipper (Martin von Haselberg), *New York Ted*; Harry Kipper (Brian Routh), *Bri and George*; Peace Pagoda, Battersea Park, 30th Anniversary, 2015.

Bottom (left to right): Reverend Nagase, *Peace Pagoda Ted*; *Liwase Ted*, Mwandi Community School, Livingstone, Zambia; an Elvis impersonator opening the exhibition of *Today's the Day*, Coleman Project Space 2005. Photo: Mai T. Seguro

When the teds returned from all these ventures, one year later, bearing the evidence of their journeys, physical or metaphysical, they were exhibited at Coleman Project Space. The private view opened with a blessing by Rev. Nagase, the Buddhist monk, as well as an Elvis impersonator repeatedly singing "Let me be your Teddy Bear".

Reverend Nagase has been involved with the peace movement for a long time, including appealing for a debt-free start to the twenty-first century for poor countries. He has made and continues to make months-long walking and drumming peace pilgrimages between significant places. In a text he wrote entitled 'IMAGINE PEACE, NAMUMYOHORENGEKYO', he states:

'Shakyamuni Buddha came upon the Pagoda shape by folding his robe as a base for his upturned begging bowl against which he leaned his stick. This gives the classic form of reliquary pagodas: a square base surmounted by a pinnacled dome. The Peace Pagoda is eternal contemporary art. In this military-industrial complex orientated world, the wandering Buddhist monk's religious mendicant life of prayer for world peace is living contemporary art with tears. I met Anne Bean and was invited to join her unique projects on a number of occasions and have fond memories of them.'

For nearly 20 years I have been involved with the Peace Day at the Pagoda in Battersea Park, which was built by Nipponzan Myohoji Buddhists, Reverend Nagase being the main keeper of the Pagoda.

On the thirtieth Anniversary of the Peace Pagoda in 2015, I read parts of Allen Ginsberg's poem *Kaddish* (1959) to the Buddhist monks and nuns and other guests:

And how Death is that remedy
all singers dream of, sing,
remember, prophesy as in
the Hebrew Anthem, or the
Buddhist Book of Answers –
and my own imagination of
a withered leaf – at dawn –

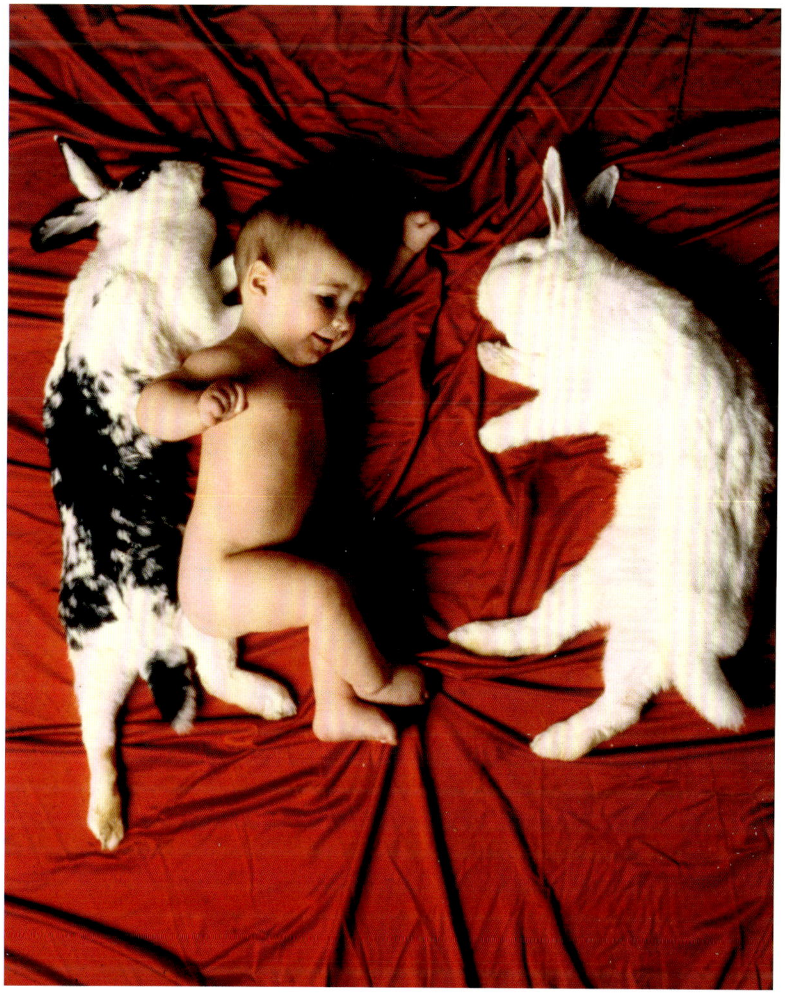

Anne Bean, *Rabbitears*, Available Resources, Derry, 1991.
A slide work with performance for a former funeral parlour

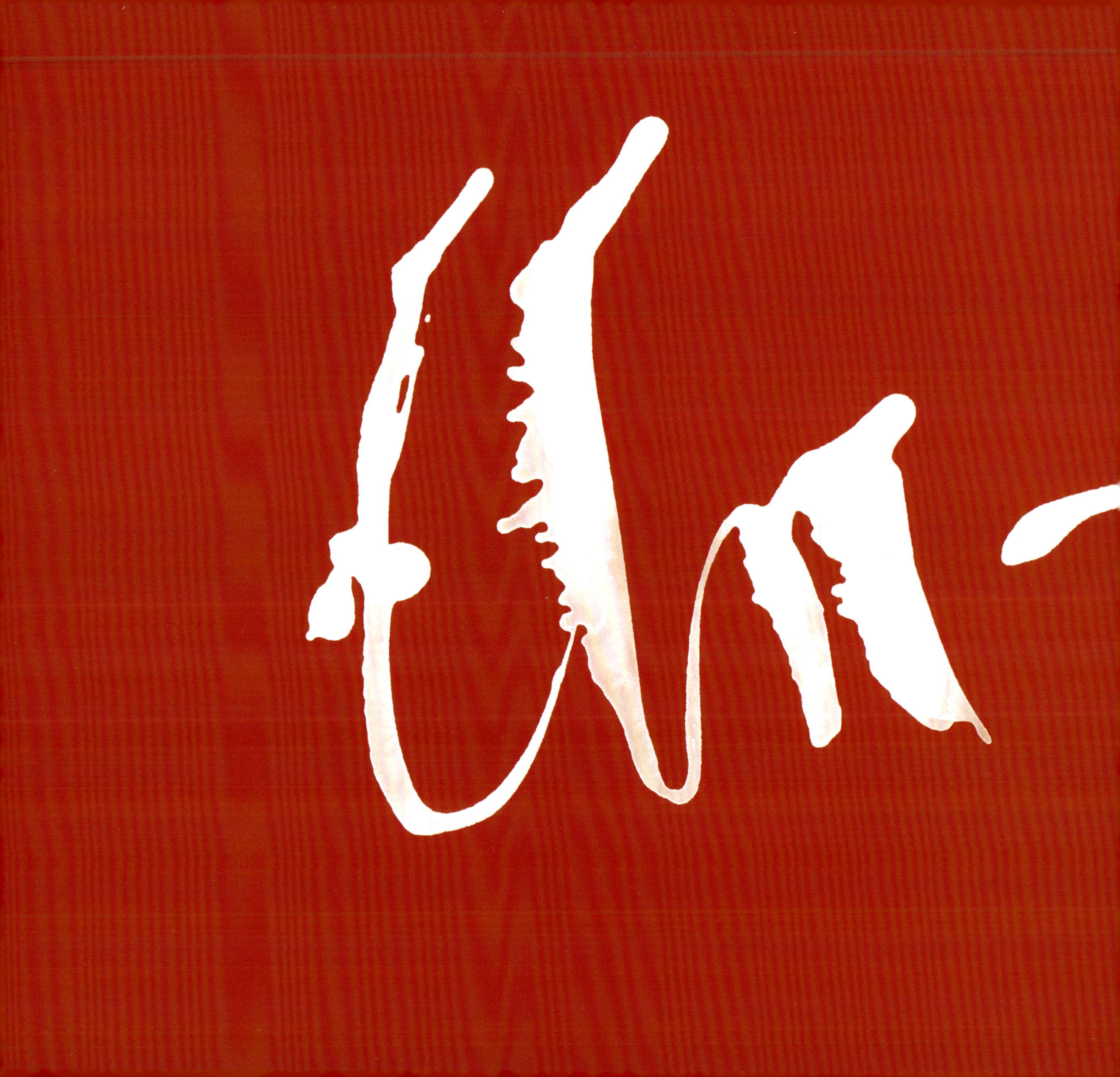

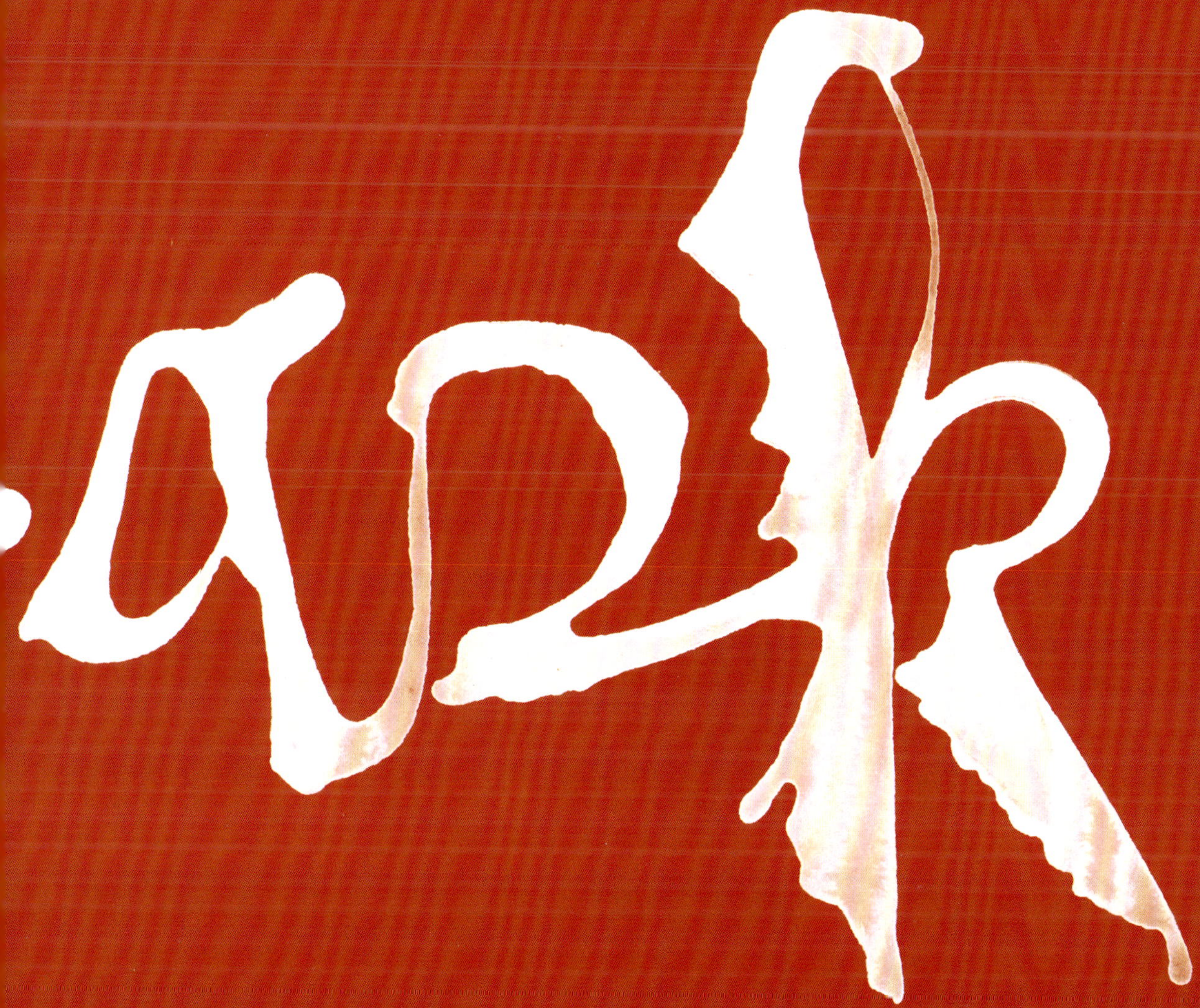

UN-ASK THE QUESTION

I met Zack Simpila and the other members of Liwase Theatre in 2000, when I returned to Zambia to make work with them for the local Livingstone festival. Since leaving in 1968, I had last visited Livingstone, Zambia in 1986, when I had been warned not to go there. I had a harrowing time seeing the beginning of the rampant devastation of HIV/AIDS, the instability caused by various guerrilla factions taking hold, including Mozambican FRELIMO, plus I was arrested and held on trumped-up charges, fortuitously briefly. I felt cautious returning years later but the Liwase group met me at the airport and called me 'our sister', which was extremely meaningful to me. The African sounding word 'Liwase' comes from funding they received from Livingstone Water and Sewage Company.

I worked with Liwase and young children orphaned and often affected by HIV/AIDS towards a performance, workshopping it in the Victoria Hall, where as a child I had been involved in several poetry readings and plays. Spontaneous actions and improvised words led to the composition of personal, heartfelt songs. In the final performance I included my own memory as a child lying on my back at night looking up at the vast star-filled blackness, overwhelmed by the sensation of falling into the sky.

I placed all the participants in configurations to form shapes of various constellations in the night sky at the time and gave them each helium balloons with sparklers attached. As they sang the songs they had composed, they lit the sparklers and released the balloons where the sparklers momentarily merged with the stars.

I asked Zack to write something about the group for this book. Liwase represents for me one of many organisations who daily transcend the huge difficulties of their lives and countries to make an incalculable difference, often unacknowledged, except by the people who most matter, the people who learn, laugh and love with them:

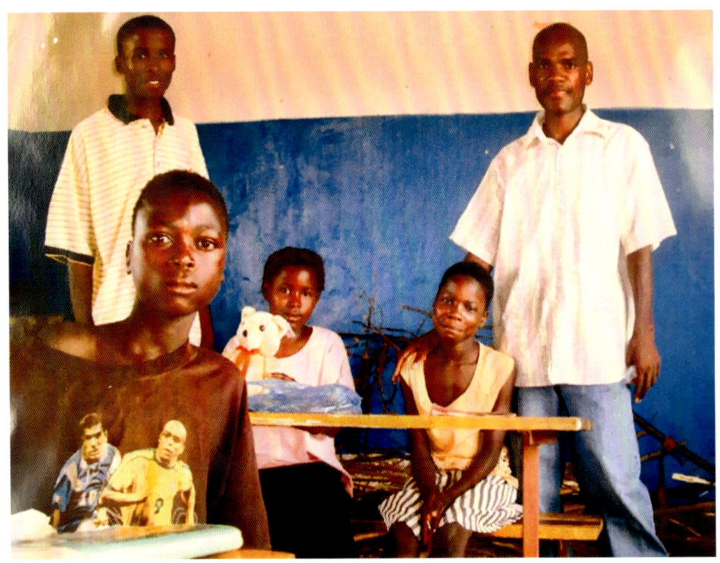

Zack Simpila and Mwandi School students and bear.
Photo: Simon Read

Liwase Theatre is a Livingstone, Zambia based theatre group. It was formed in 1998 as a community theatre group by Livingstone young people. The group is made up of seven members, five men and two women, whose names are: Zack Alston-Simpila, group leader; Ziwa Malilo-Ziwa, program coordinator; Musonda Katongo, secretary; Vincent Showa, treasurer; Bob Muleya, kit master; Alex Mudenda and Patricia Ngoma. After seeing that a lot of people in the community and rural areas of Livingstone are ignored on lots of things – e.g. their human rights and HIV/AIDS information – the group saw a cause to educate the public on matters that discuss such issues of human rights and HIV/AIDS using theatre as a medium to provide such information, as theatre attracts and compels people to come near and watch and thereafter get information. From the time the group was formed it has enjoyed support and worked closely with YWCA (Young Women Christian Association) and NGOCC (Non-Governmental Organisations' Co-ordinating Council) on gender issues, Society for Family Health and Ministry of Health on HIV/AIDS, World Vision, Culture Office and Tourism Department, Anti-Corruption Commission to mention a few. The group has also worked with individual artists: in 2000, the group was privileged to work with Anne Bean, a British artist during the Livingstone Arts Festival with some orphans. Together they put up a dance, drama and lighting event. Three years later Anne and friends raised funds for the group to carry out an awareness program on HIV/AIDS prevention in the schools of Livingstone, Kalomo, Kazungula and Sesheke district. They also participated with Anne Bean's yearlong project *REAP* when a teddy bear visited Zambia. The programme for HIV/AIDS earned the group an award at the Ngoma Award festival. During its existence it has participated in a lot of Zambian festivals. Up to date, the group is active in performing arts. It develops short plays and radio drama, dance and songs as a tool to sensitize the communities on various issues affecting the public. The group believes that through such intervention communities are able to identify their problems and hence become key players in finding the solution.

Zack Simpila, 2018

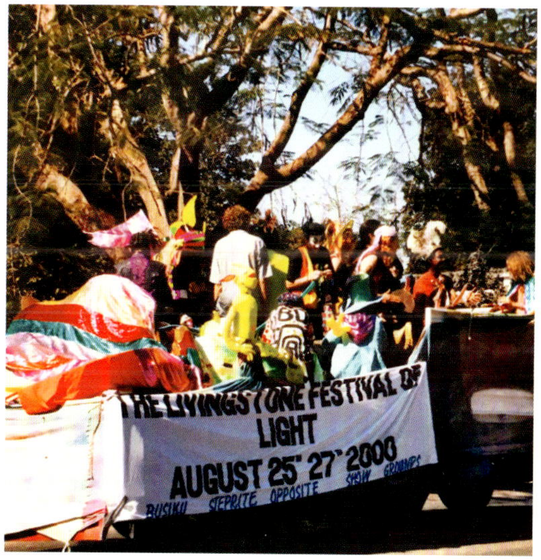

Livingstone festival of Light, street parade, 2000

Flight from Gondwanaland, 1982

I began this performance standing underneath a light bulb as the only lighting in the room., I read out on a video recording, the words below, from my teenage writings in Zambia. Paul Burwell, using an air pistol shot the light bulb so that it shattered over my head and the room went dark, apart from the video:

The tyrannical heat, the strident light, the low rumbling sound that seemed to be the sun itself, all breaking into free-fall, so my eyes weren't seeing but were what they saw, my ears weren't hearing but were what they heard. Particles simultaneously possessed and dispossessed.

My face in the video carried on saying these words whilst I bound up the monitor with black ribbon until the whole room was dark

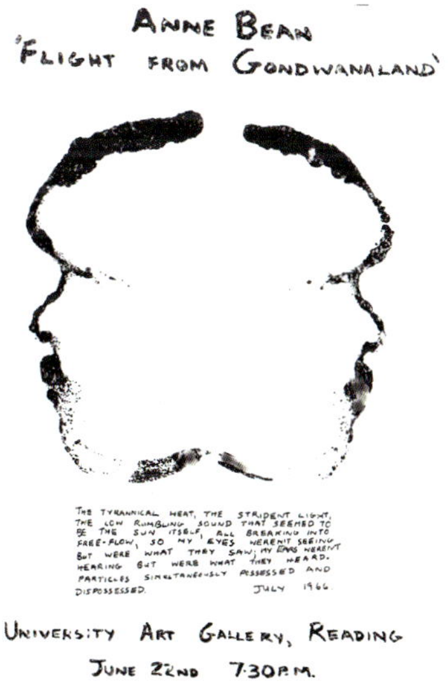

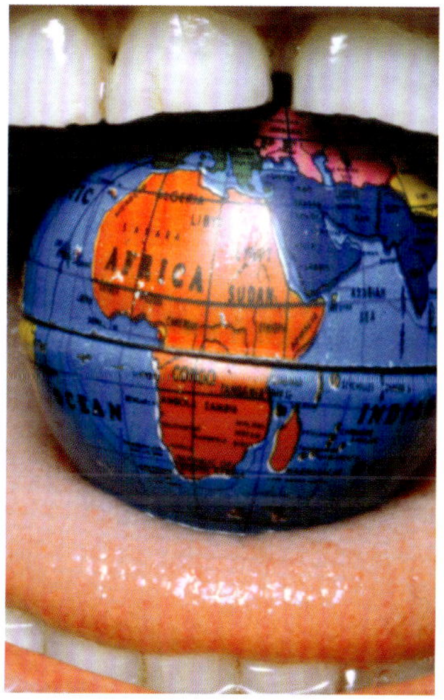

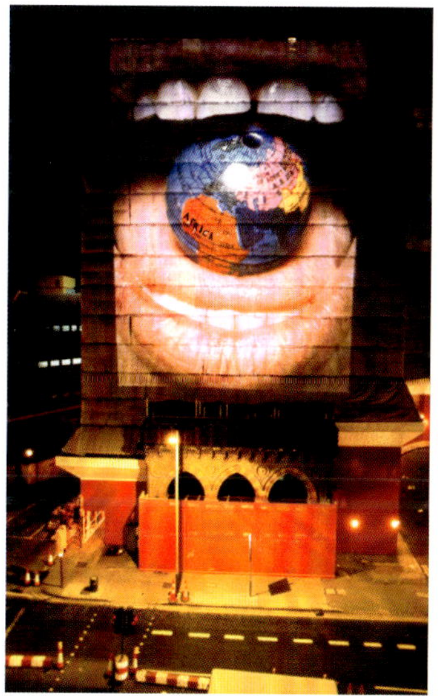

Right: Lilian and the angels, 1992
Projections onto the dust sheets during the renovation of St Pancras Station.
Image: Chris Bishop

The artist Simon Read and myself twinned Mwandi Community School with a school in Poplar, East London. They sent over gifts, including their school uniform for all the children at Mwandi and organised exchanges of letters.

In 1968, an essay I wrote called 'Impressions after visiting Luveve and Mpopoma Townships' was included in my school magazine, *Annual of the Eveline High School*. It begins:

In the bus on the way to the townships I cynically mused on Disraeli's words describing the rich and poor in England in nineteenth century: 'There are two nations between whom there is no intercourse and no sympathy; who are as ignorant of each other's habits, thoughts, and feelings, as if they were dwellers in different zones, or inhabitants of different planets: who are formed by a different breeding, are fed by different food, are ordered by different manners and not governed by the same laws.'

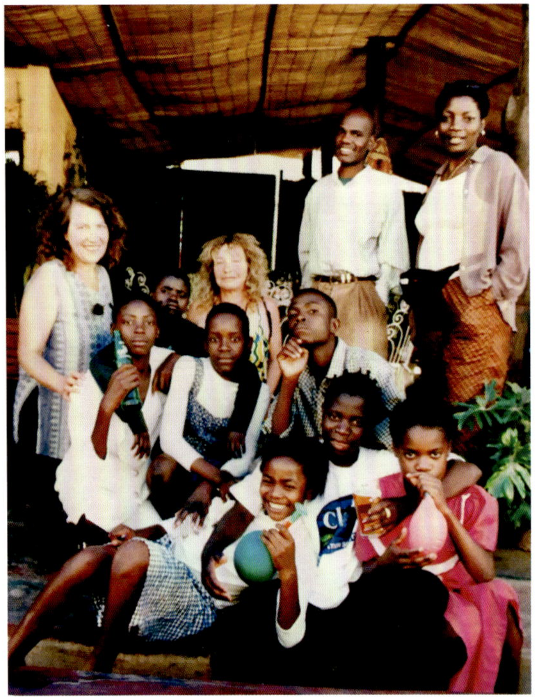

Top: With my friend and neighbour since babyhood in Livingstone, Jenya Iljon, whom I invited to join me for the Livingstone Festival of Light in 2000; Zack Simpila (standing); Vincent Showa; Maureen Lilanda, a singer who worked with the project; and the young people whose lives are affected by HIV/AIDS. Photo: Livvy Fink

Right: I jump towards Jenya in 1952 in Livingstone, Zambia. Sixty years later, the water splashes in Riverside Cottage, Newark-on-Trent: the two panels for a single work, *Jump*, part of *A Transpective: How Things Used To Be Now*, 2012

Far right: Portrait of Chana Dubinski in front of *Jump* in Riverside Cottage, 2013. Photo: Gordon Currie

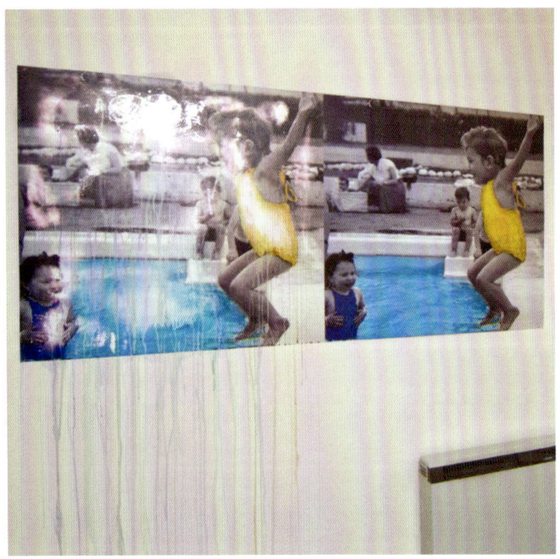

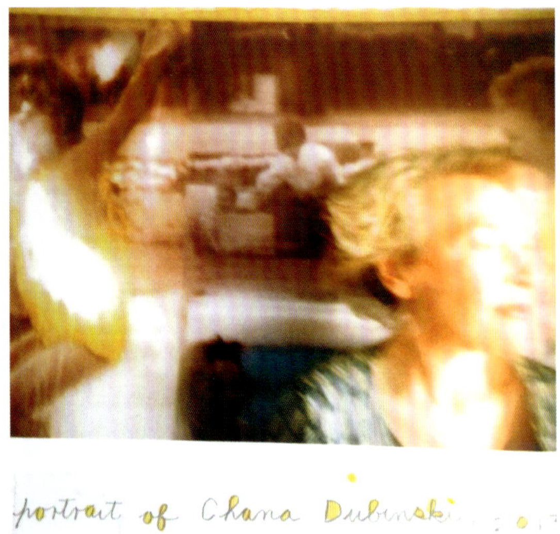

In 2012, the author Leslie Tate, with whom I had a long dialogue in Riverside Cottage, Newark, writes in the catalogue for my show, *Chana Dubinski, A Transpective: How Things Used To Be Now*:

Chana said 'I think certain ways of looking at the world are seared into us as children. They are the hot spots from which we create our own universe.' Born in 1950 and brought up in Livingstone, Northern Rhodesia (now Zambia), close to The Victoria Falls, Chana was aware of the hidden face of bigotry, in what was an apartheid system in all but name. Her work Benchmarks reflects this particular 'hot spot': 'As a young child, I was called "a white kaffir", a very offensive racist term, by some of the girls in my convent school. I was told I could not sit on the bench in the garden. These words, "white kaffir", were the words that pinpointed the complex layers of prejudice that, for me, as a child, embodied my bewilderment at the toxic society we inhabited. It gave me some pride that I straddled boundaries, but also disquiet, bewilderment and loneliness. I was aware of the "Whites Only" benches in South Africa and the "Aryan Only" benches in Germany of the thirties. I felt suspended between these poles: victim and perpetrator, both of which were unchosen, unwanted, abhorrent.'

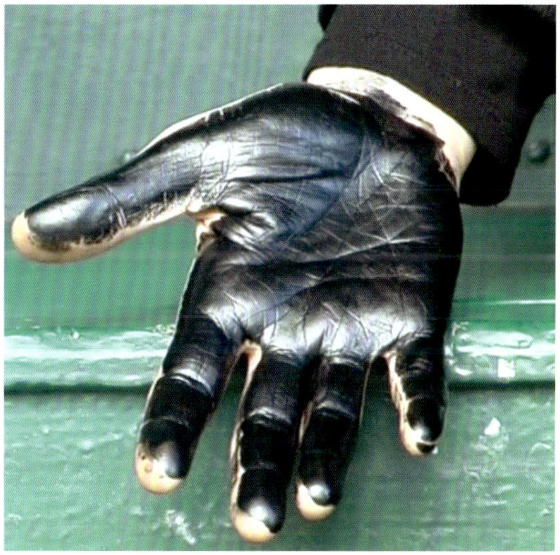

I asked Tom Barrett – my tutor at Reading University Fine Art Department in 1969 – if he recalled some of the issues we discussed. He wrote me a long letter from which the following is an extract:

'Anne told me, as her tutor, that she had been contacted by certain official government authorities in South Africa. I didn't think too much about it, as I vaguely knew that she had been involved in certain arts activities which were not exclusive to white people. It was not until she showed me letters she had received from a SA [South African] government agency (there were more than one) which stated in rather formal language that they were aware of her past associations with various groups in SA. I seem to remember that names were mentioned. There were some remarks about avoiding any provocative political activity, and that although now a student in the UK, she was under some surveillance by SA agencies.'

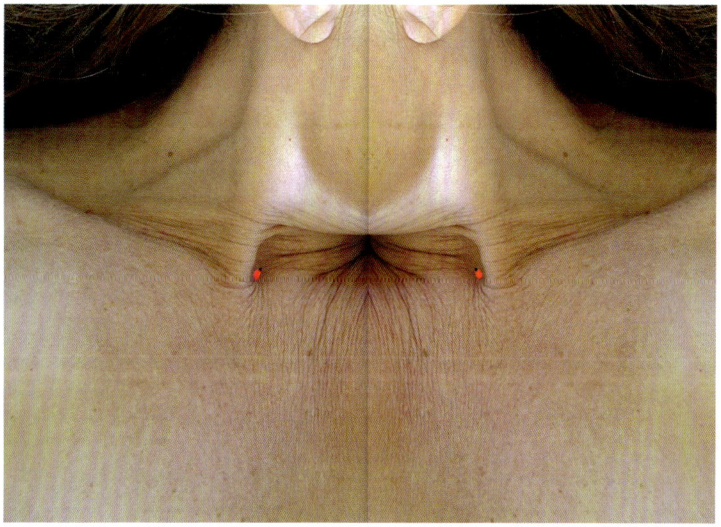

Above right: Anne Bean, *Net Blankes* reformed as a *Shadow Deed* in 1998 for *Autobituary* (2006). Still from video by Chris Bishop

Right: Chana Dubinski, *Hollow*, part of *A Transpective: How Things Used To Be Now*, 2012. As a small child, I liked to place a tiny 'lucky bean' seed in the hollow of my mother's neck

The poet and writer Mark Pearce writes in his essay 'Autobituary: Reflections' (2010):

From the ages of 12 to 20, the artist wrote a series of letters which she would read at a later age. These letters formed the series of *Excerpt from a Letter to my Older Self*. In one of these letters composed in 1964 she wrote with red and green crayon(s) and with elegant handwriting, yet nonetheless unmistakably pre-adolescent these extraordinary words which give us a glimpse into Anne Bean's artistic practice: 'I feel my body grow towards you and my gestures, thoughts and ideas/ideals becoming yours'.

Bean's constant shift of arranging/rearranging time and her own approximation with in the world both physically and imaginary are essential in her life as an artist. Life and art are blurred and any given definition will be open to interpretation. In a recent performance project PAVES, the artist was asked why she made art, she replied that as a creator you can say yes and no to the same question.

Allan Kaprow writes in his 'Un-Education of the Artist', 'I urged the artists of the world to drop out and lose their professions, lose their egos and identities.' The desire for a link between art and *life* is very much yearned for in Bean's work and it seems all of her artwork is allowing herself to be free from any constraints. An autobituary it would appear is as much a celebration of life as it rails against the limitations of death and the constraints of a rational society.

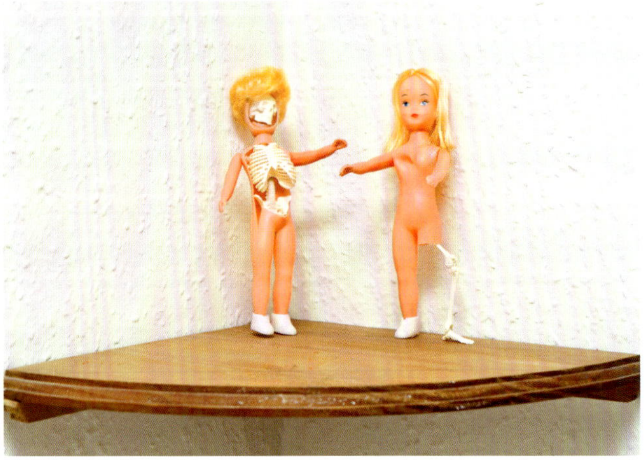

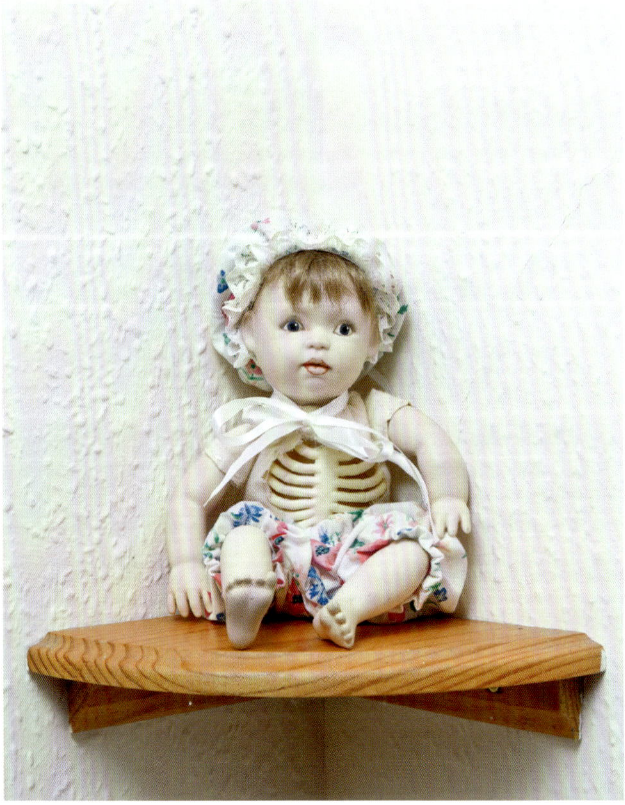

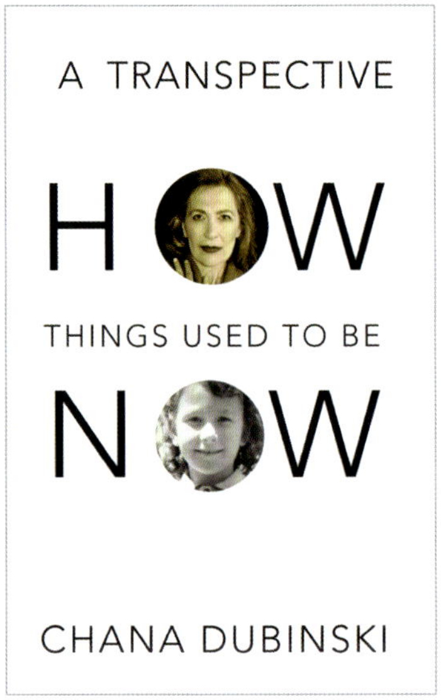

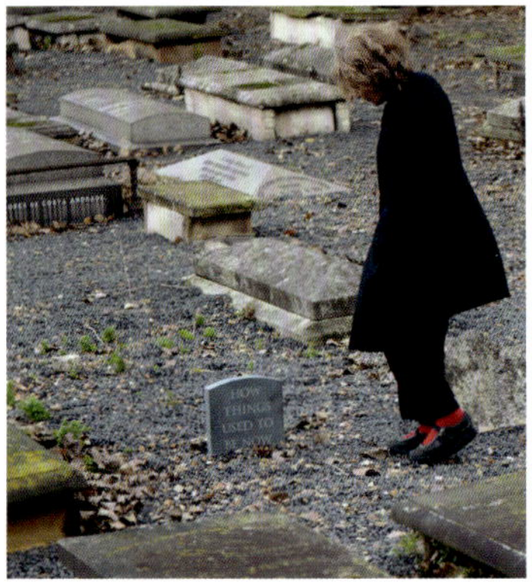

Left (top and bottom): Chana Dubinsku, *Skolls* (skeletal dolls envisioned in childhood), part of *A Transpective: How Things Used To Be Now*, 2012

Top right: exhibition catalogue cover for *A Transpective*, 2012,

Bottom right: Chana Dubinski, untitled action, Novo Jewish Cemetery, Mile End, London, 2014. Photo by Nick Evans

The artist John Latham (1921–2006) was born in the same town as I was: Livingstone, Zambia. John had coined the term 'Incidental Person,' beyond the Beuys/Cage/ Duchamp 'art-life' querying, by taking on both art and life within an 'incidental' mind-set, a reflective, intuitive response, without a particular brief or knowable result, within organisational/social structures. John and I had spoken about the idea of taking on the role of the 'incidental person' back in this Zambian town. Now, especially with the one-hundredth anniversary of his birth, 1921, coming up, I am keen to return to Livingstone as an 'incidental person', with the awareness of some outcome for 2021. In the past couple of years, I have attended several meeting of the Incidental Unit, which Barbara Steveni is still very active within. She co-founded Artists Placement Group (APG) with John and I first met them both in the mid-1970s at meetings of APG.

I wrote an email to Barbara Steveni saying:

A Livingstone/Maramba incidentalism would be meaningful to me in all the layers of that odd connection to John through shared birth soil and through the 'frisson' that the 'incidental person' has had for me as a concept – African Incidentalism would certainly have my antennae in powerful twitching mode.

Barbara Steveni's response:

Incidental Unit is being activated by Marsha (Bradfield), Gareth (Bell-Jones) and Neal (White), with me in there (they are working on applications no less!) so a Bean/Latham/Livingstone/Maramba 'Incidentalism' must be an essential African manifestation!

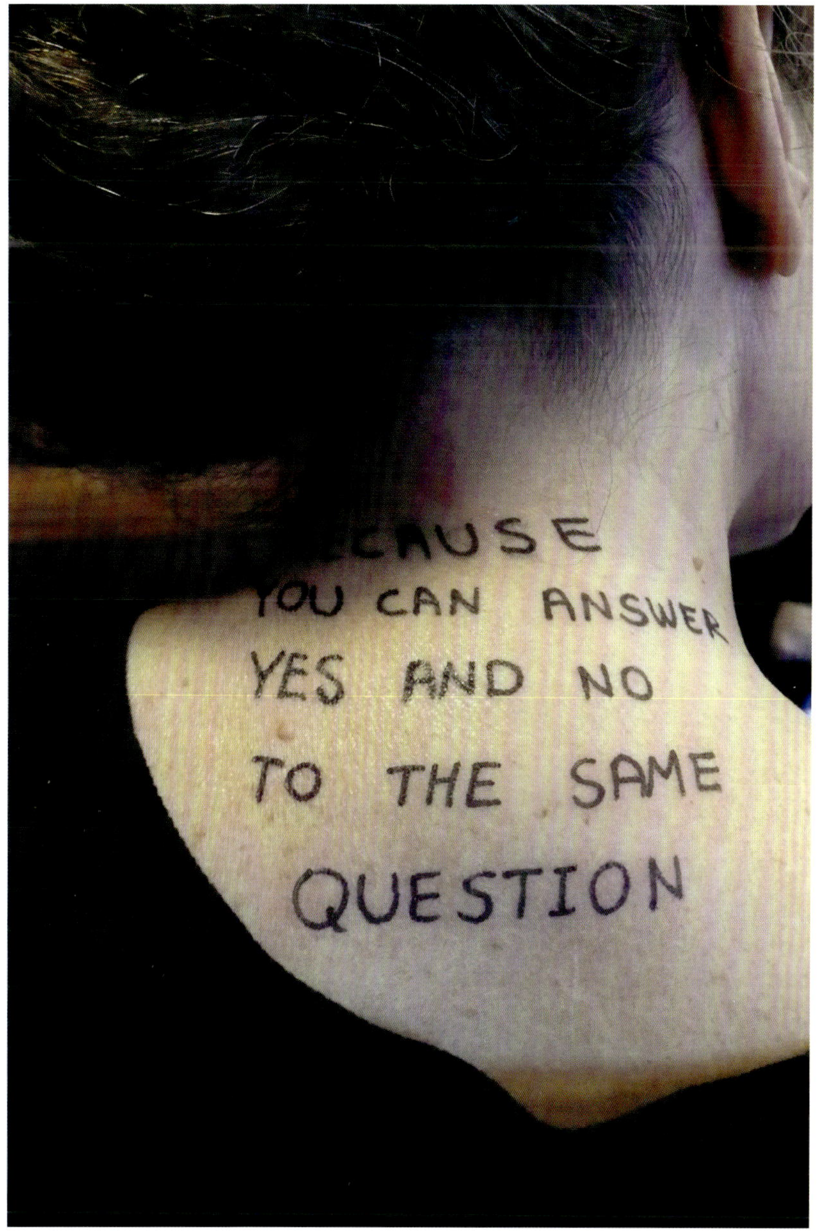

PAVES, *MU: Un-ask the Question*, *Shared Sketchbook*, Toynbee Hall, London, 2009

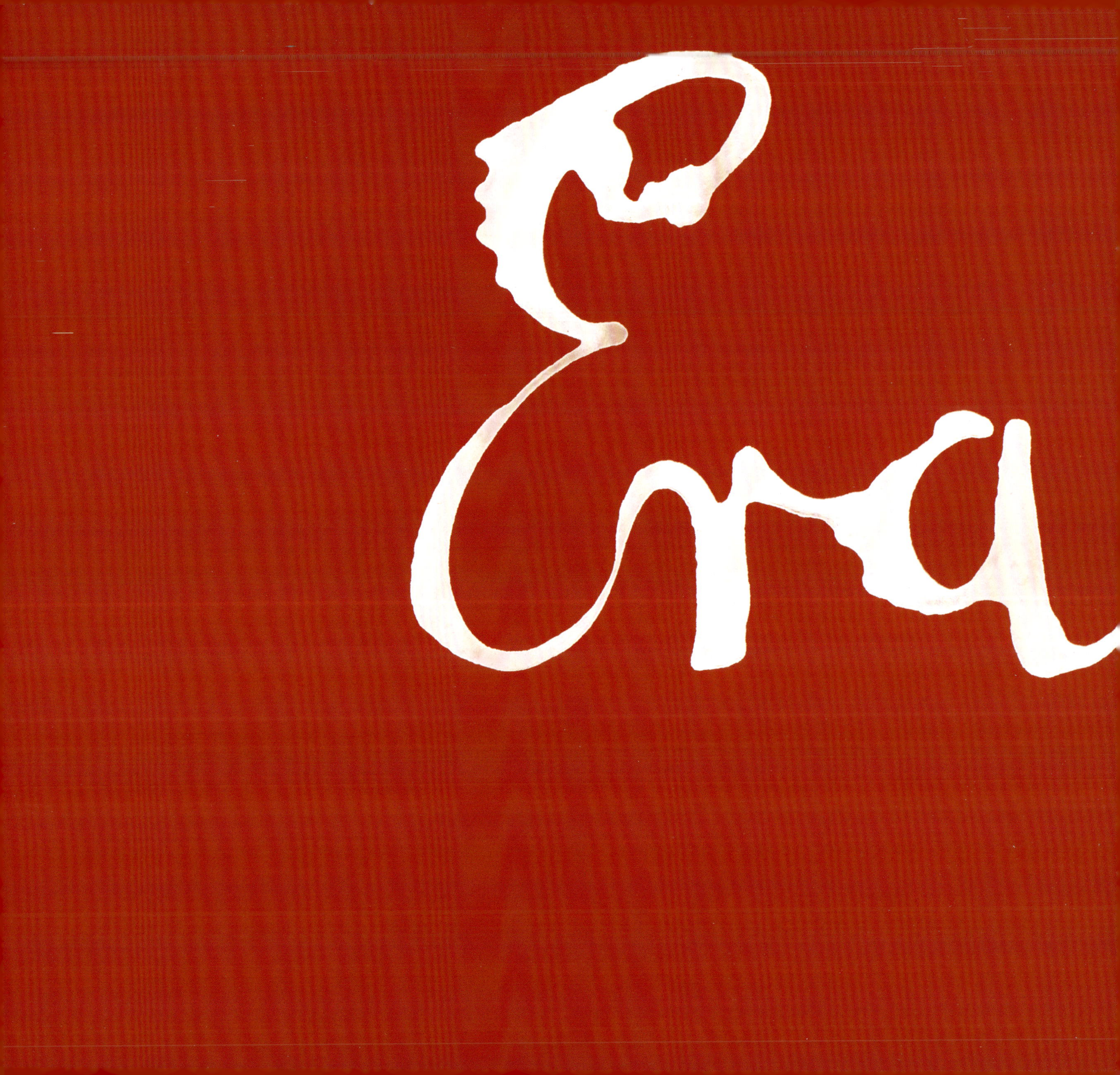
Era

ing

ERASING DISTANCES: FORGING PAVES
POSHYA KAKL

It was a hot summer in 2008. I was a junior student at the College of Fine Art in Erbil, Iraqi Kurdistan, and after finishing my classes for the day a friend told me that a group of international artists had arrived to work on art projects in the city. Anne Bean was one of them. Adalet Garmiany, an artist and curator in the UK, had invited her. When I met Anne for the first time I instantly felt a very warm and spiritual connection with her. The way she was talking with a slow and calm voice just made me feel so comfortable, and when she told me that she was a performance artist as well, I was astounded. At that time, I knew some English and I was the only woman doing performance art in Erbil, so I was eager to get involved in Anne's project. There are only a small group of artists in the region who understand the fundamentals of performance art and who perform regularly. For a woman artist, it is particularly odd and rare.

Only a few weeks before meeting Anne, I'd made my first performance *Broken Fancies* at the College of Fine Art. The concept was based on my own response to honour killings and suicides. Today, honour killings and suicides by self-burning are frequent phenomena in Iraqi Kurdistan. When women can't find solutions for their social problems in a conservative, close-minded, religious patriarchy, some become hopeless or outraged. With no agency to change the social order, women may reach the utmost despairing point where they set themselves on fire. They use petroleum oil as their only source for this type of suicide, not just because we use it to power household appliances such as stoves or heating, but also because it has become a trend. In tragic spectacles, a woman will pour a gallon of oil on her body, which turns it into a screaming fire – as a protest, or to tell a suppressed love story, or to stage her reproach for herself, her unspoken feelings, her unrealised dreams.

Oil and women have been alongside each other for so long. Sometimes I wish that Iraq would run out of oil so that no more women would burn and the war would end. Growing up in a war zone, I hated watching my country be destroyed in order to fuel the factories of other countries. Without the wars over oil perhaps we could live in peace.

As a child, I saw my mother pour oil on her body many times and threaten to commit suicide if she wasn't given her rights – but always, seeing me cry for her, she would stop. I used this trauma to try to figure out the relationships between oil, women, freedom, and fire. I wondered, what I would do if I were faced with a crisis in my life that I couldn't resolve? Would a gallon of oil be my solution? I was not allowed to date my lover (now my husband) and I was forced to break up with him many times. I was determined to keep my relationship, despite my oppression, and I was passionate to change my circumstances, by saying NO to restrictions through performance. *Broken Fancies* was my way of trying to change my family's mind – or, at least, to make them to give up and embrace as kind of freedom instead. Knowing Anne and connecting with PAVES made me feel alive and encouraged me to fight.

In *Broken Fancies*, I had a long, narrow white paper trail that made an aisle across the rooftop of the College of Fine Art. I placed glass wine bottles filled with oil a metre apart, as symbols for women's suicide. I proceeded to make a path between them with black oil paint, and when I reached the end, I returned and broke each bottle. As I made my way, I swung the oil around me as I walked across the floor, barefoot, with shards of glass beneath my feet.

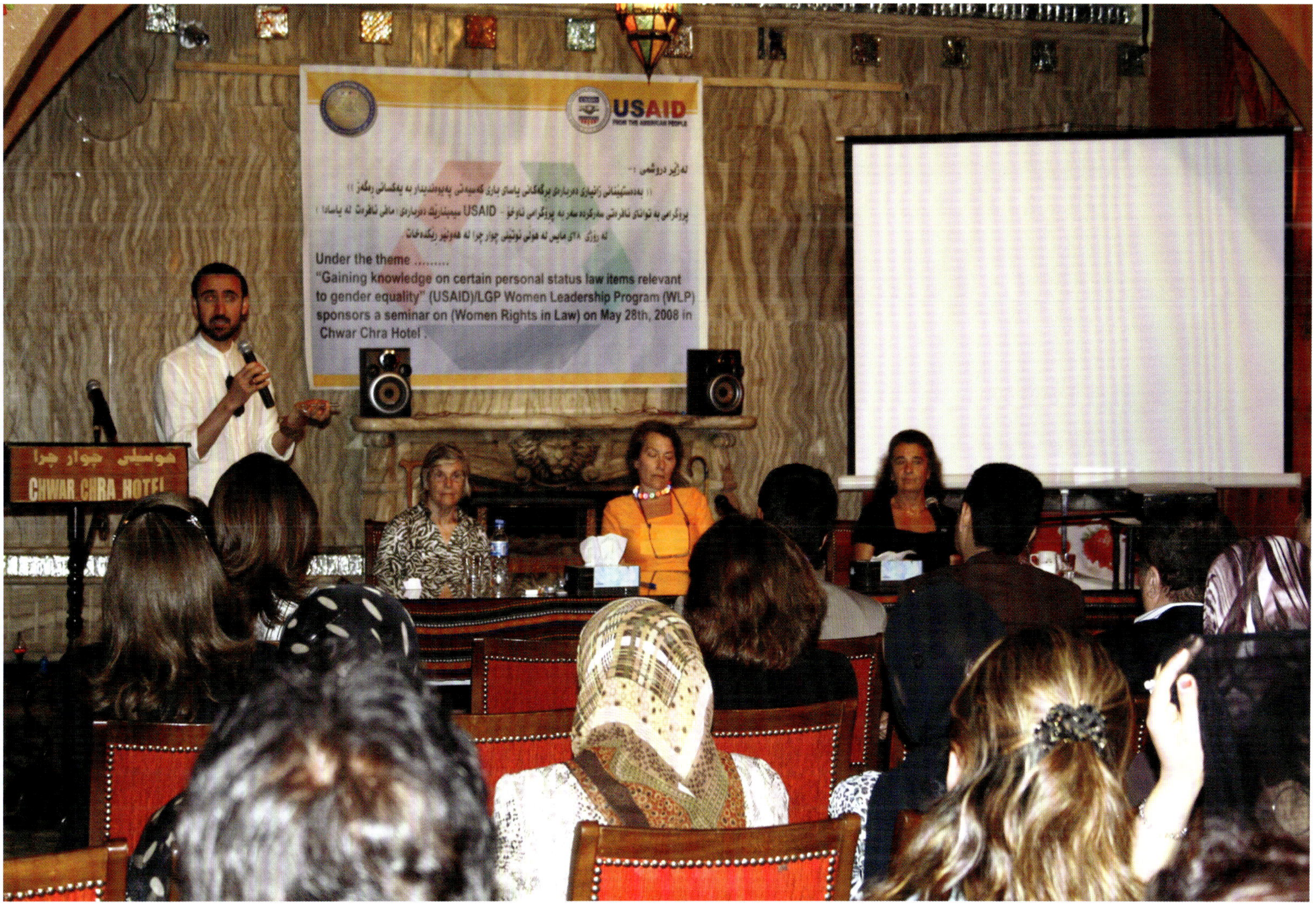

Anne Bean on a panel for a conference on women's rights in Erbil, Iraqi Kurdistan with artist Nancy Buchanan, curator Anna Bowman, and director of Artrole, Adalet Garmiany, 2008.

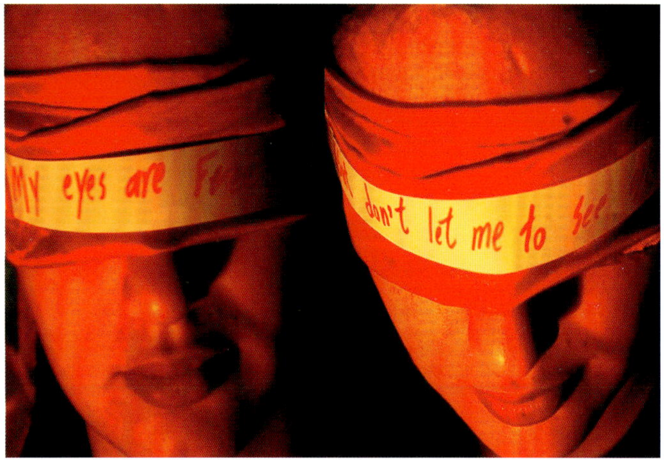
My eyes are
don't let me to see

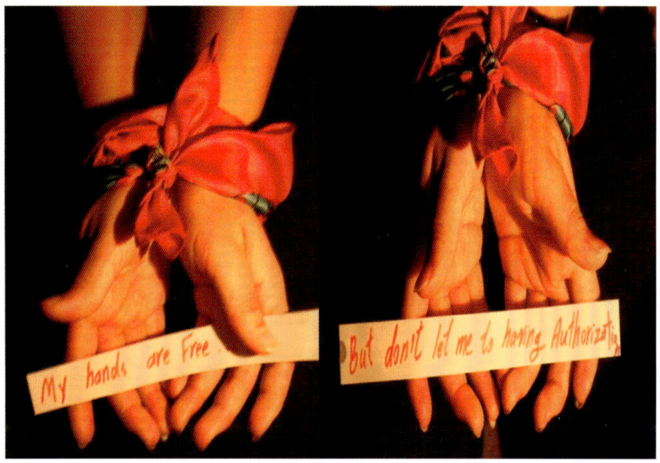
My hands are Free
But don't let me to having

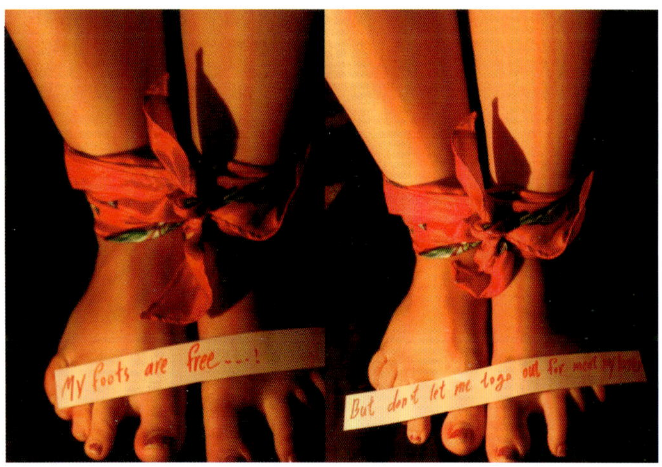
My foots are free...!
But don't let me togo out for

I experienced a feeling akin to participating in a Sufi rite of passage, where I couldn't feel any pain even though my feet were bleeding, and I was badly wounded. I set the trail on fire and let it burn. I left one unbroken bottle as a symbol of hope. People thought I was crazy. My entire audience was composed of teachers and students from the College of Fine Art, and they organised a crowded seminar afterwards to criticise me. My project had become controversial. They did not understand what performance art was. At first, they thought I was an actor, and had faked the process. Because I joined the College of Fine Art from a science high school – and without an associate degree in art – some of my teachers in the visual art and design departments looked at me as though I simply lacked the technical skills to paint or draw – as if that's why I snuck away to make art in a different way, to make up something meaningless and call it performance art. I tried to explain performance art to them.

I had started to feel fatigued in my work. I truly believe Anne came into my life to propel me into realising myself as an artist. Not only did she inspire me, but she also supported me during the worst circumstances. I knew I wasn't that much of an outsider as the way I was perceived. Anne's trips to Iraqi Kurdistan truly changed my life for the better, simply by her sharing in it with empathy. She continues to make the world a more significant and meaningful place to live for so many others just like me. Her impact is ongoing, just by being herself to others.

Going back to the first time I met her, I told myself that I could not let her leave without letting her seeing my work, whether she found it meaningful or not. She didn't have much time, so after introducing myself, I asked if she could watch a video of *Broken Fancies*. I placed my laptop on a chair and hit play. We were standing around the chair, my stomach full of unsaid words, and my brain full of unfolded ideas. I didn't know enough English to express myself to her, but I was sure I could tell her all I needed to by playing that video. When it finished, her eyes were blurry with tears, she hugged me and she was telling me *F–A–N–T–A–S–T–I–C, FANTASTIC!* I didn't know what 'fantastic' meant, but I knew it was a very powerful word, so now no matter where or how I hear or read the word '*FANTASTIC*', it directly connects me to Anne's voice as an echo in my brain; in my dictionary *FANTASTIC* means *ANNE BEAN*. If I ever were asked to describe Anne in one word, I would say F–A–N–T–A–S–T–I–C. Since then, she has become my role model. I am always amazed at how engaged she is with art.

She was one of the audience members when I performed *Mosque and Harmonica* in Erbil. I performed it in front of two different mosques. She was there for the first part. I stood in front of the mosque's door while I played a harmonica without speaking at all. The camera was hidden, and I really wanted to witness people's reaction, especially in locations that were mainly populated by men, and mostly religious or very traditional ones. I felt powerful as I stood there and played my harmonica, even though I was abused physically and emotionally by the audience – they insulted me and called me as a whore, an infidel. Someone pushed me hard and hit me in my back. I still played my harmonica, then walked away silently with a smile. It is one of the riskiest projects I have ever done. I was primed for the violence against me. The same day, after *Mosque and Harmonica*, I saw Anne and we ate together. Anne gave me hope.

Poshya Kakl, *False Democracy*, a PAVES action, Erbil, Iraqi Kurdistan, 2009.
Photographer unknown

Soon after Anne left Erbil, she formed an international group of women artists called PAVES. In the beginning I had so much difficulty with English: I didn't have access to online dictionaries, so I used to print out her emails, and highlight the words I didn't understand, then search in a very old print edition of the *Oxford English Dictionary*. Sometimes it took me days and weeks to understand an email and answer it. I kept searching in dictionaries to find the meaning of PAVES: the closest I got it was 'to pave', as in 'to make way'. After a year of working together with the women of PAVES – with Anne Bean in London and Zambia, Vlasta Delimar in Croatia, Efi Ben-David in Israel, and Sinéad O'Donnell in Northern Ireland – I realised that the name PAVES represents the first letter of each of our names: Poshya, Anne, Vlasta, Efi, Sinéad. I was too ashamed to say it, but I loved the fact that PAVES started with my name. I was truly introduced to a different world through working with the PAVES women. They impacted on me in a unique way and they are a part of my life and my history. After getting to know Sinéad, primarily through Skype meetings, my language skills started to develop and Sinéad was wonderfully supportive in bringing me to a wider international audience, for example through her *CAUTION* project in 2012, which brought us together in London for the first time.

Many times, Efi's performances made me cry. We are prohibited from visiting each other's countries. *We are supposed to be the enemy*, but we made performances simultaneously, in Iraqi Kurdistan and Israel, actions about love and peace, disregarding the meaningfulness of borders. Art has no rules, no nations, no borders: that is why artists are sometimes viewed by politicians as dangerous people, and why we are the first to be punished by those who want to suppress the voice of freedom. I think of Vlasta, an example of braveness and power. Her project about swapping identity and mopping the floor to mix our PAVES portraits showed us how we might erase the distances that separate us.

I was never an acceptable artist in my society but getting involved with PAVES helped me to create a small but sound metaphorical world inside my tiny bedroom, connected to an outside world. It is very hard to meet my collaborators physically. We all connected together telepathically: though isolated, we contact each other through Mother Nature regardless of distances, borders, barriers, the differences in spaces and duration that intervene between us. Touching the earth, looking at the moon, walking towards the sea, standing under the rain, sleeping or closing our eyes: performed simultaneously, these actions join us together. Distance made us much closer.

Anne came back to Iraqi Kurdistan one more time for a shorter visit to Suleymaniye in 2009. She emailed me to ask if we could meet. Suleymaniye is about two-and-a-half hours from where I lived in Erbil. In a conservative society it is hard for me – as a young woman – to travel alone, so I worked hard to convince my mother to travel with me to meet Anne. Finally, she agreed. Seeing Anne again was like realising a dream: I have a photograph of our hug, which my mother took. I met Anne in the Red Jail, which served as a headquarters for some of Saddam Hussein's regime's most brutal abuses: it was a jail for torturing, killing, and persecuting Kurdish civilians, politicians and activists – including my father, who was captured and held for seven years in a jail just like it for his political resistance during the revolution against Saddam's regime. From my parents' stories and their real experiences in the regime's jails,

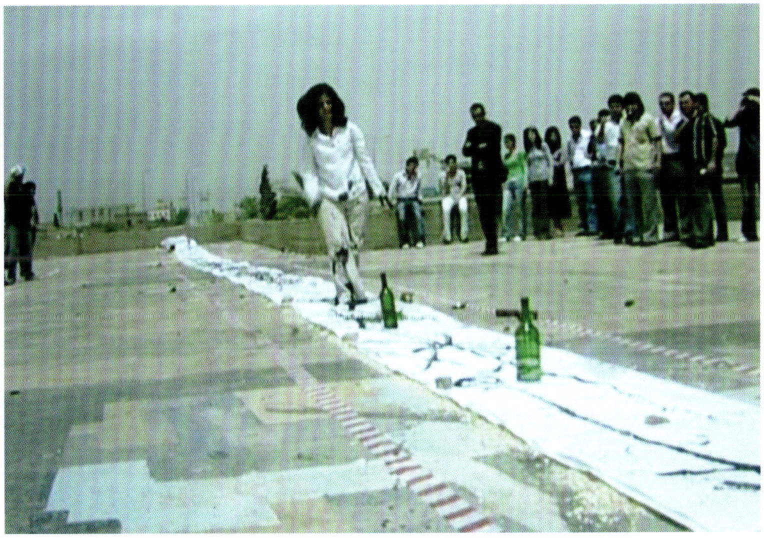

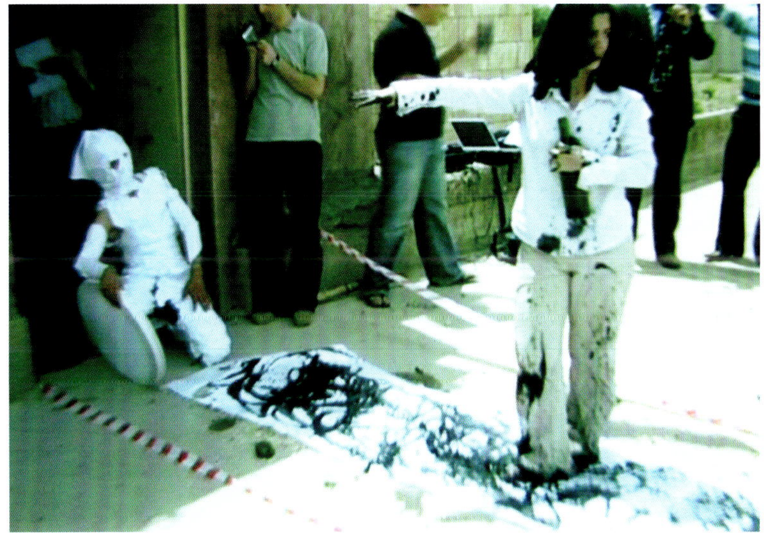

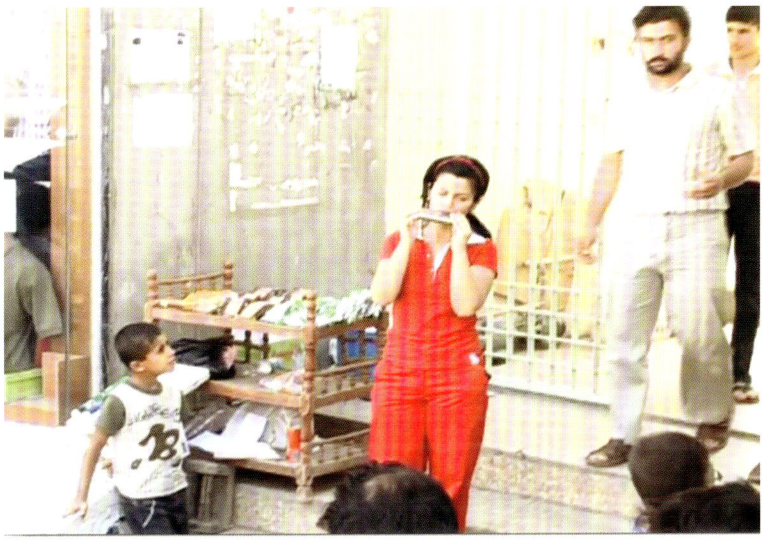

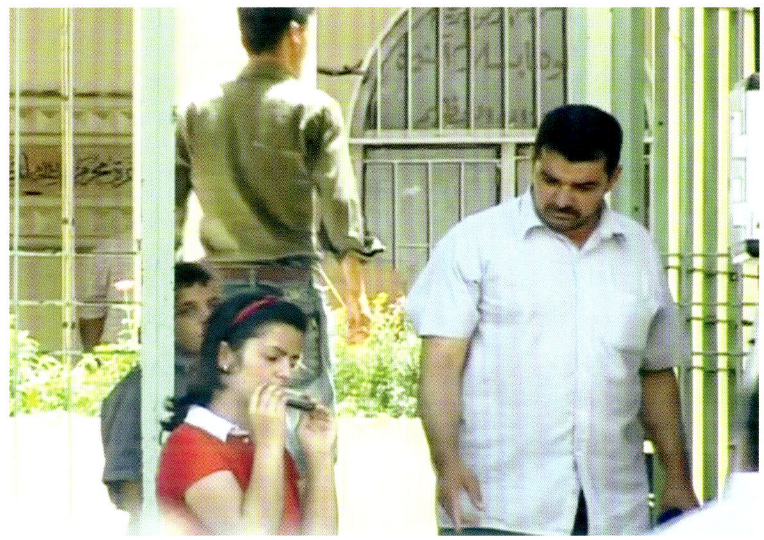

Top: Poshya Kakl, *Breaking Fancies*, video stills from performance, Erbil, Iraqi Kurdistan, 2007
Bottom: Poshya Kakl, *Mosque and Harmonica*, video stills from performance, Erbil, Iraqi Kurdistan 2008

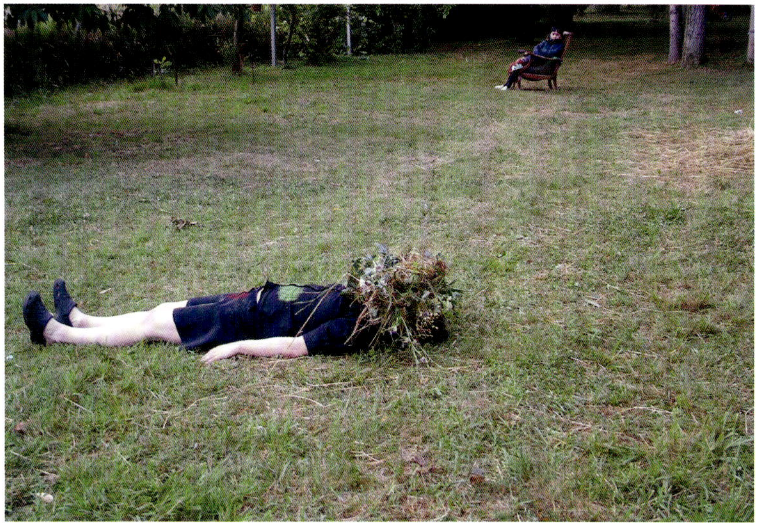

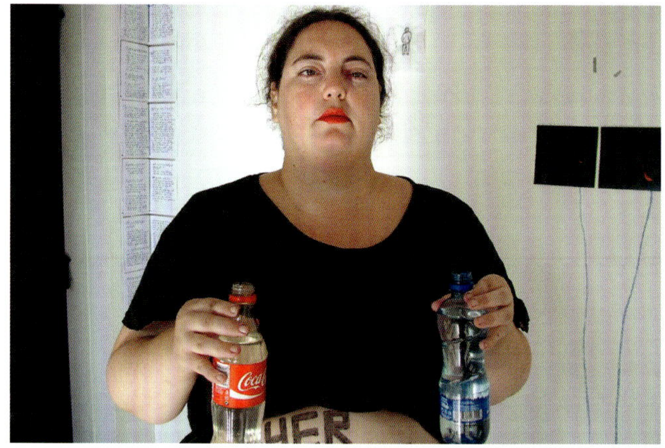

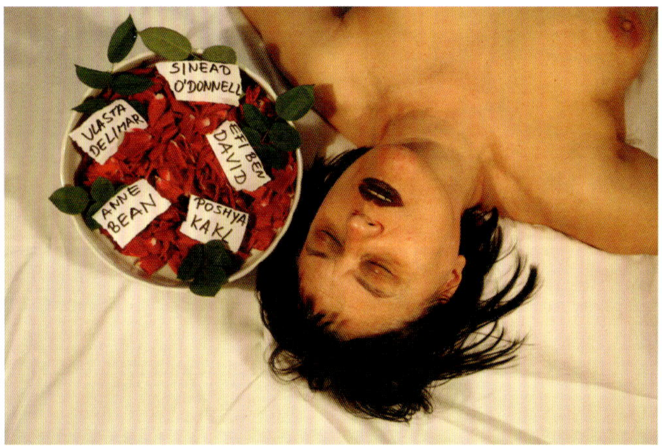

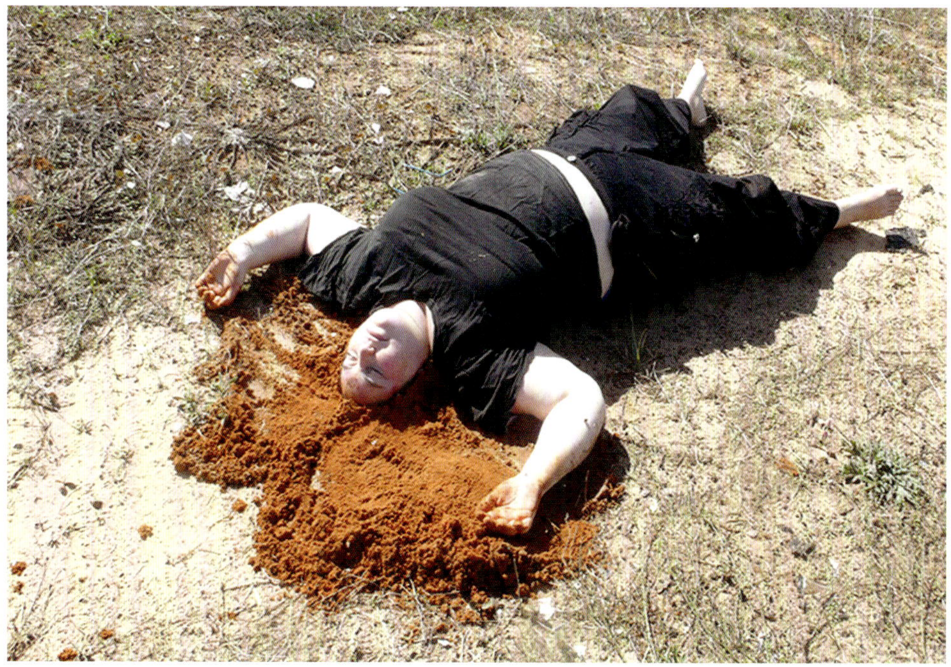

Top left: Sinead O'Donnell, PAVES action, My Land Festival, Staglinec, Croatia, 2009;
Top right: Efi Ben-David, PAVES action, Golden Threads Gallery, Belfast, 2009;
Bottom left: Vlasta Delimar, PAVES action, Croatia, 2009;
Bottom right: Efi Ben-David, PAVES action, Israel, 2009

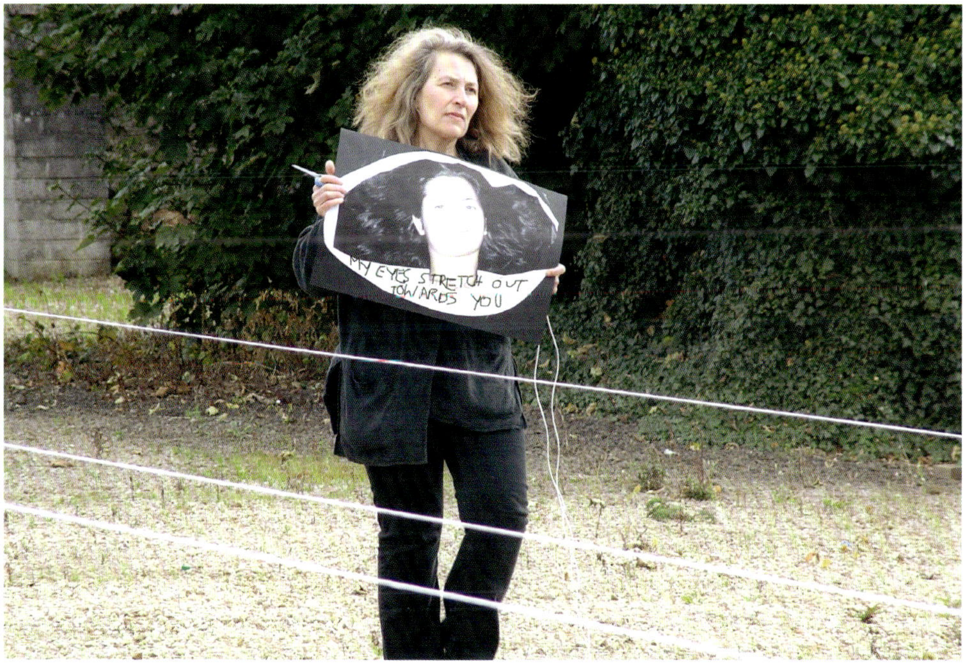

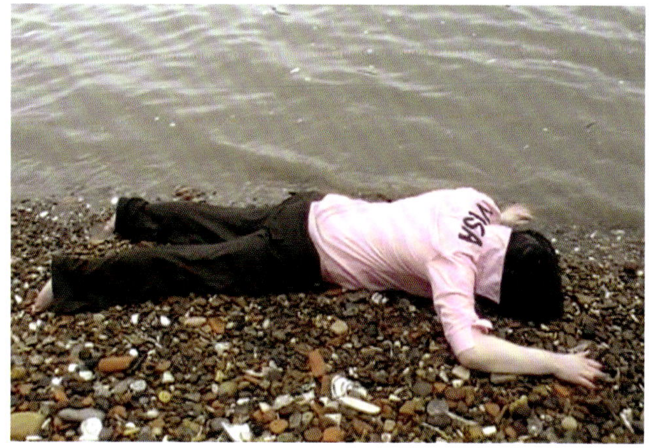

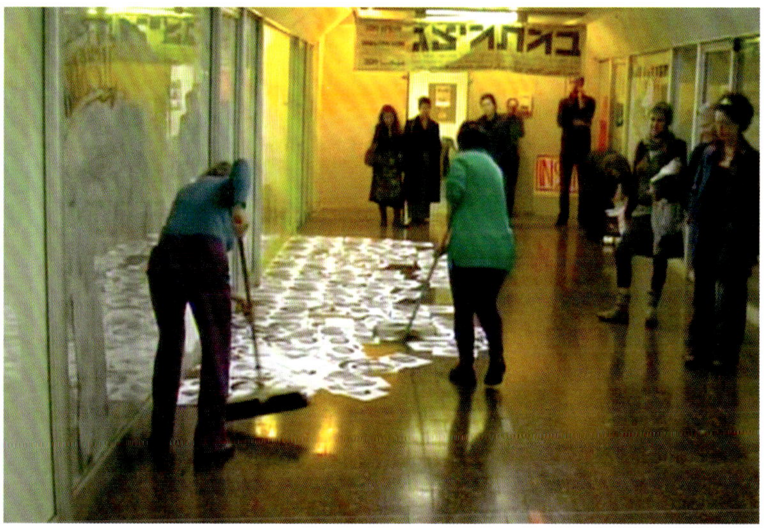

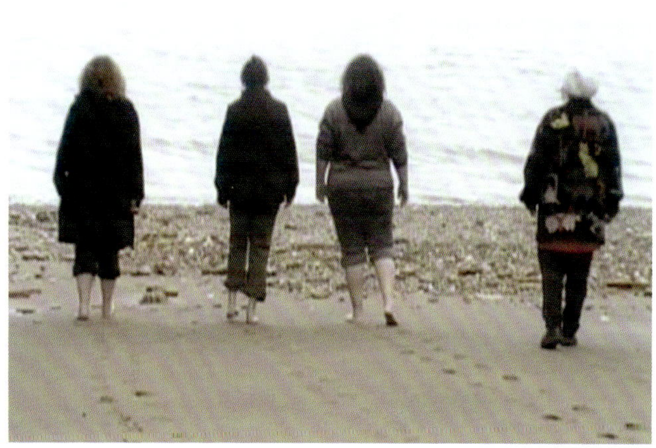

Top left: Anne Bean, PAVES action, Cavan, Eire, 2009
Top right: Sinead O'Donnell, PAVES action, London, 2009;
Bottom left: Vlasta Delimar with Gina Ben-David, PAVES action, Israel, 2009;
Bottom right: PAVES action, London, 2009

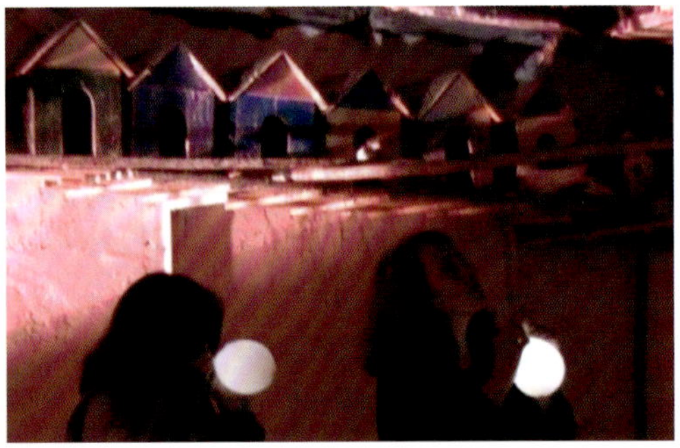

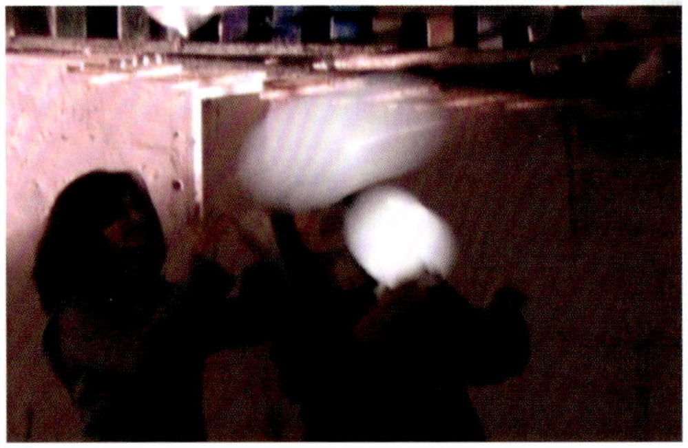

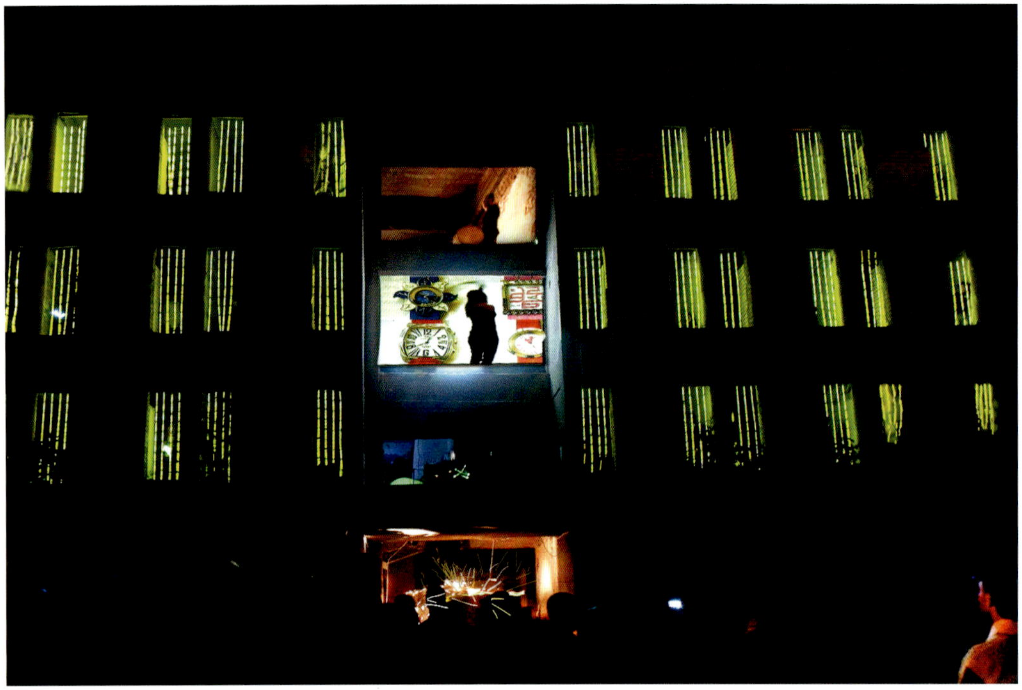

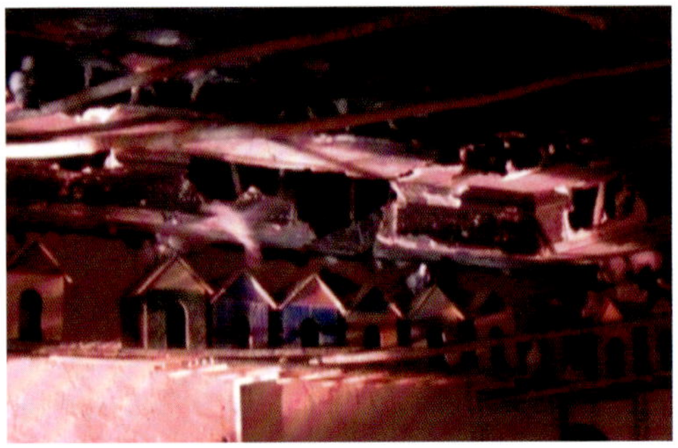

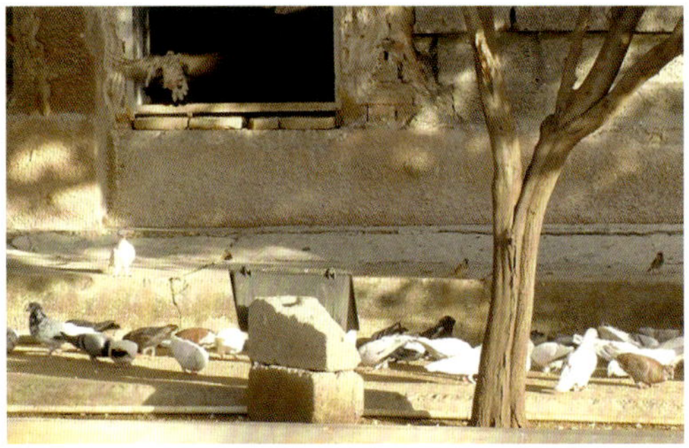

I could imagine what it felt like to walk around that frightening building during the Saddam era: if anyone went in, there was no way out until death. They used wooden rooms so that no one could hear the prisoners' screams, and dark solitary confinement rooms, until armed Kurdish fighters (the *Peshmerga*) liberated it in the early 1990s. The last 800 Iraqi soldiers in the city holed themselves up in the Red Jail. After a week of shelling, the Kurds broke in and killed them all. The tanks and artillery left by the Iraqi army still litter the courtyard of the Red Jail, and the bullet-ridden building now serves as a monument to those who lost their lives inside its pockmarked concrete walls. The building is otherwise left as it was, and it now serves as a depressing museum for history. Recently, it became a very active centre for contemporary art projects. When Anne and I walked around the building to get inspiration for working together, my mother shared her memories of the jails: how the regime tortured my father and abused her. It was late evening, the sky completely dark. Anne took me to one of the dark cells in the Red Jail, which had become a dove house as a symbol of peace and freedom: the entire room was covered with colourful tiny wooden birdhouses, and it was full of doves trying to sleep in the silence of the building. Anne whispered in my ear to suggest we could make talk with the doves by making sounds with glowing white balloons. We did. It was a very special moment when the doves answered us. We had a long peaceful conversation with the doves and balloons.

The next day, we went to the Aram Gallery to do another performance. We made a white circle with the names of the women of PAVES, as a symbol of our connection. Anne and I sat back-to-back, and my mother braided my hair with Anne's. Meanwhile, Efi buried her hair in the ground in Israel, as if to connect our heads with hers. All human beings inhabit the same ground, but we are separated by differences in the quality of our lives and by boundaries and borders that separate us. Yet we try to connect with each other, regardless of what makes us different. We created a sense of harmony despite the visual contrasts between us: Anne's blonde hair and my black hair, her white shirt and my black clothes; she speaks English, I speak Kurdish; she comes from a free and peaceful environment, while I grew up in war zones, and living in a place where women are victims of honour killings. Nevertheless, we have an inner similarity, and that is what matters most.

Opposite, top and bottom: Anne Bean and Poshya Kakl, *They are Talking to Us*, a performance in The Dove House in a former torture chamber in the Red Jail, Suleymaniye, 2009. Stills from video by Miyako Narita

Middle: Anne Bean, *Memory Game*, the Red Jail, Suleymaniye, 2009, with Adalet Garmiany, Mrs. Garmiany, Chris Gladwin, Miyako Narita, Richard Wilson, local dancers, musicians and volunteers. Photo: Mark Terry

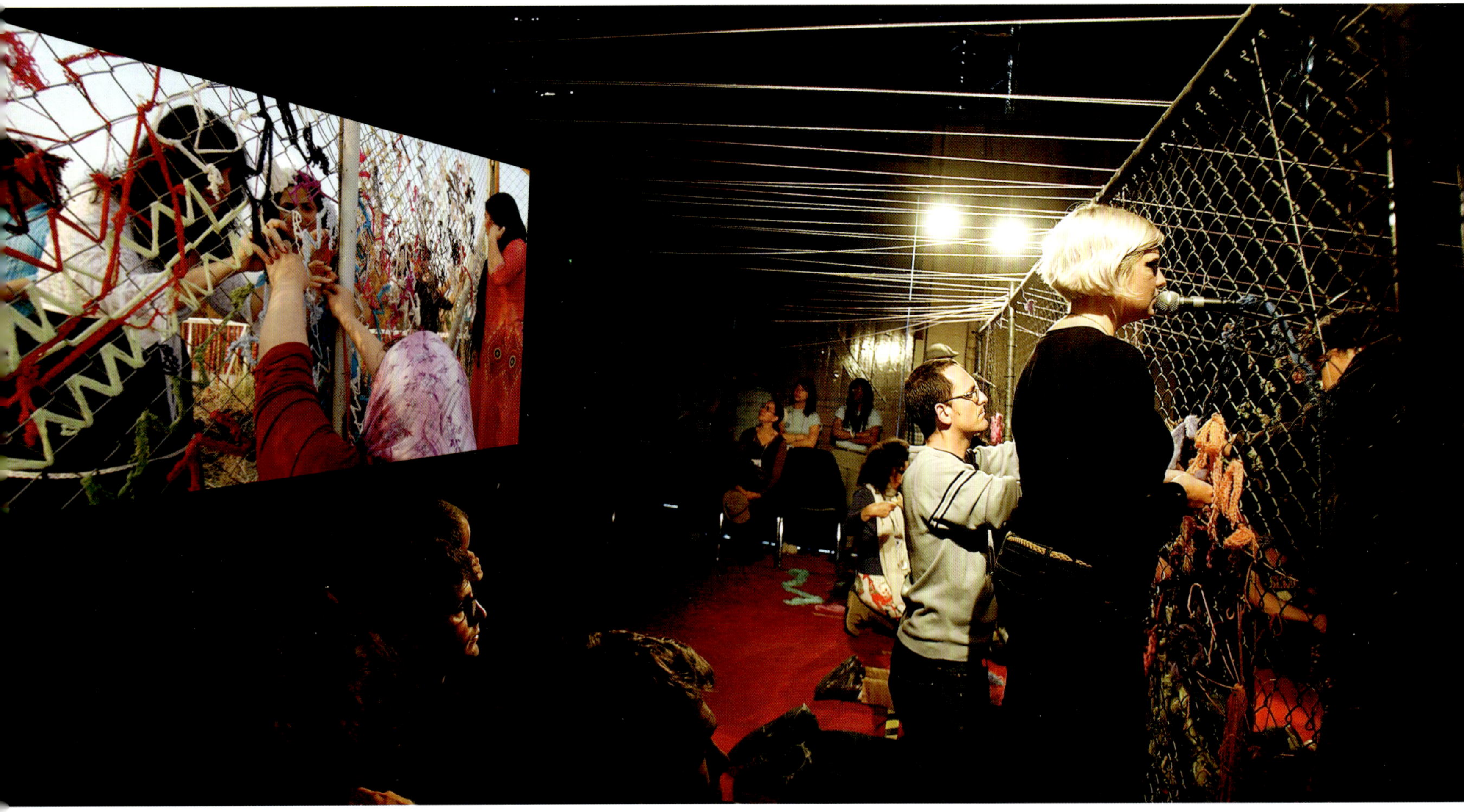

Anne Bean and Poshya Kakl, *The Unknitted Lives of Young Girls*, AE Harris Space, Birmingham European Festival, 2011. Photo: courtesy BE Festival

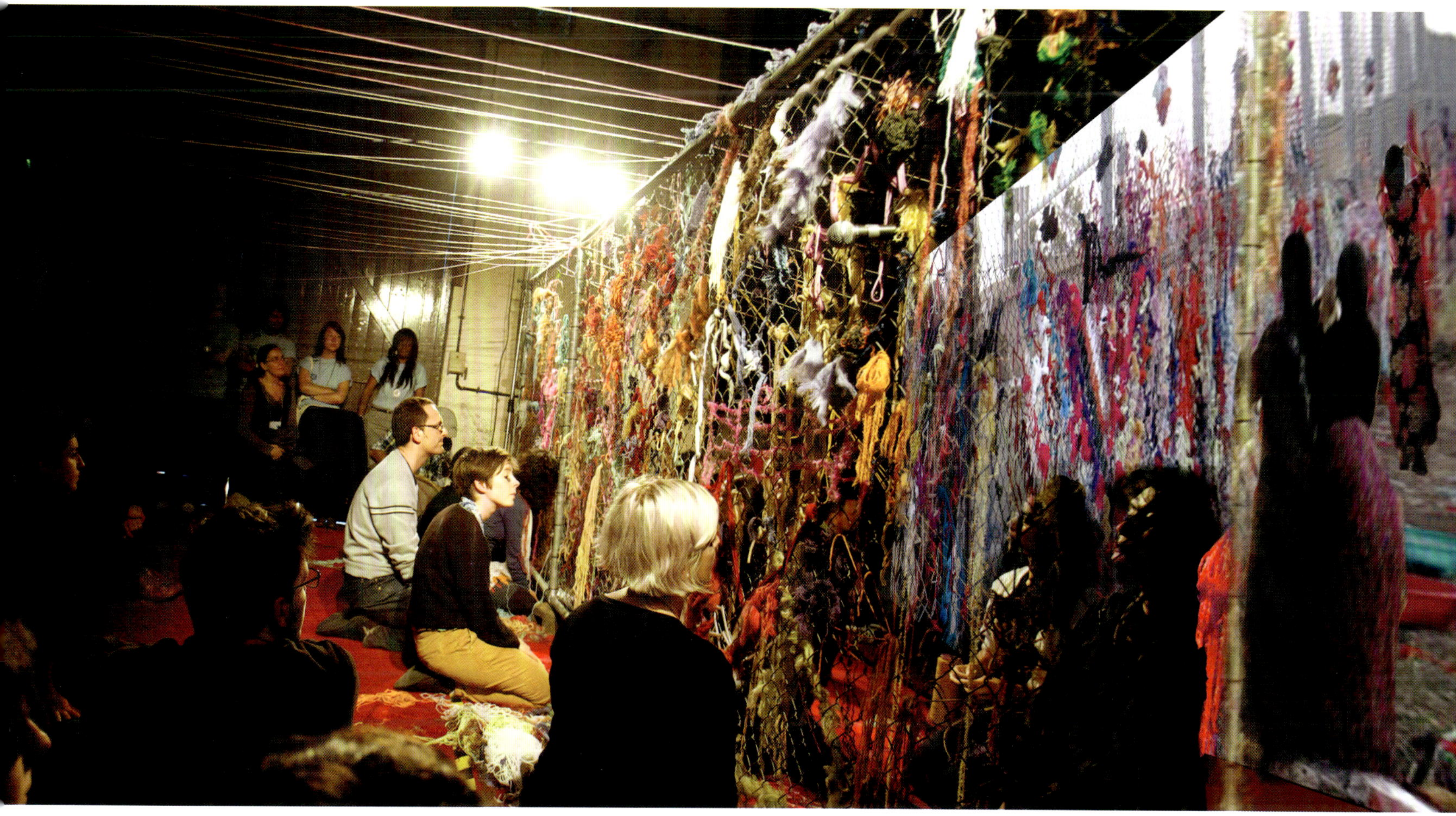

For several years I have been working with the young Iraqi artist Poshya Kakl, making several public actions together, both in Iraq and through Skype. She made a film *Knitting Iron* with women inside a jail in Iraqi Kurdistan, imprisoned for refusing arranged marriages. These women feel safer inside prison than out. Poshya wrote: 'We make pieces of Art and of cultural beauty out of the prison wire fencing with the un-knitted lives of young girls, victims of social and cultural rules. These very rules that can at any moment un-knit other lives outside the prison.' At BE Festival (Birmingham) in 2011, I interacted with the film that she made of this action, along with many participants. The audience was divided by the fence, uncertain who was on the inside or outside. This was the first screening of Poshya's film outside of Iraqi Kurdistan.

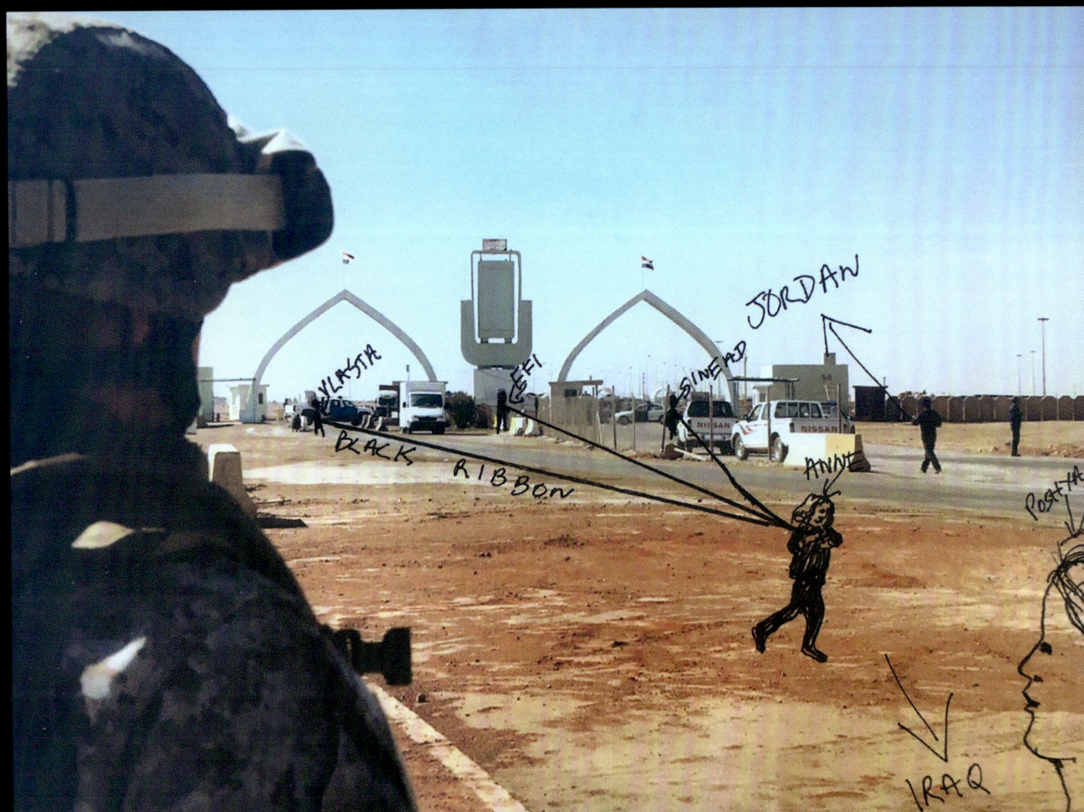

Above: Anne Bean, untitled drawing in response to the Jordanian visa experience

Opposite: Anne Bean, *I am Thirsty*, Aram Gallery, Suleymaniye, Iraqi Kurdistan, 2009. Photo: Miyako Narita

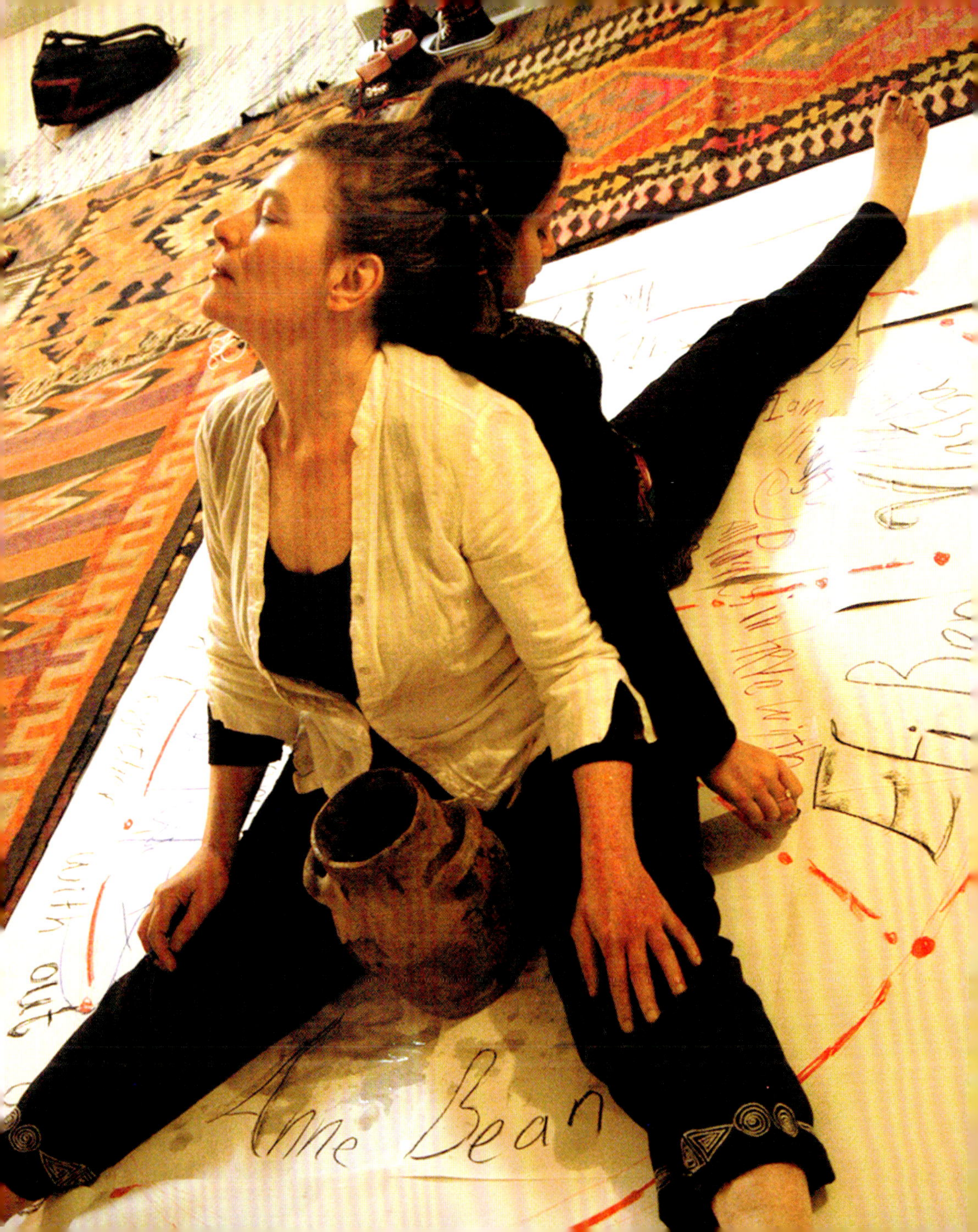
Anne Bean

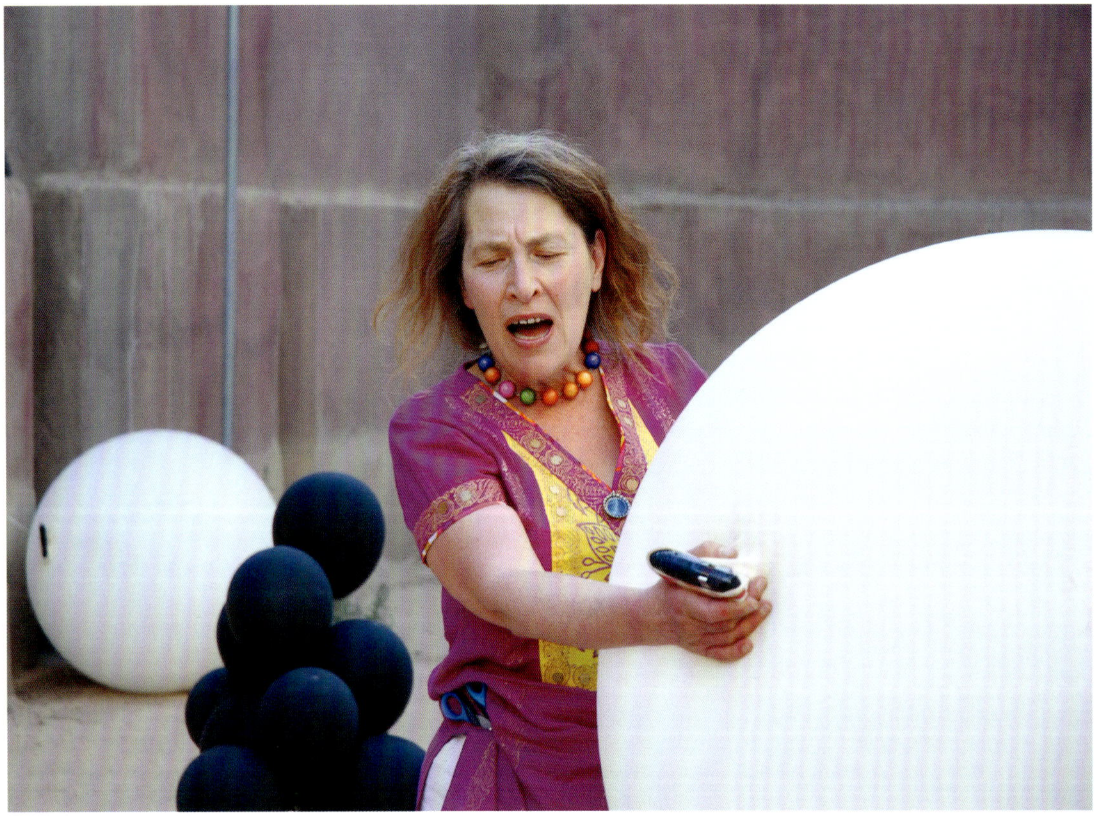

Above and opposite: Anne Bean, *MASS*, Iraqi Kurdistan, 2009

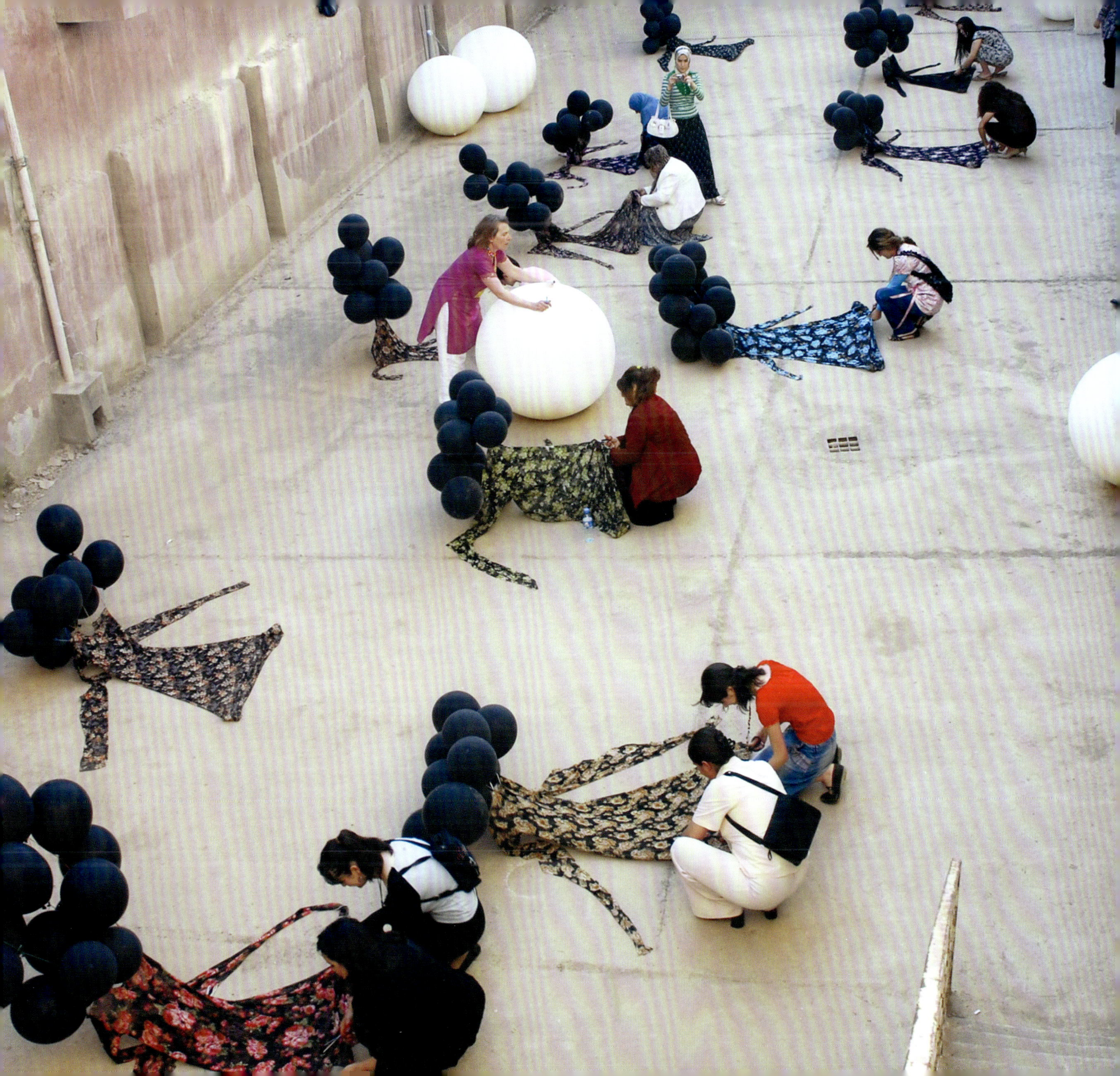

INTERVENTIONS BY ANNE BEAN

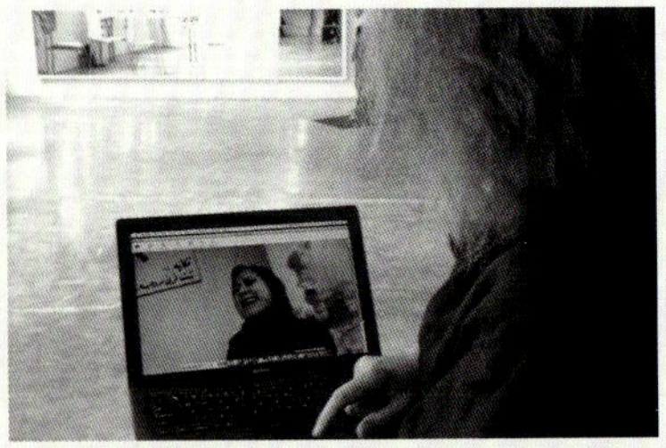

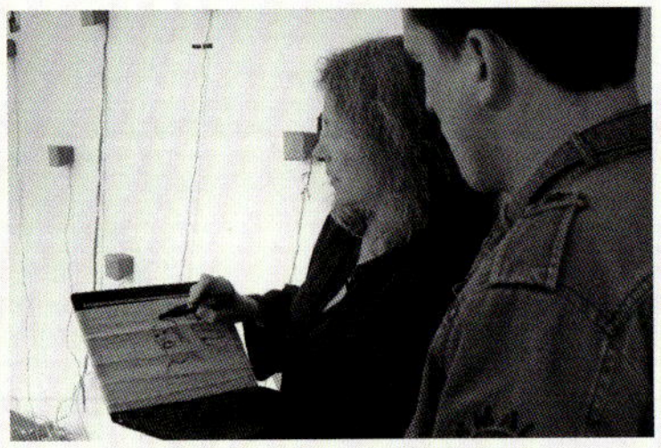

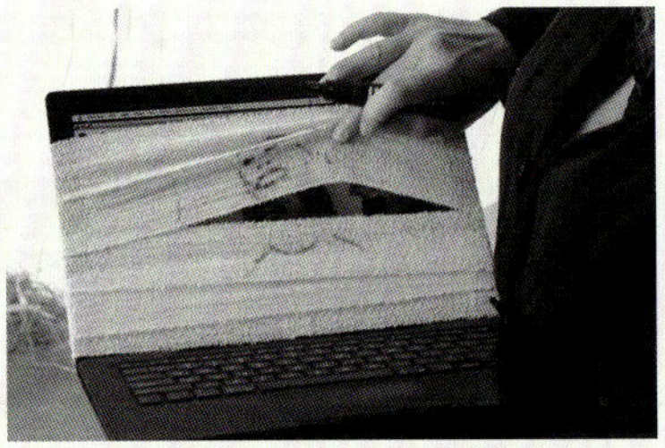

Above: PAVES actions, Golden Thread Gallery, Belfast.

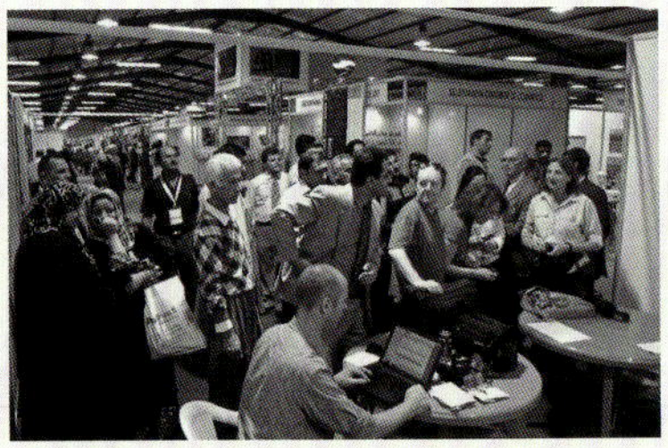

Above: Artrole at Erbil Trade Fair with Susan Meiselas, Richard Wilson and Mark Terry

When Poshya's London visa was refused for her to participate with PAVES, I emailed her:

'Dear Poshya

The refusal of your visa affects much of the work we are doing in London in terms of how political and social rules restrict each of us. It made us think about how we can include you even though you are not present.

There is a way without even relying on technology. I would like to suggest us working together in time. There is a way of being very close by sharing the space of time. Frontiers, borders, demarcations, boundaries, barriers become irrelevant.'

We decided that she would do a work at the same time as our PAVES 'Shared Sketchbook' at Toynbee Hall, 2009. She sent us an email about the work:

'It was about burning women, I tie up my body like as a women's burn, I was sit in front of hospital of burning and I wrote the number data of death by burn on problem of honor killing in Kurdistan from 1999 to 2008 nearly more than 12000.

And I made a dialogue with the women and man there who were kindredes of women"s burn and I asked them about it all. really I am so sad because so tragedy

My work successful.'

I replied: 'I saw your images in the hospital with the women and knowing that this action was happening at the same time as our actions was so powerful for me. my heart was so heavy and questioning I feel like I must wrap up my computer in bandages.'

Looking at Susan Sontag's *Regarding the Pain of Others*, I was struck by something she articulated so accurately that I have long felt and struggled with: 'So far as we feel sympathy, we feel we are not accomplices to what caused the suffering. Our sympathy proclaims our innocence as well as our impotence. To that extent, it can be (for all our good intentions) an impertinent -if not an inappropriate- response. To set aside the sympathy we extend to others beset by war and murderous politics for a consideration of how our privileges are located on the same map as their suffering, and may - in ways that we prefer not to imagine- be linked to their suffering, as the wealth of some may imply the destitution of others, is a task for which the painful, stirring images supply only the initial spark.'

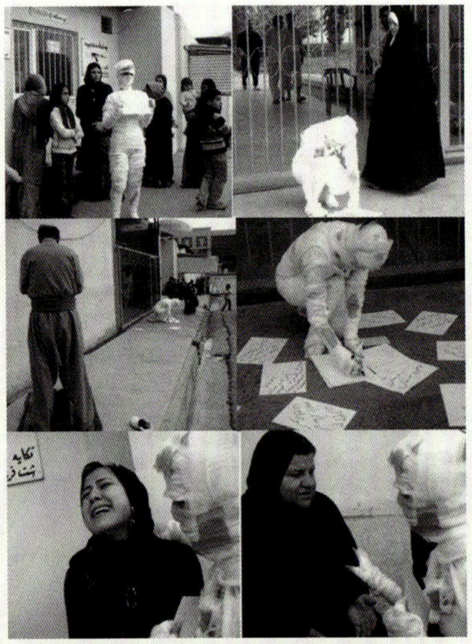

Poshya Kakl, Erbil Woman's Hospital for burns victims, simultaneous PAVES action, 2009.

In Hull, in 2000, I met Adalet Garmiany, a young, visionary refugee with a fervent desire to activate exchange projects between artists in the UK and USA and Iraq. He subsequently formed the organisation Artrole and I visited Kurdistan-Iraq with this group. The performance *MASS* was stimulated by interactions with women in Iraq and by visiting sites, particularly those related to the Anfal campaign against the Kurds. I decided to work with Kurdish women directly affected by the Anfal campaign. I developed ideas for *MASS* and returned to Kurdistan in May 2008 to find a space and work with local women towards the piece, which was then performed in a disused Ba'thist prison compound. Poshya assisted me on many aspects of this.

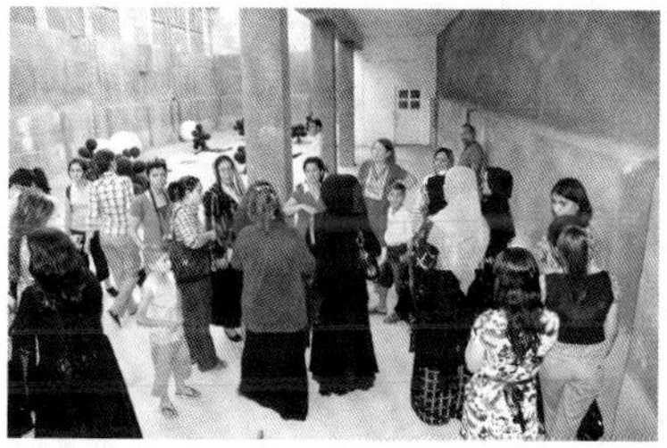

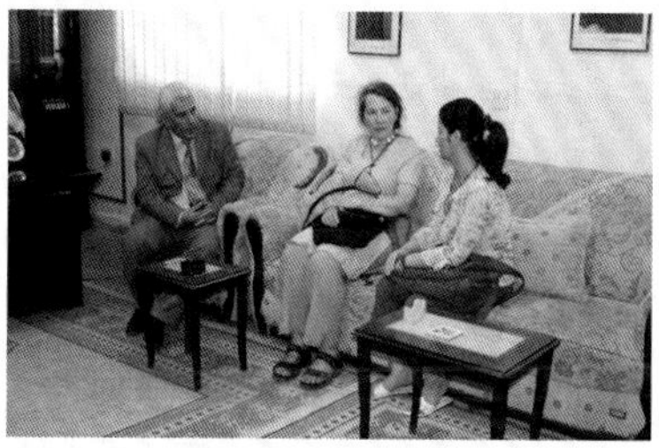

Above: Organising MASS together, Erbil, 2008. Photo: Mark Terry

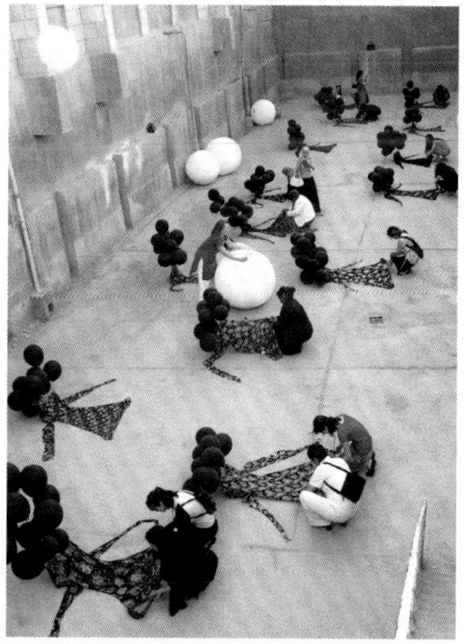

Above: MASS, Erbil, Iraqi Kurdistan Photo: Sarbest Raza

PAVES heard that Poshya's visa had been refused on the first day we met all together in London in 2009. I had arranged for us to go to the ICA that night to see the film Afghan Star about the risk women take to be part of public events in Afghanistan. As the first PAVES action, I made a leaflet about Poshya's situation, mirroring the poster, to put on people's seats in the cinema. Sinead O'Donnell's action,2009, with her shirt saying visa, lying on a beach, almost exactly mirrors the famous photo of the young Syrian-Kurdish boy, Alan Kurdi, drowned because of visa restrictions, on a Turkish beach 6 years later, in 2015. We made many actions in each other's countries, in which we reached out to Poshya

"Poshya's absence became symbolic of the women's encounter with political antagonism. It became necessary to find strategies to make Poshya present across political territories in order to overcome her reclusion. This was achieved through the actions of the other members of the collective...

The work of PAVES articulates the continuing consequences of national borders. It is often said that the world is getting smaller, that we live as one multilateral community, however these individuals have strived to be with one another despite great adversity, leading them to focus upon the transcendental medium of time when most else fails. Prioritising the private physical experience, each artist employs their body as a locality for empathy and estrangement from place."

Extract PAVES dvd text, Helen Kaplinsky.

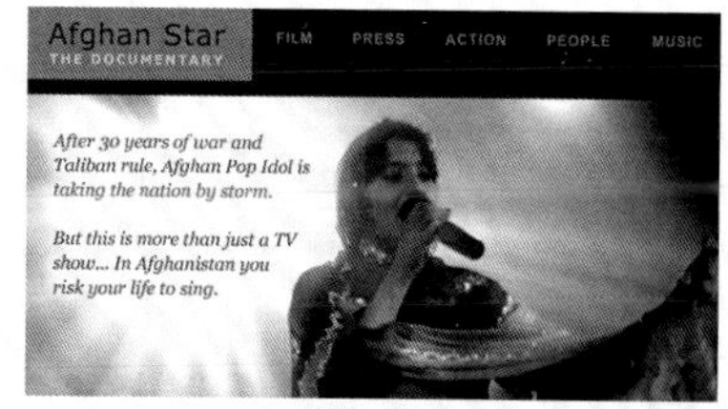

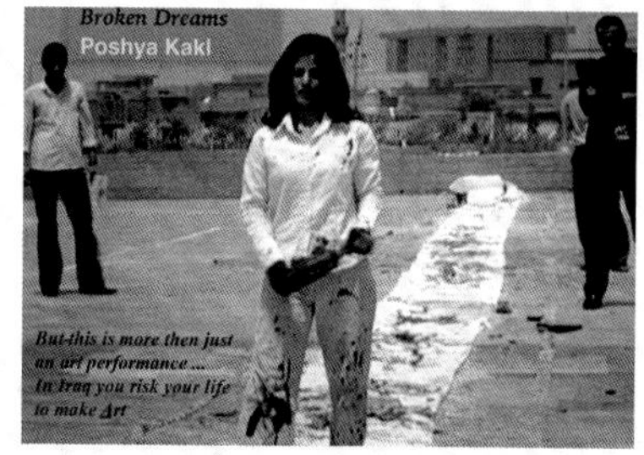

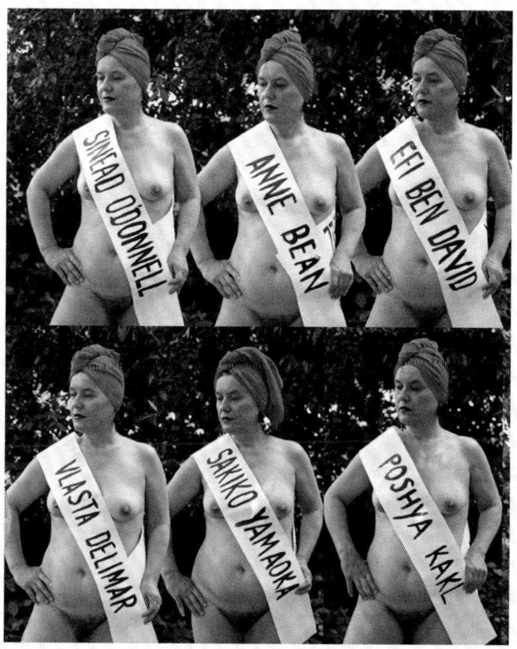

Left: Vlasta Delimar, *PAVES action*, Croatia, 2009

We made many attempts to meet up with Poshya during 2009, as we hadn't met all as a group. Jordan became the most possible because Efi from Israel and Poshya could potentially get access. PAVES travelled to Amman through Israel and Poshya took a flight. We went to the airport, but although Poshya had a visa and landed, she was not allowed to enter. A man called Mr Chance gave her a great deal of help, as she was very stressed.

I emailed Poshya:

'The fact that someone called Chance helped you and was inspired by you makes it all feel like strange destinies are with us. BUT as I wrote to you on the night that we were all in Amman, the sadness was so strong. There was an emptiness after coming back from the airport . It was such a primal feeling sensing you through the few walls separating us ... On top of everything the bright, open and innovative thinking people in the art gallery in Amman where we were about to work, said Efi is not welcome there because she is from Israel. In the airport I thought of a work in which Efi is at the Jordanian border with Iraq and you, Poshya at the Iraqi border with Jordan and I would walk between you with a piece of ribbon connecting you both and then you would tug on it and feel each other.'

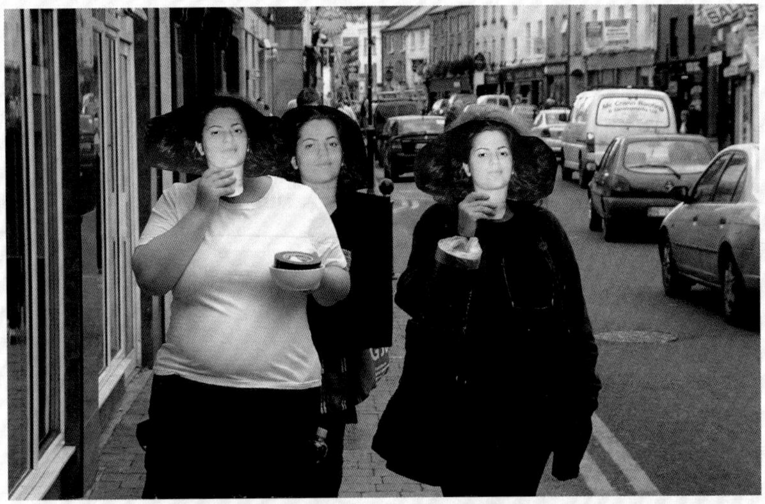

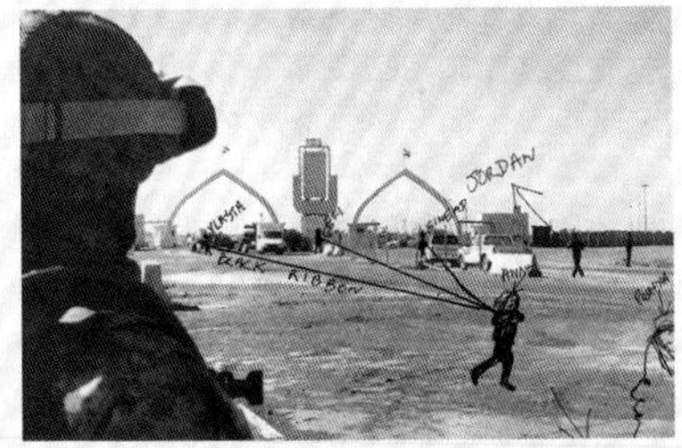

Email to friend and artist, Carlyle Reedy, explaining the day at the Amman gallery and then the night at Amman airport:

'It is really a desperate night here in Amman, Jordan...

These underlying fears of other ways and other cultures, often primitive feelings of apprehension, strongly bring back to me that piece I mentioned to you ages ago that I wrote as a teenager about my conflicted feelings in relation to Virginia Woolf--- called V W's daughter. Virginia has a daughter with Leonard Woolf and this little girl looks very like his family with her obviously semitic features. This nagging feeling of the baby's otherness slowly muddies Virginia's great outpourings of sensual love and unbounded joy on first seeing her tiny daughter. The very being who has finally given her a connection to flesh in the world, also inhabits a painfully mistrusted space. Virginia's bond and love is tainted and there is caution about who this small being is and that this little girl possesses something Virginia cannot access. She has terrifying misgivings about her half Jewish baby.

It is so easy to see these misgivings within families, so the bigger picture is overwhelming.'

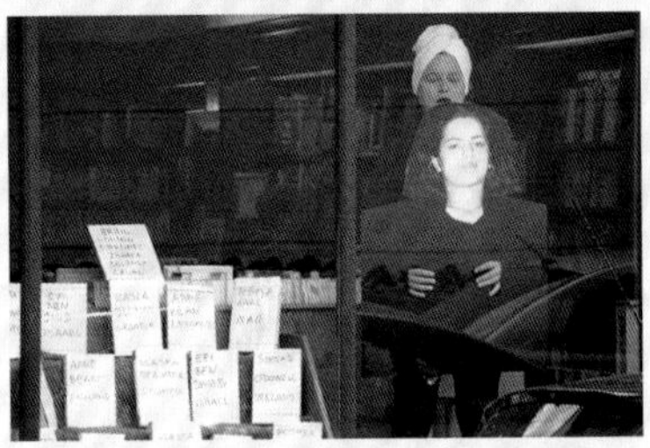

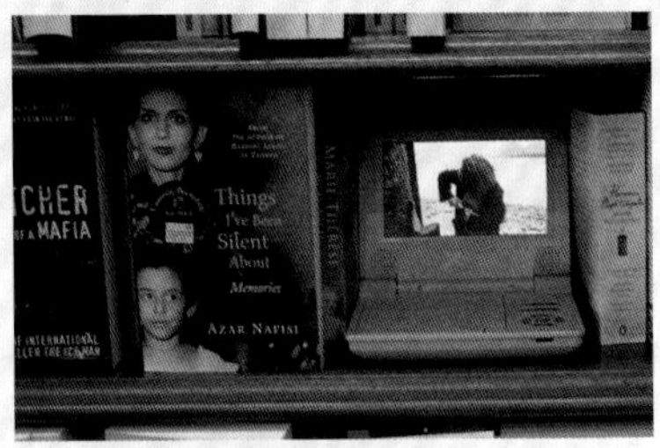

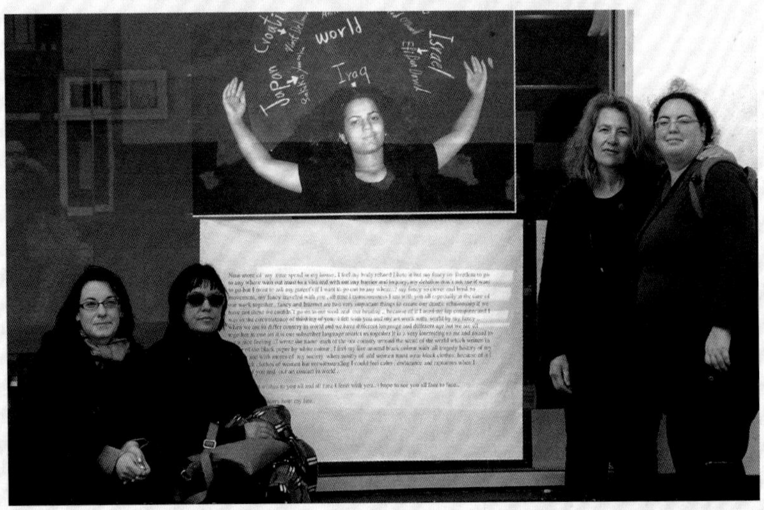

Right: PAVES actions inclusive of the physically absent Poshya, in department stores, bookshops and on the streets of Cavan, Ireland, 2009.

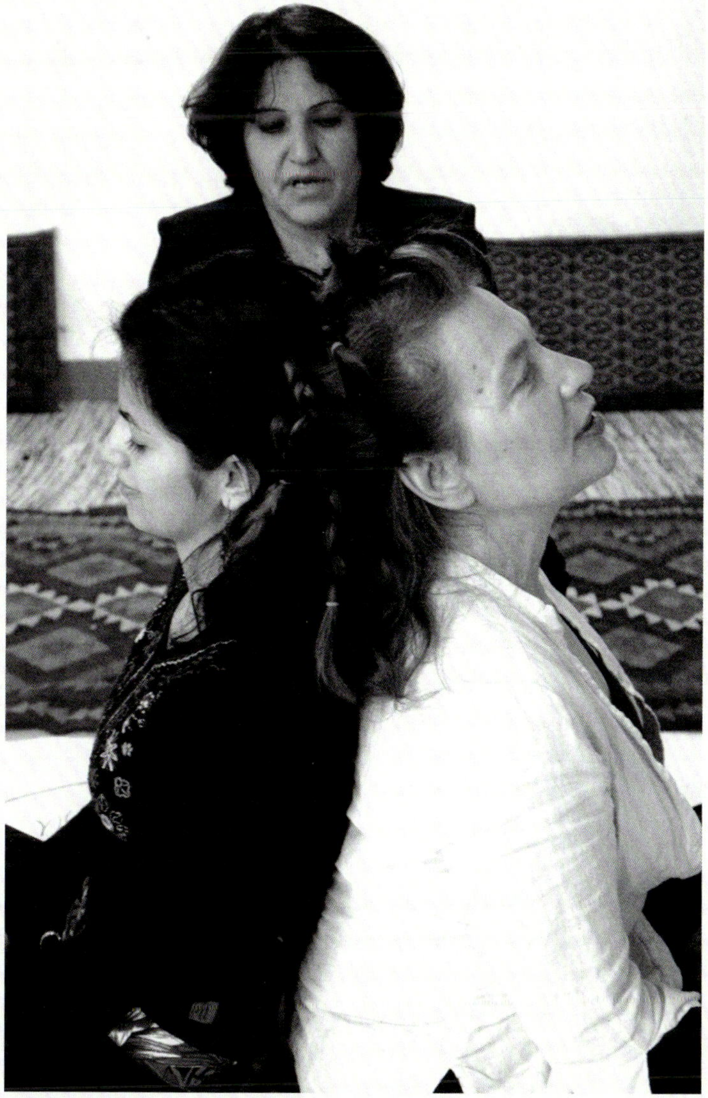

I asked Poshya what her mother thinks of PAVES. She translated the reply: 'She is very happy. She thinks it is a new art and a new way of living.'

Right: 'A solution to concerns about modesty.' A drawing in response to Poshya's work 'Mosque and Harmonica', 2008.

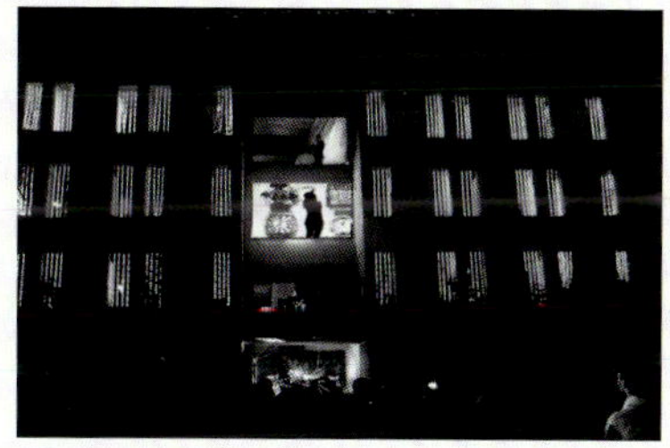

The Red Jail

The Red Jail, scarred and wounded by war has such a massive presence that it felt like the building itself had to be the 'star' of the work. We decided to make an architectural installation initially led by what the building's physicality suggested with a low pulsing sound rumbling through it. I asked each of the students working with us to stand behind a window and, just as the performance began, to hang up previously prepared 'bars' of light, so that the performance started as an installation of these barred windows and deeply rumbling sounds. I also projected *Watch*, a film I made with Miyako Narita responding to images from the genocide seen in a Kurdish museum where watches were displayed which had been dug out the ground of mass graves, having been buried with the victims.

Heartbeats and watch beats aurally pulsated so the installation became more complex with the low echoing breath. Sounds became more and more rhythmically complex as the students each joined in rolling marbles in large water bottles and Kurdish drummers added traditional rhythms. I did a duet with Mrs. Garmiany speaking of the time she spent in the jail with her young family whilst the students each rang a small bell. Large percussive sounds from Richard Wilson's huge spring gong tank with accompanying welding light, Chris Gladwin's sound sculptings and Miyako Narita's projections of her images of the building's scars, all augmented the building's presence as the central component. The event ended with the students making circles of light out of the bars and throwing them into the audience.

This event happened as a part of the Post-War Art & Culture Festival, a 3-day celebration of Art and Culture in November, 2009, Iraq initiated and organized by Adalet Garmiany

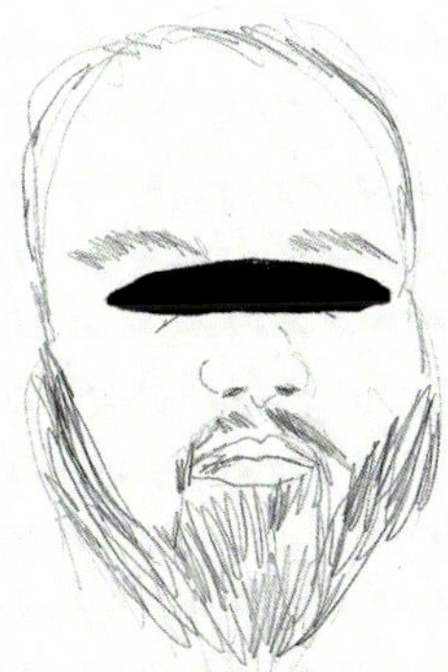

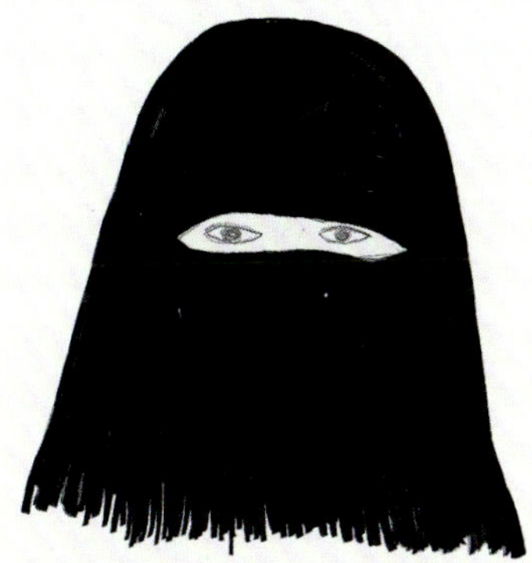

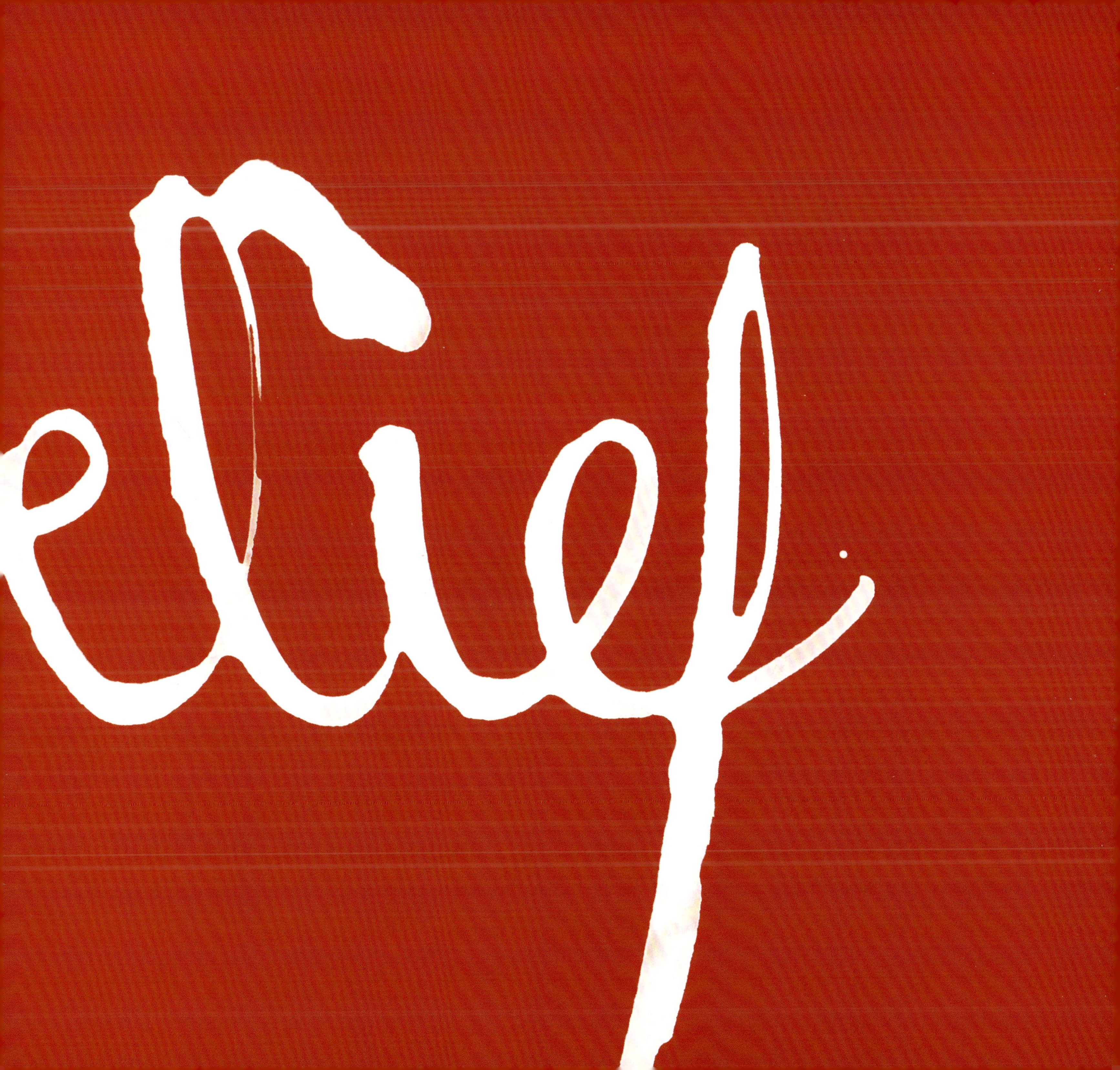
elief

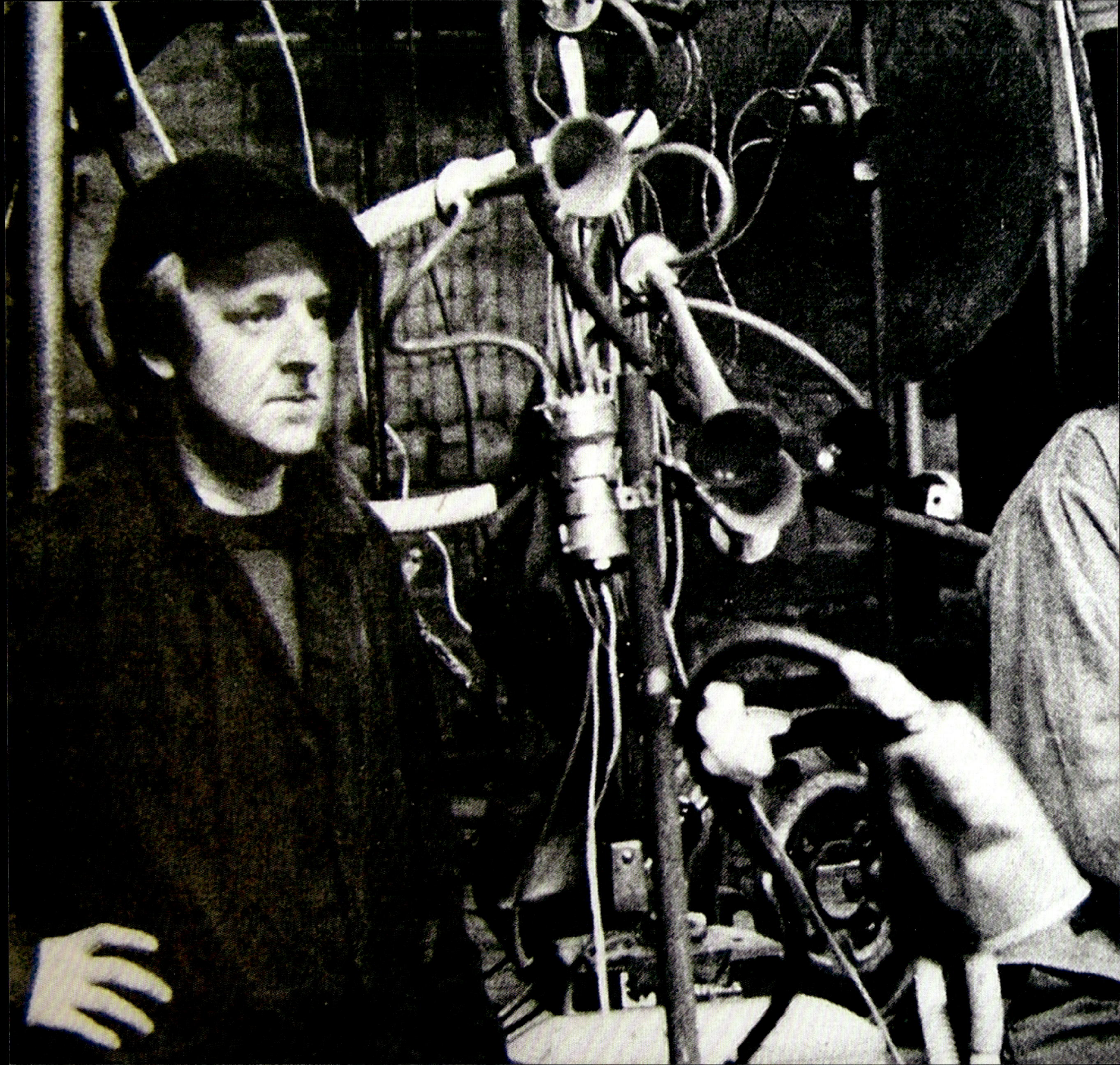

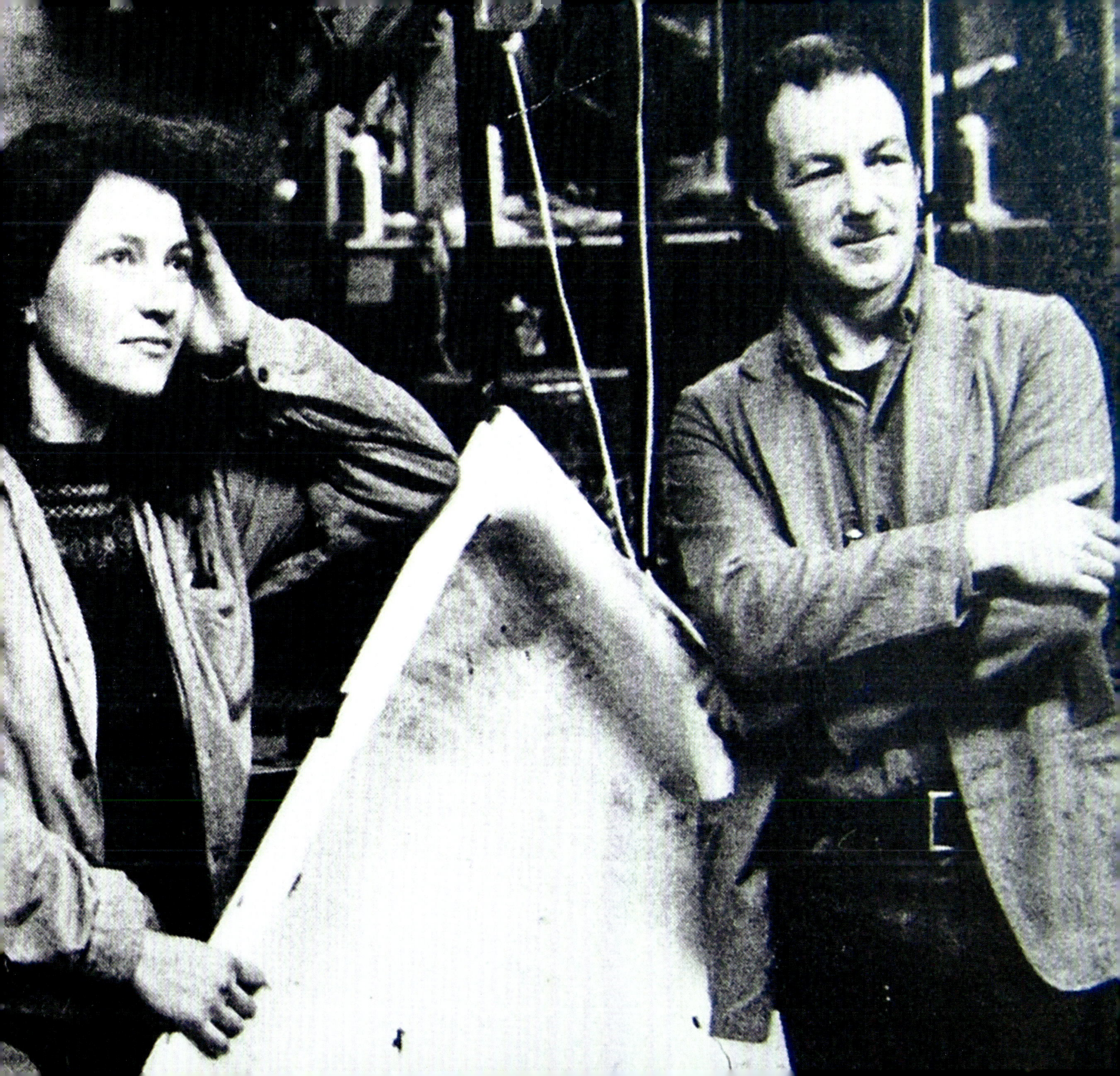

DISBELIEF SYSTEMS: AN INTERVIEW WITH BOW GAMELAN ENSEMBLE

ROB LA FRENAIS

The Bow Gamelan Ensemble was founded in 1983 by Anne Bean, Paul Burwell and Richard Wilson during a boat trip up Bow Creek.[1] Over the next eight years they created a dynamic experience using sound, light and performance which went beyond the conventional definitions of music event. Since their first performance at the London Musicians Collective (which was intended to be their only performance), the Bow Gamelan Ensemble made dozens of performances, actions, events and specially commissioned works throughout Europe and North America, as well as in Mexico and Japan. The name 'Bow Gamelan' derives from the area of East London where they lived and worked, and the Indonesian metallophone ensembles.

The Bow Gamelan Ensemble grew from intimate indoor performances to large outdoor events, which created new orchestras out of discarded materials around the world. Their instruments were all specially constructed, mostly from scrap metal, electric motors and glass, and produced a wide variety of sounds ranging from the deep, organ-like sounds of pyrophones through a gamut of percussive timbres and dynamic ranges. Both the sound sources and the musical structures generated were unusual because of the physical relationship between the way instruments work and how they had to be played. The unique sensibilities of the individual members combined with their long and varied experience in the areas of performance art, drumming, sculpture, environments and multimedia practices, which made the collaboration remarkably creative and fruitful.

The Bow Gamelan Ensemble gave their last performance together in 1990. Paul Burwell died of hypothermia on 4 February 2007. In the interview below, 11 years after Burwell's death, the surviving members Anne Bean and Richard Wilson reminisce about Bow Gamelan Ensemble and discuss their performances together since, often inhabited by the spirit of Burwell. The interview is followed by a short afterword by Rose Fenton and Lucy Neal, co-founders of London International Festival of Theatre (LIFT), who commissioned *Offshore Rig* and Bow Gamelan Ensemble's major performance at Bankside Power Station.

Rob La Frenais *Working backwards through the timeline, when was the last time you did something you could call Bow Gamelan Ensemble?*

Richard Wilson Well it is an interesting question because you're working backwards and we did a back-to-front Bow Gamelan at the 2015 London Contemporary Music Festival at Ambika 2. Obviously, Paul's not around – we don't want to repeat the Gamelan – so we turned the name back-to-front and we became WOB, rather than BOW Gamelan. We performed a piece called *Nalemag*, Gamelan backwards. I wouldn't say we were doing it strictly as Bow Gamelan, but we certainly cannot say we weren't affected by working together for – what was it? – 9 or 10 years and then Anne and I continued. We'd done various bits and pieces but it's always had a very, very strong mix of the Gamelan in what we do. We've not gone digital, we're still natural acoustic ... therefore working with those themes of the gamelan. It's just that Paul's not there and that makes it very difficult to say it's the Gamelan.

1. The bulk of this introductory text reproduces a statement written by Bean, Burwell and Wilson for a publicity sheet to accompany performances by Bow Gamelan Ensemble in the 1980s.

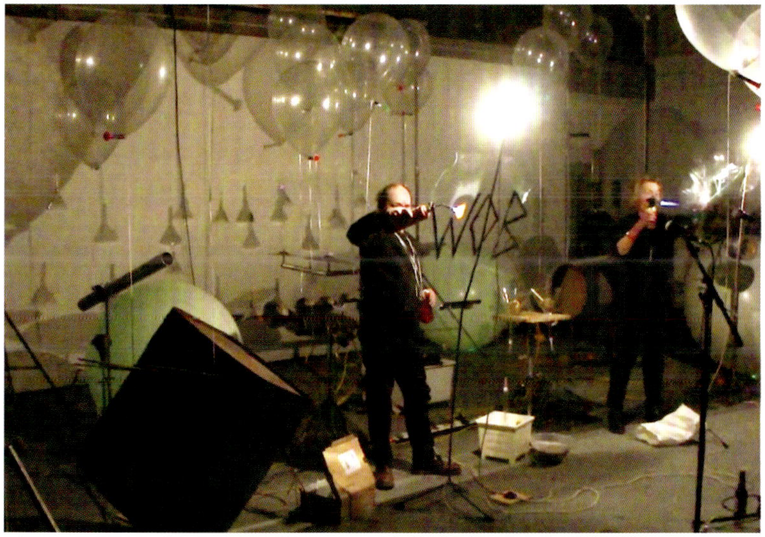

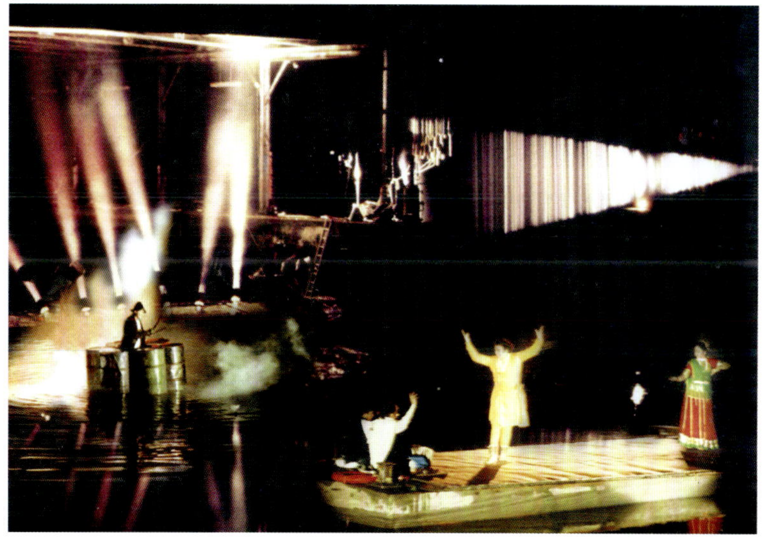

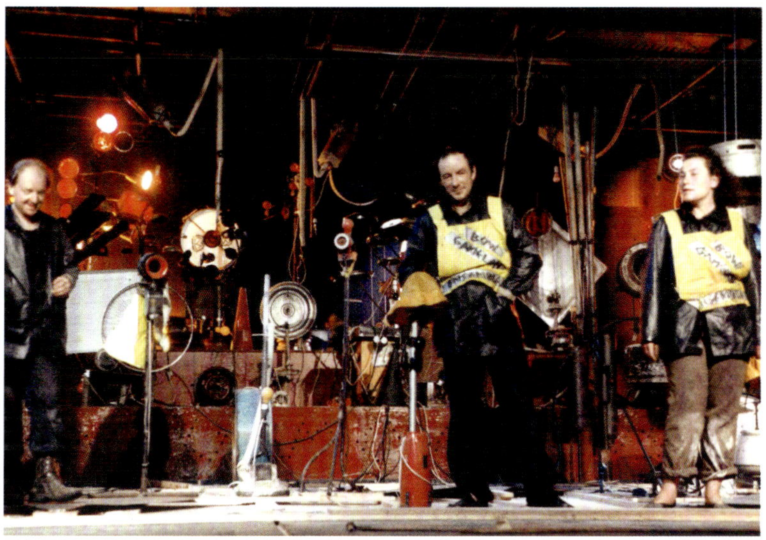

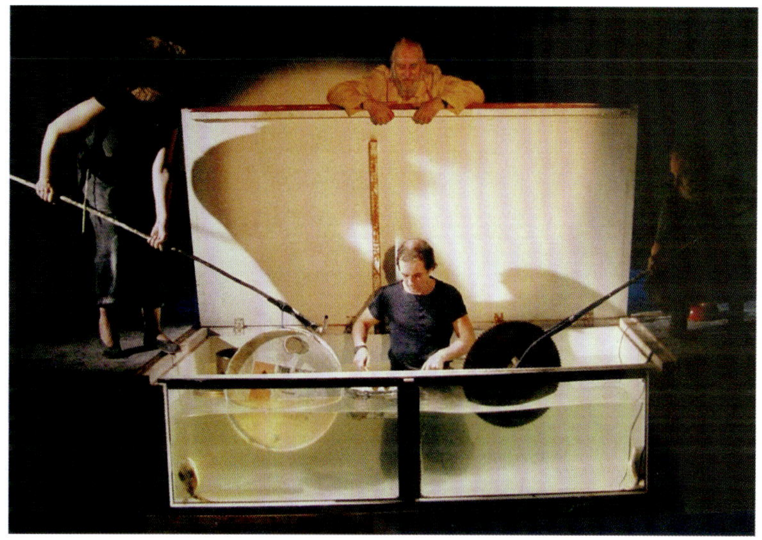

Top left: WOB (Anne Bean and Paul Burwell), *Nalemag*, London Contemporary Music Festival, Ambika, London, 2015. Still from video by Miyako Narita

Top right: Bow Gamelan Ensemble (with Z'EV, Treveni Kathak Dance Troupe, Thames Steam Launch Company, and Eel Pie Marine), *Offshore Rig*, Lot's Ait, 1987. Photo: Jim Harold

Bottom left: Bow Gamelan Ensemble, untitled performance, Dowanhill Church, Glasgow 1986. Photographer unknown

Bottom right: Bow Gamelan Ensemble (with Bob Cobbing), *In C and Air*, Institute of Contemporary Arts, London, 1986. Photo: Jim Harold

pp. 252-3: Bow Gamelan Ensemble, untitled performance, Dowanhill Church, Third Eye Centre, Glasgow, 1986 Photo: courtesy *The Scotsman*

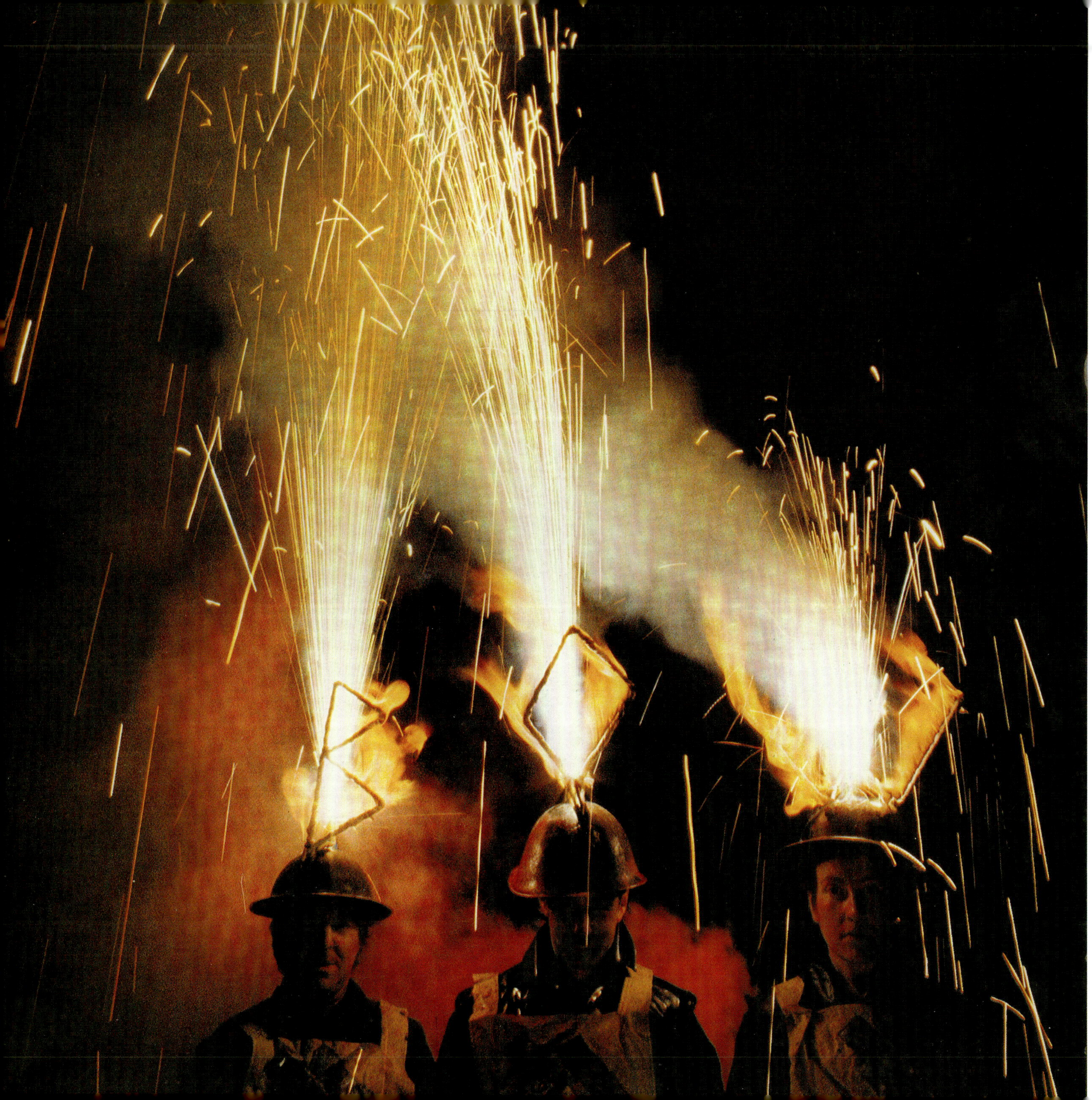

RLF *Who was there?*

RW The presence of Anne and me – but we've always believed there is the 'other' presence.

Anne Bean What I find really interesting is that– whether it's WOB or BOW – it contains Bean – Zero – Wilson. Paul's become this circular zero. So within the name itself, the B and the W are holding this zero between them. The zero is both a great circularity and a void. So it's a very beautiful space, I feel the name BOW then becomes prescient in a different way. Initially, Bow was used because it was where we were from, where Paul and I lived for a very long time, where there were several scrap yards and bits of scrap lying about on the street, where the three of us made the Gamelan together.

RLF *Without trying to be totally spooky about it, I've heard some of the stories about Paul manifesting himself. When you do these performances, do you feel the presence of Paul still?*

RW I think so – they're not done without Paul – I say that but I mean we always go into it talking about him – we always go into it with his drive and spirit in the background with whatever the performance is. You know, in that way there is a presence. He's been present in the form of ashes, in forms of re-incarnation through some of the instruments that he made – we made together – possibly even the way we script stuff follows very much how the three of us did things, and I think that the three of us influences the two of us. In that statement obviously the third person is there.

AB When we were doing *TAPS*, which was the piece with 80 people who had known or collaborated with Paul, newly improvising with him, in whatever way they wanted the word 'with' to mean, the fire alarms kept going off in the building, for no reason – whether it's symbolic, whether its imagination – whatever it is, it's very present and very potent.

Bow Gamelan Ensemble, *Damned Near Run Thing*, Southbank, London, 1988. Photo: Ed Sirrs

RW Basically all the fire safety equipment in Dilston Grove was triggering itself for no obvious reason – which it hadn't done before. It just seemed co-incidental and unusual that it happened to be during *TAPS*. It was a three-day event. We weren't doing anything that would specifically trigger the alarm system in the building.

RLF *This and some of the incidents you've described do give you the sense – in the classic ghost-hunting literature – of a version of the poltergeist.*

RW Yes, but I don't think we worked with a poltergeist. I think we worked with the spirit of ... That's open to interpretation. I think it's just a feeling, personally, I don't believe myself that Paul is present in us when we are doing things – I mean I did not feel him alongside – but I know the presence of the way we got to where we were somehow was inclusive of Paul.

RLF *Anne, do you agree with that?*

AB Well, as Richard was talking I was thinking of a conversation we had this morning. Basically, someone was taking Paul's archives to catalogue them and Richard was talking about some particular bits that we weren't sure we should include for various reasons. I felt I couldn't throw them away because of a feeling of Paul watching – it is like some trust or honouring you made in life exists through time and remains fully *present*, whatever then happens. What is that?

RW I know, I know.

RLF *Given that you both feel this presence of Paul, you were both very close to him and worked together, it seems to me, that you are interpreting the presence of Paul through different belief systems between the two of you.*

AB I think we're probably in complete agreement in our belief systems in that it's a very rich and vivid triggering of being, of vision, and that it doesn't matter if you believe or disbelieve anything. It really is irrelevant, it's very present and very alive.

RLF *Is that something about art? About what artists do?*

AB I think it is in terms of that very open imagination, that includes a lot of belief systems and kind of hoovers up bits and pieces from all of them, sometimes contradictory.

RLF *To some extent art is a belief system in its own right.*

AB In many ways art is a *disbelief* system.

RLF *It's a disbelief system that allows more latitude for the imagination to come in. Does this allow for a more physical manifestation? You're opening a portal?*

RW It can be an attitude as well. Sometimes I have to sit back and think – what would Paul do in this situation, or this scenario? It's that sort of vital way in which he'd improvise his way through something. It wasn't over-calculated, it wasn't driven into the ground and crucified, taken too far and just died because you'd done just too much with it. It held on to something that was very, very natural and spontaneous – I don't know if 'raw' is the right word but it had guts to it – visceral.

AB Intestinal.

RW In that sense it's not a poltergeist around, it's like you're keeping that person's unique attitude towards creativity. Because you have to say there's been a real dumbing down in the approach to making a work nowadays. The way it's processed, the way it's done, the professionalism ... it's driven by certain criteria that weren't around when we were doing this stuff in the 1980s with Bow Gamelan. It came out of nothing, like rubbish, like junk, the written-off and the discarded. You don't get a real sense of magic any more – I suppose the word is 'transported'.

RLF *That connects with a question I had about the Bow Gamelan being part of a landscape of an older London, when Tate Modern was just an abandoned power station. What is the place of Bow Gamelan in this new, brash version of London?*

RW It's an interesting question. Aside from Paul dying it would now be physically impossible to do what we did back then. The very simplistic point is that incandescent light is dying out and it would be very difficult to get the self-illuminations we did, then if you go to the extreme other range in terms of the practicalities of Bow Gamelan, you're just not allowed to do anything of those health and safety aspects, anymore. Risk was part of what we used to use and what you can actually get hold of now.

RLF *I suppose that if you throw money at things you can avoid those health and safety issues.*

AB Kind of ... but at the Contemporary Music Festival [in 2015], Richard and I decided to just go ahead. I just said that we'd take responsibility. We knew we could. It is often more dangerous trying to compromise ideas, physically and metaphysically.

RW No one in the 1980s had ever asked us for a comprehensive risk assessment. Risk was part of getting on with living. Now, you can't open the door without declaring an element of danger in that act. Should we wish to undertake any part of those performances from back then we would have to fill out an assessment form at the outset. We have the history but now there is a nervousness about that.

RLF *In those early performances were there any life threatening moments?*

RW Yes and no. I mean everything has the potential to be life threatening. Paul said, plugging into a socket is life threatening, crossing the road is life threatening.

RLF *Is there any point at which you felt, maybe we've bitten off a bit more than we can chew?*

RW I don't think anything got so completely out of control where we felt our lives were on the line – it wasn't so dangerous! More a sleight of hand that appeared to be risky. There were small occurrences but they were manageable. One just dealt with them, in the same way you'd extinguish a fire. I'll give an example, we went to Bretton Hall

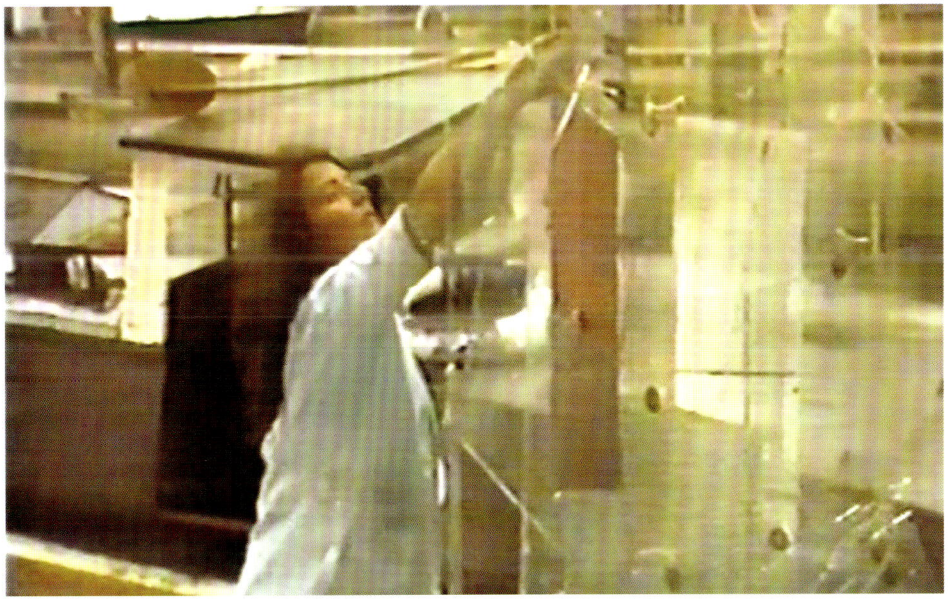

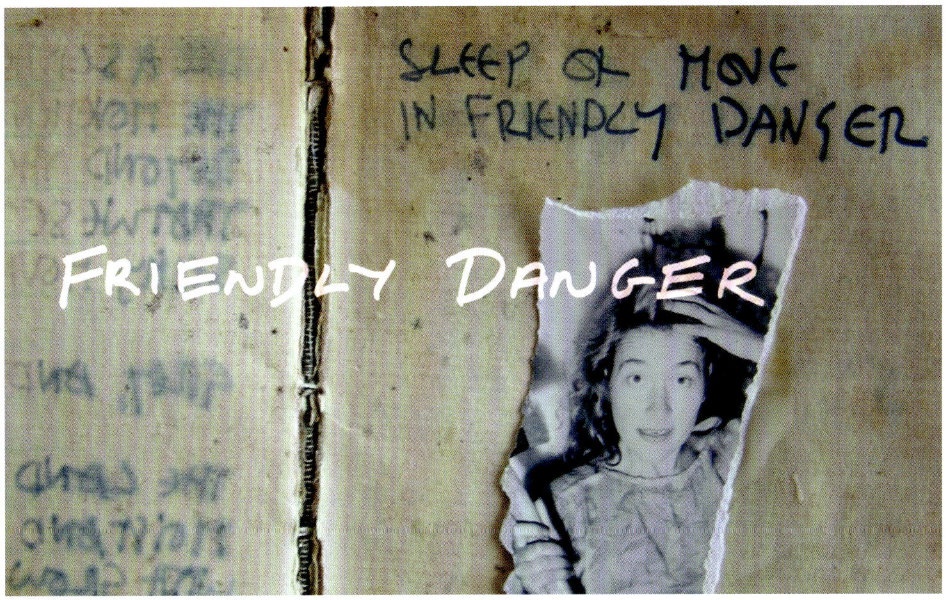

Top: Anne Bean hanging glass chimes in *Offshore Rig*, Lot's Ait, 1987.
Still from a video. Photo: courtesy After Image Production

Bottom: Anne Bean and Paul Burwell, shared notebook, 1978

pp. 260-1: Bow Gamelan Ensemble, *Earth Celebrations*, KODO Drummers International Percussion Festival, Sado Island, Japan, 1988. Photo: courtesy KODO Drummers

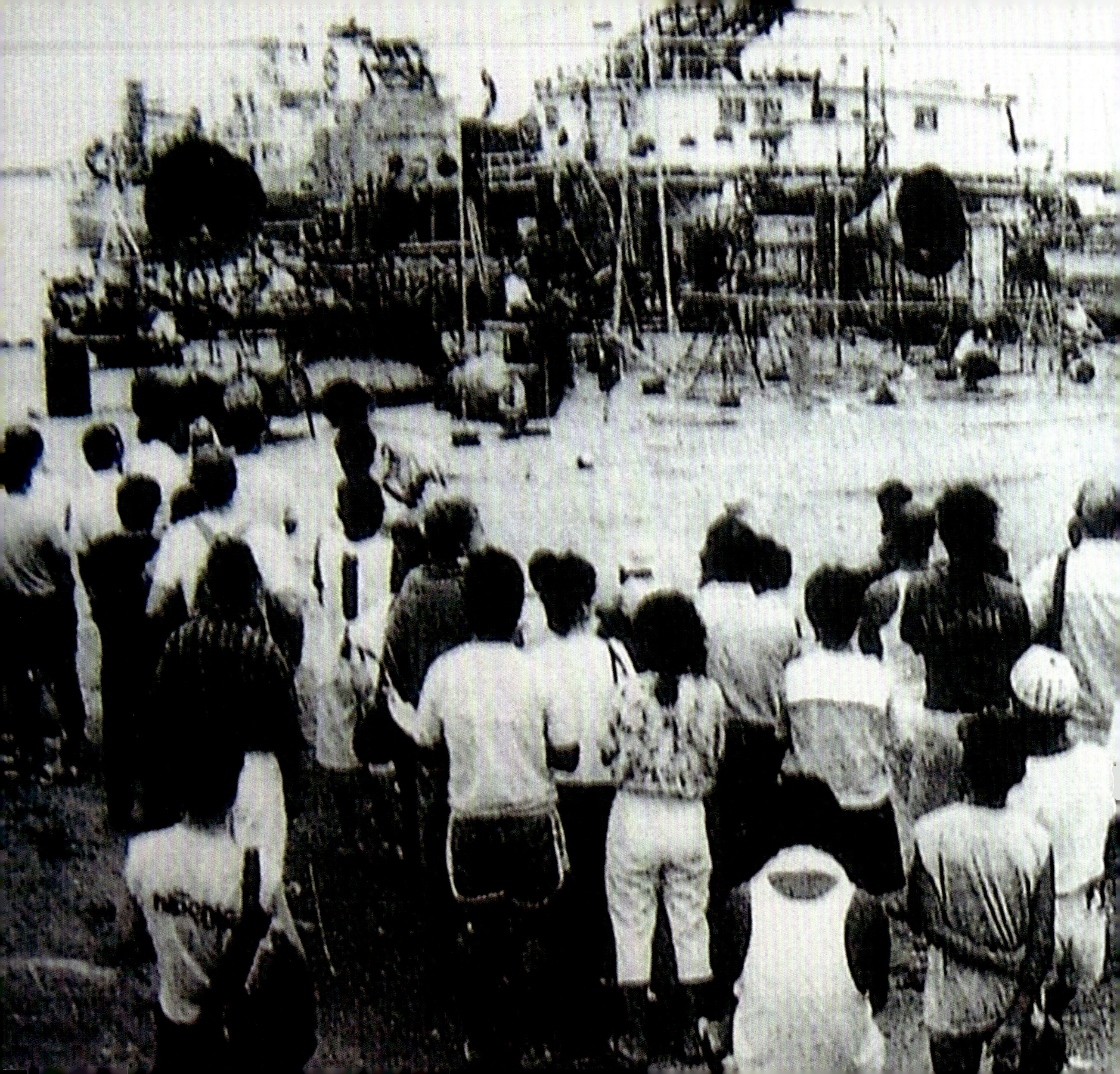

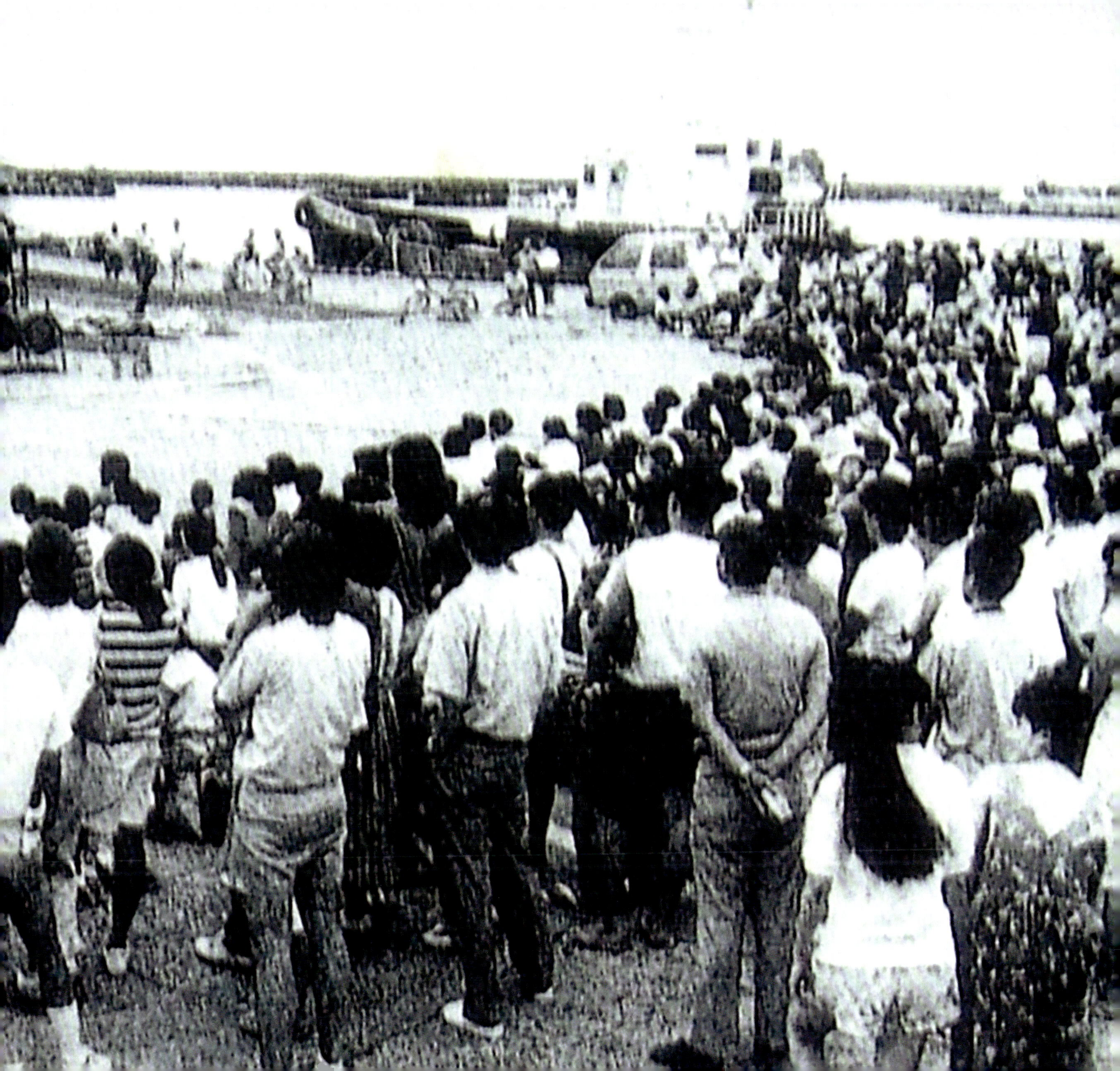

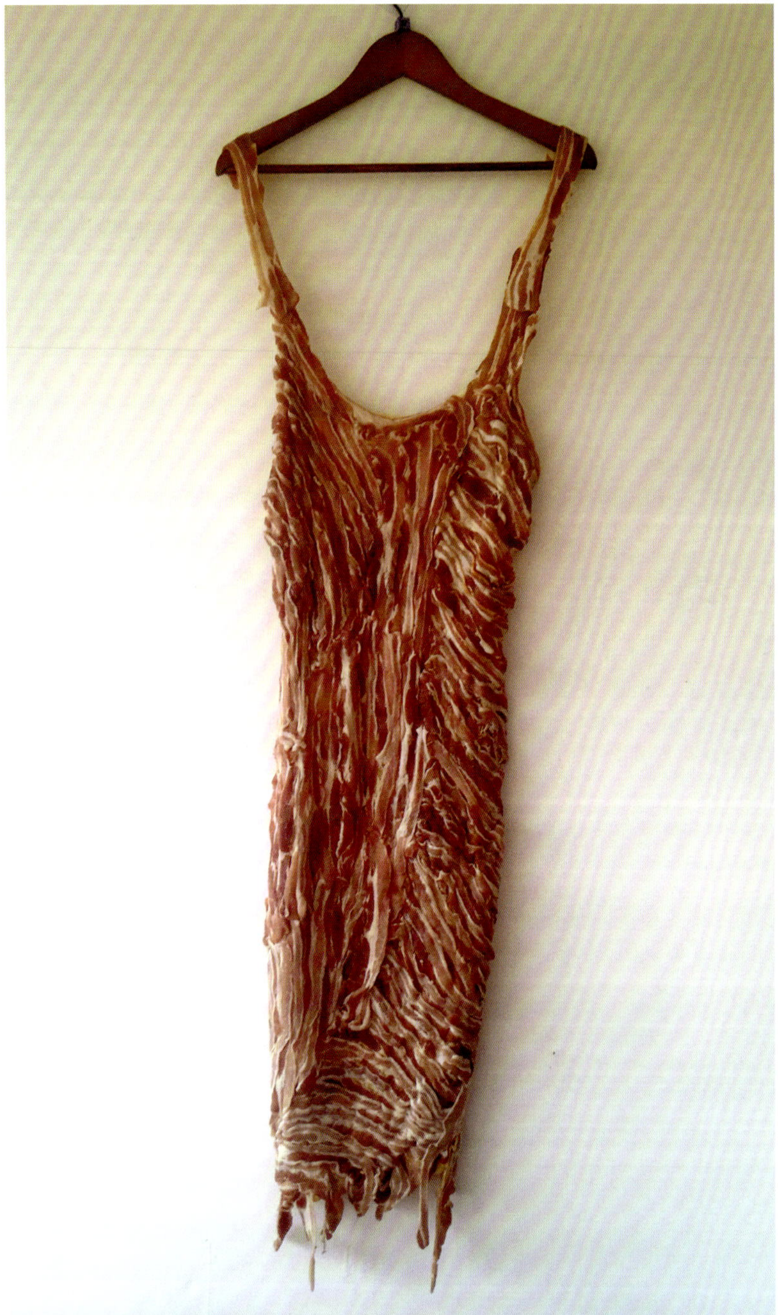

Anne Bean, *Bacon Dress*, PART Y, C4 Butlers Wharf, London, 1977

to give a talk and there was an occurrence – a flame that set the curtains alight [*laughter*]. But that was dealt with immediately. The thing is, if the work was on the very edge anyway, you became more aware of the risk factor. If you weren't familiar with it you wouldn't be able to deal with it.

RLF *I suppose it's this interplay between risk and control – Anne in her work has gone into areas I think are pretty risky such as in Chana Dubinski, living completely outside, starting off from living on the road, being more or less homeless and seeing what's going to happen. That's almost more risky than what you were doing with pyrotechnics.*

RW I would agree with that because the three of us, collectively, were able to share in dealing with it – but you were on your own with it.

AB There is that existential risk, which I think is always the most fundamental. Going back to the physical risk, the thing that sticks with me, just pre-Gamelan, was Steve Cripps.

Paul had this horror moment with the big glass chimes that I set up, like a chandelier of sound and light played with different settings of a wind machine. I was hanging it on the island at Lot's Ait [a river island in the Thames], with these sharp shards of glass and mirror. I was poking at them and Paul thought that I could easily have been beheaded. I didn't have that frisson. But once, with Paul and Steve at the London Musicians Collective, I put several record players on top of flaming Bunsen burners – I don't know what possessed me, when I think back. The record players, playing Paul's and my single *Low Flying Aircraft* caught fire, so the sound juddered to a halt, ghostily returning, entering and exiting through the flames. All this burning plastic was surrounding the cylinder of propane. I mean, utterly, a bomb. I suddenly looked at it and I thought that this is beyond frisson. In a wooden building. It was embracing a very edgy, frightening moment, although in my gut I knew we would be able to control it — a palpable awareness kicks in, maybe addictive in some way.

RLF *That glass chandelier was* Offshore Rig? *That was Bow Gamelan at its height, in a sense.*

AB It was outdoor with huge elements. It was an almighty taking-on of a space, reanimating an industrial part of London, the continual tidal rejigging of space, the old boat repair and boat building yard, all the old machinery which had been working on compressed air ... deep breathy sounds, spawning this sound-visual piece. Again, in terms of ghosts – but not ghosts ... It's an actual recognition of spaces that had incredible dynamism and energy, an embrace and capturing of that in what we were doing in the present.

RW I mean, one had to change one's direction slightly when the Gamelan worked outdoors. Indoors, as Paul would say in interviews, our canvas is one of darkness and silence – in churches or theatre spaces, the hull of a ship, a cave – those spaces work, but once you go outside it's not just a canvas of darkness and silence but other things as well, to do with the built environment, the way you animate that. You transgress it, you transform it, you have to throw sound at it. You could whisper but you had to also find ways to shout.

RLF *I always felt that Bow Gamelan worked better in those constricted spaces where you felt slightly unsafe.*

RW It meant that the audience was closer, obviously.

RLF *Like the Diorama. But there came this trend towards large-scale outdoor performances that were very well financed. There became a point where people expected too much – fireworks and big bangs, massive theatrical things.*

RW It gave an opportunity to areas that we wanted to travel to. For example, big pyrotechnical sound, and also the whole notion of air hooters and steam whistles, boilers, vast amounts of compressed air to give us very loud and dense sounds.

AB A lot of people on the river started to work with us, including Tom Leadlay and his Thames Steam Launch Company. It was very much part of that Gamelan ethos – because it started on the river, an animation of vast urbanscapes.

RLF *The River Thames kind of flows through the history of the Bow Gamelan. All the way through the things I remember from* Offshore Rig *to the famous picture of the boat nearly capsizing under Blackfriars Bridge – one of the iconic images, with Anne blowing through the tube and the ship listing. And also the lifeboat you co-owned with Ron Haselden.*

RW The *Coral Star* – Ron owned half of it then moved to France and Paul came on board.

RLF *I remember an early performance art journey on the* Coral Star, *more a social event, with my son Max, now 28, who was a newborn baby. We were going up the Thames at Barnes and Jock McFadyen's dog escaped.*

RW We jumped in the river.

RLF *We had a newborn and his mother on board and you and Paul swam after Jock's dog. Nobody quite knew how to navigate. A typical example of the anarchy of that time* [laughter].

RW I didn't even have time to get rid of the camera round my neck. I wonder why? But we did rescue the dog.

RLF *The giant poodle, yes. I remember saying, does anyone know how to steer this thing?*

RW Can anyone steer this thing? Can anyone rescue the dog? We were so sort of versatile in all territories really. OK, suck it and see, we'll try this, we'll do that. That was really the attitude of the Bow Gamelan, to find what it was we were doing.

AB That was it, very much – whatever is chucked at us has potential.

RW It wasn't just structurally daring, health and safety and everything, it was also the territory of where the art was. Paul once stated in an interview that 'we were almost rejected by the avant-garde musicians – we were too avant-garde'.

AB Paul liked what Spike Jones said – 'too sophisticated for the corny and too corny for the sophisticated'. He loved that quote.

RW It didn't fit anywhere at that specific time. In a way it was sound-making, it wasn't music.

RLF *That brings me on to these three individuals, we have Paul, who was kind of at the heart of London's avant-garde music scene, there's Anne, whose career was building as a performance artist, and Richard, who was becoming a relatively famous mid-career sculptor, coming together in the group of the Bow Gamelan. How did that resonate? How did that work?*

RW Well to go back in history, we came together not because of those reasons, we came together because we were friends at Butlers Wharf. We all seemed to get on with each other, tolerate each other. Paul and Anne were working together anyway. They'd been working with Steve Cripps, who was a sculptor working with issues of sound as a physical element. I had done little bits and pieces as a postgraduate at Reading with sound and stuff. Paul was intrigued by my workshop and just my attitude. He came to me and said, listen, let's respond to this invitation to the New Musics Festival at London Musicians Collective.

AB Although we'd had history before that...

RW Yes, we'd been going on the boat, a couple of Anne's parties, collaborating on bits and pieces. So, I was just kind of called in, because Steve wasn't there. Which I was willing to do. I was familiar with the territory, I liked it. We just got going, from that.

RLF *So you think that Steve Cripps might have been the natural third member of the Bow Gamelan?*

RW I think he was the third member and I probably wouldn't have been the fourth.

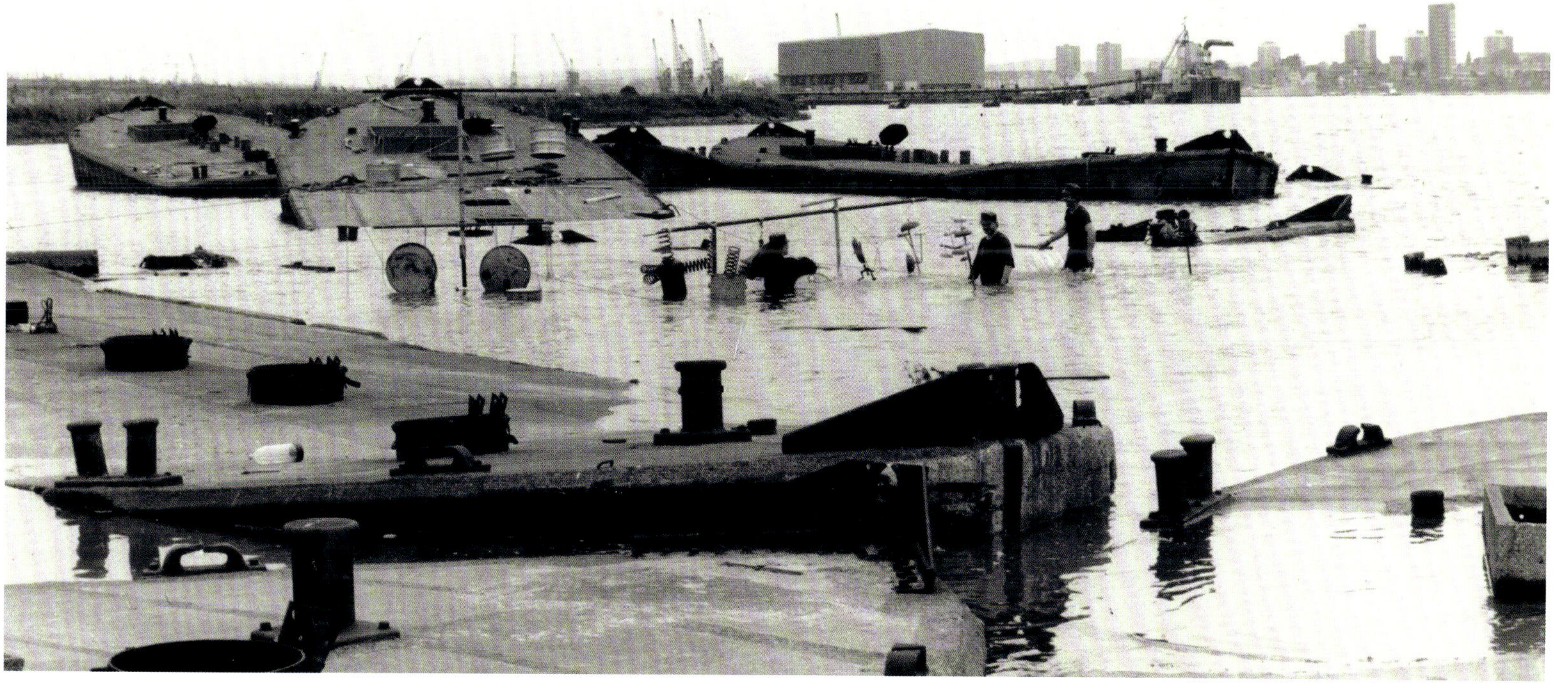

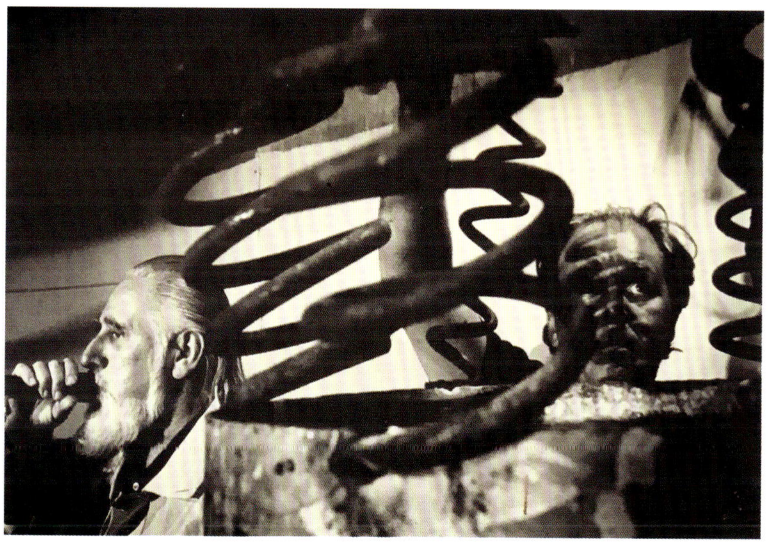

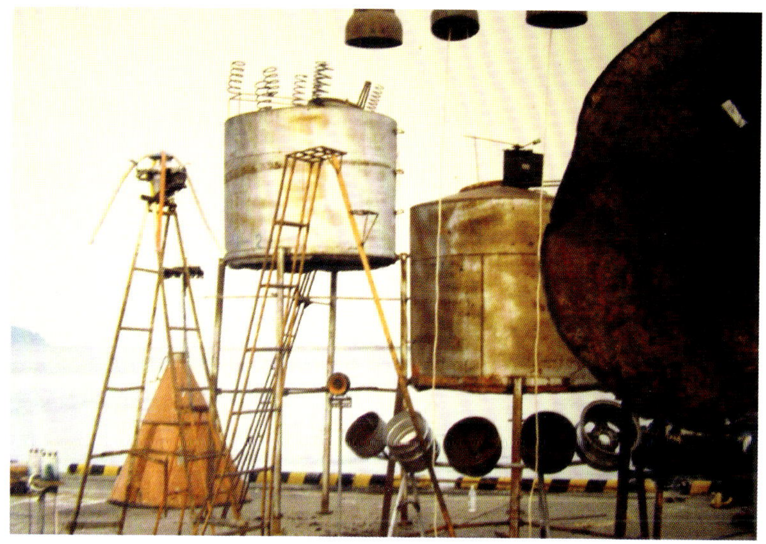

Top: Bow Gamelan Ensemble, *51° 29'.9" North – 0°11' East*,
Rainham Concrete Barges, Essex, 1987. Photo: After Image Productions

Bottom left: Bow Gamelan Ensemble (with Bob Cobbing), *In C and Air*,
Institute of Contemporary Arts, London, 1986. Photo: Jim Harold

Bottom right: Bow Gamelan Ensemble, *Earth Celebrations*, KODO Drummers
International Percussion Festival, Sado Island, Japan, 1988. Photo: Paul Burwell

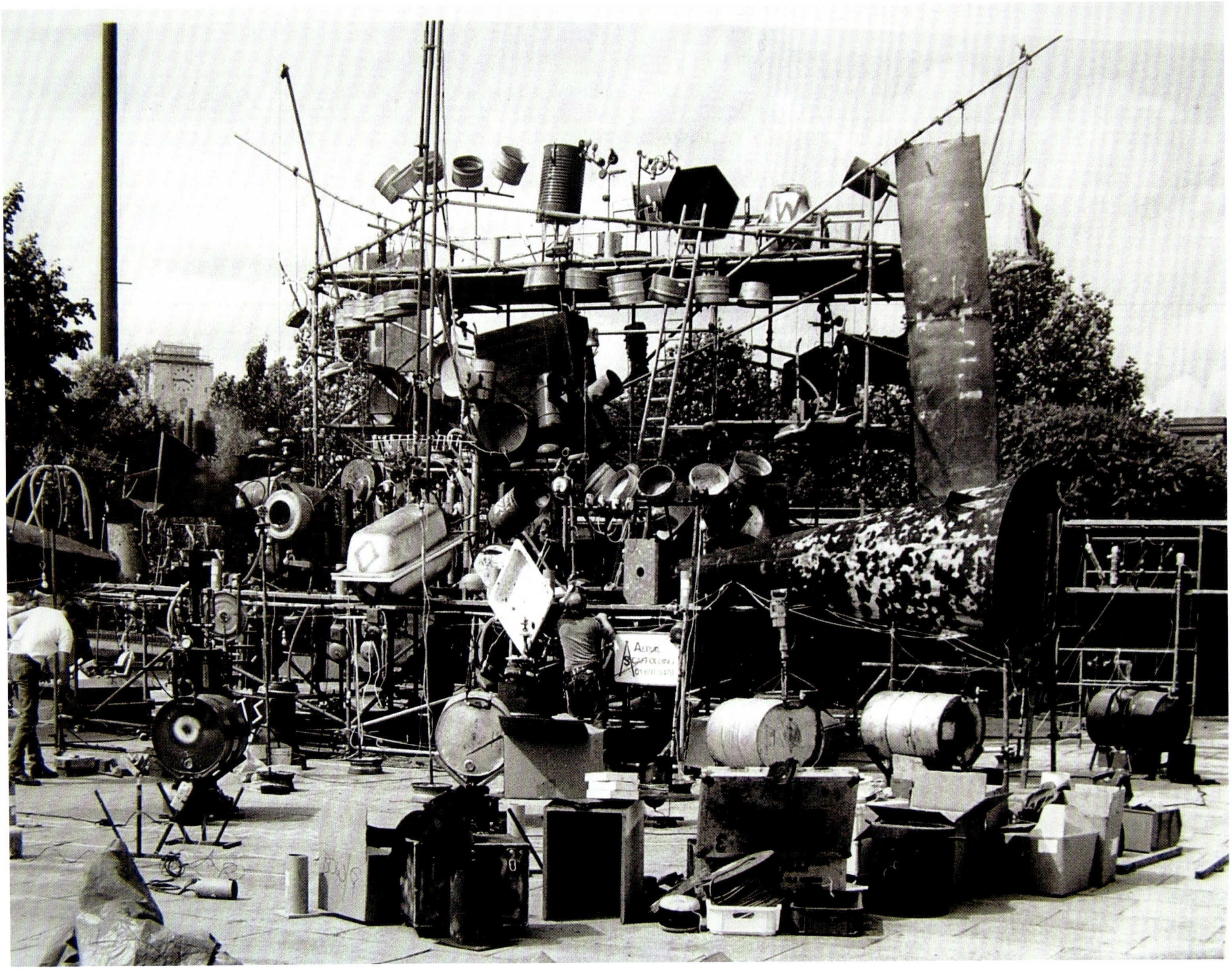

Bow Gamelan Ensemble, *Damned Near Run Thing*, Southbank, London, 1988. Photo: Ed Sirrs

pp. 268-9: Bow Gamelan Ensemble, *Damned Near Run Thing*, Southbank, London, 1988. Photo: Ed Sirrs

RLF *You were the Ringo Starr...* [laughter].

RW I was around and I just kind of came in...

AB No, I think your ingenuity and skills in analysing how to juggle certain things into action, how to make almost impossible visions work, was a very different input and a really pivotal influence. I think we just came together so organically, because we were all utterly thrilled by watching what was going-on on the river – we were all totally excited by it and every bridge that resonated and echoed and every welder that sparked across the water and every forklift truck that dropped a whole load of stuff and every magnetic lifter just absolutely inspired and triggered us. We weren't thinking of coming together at all.

RLF *Hypothetically speaking, if I was a historian 50 years in the future and was looking back at this, I might be thinking of Dada and the Surrealists as precedents, I might be thinking of the Futurists...*

AB ... or the Russian Constructivists' ideas for urban landscape and exalting industrial workers, so that events like the extraordinary *Concert for Factory Sirens* in Baku could take place in 1922. It's all in the DNA. I mean that it isn't academically there.

RW I think what's great about all three of us is that we're coming from left of centre. If we had to think about a new musical instrument, it wasn't a re-invention of the guitar or a re-invention of the hooter. I remember the first instrument we made. We worked with blowlamps, we put tins together, we heated water, we used the whistles off kettles. I made this stand out of a massive piece of RSJ [rolled steel joist] with three legs on it – it basically weighed two sacks of cement – welded together so you couldn't break it down like a drum kit. I know Paul was fascinated by the fact that we'd all built this thing but the stand was a bit crazy as well. We played it and it was perfect and it wasn't like any instrument we knew, other than if you compared it to, let's say, a whistle on a locomotive or whatever. It had the essence of that, which was closer to designing locomotives than a musician playing an instrument. I think that Brunel attitude that we had, where basically sound was the lively thing that kept us all going, we all bounced off the sheer hilarity of it, but at the same time, there was something very genuine and positive and the outcomes were always extraordinary, Anne with a big funnel throwing beans onto a fan, throwing themselves around a room when we were performing. There is no instrument that I can think of that is like that.

AB I think that we were freed of that history. I think Paul, who had been very much involved with the London Musicians Collective – even though it was a radical knowledge of instrumentation, it still had coherence and agreements. Richard and I genuinely were completely freed up from any sense of what that history was. So, we could think – could we fill a saucepan with dried chickpeas and put water in so they would slowly swell and spill over onto a thin aluminium sheet below to bounce and resonate for a long and intermittent chickpea percussion concerto? You know, we could look at anything on the table and just ...

RW ... find another purpose – like eating your famous dress made of bacon after that 1970s party in Butlers Wharf. A dress becomes a damn fine breakfast. Also, I think the thing about the ergonomics of playing – Paul always said trombones, drums, bell ringing, you could *see* where the sound is coming from – the ergonomics was very much part of the instrument. They became beautifully animated by the way we actually moved the things, played with them in a way and also were technicians for them. That's why Anne's beautiful glass chime outdoors was wonderful because of the ergonomics of that, her in there clunking away. Fuck! It was thunderous! It was like gas bottles banging, cabinets being blasted by jets of water from a Merryweather fire engine pump so they were smashed into each other. All that is not how an instrument is conventionally played but it's a damned good way of getting a sound. I mean, I'm not saying, when you listen to a car crash ... but it's this idea of the implosion of

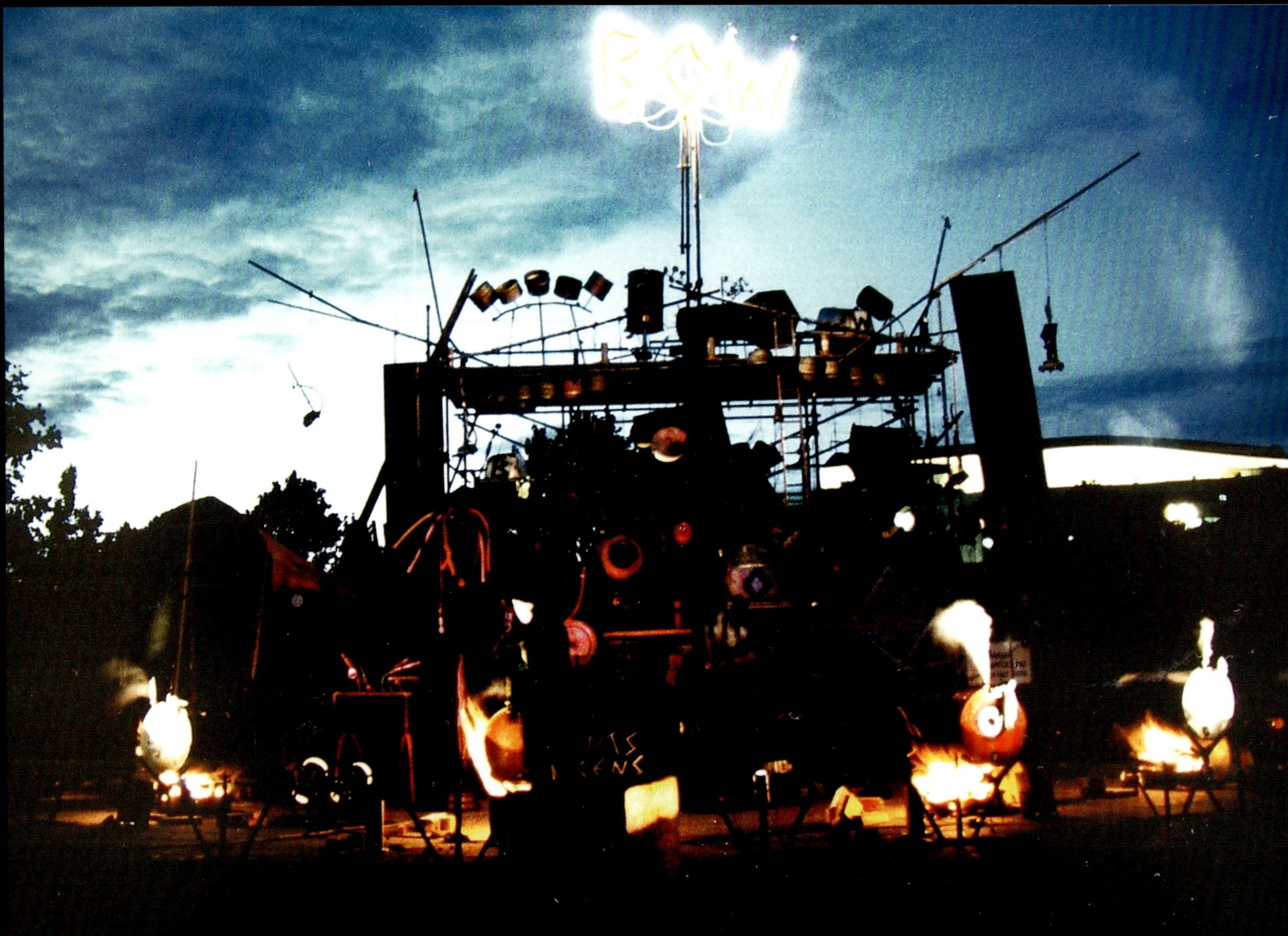

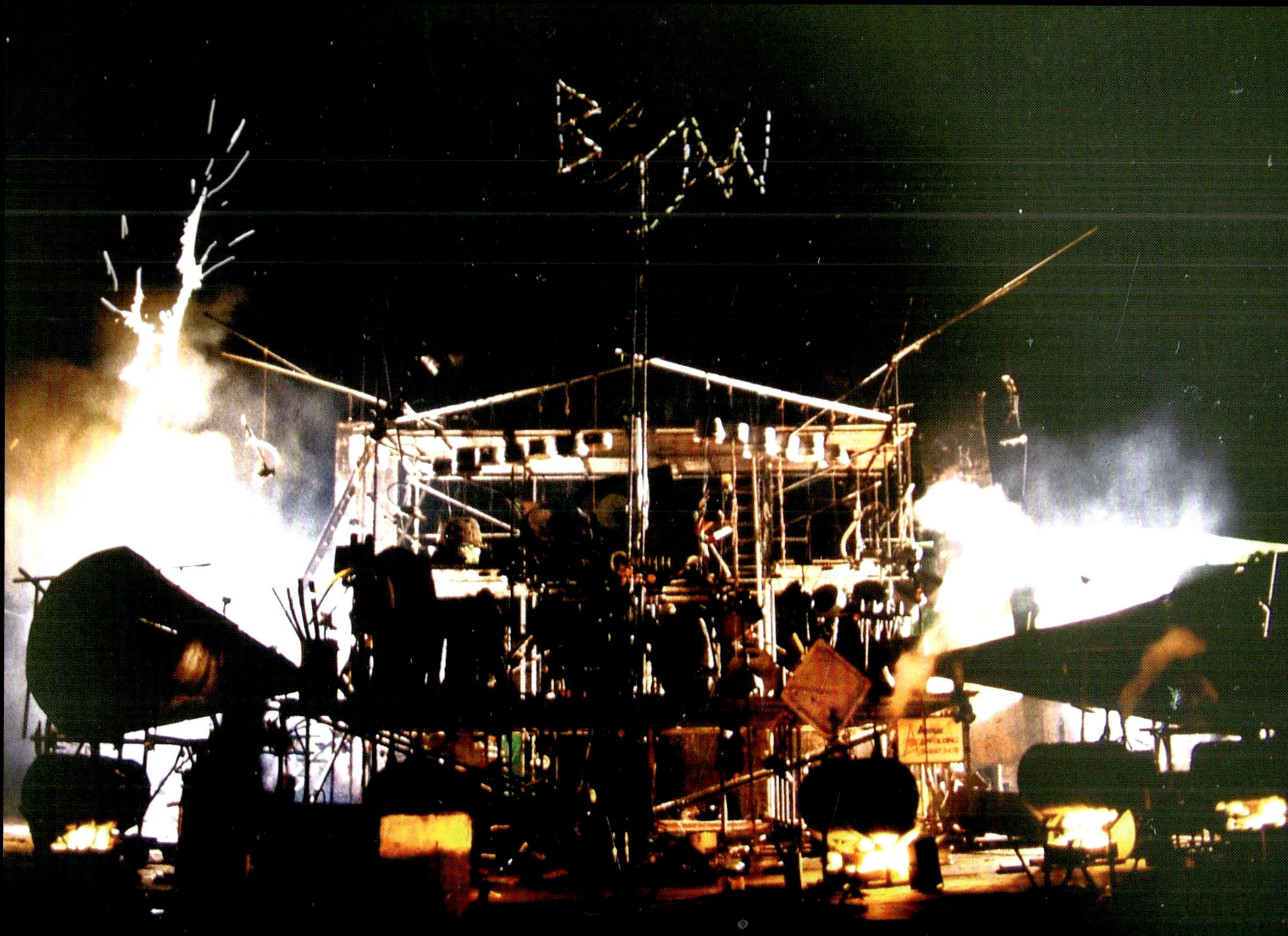

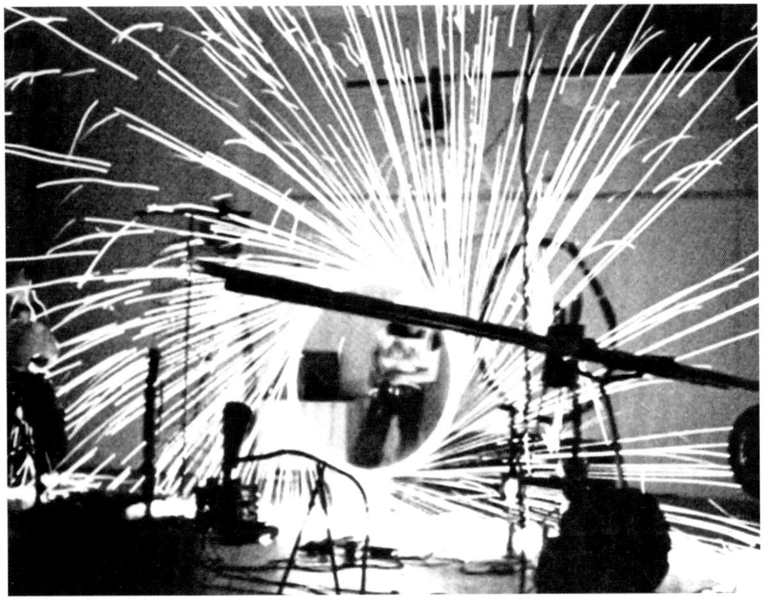

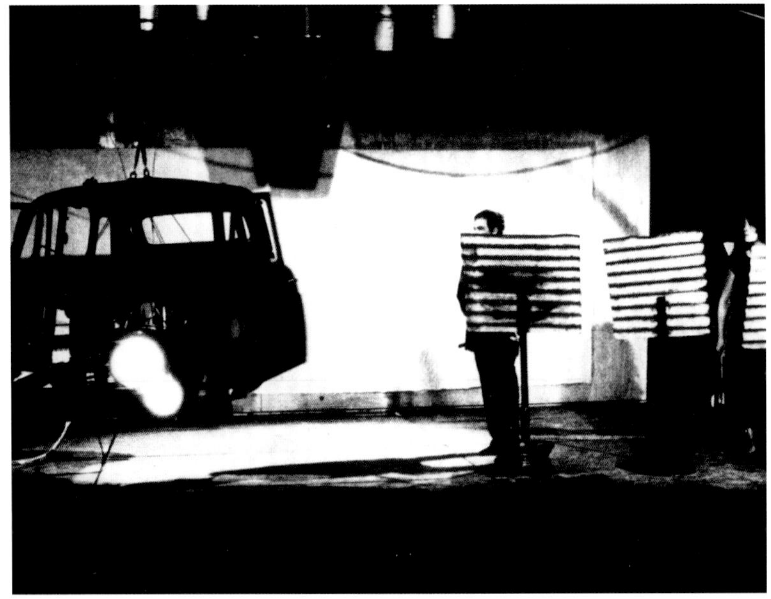

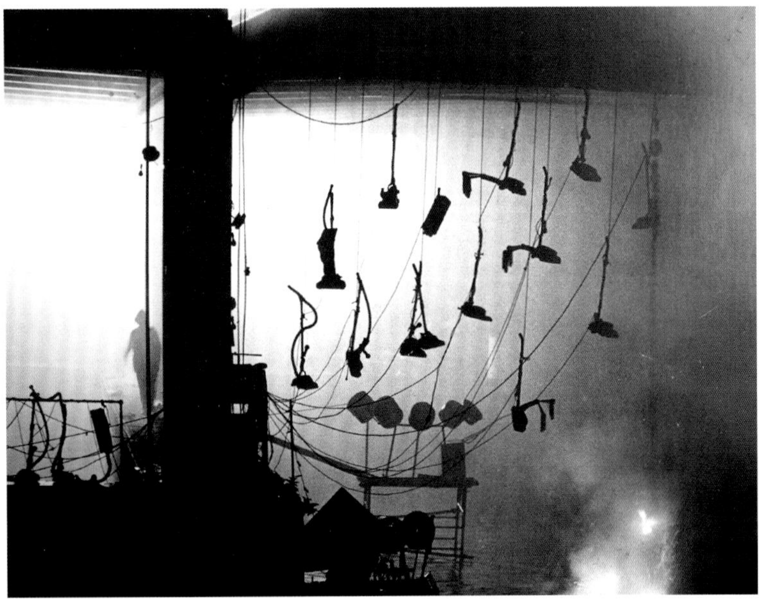

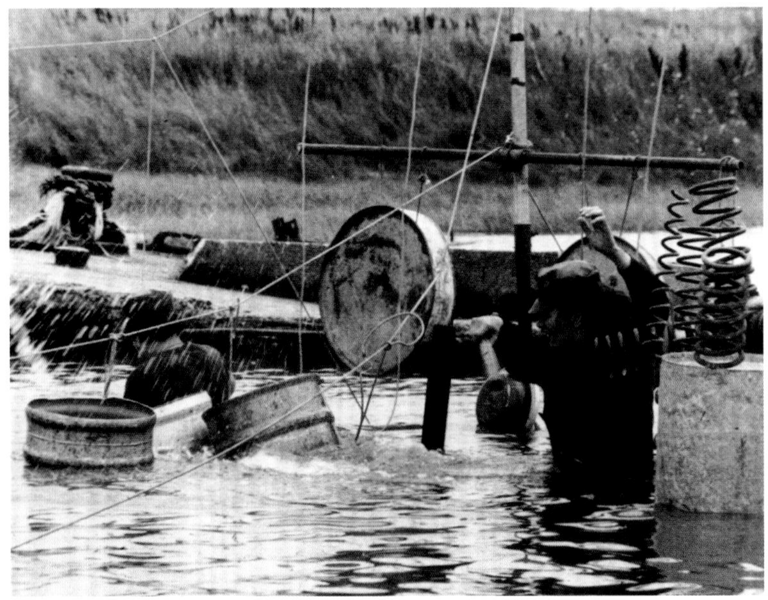

Top left: Bow Gamelan Ensemble, untitled performance, The Place Theatre, London 1985. Photo: Peter Kosminsky

Top right: Bow Gamelan Ensemble (with Bob Cobbing), *In C and Air*, Institute of Contemporary Arts, London, 1986. Photo: Jim Harold

Bottom left: Bow Gamelan Ensemble, *Offshore Rig*, Lot's Ait, 1987. Photo: Jim Harold

Bottom right: Bow Gamelan Ensemble, *51° 29'.9" North – 0°11' East*, Rainham Concrete Barges, Essex, 1987. Photo: courtesy After Image Productions

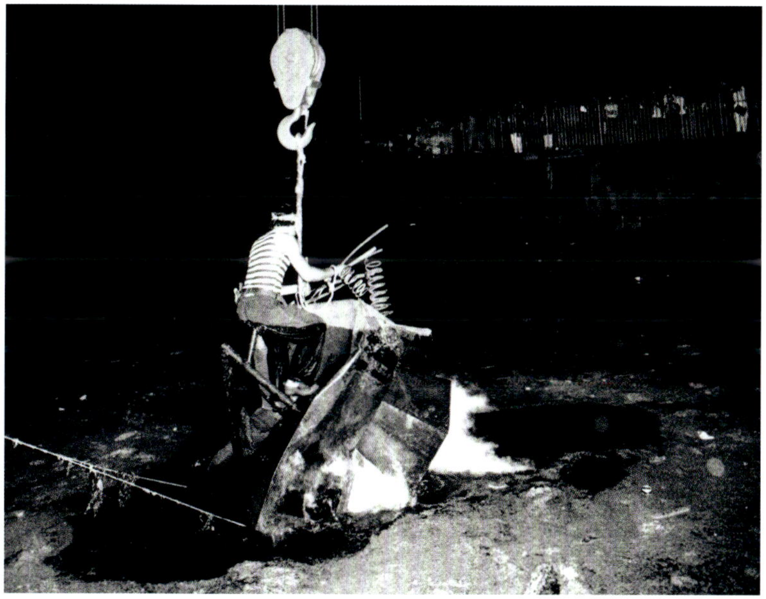

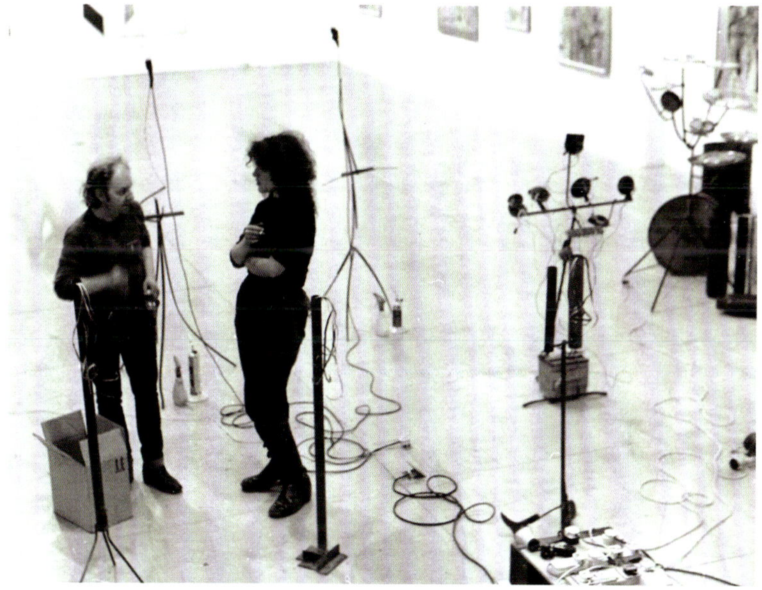

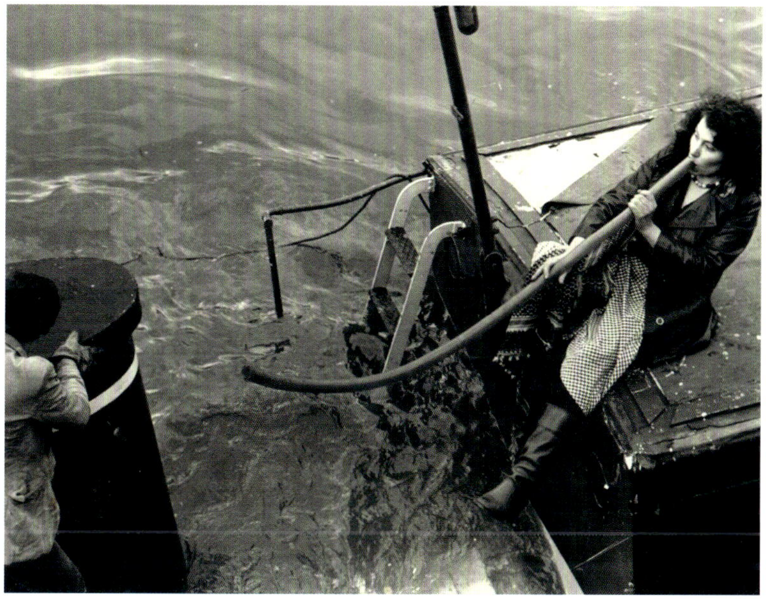

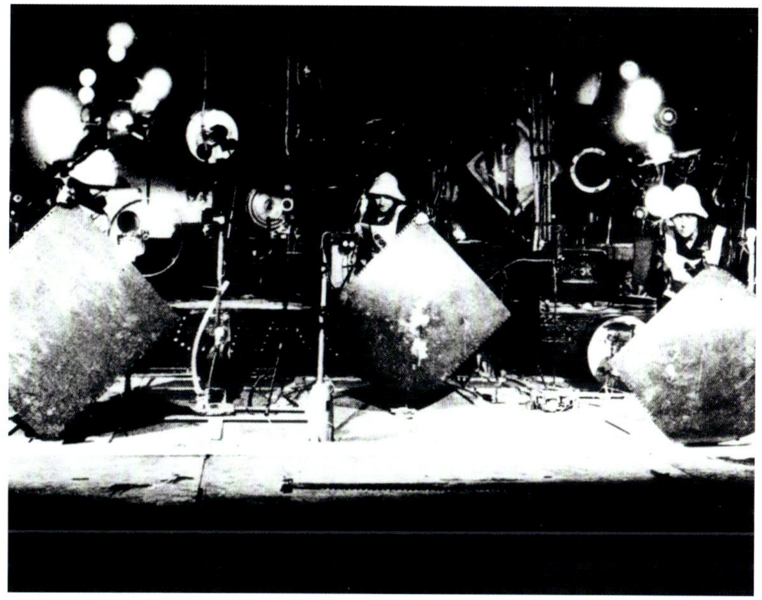

Top left: Bow Gamelan Ensemble, *The Navigators/Port of Calls*, a series of waterborne performances on the Thames, 1988. Photographer unknown

Top right: setting up for Bow Gamelan Ensemble, untitled performance, Museum of Modern Art, Oxford, 1984. Photo: Paul Burwell

Bottom left: Anne Bean and Paul Burwell, *Sunken Boat*, River Thames, 1978. Photo: Chris Bishop

Bottom right: Bow Gamelan Ensemble (with Bob Cobbing), *In C and Air*, Institute of Contemporary Arts, London, 1986. Photo: Jim Harold

"A DAMMED NEAR RUN THING".

Basic scaffolding structure is overlaid with our equipment. Overall effect is of a Tower of Babel/Building site/deck of Destroyer during Refit. The Rig is one big instrument and one big firework.

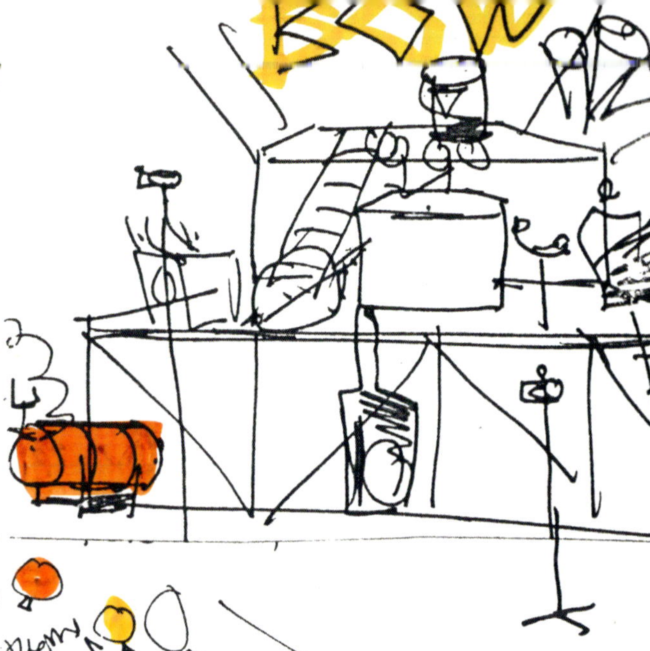

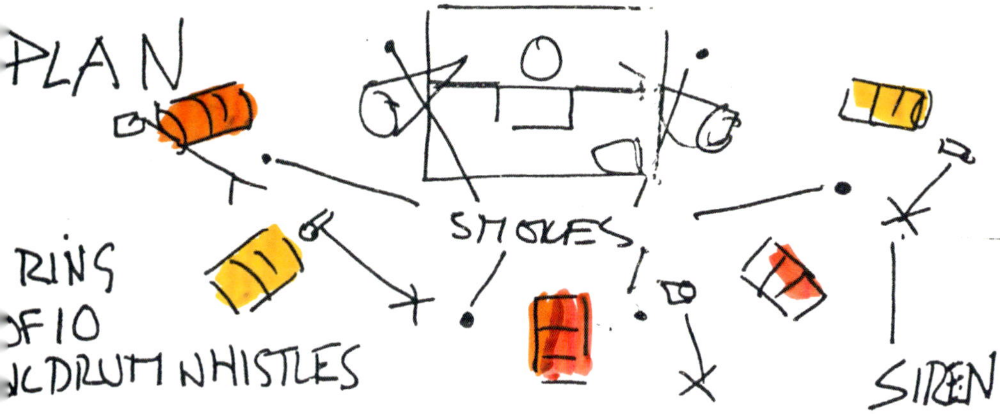

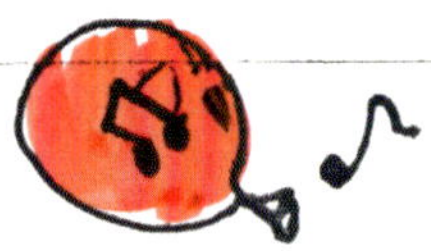

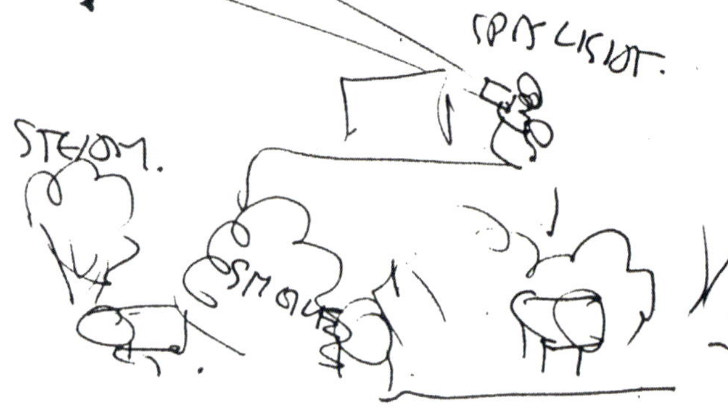

Steam whistle OVERTURE.
the ring of steam whistles plays prior to the performance, getting louder.
theactual start is signalled by a large steam whistle, and pyrotechnic bangs+large flame.

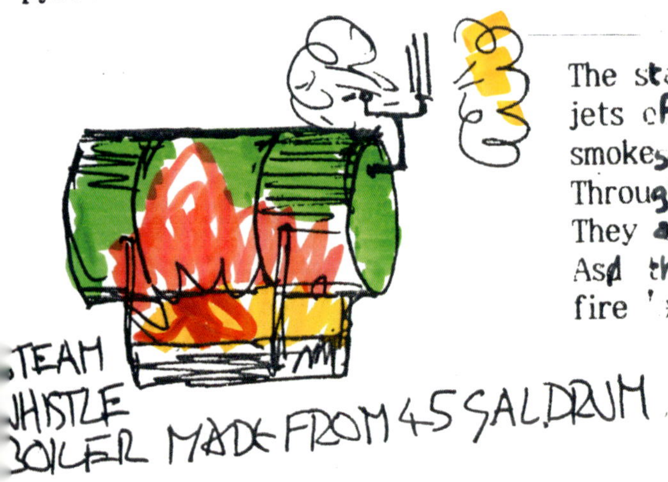

The steam whistles finish, and are switched to producing jets of steam, shot through with coloured lights, and 7 and 30 sec. colou smokes, fired sporadically.
Through this, helium filled balloons playing toy trumpets are launch
They are followed by follow spots.
As they dissapear/become inaudible, Coloured Balls (Roman Candles) co fire 'after' them.

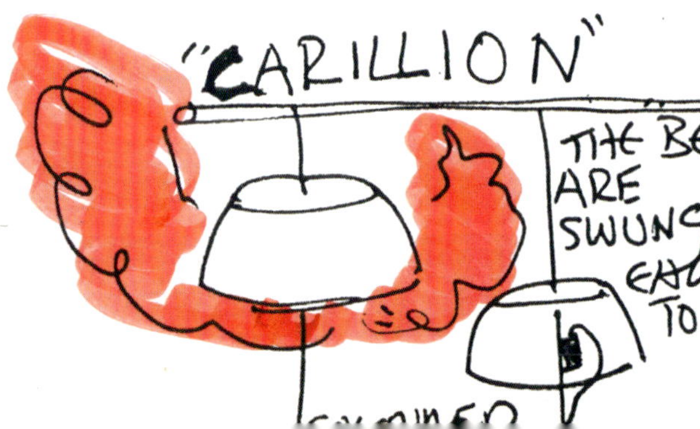

HAND CRANKED PERCUSSION SECTION.
there are various percussion instruments being made that rely on circular movement, and if possible, this could be echoed pyrotechnically by various small wheels/spinners.

objects, touching and banging and moving, doing things that create sounds that no one's really looked at. Just two barges, empty barges on the river going *boomp boomp, crump*! Big resonating chambers, they would have a sound unique to themselves. There's no way, other than if you did it digitally, that you could ever do that. Digital wasn't around then. Our way of thinking for Bow Gamelan was how could you get two barges into this space and get them colliding. It's a bit like Fitzcarraldo's answer in Werner Herzog's film when he's asked how he would get his ship from one river to another: 'Like the cow jumps over the moon'. We were in that territory.

RLF *What I wanted to finally ask you is, whether, during the Bow Gamelan performance,* Adventures In The House of Memory *(2009) in Liverpool, when you brought in a spirit medium, Phil the Messenger to somehow invoke Paul, what were you trying to do, what happened that night and whether it worked? I was there, I have my own memories of it, but can I have your memory of this?*

AB Well I don't really see that as a Bow Gamelan performance, I see it as an aftermath of trying to reach Paul in a charged set-up ... We'd gone through a long and very complex process of his burial, trying to fulfil his last wishes about how his body was to be disposed of. We organised a massive wake where we'd had about 30 people doing short works together or solo, including a pibroch player playing Paul's favourite piece, *The Old Men of the Shells*. In Liverpool, we were trying to get in touch with Paul as a being, not just necessarily as the Gamelan. Because of *TAPS*, which was a commission about how you look at 'legacy' in various different ways, I had wanted to involve many different people in a collaboration with Paul, because I realised so many people had a different vision of how they perceived him. One of the pieces I wanted to do was to go to a spirit medium – whether you see it as an imaginative exercise or whatever – and see if he contacted Paul. So, this guy, Phil the Messenger, seemed perfect. He was very keen on doing this and he happened to be in Liverpool. So, I went along and Brian [Routh aka Harry Kipper] and Patricia [Routh] filmed him. There was one moment that was incredibly beautiful – where we heard *Greensleeves* from an ice cream van outside. He said, just at that moment, 'Paul is the wings of an eagle flapping'. It was so beautiful, for me, this image. I said to Phil the Messenger that we're meant to be doing something in Liverpool and would he be prepared to be there as the third person, as the evocation of Paul, whether it was from his imagination or his 'channelling'. He said he would, so Richard and I saw this piece as an invocation – an evocation. We used lots of different moments – like a video of Paul drumming in the disused swimming pool at Dilston Grove for Richard's installation. It felt very real. We'd prepared by drinking Four Roses bourbon – which was one of his favourite tipples – and we washed down his ashes with it.

RLF *You consumed Paul's ashes?*

AB We consumed Paul's ashes. We embodied him literally. And kicked of the performance with that moment.

RLF *So you're cannibals as well?*

AB We're cannibals! [*Laughter*]

RW It wasn't the first time! I think we've eaten the lot now.

Opposite: Part of a score for Bow Gamelan Ensemble, *A Damned Near Run Thing*, South Bank, London, 1988. Peter Hewison's *Future Tense: A New Art for the Nineties* quotes Bow Gamelan: 'They contrast the work of the "junk sculptors", where the emphasis is on transformation, with their own aim, "to release the hidden potential of things"'

pp. 274: Bow Gamelan Ensemble, *Offshore Rig*, Lot's Ait, 1987. Photo: Jim Harold

pp. 275: Bow Gamelan Ensemble, *Damned Near Run Thing*, Southbank, London, 1988. Photo: Ed Sirrs

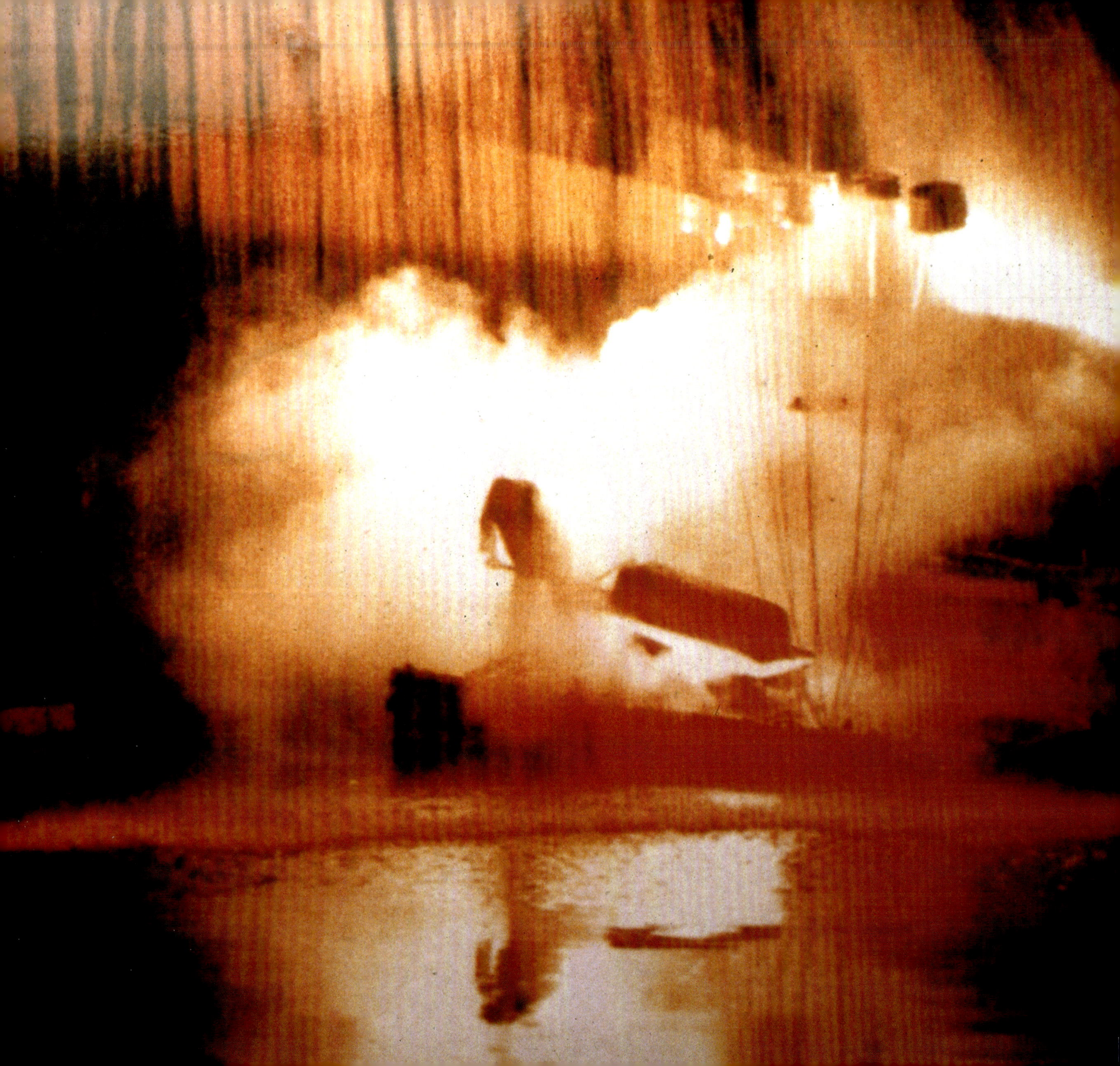

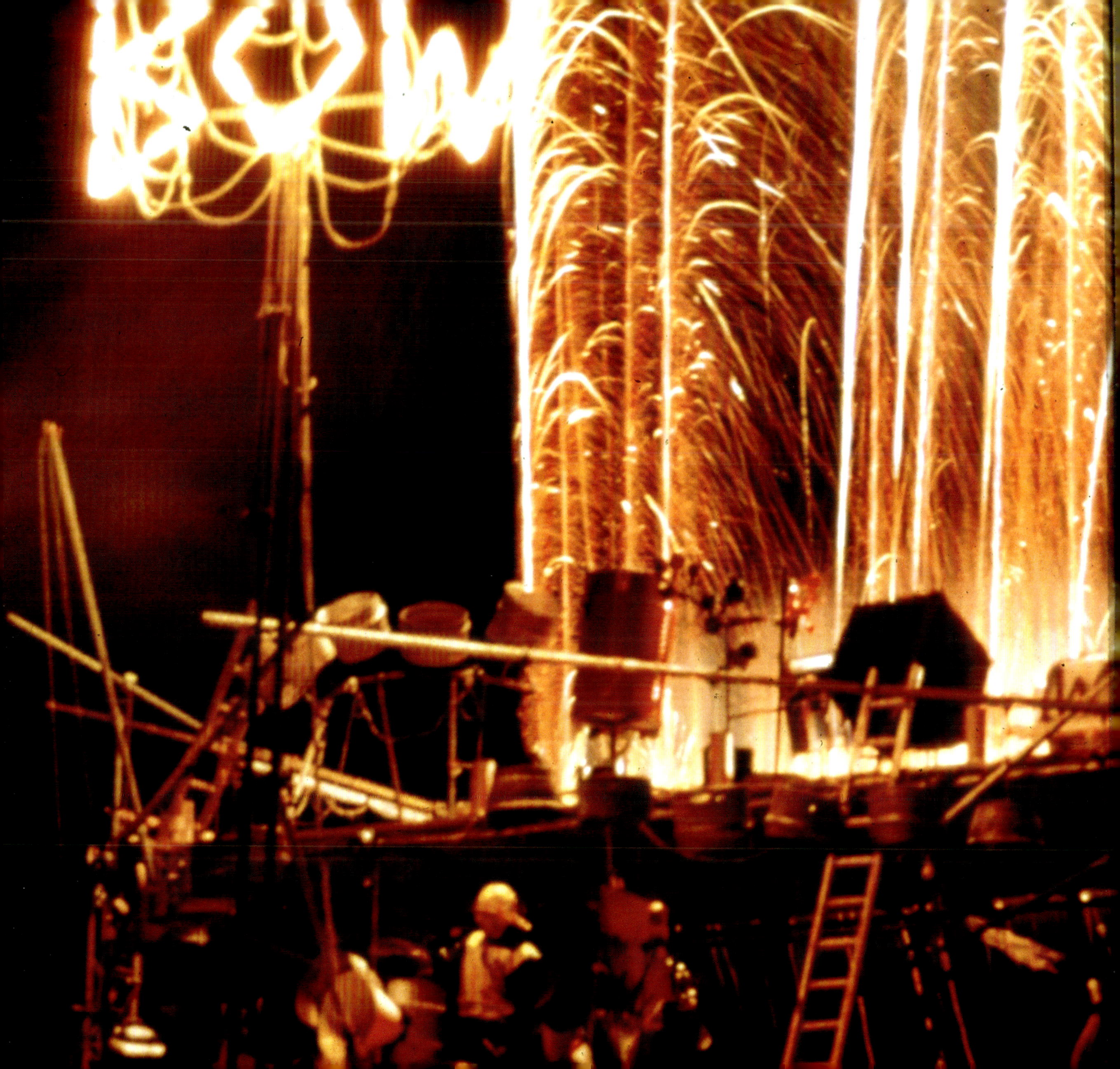

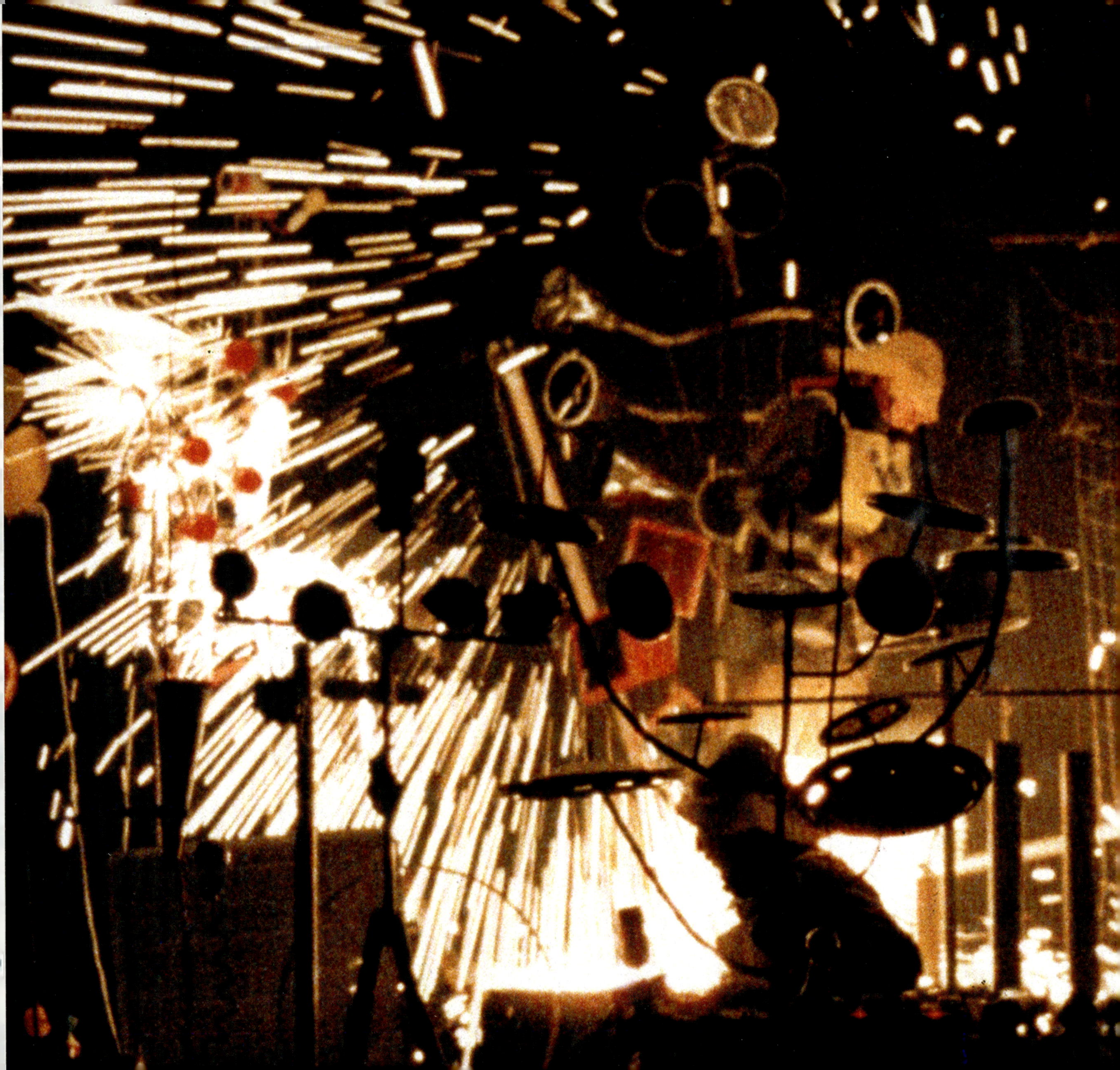

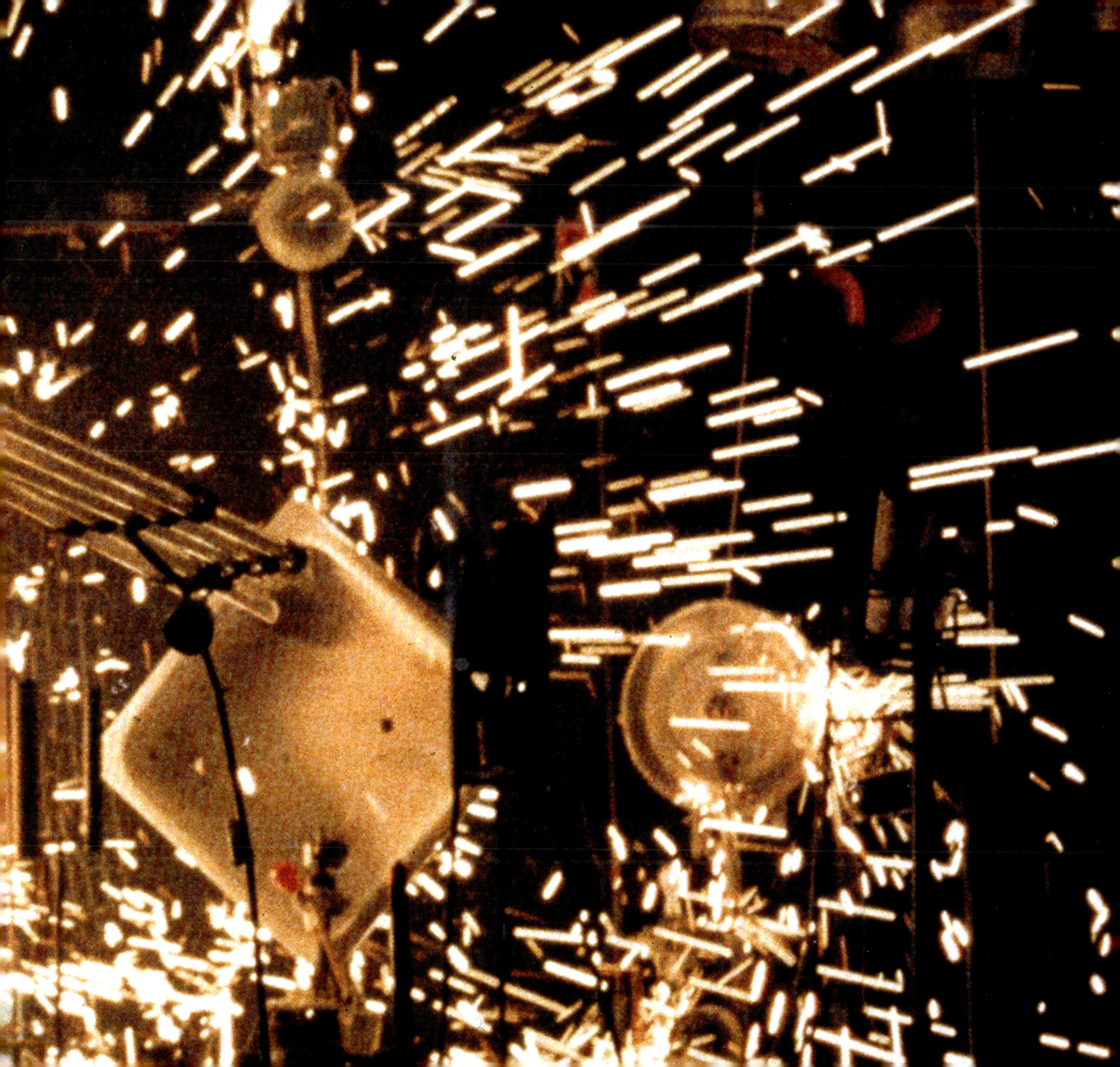

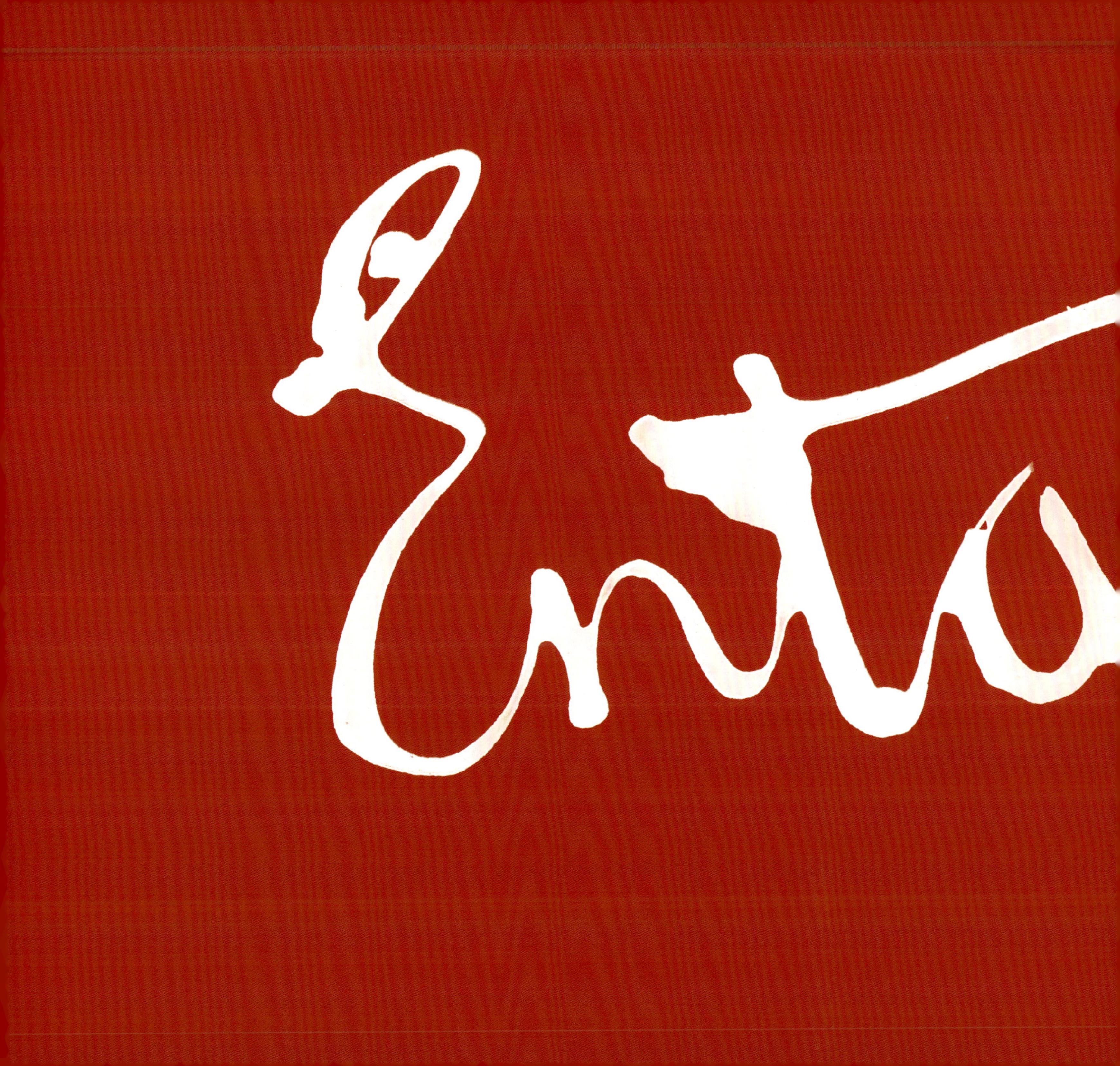

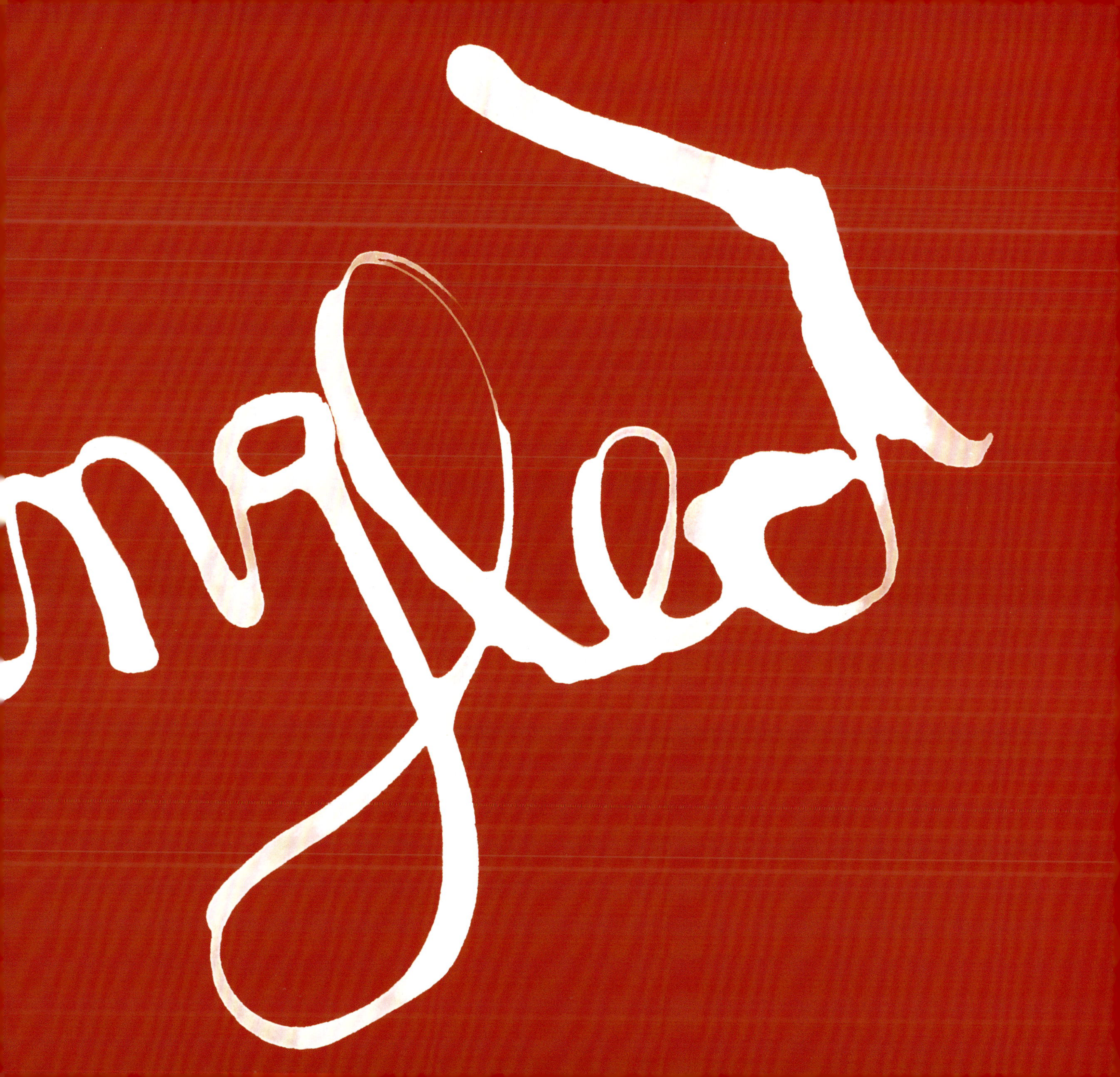

THE ENTANGLED SELF: THE ART OF LIFE IN THE OPEN AIR

EZRA RUBENSTEIN

One of the most surprising phenomena to be discovered by modern physics is entanglement. When it was first predicted by quantum mechanics, many physicists thought that the new theory must be missing something. Even Einstein – who had already profoundly reimagined space and time – found its consequences too counterintuitive to accept. Yet experiments later verified the prediction, and entanglement is now widely embraced as a ubiquitous and foundational phenomenon.

The situation is something like this. Imagine that you and a friend of yours on the other side of the world are simultaneously tossing ordinary coins, and suppose that whichever way your coin comes up, so does your friend's. Such a perfectly reliable correlation would be very curious indeed: it would be as if the coins were communicating instantaneously, or had agreed in advance exactly how they would come up.

Quantum physics has revealed analogous behaviour in 'entangled' particles. Measuring particles interferes with them, and there is no way for them to 'know' in advance how they will be measured, just as the coins cannot 'know' in advance how they will be tossed. Yet whenever we measure two entangled particles simultaneously, we get correlated results, and this correlation remains intact even when the particles are separated by implausibly large distances. It is this violation of locality – the principle that all causal connections stretch continuously and unbroken through space and time – which famously spooked Einstein.

Just in the last few months, a Chinese research team has verified entanglement effects between a photon on Earth and a photon on an orbiting satellite. These effects apply not only across space but also across time. It is thought, for example, that a pair of photons can be entangled despite never having coexisted.

This non-locality is not the only strange consequence of entanglement. Perhaps even more intriguing is non-separability. It has been a common and apparently innocent assumption in the history of physics that a system's state can be separated out into the states of its subsystems. For example, to fully characterize the instantaneous state of a cat, it is enough to fully characterize the positions and properties of all the particles which jointly constitute it.

This eminently reasonable assumption is threatened by quantum physics. When two particles are entangled, the two-particle system is in an overall quantum state which does not consist in a combination of two single-particle quantum states. Consider the coin analogy again: their joint propensity to be perfectly correlated transcends their individual propensities to come up Heads half the time. The probability distributions for the individual coins do not capture the probabilities governing the behaviour of the two-coin system. As it turns out, almost every physical system is like the pair of coins: its quantum state cannot be described fully by describing the states of its individual components. Almost everything is entangled with almost everything else.

As I hope to articulate, the abstract concept of entanglement – and in particular, this strange consequence of non-separability – provides an oddly apt lens through which to view two central and interconnected themes of Anne Bean's incredibly rich and varied life-work: selfhood and collaboration.

Opposite: Anne Bean, *Water Drop and Flame*, 1990. I worked with Oxford Scientific Films to create a series of images of a drop of water falling into a flame and extinguishing it, towards slide and photographic works

pp. 286-7: Anne Bean, *Chances Are*, a DIY workshop project supported by the Live Art Development Agency, 2014. Sleeping out with participants on Holkham Beach, Norfolk, on the evening of the Perseid meteor showers and the perigee moon. Photo: Ezra Rubenstein

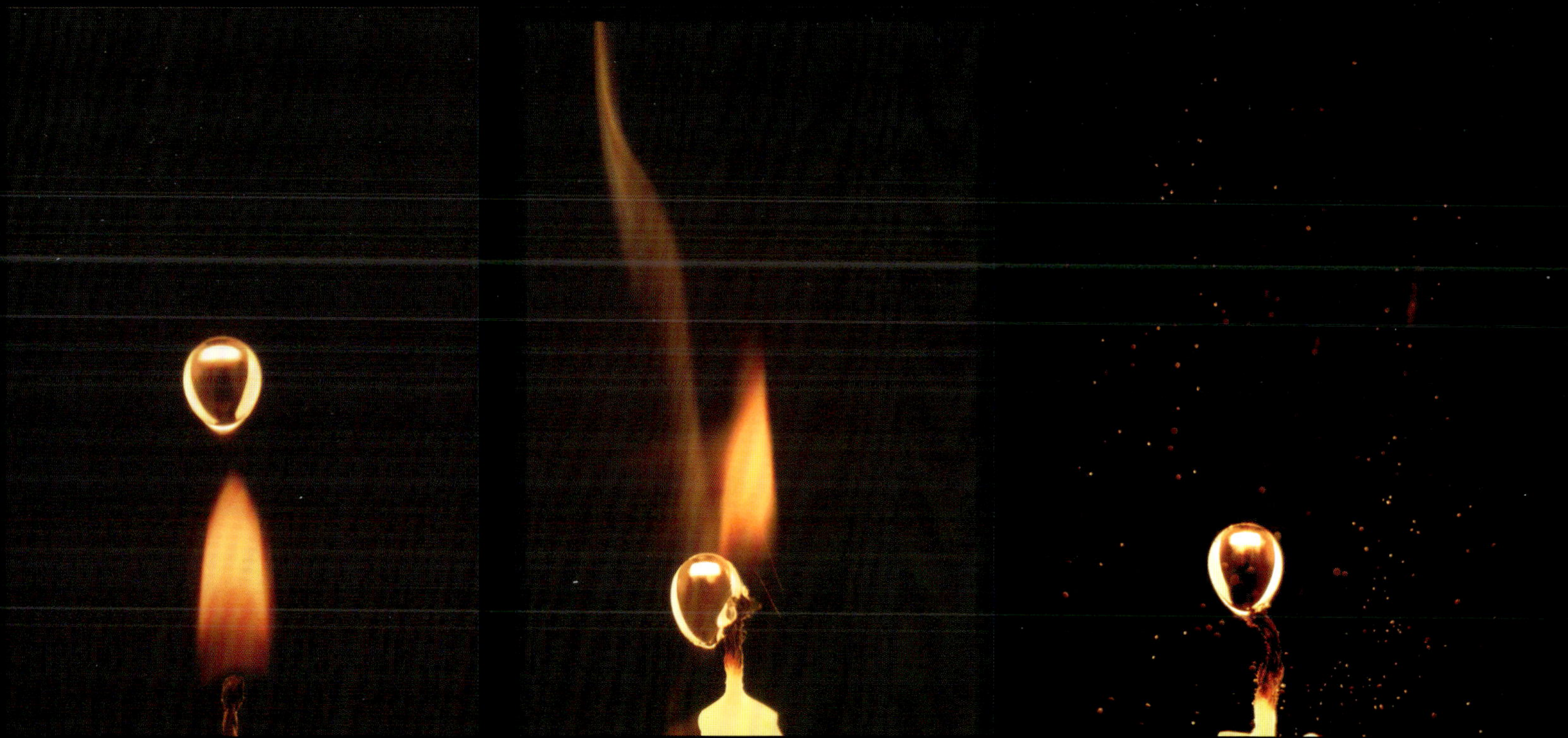

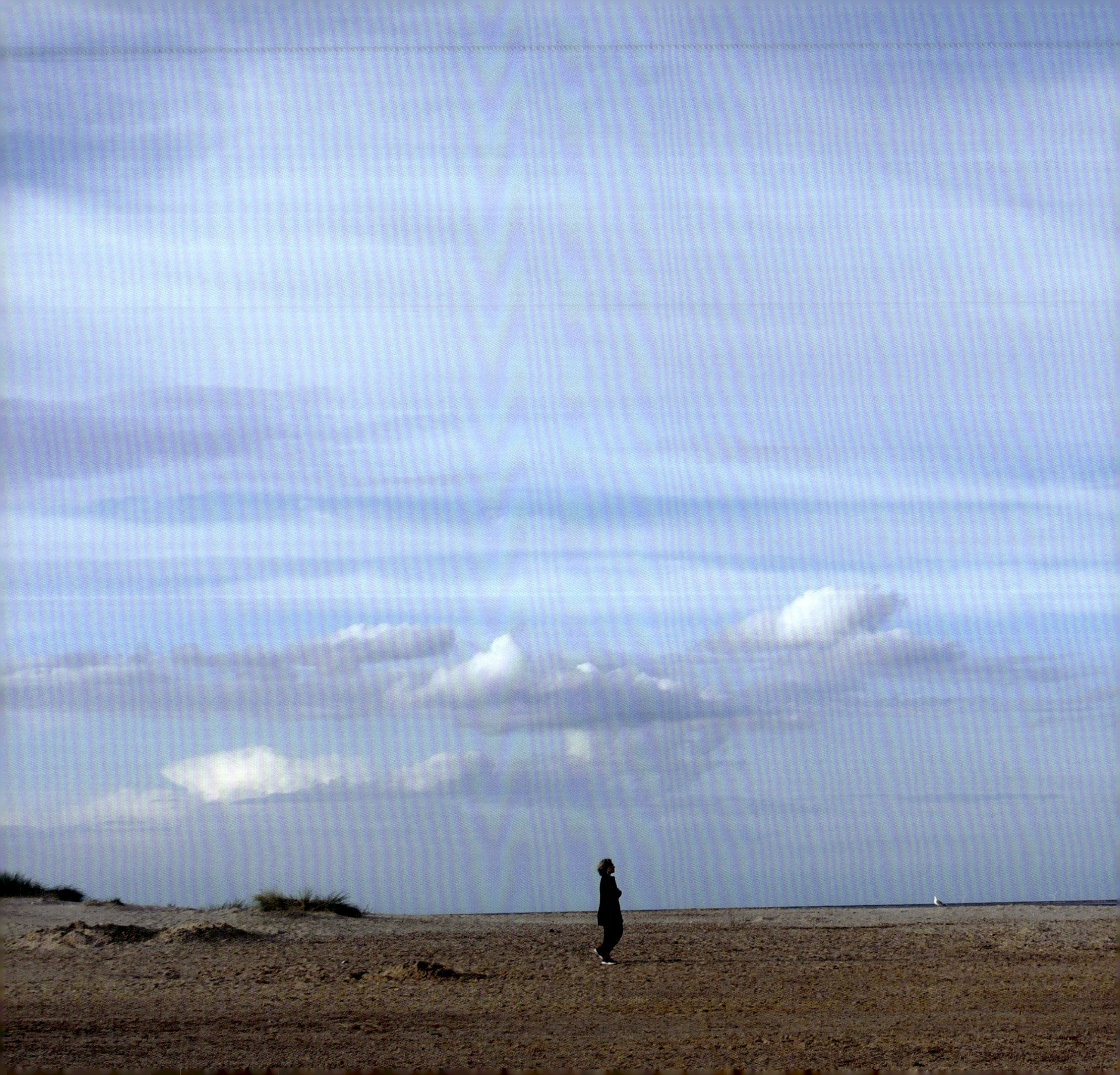

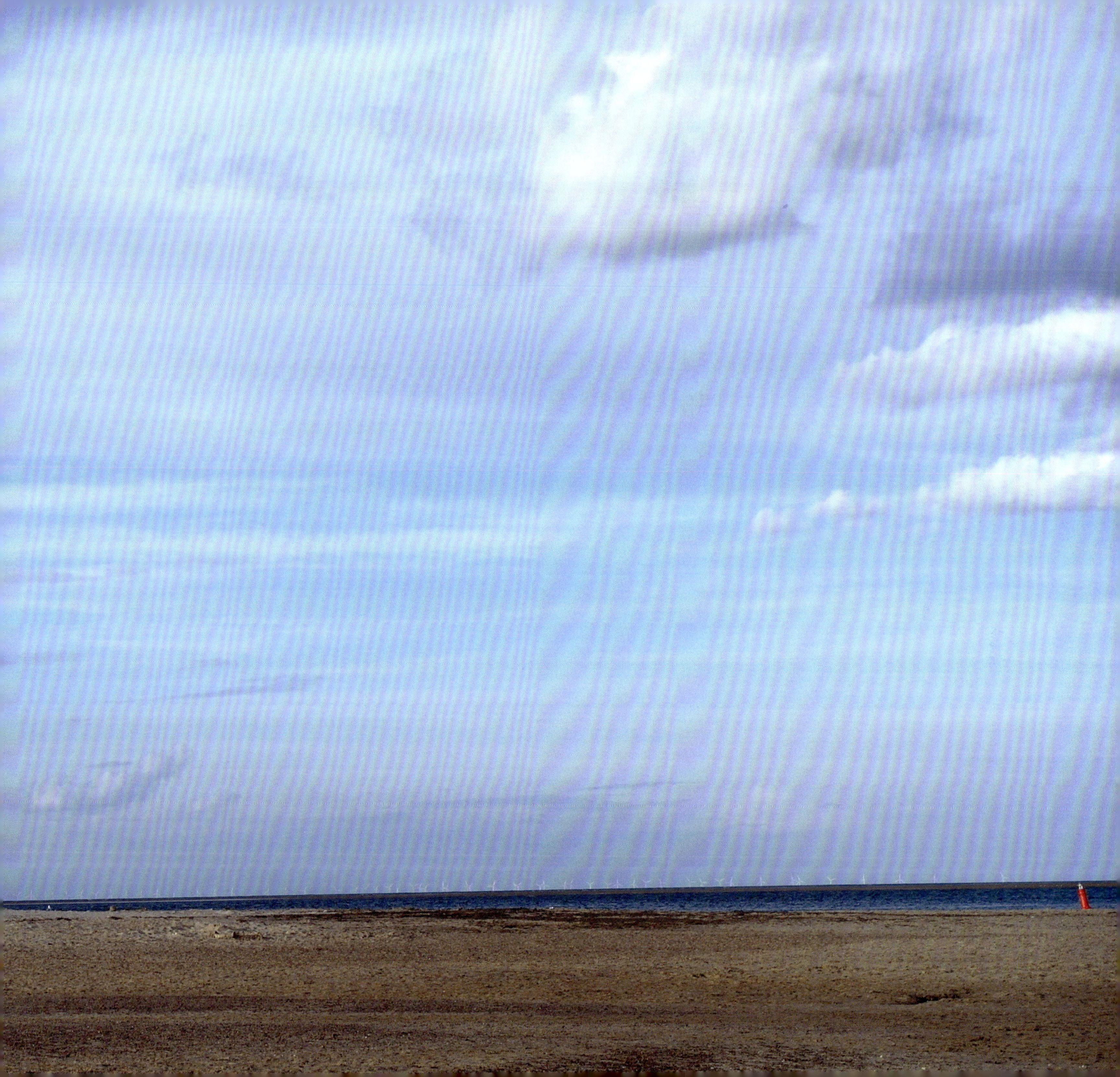

The history we absorb often comes dominated by The Great Man: a lone figure of maverick and brilliant genius who single-handedly shapes events, acting with a decisively masculine agency. It is a tempting vision; and nowhere more so, perhaps, than in the history of art. One thinks of Michelangelo and da Vinci, Rembrandt and Caravaggio, Picasso and van Gogh, Warhol and Duchamp ... Each are of course situated alongside their contemporaries, the lineage of their influences meticulously drawn, but each remains unabashedly individual: their contributions emerging as transcendently unique. Their work is undeniably their own, bearing iconic signatures and handed down to posterity as shining proof of their value. Duchamp's most famous work, *Fountain* (1917), is variously hailed and derided as the end of this line. It bears witness, finally, to the great irony of the signature as a mark of Authenticity. I treasure these men and their work; but it is right, I think, to challenge the warped view of art that this 'history' engenders.

If the category of art succumbs to any crude and general truth, it is surely that it is at bottom a relational activity. An artwork is always about and for and exists between us: those that inspire and conspire, those that witness and (re-)create. If art is to exist then it must carry meaning, and to carry meaning it must always be a matter of dialogue, of openness, of gifting and exchange.

At the core of Bean's practice seems to lie a vigorous and authentic awareness of this truth, and with it a rejection of the commonplace assumption that the artist exists as an individual – indeed, that the artist should even be capable of working alone. In a recent interview, she remarks:

I am more and more aware of the subtleties involved in determining what collaboration actually means, to the extent that I am no longer clear about what working alone constitutes. We are 'inhabited' by so many consciousnesses, that the idea of work done alone seems to have an almost paradoxical quality.[1]

1. Anne Bean, transcript of unpublished interview for CAMP residency programme, Pyrenees, France, 2018.

There is an illuminating parallel between the principle she observes and the similarly paradoxical 'non-separability' of contemporary physics. Like quantum systems, art is not constituted by a vast network of contributions interacting and connecting with each other but belonging nonetheless to certain notable individuals. Art does not so belong. It cannot cleanly be divided between the artist that creates it, the world that inspires it and the audience that absorbs it. Art is much more entangled and mysterious than that. It is always and necessarily a collaboration: a matter of open-ended consciousness whose content cannot be described in isolation but only as it relates to the consciousness of others; of mediating voyages between minds; of co-incidence.

This yields an anonymity which does not serve to downplay the creative role of the artist, but rather to imbue it with a fitting magic and mystery. In the same interview, Bean likens one of the artist's central roles to that of the dream-agent in Richter's film *Dreams That Money Can* Buy (1947), collaborating with all comers on the creation of new possibilities for the world they inhabit. She takes up this role with a contagious zest. Her art-life is characterized above all by a generous, courageous and uncompromising openness to co-creation. 'Her work' is constituted by a dizzying array of collaborations – with very close friends and complete strangers, young and old, alive and dead, blind and sighted, well-established and unknown, invited guests and passers-by, witnesses and participants – frequently blurring and transcending these distinctions in the process.

In a recent lecture at the ICA, Bean asked her audience to spend some time mentally recreating, from just a couple of visual clues, a piece of hers entitled *An Angel Called Gravity*, performed in the same building over 20 years earlier, and purposefully undocumented. Few of them had witnessed the original performance, but each became a co-conspirator, some influenced more directly than others by the event itself, all breathing a life into it, and providing a home for it to inhabit.

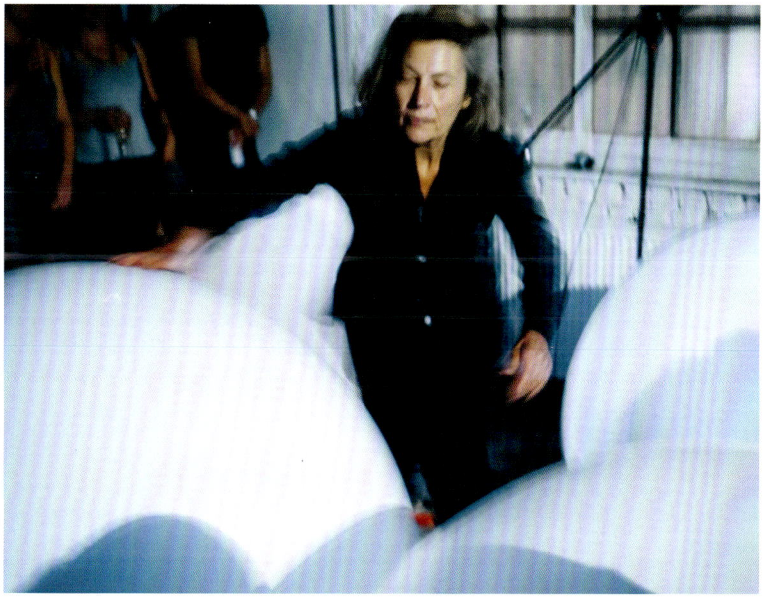

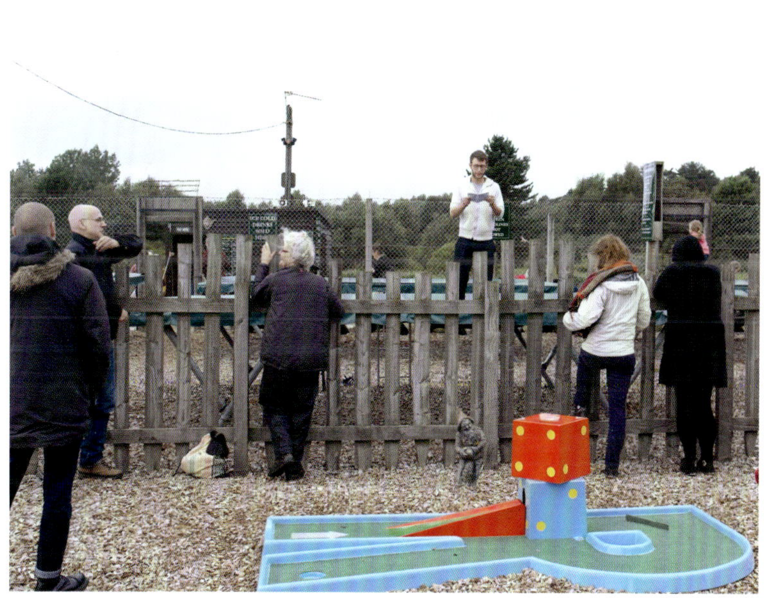

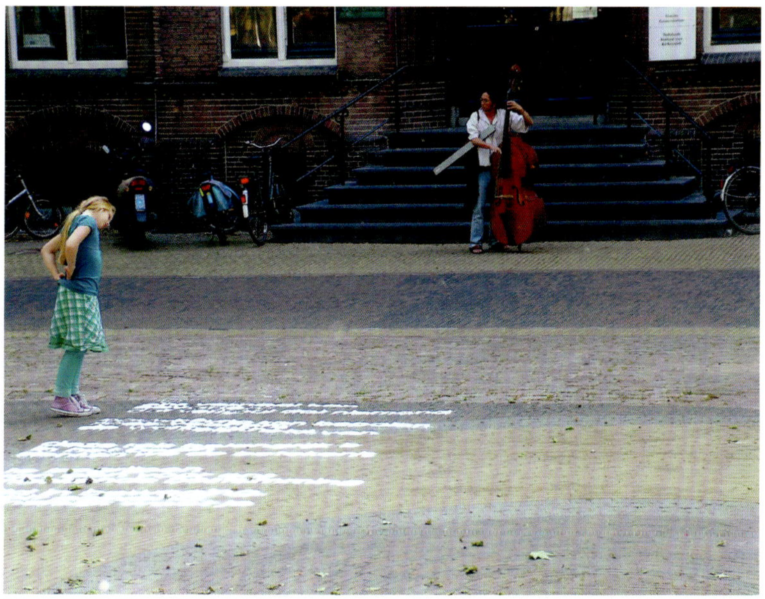

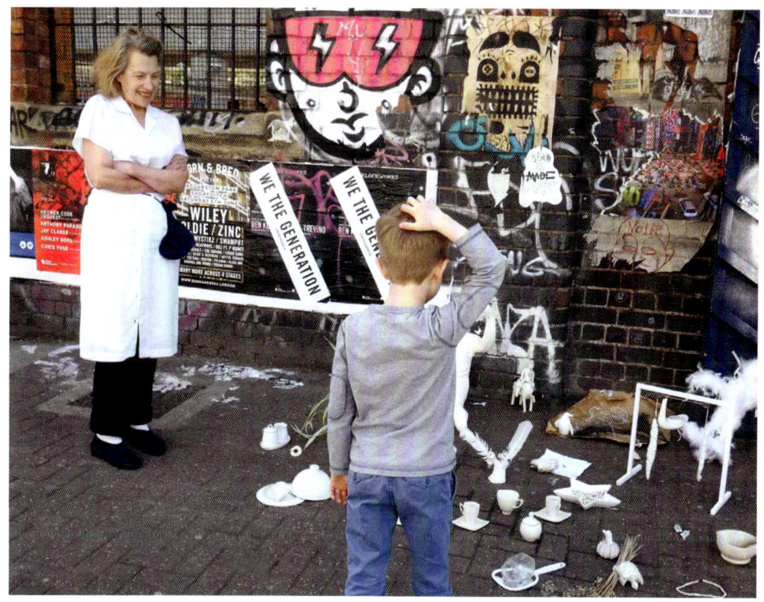

Top left: Anne Bean, collaborating with the as-yet-unborn baby of Manuel Vason and Rubiane Maia, London, 2017. Photo: Manuel Vason

Top right: Anne Bean, *Chances Are*, a DIY workshop project supported by the Live Art Development Agency, 2014. A trampolining lecture with Thomas John Bacon, Katy Baird, Daniel Gosling, Siriol Joyner, Elspeth Owen, Ezra Rubenstein and Yol, Wells-next-the-Sea, Norfolk

Bottom left: Anne Bean, *Whoseywhats* Festival a/d Werf, Utrecht, 2010. A travelling poem from Utrecht's immigrant population, written in salt, with a specially commissioned machine by local artist Gijs van Bon

Bottom right: Anne Bean, *Is it a Stall?* Brick Lane, 2015. A market stall of white objects that were not for sale. Photo: Markéta Luskačová

pp. 290-1: Anne Bean, *Eclipse*, 2004-5. A 12-months-long drawing capturing the shadow of a globe of the earth

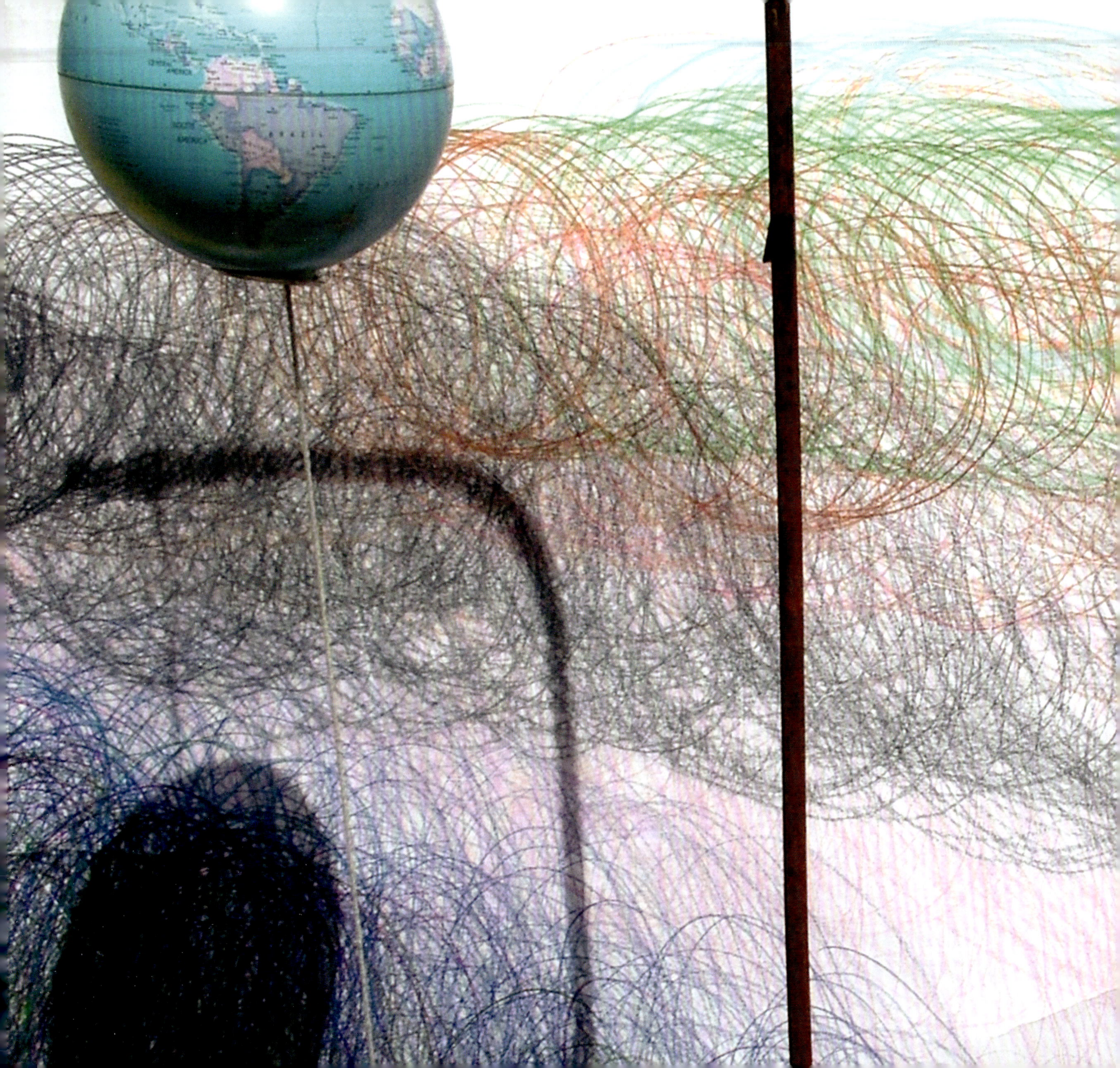

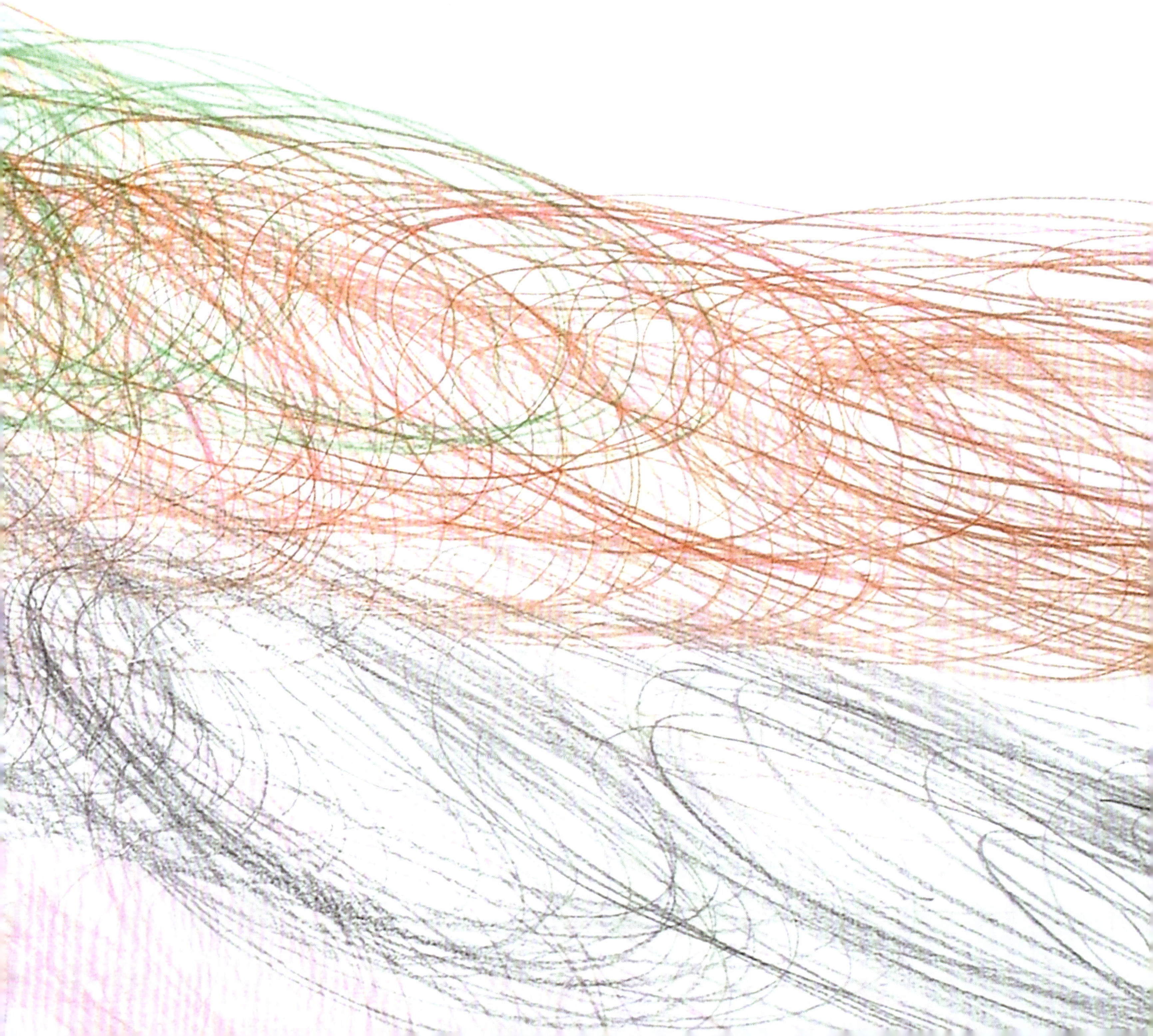

Art's relational character is especially vivid in the particular case of performance. Of course, a performance is ostensibly an event, just as a painting or sculpture is ostensibly an object; but if they consist in anything at all as authentic artworks, it is in the mediated connectivity between the thoughts they produce and the thoughts that produced them, in the moments of recognition that both artist and witness are bouncing off the same thing. Performances cannot be reduced to any preserved archive of footage, photographs or texts, nor even to an accumulation of conscious experiences, since these things, being inherently perspectival and one-sided, lack the right form. The situation does not allow for any full description in terms of separable components; it might therefore aptly be called an 'entanglement' of consciousnesses.

This dissipation of the individual into connections subsumes not only the artwork but the artist too. Selfhood consists also in the connections between experiences, rather than in some archive of experiences belonging separately to it. And with openness, this self becomes fluid and expansive, inhabiting many other consciousnesses, as it too is inhabited. As Bean puts it, 'if one is open, one can freefall into the territories existing "between" us', thereby exploring what she calls 'an ecstatic reality'.

In the midst of a recent year-long project in which Bean explored the possibilities of a new identity, leaving home, name, history and reputation behind her, she wrote:

> The more provocative and stimulating position is not that 'everyone is an artist' but 'no-one is an artist' and that the 'art' space is implicitly part of living. This undefined, open, permissive exploration that art claims then becomes part of the everyday.

I take this position to be that the notion of a coherent self to which a distinctively artistic activity belongs is a myth. Underlying the necessity of useful conventions, there may be no such artist to be individuated or distilled; just the 'great blooming, buzzing confusion' of life, and all of us living it, entangled and inseparable.[2]

In a passage entitled 'Liberation from the Self', the brilliant philosopher Derek Parfit describes his own experience of coming to the view that selfhood is no further fact beyond certain relations of physical and psychological continuity holding between all of our experiences. He finds this view 'liberating, and consoling':

> When I believed that my existence was such a further fact, I seemed imprisoned in myself. My life seemed like a glass tunnel, through which I was moving faster every year, and at the end of which there was darkness. When I changed my view, the walls of my glass tunnel disappeared. I now live in the open air. There is still a difference between my life and the lives of other people. But the difference is less...
>
> After my death, there will [be] no one living who will be me. I can now redescribe this fact. Though there will later be many experiences, none of these experiences will be connected to my present experiences by chains of such direct connections as those involved in experience-memory, or in the carrying out of an earlier intention. Some of these future experiences may be related to my present experiences in less direct ways. There will later be some memories about my life. And there may later be thoughts that are influenced by mine, or things done as the result of my advice. My death will break the more direct relations between my present experiences and future experiences, but it will not break various other relations. This is all there is to the fact that there will be no one living who will be me.[3]

I find that this 'open air' captures, in a moving and precise way, Bean's own ecstatic vision of the entangled self.

2. As William James famously described the world as viewed by an infant, in *Principles of Psychology* (1890, Cambridge, MA: Harvard University Press, 1981), p. 462.

3. Derek Parfit, *Reasons and Persons* (Oxford and New York: Oxford University Press, 1987), p. 281.

PULp MUSIC (Anne Bean and Paul Burwell), *Her voice is pollen as she was placed*, South Hill Park, Bracknell, 1983. Photo: Guy Brett

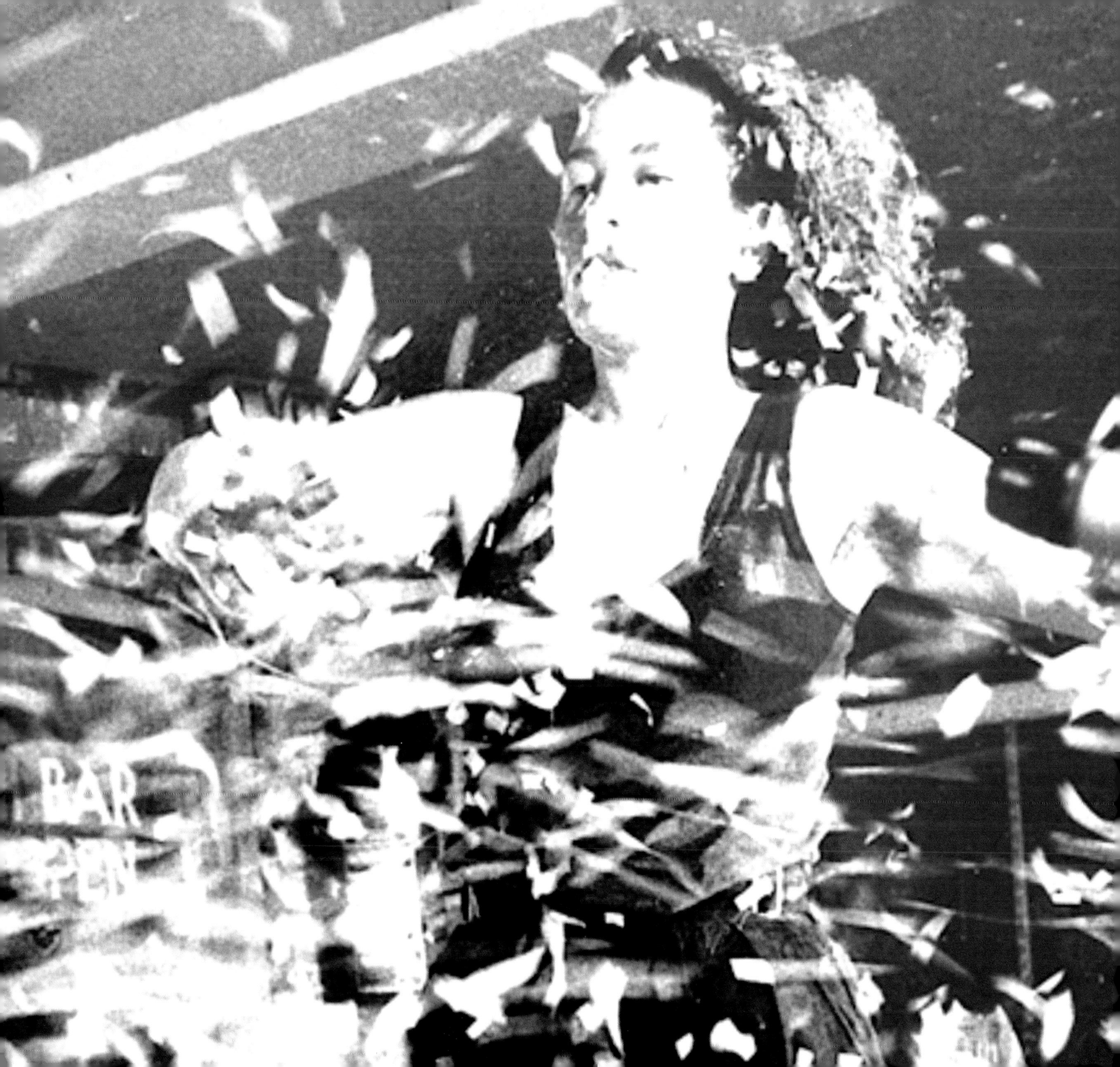
BAR

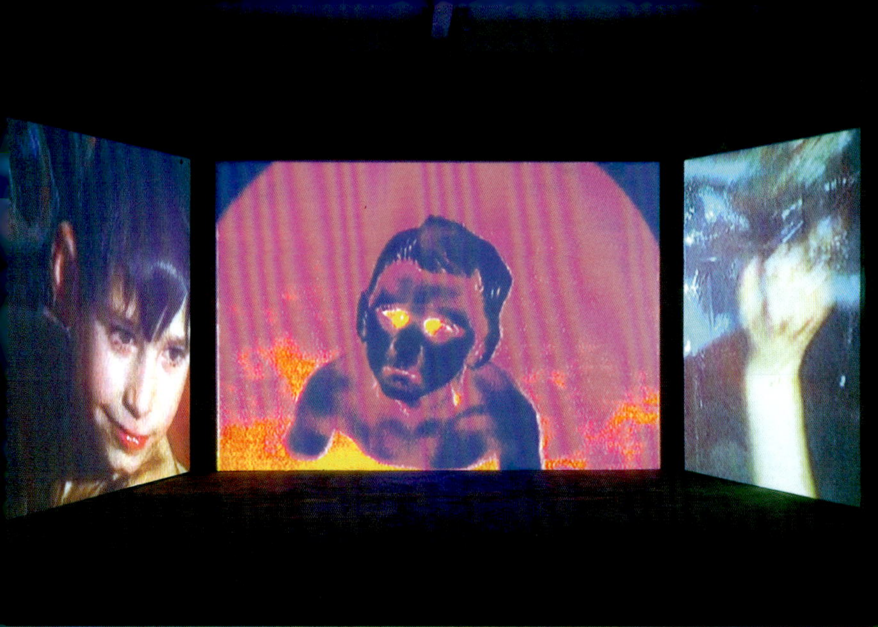

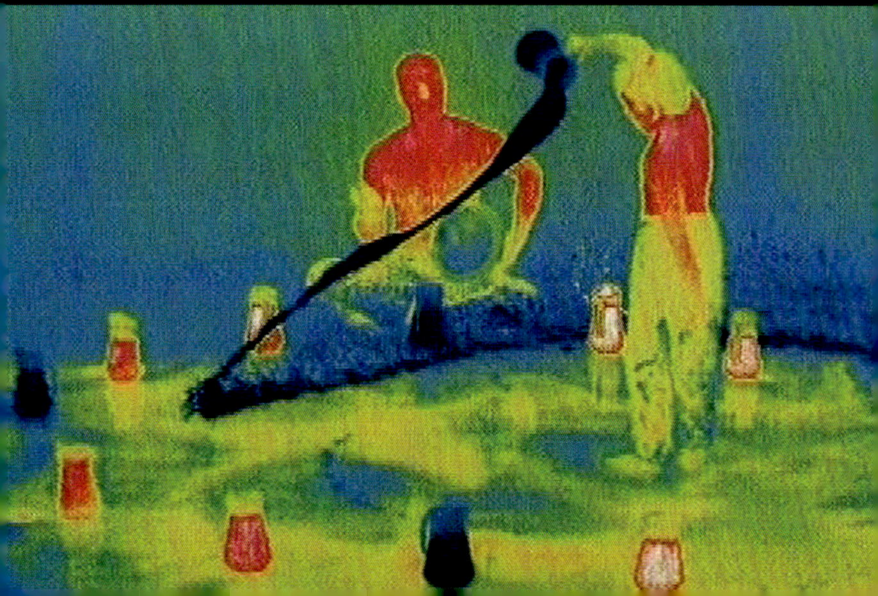

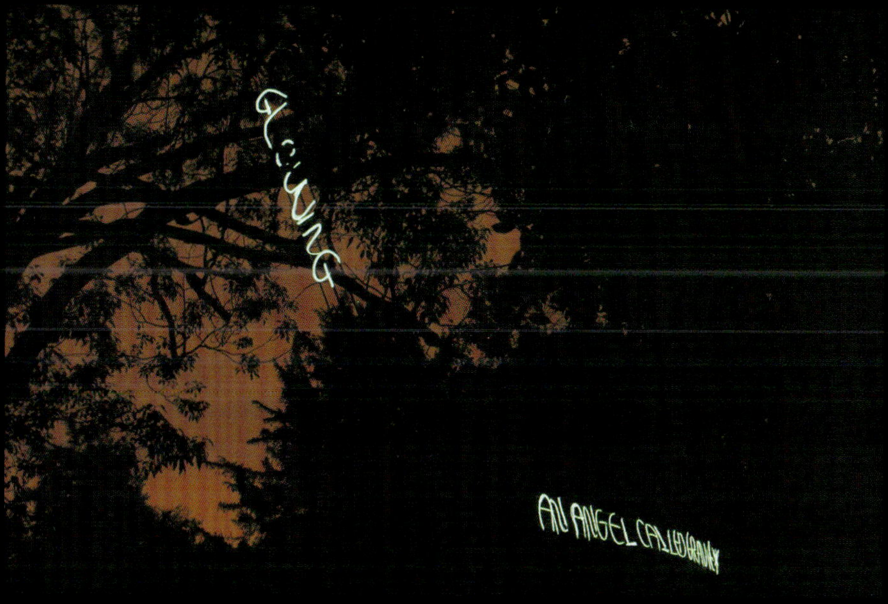

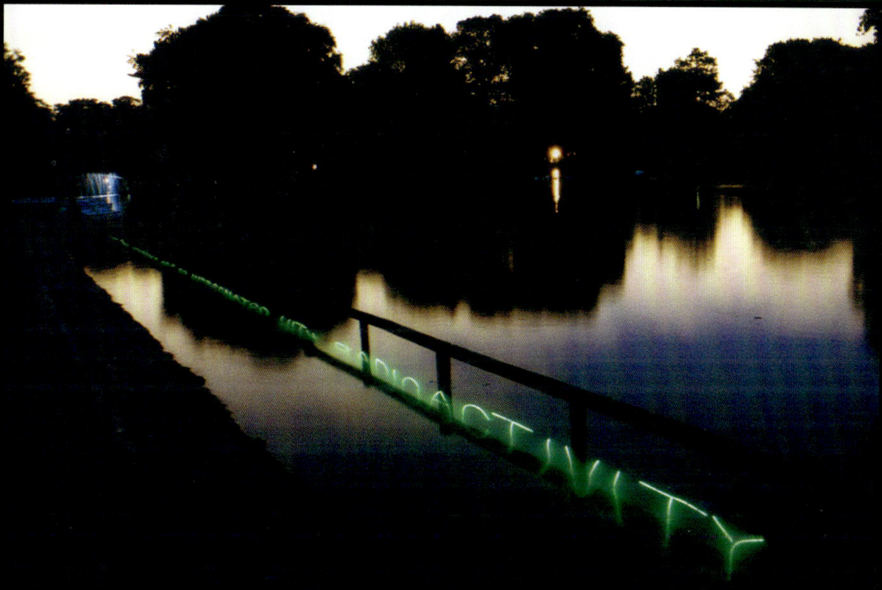

Top: Anne Bean, *Many Hands*, installation, Battersea Park, London, 2002. A work with audience creating luminescent words, hung in trees by tree climbers throughout midsummer night, and a dawn greeting by Rev. Nagase.

Bottom: Anne Bean, *CHARGE*, installation, West Park, Wolverhampton, 2000. Luminescent writing around the lake edge reads: 'Madam Curie's notebooks are so impregnated with radioactivity that if you place photographic paper between the pages and then print it, her ghostly fingerprints swim into view.' Photo: Mark Anderson

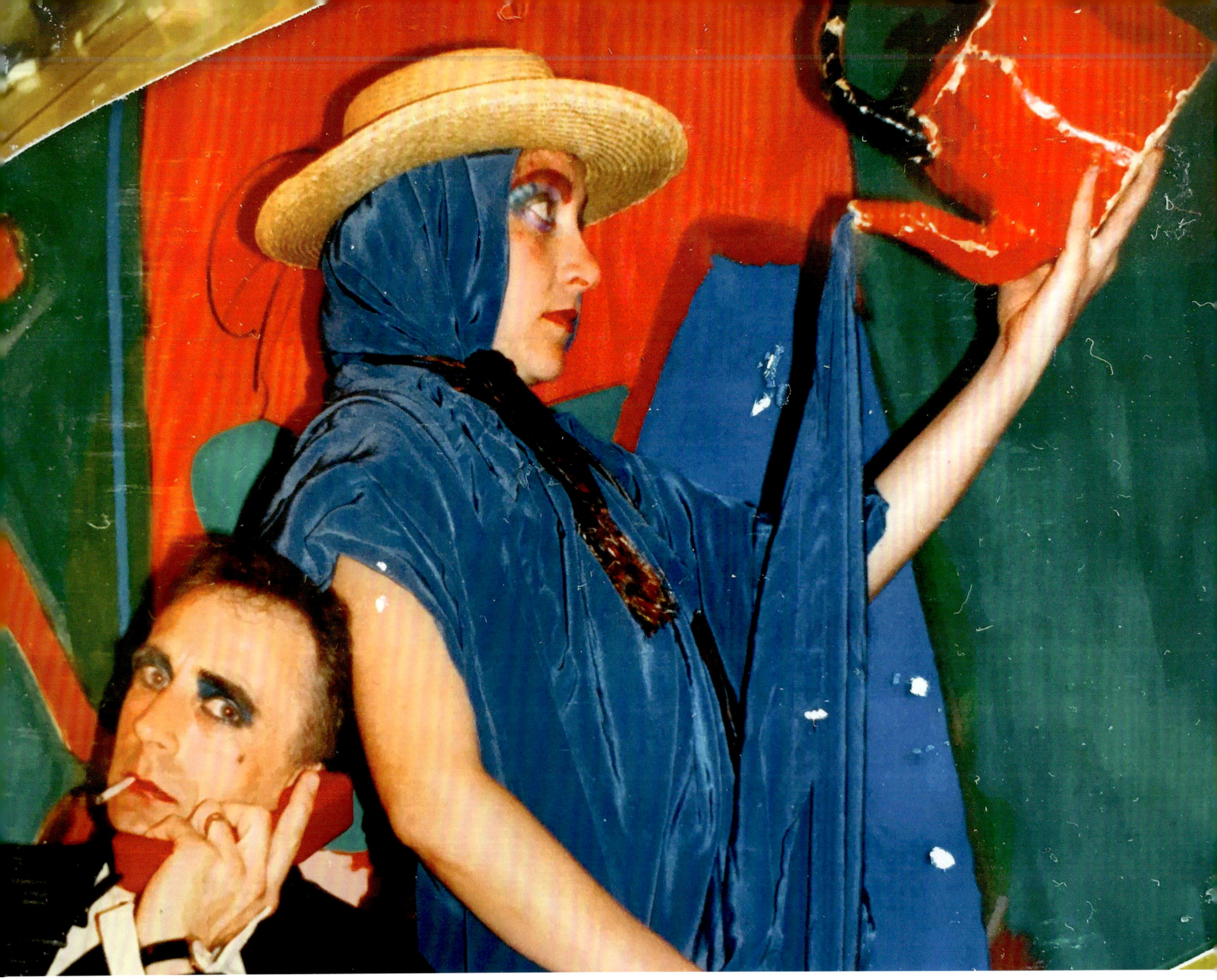

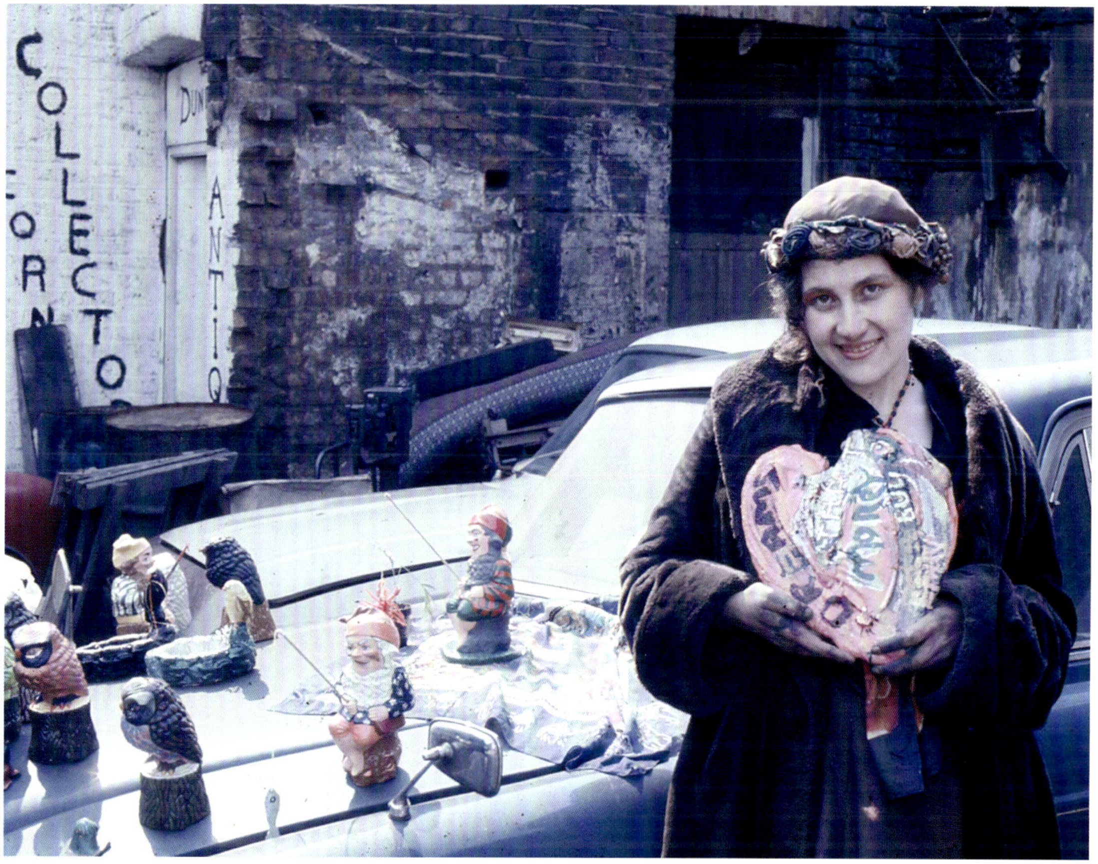

Above: Anne Bean selling *Dreams that Money can Buy* plaques, Brick Lane, London, 1973. Photo: Malcolm Jones

Opposite: Anne Bean pouring her cloak with Peter Davey, 1980. Photographer unknown

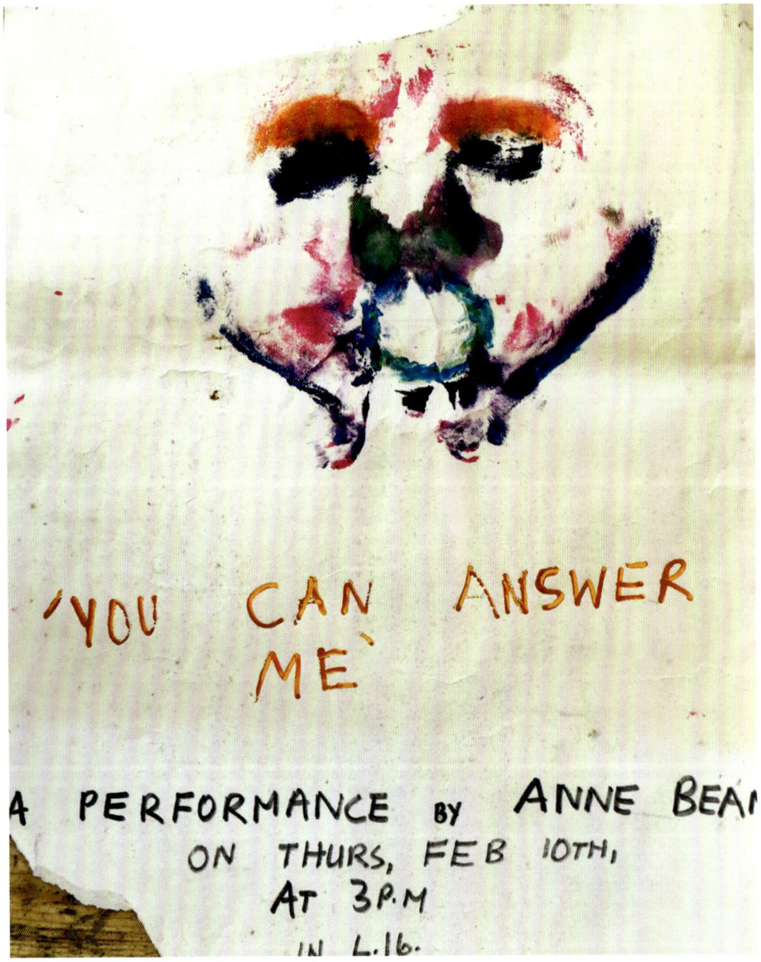

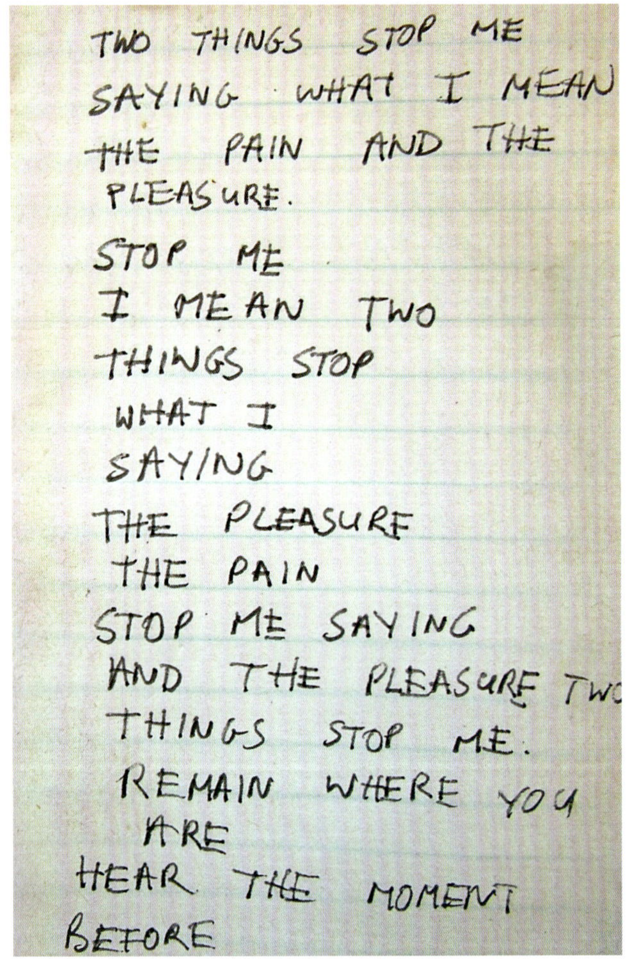

Left: Anne Bean, poster with Rorschach drawing for *You Can Answer Me*, 1972/1986
Right: Anne Bean and Paul Burwell, page from shared notebook, 1978

INTERVENTIONS BY ANNE BEAN

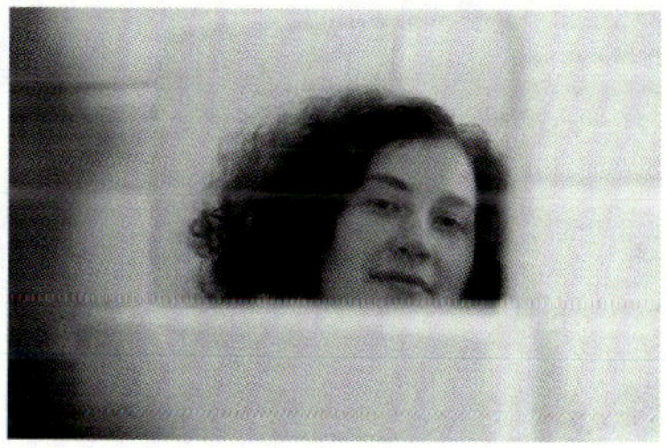

Communicating only through our Reflections, Reading, 1970. I am a meeting point Not even I am me. Photo: Phil Winder

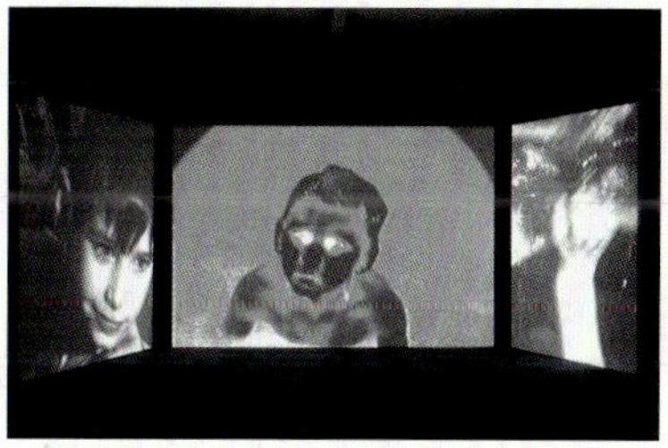

The Waxman, part of *Radiant Fields*, a three-screen video installation, Matt's Gallery, London, 2000. Photo: courtesy Matt's Gallery

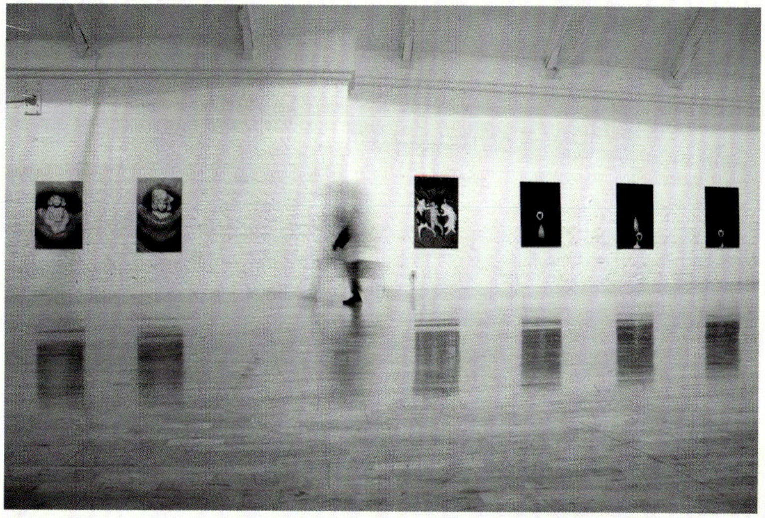

Everybody went back home to go to sleep, everyone but the Waxman, for he did not have a home, so he just walked on and on into the new blue sheet of the night sky, which got dark and the Waxman was growing tired. Soon he came to an oak tree. Taking full advantage of the shelter, he lay down under it. He couldn't get to sleep that night, he kept wondering about the strange happenings of the day, so he just sat there thinking silently as the moon glowed upon him. But, In the middle of his deep thoughts the Waxman was getting lonely and was getting fearful of the world around him. He had only just realised that he was in the middle of the dark woods. His wonders became fears and out of his fears, the only comfort he could think of was to edge towards the oak tree and huddle up and try to get to sleep. The Waxman's thoughts got twisted round and round and soon the only thing the Waxman could think of was to explore.

He had a memory of this thought, it had been lying at the back of his head, disguised as another thought, all that time. He pictured himself playing by a river, under the tree. The Waxman's imagination was getting wider and wider, as his wonders grew and grew. He stopped exploring and like a bubble, all his imagination popped. Now he remembered everything. He remembered being born out of a tree. He remembered exploring the world around him and how it had led to this. There was one thought that had remained in his head for a long time, that had been trapped in a part of his brain all alone and now he had the key to open the door and rescue it. If I was born out of a tree he thought, the tree would be my mother

Waxman text, part of *Radiant Fields* Ezra Rubenstein 1996

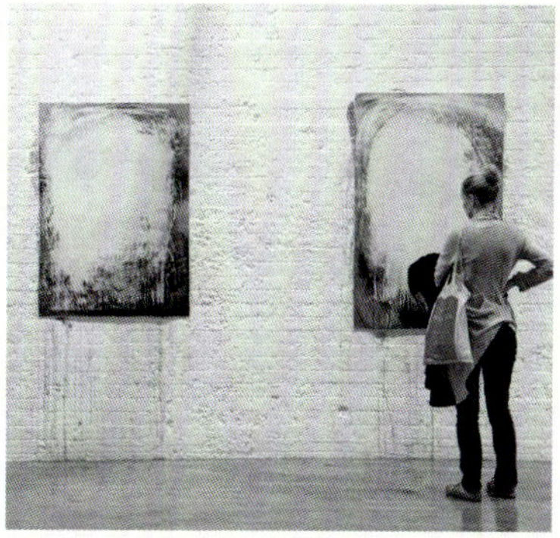

Above: *I'd Rather Go Blind*, part of *SOLO*, curated by Brian Catling at Modern Art Oxford. This photographic exhibition – including *Flame and Water Droplet* printed with special water-based inks – was literally washed away during the performance, becoming more and more painterly and finally leaving merely 'frames' around emptinesses, with dripping colours below on the gallery walls. I asked the musician Chris Gladwin to work on the song *I'd Rather Go Blind*, sung by Etta James, in a similarly disintegrating way; a laundered, scrubbed, dripping, song, forming its own whirls and emptiness. As I washed the photographs, I improvised with the scoured voice of Etta James. Photo: courtesy Modern Art Oxford

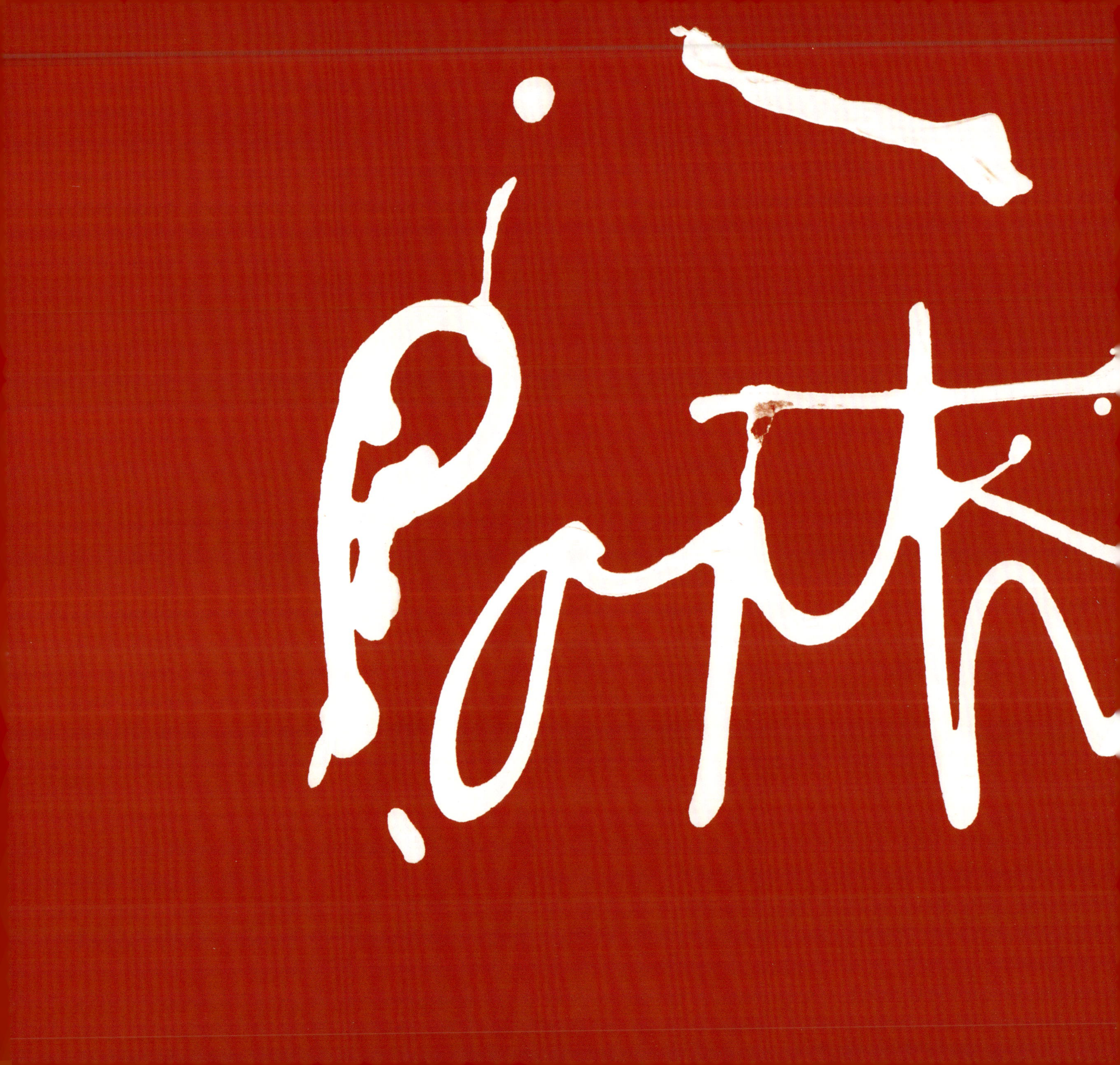

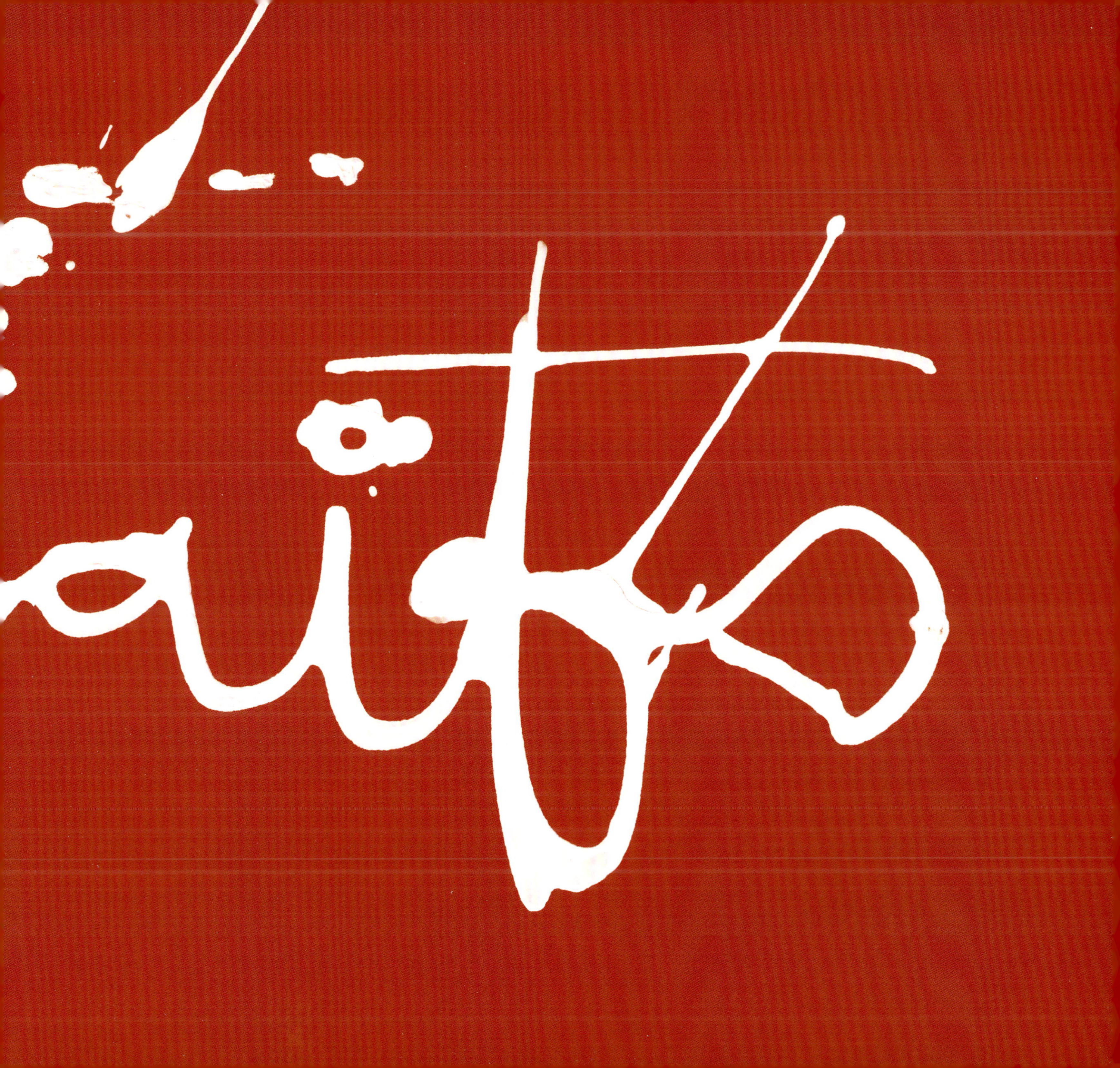

CONVERSATION PORTRAITS

Conversation Portraits
Franklin Furnace Fellowship, New York, 2007

In 2007, during a fellowship at Franklin Furnace Archives, groping for ways of animating the archive, my thoughts focussed on questions about collaboration, documentation, spontaneity and the original radical stance of performance art.

Collaboration: What is the space between us? How can we enter that most profoundly? Can we foment a strong unique sensibility only existing between ourselves?

Spontaneity: Can spontaneous action break down some defences and make it more possible to venture into unknown territory?

Documentation: Is a painting or sculpture inevitably its own document: an archiving of its live process? Was performance art initially a radical response in order to share the live and ditch the archive?

Eighteenth-century British painters used the word "Conversation Pieces," or "Conversation Portraits", to describe informal group portraits as well as views of daily life. I invited 9 artists, all of whom had been involved in the Franklin Furnace performance programme, to have a dialogue with me about their work and together to try and 'capture' this interaction within the time frame of the conversation, using a mix of media as part of this 'visual' exchange, in which we could doodle, draw, collage and chat together. The invited artists were Lenora Champagne, Diego Cortez, Mary Beth Edelson, Karen Finley, Donna Henes, Kim Jones, Harry Kipper (Martin von Haselberg), Nina Sobell and Fiona Templeton.

Immediately after each of our dialogues, I also created an image with the sense of each different encounter, trying to encapsulate the nub of our exchanges.

These works and further manifestations from them, were exhibited at Space Gallery, New York, 2007 curated with the director Jim Wintner.

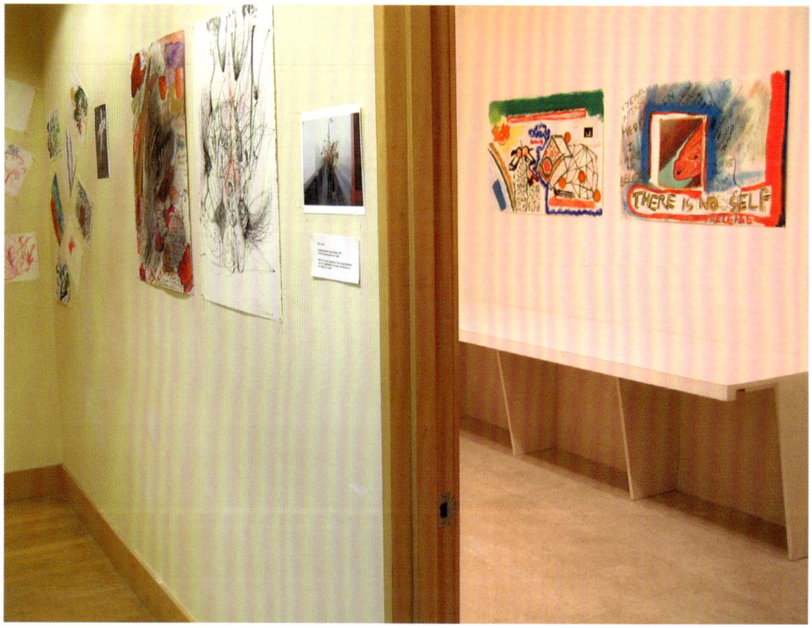

Exhibition view Space Gallery, New York

Anne Bean/Kim Jones room and Anne Bean/Martin von Haselberg, (Harry Kipper) *Peering Out: There Is No Self*

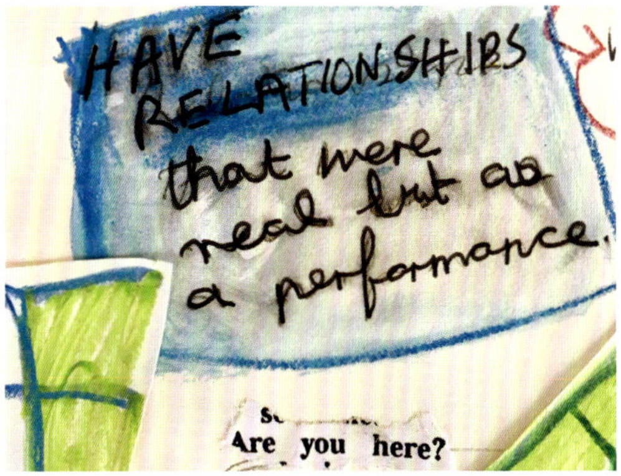

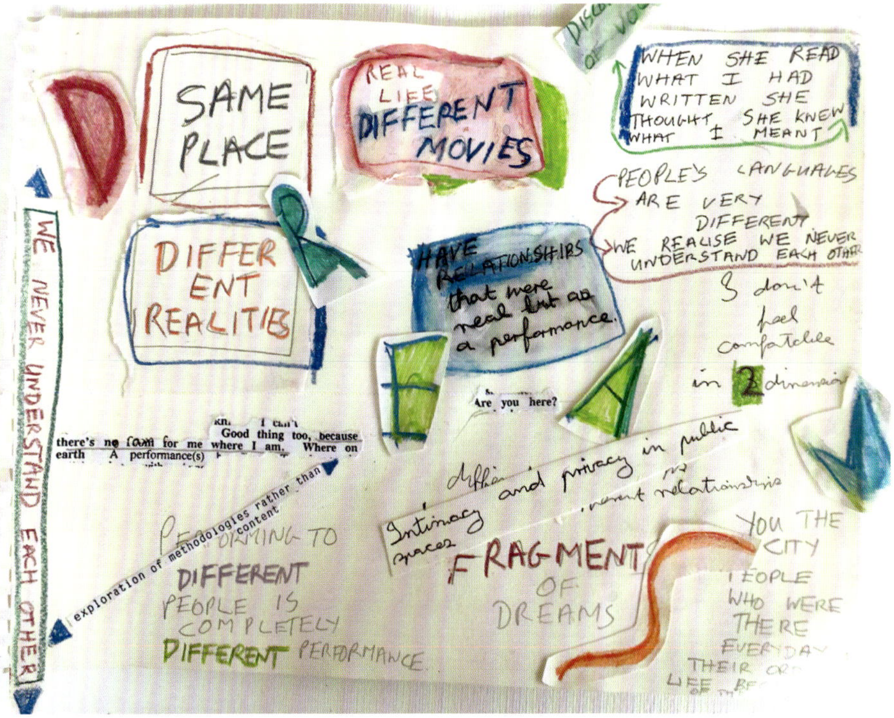

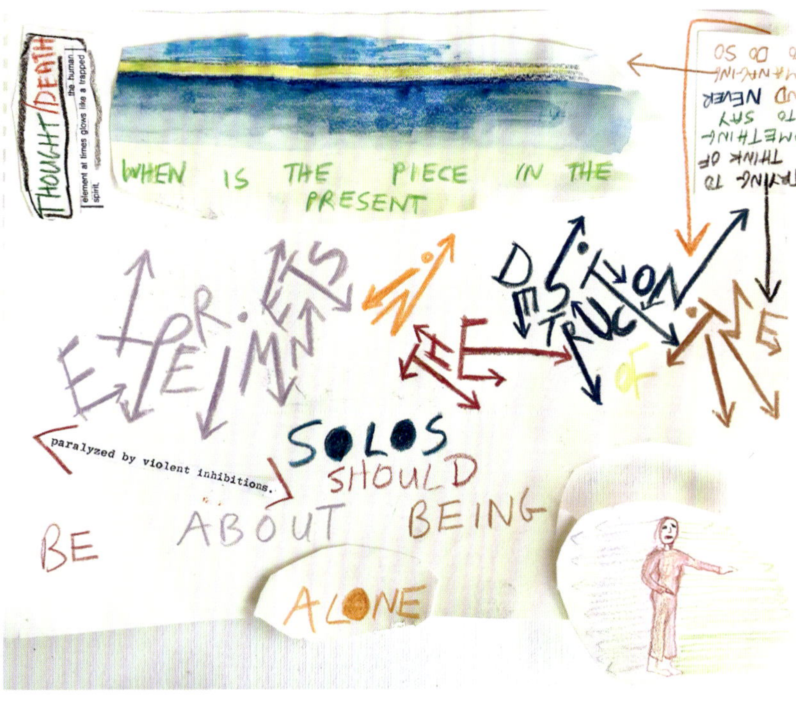

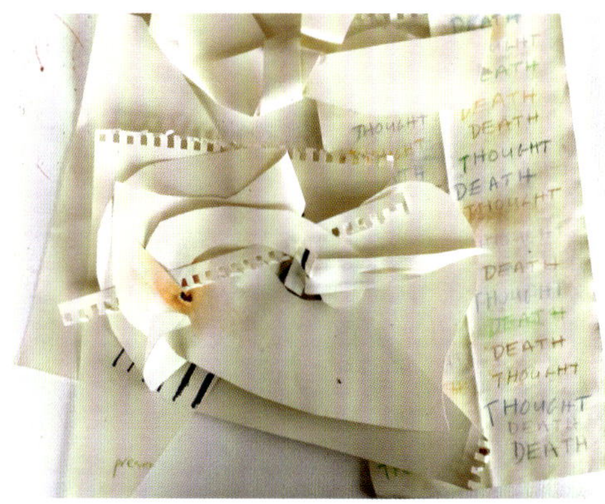

Experiments in the Destruction of Time
with Fiona Templeton

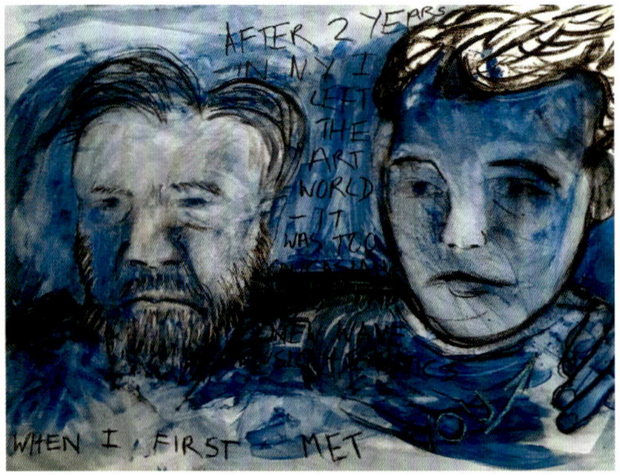

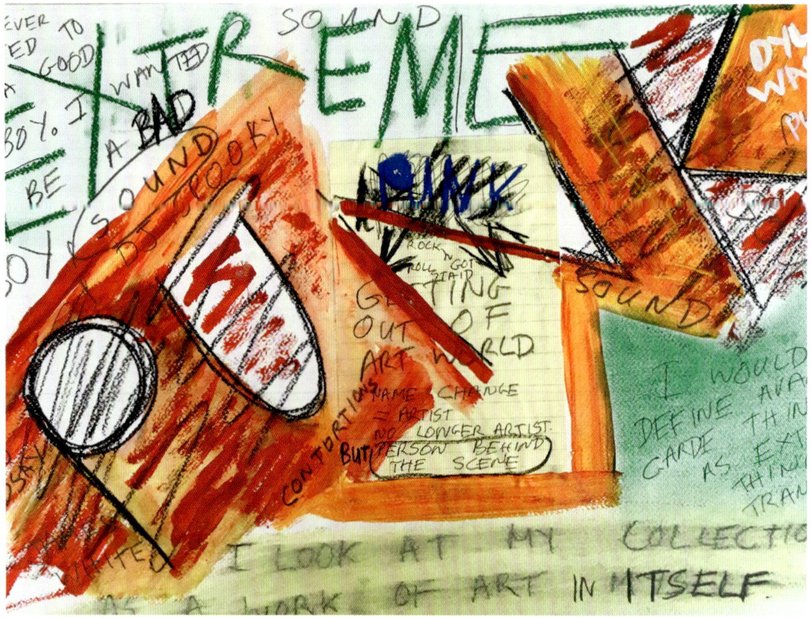

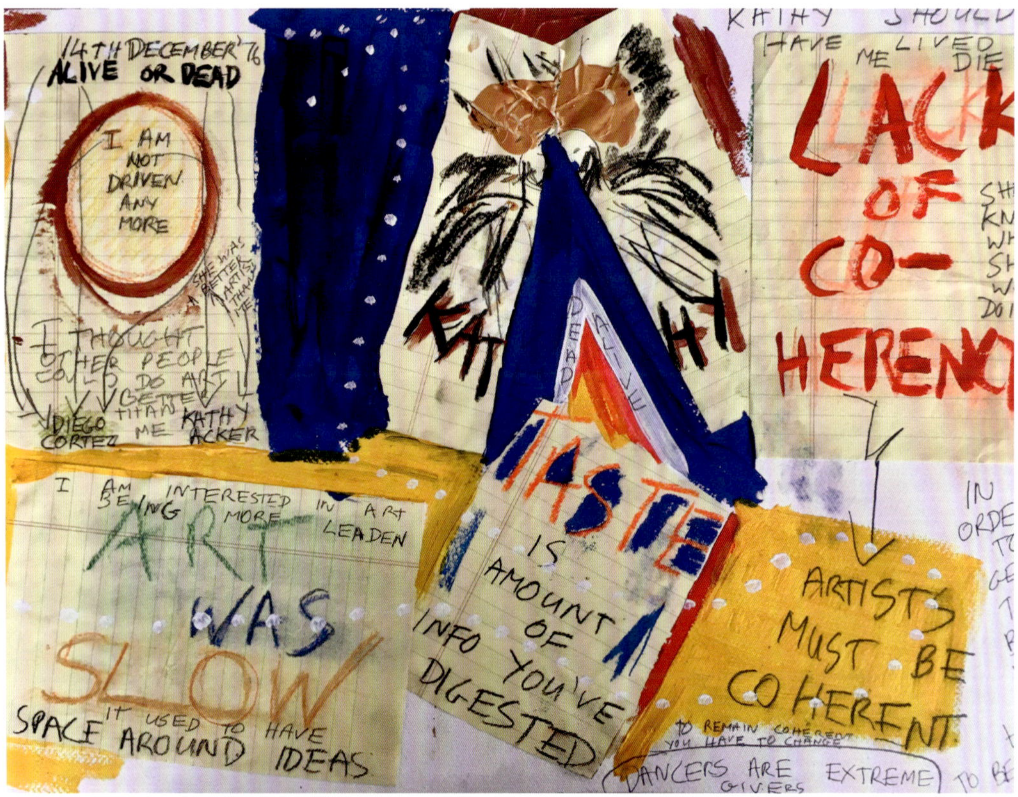

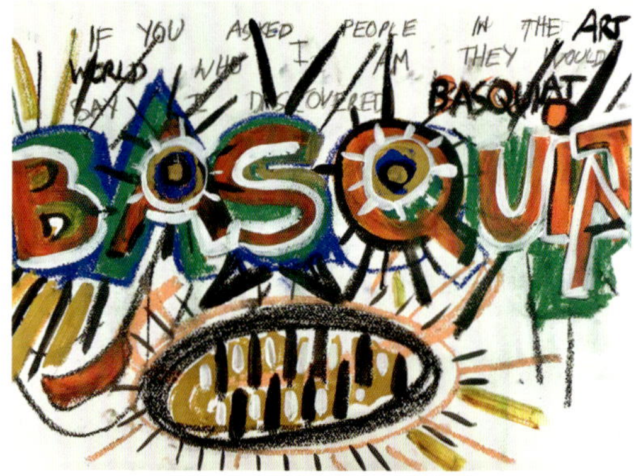

Opposite page: Killed, Erased, Redrawn with Kim Jones
This page: Speed is the Enemy of Art with Diego Cortez

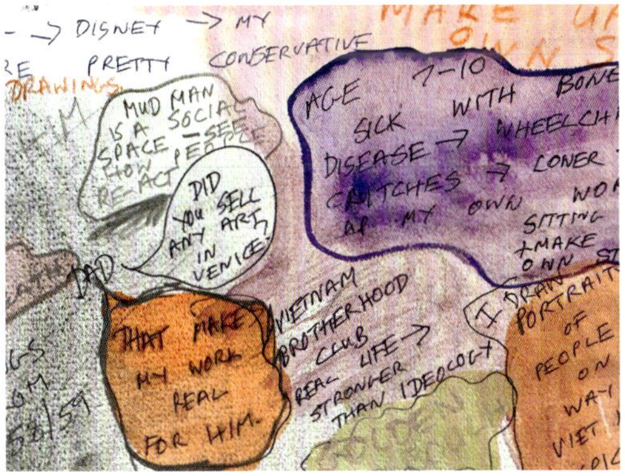
DISNEY → MY
PRETTY CONSERVATIVE
MUD MAN IS A SOCIAL SPACE
DID YOU SELL ANY ART IN VENICE
AGE 7-10
SICK WITH
DISEASE →
CRUTCHES
THAT MADE MY WORK REAL FOR HIM
VIETNAM BROTHERHOOD CLUB

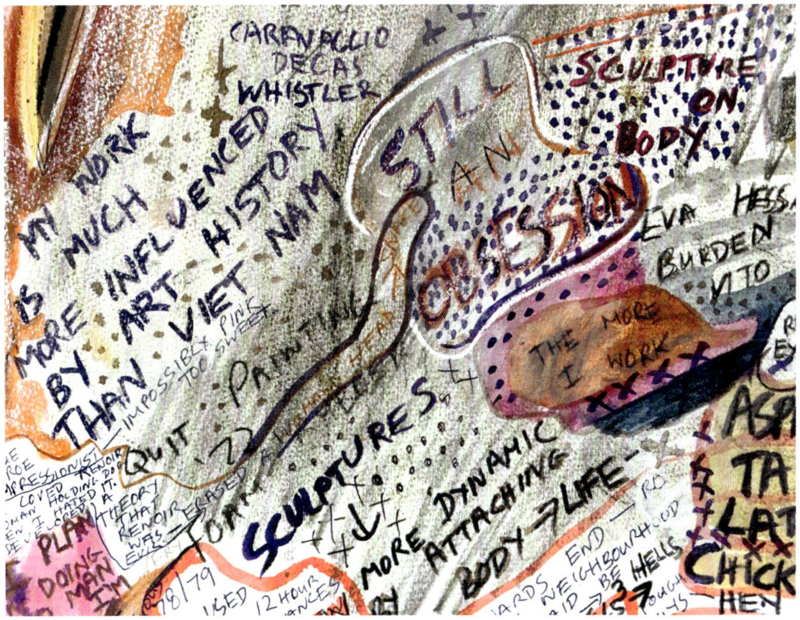
CARAVAGGIO
DEGAS
WHISTLER
MY WORK IS MUCH MORE INFLUENCED BY ART HISTORY THAN VIET NAM
STILL AN OBSESSION
SCULPTURE ON BODY
SCULPTURES
MORE DYNAMIC
ATTACHING BODY → LIFE

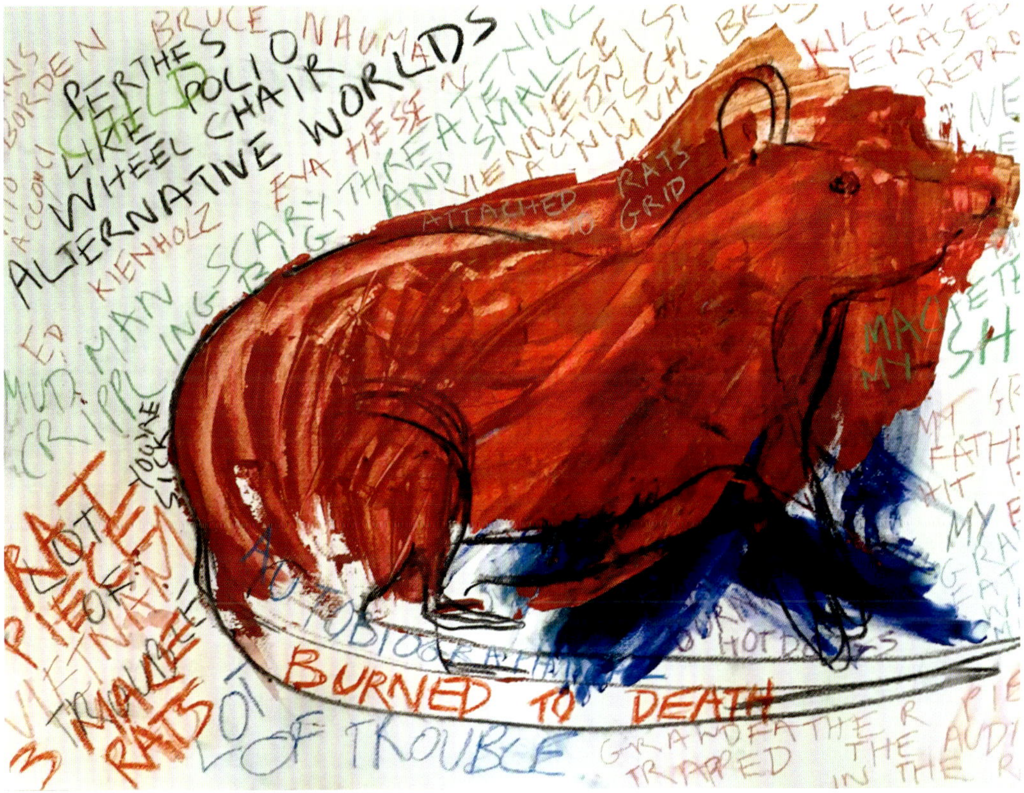
PERTHES
LIKE POLIO
WHEEL CHAIR
ALTERNATIVE WORLDS
EVA HESSE
KIENHOLZ
ATTACHED RATS TO GRID
BURNED TO DEATH
OF TROUBLE

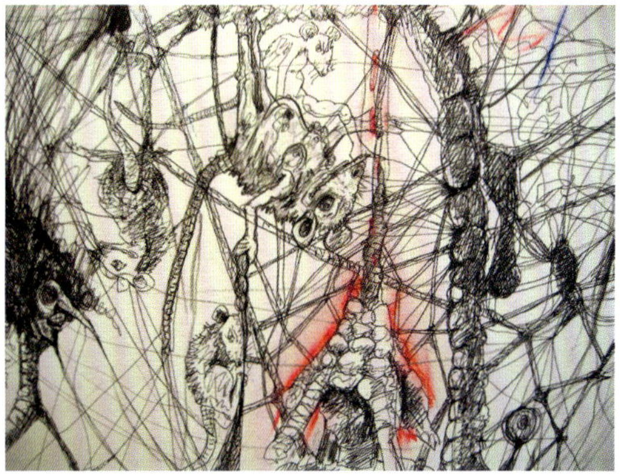

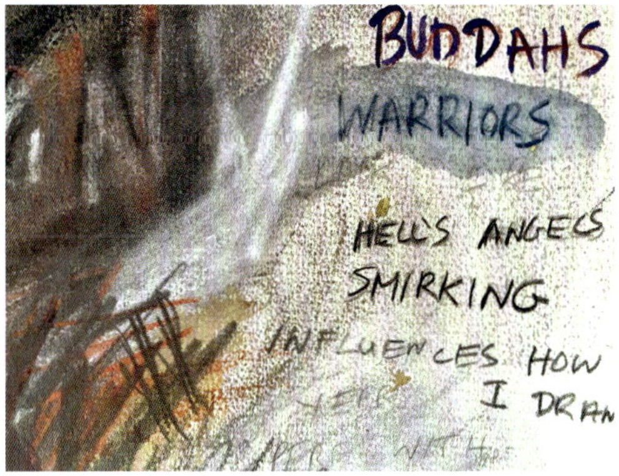
BUDDAHS
WARRIORS
HELL'S ANGELS
SMIRKING
INFLUENCES HOW

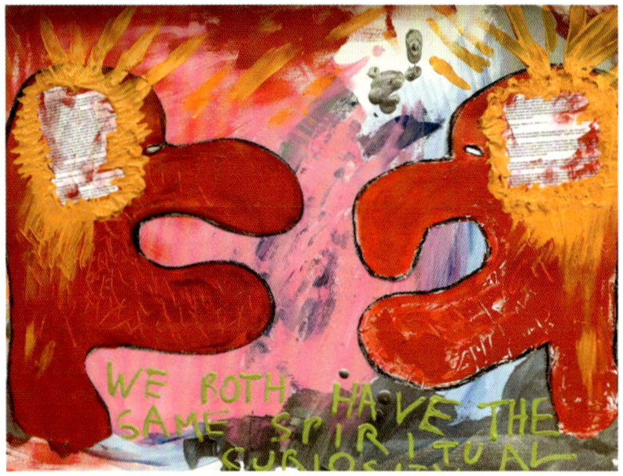

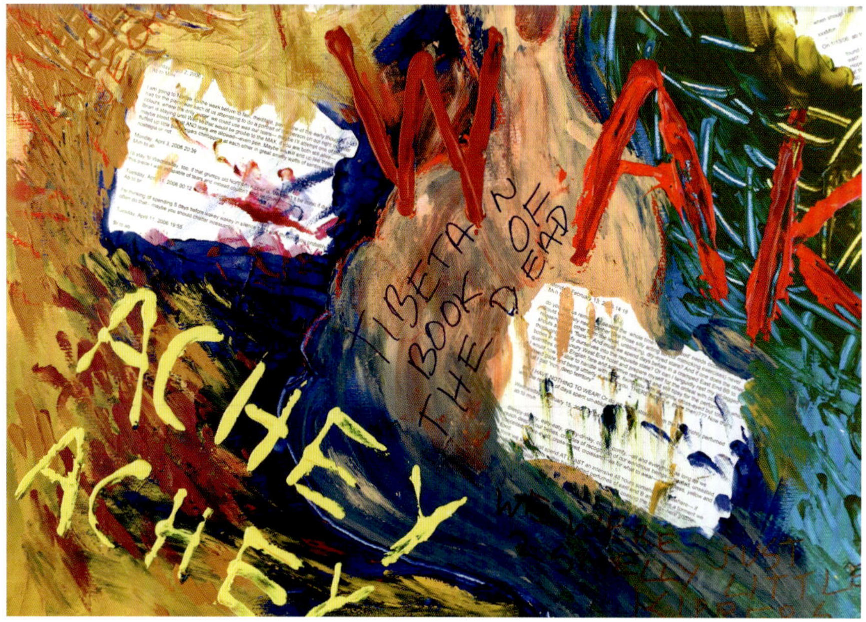

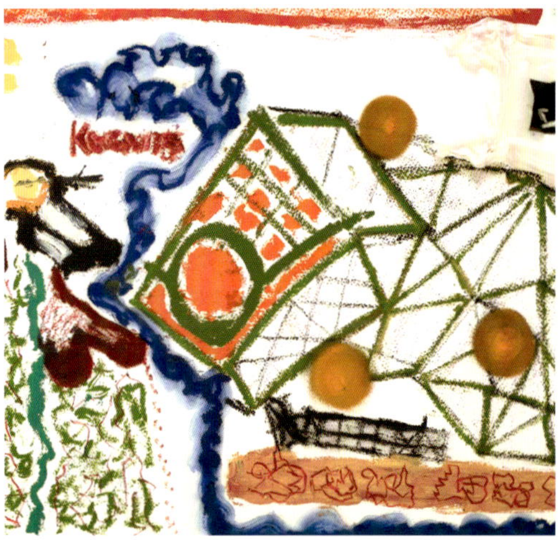

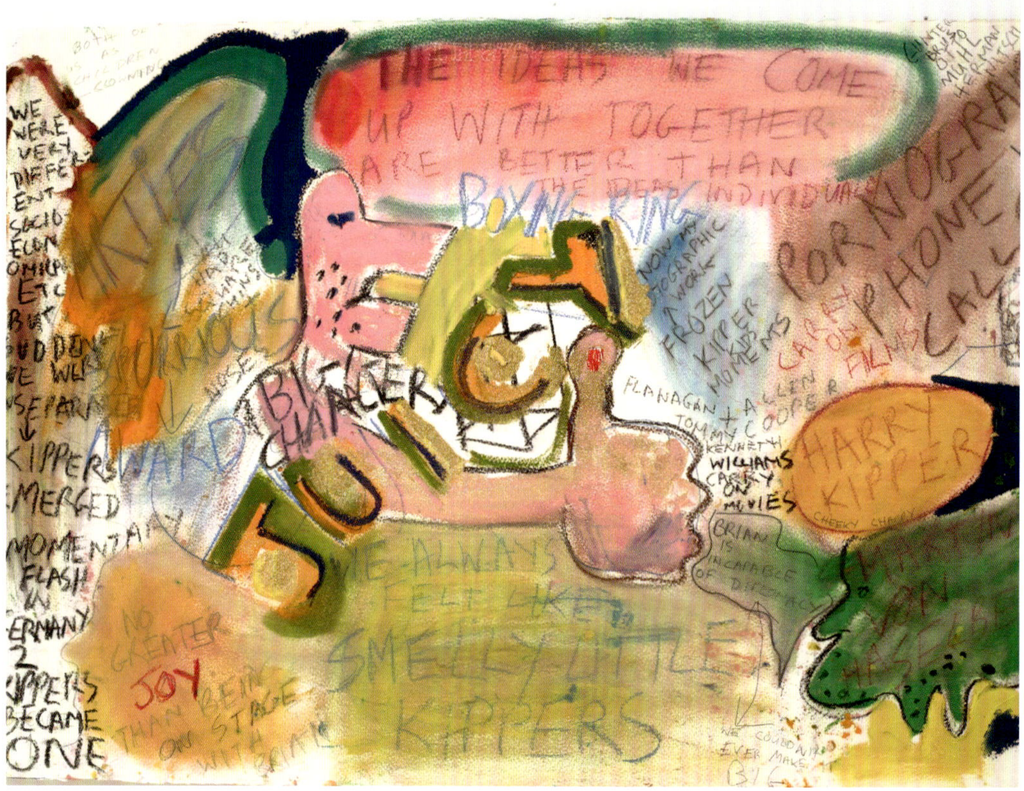

This page: Achey Achey with Martin von Haselberg (Harry Kipper)

Opposite page: As Above, So Below with Donna Henes

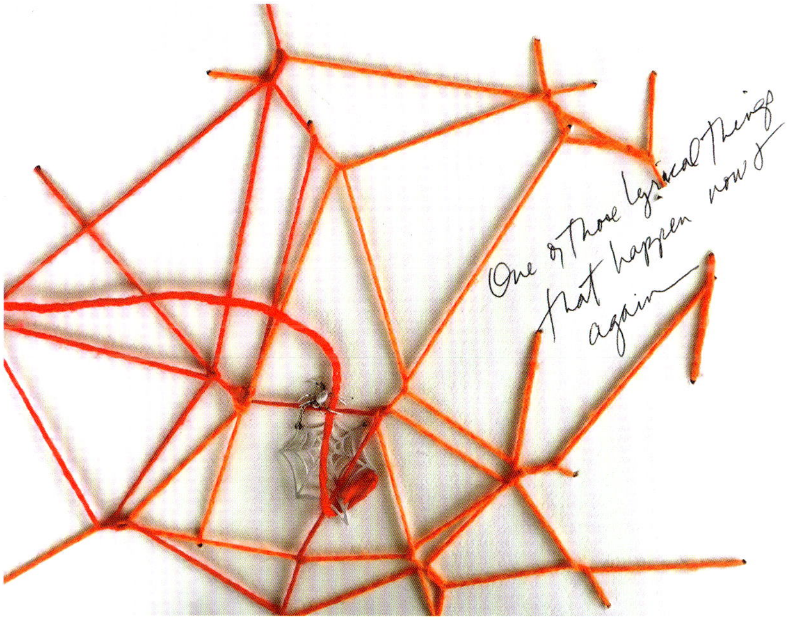
One of those lyrical things
that happen now &
again

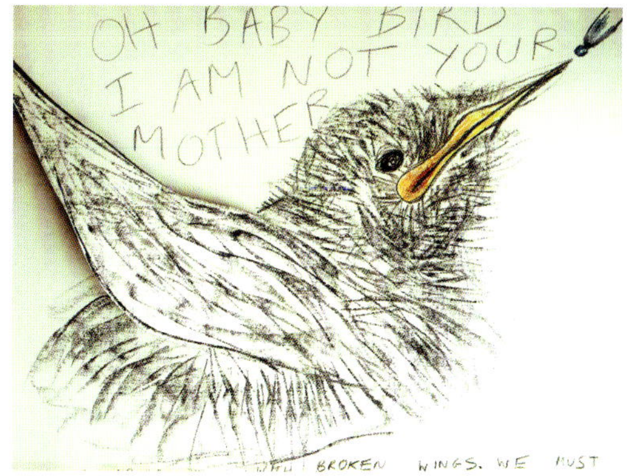
OH BABY BIRD
I AM NOT YOUR
MOTHER
BROKEN WINGS. WE MUST

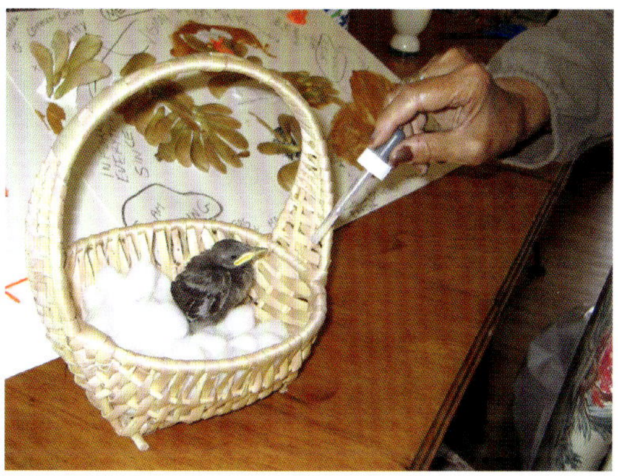

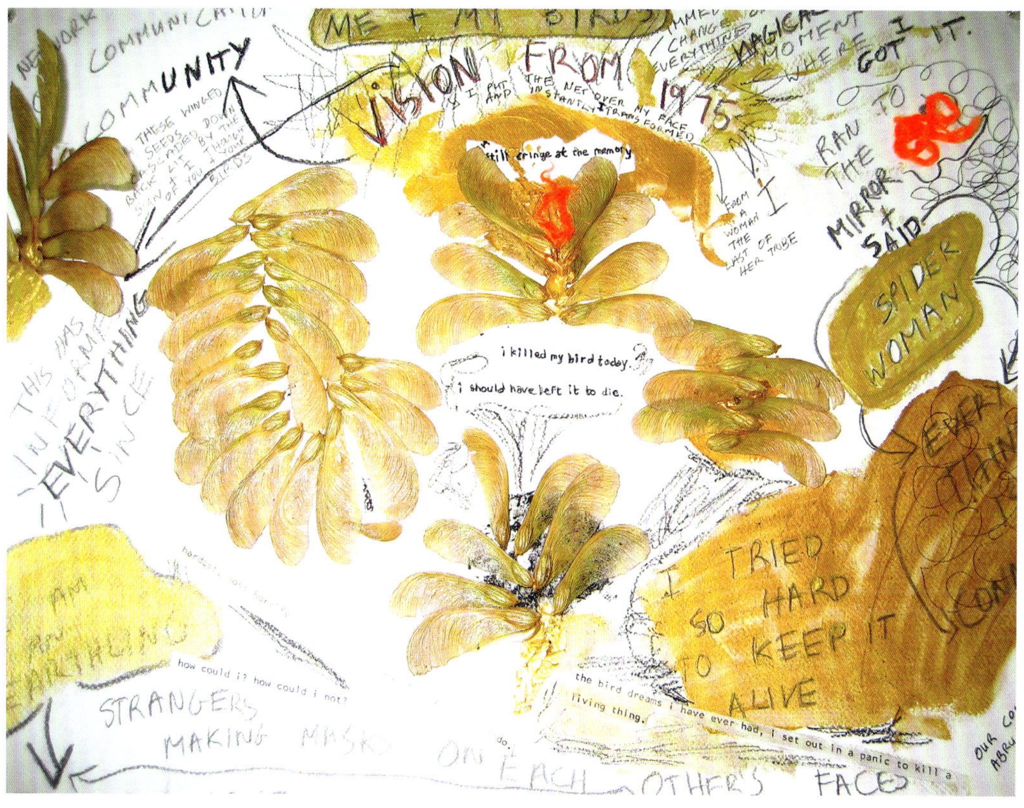
ME + MY BIRDS
COMMUNITY
VISION FROM 1975
MAGICAL MOMENT WHERE I GOT IT.
i still cringe at the memory
I RAN TO THE MIRROR + SAID
SPIDER WOMAN
i killed my bird today.
i should have left it to die.
THIS HAS INFORMED EVERYTHING SINCE
I TRIED SO HARD TO KEEP IT ALIVE
how could i? how could i not?
STRANGERS MAKING MASKS ON EACH OTHER'S FACES

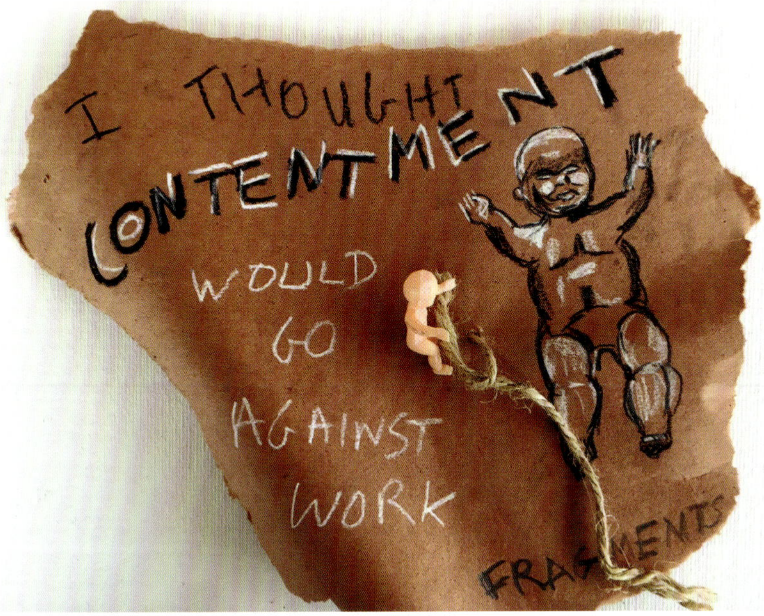
I THOUGHT
CONTENTMENT
WOULD
GO
AGAINST
WORK
FRAGMENTS

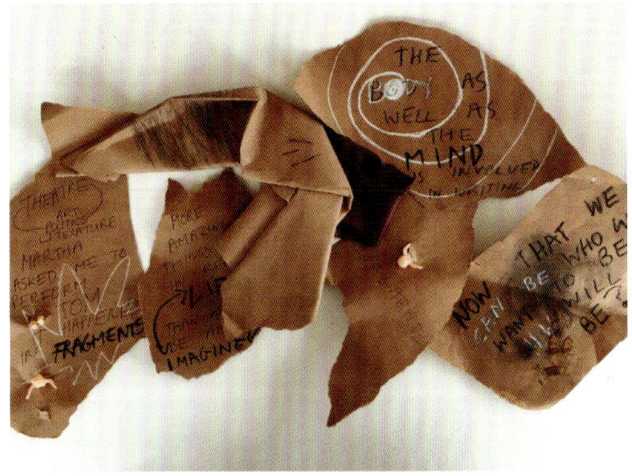
THE BODY AS WELL AS THE MIND
FRAGMENTS

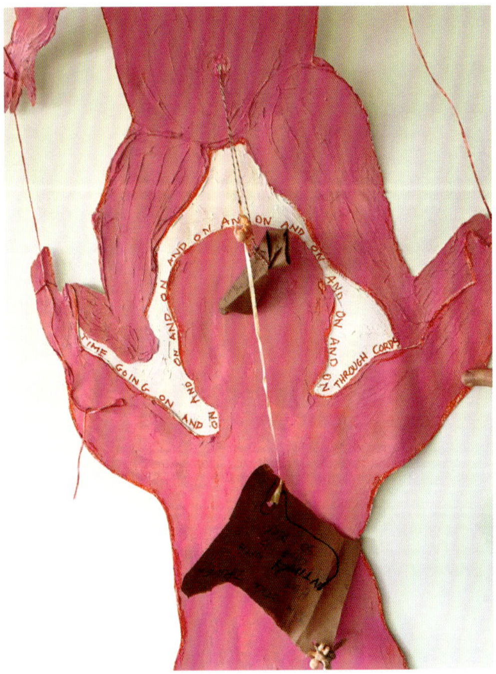

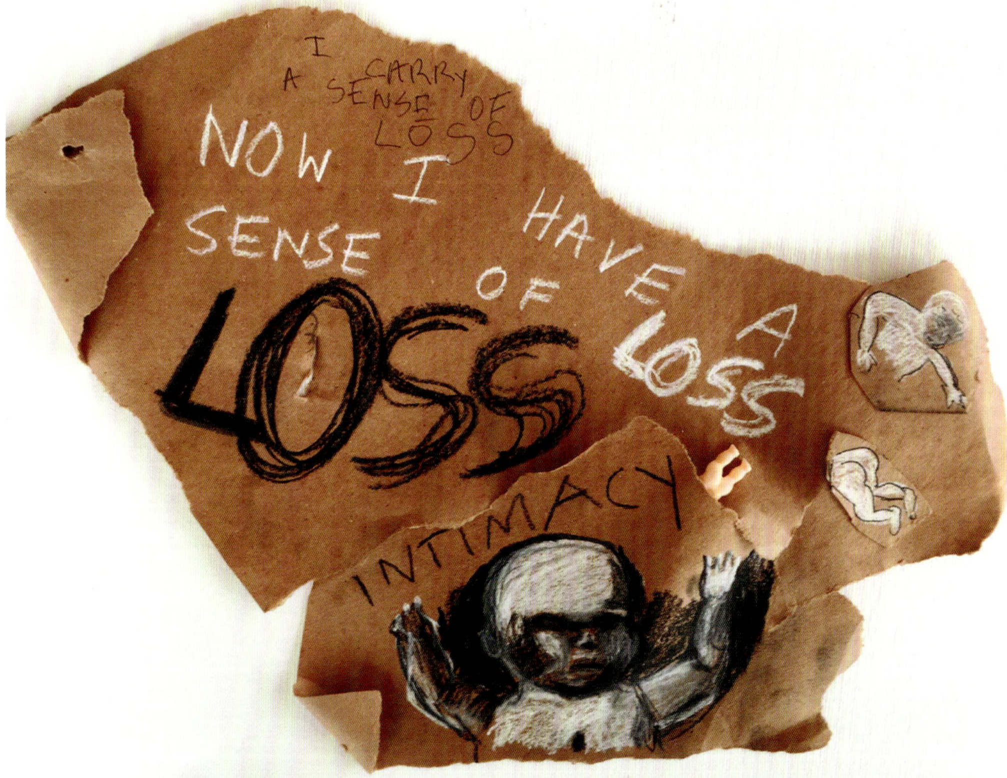
I CARRY A SENSE OF LOSS
NOW I HAVE A SENSE OF LOSS
LOSS
INTIMACY

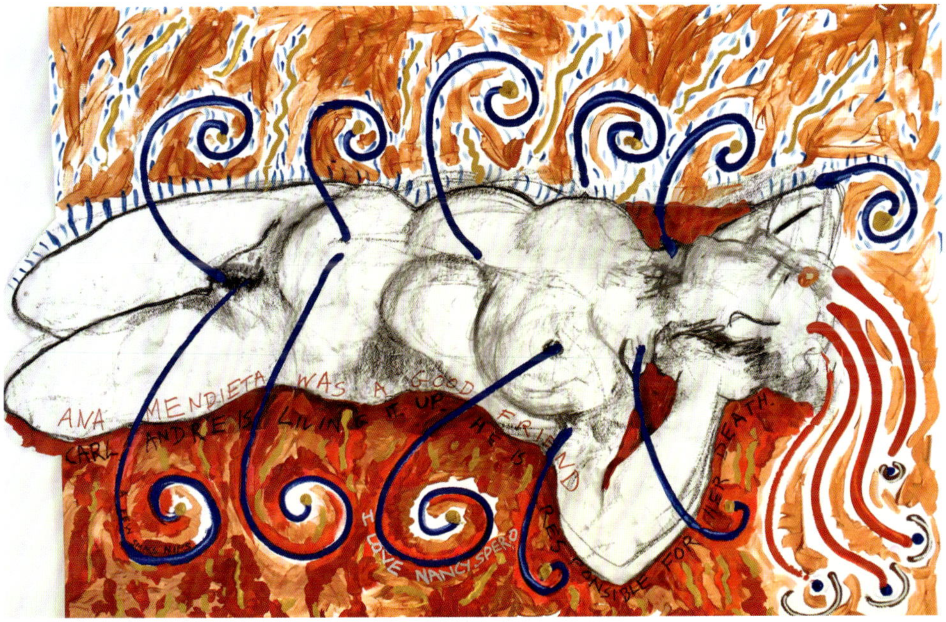

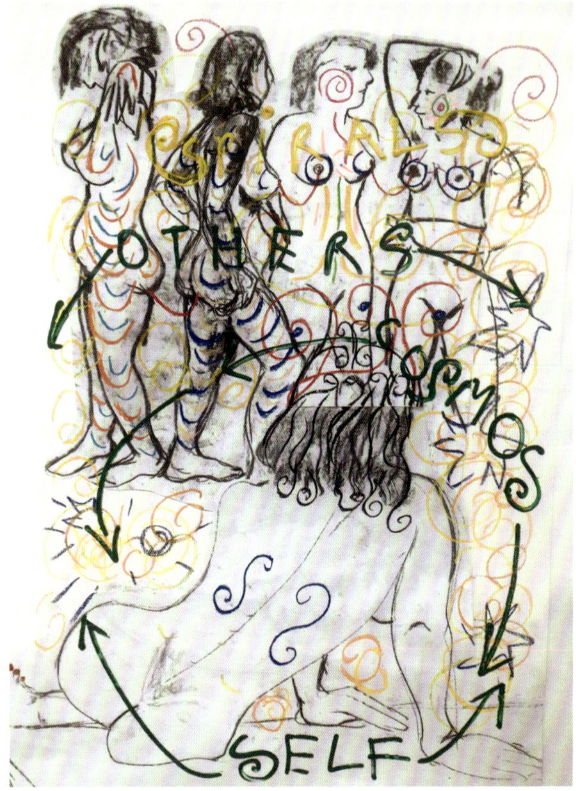

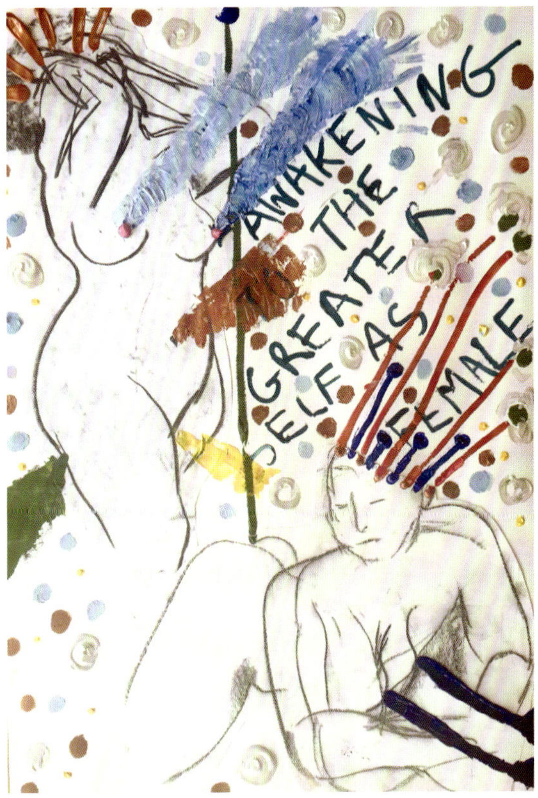

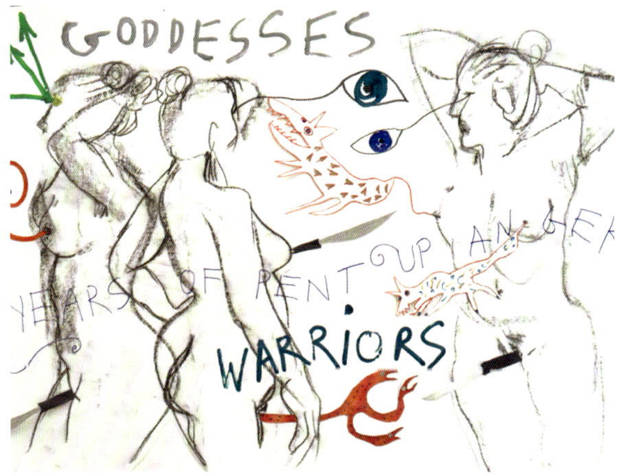

This page: Awakening to the Greater Self as Female with Mary Beth Edelson

Opposite page: I need to get Lost but I Fear with Lenora Champagne

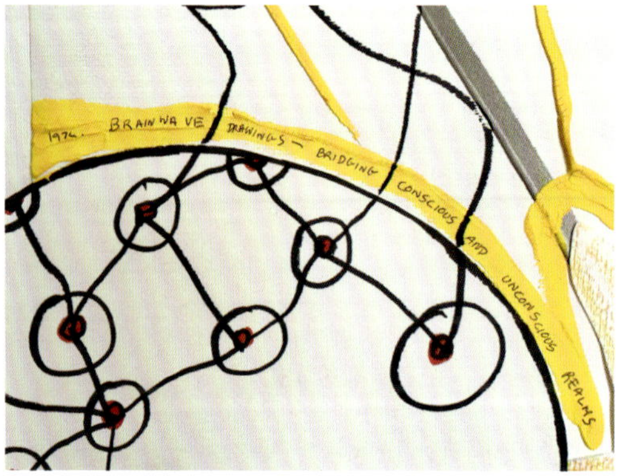

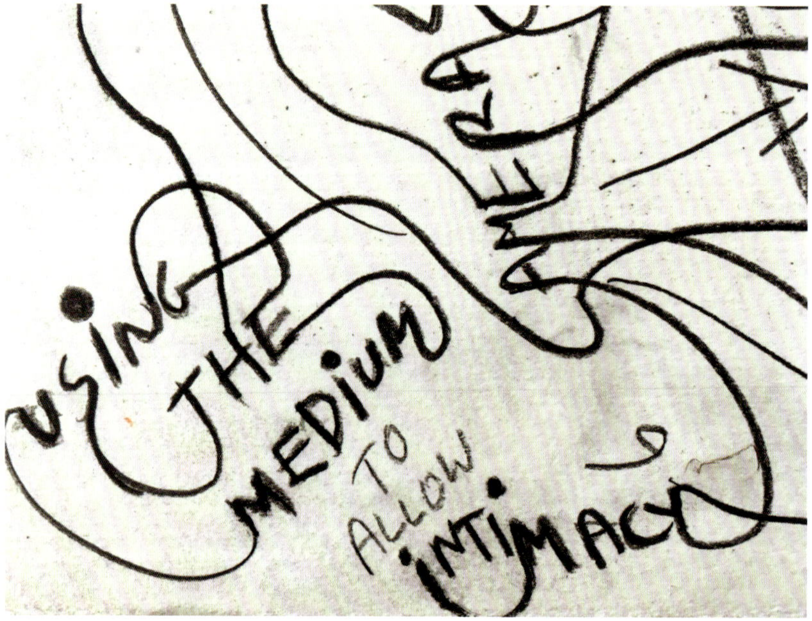

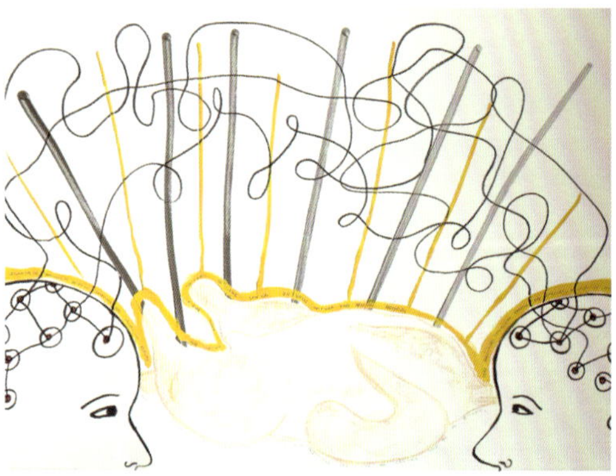

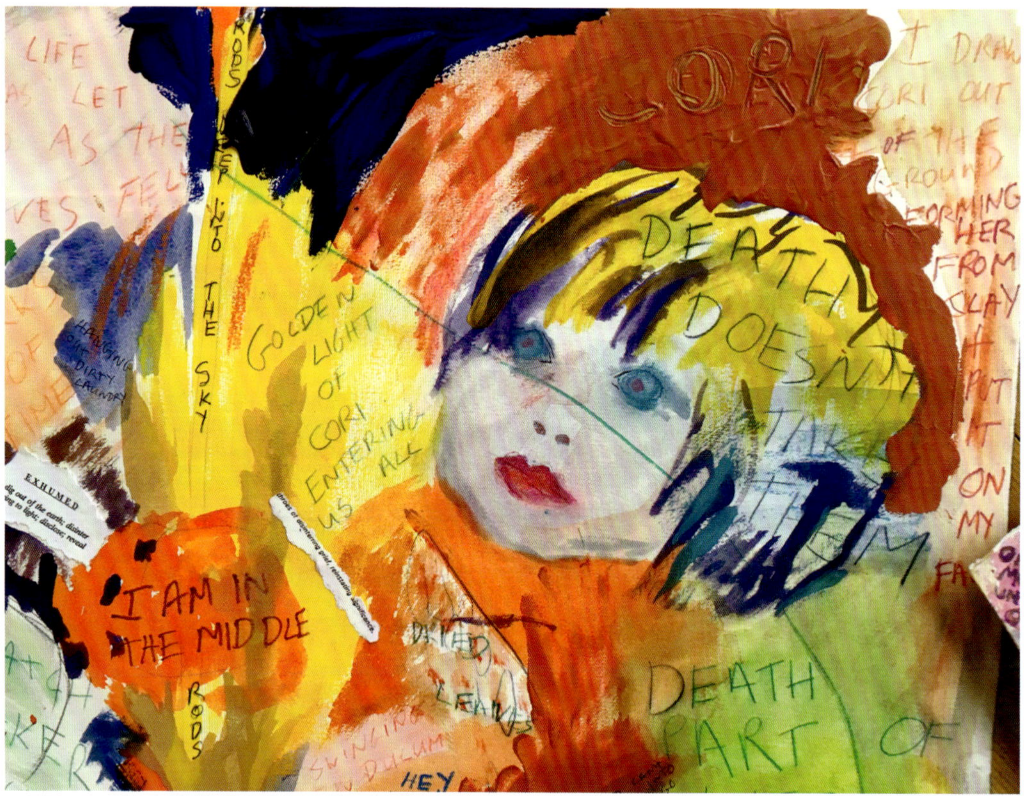

This page: Using the Medium to Allow Intimacy with Nina Sobell

Opposite page: Bath in a Suitcase with Karen Finley

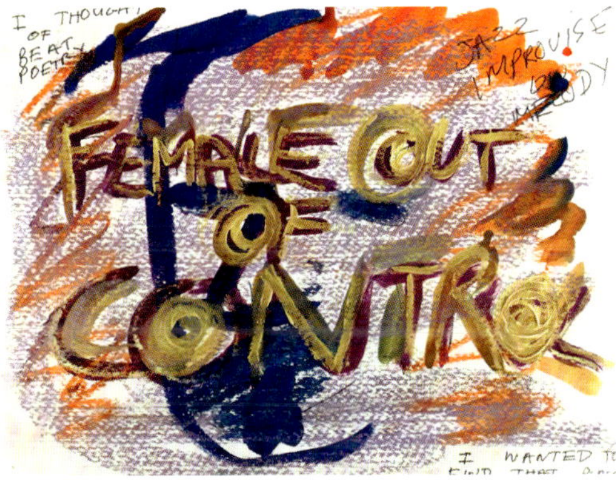
FEMALE OUT OF CONTROL
JAZZ IMPROVISE
I WANTED TO

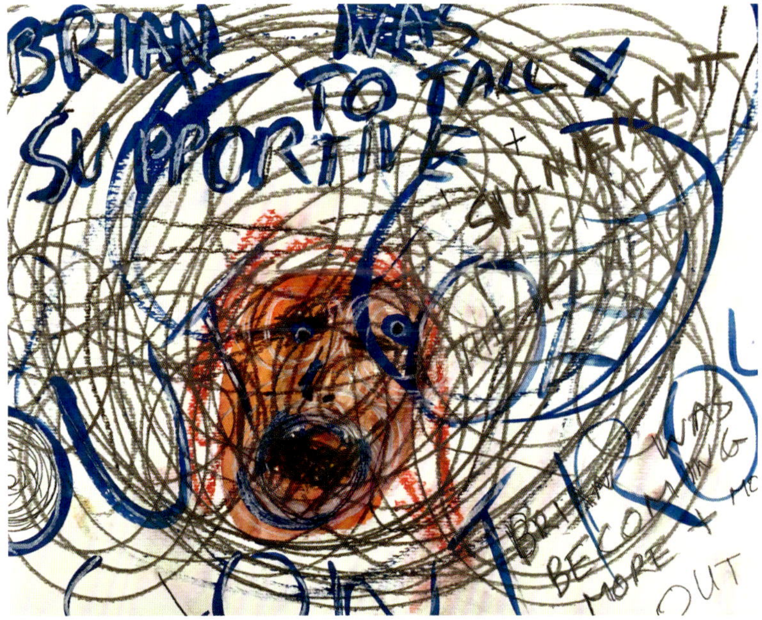
BRIAN WAS
SUPPORTIVE
BECOMING
MORE
OUT

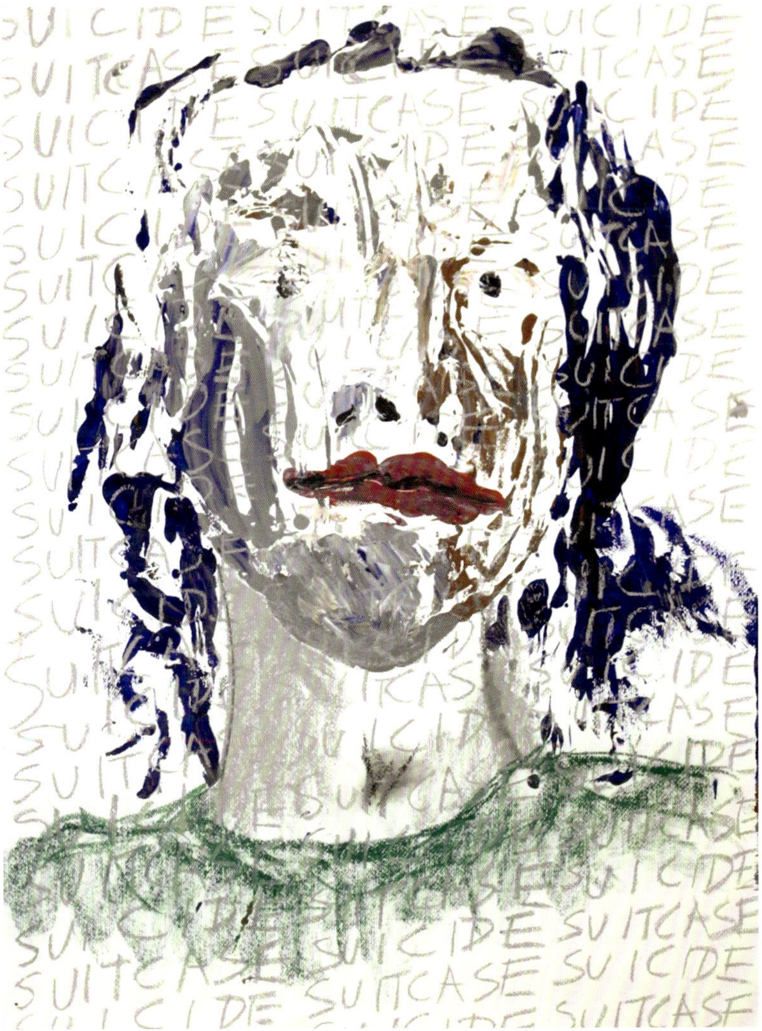
SUICIDE SUITCASE SUICIDE
SUITCASE
SUICIDE SUITCASE
SUITCASE SUICIDE
SUICIDE SUITCASE SUICIDE
SUITCASE SUICIDE SUITCASE

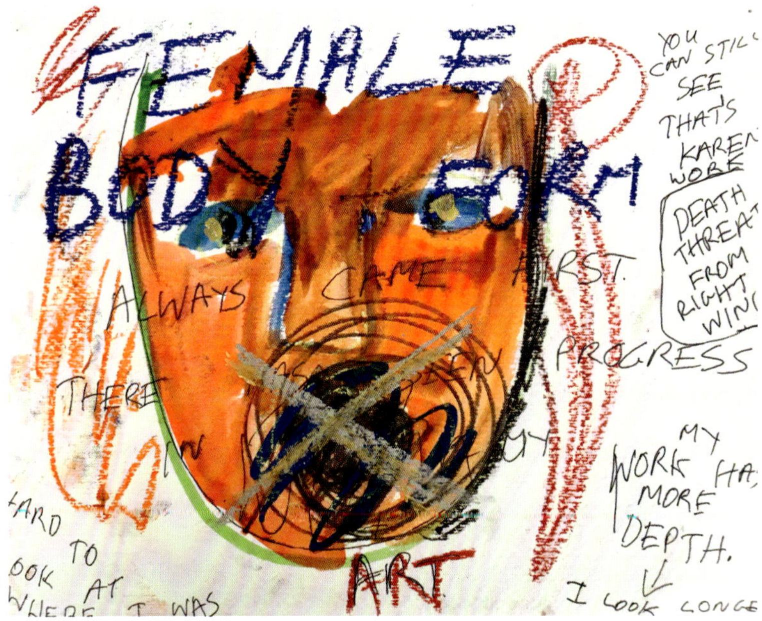
FEMALE
BODY FORM
SEE
THAT'S
DEATH
FROM
RIGHT
ALWAYS CAME FIRST.
PROGRESS
THERE
MY
WORK
MORE
DEPTH.
TO
AT
WAS
ART

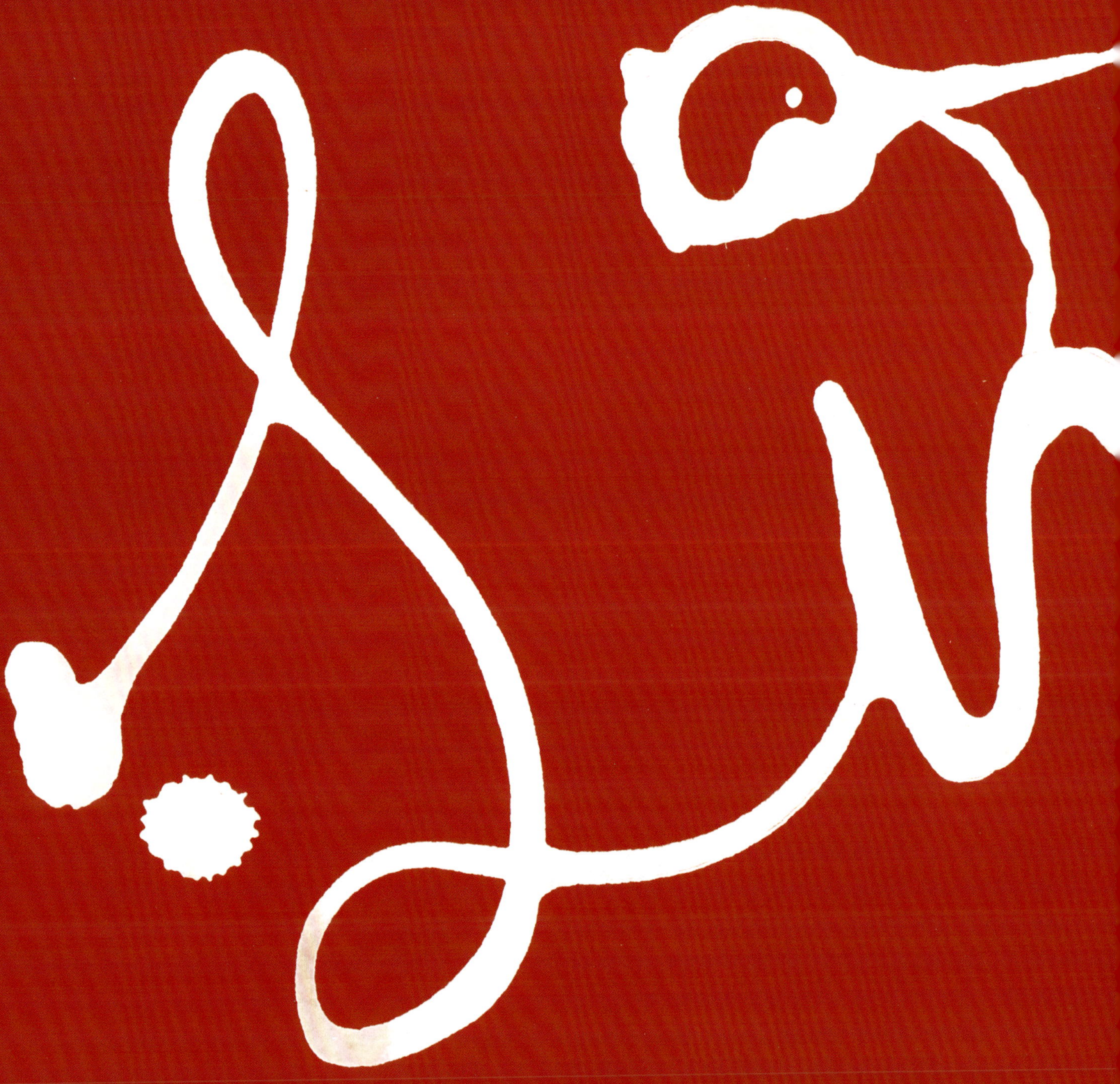

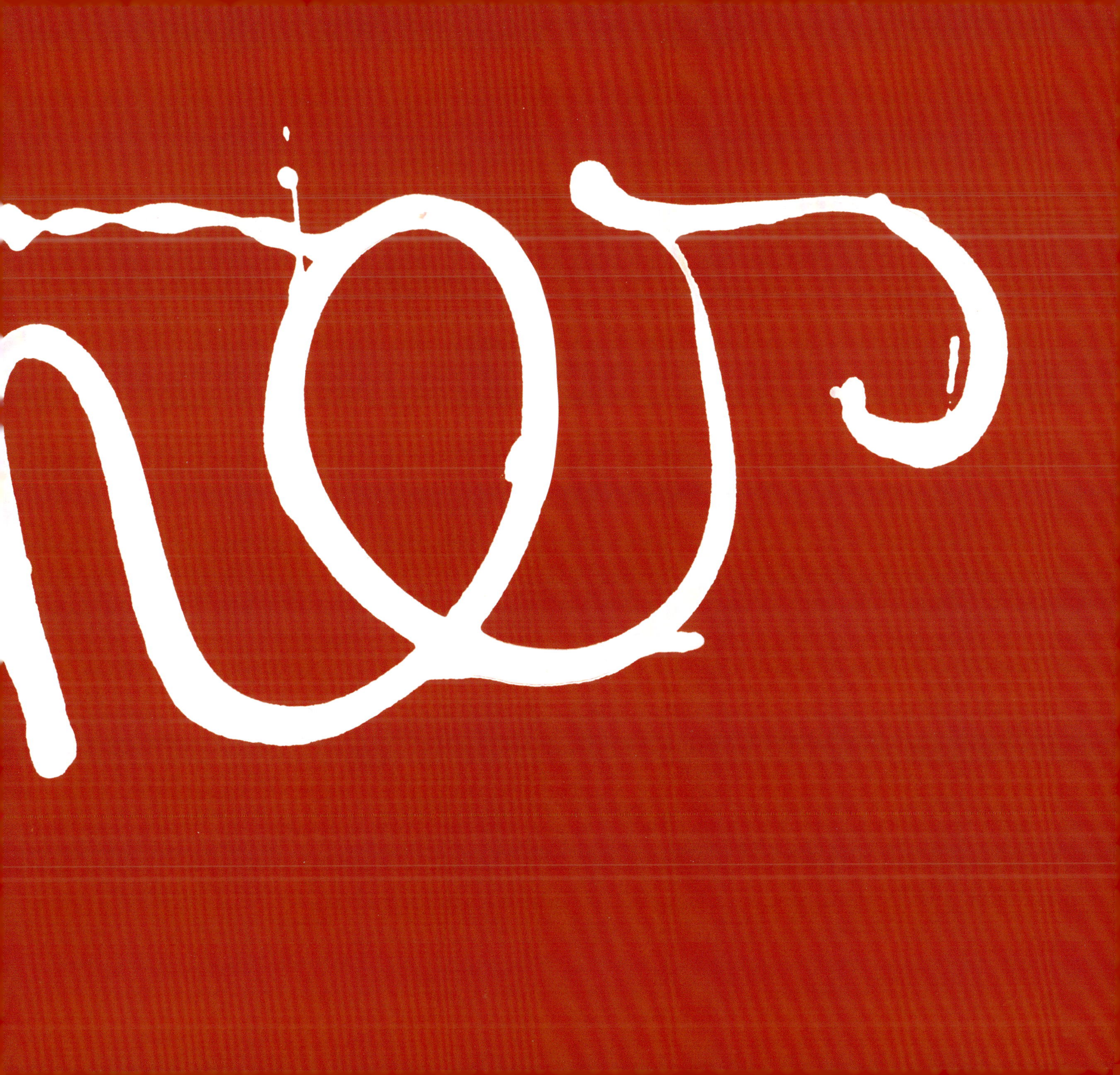

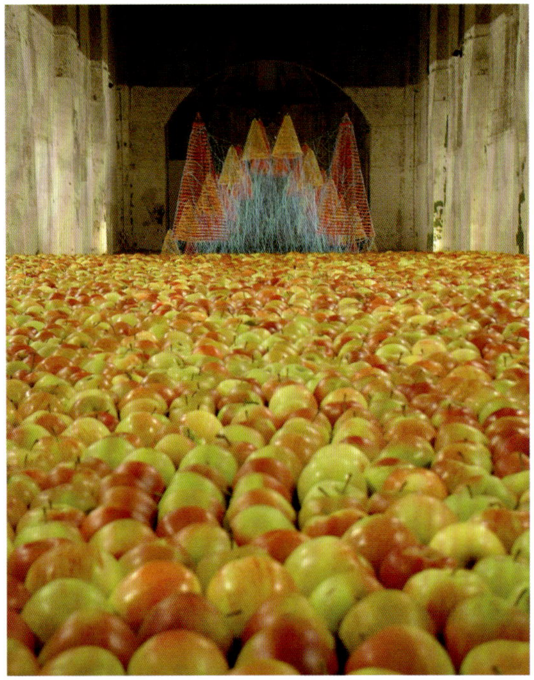

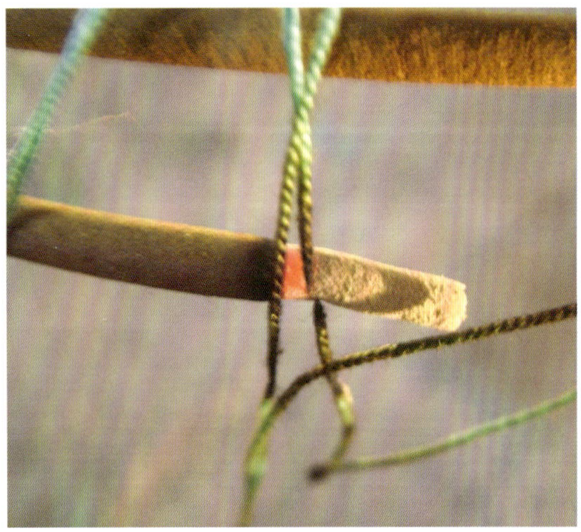

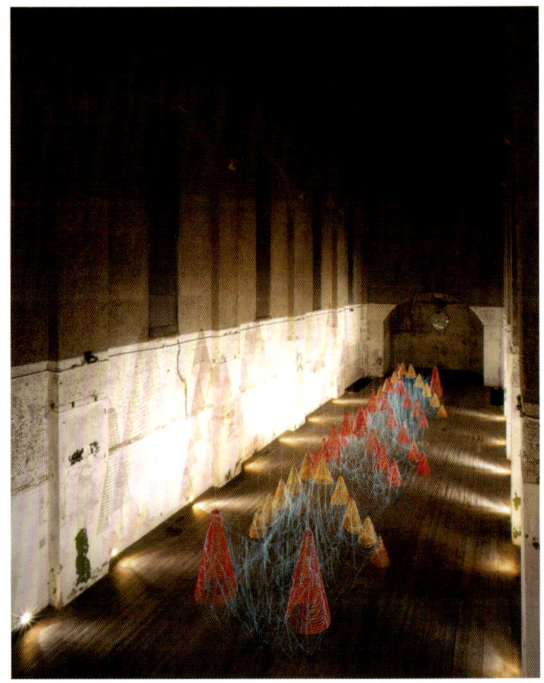

ASHES and THREADS, Dilston Grove, London 2004/2005 (part of Reap)

Coils of incense for Buddhist temples, calculated to last altogether for one year of constant burning, were suspended in a former church. I looped turquoise threads through the coils. Finally, at the end of the year, all that remained was a floor piece of ashes and threads, the shape of which echoed the former installation. Photos: Mark Anderson, Brent Helsel, Anne Bean

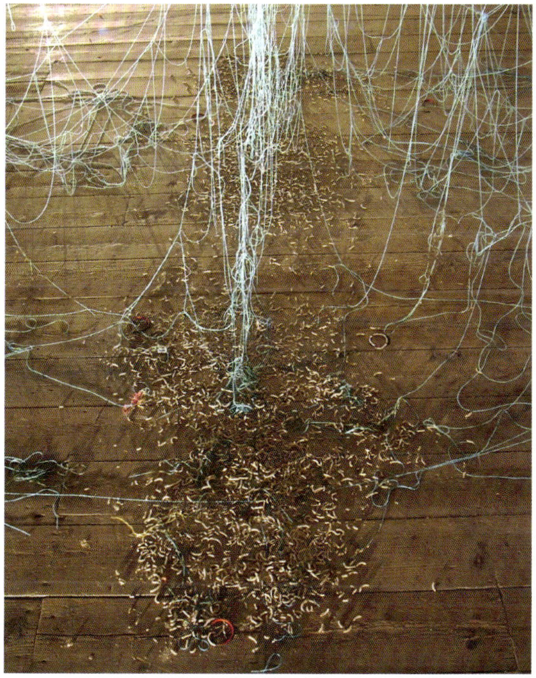

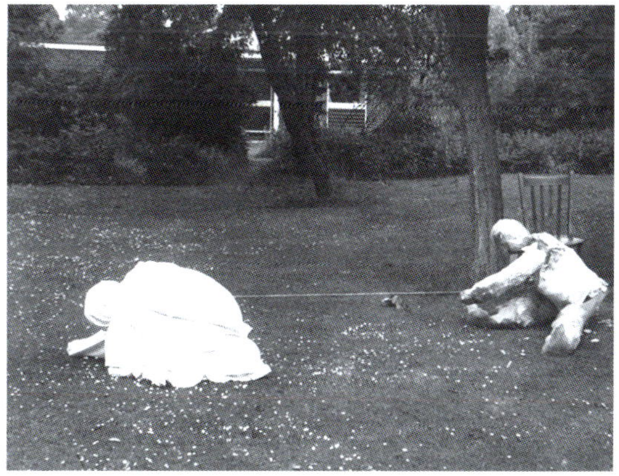

Self-Taut, Reading University 1970

I used the weight of my body, under a sheet, with a counter-balance approximately the same weight and size as me and a string taut between us. I stayed with this tension for a few hours. Photo: Graham Challifour

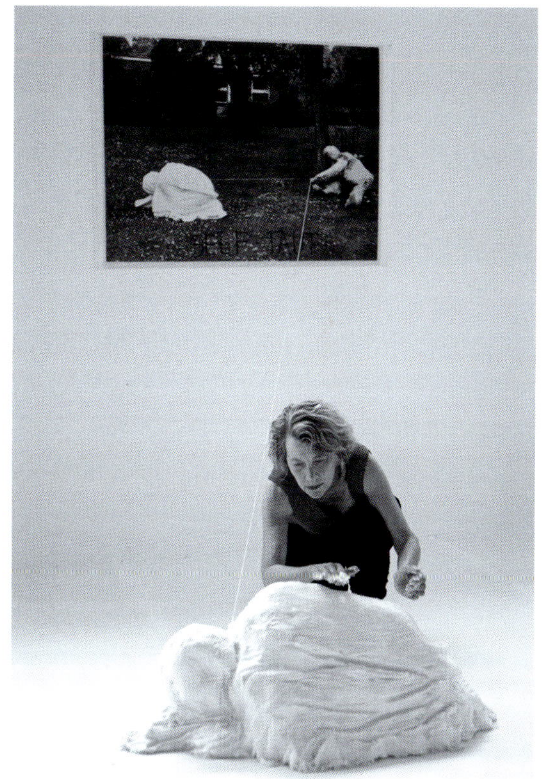

Self-Taut, Sculpture-Performance: Acme Artists Now 2014

Using the *Self-Taut* 1970 image I remade 'myself' as a sculptured crouching figure attached to the original counter balance (in the photograph), again the same weight. Photo: Nick Evans

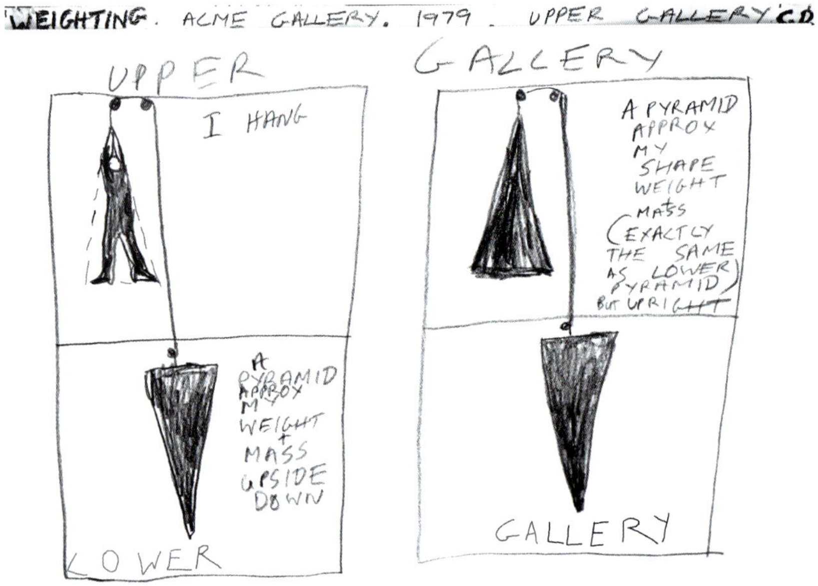

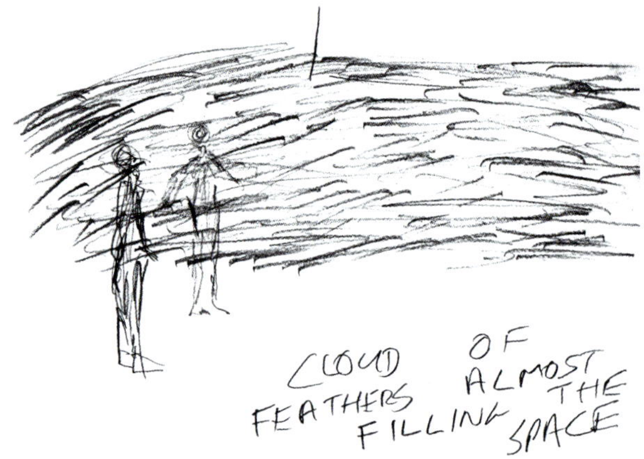

Anne Bean, idea proposals for Acme Gallery, London, 1979. Photos: Graham Challifour

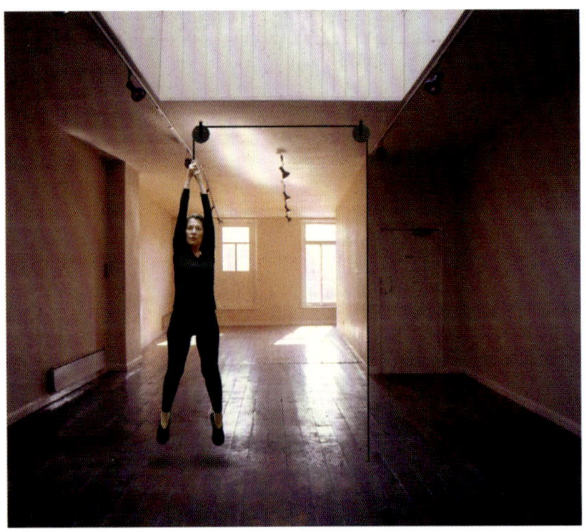

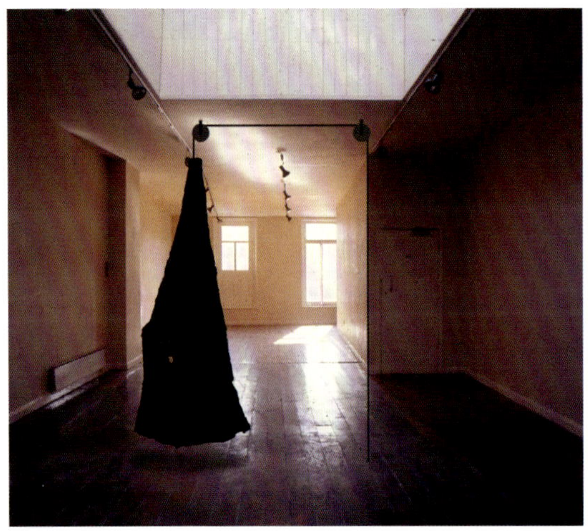

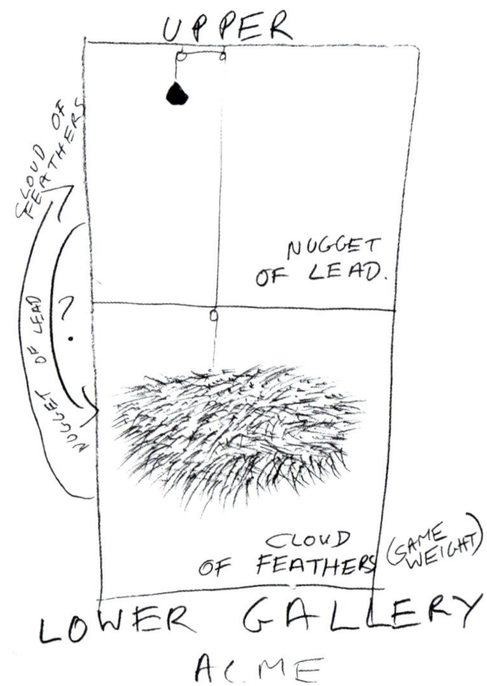

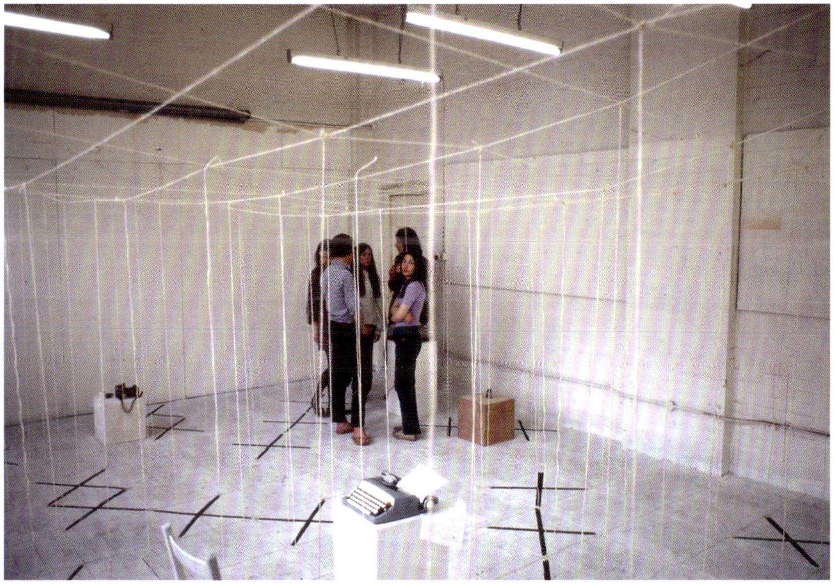

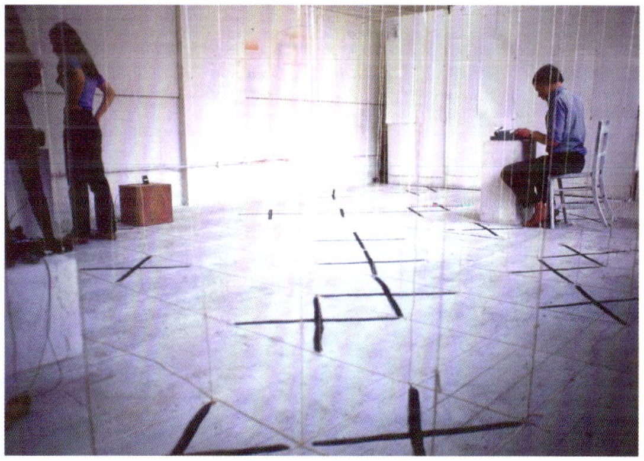

The White Room, 1970

This project was instigated by the artist/tutor Rita Donagh. It articulated and extended for me ideas of the crossover of art/life, private action/shared space, personal/global, as well as the multiple 'others' that are created through collaboration. Beginning as a life-drawing class, it evolved into a drawing-life action, as the life model became a part of the group. We devised systems and ways of operating and more-or-less lived in the space for three weeks. I suggested extending the floor grid devised by Graham Challifour, into 3 dimensions as string into the air, to cause different kinds of obstacles and strategies in the space.

Above: Rita Donagh talking with several participants including Graham Challifour and Rod Melvin. Photo: Phil Winder

Right: Other *Self-Taut* manifestations included putting tension on my lips whilst singing

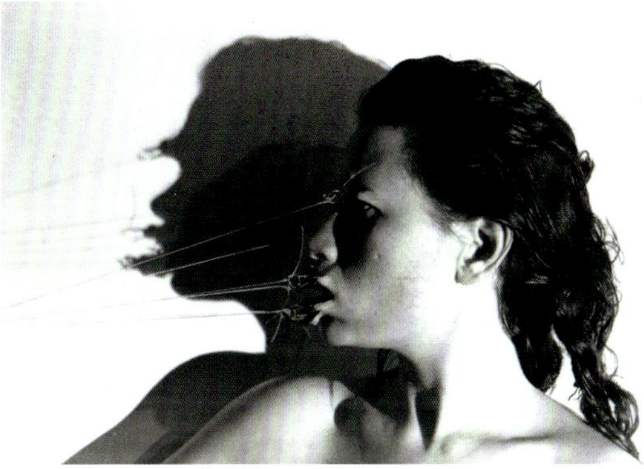

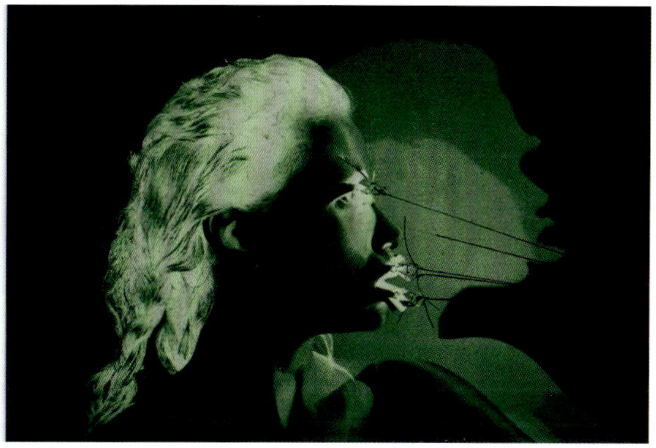

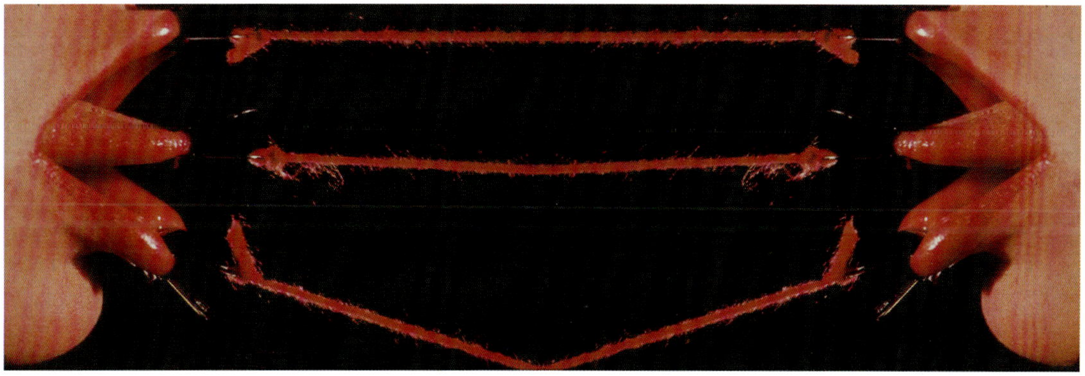

Vanishing Points, 2009

As part of PAVES I did many works about vanishing points, verbally improvising, alongside the actions, about borders and vanishings. In Staglinec, Croatia, I disappeared into the vanishing point on a railway track from Croatia walking towards Bosnia with a ball of 1 km of string held by the audience to tug me back when it was at the end. In Tel Aviv bus station, I asked people to hold the spool of ribbon, whilst I ran into the vanishing point. In the small town of Cavan, Ireland, just over the border from Northern Ireland, I invited people to tie the ends to the railings.

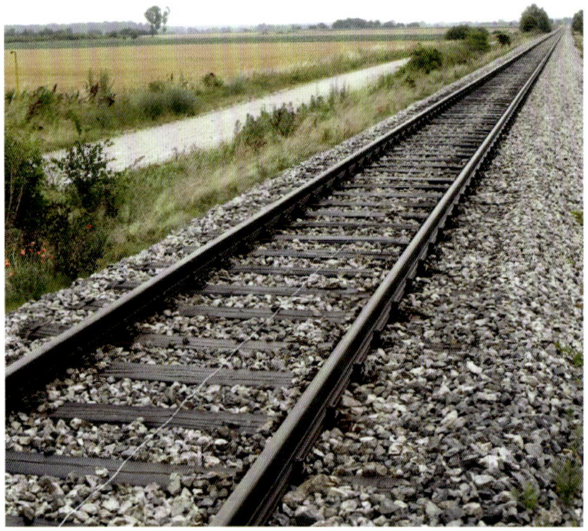

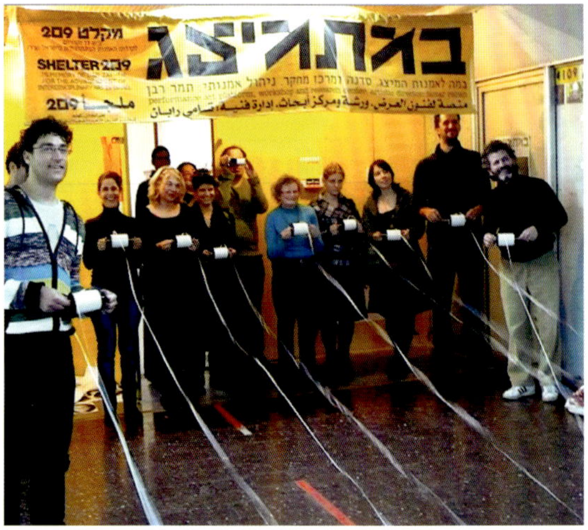

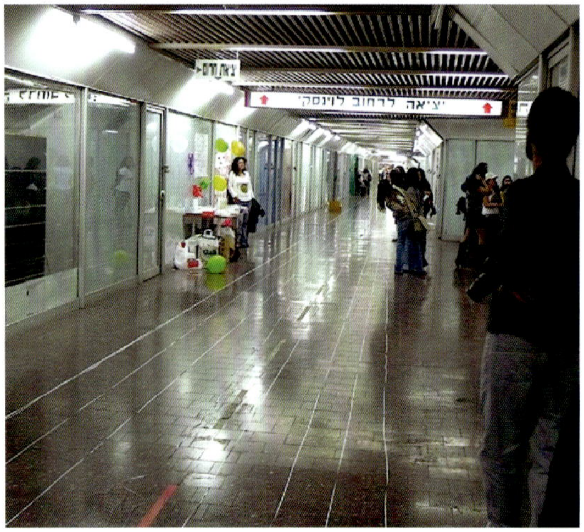

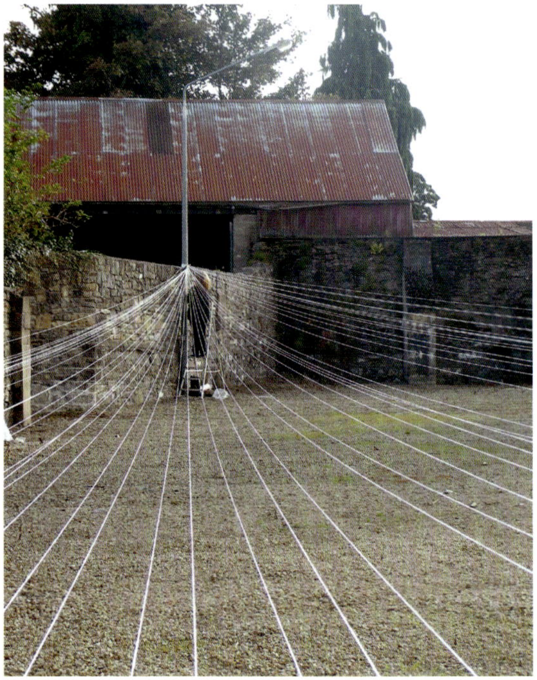

Anne Bean, *Vanishing Points*, 2009. Photos: PAVES

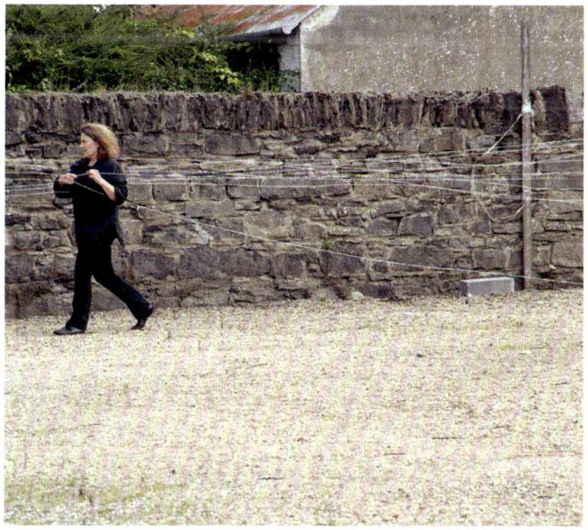

The Art of Living, 2015
Book launch, King's College Chapel

I was invited to make a performance for the launch of Dominic Johnson's book, a collection of interviews with a variety of artists involved in performance art. I made an action, simultaneously destroying and liberating the book, as I ripped arbitrary pages out, singing out their contents, making the book light enough to launch up, suspended on ribbons from helium filled balloons, to be received by the angelic chorus on the ceiling and to subsequently slowly descend once more to earth. Rod Melvin accompanied me on piano, improvising with my voice, singing out the scattered book texts, filling the chapel as the book ascended.

Top: Photo: Peter Fink
Bottom: Photo: Eoin Richford

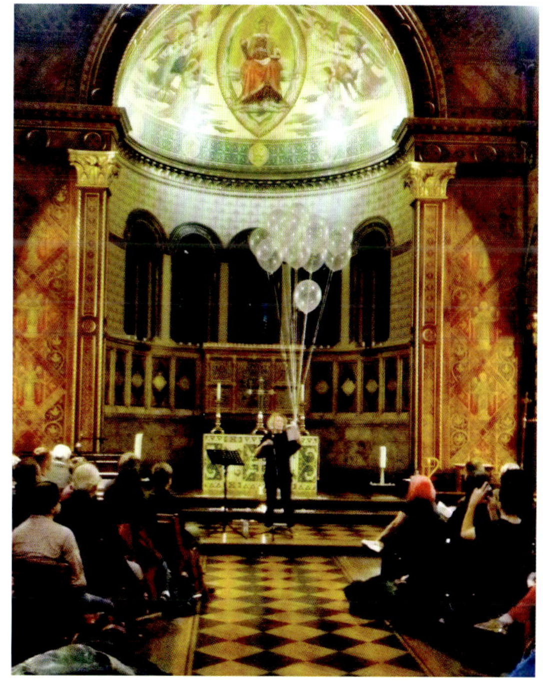

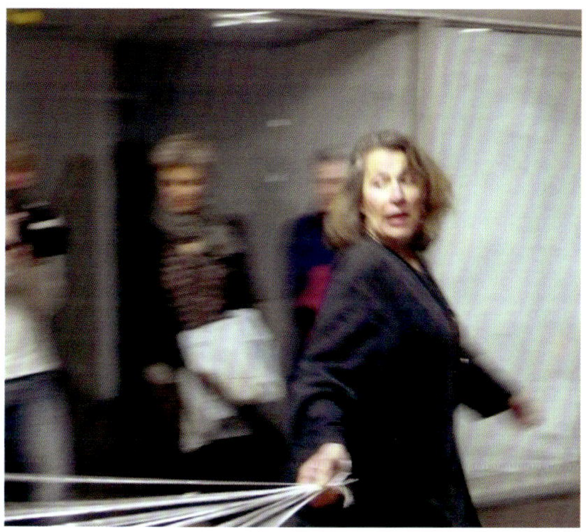

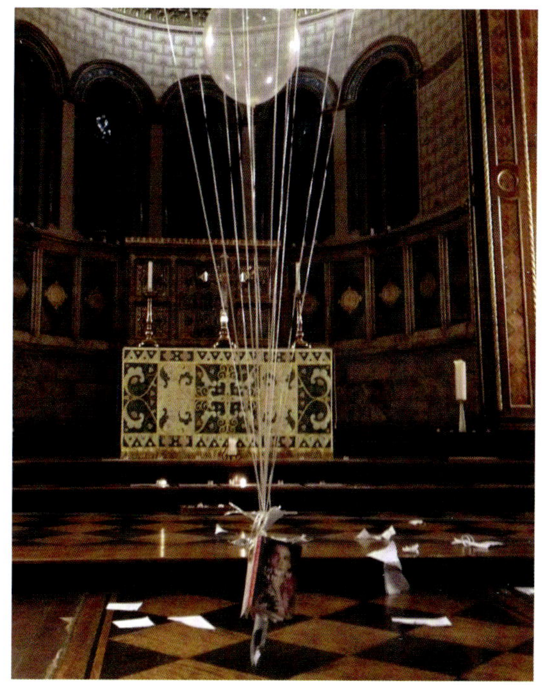

Email to Marcus Chown, Cosmology consultant for *New Scientist* Magazine, 7th Feb 2011

Hi Marcus,

...I am just embarking on a project, WAKE, that is about materials and transformations.

The press release reads:

'Anne Bean aims to liberate these exhibitions from the usual conventions of curated shows. Ignoring the traditions of themes or commissions she has instead opted for a way of interrogating materiality itself, as well as ownership, collaborative process and transmissions of ideas, towards a final outcome that is a complete unknown."

The memory came back to me from discussions we had had many years ago about how the entire human race could fit in the volume of a sugar cube because matter is so astonishingly empty. I have noticed this statement again in a couple of your books.

In your new publication, I like that you describe your book as a ghost book and us as ghosts reading it and the ground we are standing on as "more tenuous than the most tenuous morning mist.'

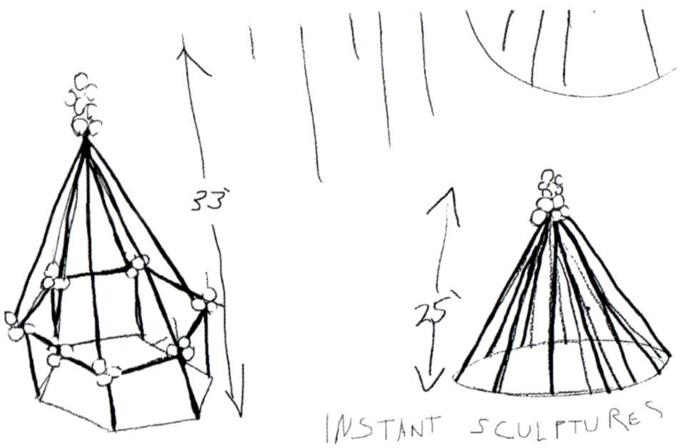

Out of Control, Ars Elecronica, Linz, 1991

The artist musicians Z'EV, Erik Hobijn and Lydia Lunch invited several artists to work on individual pieces which together would create a huge event in a vast steelwork in Linz. I made three works, the first of which was to install instant sculptures in the space made by releasing weighted down helium balloons with wide ribbons attached to suddenly appear in the space making various configurations.

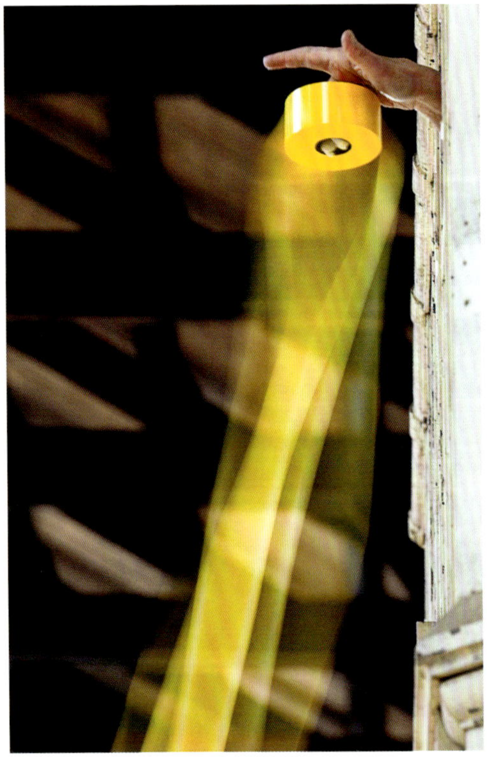

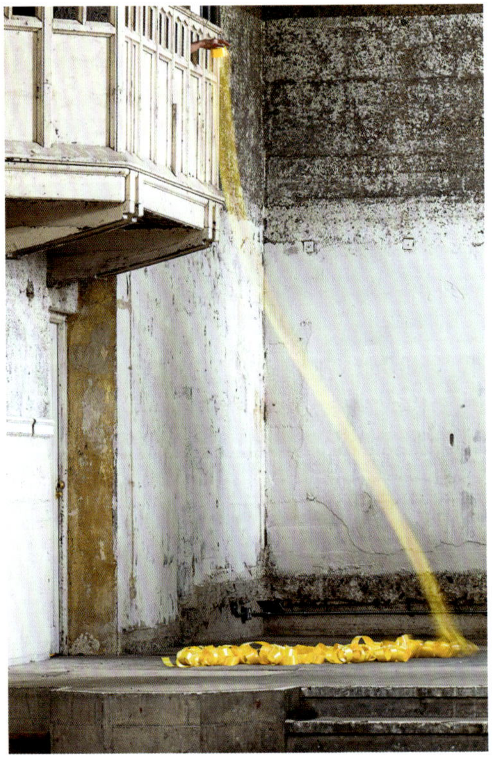

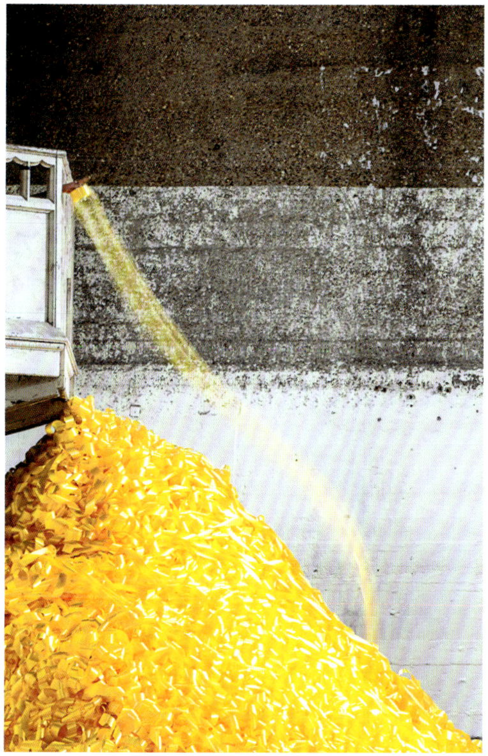

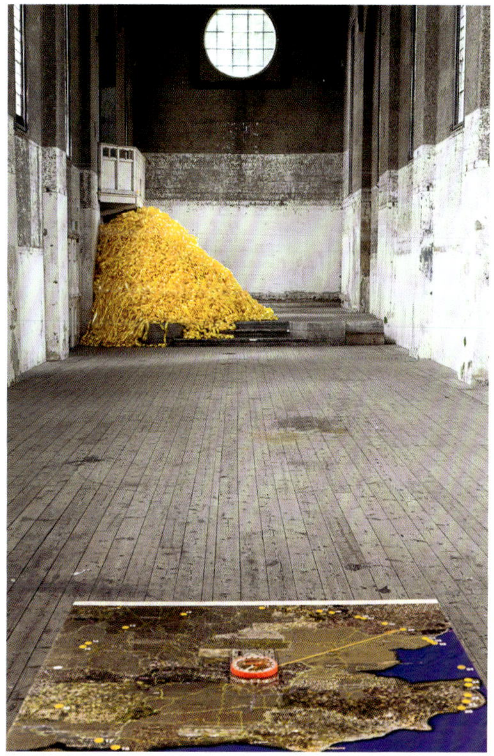

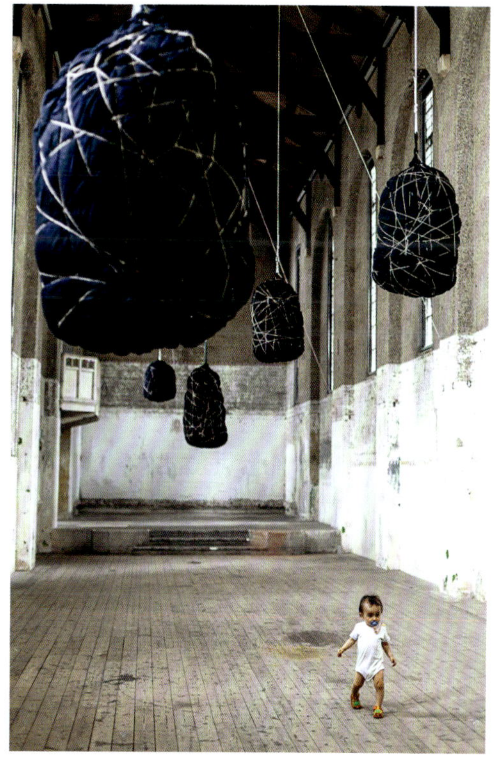

Rachel Withers, On *WAKE*, Dilston Grove, 2011

...Bean proposed that six artists develop work there sequentially, in one another's "wake", across a series of six week long residencies. Crucially, she also chose to relinquish control over the list of participants, inviting each to select his or her successor. She chose Will Cobbing to follow her own Week One project, not least, she says, because she had no idea who he would bring on board. That person turned out to be David Cotterell. Cotterell recruited Carl von Weiler. Von Weiler handed the space over to Rachel Lowe, and Lowe invited Bronwen Buckeridge to bring the project to a close. The six had just five days to realise their individual plans and one weekend to exhibit them.

Contextualising the slow unfurling of hundred kilometres of shining golden gift-wrapping ribbon..., Anne Bean's simple, mesmerising two-day-long performance poetically translated "Planet Dilston's" terrestrial location into an episode in time...

Carl von Weiler wrestled the ribbon into five capacious black sacks, and hoisted them into the air. Dangling from the roof on ropes tethered to the walls, the lumpy, pendulous, boulder-like sacks infused the space with powerful feelings of tension and suspense — even a hint of threat.

Photos: Hydar Dewachi

McCracken is Flying South,
Kitchen Gallery, New York, 1978

Extract from the Kitchen Gallery publicity:

I worked with John McKeon, violinist, poet, playwright, novelist, painter on several works, trying to untangle where our very different sensibilities 'crossed over' to forge a production that could accommodate both.

His subtitle: A laugh a minute

Her subtitle: A painting in several acts

...He thinks they're experimenting with a risky, decadent, gutsy entertaining lie. She thinks they're experimenting with a wholesome, courageous, paradoxical, entertaining truth... He accepts the human lot as a delightful but hopeless joke. She is totally without cynicism...

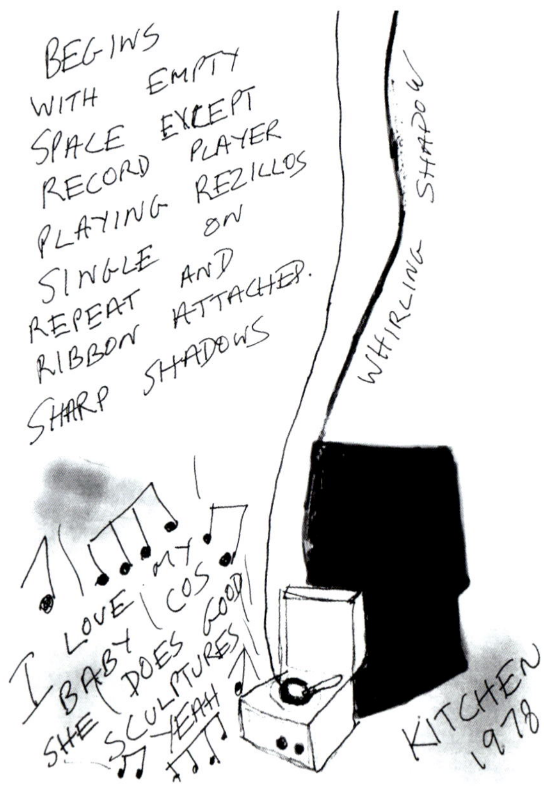

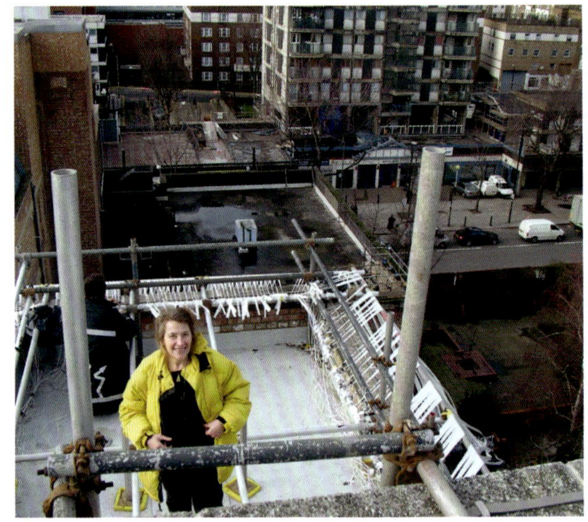

Toynbee Studios Launch Event, 2007

I used the imagery and symbolism of cutting ribbon to create an installation that then became a celebratory event. I installed, with the pyrotechnicians and artists Nick Sales and Mark Anderson, over 100 ribbons of 100 metres, each with an electrically detonated explosive charge to ignite and cut through them to finally release the new building. During the days before the event, the ribbons acted as a gigantic aeolian harp, playing mysterious hummings and throbbings in the wind.

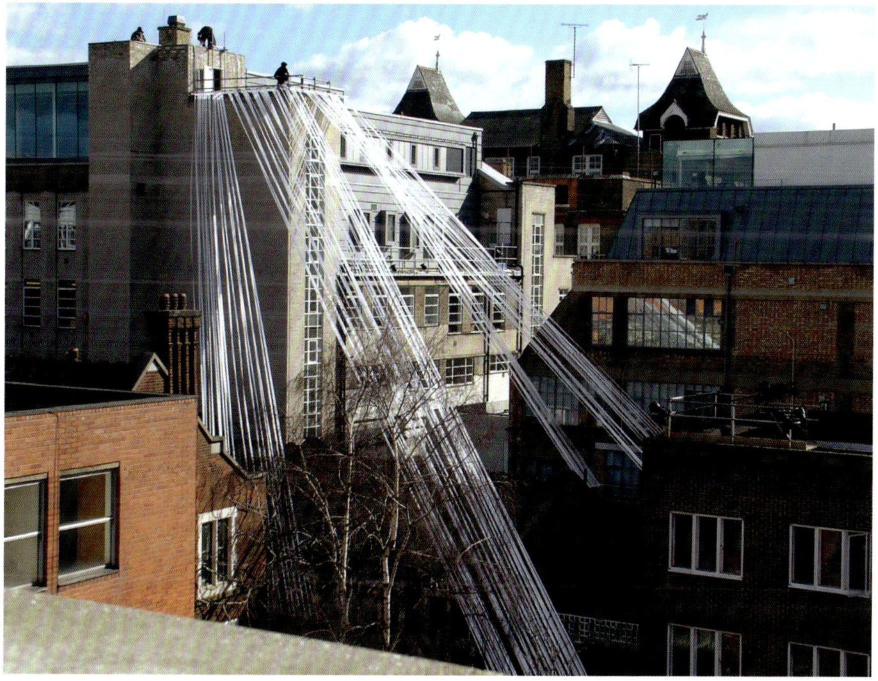

Below: Artists Airshow, 2004, commissioned by The Arts Catalyst

Airshow used the deserted research facility and airfields, Farnborough, Europe's largest wind tunnel, where supersonic flight was developed and the ghosts of sixties rocket projects linger.

I asked Mark Anderson and Nick Sales, to work with me to find ways to adapt parachute rockets to be able to carry into the sky 100 metres of ribbon attached to each. One hundred rockets were launched and the 10,000 metres of ribbon danced between sparks and smoke trails for several minutes, until the ribbons gently drifted to earth.

Photos: courtesy The Art Catalyst

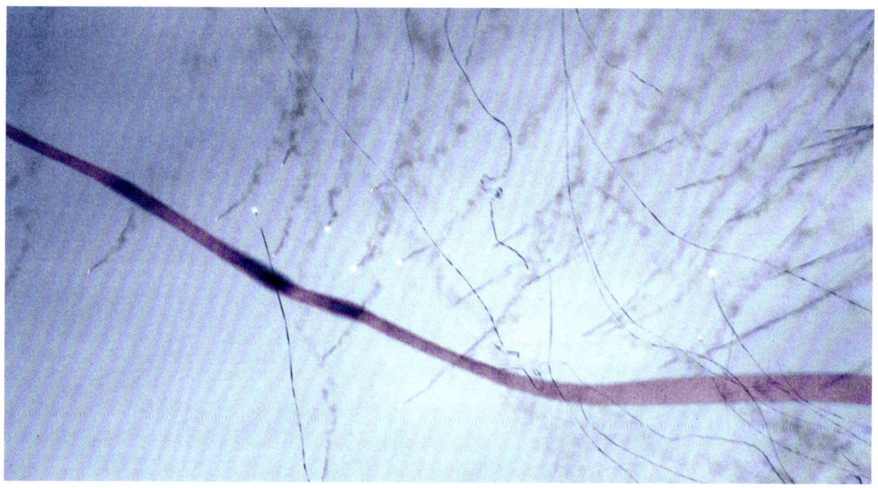

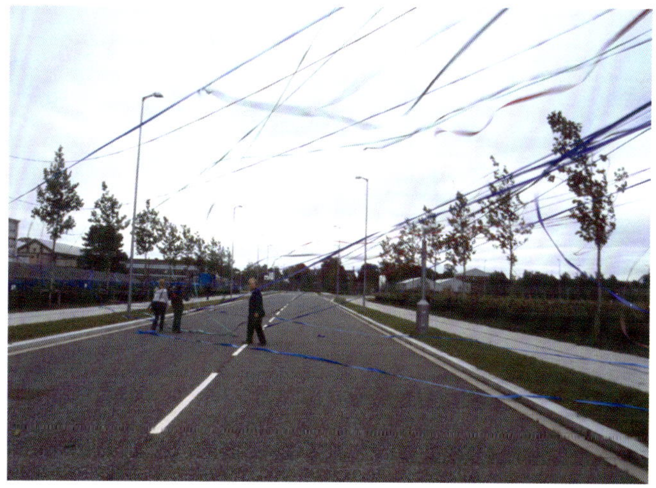

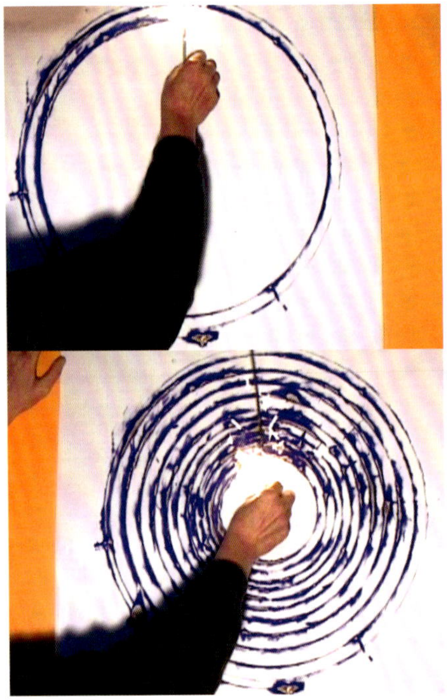

Above: A spiralling line, sparkler drawing on thermally responsive paper.
Stills from *Five Drawings* shown at Royal Academy Summer Show 2009

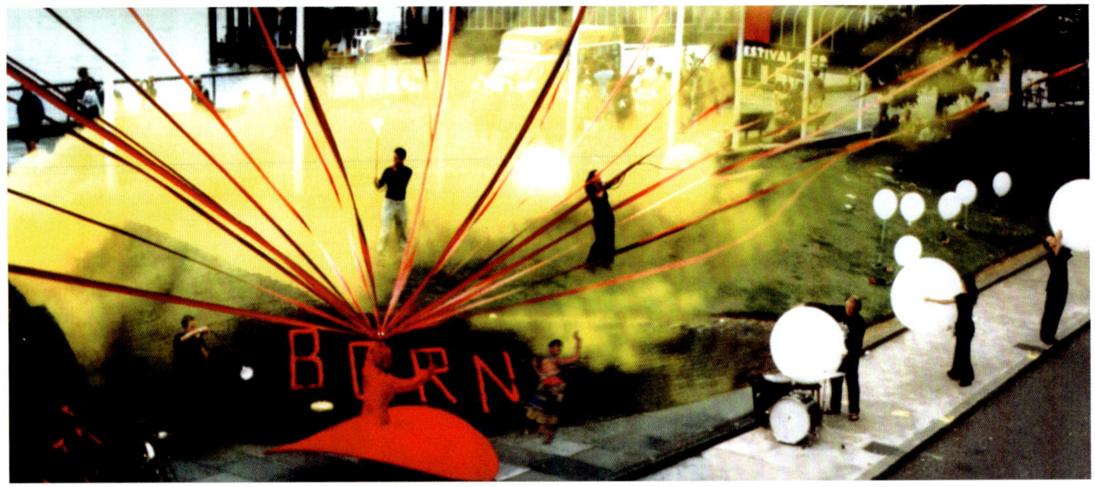

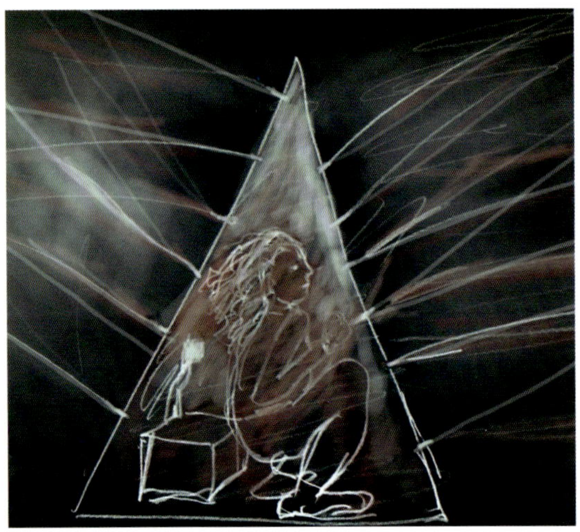

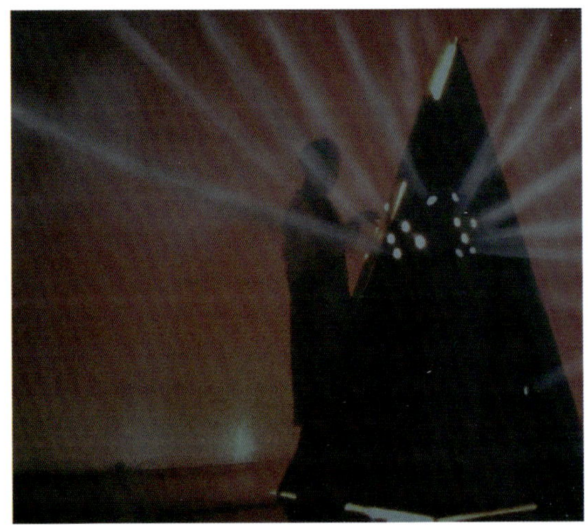

Right: Double Being,1985

I made numerous works with Giles Thomas in Butlers Wharf 1977-1979. For a couple of years we made improvised works, both sound and visually based, often daily and non-audience based. I sometimes used motorised tools to make visual and aural interventions, with Giles on guitar or other instruments. At the Zap Club I had a bright spotlight and a wallpaper steam remover machine creating plumes of steam inside an enclosed pyramid so that as I drilled solid lines of light and plumes of steam shot-out into the space.

Left: Air Born, South Bank, 1998

In *Air Born* the rhythms from the bells of dancer, Swarup Menon and drummers of Bharat Natyam style intersected with the drones accompanying a whirling dervish dancer, Charlie Morrissey, continuously twirling with red ribbons attached to his head, on a joint clamp, which originated from many of the poles and balconies around the South Bank. The animated ribbons gave a huge breadth to the event drawing the surrounding architectural space, the river, the bridges and the audience into the whirling centre of the performance. Photo: Peter Fink

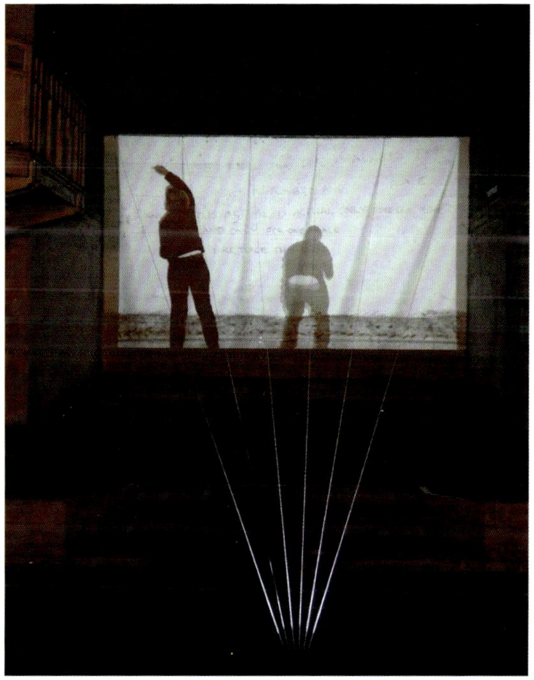

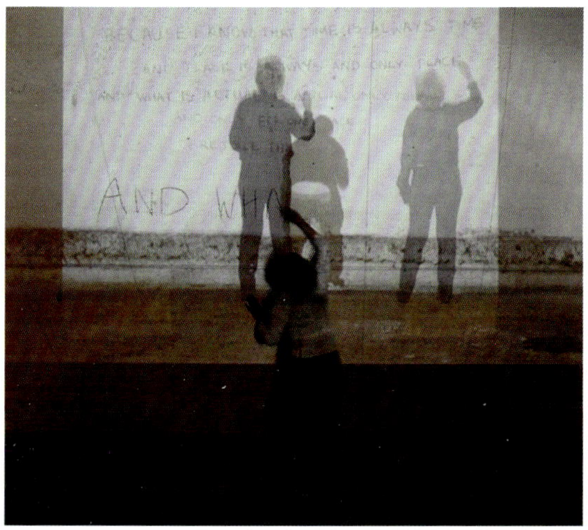

Left: Retracing, Decade, Dilston Grove, 2015

Yearnings was a solo performance of mine shown only to five artists Lucy Cash, Holly Darton, Meg Mosley, Miyako Narita, and Lucille Power in the Scout Hut on the edge of Southwark Park in September 2004. No documentation was permitted to ensure the original event existed only as an 'electro-chemical trace' within the consciousness of each artist. Exactly a year later, this memory was publicly revealed by each artist, performing her own memory in all of the mutations, fragilities and uneasiness of recall.

Ten years' later, I asked these same five artists, to take this shared memory as a launch for individual works to be woven together. This experiment in 'carrying' the 'electro-chemical trace' was even more resonant a decade later. The artists each produced a new video from fragments of memory. In a live opening performance all together, the artists created shadows that worked with the projection as well as creating layers of interactions. During the opening performance, I put strings from the projector to the screen to produce shadows and play of light that worked with the imagery in the edited collaborative film that then remained throughout the installation.

Photos: Miyako Narita

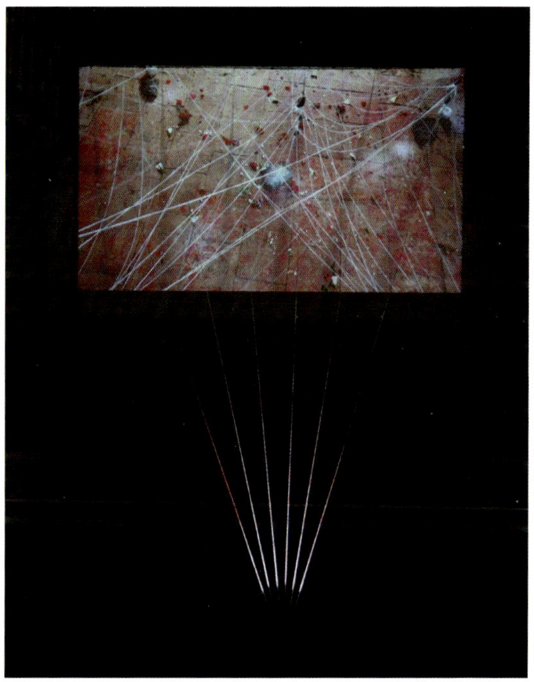

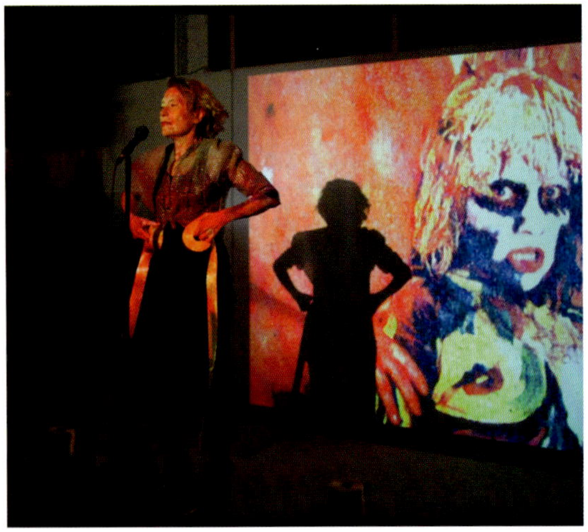

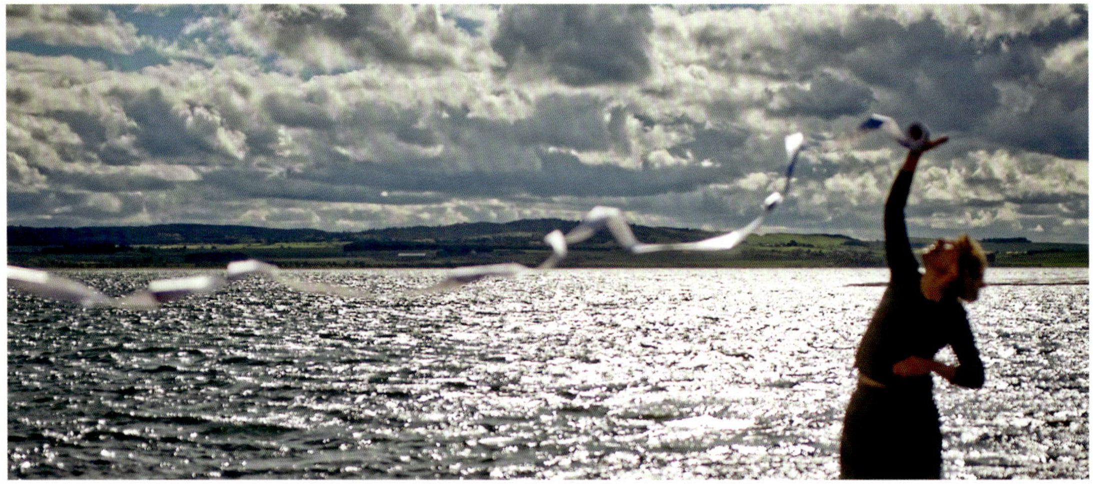

WILD THINGymajik, Matts Gallery, 2014

The whirling sound of unfurling ribbons conjure up my younger demonic self. Photo: Dafydd Jones.

Holy Island, 2015

On the summer solstice, 2015, I organised a trip to Holy Island with the artists Shaun Caton, Brian Gilson, Sinead O'Donnell and Yol. Our mutual friend, the artist, Sue Arrowsmith (1950-2014) had always wanted to visit Holy island, so we decided to bring her ashes there and make a ritual piece together. I wrote the words from her writings onto ribbon and let them fly in the air. This led to me to using her words on ribbon flying over the Thames where we had often beach-combed together, in a work with Manuel Vason. Later, in 2017 in Hull, where she died, I did a work again incanting her words with Yol, whilst Ansuman Biswas and Richard Wilson drummed. Photos top: Julius Beltrame Right: Manuel Vason

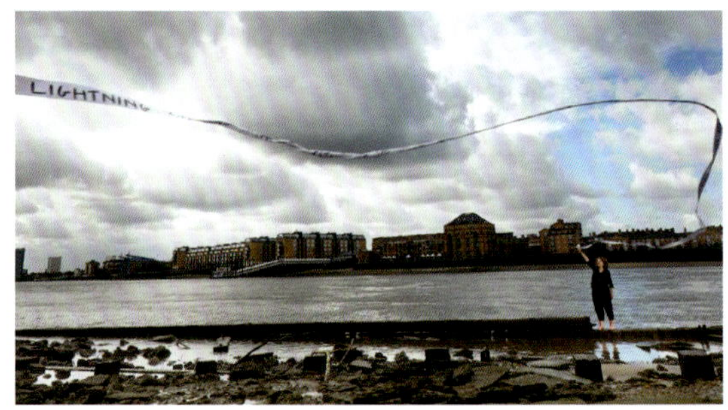

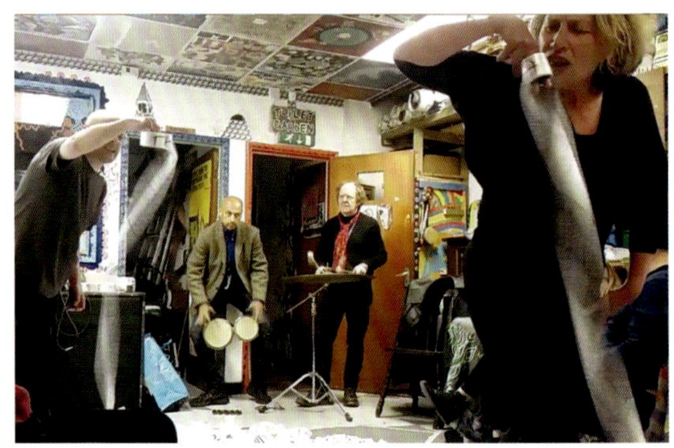

Right: *Zero Degrees*

In 1992 I conceived the idea of a laser originating at the Greenwich Observatory designating the meridian line which crosses the Thames three times. I worked with artist Peter Fink, to realise the project and the laser was switched on with a huge event of numerous vessels, over 100 musicians, projections, the Thames fire brigade boat with spraying hoses and a lightning machine used in feature films to simulate storms, as well as a remote control model helicopter spewing smoke into the laser. The projection surfaces included the power station façade on the South Bank, the fine spray from the fireboat and the sails of yachts from the Greenwich sailing club. There were several other barges with various events including one with 20' high poles covered in paraffinned cloth set alight as it floated across. The laser has become a permanent installation. Photo: Sagerhead

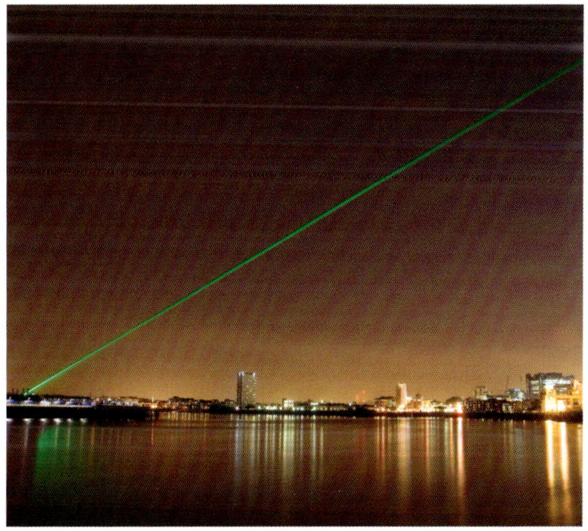

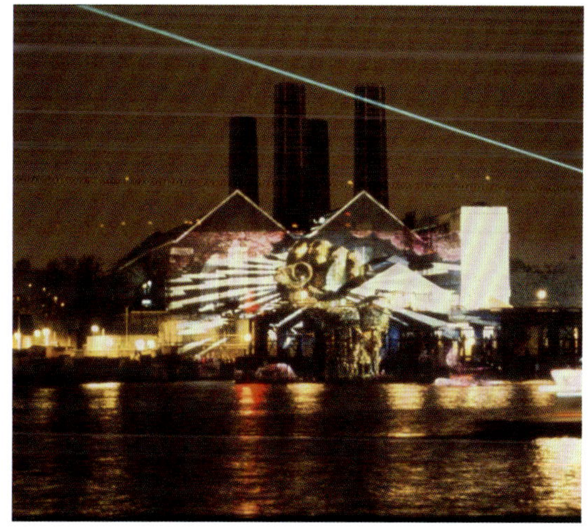

Right: Regarding the Pain of Others, Image by Meg Mosley 2009

Below: Stills from Video *Song with Sue*, Hull 2017

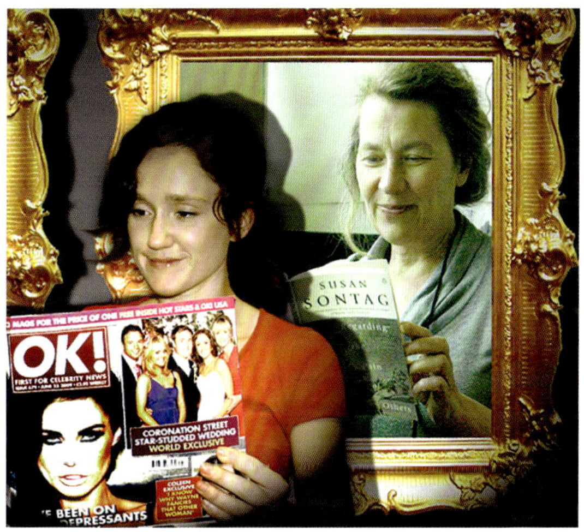

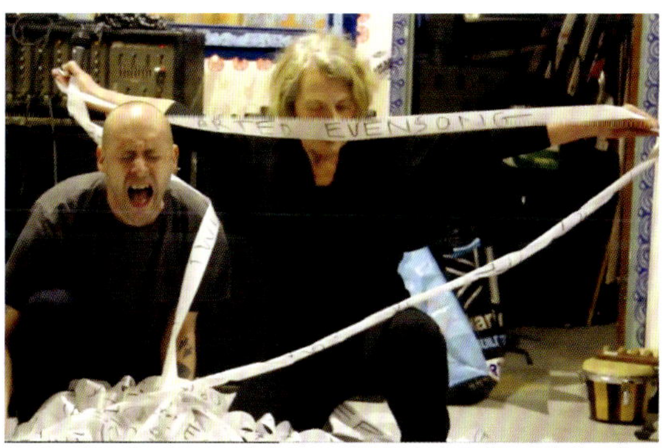

Left: *The Worms*

In a solution known to string theory as a wormhole, two points in space-time could be connected by a shortened path. In some special cases, a wormhole may actually allow for time travel. Instead of connecting different regions of space, the wormhole could connect different regions of time. Calling ourselves 'The Worms,' the artist Meg Mosley and myself have explored these potential connections on several occasions, including during *Notes on a Return*, Laing Gallery, 2009, Regarding the Pain of Others, as a part of my work *Pain tings* and during my time at MoCa Trowbridge and Meg's *Trow Vegas*, her home town. In 2018, MoCa Trowbridge was the gathering point and first stop for the Megastar guided tour of *Trow Vegas*, when we both again leapt through the looking glass.

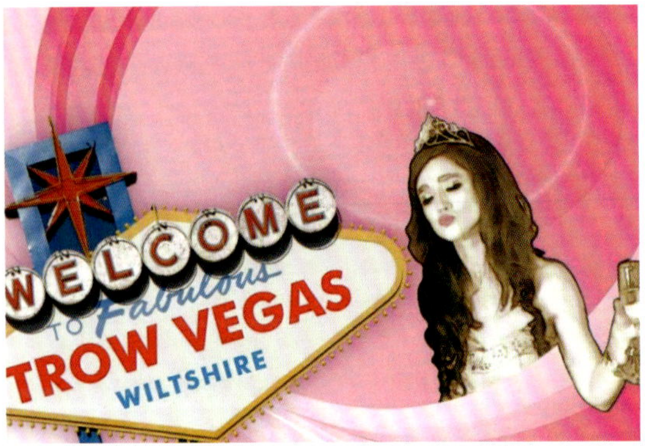

The writer Mark Pearce wrote of the Trowbridge/*Trow Vegas* event *MoCa to Mega*:

A tour of the town, with much mirth and offbeat humour brought the place to life, awaking old ghosts perhaps, mimicking the spirit of a circus troupe, peculiarly cinematic and theatrical.

There was an exciting feeling of chance, improvisation, connections and new possibilities which bubbled fiercely and brightly for all of us.

On Feb 27th in email response to Rob LF asking how *MoCa to Mega* had gone, I wrote:

...forces fizzed and worlds whirled – I leapt through the looking glass and a great venture unfurled with multiple local interventions including digital shop signs programmed to say 'VIVA Trow Vegas'.

The 'show girl' (in sequinned union jack costume – totally incredible performance) left saying 'Now all you artists don't rack your brains what it's all about'and so we won't.

Top: Trow Vegas poster by Meg Mosley
Right: Photos by Lucy Rose Tindal and Jane England

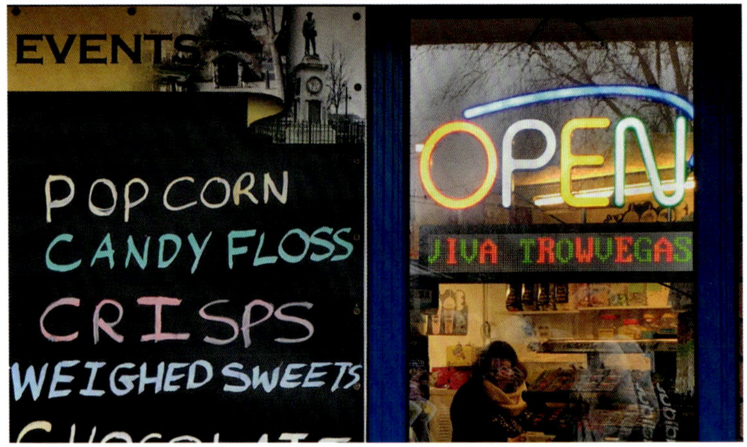

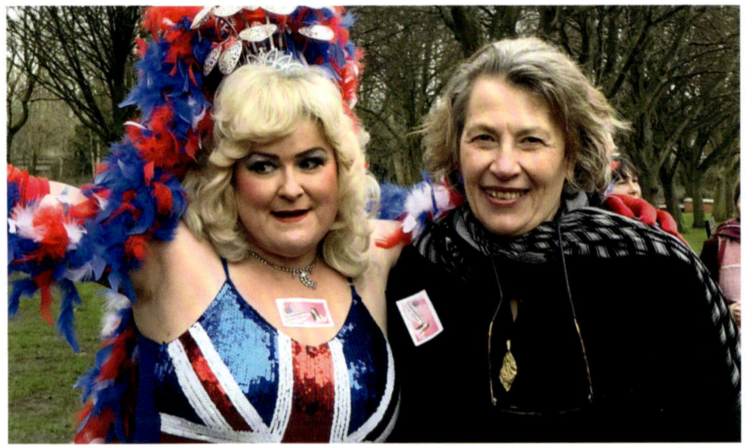

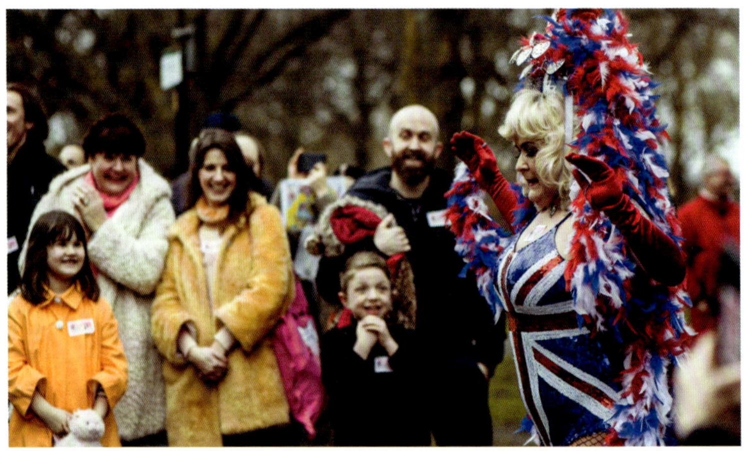

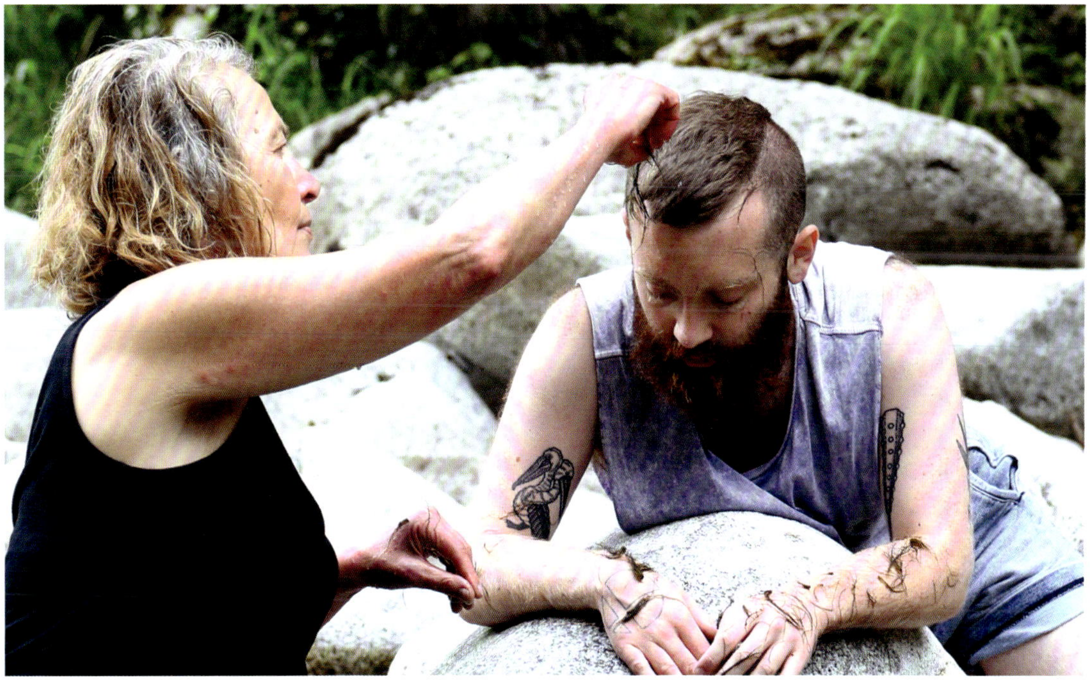

A River Yarn, 2018

A work in collaboration with artist Conor Baird, mingling textural land and bodyscapes at CAMP, a revolutionary arts centre, in the French Pyrenees. Photos: Sarah Faraday at CAMP.

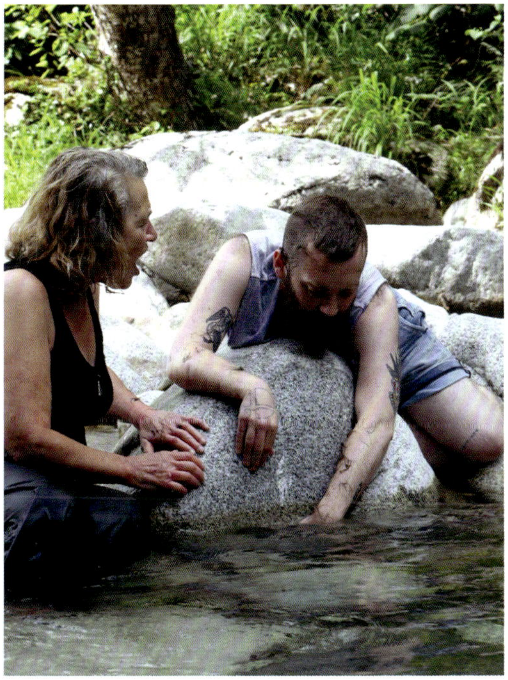

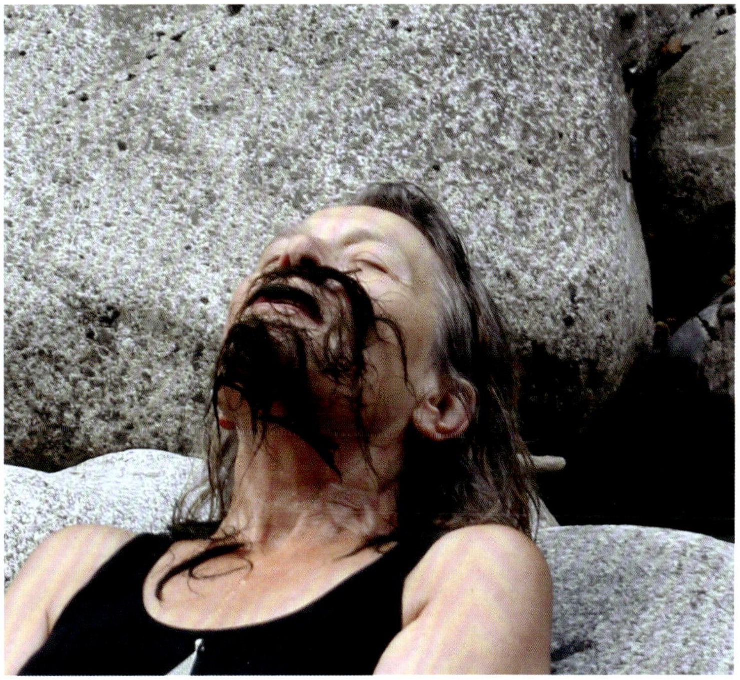

CONTRIBUTOR BIOGRAPHIES

Guy Brett is a London-based art critic, curator and lecturer on art. His books include *Kinetic Art: the Language of movement* (1968), *Through Our Own Eyes: Popular Art and Modern History* (1986), *Transcontinental* (1990), *Exploding Galaxies: The Art of David Medalla* (1995), *Mona Hatoum* (1997) and *Li Yuan-chia: Tell me what is not yet said* (2001). Brett was the art critic for *The Times* newspaper from 1964-75; and Visual Arts Editor of *City Limits* from 1981-83. He has written for *Art in America*, *Artforum*, *Art & Text*, *Third Text*, *Studio International*, *Signals*, *Artscribe*, *Art Monthly*, *Black Phoenix*, *Performance Magazine*, *Parkett* and others, and has published essays in numerous books and exhibition catalogues. He has curated influential exhibitions such as *In Motion*, an international exhibition of kinetic art for the Arts Council of Great Britain (1966); and *Force Fields: Phases of the Kinetic* for MACBA in Barcelona and the Hayward Gallery in London (2001).

David Caines is a graphic designer and visual artist based in London. Other books he has designed include *Kira O'Reilly: Untitled (Bodies)* (2017), *People Show: Nobody Knows but Everybody Remembers* (2016), *The Only Way Home Is Through the Show: Peformance Work of Lois Weaver* (2015), and *Out of Now: The Lifeworks of Tehching Hsieh* (2009/2015). David also makes paintings and in 2015 was shortlisted for the East London Painting Prize. www.davidcaines.co.uk

Poshya Kakl was born in Erbil, Iraqi Kurdistan in 1989. She received a BA from the College of Fine Art, Erbil in 2012; and a MA in Architecture at Marywood University, PA in 2016. Her work has been shown internationally, including *Caution* with Sinéad O'Donnell at Southbank Centre, London, and Golden Thread Gallery, Belfast in 2012; and a solo exhibition *The Shadow of ISIS* in Scranton, PA. Kakl is a member of the art-collaborative project PAVES, who have exhibited in UK, Croatia, Israel, Canada, Taiwan, Germany and Iraqi Kurdistan since 2008. Kakl's collaborations with Anne Bean include *The Un-knitted Lives of Young Girls*, BE Festival, 2011; *Sacred Places: Performances, Politics and Ecologies*, Liverpool Hope University, 2017; and *Two Nineteen-Year-Old Girls*, Phoenix Brighton, 2018. Kakl received the Artiste International Award for *Tawa Malak: Peacock Angel*, her contribution to the juried exhibition *Transformation* at Gallery MC, New York, 2017. A DVD anthology of her works, *Knitting Iron* was published by Live Art Development Agency in 2012.

Dominic Johnson is a Reader in Performance and Visual Culture in the School of English and Drama, at Queen Mary University of London. He is the author of *Glorious Catastrophe: Jack Smith, Performance and Visual Culture* (2012); *Theatre & the Visual* (2012); *The Art of Living: An Oral History of Performance Art* (2015); and *Unlimited Action: The Performance of Extremity in the 1970s* (2018). He is the editor of five books, including most recently *Pleading in the Blood: The Art and Performances of Ron Athey* (2013); and *It's All Allowed: The Performances of Adrian Howells* (with Deirdre Heddon, 2016). He is a co-editor (with Lois Keidan and CJ Mitchell) of the book series *Intellect Live* and serves on the Board of Directors of the Live Art Development Agency.

Rose Fenton is a founding director of the LIFT Festival (1981-2005) and co-author (with Lucy Neal) of *The Turning World: Stories from the London International Festival of Theatre* (2005). She was the director of Freeword (2011-2016), an international centre for literature, literacy and free expression, exploring and celebrating the power of words to change lives. She continues to work internationally and is currently researching a book about an evolving Europe. She serves on the board of Airwaves/Dance Across Europe.

Rob La Frenais is a curator and critic who has worked in the arts since 1972. He received a PhD from Brunel University and an Honorary Doctorate from Dartington College of Arts. He was a member of the Action Space arts group from 1972-78. Between 1979-1987 he founded and edited *Performance Magazine*, which published exclusive interviews with Joseph Beuys, John Cage, Robert Wilson, Laurie Anderson, Yoko Ono and Marina Abramović among many others. He has curated a number of projects with Anne Bean, both as an independent curator and The Arts Catalyst, where he was curator from 1997-2014, as well as collaborating with her on performances. His recent curated exhibitions have taken place in El Paso and White Sands New Mexico, Liverpool, France, Dundee and Taiwan. He is a regular contributor to *Art Monthly* and *Makery.info*, France and is a member of the Association of International Critics of Art. He is also a single-scull rower. www.roblafrenais.info

Lynn MacRitchie is an artist and writer based in London. Born in Glasgow, she studied art history at Edinburgh University and drawing and painting at Edinburgh College of Art. As a student, she attended Joseph Beuys' famous lectures in Edinburgh and organized the controversial Participation Art Event at Edinburgh College of Art, featuring the Artists Placement Group and David Medalla. Moving to London, she became a founder member of the Poster Film Collective and of Artists for Democracy. After completing a post-graduate degree in architectural studies at University College, London, she became a writer, contributing to many art magazines including editing *Performance Magazine*. As a business journalist she worked for Financial Times Business Publishing before becoming a regular contributor on contemporary art for the *Financial Times* newspaper. She returned to art making in the late 1990s. www.lynnmacritchie.com

Lucy Neal is a theatre maker and writer, a founding director of the LIFT Festival (1981-2005), and co-author (with Rose Fenton) of *The Turning World: Stories from the London International Festival of Theatre* (2005). She is the author of *Playing for Time: Making Art As If The World Mattered* (2015), which maps emergent arts practices responding to planetary challenges. She is Creative Associate of Devon-based Encounters, Happiness Associate of the Happy Museum, and a Trustee of the Aluna Foundation.

Ezra Rubenstein was involved in a number of Anne Bean's projects as a young writer, including *Seaclipse*, *An Angel Called Gravity*, *Radiant Fields*, *TAPS*, and most recently at the ICA, London as part of Bean's Stanley Picker Lecture in 2017. He studied Mathematics and Philosophy at Oxford University and is currently working towards a PhD in Philosophy at Rutgers University, with a focus on the interpretation of Quantum Mechanics.

Richard Wilson is one of Britain's most renowned sculptors. His seminal installation *20:50* (1987), a sea of reflective sump oil, is permanently installed in the Saatchi Collection. He has exhibited widely for over thirty years and has made major museum exhibitions and public works in Japan, USA, Brazil, Mexico, Russia, Australia and throughout Europe. Wilson represented Britain in the Sydney, Sao Paulo and Venice Biennials and the Yokohama and Echigo-Tsumari Art Triennials, Japan; he was nominated for the Turner Prize on two occasions; and was awarded the prestigious DAAD residency in Berlin. Major recent works include *Turning the Place Over* at Liverpool's European Capital of Culture 2008; *The Italian Job* as part of his regional cultural Olympic exhibition at the De La Warr Pavilion, Bexhill in 2012; and a major commission for Heathrow's Terminal 2 in 2014. In 2006, he was elected as a member of the Royal Academy and in 2008 was awarded an Honorary Doctorate by University of Middlesex. He is a Visiting Research Professor at the University of East London, and Honorary Professor of Sculpture at the Royal Academy Schools, London.

ACKNOWLEDGEMENTS

Anne Bean My special thanks for the long haul with *Self Etc.* go to Rob La Frenais, Dominic Johnson, David Caines, Lois Keidan, CJ Mitchell, and Jane England. I deeply appreciate the generosity shown by the writers of the essays and shorter texts, including Rob and Dominic, as well as Guy Brett, Poshya Kakl, Lynn MacRitchie, Rev. Nagase, Lucy Neal and Rose Fenton, Mark Pearce, Ezra Rubenstein, and Zack Simpila, who enabled these ciphers to emerge between us:

ERASING IMPOSSIBLE POSSESSED UN-ASK
ENTANGLED BATTERY REFLECT
MEMENTO PORTRAITS LINES TODAY
THRESHOLD LIVING DISBELIEF

I recognise, in everyone who appears in this book, that our shared lives at various junctures, from momentary to life-long, have shifted parameters and amplified perspectives for me. Thank you all. I would also like to warmly acknowledge the support and vision of several organisations, including Artsadmin, Arts Catalyst, Artrole, CGP London: Dilston Grove, Coleman Project Space, Cooper Gallery, England & Co, Franklin Furnace, LIFT, Live Art Development Agency, and Matt's Gallery.

Rob La Frenais I'd like to thank Anne Bean and Live Art Development Agency (Lois Keidan, CJ Mitchell and their colleagues) for inviting me to edit and write for this book; and Dominic Johnson for his editorial guidance. I'd like to thank Sophia Yadong Hao for inadvertently starting me on this journey. I would like to thank all the writers and artists and friends of Anne involved in this process, particularly Richard Wilson for his time and energy in undertaking the interviews and reminiscing about Paul Burwell and days past. I'd like to thank Lynn MacRitchie for coming back into the fray many years since we last worked together. Finally, I thank Anne Bean for forcing me to shed my skin as a curator and writer and become a performance artist for a day or two.

'The finished work is... a lie.' – Theodor W. Adorno

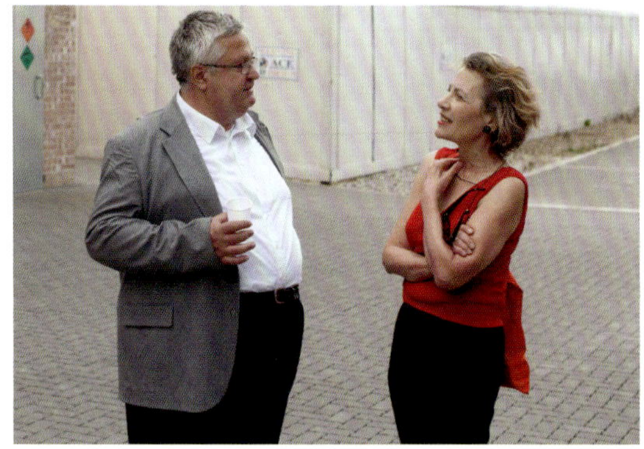

My friend, Dr Thomas Frangenberg, (1957–2018), the Renaissance art historian and collector of contemporary art, died before this book was completed. He was excited that it was happening.

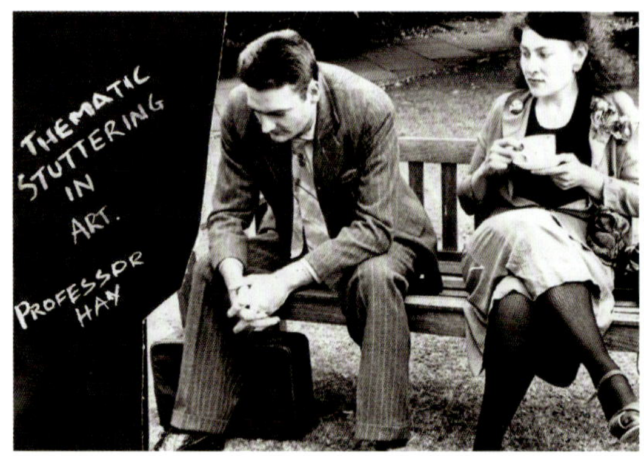

In the 70's, Brian Routh aka Harry Kipper (1948–2018) and I did several performances together as Prof Hay and his wife, giving lectures on 'Thematic Stuttering in Art.' On the day Brian died I went past some graffiti saying 'Everyone dies but not everyone lives'. He lived.

First published in the UK in 2018 by

Live Art Development Agency
The Garrett Centre
117 Mansford Street
London, E2 6LX, UK
www.thisisLiveArt.co.uk

and

Intellect, The Mill, Parnall Road,
Fishponds, Bristol, BS16 3JG, UK
www.intellectbooks.com

First published in the USA in 2018 by

Intellect, The University of Chicago Press,
1427 E. 60th Street, Chicago, IL 60637, USA

Edited by Rob La Frenais, 2018

Front cover image: Anne Bean, *Self Etc.*, 2017
Photos: Hugo Glendinning

Designed by David Caines Unlimited
www.davidcaines.co.uk

Printed and bound by Gomer Press, UK

ISBN 978-1-78320-946-0

ePDF ISBN 978-1-78320-947-7

epub ISBN 978-1-78320-980-4

A catalogue record for this book is available from the British Library.

INTELLECT LIVE

Anne Bean: Self Etc. is part of Intellect Live – a series of publications on influential artists working at the edges of performance. Intellect Live is a collaboration between Intellect Books and the Live Art Development Agency. The series is characterised by lavishly illustrated and beautifully designed books, each of which is the first substantial publication dedicated to an artist's work.

Series Editors: Dominic Johnson, Lois Keidan and CJ Mitchell

ISSN 2052-0913

Live Art Development Agency

intellect live

intellect
publishers of original thinking

LOTTERY FUNDED

Supported using public funding by
ARTS COUNCIL ENGLAND

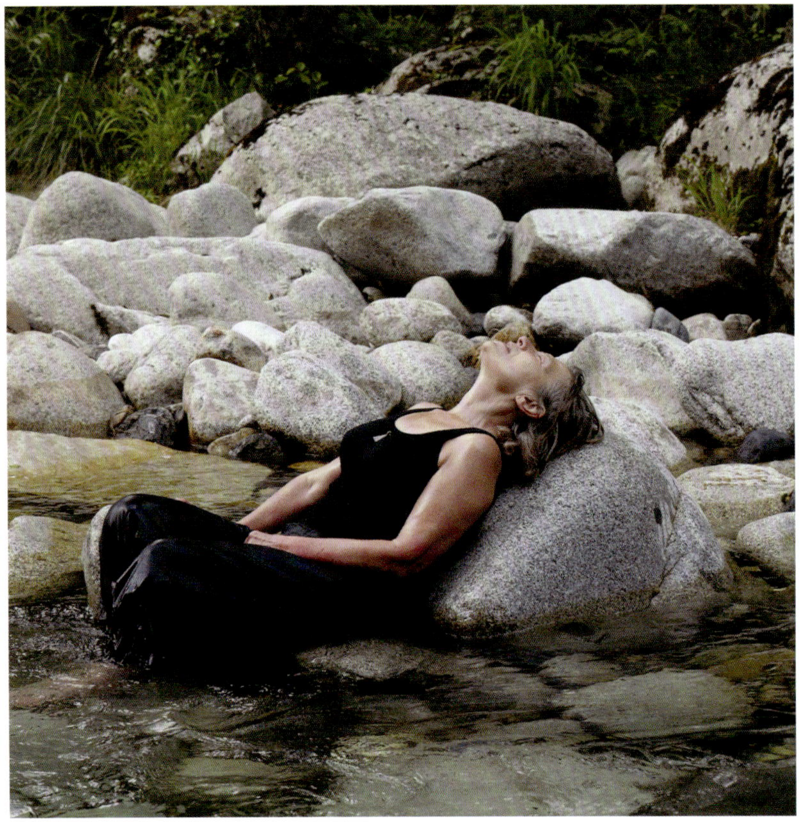

Photo: Sarah Faraday at CAMP, Pyrenees

Page 336: Same River, A work in collaboration with artist Rachel Gomme. Photo: Sarah Faraday at CAMP, Pyrenees

BECAME THOSE WHO BECAME THOSE
WHO BECAME THOSE WHO BECAME THOSE WHO
RAN FROM THE THOUGHT OF THE LOST AND
CAME FINALLY
TO THE PLACE WHERE THE WATER MEETS THE BANKS AND
THE PLACE WHERE THE SKY MEETS THE CLOUDS AND
THE PLACE WHERE THE SKIN MEETS THE AIR AND
THE BOOK MEETS THE TABLE
AND INHABITED THE SPACES

ADVENTURES IN THE HOUSE OF MEMORY
PULp MUSIC, 1982

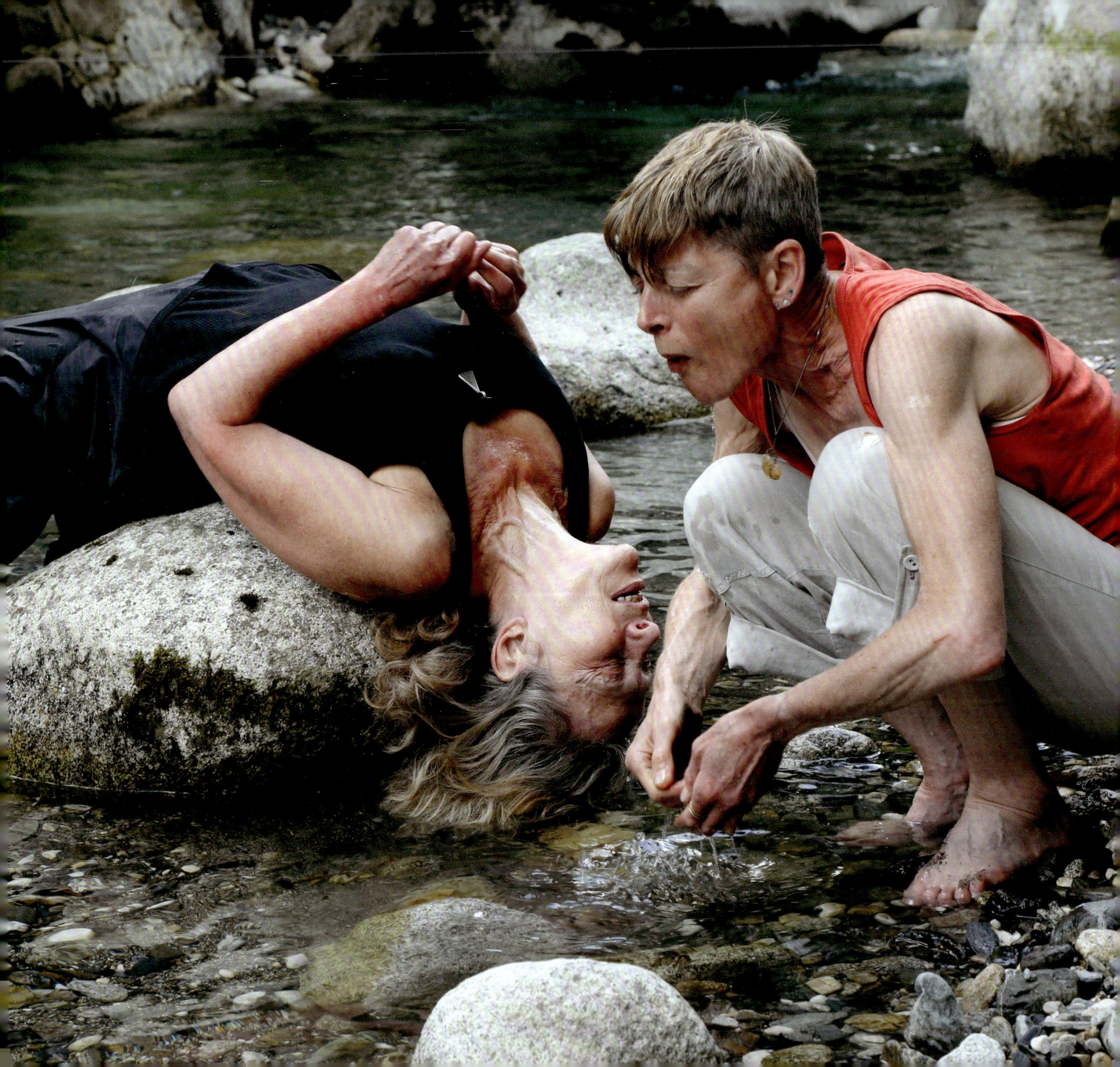